Formal Approaches to Computing and
Information Technology

FACIT

Springer
*London
Berlin
Heidelberg
New York
Barcelona
Hong Kong
Milan
Paris
Santa Clara
Singapore
Tokyo*

Also in this series:

Proof in VDM: A Practitioner's Guide
J.C. Bicarregui, J.S. Fitzgerald, P.A. Lindsay, R. Moore and B. Ritchie
ISBN 3-540-19813-X

The B Language and Method
K. Lano
ISBN 3-540-76033-4

A Theory and Practice of Program Development
D. Andrews
ISBN 3-540-76162-4

Constructing Correct Software: *the basics*
J. Cooke
ISBN 3-540-76156-X

Formal Methods in Human-Computer Interaction
P. Palanque and F. Paternò (Eds)
ISBN 3-540-76158-6

Proof in VDM: Case Studies
J.C. Bicarregui (Ed.)
ISBN 3-540-76186-1

Program Development by Refinement
E. Sekerinski and K. Sere (Eds)
ISBN 1-85233-053-8

Jonathan P. Bowen and Michael G. Hinchey

High-Integrity System Specification and Design

Springer

Jonathan P. Bowen, BA, MA
Department of Computer Science, University of Reading, P.O. Box 225, Whiteknights,
Reading, Berkshire, RG6 6AY, UK

Michael G. Hinchey, BSc, MSc, PhD
Department of Computer Science, University of Nebraska-Omaha,
College of Information Science and Technology, 6001 Dodge Street, Omaha,
NE 68182-0500, USA

Series Editor
S.A. Schuman, BSc, DEA, CEng
Department of Mathematical and Computing Sciences
University of Surrey, Guildford, Surrey GU2 5XH, UK

ISBN 3-540-76226-4 Springer-Verlag Berlin Heidelberg New York

British Library Cataloguing in Publication Data
A catalogue record for this book is available from the British Library

Library of Congress Cataloging-in-Publication Data
High-integrity system specification and design / Jonathan P. Bowen and
  Michael G. Hinchey.
  p.   cm. -- (Formal approaches to computing and information
technology)
  Includes bibliographical references and index.
  ISBN 3-540-76226-4 (alk. paper)
  1. System design.   2. System analysis.   I. Bowen, J.P. (Jonathan
Peter), 1956-   . II. Hinchey, Michael G. (Michael Gerard), 1969-
. III. Series.
QA76.9.S88H52 1998   98-50694
004.2'1--dc21   CIP

Apart from any fair dealing for the purposes of research or private study, or criticism or review, as permitted under the Copyright, Designs and Patents Act 1988, this publication may only be reproduced, stored or transmitted, in any form or by any means, with the prior permission in writing of the publishers, or in the case of reprographic reproduction in accordance with the terms of licences issued by the Copyright Licensing Agency. Enquiries concerning reproduction outside those terms should be sent to the publishers.

© Springer-Verlag London Limited 1999
Printed in Great Britain

The use of registered names, trademarks etc. in this publication does not imply, even in the absence of a specific statement, that such names are exempt from the relevant laws and regulations and therefore free for general use.

The publisher makes no representation, express or implied, with regard to the accuracy of the information contained in this book and cannot accept any legal responsibility or liability for any errors or omissions that may be made.

Typesetting: Camera ready by authors
Printed and bound at the Athenæum Press Ltd., Gateshead, Tyne & Wear
34/3830-543210 Printed on acid-free paper

There are two ways of constructing a software design. One way is to make it so simple that there are obviously no deficiencies. And the other way is to make it so complicated that there are no obvious deficiencies.

— C.A.R. Hoare

Preface

> *Errata, detected in Taylor's* Logarithms. *London: 4to, 1792.* [sic]
> ...
> 6   Kk   Co-sine of   14.18. 3   —   3398   —   3298
> ...
> — *Nautical Almanac* (1832)
>
> In the list of ERRATA detected in Taylor's *Logarithms*, for cos. 4° 18′ 3″, read cos. 14° 18′ 2″.   — *Nautical Almanac* (1833)
>
> ERRATUM of the ERRATUM of the ERRATA of TAYLOR'S *Logarithms*. For cos. 4° 18′ 3″, read cos. 14° 18′ 3″.
> — *Nautical Almanac* (1836)

In the 1820s, an Englishman named Charles Babbage designed and partly built a calculating machine originally intended for use in deriving and printing logarithmic and other tables used in the shipping industry. At that time, such tables were often inaccurate, copied carelessly, and had been instrumental in causing a number of maritime disasters.

Babbage's machine, called a 'Difference Engine' because it performed its calculations using the principle of partial differences, was intended to substantially reduce the number of errors made by humans calculating the tables. Babbage had also designed (but never built) a forerunner of the modern printer, which would also reduce the number of errors admitted during the transcription of the results.

Nowadays, a system implemented to perform the function of Babbage's engine would be classed as *safety-critical*. That is, the failure of the system to produce correct results could result in the loss of human life, mass destruction of property (in the form of ships and cargo) as well as financial losses and loss of competitive advantage for the shipping firm.

Computer systems now influence almost every facet of our lives. They wake us up in the morning, control the cooking of our food, entertain us, help in avoiding traffic congestion and control the vehicles in which we travel, they wash our clothes, and even give us cash from our bank accounts (sometimes!). Increasingly, they are being used in systems where they can have a great influence over our very existence. They control the flow of trains in the subway, signaling on railway lines, even traffic lights on the street. The failure of any of these systems would cause us great inconvenience, and could conceivably result in accidents in which lives may be lost. As they control the actual flight of an airplane, cooling systems in chemical plants, feedback loops in nuclear power stations, etc., we can see that they allow the possibility of great disasters if they fail to operate as expected.

In recent years, the media, in the form of both television news and the popular science journals, have become very preoccupied with the failures of a number of safety-critical computer systems. A number of systems, or classes of system, seem to have particularly caught their attention; chief amongst these are various nuclear power plants where the cooling systems or shutdown loops have been demonstrated to be inconsistent, and recent air crashes which cannot be convincingly blamed on pilot error.

The introduction of computer systems to replace more traditional mechanical systems (consider, for example, Boeing's fly-by-wire system in the 777 jet, and the disastrous baggage-handling system at Denver airport) has made both the system development community and the general public more aware of the unprecedented opportunities for the introduction of errors that computers admit.

Many journalists have become self-styled authorities on techniques that will give greater confidence in the correctness of complex systems, and reduce the number and frequency of computer errors. *High-Integrity Systems*, or systems whose code is relied upon to be of the highest quality and error-free, are often both security- and safety-critical in that their failure could result in great financial losses for a company, mass destruction of property and the environment, and loss of human life. *Formal Methods* have been widely advocated as one of those techniques which can result in high-integrity systems, and their usage is being suggested in an increasing number of standards in the safety-critical domain. Notwithstanding that, formal methods remain one of the most controversial areas of modern software engineering practice. They are the subject of extreme hyperbole by self-styled 'experts' who fail to understand what formal methods actually are, and of deep criticism by proponents of other techniques who see formal methods as merely an opportunity for academics to exercise their intellects over whichever notation is the current 'flavor-of-the-month'.

This book serves as an introduction to the task of specification and design of high-integrity systems, with particular attention paid to formal methods throughout, as these (in our opinion) represent the most promising development in this direction. We do not claim that this book will tell the reader *everything* he/she needs to know, but we do hope that it will help to clarify the issues, and give a good grounding for further investigation.

Each of the major Parts of the book consists of expository material, couched at levels suitable for use by computer science and software engineering students (both undergraduate and graduate), giving an overview of the area, pointers to additional material, and introductions to the excellent papers which are reprinted in this volume.

For practicing software engineers too, both industrialists and academics, this book should prove to be of interest. It brings together some of the 'classic' works in the field, making it an interesting book of readings for self-study, and a convenient, comprehensive reference.

Part 1 introduces the many problems associated with the development of large-scale systems, describes the system life-cycle, and suggests potential solutions which have been demonstrated to be particularly promising.

Traditionally, computer systems have been analyzed, specified and designed using a number of diagrammatic techniques. Over the years, different techniques and notations have been combined into various structured methods of development. These are introduced in Part 2, and a number of the more popular methods are described.

Part 3 goes on to describe formal methods, the major focus of this collection. The components of a formal method are identified; overviews of several representative formal methods are given, and major misconceptions regarding formal methods are identified and dispelled.

Object-Orientation has often been cited as a means of aiding in reducing complexity in system development. Part 4 introduces the subject, and discusses issues related to object-oriented development.

With increased performance requirements, and greater dispersal of processing power, concurrent and distributed systems have become very prevalent. Their development, however, can be exponentially more difficult than the development of traditional sequential systems. Part 5 discusses such issues, and describes two diverse approaches to the development of such systems.

Increasingly, complex concurrent and distributed systems are employed in areas where their use can be deemed to be *safety-critical*, and where they are relied upon to perform within strict timing constraints. Part 6 identifies the relationship of formal methods to safety-critical standards and the development of safety-critical systems. The appropriateness of a number of formal methods is discussed, and some interesting case studies are presented.

While formal methods have much to offer, many fail to address the more methodological aspects of system development. In addition, there has been considerable effort invested in the development of appropriate structured methods which it would be foolhardy to ignore. Part 7 presents the motivation for integrating structured and formal methods, as a means of exploiting the advantages of each.

Clearly the aim of system development is to derive a sensible implementation of the system that was specified at the outset. Part 8 introduces refinement of formal specifications, rapid prototyping and simulation, and the relative merits of executable specifications.

Part 9 addresses the mechanization of system development, and tool support via Computer-Aided Software Engineering (CASE). The future of CASE, and the advent of 'visual formalisms', exploiting graphical representation with formal underpinnings, is postulated.

Finally, a bibliography with recent references is included for those wishing to follow up on any of the issues raised in more depth. We hope this collection of papers and articles, together with the associated commentary, provide food for thought to all those actively involved in or contemplating the production of computer-based high integrity systems.

Information associated with this book will be maintained on-line under the following URL (Uniform Resource Locator):

```
http://www.fmse.cs.reading.ac.uk/hissd/
```

Relevant developments subsequent to publication of this collection will be added to this resource.

J.P.B.   M.G.H.
Reading   Omaha

Table of Contents

Acknowledgements xv

List of Reprints xvii

1. **Specification and Design** 1
   1.1 An Analogy 1
   1.2 The Development Life-Cycle 3
   1.3 The Transformational Approach 6
   1.4 Silver Bullets 8

   No Silver Bullet: Essence and Accidents of Software Engineering (Brooks) 11

   Biting the Silver Bullet: Toward a Brighter Future for System Development (Harel) 29

2. **Structured Methods** 53
   2.1 Structured Notations 53
   2.2 The Jackson Approach 54

   Methodology: The Experts Speak (Orr, Gane, Yourdon, Chen & Constantine) 57

   An Overview of JSD (Cameron) 77

3. **Formal Methods** 127
   3.1 What are Formal Methods? 128
   3.2 Formal Specification Languages 128
   3.3 Deductive Apparatus 129
   3.4 Myths of Formal Methods 130
   3.5 Which Formal Method? 131

   Seven Myths of Formal Methods (Hall) 135

   Seven More Myths of Formal Methods (Bowen & Hinchey) 153

   A Specifier's Introduction to Formal Methods (Wing) 167

   An Overview of Some Formal Methods for Program Design (Hoare) 201

   Ten Commandments of Formal Methods (Bowen & Hinchey) 217

xii High-Integrity System Specification and Design

4. Object-Orientation 231
    4.1 The Object Paradigm 231
    4.2 Modularization 232
    4.3 Information Hiding 232
    4.4 Classes 233
    4.5 Genericity and Polymorphism 233
    4.6 Object-Oriented Design 234

Object-Oriented Development (Booch) 237

Object-Oriented and Conventional Analysis and Design Methodologies: Comparison and Critique (Fichman & Kemerer) 261

5. Concurrent and Distributed Systems 295
    5.1 Concurrent Systems 296
    5.2 Distributed Systems 297
    5.3 Models of Computation 297
    5.4 Naming Considerations 298
    5.5 Inter-Process Communication 298
    5.6 Consistency Issues 299
    5.7 Heterogeneity and Transparency 300
    5.8 Security and Protection 300
    5.9 Language Support 301
    5.10 Distributed Operating Systems 301

Communicating Sequential Processes (Hoare) 303

A Simple Approach to Specifying Concurrent Systems (Lamport) 331

6. Real-Time and Safety-Critical Systems 359
    6.1 Real-Time Systems 359
    6.2 Safety-Critical Systems 360
    6.3 Formal Methods for Safety-Critical Systems 361
    6.4 Standards 362
    6.5 Legislation 363
    6.6 Education and Professional Issues 363
    6.7 Technology Transfer 365

Formal Methods for the Specification and Design of Real-Time Safety-Critical Systems (Ostroff) 367

Experience with Formal Methods in Critical Systems (Gerhart, Craigen & Ralston) 413

Regulatory Case Studies (Gerhart, Craigen & Ralston) 429

Medical Devices: The Therac-25 Story (Leveson) 447

Safety-Critical Systems, Formal Methods and Standards (Bowen & Stavridou) 485

7.	**Integrating Methods**	529
	7.1 Motivation	529
	7.2 Integrating Structured and Formal Methods	530
	7.3 An Appraisal of Approaches	532

Integrated Structured Analysis and Formal Specification Techniques (Semmens, France & Docker) 533

8.	**Implementation**	557
	8.1 Refinement	557
	8.2 Rapid Prototyping and Simulation	559
	8.3 Executable Specifications	560
	8.4 Animating Formal Specifications	560

Specifications are not (Necessarily) Executable (Hayes & Jones) 563

Specifications are (Preferably) Executable (Fuchs) 583

9.	**CASE**	609
	9.1 What is CASE?	609
	9.2 CASE Workbenches	610
	9.3 Beyond CASE	610
	9.4 The Future of CASE	611

CASE: Reliability Engineering for Information Systems (Chikofsky & Rubenstein) 613

On Visual Formalisms (Harel) 623

Glossary 659

Bibliography 665

Author Biographies 679

Index 681

Acknowledgements

We are grateful for the permissions to reprint the papers and articles included in this volume provided by authors and publishers. Full details of the original published sources is provided overleaf on page xvii. We are also grateful to all the authors whose work is reproduced in this collection. Robert France, Ian Hayes, Leslie Lamport, Nancy Leveson, Jonathan Ostroff and Jeannette Wing provided original LaTeX format sources for their contributions which helped tremendously in the preparation of the book. Norbert Fuchs, David Harel and Ian Hayes helped with proof reading of their contributions.

Angela Burgess and Michelle Saewert were very helpful in providing sources and scanning some of the IEEE articles in this collection which aided their preparation. The IEEE, through William Hagen, generously allowed all the contributions originally published in IEEE journals to be included in this collection for no payment. Deborah Cotton of the ACM allowed the contributions originally published by the ACM to be included at a very reasonable cost. Jonathan Ostroff contributed to the payment of the reproduction fee for his paper, which otherwise could not have been included.

Some of the material in Part 5 is based on parts of [34] and Part 6 is adapted from parts of [45].

The book has been formatted using the excellent (and free) $\text{LaTeX} 2_\epsilon$ Document Preparation System [154]. Many of the diagrams have been prepared using the xfig package. Thank you in particular to Mark Green for preparing many of the Cameron paper diagrams, John Hawkins for transcribing the Orr *et al.* diagrams and some of the Cameron diagrams, and Ken Williams for expertly reconstructing some of the diagrams for the Booch, Chikofsky & Rubenstein and Harel 1992 articles (all at The University of Reading).

Finally thank you to Rosie Kemp together with her assistants, Vicki Swallow and Karen Barker, at Springer-Verlag, London, for bringing this project to fruition in print. Rosie generously organized initial typing of many of the articles and was very helpful in organizing copyright permissions. Without her friendly reminders this book would probably never have reached completion.

List of Reprints

Grady Booch. 237
Object-Oriented Development.
IEEE Transactions on Software Engineering, 12(2):211–221, February 1986.

Jonathan P. Bowen and Michael G. Hinchey. 217
Ten Commandments of Formal Methods.
IEEE Computer, 28(4):56–63, April 1995.

Jonathan P. Bowen and Michael G. Hinchey. 153
Seven More Myths of Formal Methods.
IEEE Software, 12(4):34–41, July 1995.

Jonathan P. Bowen and Victoria Stavridou. 485
Safety-Critical Systems, Formal Methods and Standards.
Software Engineering Journal, 8(4):189–209, July 1993.

Frederick P. Brooks, Jr. 11
No Silver Bullet: Essence and Accidents of Software Engineering.
IEEE Computer, 20(4):10–19, April 1987.
Originally published in H.-J. Kugler, editor, *Information Processing '86*.
Elsevier Science Publishers B.V. (North-Holland), 1986.

John R. Cameron. 77
An Overview of JSD.
IEEE Transactions on Software Engineering, 12(2):222–240, February 1986.

Eliott J. Chikofsky and B.L. Rubenstein. 613
CASE: Reliability Engineering for Information Systems.
IEEE Software, 5(2):11–16, March 1988.

Robert G. Fichman and Chris F. Kemerer. 261
Object-Oriented and Conventional Analysis and Design Methodologies: Comparison and Critique.
IEEE Computer, 25(10):22–39, October 1992.

Norbert E. Fuchs. 583
Specifications are (Preferably) Executable.
Software Engineering Journal, 7(5):323–334, September 1992.

Susan Gerhart, Dan Craigen and Ted Ralston. 413
Experience with Formal Methods in Critical Systems.
IEEE Software, 11(1):21–28, January 1994.

Susan Gerhart, Dan Craigen and Ted Ralston. 429
Regulatory Case Studies.
IEEE Software, 11(1):30–39, January 1994.

J. Anthony Hall. 135
Seven Myths of Formal Methods.
IEEE Software, 7(5):11–19, September 1990.

David Harel. 623
On Visual Formalisms.
Communications of the ACM, 31(5):514–530, May 1988.

David Harel. 29
Biting the Silver Bullet: Toward a Brighter Future for System Development.
IEEE Computer, 25(1):8–20, January 1992.

Ian J. Hayes and Cliff B. Jones. 563
Specifications are not (Necessarily) Executable.
Software Engineering Journal, 4(6):330–338, November 1989.

C.A.R. Hoare. 303
Communicating Sequential Processes.
Communications of the ACM, 21(8):666–677, August 1978.

C.A.R. Hoare. 201
An Overview of Some Formal Methods for Program Design.
IEEE Computer, 20(9):85–91, September 1987.

Leslie Lamport. 331
A Simple Approach to Specifying Concurrent Systems.
Communications of the ACM, 32(1):32–45, January 1989.

Nancy G. Leveson. 447
Medical Devices: The Therac-25 Story.
Safeware: System Safety and Computers, Addison-Wesley Publishing Company, Inc., 1995, Appendix A, pages 515–553.

Ken Orr, Chris Gane, Edward Yourdon, Peter P. Chen and Larry L. Constantine. 57
Methodology: The Experts Speak.
BYTE, 14(4):221–233, April 1989.

Jonathan S. Ostroff. 367
Formal Methods for the Specification and Design of Real-Time Safety-Critical Systems.
Journal of Systems and Software, 18(1):33–60, April 1992.

Lesley T. Semmens, Robert B. France and Tom W.G. Docker. 533
Integrated Structured Analysis and Formal Specification Techniques.
The Computer Journal, 35(6):600–610, December 1992.

Jeannette M. Wing. 167
A Specifier's Introduction to Formal Methods.
IEEE Computer, 23(9):8–24, September 1990.

1. Specification and Design

Computers do not make mistakes, or so we are told; but computer software is written by human beings, who certainly *do* make mistakes. Errors may occur as a result of misunderstood or contradictory requirements [77, 234, 265], unfamiliarity with the problem, or simply due to human error during coding. Whatever the cause of the error, the costs of software maintenance (rectifying errors and adapting the system to meet changing requirements or changes in the environment) have risen dramatically over recent years. Alarmingly, these costs now greatly exceed the original programming costs.

The media have recently shown a great interest in computer error, in particular where *safety-critical systems* are involved. These are systems where a failure could result in the loss of human life, or the catastrophic destruction of property (e.g., flight-controllers, protection systems of nuclear reactors). Lately, however, many financial systems are being classed as 'safety-critical' since a failure, or poor security arrangements, could result in great financial losses or a breach of privacy, possibly resulting in the financial ruin of the organization.

Most major newspapers have at some time or other carried articles on Airbus disasters, or discussing fears regarding the correctness of the software running nuclear reactor control systems. The problem with the latter is that since the software is so complex, consisting of hundreds of thousands, or even millions, of lines of code, it can never be fully tested. Reading these articles, it appears that a number of journalists have set themselves up as self-appointed experts on the subject. The most common claim that they make is that had particular techniques been used at the outset, these problems could have been avoided completely. These claims are often completely without justification.

But how then are we to develop computer systems that will operate as expected, i.e., predictably or 'correctly'?

1.1 An Analogy

As complex computer systems influence every facet of our lives, controlling the cars we drive, the airplanes and trains we rely on others to drive for us, and even in everyday machinery such as domestic washing machines, the need for *reliable* and *dependable* systems has become apparent.

With systems increasing rapidly both in size and complexity, it is both naïve and ludicrous to expect a programmer, or a development team, to write a program or system without stating clearly and unambiguously what is required of the program or suite of programs.

Surely nobody would hire a builder and just ask him to build a house. On the contrary, they would first hire an architect, state the features of the house that are *required* and those that are *desired* but not essential. They are likely to have many conflicting goals in terms of the features that are required and what is actually possible. There may be environmental constraints (e.g., the ground is too water-logged for a basement), financial constraints, governmental regulations, etc., all of which will influence what can actually be built.

Different members of the family are likely to have different requirements, some of which will be compatible, others which will not be. Before the house can be built, the family must come to agreement on which features the finished house will have. The architect will formulate these in the form of a set of blueprints, and construction can begin.

Often the construction team will discover errors, omissions and anomalies in the architect's plans, which have to be resolved in consultation with the architect and the family. These may be as a result of carelessness, or sometimes due to unexpected conditions in the environment (e.g., finding solid rock where the foundations should be laid). The problems will be resolved by changing the plans, which sometimes will require modifying other requirements and other aspects of the building.

Finally, when the house has been built, the architect will inspect the work, ensuring that all the relevant building quality standards have been adhered to and that the finished building corresponds to the plans that were drawn up at the outset. Assuming that everything is satisfactory, final payments will be made, and the family can move into their new home.

However, they will often uncover deficiencies in the work of the construction team: faulty wiring, piping, etc. that needs to be replaced. They may also find that the house does not actually meet their requirements; for example, it may be too small for their family meaning that eventually they need to add an extra room.

Even if they find that the house is ideal for their requirements at the outset, over time they will decide that they want changes made. This may mean new fixtures and fittings, new furniture, re-decorating, etc., all of which is a natural part of the existence of a house.

Developing a complex computer system follows a similar development process, or *life-cycle*, except that the development is likely to be less well understood, far more complex, and considerably more costly.

1.2 The Development Life-Cycle

Just as there is a set ordering of events in the construction of a house, similarly there is a set ordering of stages in the 'ideal' system development. We use the word 'ideal' advisedly here, as we will see shortly.

The software development life-cycle is usually structured as a sequence of phases or stages, each producing more and more detailed tangible descriptions of the system under consideration. These are often ordered in a 'waterfall' style as identified by Royce [223], and as illustrated in Figure 1.1, with each phase commencing on the completion of the previous phase.

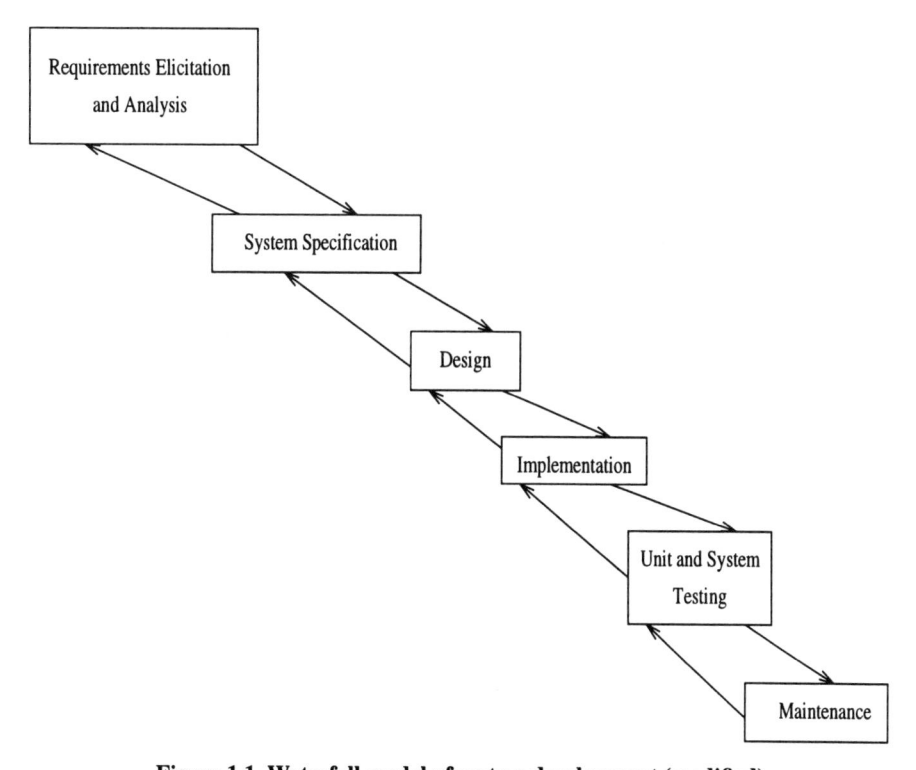

Figure 1.1. Waterfall model of system development (modified)

The first phase, *Requirements Elicitation and Analysis* involves the determination of the exact requirements of the system. It involves talking to end-users and system procurers (those actually contracting the development, and usually incurring the cost), both informally and in arranged interviews. It is likely than many inconsistencies and contradictions will be identified at this point, and these must be resolved. Some of these problems will be very obvious, others not so.

The deliverable at the end of this phase is the requirements specification, a document detailing the system requirements, be they functional (i.e., services which the system is expected to perform) or non-functional (i.e., restrictions or constraints placed on the system's provision of services). The specification is usually written in natural language, augmented as necessary with tables, diagrams, etc., and sometimes with the more precise parts of the requirements expressed in the notation of a structured development method (see Part 2) or a more rigorous formal specification language (see Part 3) [210].

The deliverable is the input to the next stage of the development, *System Specification*. At this stage, it is used in deriving an unambiguous specification of *what* the system should do, without saying *how* this is to be achieved [232]. This will almost certainly be written in the notation of a structured method, such as SA/SD [67, 261], Yourdon [262], SSADM [56], Mascot [222], or JSD [143], etc., or more commonly using the specification language of one of the more popular formal methods, such as VDM [141] or Z [268].

The System Specification, or *functional specification* is generally written in a highly abstract manner, constraining the implementation as little as possible. That is to say, any implementation that satisfies the specification should be acceptable, with no obligation on the way any particular constructs should be implemented. The object at this point is rather to develop an explicit model of the system that is clear, precise and as unambiguous as possible; the final implementation may bear no obvious resemblance to the model, with the *proviso* that it satisfies all of the constraints and all of the functionality of the model.

The intention is that specification and implementation are separated, and implementation issues are only considered at the appropriate juncture. Unfortunately, such a separation, although logical, is unrealistic. Phases of the life-cycle inevitably overlap; specification and implementation are the *already-fixed* and *yet-to-be-done* portions of the life-cycle [241], in that every specification, no matter how abstract, is essentially the implementation of some higher level specification. As such, the functional specification is an implementation of the requirements specification, which is itself implemented by the design specification.

The reader should understand, as a consequence, the difficulty of producing a good functional specification – that is, one that is both high-level enough to be readable and to avoid excluding reasonable implementations, and yet low-level enough to *completely* and *precisely* define the behavior of the implementation.

At the System Specification phase, the intention is to state *what* is required. This generally makes extensive use of implicit (functional) definition, where precise orderings are not specified. At the *Design* phase, however, the aim is to reduce the level of abstraction and to begin addressing *how* the system is to be implemented. This involves considering how various data are to be represented (e.g., considering the efficiency of various data structures), more explicit definition, and how various constructs may be decomposed and structured.

Again, the notation of a structured method or a formal specification language may be used at this point, but using a more operational style, using more realistic data representations, such as files, arrays and linked-lists, and lower level constructs.

The Design Specification (or simply 'Design') is used in deriving the actual implemented program. A program is itself just a specification, albeit an executable one. It is also the most accurate description of the system, as the execution of the system is based on the microcode that corresponds *directly* to the program. The program must, however, address many more issues than those dealt with in the more abstract specifications. It must consider interaction with the underlying hardware and operating system, as well as making efficient use of resources. In fact, the major distinction between an executable specification and an actual program is resource management [266].

At the design phase, the level of abstraction is reduced gradually in a process known as *stepwise refinement*, with more and more detail introduced at each step, the description at each step becoming a more low-level specification of the system. This process continues until the design is in a format where it can be almost transliterated into a programming language by a competent programmer in the *Implementation* phase.

The Implementation Phase, or what is traditionally described as 'programming', is no longer the major contributor to development costs. While programmers still make errors, and the program 'bug' is something that will always be familiar to us, the major cost of software development comes *after* the system has been implemented. It is then that the system is subjected to *Unit* and *System Testing* which aims to trap 'bugs'. However this increasingly tends to highlight inconsistencies and errors in the requirements specification, or in mapping these to the functional specification.

As much as 50% of the costs of system development may be due to the costs of system maintenance. Of this, only 17% is likely to be *corrective* (i.e., removing 'bugs'), just 18% is *adaptive* (i.e., modifying the software to add extra functionality, or to deal with changes in the environment), with a phenomenal 65% being due to *perfective* maintenance [171], much of which is due to errors at the earlier stages of development, such as incomplete and contradictory requirements, imprecise functional specification and errors in the design.

As anyone who has had experience of software development will quickly realize, such a view of the development cycle is very simplistic. As one can even see from the house-building analogy given in the previous section, the distinction between the various phases of development is not clear. System development is not a straightforward process, progressing from one stage to another in a linear fashion. Rather, it is an iterative process, whereby various stages may be repeated a number of times as problems and inconsistencies are uncovered, and as requirements are necessarily modified.

Royce's model [223] holds that system requirements and the system specification are frozen before implementation. However, at implementation, or during post-implementation testing, or in an extreme case, at some point during post-implementation execution, errors in the system specification are often uncovered. Such errors require corrections to be made to the specification, or sometimes a reappraisal of the system requirements. One would hope that using (relatively) more recent developments such as formal specification techniques, such errors would be detected during system specification; unfortunately, although such techniques are often augmented with theorem provers and proof-checkers, errors may still be made in proofs, and system development remains a human activity which is prone to error.

It is not surprising then that Royce's 'waterfall' model has been criticized [93, 175] as being unrepresentative of actual system development. Nowadays, the more accepted model of the system life-cycle is one akin to Boehm's 'spiral' model [19] (as illustrated in Figure 1.2), which takes more account of iteration and the non-linear nature of software development, and allows for the re-evaluation of requirements and for alterations to the system specification even after the implementation phase.

1.3 The Transformational Approach

It should be pointed out that there is no definitive model of the system life-cycle, and the development process employed is likely to vary for different organizations and even for different projects within a given organization. An alternative approach to the life-cycle model is what has come to be known as the *transformational* or *evolutionary* approach to system development. This begins with a very simple, and inefficient, implementation of the system requirements, which is then transformed into an efficient program by the application of a sequence of simple transformations. The intention is that libraries of such transformations, which are known to preserve semantics and correctness, should be built up.

There are however, a number of flaws in the approach [95]:

- there are tasks for which even the simplest and most inefficient program is complex, whereas a specification of the task could easily be realized;
- to demonstrate the correctness of the transformation, it is necessary to verify that certain properties hold before the transformation may be applied, and after its completion; a specification of how the program is to function is required in order to verify these conditions;
- transformations are applied to parts of programs and not to entire systems; to ensure that transformations do not have side-effects, specifications of program parts are required;
- the idea of building up libraries of transformations is attractive, but has not worked in practice; transformations tend to be too specialized to be applicable to other systems, the resulting libraries becoming too large to be manageable.

The approach is not incongruous with the more traditional development life-cycle, but rather specifications are required if transformations are to be used to derive correct programs. In more recent years, the proponents of the transformational

Part 1   Specification and Design   7

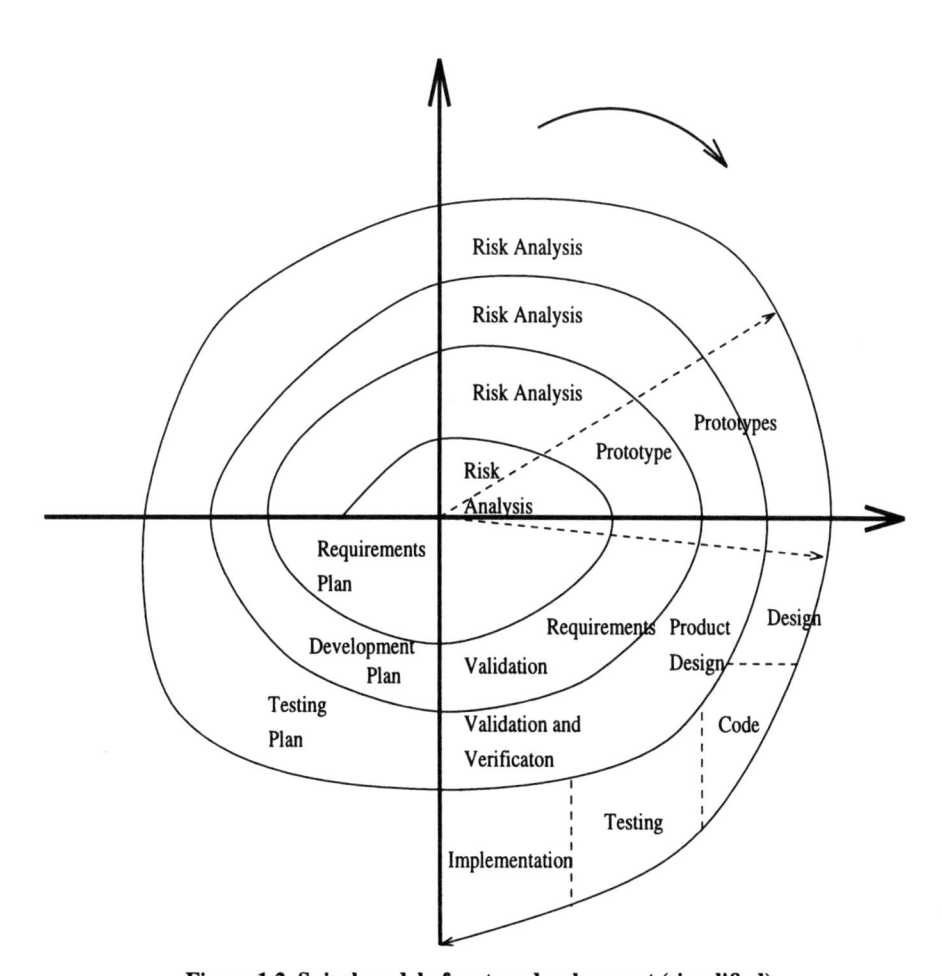

Figure 1.2. Spiral model of system development (simplified)

approach have come to realize the dependency, and *transformational programming* has come to refer to the application of correctness-preserving transformations to formal specifications, in a constructive approach to system development.

1.4 Silver Bullets

With computer systems being applied in more and more 'safety-critical' domains, the need to be assured of the 'correctness' of the system has become increasingly vital. When system failures can result in large-scale destruction of property, great financial loss, or the loss of human life, nothing can be left to chance. In the development of such complex systems, informal inferences are not satisfactory. Firstly, we require a definite means of *proving* that the system we are building adequately reflects all of the requirements specified at the outset. We must validate these requirements and determine that they do not conflict, and ensure that realizing those requirements would result in a satisfactory system. Secondly we must determine that these requirements are complete, and be able to demonstrate that all potential eventualities are covered. Finally, we must be able to *prove* that a particular implementation satisfies each of the requirements that we specified.

We have seen that system development is not a one-pass process, but rather involves multiple iterations, subject as it is to the imprecision of natural language and the indecision and whim of procurers and end-users. Even with increased levels of automation, Computer-Aided Software Engineering (CASE) workbenches (see Part 9), more precise specifications (see Part 2) and more appropriate design methods (see Parts 2, 4, 5 and 6), system development will remain an imprecise process, subject to human input, and human error. As such, the system development process will always be the subject of further research, and a source of possible improvements.

In his widely-quoted and much-referenced article, *No Silver Bullet* (reprinted in this volume), Fred Brooks, also of *Mythical Man-Month* fame [51], warns of the dangers of complacency in system development [50]. He stresses that unlike hardware development, we cannot expect to achieve great advances in productivity in software development unless we concentrate on more appropriate development methods. He highlights how software systems can suddenly turn from being well-behaved to behaving erratically and uncontrollably, with unanticipated delays and increased costs (e.g., for a spectacular and expensive example, see the ARIANE 5 failure in 1996 [174]). Brooks sees software systems as 'werewolves', and rightly points out that there is no single technique, no 'Silver Bullet', capable of slaying such monsters.

On the contrary, more and more complex systems are run on distributed, heterogeneous networks, subject to strict performance, fault tolerance and security constraints, all of which may conflict. Many engineering disciplines must contribute to the development of complex systems in an attempt to satisfy all of these requirements. No single technique is adequate to address all issues of complex system development; rather, different techniques must be applied at different stages of development to ensure unambiguous requirements statements, precise specifications that are amenable to analysis and evaluation, implementations that satisfy the requirements and various goals such as re-use, re-engineering and reverse engineering of legacy code, appropriate integration with existing systems, ease of use, predictability, dependability, maintainability, fault-tolerance, etc.

Brooks differentiates between the *essence* (i.e., problems that are necessarily inherent in the nature of software) and *accidents* (i.e., problems that are secondary and caused by current development environments and techniques). He points out the great need for appropriate means of coming to grips with the conceptual difficulties of software development – that is, for appropriate emphasis on specification and design; he writes:

> *I believe the hard part of building software to be the specification, design, and testing of this conceptual construct, not the labor of representing it and testing the fidelity of the representation.*

In his article he highlights some successes that have been achieved in gaining improvements in productivity, but points out that these address problems in the current development process, rather than those problems inherent in software itself. In this category, he includes: the advent of high-level languages (such as Ada [8]), time-sharing, unified programming environments, object-oriented programming, techniques from artificial intelligence, expert systems, automatic programming, , program verification, and the advent of workstations. These he sees as 'non-bullets' as they will not help in slaying the werewolf.

He sees software reuse [88], rapid prototyping (discussed in Part 8), incremental development (akin to the transformational approach described earlier) and the employment of top-class designers as potential starting points for the 'Silver Bullet', but warns that none in itself is sufficient.

Brooks' article has been very influential, and remains one of the 'classics' of software engineering. His viewpoint has been criticized, however, as being overly pessimistic and for failing to acknowledge some promising developments.

Harel, in his article *Biting the Silver Bullet* (also reprinted in this Part), points to developments in CASE and Visual Formalisms (see Part 9) as potential 'bullets' [109]. Harel's view is far more optimistic. He writes five years after Brooks, and has seen the developments in that period. The last forty years of system development have been equally difficult, according to Harel, and using a conceptual 'vanilla' framework, we devised means of overcoming many difficulties. Now, as we address more complex systems, we must devise similar frameworks that are applicable to the classes of systems we are developing.

Concentrating on reactive systems (see Part 6), he describes one such 'vanilla' framework, with appropriate techniques for modeling system behavior and analyzing that model. Harel, as many others, believes that appropriate techniques for modeling must have a rigorous mathematical semantics, and appropriate means for representing constructs (disagreeing with Brooks, who sees representational issues as primarily *accidental*), using visual representations that can be meaningful to engineers and programmers; he says:

It is our duty to forge ahead to turn system modeling into a predominantly visual and graphical process.

He goes on to describe his concepts in more detail in his paper *On Visual Formalisms* [108], reprinted in Part 9.

Software engineering is a wide-ranging discipline in general requiring expertise in a number of related areas to ensure success. Software quality is of increasing importance as the use of software becomes more pervasive. Formal example, the Software Engineering Institute (SEI, based at Carnegie-Mellon University, Pittsburg) and Mitre Corporation have proposed a Capability Maturity Model (CMM) for assessing an organization's software process capability [82].

Those interested in exploring the topic of software engineering further are recommended to read one of the comprehensive reference sources on this subject (e.g., see [176, 181, 217]). For the future, software architecture [231] is emerging as an approach in which typically software components are designed to interface with each other in a similar way that hardware components are designed to fit together in other engineering disciplines. This has proved to be a difficult problem, but may improve the hope for more software reuse in future products [88]. However software reuse should be undertaken with caution, since when misapplied, disastrous consequences can result (e.g., see [174]). In the industrial application of any technique to aid software development, including for high-integrity systems, adequate and dependable tool support is vital for success [245].

No Silver Bullet

Essence and Accidents of Software Engineering

Frederick P. Brooks, Jr.

Summary.

Fashioning complex conceptual constructs is the *essence*; *accidental* tasks arise in representing the constructs in language. Past progress has so reduced the accidental tasks that future progress now depends upon addressing the essence.

O f all the monsters that fill the nightmares of our folklore, non terrify more than werewolves, because they transform unexpectedly from the familiar into horrors. For these, one seeks bullets of silver that can magically lay them to rest.

The familiar software project, at least as seen by the nontechnical manager, has something of this character; it is usually innocent and straightforward, but is capable of becoming a monster of missed schedules, blown budgets, and flawed products. So we hear desperate cries for a silver bullet – something to make software costs drop as rapidly as computer hardware costs do.

But, as we look to the horizon of a decade hence, we see no silver bullet. There is no single development, in either technology or in management technique, that by itself promises even one order-of-magnitude improvement in productivity, in reliability, in simplicity. In this article, I shall try to show why, by examining both the nature of the software problem and the properties of the bullets proposed.

Skepticism is not pessimism, however. Although we see no startling breakthroughs – and indeed, I believe such to be inconsistent with the nature of software – many encouraging innovations are under way. A disciplined, consistent effort to develop, propagate, and exploit these innovations should indeed yield an order-of-magnitude improvement. There is no royal road, but there is a road.

© 1986 Frederick P. Brooks, Jr.. Reprinted by permission.
Reprinted from *IEEE Computer*, 20(4):10–19, April 1987.
Originally published in H.-J. Kugler (ed.), *Information Processing '86*, Elsevier Science Publishers B.V. (North-Holland), 1986.

The first step toward the management of disease was replacement of demon theories and humours theories by the germ theory. That very step, the beginning of hope, in itself dashed all hopes of magical solutions. It told workers that progress would be made stepwise, at great effort, and that a persistent, unremitting care would have to be paid to a discipline of cleanliness. So it is with software engineering today.

Does it Have to be Hard? – Essential Difficulties

Not only are there no silver bullets now in view, the very nature of software makes it unlikely that there will be any – no inventions that will do for software productivity, reliability, and simplicity what electronics, transistors, and large-scale integration did for computer hardware. We cannot expect ever to see twofold gains every two years.

First, one must observe that the anomaly is not that software progress is so slow, but that computer hardware progress is so fast. No other technology since civilization began has seen six orders of magnitude in performance-price gain in 30 years. In no other technology can one choose to take the gain in *either* improved performance *or* in reduced costs. These gains flow from the transformation of computer manufacture from an assembly industry into a process industry.

Second, to see what rate of progress one can expect in software technology, let us examine the difficulties of that technology. Following Aristotle, I divide them into *essence*, the difficulties inherent in the nature of software, and *accidents*, those difficulties that today attend its production but are not inherent.

The essence of a software entity is a construct of interlocking concepts: data sets, relationships among data items, algorithms, and invocations of functions. This essence is abstract in that such a conceptual construct is the same under many different representations. It is nonetheless highly precise and richly detailed.

I believe the hard part of building software to be the specification, design, and testing of this conceptual construct, not the labor of representing it and testing the fidelity of the representation. We still make syntax errors, to be sure; but they are fuzz compared with the conceptual errors in most systems.

If this is true, building software will always be hard. There is inherently no silver bullet.

Let us consider the inherent properties of this irreducible essence of modern software systems: complexity, conformity, changeability, and invisibility.

Complexity. Software entities are more complex for their size than perhaps any other human construct because no two parts are alike (at least above the statement level). If they are, we make the two similar parts into a subroutine – open or closed. In this respect, software systems differ profoundly from computers, buildings, or automobiles, where repeated elements abound.

Digital computers are themselves more complex than most things people build: They have very large numbers of states. This makes conceiving, describing, and testing them hard. Software systems have orders-of-magnitude more states than computers do.

Likewise, a scaling-up of a software entity is not merely a repetition of the same elements in larger sizes, it is necessarily an increase in the number of different elements. In most cases, the elements interact with each other in some nonlinear fashion, and the complexity of the whole increases much more than linearly.

The complexity of software is an essential property, not an accidental one. Hence, descriptions of a software entity that abstract away its complexity often abstract away its essence. For three centuries, mathematics and the physical sciences made great strides by constructing simplified models of complex phenomena, deriving properties from the models, and verifying those properties by experiment. This paradigm worked because the complexities ignored in the models were not the essential properties of the phenomena. It does not work when the complexities are the essence.

Many of the classic problems of developing software products derive from this essential complexity and its nonlinear increases with size. From the complexity comes the difficulty of communication among team members, which leads to product flaws, cost overruns, schedule delays. From the complexity comes the difficulty of enumerating, much less understanding, all the possible states of the program, and from that comes the unreliability. From complexity of function comes the difficulty of invoking function, which makes programs hard to use. From complexity of structure comes the difficulty of extending programs to new functions without creating side effects. From complexity of structure come the unvisualized states that constitute security trapdoors.

Not only technical problems, but management problems as well come from the complexity. It makes overview hard, thus impeding conceptual integrity. It makes it hard to find and control all the loose ends. It creates the tremendous learning and understanding burden that makes personnel turnover a disaster.

Conformity. Software people are not alone in facing complexity. Physics deals with terribly complex objects even at the "fundamental" particle level. The physicist labors on, however, in a firm faith that there are unifying principles to be found, whether in quarks or in unified-field theories. Einstein argued that there must be simplified explanations of nature, because God is not capricious or arbitrary.

No such faith comforts the software engineer. Much of the complexity that he must master is arbitrary complexity, forced without rhyme or reason by the many human institutions and systems to which his interfaces must conform. These differ from interface to interface, and from time to time, not because of necessity but only because they were designed by different people, rather than by God.

In many cases, the software must conform because it is the most recent arrival on the scene. In others, it must conform because it is perceived as the most conformable. But in all cases, much complexity comes from conformation to other interfaces; this complexity cannot be simplified out by any redesign of the software alone.

Changeability. The software entity is constantly subject to pressures for change. Of course, so are buildings, cars, computers. But manufactured things are infrequently changed after manufacture; they are superseded by later models, or essential changes are incorporated into later-serial-number copies of the same basic design. Call-backs of automobiles are really quite infrequent; field changes of computers somewhat less so. Both are much less frequent than modifications to fielded software.

In part, this is so because the software of a system embodies its function, and the function is the part that most feels the pressures of change. In part it is because software can be changed more easily – it is pure thought-stuff, infinitely malleable. Buildings do in fact get changed, but the high costs of change, understood by all, serve to dampen the whims of the changers.

All successful software gets changed. Two processes are at work. First, as a software product is found to be useful, people try it in new cases at the edge of or beyond the original domain. The pressures for extended function come chiefly from users who like the basic function and invent new uses for it.

Second, successful software survives beyond the normal life of the machine vehicle for which it is first written. If not new computers, then at least new disks, new displays, new printers come along; and the software must be conformed to its new vehicles of opportunity.

In short, the software product is embedded in a cultural matrix of applications, users, laws, and machine vehicles. These all change continually, and their changes inexorably force change upon the software product.

Invisibility. Software is invisible and unvisualizable. Geometric abstractions are powerful tools. The floor plan of a building helps both architect and client evaluate spaces, traffic flows, views. Contradictions and omissions become obvious.

Scale drawings of mechanical parts and stick-figure models of molecules, although abstractions, serve the same purpose. A geometric reality is captured in a geometric abstraction.

The reality of software is not inherently embedded in space. Hence, it has no ready geometric representation in the way that land has maps, silicon chips have diagrams, computers have connectivity schematics. As soon as we attempt to diagram software structure, we find it to constitute not one, but several, general directed graphs superimposed one upon another. The several graphs may represent the flow of control, the flow of data, patterns of dependency, time sequence, name-space relationships. These graphs are usually not even planar, much less hierarchical. Indeed, one of the ways of establishing conceptual control over such structure is to enforce link cutting until one or more of the graphs becomes hierarchical [1].

In spite of progress in restricting and simplifying the structures of software, they remain inherently unvisualizable, and thus do not permit the mind to use some of its most powerful conceptual tools. This lack not only impedes the process of design within one mind, it severely hinders communication among minds.

Past Breakthroughs Solved Accidental Difficulties

If we examine the three steps in software-technology development that have been most fruitful in the past, we discover that each attacked a different major difficulty in building software, but that those difficulties have been accidental, not essential, difficulties. We can also see the natural limits to the extrapolation of each such attack.

High-level languages. Surely the most powerful stroke for software productivity, reliability, and simplicity has been the progressive use of high-level languages for programming. Most observers credit that development with at least a factor of five in productivity, and with concomitant gains in reliability, simplicity, and comprehensibility.

What does a high-level language accomplish? It frees a program from much of its accidental complexity. An abstract program consists of conceptual constructs: operations, data types, sequences, and communication. The concrete machine program is concerned with bits, registers, conditions, branches, channels, disks, and such. To the extent that the high-level language embodies the constructs one wants in the abstract program and avoids all lower ones, it eliminates a whole level of complexity that was never inherent in the program at all.

The most a high-level language can do is to furnish all the constructs that the programmer imagines in the abstract program. To be sure, the level of our thinking about data structures, data types, and operations is steadily rising, but at an ever-decreasing rate. And language development approaches closer and closer to the sophistication of users.

Moreover, at some point the elaboration of a high-level language creates a tool-mastery burden that increases, not reduces, the intellectual task of the user who rarely uses the esoteric constructs.

Time-sharing. Time-sharing brought a major improvement in the productivity of programmers and in the quality of their product, although not so large as that brought by high-level languages.

Time-sharing attacks a quite different difficulty. Time-sharing preserves immediacy, and hence enables one to maintain an overview of complexity. The slow turnaround of batch programming means that one inevitably forgets the minutiae, if not the very thrust, of what one was thinking when he stopped programming and called for compilation and execution. This interruption is costly in time, for one must refresh one's memory. The most serious effect may well be the decay of the grasp of all that is going on in a complex system.

Slow turnaround, like machine-language complexities, is an accidental rather than an essential difficulty of the software process. The limits of the potential contribution of time-sharing derive directly. The principal effect of time-sharing is to shorten system response time. As this response time goes to zero, at some point it passes the human threshold of noticeability, about 100 milliseconds. Beyond that threshold, no benefits are to be expected.

Unified programming environments. Unix and Interlisp, the first integrated programming environments to come into widespread use, seem to have improved productivity by integral factors. Why?

They attack the accidental difficulties that result from using individual programs *together*, by providing integrated libraries, unified file formats, and pipes and filters. As a result, conceptual structures that in principle could always call, feed, and use one another can indeed easily do so in practice.

This breakthrough in turn stimulated the development of whole toolbenches, since each new tool could be applied to any programs that used the standard formats.

Because of these successes, environments are the subject of much of today's software-engineering research. We look at their promise and limitations in the next section.

Hope for the Silver

Now let us consider the technical developments that are most often advanced as potential silver bullets. What problems do they address – the problems of essence, or the remaining accidental difficulties? Do they offer revolutionary advances, or incremental ones?

Ada and other high-level language advances. One of the most touted recent developments is Ada, a general-purpose high-level language of the 1980's. Ada not only reflects evolutionary improvements in language concepts, but indeed embodies features to encourage modern design and modularization. Perhaps the Ada philosophy is more of an advance than the Ada language, for it is the philosophy of modularization, of abstract data types, of hierarchical structuring. Ada is over-rich, a natural result of the process by which requirements were laid on its design. That is not fatal, for subsetted working vocabularies can solve the learning problem, and hardware advances will give us the cheap MIPS to pay for the compiling costs. Advancing the structuring of software systems is indeed a very good use for the increased MIPS our dollars will buy. Operating systems, loudly decried in the 1960's for their memory and cycle costs, have proved to be an excellent form in which to use some of the MIPS and cheap memory bytes of the past hardware surge.

Nevertheless, Ada will not prove to be the silver bullet that slays the software productivity monster. It is, after all, just another high-level language, and the biggest payoff from such languages came from the first transition – the transition up from the accidental complexities of the machine into the more abstract statement of step-by-step solutions. Once those accidents have been removed, the remaining ones will be smaller, and the payoff from their removal will surely be less.

I predict that a decade from now, when the effectiveness of Ada is assessed, it will be seen to have made a substantial difference, but not because of any particular language feature, nor indeed because of all of them combined. Neither will the new Ada environments prove to be the cause of the improvements. Ada's greatest contribution will be that switching to it occasioned training programmers in modern software-design techniques.

Object-oriented programming. Many students of the art hold out more hope for object-oriented programming than for any of the other technical fads of the day [2]. I am among them. Mark Sherman of Dartmouth notes on CSnet News that one must be careful to distinguish two separate ideas that go under that name: *abstract data types* and *hierarchical types*. The concept of the abstract data type is that an object's type should be defined by a name, a set of proper values, and a set of proper operations rather than by its storage structure, which should be hidden. Examples are Ada packages (with private types) and Modula's modules.

Hierarchical types, such as Simula-67's classes, allow one to define general interfaces that can be further refined by providing subordinate types. The two concepts are orthogonal – one may have hierarchies without hiding and hiding without hierarchies. Both concepts represent real advances in the art of building software.

Each removes yet another accidental difficulty from the process, allowing the designer to express the essence of the design without having to express large amounts of syntactic material that add no information content. For both abstract types and hierarchical types, the result is to remove a higher-order kind of accidental difficulty and allow a higher-order expression of design.

Nevertheless, such advances can do no more than to remove all the accidental difficulties from the expression of the design. The complexity of the design itself is essential, and such attacks make no change whatever in that. An order-of-magnitude gain can be made by object-oriented programming only if the unnecessary type-specification underbrush still in our programming language is itself nine-tenths of the work involved in designing a program product. I doubt it.

Artificial intelligence. Many people expect advances in artificial intelligence to provide the revolutionary breakthrough that will give order-of-magnitude gains in software productivity and quality [3]. I do not. To see why, we must dissect what is meant by "artificial intelligence."

D.L. Parnas has clarified the terminological chaos [4]:

> *Two quite different definitions of AI are in common use today. AI-1: The use of computers to solve problems that previously could only be solved by applying human intelligence. AI-2: The use of a specific set of programming techniques known as heuristic or rule-based programming. In this approach human experts are studied to determine what heuristics or rules of thumb they use in solving problems.... The program is designed to solve a problem the way that humans seem to solve it.*
>
> *The first definition has a sliding meaning.... Something can fit the definition of AI-1 today but, once we see how the program works and understand the problem, we will not think of it as AI any more.... Unfortunately I cannot identify a body of technology that is unique to this field.... Most of the work is problem-specific, and some abstraction or creativity is required to see how to transfer it.*

I agree completely with this critique. The techniques used for speech recognition seem to have little in common with those used for image recognition, and both are different from those used in expert systems. I have a hard time seeing how image recognition, for example, will make any appreciable difference in programming practice. The same problem is true of speech recognition. The hard thing about building software is deciding what one wants to say, not saying it. No facilitation of expression can give more than marginal gains.

Expert systems technology, AI-2, deserves a section of its own.

Expert systems. The most advanced part of the artificial intelligence art, and the most widely applied, is the technology for building expert systems. Many software scientists are hard at work applying this technology to the software-building environment [3, 5]. What is the concept, and what are the prospects?

An *expert system* is a program that contains a generalized inference engine and a rule base, takes input data and assumptions, explores the inferences derivable from the rule base, yields conclusions and advice, and offers to explain its results by retracing its reasoning for the user. The inference engines typically can deal with fuzzy or probabilistic data and rules, in addition to purely deterministic logic.

Such systems offer some clear advantages over programmed algorithms designed for arriving at the same solutions to the same problems:

- Inference-engine technology is developed in an application-independent way, then applied to many uses. One can justify much effort on the inference engines. Indeed, that technology is well-advanced.
- The changeable parts of the application-peculiar materials are encoded in the rule base in a uniform fashion, and tools are provided for developing, changing, testing and documenting the rule base. This regularizes much of the complexity of the application itself.

The power of such systems does not come from ever-fancier inference mechanisms, but rather from ever-richer knowledge bases that reflect the real world more accurately. I believe that the most important advance offered by the technology is the separation of the application complexity from the program itself.

How can this technology be applied to the software-engineering task? In many ways: Such systems can suggest interface rules, advise on testing strategies, remember bug-type frequencies, and offer optimization hints.

Consider an imaginary testing advisor, for example. In its most rudimentary form, the diagnostic expert system is very like a pilot's checklist, just enumerating suggestions as to possible causes of difficulty. As more and more system structure is embodied in the rule base, and as the rule base takes more sophisticated account of the trouble symptoms reported, the testing advisor becomes more and more particular in the hypotheses it generates and the tests it recommends. Such an expert system may depart most radically from the conventional ones in that its rule base should probably be hierarchically modularized in the same way the corresponding software product is, so that as the product is modularly modified, the diagnostic rule base can be modularly modified as well.

The work required to generate the diagnostic rules is work that would have to be done anyway in generating the set of test cases for the modules and for the system. If it is done in a suitably general manner, with both a uniform structure for rules and a good inference engine available, it may actually reduce the total labor of generating bring-up test cases, and help as well with lifelong maintenance and modification testing. In the same way, one can postulate other advisors, probably many and probably simple, for the other parts of the software-construction task.

Many difficulties stand in the way of the early realization of useful expert-system advisors to the program developer. A crucial part of our imaginary scenario is the development of easy ways to get from program-structure specification to the automatic or semiautomatic generation of diagnostic rules. Even more difficult and important is the twofold task of knowledge acquisition: finding articulate, self-analytical experts who know *why* they do things, and developing efficient techniques for extracting what they know and distilling it into rule bases. The essential prerequisite for building an expert system is to have an expert.

The most powerful contribution by expert systems will surely be to put at the service of the inexperienced programmer the experience and accumulated wisdom of the best programmers. This is no small contribution. The gap between the best software engineering practice and the average practice is very wide – perhaps wider than in any other engineering discipline. A tool that disseminates good practice would be important.

"Automatic" programming. For almost 40 years, people have been anticipating and writing about "automatic programming," or the generation of a program for solving a problem from a statement of the problem specifications. Some today write as if they expect this technology to provide the next breakthrough [5].

Parnas [4] implies that the term is used for glamor, not for semantic content, asserting:

> *In short, automatic programming always has been a euphemism for programming with a higher-level language than was presently available to the programmer.*

He argues, in essence, that in most cases it is the solution method, not the problem, whose specification has to be given.

One can find exceptions. The technique of building generators is very powerful, and it is routinely used to good advantage in programs for sorting. Some systems for integrating differential equations have also permitted direct specification of the problem, and the systems have assessed the parameters, chosen from a library of methods of solution, and generated the programs.

These applications have very favorable properties:

- The problems are readily characterized by relatively few parameters.
- There are many known methods of solution to provide a library of alternatives.
- Extensive analysis has led to explicit rules for selecting solution techniques, given problem parameters.

It is hard to see how such techniques generalize to the wider world of the ordinary software system, where cases with such neat properties are the exception. It is hard even to imagine how this breakthrough in generalization could occur.

Graphical programming. A favorite subject for PhD dissertations in software engineering is graphical, or visual, programming – the application of computer graphics to software design [6, 7]. Sometimes the promise held out by such an approach is postulated by analogy with VLSI chip design, in which computer graphics plays so fruitful a role. Sometimes the theorist justifies the approach by considering flowcharts as the ideal program-design medium and by providing powerful facilities for constructing them.

Nothing even convincing, much less exciting, has yet emerged from such efforts. I am persuaded that nothing will.

In the first place, as I have argued elsewhere [8], the flowchart is a very poor abstraction of software structure. Indeed, it is best viewed as Burks, von Neumann, and Goldstine's attempt to provide a desperately needed high-level control language for their proposed computer. In the pitiful, multipage, connection-boxed form to which the flowchart has today been elaborated, it has proved to be useless as a design tool – programmers draw flowcharts after, not before, writing the programs they describe.

Second, the screens of today are too small, in pixels, to show both the scope and the resolution of any seriously detailed software diagram. The so-called "desktop metaphor" of today's workstation is instead an "airplane-seat" metaphor. Anyone who has shuffled a lap full of papers while seated between two portly passengers will recognize the difference – one can see only a very few things at once. The true desktop provides overview of, and random access to, a score of pages. Moreover, when fits of creativity run strong, more than one programmer or writer has been known to abandon the desktop for the more spacious floor. The hardware technology will have to advance quite substantially before the scope of our scopes is sufficient for the software-design task.

More fundamentally, as I have argued above, software is very difficult to visualize. Whether one diagrams control flow, variable-scope nesting, variable cross-references, dataflow, hierarchical data structures, or whatever, one feels only one dimension of the intricately interlocked software elephant. If one superimposes all the diagrams generated by the many relevant views, it is difficult to extract any global overview. The VLSI analogy is fundamentally misleading – a chip design is a layered two-dimensional description whose geometry reflects its realization in 3-space. A software system is not.

Program verification. Much of the effort in modern programming goes into testing and the repair of bugs. Is there perhaps a silver bullet to be found by eliminating the errors at the source, in the system-design phase? Can both productivity and product reliability be radically enhanced by following the profoundly different strategy of proving designs correct before the immense effort is poured into implementing and testing them?

I do not believe we will find productivity magic here. Program verification is a very powerful concept, and it will be very important for such things as secure operating-system kernels. The technology does not promise, however, to save labor.

Verifications are so much work that only a few substantial programs have ever been verified.

Program verification does not mean error-proof programs. There is no magic here, either. Mathematical proofs also can be faulty. So whereas verification might reduce the program-testing load, it cannot eliminate it.

More seriously, even perfect program verification can only establish that a program meets its specification. The hardest part of the software task is arriving at a complete and consistent specification, and much of the essence of building a program is in fact the debugging of the specification.

Environments and tools. How much more gain can be expected from the exploding researches into better programming environments? One's instinctive reaction is that the big-payoff problems – hierarchical file systems, uniform file formats to make possible uniform program interfaces, and generalized tools – were the first attacked, and have been solved. Language-specific smart editors are developments not yet widely used in practice, but the most they promise is freedom from syntactic errors and simple semantic errors.

Perhaps the biggest gain yet to be realized from programming environments is the use of integrated database systems to keep track of the myriad details that must be recalled accurately by the individual programmer and kept current for a group of collaborators on a single system.

Surely this work is worthwhile, and surely it will bear some fruit in both productivity and reliability. But by its very nature, the return from now on must be marginal.

Workstations. What gains are to be expected for the software art from the certain and rapid increase in the power and memory capacity of the individual workstation? Well, how many MIPS can one use fruitfully? The composition and editing of programs and documents is fully supported by today's speeds. Compiling could stand a boost, but a factor of 10 in machine speed would surely leave think-time the dominant activity in the programmer's day. Indeed, it appears to be so now.

More powerful workstations we surely welcome. Magical enhancements from them we cannot expect.

Promising Attacks on the Conceptual Essence

Even though no technological breakthrough promises to give the sort of magical results with which we are so familiar in the hardware area, there is both an abundance of good work going on now, and the promise of steady, if unspectacular progress.

All of the technological attacks on the accidents of the software process are fundamentally limited by the productivity equation:

$$time\ of\ task = \sum_i (frequency)_i \times (time)_i$$

22   High-Integrity System Specification and Design

If, as I believe, the conceptual components of the task are now taking most of the time, then no amount of activity on the task components that are merely the expression of the concepts can give large productivity gains.

Hence we must consider those attacks that address the essence of the software problem, the formulation of these complex conceptual structures. Fortunately, some of these attacks are very promising.

Buy versus build. The most radical possible solution for constructing software is not to construct it at all.

Every day this becomes easier, as more and more vendors offer more and better software products for a dizzying variety of applications. While we software engineers have labored on production methodology, the personal-computer revolution has created not one, by many, mass markets for software. Every newsstand carries monthly magazines, which sorted by machine type, advertise and review dozens of products at prices from a few dollars to a few hundred dollars. More specialized sources offer very powerful products for the workstation and other Unix markets. Even software tools and environments can be bought off-the-shelf. I have elsewhere proposed a marketplace for individual modules [9].

Any such product is cheaper to buy than to build afresh. Even at a cost of one hundred thousand dollars, a purchased piece of software is costing only about as much as one programmer-year. And delivery is immediate! Immediate at least for products that really exist, products whose developer can refer products to a happy user. Moreover, such products tend to be much better documented and somewhat better maintained than home-grown software.

The development of the mass market is, I believe, the most profound long-run trend in software engineering. The cost of software has always been development cost, not replication cost. Sharing that cost among even a few users radically cuts the per-user cost. Another way of looking at it is that the use of n copies of a software system effectively multiplies the productivity of its developers by n. That is an enhancement of the productivity of the discipline and of the nation.

The key issue, of course, is applicability. Can I use an available off-the-shelf package to perform my task? A surprising thing has happened here. During the 1950's and 1960's, study after study showed that users would not use off-the-shelf packages for payroll, inventory control, accounts receivable, and so on. The requirements were too specialized, the case-to-case variation too high. During the 1980's, we find such packages in high demand and widespread use. What has changed?

Not the packages, really. They may be somewhat more generalized and somewhat more customizable than formerly, but not much. Not the applications, either. If anything, the business and scientific needs of today are more diverse and complicated than those of 20 years ago.

The big change has been in the hardware/software cost ratio. In 1960, the buyer of a two-million dollar machine felt that he could afford $250,000 more for a customized payroll program, one that slipped easily and nondisruptively into the computer-hostile social environment. Today, the buyer of a $50,000 office machine cannot conceivably afford a customized payroll program, so he adapts the payroll procedure to the packages available. Computers are now so commonplace, if not yet so beloved, that the adaptations are accepted as a matter of course.

There are dramatic exceptions to my argument that the generalization of software packages has changed little over the years: electronic spreadsheets and simple database systems. These powerful tools, so obvious in retrospect and yet so late in appearing, lend themselves to myriad uses, some quite unorthodox. Articles and even books now abound on how to tackle unexpected tasks with the spreadsheet. Large numbers of applications that would formerly have been written as custom programs in Cobol or Report Program Generator are now routinely done with these tools.

Many users now operate their own computers day in and day out on various applications without ever writing a program. Indeed, many of these users cannot write new programs for their machines, but they are nevertheless adept at solving new problems with them.

I believe the single most powerful software-productivity strategy for many organizations today is to equip the computer-naive intellectual workers who are on the firing line with personal computers and good generalized writing, drawing, file, and spreadsheet programs and then to turn them loose. The same strategy, carried out with generalized mathematical and statistical packages and some simple programming capabilities, will also work for hundreds of laboratory scientists.

Requirements refinement and rapid prototyping. The hardest single part of building a software system is deciding precisely what to build. No other part of the conceptual work is as difficult as establishing the detailed technical requirements, including all the interfaces to people, to machines, and to other software systems. No other part of the work so cripples the resulting system if done wrong. No other part is more difficult to rectify later.

Therefore, the most important function that the software builder performs for the client is the iterative extraction and refinement of the product requirements. For the truth is, the client does not know what he wants. The client usually does not know what questions must be answered, and he has almost never thought of the problem in the detail necessary for the specification. Even the simple answer – "Make the new software system work like our old manual information-processing system" – is in fact too simple. One never wants exactly that. Complex software systems are, moreover, things that act, that move, that work. The dynamics of that action are hard to imagine. So in planning any software-design activity, it is necessary to allow for an extensive iteration between the client and the designer as part of the system definition.

I would go a step further and assert that it is really impossible for a client, even working with a software engineer, to specify completely, precisely, and correctly the exact requirements of a modern software product before trying some versions of the product.

Therefore, one of the most promising of the current technological efforts, and one that attacks the essence, not the accidents, of the software problem, is the development of approaches and tools for rapid prototyping of systems as prototyping is part of the iterative specification of requirements.

A *prototype software system* is one that simulates the important interfaces and performs the main functions of the intended system, while not necessarily being bound by the same hardware speed, size, or cost constraints. Prototypes typically perform the mainline tasks of the application, but make no attempt to handle the exceptional tasks, respond correctly to invalid inputs, or abort cleanly. The purpose of the prototype is to make real the conceptual structure specified, so that the client can test it for consistency and usability.

Much of present-day software-acquisition procedure rests upon the assumption that one can specify a satisfactory system in advance, get bids for its construction, have it built, and install it. I think this assumption is fundamentally wrong, and that many software-acquisition problems spring from that fallacy. Hence, they cannot be fixed without fundamental revision – revision that provides for iterative development and specification of prototypes and products.

Incremental development – grow, don't build, software. I still remember the jolt I felt in 1958 when I first heard a friend talk about *building* a program, as opposed to *writing* one. In a flash he broadened my whole view of the software process. The metaphor shift was powerful, and accurate. Today we understand how like other building processes the construction of software is, and we freely use other elements of the metaphor, such as *specifications, assembly of components*, and *scaffolding*.

The building metaphor has outlived its usefulness. It is time to change again. If, as I believe, the conceptual structures we construct today are too complicated to be specified accurately in advance, and too complex to be built faultlessly, then we must take a radically different approach.

Let us turn to nature and study complexity in living things, instead of just the dead works of man. Here we find constructs whose complexities thrill us with awe. The brain alone is intricate beyond mapping, powerful beyond imitation, rich in diversity, self-protecting, and self-renewing. The secret is that it is grown, not built.

So it must be with our software systems. Some years ago Harlan Mills proposed that any software system should be grown by incremental development [10]. That is, the system should first be made to run, even if it does nothing useful except call the proper set of dummy subprograms. Then, bit by bit, it should be fleshed out, with the subprograms in turn being developed – into actions or calls to empty stubs in the level below.

I have seen most dramatic results since I began urging this technique on the project builders in my Software Engineering Laboratory class. Nothing in the past decade has so radically changed my own practice, or its effectiveness. The approach necessitates top-down design, for it is a top-down growing of the software. It allows easy backtracking. It lends itself to early prototypes. Each added function and new provision for more complex data or circumstances grows organically out of what is already there.

The morale effects are startling. Enthusiasm jumps when there is a running system, even a simple one. Efforts redouble when the first picture from a new graphics software system appears on the screen, even if it is only a rectangle. One always has, at every stage in the process, a working system. I find that teams can *grow* much more complex entities in four months than they can *build*.

The same benefits can be realized on large projects as on my small ones [11].

Great designers. The central question in how to improve the software art centers, as it always has, on people.

We can get good designs by following good practices instead of poor ones. Good design practices can be taught. Programmers are among the most intelligent part of the population, so they can learn good practice. Hence, a major thrust in the United States is to promulgate good modern practice. New curricula, new literature, new organizations such as the Software Engineering Institute, all have come into being in order to raise the level of our practice from poor to good. This is entirely proper.

Nevertheless, I do not believe we can make the next step upward in the same way. Whereas the difference between poor conceptual designs and good ones may lie in the soundness of the design method, the difference between good designs and great ones surely does not. Great designs come from great designers. Software construction is a *creative* process. Sound methodology can empower and liberate the creative mind; it cannot inflame or inspire the drudge.

The differences are not minor – they are rather like the differences between Salieri and Mozart. Study after study shows that the very best designers produce structures that are faster, smaller, simpler, cleaner, and produced with less effort [12]. The differences between the great and the average approach an order of magnitude.

A little retrospection shows that although many fine, useful software systems have been designed by committees and built as part of multipart projects, those software systems that have excited passionate fans are those that are the products of one or a few designing minds, great designers. Consider Unix, APL, Pascal, Modula, the Smalltalk interface, even Fortran; and contrast them with Cobol, PL/I, Algol, MVS/370, and MS-DOS. (See Table 1.)

| Exciting Products ||
Yes	No
Unix	Cobol
APL	PL/1
Pascal	Algol
Modula	MVS/370
Smalltalk	MS-DOS
Fortran	

Table 1. Exciting vs. useful but unexciting software products.

Hence, although I strongly support the technology-transfer and curriculum-development efforts now under way, I think the most important single effort we can mount is to develop ways to grow great designers.

No software organization can ignore this challenge. Good managers, scarce though they be, are no scarcer than good designers. Great designers and great managers are both very rare. Most organizations spend considerable effort in finding and cultivating the management prospects; I know of none that spends equal effort in finding and developing the great designers upon whom the technical excellence of the products will ultimately depend.

My first proposal is that each software organization must determine and proclaim that great designers are as important to its success as great managers are, and that they can be expected to be similarly nurtured and rewarded. Not only salary, but the perquisites of recognition – office size, furnishings, personal technical equipment, travel funds, staff support – must be fully equivalent.

How to grow great designers? Space does not permit a lengthy discussion, but some steps are obvious:

- Systematically identify top designers as early as possible. The best are often not the most experienced.
- Assign a career mentor to be responsible for the development of the prospect, and carefully keep a career file.
- Devise and maintain a career-development plan for each prospect, including carefully selected apprenticeships with top designers, episodes of advanced formal education, and short courses, all interspersed with solo-design and technical-leadership assignments.
- Provide opportunities for growing designers to interact with and stimulate each other.

Acknowledgements. I thank Gordon Bell, Bruce Buchanan, Rick Hayes-Roth, Robert Patrick, and, most especially, David Parnas for their insights and stimulating ideas, and Rebekah Bierly for the technical production of this article.

References

1. D.L. Parnas, "Designing Software for Ease of Extension and Contraction," *IEEE Trans. Software Engineering*, Vol. 5, No. 2, Mar. 1979, pp. 128–138.
2. G. Booch, "Object-Oriented Design," *Software Engineering with Ada*, 1983, Benjamin/Cummings, Menlo Park, Calif.
3. *IEEE Trans. Software Engineering* (special issue on artificial intelligence and software engineering), J. Mostow, guest ed., Vol. 11, No. 11, Nov. 1985.
4. D.L. Parnas, "Software Aspects of Strategic Defense Systems," *American Scientist*, Nov. 1985.
5. R. Balzar, "A 15-Year Perspective on Automatic Programming," *IEEE Trans. Software Engineering* (special issue on artificial intelligence and software engineering), J. Mostow, guest ed., Vol. 11, No. 11, Nov. 1985, pp. 1257–1267.

6. *Computer* (special issue on visual programming), R.B. Graphton and T. Ichikawa, guest eds., Vol. 18, No. 8, Aug. 1985.
7. G. Raeder, "A Survey of Current Graphical Programming Techniques," *Computer* (special issue on visual programming), R.B. Graphton and T. Ichikawa, guest eds., Vol. 18, No. 8, Aug. 1985, pp. 11–25.
8. F.P. Brooks, *The Mythical Man-Month*, 1975, Addison-Wesley, Reading, Mass., New York, Chapter 14.
9. Defense Science Board, *Report of the Task Force on Military Software*, in press.
10. H.D. Mills, "Top-Down Programming in Large Systems," in *Debugging Techniques in Large Systems*, R. Ruskin, ed., Prentice-Hall, Englewood Cliffs, N.J., 1971.
11. B.W. Boehm, "A Spiral Model of Software Development and Enhancement," 1985, TRW tech. report 21-371-85, TRW, Inc., 1 Space Park, Redondo Beach, CA 90278.
12. H. Sackman, W.J. Erikson, and E.E. Grant, "Exploratory Experimental Studies Comparing Online and Offline Programming Performance," *CACM*, Vol. 11, No. 1, Jan. 1968, pp. 3–11.

Biting the Silver Bullet

Toward a Brighter Future for System Development

David Harel

Summary.

A "vanilla" approach to modeling, together with powerful notions of executability and code generation, may have a profound impact on the "essence" of developing complex systems.

In an eloquent and thoughtful 1986 article, Frederick Brooks expresses his feelings about the illusions and hopes software engineering offers [1]. He argues that many proposed ideas are not "silver bullets" that will deliver us from the horrors of developing complex systems.

Brooks' article is reminiscent of Parnas' series of minipapers [2] that accompanied his widely publicized resignation from the Strategic Defense Initiative Organization (SDIO) Panel on Computing in 1985. Parnas claims that current proposals are vastly inadequate to build reliable software as complex as that required for the SDI project.

We thus have two rather discouraging position papers, authored by two of the most influential figures in the software world. Neither is a critique of software engineering per se, although both make an effort to dissolve myths of magical power that people have cultivated concerning certain trends in the field.

This article was triggered by those of Brooks and Parnas. It is not a rebuttal. Indeed, I agree with most of the specific points made in both papers. Instead, the goal of this article is to illuminate the brighter side of the coin, emphasizing developments in the field that were too recent or immature to have influenced Brooks and Parnas when they wrote their manuscripts.

© 1992 IEEE. Reprinted by permission.
Reprinted from *IEEE Computer*, 25(1):8–20, January 1992.

The two main aspects of these developments have to do with a carefully wrought "vanilla" approach to system modeling and the emergence of powerful methods to execute and analyze the resulting models. It can be argued that the combined effect of these and other ideas is already showing positive signs and appears to have the potential to provide a truly major improvement in our present abilities – profoundly affecting the essence of the problem. This might take more than the 10 years Brooks focuses on. It will surely be a long time before reliable software for the likes of the SDI project can be built. Such a system remains an order of magnitude too large and too critical to construct today, mainly because of its first-time-must-work nature. But I also believe that we are on the royal (main) road and that the general impression you get from reading the Brooks and Parnas articles is far too bleak.

On Biting Bullets

There are two opinions about the origin of the phrase "Biting the bullet." One is that it came from the need to bite the top off the paper cartridge prior to firing a certain kind of British rifle used in the mid 19th century. This often had to be done under enemy fire and required keeping a cool head.

The other is that it is an old American phrase, rooted in the folklore of the US Civil War. It supposedly emerged from the practice of encouraging a patient who was to undergo field surgery to bite down hard on a lead bullet to "divert the mind from pain and prevent screaming" (R.L. Chapman, *American Slang*, Harper and Row, New York, 1986).

In more recent years, the phrase has come to signify having to do something painful but necessary, or to undertake an activity despite criticism or opposition, while exhibiting a measure of courage and optimism.

Past Versus Present

Brooks' arguments. The main problem, as Brooks rightly sees it, is in specifying, designing, and testing the "conceptual construct" underlying the system being developed, and not in "the labor of representing it and testing the fidelity of the representation."

"The hard thing about building software," he claims "is deciding what one wants to say, not saying it." In elaborating, he mentions the superlinear growth in the number of system states, the difficulty of comprehending the conceptual construct and communicating it to others, and what he believes to be its inherent unvisualizable character.

Brooks further argues that, in contrast to their apparent appeal, several proposed ideas in the field do not constitute magical solutions to the essential problems.

Among the "nonbullets" he discusses are high-level languages, object-oriented programming, artificial intelligence and expert systems, automatic programming, graphical languages, program verification, and hardware improvements.

In his introduction, Brooks says that although he sees no startling breakthroughs in the next decade, "many encouraging innovations are under way," and eventually they will be exploited to "yield an order-of-magnitude improvement."

Brooks mentions two sets of innovations. The first set includes those of the above proposals that he doesn't totally discard (for example, high-level languages and object oriented programming). However, he claims that they deal only with representation issues, which constitute the accidental part of the problem.

The second set of innovations, the ones Brooks claims *will* influence the essence, include

- buying sufficiently general ready-made software, instead of having it tailor-made;
- refining the requirements iteratively and interactively with the client, using increasingly better prototypes;
- enhancing the design in an iterative, top-down fashion, adding lower-level details at each step; and
- finding, hiring, and cultivating extremely talented designers.

Despite the encouraging way the points are expressed, we come away feeling distinctly uncomfortable. Apart from ideas that deal with the accidental parts of the problem, we are told to buy good software from others, hire better people than we already have, and continue with the well-established practices of prototyping and iterative design. All the rest is marginal.

I have discussed Brooks' article with many people over the last few years. Most stated that while they agree with many of its individual points, the paper presents a far gloomier assessment of the situation than seems appropriate. I feel that this is rooted in some of its underlying adopted themes.

The first is the sharp separation between the accidental and essential aspects of the problem, relegating everything related to representation, language, and levels of abstraction to the former and only the process of thinking about the concepts to the latter.

The second is the treatment of each proposed idea in isolation, with the accompanying claim that most of the proposals address representation, so that they cannot help with the essence.

The third involves concentrating on only 10 years of the future, which is probably too short a period in which to expect any significant improvement. (About half of this period is already behind us.)

Finally the discussion is presented as a search for a miracle-working silver bullet that will slay the werewolf of constructing complex software. By arguing that current motifs will not bring about that miracle, at least not within the next few years, we are left with the troubling feeling that the werewolf is here to stay.

We've been there before. Since this article takes a longer term point of view, it is instructive to carry out a brief thought experiment. Let's go back, say 40 years.

That was the time when instead of grappling with the design of large, complex systems, programmers were in the business of developing conventional one-person programs (which would be on the order of 100–200 lines in a modern programming language) that were to carry out limited algorithmic tasks. Given the technology and methodology available then, such tasks were similarly formidable. Failures, errors, and missed deadlines were all around.

Imagine an article appearing then and claiming the essence of the problem to be deciding what one wants to say, that is, conceiving the algorithm. Writing the program is the accidental part. Such an article might have asked about the availability of a one-stroke solution that deals with the essence. From the way the issue is presented, it would follow that any ideas that relate to representation and levels of detail can be discounted, because they deal with the nonessential parts of the problem. The article could very well go on to argue that ideas like high-level programming languages, compilation, and algorithmic paradigms can be safely set aside, since they do not deal with the essence.

However, while none of these ideas alone has solved the problem, and while it did take more than 10 years for the situation to change, we have indeed witnessed an order-of-magnitude advance in our ability to tackle the very essence of designing one-person programs. There is absolutely no comparison between the process of writing a correct and efficient one-person program 40 years ago and now. (Actually, we need not come all the way to 1992; it suffices to compare 1950 with, say, 1975.) The grand sum of the many innovations that have been suggested and pursued in the interim has worked wonders!

Of course the situation isn't perfect. There still is a great deal of bad programming around, and there are lots of incompetent programmers, some terrible programming languages, many misleading methods and guidelines, and widespread ignorance of the fundamentals. Nevertheless, most people would agree that the werewolves of one-person programs are gone, never to return.

Vanilla frameworks. Most instrumental in triggering the revolution in one-person programming has been the evolution of a fitting, general-purpose conceptual framework, which we shall call "vanilla." Its main contribution was to free the programmer from having to think on an inappropriate level of detail, enabling him or her to conceive of an idea for solving an algorithmic problem and to map it easily from the mind into an appropriate high-level medium.

The cornerstone of this framework is a collection of fundamental notions and concepts that includes the basic dichotomy between data and control and convenient means for structuring and combining them into an algorithmic whole. Thus, elementary control structures, data types and data structures were identified, and we learned how to wield them. A rich variety of algorithmic methods was devised, including divide and conquer, dynamic programming, and greedy paradigms; these were adapted to fit a variety of problem sets. Notions of correctness and efficiency were introduced, together with methods for establishing the former and estimating the latter.

In parallel, and based on these concepts, a corresponding set of vanilla high-level programming languages evolved, supported by powerful and sophisticated tools for testing and analyzing. We learned to rely on the theory of computational complexity to help us find efficient algorithms or to detect our stumbling upon an intractable problem; we have begun to understand the great virtues of parallelism, approximation, and randomization in obtaining even better solutions.

Thus, for one-person programs, accidental and essential issues were intimately and unavoidably intertwined.

Of course, as time went by, other flavors, more exotic than vanilla, naturally emerged, such as applicative, functional and, logic programming styles, as well as more esoteric approaches like systolic arrays and neural nets. For each, the basic notions and concepts have had to be redefined, and new languages and tools have been developed. The arsenal has thus grown considerably and has become richer and more varied – a sure sign of healthy evolution.

Back to the future. I believe the current situation is similar, except that we are now in the business of developing very complex systems. These systems are to consist of large amounts of software and hardware and are often of a distributed nature. Their size and complexity, as Brooks and Parnas observe, is formidable when compared to one-person programs. By their very nature they also involve large numbers of technical personnel.

The rest of this article is restricted to a class of systems that has been termed *reactive* [5, 6]. This class includes many kinds of embedded, concurrent, and real-time systems, but excludes data-intensive ones such as databases and management information systems. Reactive systems are widely considered to be particularly problematic, posing some of the greatest challenges in this field.

Building on a solid foundation of time-honored work in software and systems engineering, a number of developments have taken place in the past several years. Although not yet universally accepted as such, I submit that they combine to form the kernel of a solid general-purpose vanilla approach (see the box) to the development of complex reactive systems. Moreover, encouraging research is under way in a number of related fields that has fundamental implications regarding these ideas.

The climate suggests that we stand to witness a grand-scale improvement in the process of constructing such systems. It is hard to predict a time frame for this, but the scope of the benefits it will bring about could very well match the striking changes we have witnessed in solving one-person algorithmic problems.

We now discuss the two components of these developments: means for modeling the system, and techniques for inspecting and analyzing the model.

Modeling the System

To model systems, we need an underlying set of fundamental concepts and notions – some call them "abstractions" – that, in Brooks' terminology, capture the "conceptual construct" of complex systems. Deciding what they are and how they relate is

More on the Vanilla Approach

It is impossible to provide a detailed account of the vanilla approach to modeling in this article. The discussion of it in the text is thus extremely brief. As mentioned, the ideas are based on much early work on the specification and design of nonreactive systems, suitably extended.

The three independent efforts that led to this approach are described, respectively, in the Ward and Mellor book [3], the Hatley and Pirbhai book [4], and in the Harel et al. [5] publication related to the Statemate system.

The latter is less informative on the modeling aspects of the approach than the two books: its main intention was to describe the supporting tool. However, a more detailed description of this modeling framework appears in the following book:

> Harel, D., and M. Politi, "Modeling Reactive Systems with Statecharts: The STATEMATE Approach," McGraw-Hill, New York, 1998.

The following paper compares and evaluates these three research efforts (as well as a related fourth one). It is quite illuminating and emphasizes the differences between them, particularly those relevant to modeling behavior:

> Wood, D.P., and W.G. Wood, "Comparative Evaluations of Four Specification Methods for Real-Time Systems," Tech. Report CMU/SEI-89-TR-36, Software Eng. Inst., Carnegie Mellon Univ., Pittsburgh, 1989.

The following book contains interesting discussions and comparisons of these and other modeling approaches. It also features a valuable annotated bibliography of some 600 items:

> Davis, A.M., *Software Requirements: Analysis and Specification*, Prentice Hall, Englewood Cliffs, N.J., 1990.

analogous to the separation of data and control in the vanilla approach to one-person programs and the identification of appropriate ways of structuring, expressing and combining them. For a nonexotic first cut at the problem, these concepts must be sufficiently general to be widely applicable, even at the expense of being somewhat mediocre. To be amenable to inspection and analysis, they must also be rigorous and precise, with underlying formal semantics.

The vanilla approach is rooted in the early work of Parnas and others on modularization and information hiding [7], and in that of several researchers on structured analysis and structured design [8, 9] that dealt mainly with data-intensive systems. The backbone of the system model should be a hierarchy of *activities*, as we'll call them, that capture the functional capabilities of the system – suitably decomposed to a level with which the designer is happy. (The activities need not be arranged in strict hierarchies. The break-up, or decomposition, may have overlappings, with elements on any level being shared by multiple parent elements. The term "hierarchy" used here thus carries a more flexible connotation.)

Data elements and data stores are also specified therein, and are associated as inputs and outputs that flow between the activities on the various levels. The semantics of this kind of functional description is dynamically non-committing in that it merely asserts that activities *can* be active, information *can* flow, and so on. It does not contain information about what *will* happen, *when* it will happen, or *why* it will happen. As a consequence, this hierarchy can only serve as *part* of a conceptual model for truly reactive systems – such as control and communication systems or embedded real-time systems, which have a crucial behavioral side that has to be addressed, too.

Some time ago, a number of independent research groups extended these widely accepted ideas to deal with reactive systems [3–5]. Their efforts resulted in a surprisingly similar set of conclusions. Using their own terminology and emphasis, they each recommended that the hierarchy of activities be enriched with behavioral descriptions we'll call *control activities*, which potentially appear on all levels.

Control activities serve as the central nervous system, so to speak, of the model. They are meant to sense and control the dynamics of that portion of the functional description on their level. This includes the ability to activate and deactivate activities, cause data to be read and written, and sense when such things have happened – thus affecting subsequent behavior. The resulting combination is the system's *conceptual model*.

The recommendations also call for a structural, or architectural, description of the system to deal with such notions as subsystems and modules, channels and physical links, and storage components. This description can thus be considered the system's *physical model*. The conceptual and physical models are related by a mapping that assigns implementational responsibility for the various parts of the former to those of the latter.

Modeling behavior. While the functional description is the backbone of the conceptual model, the behavioral descriptions (that is, the control activities) are, in a crucial sense, its heart and soul. Behavior over time is much less tangible than either functionality or physical structure, and more than anything else, this is the aspect that renders reactive systems so slippery and error-prone.

In the realm of dynamic behavior, there is a particularly dire need for approaches that are sufficiently clear and well-structured to enable designers to capture their thinking in a coherent and comprehensive fashion. Moreover, behavioral descriptions must possess rigorous underlying semantics; all too often, insufficient attention has been paid to semantics. The discussion of analysis below will show how important this is.

The aforementioned research groups [3-5] more or less agree that behavioral controllers should be described using modes, or states, together with control elements, such as events and conditions, that trigger transitions between them. Implicitly, they have also adopted a subtle abstraction, termed the *synchrony hypothesis* [10], according to which everything takes zero time unless explicitly prescribed otherwise. However, there is no agreement as to exactly how this is to be turned into a workable medium for modeling reactive behavior. It is clear that conventional finite-state machines will not do, due to their lack of structure, their verbosity, and the notorious state-explosion phenomenon.

The basic elements of reactive behavior (states, transitions, events, conditions, and time) must be allowed to be properly and naturally conceptualized, structured, and combined so that fundamental patterns of reactive behavior – like sequentiality, concurrency, and synchronization – will mesh smoothly with the functional decomposition.

A number of solutions have been suggested by these groups. They range from variants of communicating finite-state machines [3, 4], through combinational decision tables and other similar means [4], to a relative newcomer – statecharts [5, 11]. Other formalisms, such as Petri nets, temporal logic [6], or certain languages especially tailored for real-time systems [10], would be reasonable choices too.

Modeling data. Although data-intensive systems are not the subject of this article, a few words regarding the issue of incorporating data modeling into the vanilla framework are in order.

Conventional data elements and data structures can be specified and manipulated in standard ways within behavioral descriptions or in bottom-level activities. To deal with large-scale pools of data such as databases or knowledge-bases, we would have to use a separate data-modeling medium, such as a suitably adapted version of Chen's entity-relationship approach [3, 4, 12]. The resulting descriptions would then be associated with the data stores.

Incorporating data-modeling techniques into the present framework could serve as an excellent melting pot for combining ideas from the world of data-intensive systems with ones from the world of reactive systems.

Strata of conceptual models. Brooks states that descriptions of software that abstract away its complexity often also abstract away its essence – the complexity itself being part of the essence. Obviously, he is right. Indeed, it is important to use the vanilla approach in a way that does not hide the system's essential complexity.

Proper use actually enables harnessing and taming that complexity by allowing the designer to capture the system's inherent conceptual structure in a natural way.

Regardless of how well devised it might be, one conceptual model might not be enough to take us from our initial thoughts to a final working implementation. While it is possible to construct a good functional hierarchy, interweaved with its controlling activities, the mapping we specify between that model and the physical model often turns out to be naive, rarely constituting a satisfactory full-fledged implementation. Consequently, we must often add a new dimension to the modeling process by repeatedly refining the conceptual model.

This can be done by preparing a new tier, or stratum, of functional hierarchies, one for each of the subsystems appearing in the structural view, and providing a lower-level mapping between these refined models and the subsystems themselves. This process may continue downward until a satisfactory level of design is reached.

These ideas are quite in line with Brooks' sympathetic discussion of top-down design. Of course, two crucial parts of this process concern the methodological issue of providing guidelines and heuristics for actually carrying it out, and the technical issue of showing consistency between the resulting strata. These are briefly discussed below.

Visual representation. Most issues of representation have been skirted above; indeed, some justification could be found in giving them second-class status. However, I believe that convenient media for representing the concepts and structures inherent in a model impact the very thinking that goes into constructing that model. In the one-person programming world, the availability of programming languages such as Pascal and C and even their precursors like Fortran, Algol, and PL/I has had a profound influence on a programmer's ability to conceive of good algorithms. Moreover, good representation is also instrumental in communicating those algorithms and their underlying ideas to others.

I agree with Brooks that flowcharts have become pitiful visualizations of programs, and even with a more general claim concerning the hopelessness of finding a general-purpose visual programming language that could replace conventional languages. But this opinion comes to a screeching halt where complex reactive systems are concerned.

Much of the conceptual construct underlying a complex reactive system is inherently topological in nature, and this is reflected in the vanilla approach outlined above. Hierarchies, with or without overlapping, and multilevel relationships, whether they concern structure, function, or behavior, can be captured naturally by simple, rigorous, and well-known notions from set theory and topology: these, in turn, have natural counterparts as spatial/graphical representations.

As argued elsewhere [12], this fact gives rise to *visual formalisms*, in which encapsulation, connectedness, and adjacency play central roles, and lesser features, such as size, shape, and color, can also be exploited. Furthermore, all these graphical features come complete with rigorous mathematical semantics.

Visual formalisms have indeed been proposed for representing the various aspects of vanilla models [3–5, 11, 12]. From several years of following their application in large real-world projects, I have become convinced that using appropriate visual formalisms can have a spectacular effect on engineers and programmers. (An example of this is the avionics system for the state-of-the-art Lavi fighter at Israel Aircraft Industries, where the visual language of statecharts [11] was used for specification. Although these experiences are too recent to have yielded statistics, some comparisons and evaluations have already appeared.)

Moreover, this effect is not limited to mere accidental issues: the quality and expedition of their very *thinking* was found to be improved. Successful system development in the future will revolve around visual representations. We will first conceptualize, using the "proper" entities and relationships, and then formulate and reformulate our conceptions as a series of increasingly more comprehensive models represented in an appropriate combination of visual languages. A combination it must be, since system models have several facets, each of which conjures up different kinds of mental images.

Of course, the job is far from complete. Some aspects of the modeling process have not been as forthcoming as others in lending themselves to good visualization. Algorithmic operations on variables and data structures, for example, will probably remain textual. In addition, as Brooks aptly observes, some of the less obvious connections between the various parts of system models are not easily visualized. However, for a number of years, we have been doing far, far better than the "several, general directed graphs superimposed one upon another" Brooks describes. The graphical languages currently used are still two-dimensional, whereas some of the concepts could definitely do with higher dimensional visualization. This may still happen. In fact, realistic motion-based 3D techniques are rapidly coming into reach. A new aspect of visual languages that will have to be addressed is computerized support for the "nice looking" layout of diagrams. This is a difficult and challenging problem in which only marginal progress has been made.

Regarding hardware, our scopes are currently of limited scope, to use Brooks' captivating phrase, making the extent to which we can comfortably display very large visual models dependent on the availability of dramatically improved graphical hardware. Rather than taking this as a reason to abandon visual approaches, we should find it enlightening. For once, concepts and software ideas are ahead, waiting for the development of matching hardware. If the past record of hardware improvements is any measure, these developments will not be long in coming.

It is our duty to forge ahead to turn system modeling into a predominantly visual and graphical process. I believe this is one of the most promising trends in our field.

Methods and guidelines. In addition to thinking with the "right" concepts and representing the resulting thoughts in appropriate programming languages, a programmer can call on a variety of well-established methods, guidelines, and techniques to help formulate a good solution to a one-person algorithmic problem. These constitute a large reservoir of knowledge accumulated over years, embodying the experience and expertise of generations of programmers, algorithmic designers, and computer scientists. As might be expected, there has always been a great deal of cross fertilization between the world of methods and techniques and the world of concepts and languages.

The story for complex reactive systems is no different, except that it is at a far more embryonic stage. Despite the proliferation of so-called methodologies, it is still too early to see a wide-ranging and well-understood collection of guidelines and techniques for the step-by-step process of system development.

Many of the proposed methodologies are not methodologies at all in that they do not contain recommendations about how to actually do things. For that matter, the vanilla approach described here is not a methodology either. However, what is worse is that many *do* prescribe recipes, but these often suffer from being too restrictive, hard to apply, or downright wrong.

One of the most unfortunate trends has been in presenting a method as exclusive, that is, preaching about its being *the* step-by-step way to develop entire systems. This can be compared in naiveté to someone advocating divide-and-conquer or branch-and-bound as *the* method to write programs.

The availability of a solid, general-purpose framework within which one can conceptualize, capture, and represent a system model seems to be far more important right now. All-encompassing recipes for how to get the work done simply do not exist; guidelines and techniques that work in special cases do exist, and more will surface in time. Obviously, they will be influenced by the choice of the framework and will, in turn, influence that framework and its evolution. And they will draw heavily on our experience in wielding the notions, concepts, languages, and tools.

Among the guidelines suggested are top-down and bottom-up approaches, which prescribe the raw order of things, as well as approaches related to the nature of the elements that are to drive the process, such as state-driven, function-driven, or data driven techniques.

In principle, all of these can be followed quite smoothly within the vanilla framework, though constructing really good models, as well as choosing which of these guidelines to use for what systems, will obviously remain something of an art.

Some methods are further removed from the vanilla framework, since they advocate a somewhat different set of basic concepts. One of the better-known examples is the object-oriented approach, in which objects and their capabilities take precedence over activities and states. While it *is* possible to follow this approach within the confines of our basic framework, it's perhaps not as smooth-going as one would like. This is an excellent example of a more specialized, or exotic, flavor, which is already resulting in correspondingly specialized advances in languages and tools.

In addition to guidelines for the overall process of development, a number of heuristics have been addressed at the nontrivial process of mapping the conceptual model onto the physical one. They are often based on taking subtle advantage of the cohesion and coupling of activities [4, 7].

For pure software systems, this task is usually less perplexing, since the structure of the final product can be taken to correspond reasonably well with that of the conceptual model. However, embedded systems are different. In them, the physical break-up into components and subcomponents might be acutely orthogonal to the conceptual structure. These cases require more iterations in the design process, giving rise to several strata of physical and conceptual models, as discussed above. The importance of such heuristics stems from such cases. (These heuristics could well find their way into useful expert-system support tools, as envisioned by Brooks.)

Designers would do well to master all of these techniques, guidelines, and heuristics and to use them to devise models in a manner that they deem most natural. In time, I'm certain we will outgrow the deep convictions we have cultivated around the various methodologies. We will stop trying to get everyone to use them exclusively for all systems, and they will reduce to their proper dimensions – taking their place side by side in our bag of tricks, just as conventional algorithmic methods have for one-person programs.

Analyzing the Model

The preceding sections have repeatedly invoked the analogy between conventional algorithms and models of complex systems. When it comes to semantics and analysis, this analogy takes on a particularly interesting twist.

Although the importance of testing and analyzing one-person algorithms has always been acknowledged, the world of complex systems has long suffered from something of an indifference to such needs. By analogy, the situation was as if we were asked to solve one-person algorithmic problems without the possibility of running programs, and hence without being able to test and debug them at all.

Indeed, many past approaches to system development provided no means for capturing behavior, being centered instead on the functional aspects and dataflow. The approaches that did provide such means were informal, lacking the rigorous semantics necessary for even beginning to analyze the dynamics. Hence, it was impossible to predict in early stages how the system would behave if constructed according to the model.

Not until actual code was written – usually at a very late stage in the project by people other than those responsible for and capable of developing the "conceptual construct" and at much greater expense – could one expect to get reliable answers to "what if?" questions. This, of course, has had a deplorable effect on the expedition and quality of development efforts for large and complex systems.

As a consequence, most computerized tools that flourished around such methods (computer-aided software engineering – CASE – tools, as they are often called) concentrated on providing mere graphic-editing capabilities, sometimes accompanied by document generation, version control and project management facilities. Their proponents heralded the ability of these tools to check model "consistency and completeness," which is really just a grand form of syntax checking.

To use my analogy again, it is like making sure, in a conventional program, that the begins and ends match, that procedure calls have the right number and types of parameters, and that all declared variables are indeed used. In the complex system arena, such checking includes the consistency of level-labeling schemes and of inputs and outputs within the hierarchies, the nonredundancy of flow elements, and so on; it is analogous to the checking carried out in one-person programming environments on-the-fly or in simple precompilation stages.

Since designing a complex reactive system is so much more massive and intricate an undertaking than writing a conventional one-person program, testing for consistency and completeness in system modeling is far more important than syntax checking in programs. Nevertheless, it remains a mere test of the syntactic integrity of the model and has very little to do with that model's conceptual and logical aspects.

Checking that a model is consistent and complete cannot prevent logical errors that cause a missile to fire unintentionally or a stock market system to run amok – exactly the kinds of mishaps that are at the heart of our problem. For this, we need the ability to carry out *real* testing and analysis.

You may feel that the following discussion is unrealistically futuristic. Not so. All the possibilities we mention have been implemented in a computerized tool that supports the vanilla approach and that is being used in the development of real systems [5]. Several other tools also support some of these possibilities (see the "Tools for Model Execution" box.)

None of the implementations is perfect; each requires improvements and extensions. However, they do corroborate the feasibility of the ideas summarized below. In fact, since many of these ideas are standard practice in the world of conventional programming, the tools appear to be the first complex system analogs of useful general-purpose programming environments.

Model execution. One of the most interesting notions to come out of recent work in systems engineering is that of *executable specifications* or, to fit in better with the terminology used here, *executable models*. Executing a model is analogous to running a program directly, with the aid of an interpreter. Unfortunately, the term has been erroneously equated with the animation of diagrams only. However, executability is in fact many-sided and far more significant.

A prerequisite to executing complex system models is the availability of a formal semantics for those models – most notably, for the medium that captures the behavioral view. Thus, while the adjective "visual" in the term "visual formalism" [12] was justified earlier on grounds pertaining to model representation, the word "formalism" is justified now on grounds pertaining to model analysis.

The core of model execution is the ability to carry out a single step of the system's dynamic operation, with all consequences taken into account. During a step, the environment can generate external events, change the truth values of conditions, and update variables and other data elements. Such changes then affect the status of the system; they trigger state changes in the controllers, activate and deactivate activities, modify conditions and variables, and so on. In turn, each of these changes can cause many others, often yielding intricate chain reactions.

A semantics for the model must contain sufficient information to capture these ramifications precisely. Given the current status and the changes made by the environment, calculating the effect of a step usually involves complicated algorithmic procedures, which are derived from, and reflect, that semantics.

Tools for Model Execution

Although model execution is not a new idea, its vast potential has not yet been fully exploited. All the executability features discussed in the text are available in the Statemate tool [5], the first release of which was developed between 1984 and 1987. It is currently being used mainly in the areas of avionics, telecommunications, and process control.

A number of additional tools support some of these features. A couple of them are commercially available, and others are still in research and development stages. Here are a few additional publications describing techniques and tools for executing models:

Diaz-Gonzalez, J., and J. Urban, "Prototyping Conceptual Models of Real-Time Systems: A Visual Perspective," *Proc. 22nd Hawaii Int'l Conf. System Sciences*, IEEE CS Press, Los Alamitos, Calif., Order No. 1912, 1989, pp. 358–367.

Jensen, K., "Computer Tools for Construction, Modification, and Analysis of Petri Nets," *Advances in Petri Nets, Part II,* W. Brauer, W. Reisig, and G. Rozenberg, eds., Lecture Notes in Computer Science, Vol. 255, Springer-Verlag, New York, 1987, pp. 4–19.

Pulli, P.J., "Pattern-Directed Real-Time Execution of SA/RT Specifications", *Proc. Euromicro Workshop on Real-Time*, IEEE CS Press, Los Alamitos, Calif., Order No. 1956, 1989, pp. 3–9.

Wang, Y., "A Distributed Specification Model and its Prototyping," *IEEE Trans. Software Eng.*, Vol. 14, No. 8, Aug. 1988, pp. 1,090–1,097.

Zave, P., and W. Schell, "Salient Features of an Executable Specification Language and its Environment," *IEEE Trans. Software Eng.*, Vol. 12, No. 2, Feb. 1986, pp. 312–325.

Interactive and batch execution. The simplest way to execute, or "run," the model using a computerized tool is in a step-by-step interactive fashion. At each step, the user emulates the system's environment by generating events and changing values. The tool, in turn, responds by transforming the system into the new resulting status. If the model is represented visually, the change in status will also be reflected visually, say, by changes in color or emphasis in the diagrams.

Once we have the basic ability to execute a step, our appetite grows. We might now want to see the model executing noninteractively. To check, for example, that a telephone call connects when it should, we can prepare the relevant sequence of events and signals in a batch file, set up the model to start in the initial status, and ask our tool to execute steps iteratively, reading in the changes from the file. The graphic feedback from such a batch execution becomes an (often quite appealing) animation of the diagrams.

By executing scenarios that reflect the way we expect our system to behave, we are able to verify that it will indeed do so – long before final implementation. If we find that the system's response is not as expected, we may go back to the model, change it, and run the same scenario again. This is analogous to single-step – or batch – debugging of conventional programs.

It should be emphasized that scenarios can be run at any time in the development effort, as long as the portion of interest is syntactically legal. During an execution, the user plays the role of all parts of the model that are external to the portion being executed, even if those parts will eventually be specified and thus become internal.

Again, from several years of seeing such execution capabilities used, mainly in large aerospace and electronic industries, I have become convinced of their value (again, no statistics are yet available to quantify this impression, although a couple of preliminary case studies have appeared). These execution capabilities appear to introduce an entirely new and powerful dimension into the task of verifying and debugging system models.

I have seen model executions uncovering hitherto unknown patterns of behavior, when the members of the development team thought they had covered everything. As a result, these people were able to discuss deep behavioral issues that would otherwise have been swept under a rug of enormous unreadable specification documents.

I have seen engineers use executability to tackle crucial problems and, very early in the project, correct subtle conceptual errors – ones that could otherwise go undiscussed or undetected until it was too late. And typically, all these phenomena start to take place as soon as the first executions are run.

Customer representatives are often involved in these stages, which further supports what Brooks and others have urged: extensive prototyping and simulation of the system early on with the client.

Programmed execution. Our appetite now becomes even greater. We now might ask ourselves: If the tool can execute the model in detail, reading events in from a file, why should we be satisfied with merely witnessing the run in action and inspecting the final status? We would like to be able to incorporate breakpoints, causing the execution to suspend and the tool to take certain actions when particular situations come up. These actions can range from temporarily entering interactive mode (in order to monitor careful step-by-step progress) to executing a piece of ready-made code that describes a bottom-level activity.

In fact, we need not restrict ourselves to running self-devised scenarios. We might want to see the model executing under circumstances that we do not care to specify in detail. We might like to see its performance under *random* conditions and in both typical and less-than-typical situations. Such a capability gets to the heart of the need for an executable model: to minimize the unpredictable in the development of complex systems.

This more powerful notion of inspecting a model is achieved by the idea of *programming executions*, using a special metalanguage supported by the tool. Programs in this language (which might be appropriately termed an *execution control language*) can be set up to look out for predefined breakpoints and accumulate information regarding the system's progress as it takes place.

As a simple example, in a typical flight of an aircraft we are specifying, we might want to know how many times the radar loses a locked-on-target. Since it might be difficult for the engineer to put together a typical flight scenario, we can tap the power of our tool by instructing it to run many typical scenarios, using the accumulated results to calculate average-case information.

The tool follows typical scenarios by generating random numbers to select new events according to predefined probability distributions. The statistics are then gathered using appropriate breakpoints and simple arithmetical operations. The ideas behind these techniques are, of course, well known. However, the point is to extend them to conceptual models of complex systems, long before the costly final-implementation stages.

In a similar vein, we can use programmed executions to apply other, more powerful kinds of dynamic tests to system models. For example, we might set up an execution control program to carry out performance analysis. If we want to check whether an operating system we are modeling will ever require more main memory than some maximum allowed value, we can associate with the relevant activities in the functional view values that represent our knowledge about their memory consumption. We can then program the tool to run many typical scenarios, calculating the maximum memory consumption of all activities that are active simultaneously.

Despite its being applied to a system model, and not to a final implementation, this approach to analysis is far more informative than the extraction of worst-case estimates from simple graphs of process dependencies. The model being analyzed will (hopefully) be realistic and detailed, and executing it reflects precisely what would have happened had we run the real system instead.

If our analysis shows that the memory limit might indeed be exceeded, the tool can support that prediction by supplying the actual sequence of events that would cause it. Clearly, by replacing memory values with time information, similarly meaningful timing analysis can be carried out as well.

In general, then, carefully programmed executions can be used to inspect and debug the system model under a wide range of test data to emulate both the environment and the as-yet-unspecified parts of the system and to analyze the model for performance and efficiency.

Exhaustive executions. When executing the model, we might detect such unpleasant anomalies as deadlocks or behavioral ambiguities (nondeterminism). However, finding and eliminating these in the cases that we happen to encounter does not ensure they will never occur in the lifetime of the system. It would be extremely useful to be able to run through all possible scenarios in search of such situations, by generating all possible external events and all changes in the values of conditions and variables.

We might also be interested in *reachability tests*, which would determine whether – when started in some given initial situation – the system can ever reach a situation in which some specified condition becomes true. This condition can be made to reflect desired or undesired situations. Moreover, we could imagine the test's being set up to report on the first scenario it finds that leads to the specified condition, or to report on all possible ones, producing the details of the scenarios themselves. We thus arrive at the idea of *exhaustive executions*.

Are such tests realistic? Could we subject the model to an exhaustive reachability test, for example, after which we will know for sure whether there is any possibility of its occurring under any possible circumstances? The answer, in principle, is yes, but with serious reservations. The number of possibilities that might have to be considered in an exhaustive execution can easily become incredibly large, even if we ensure that it is finite by limiting the possible values of the variables.

To get a feel for the size involved, a behavioral model that contains about 40 concurrent components, each with about 10 states, has more state configurations and, hence, might have more possible scenarios than the number of elementary particles in the entire universe. There can never be a language, method, or tool with which one can, in general, consider all of these in any reasonable amount of time.

This doesn't mean, however, that such tests are a bad idea.

First, the above numbers denote worst-case asymptotic estimates; a real system might very well have far fewer scenarios that can actually happen, and a careful process of considering only those that are feasible will take far less time than the worst-case estimate.

In fact, just such a reachability test was recently applied to a model of the firing mechanism of a certain, already deployed, ballistic missile system. (The Statemate system [5] was used for this. The main part of the underlying model consisted of a statechart [11] with about 80 states. However, since these included parallel state components, the real number of states was much larger.) In less than three hours on a standard workstation, the test terminated, in the process discovering a new sequence of events, unknown to the design team, that leads to the firing of the missile!

Second, exhaustive tests can be run on small, critical, and well-isolated parts of the model. We can instruct the tool to ignore some of the external events or to avoid simulating the details of certain activities. Clearly, this can cause it to overlook crucial situations, but the advantage is that the set of scenarios it considers is greatly reduced. To maximize the test's effectiveness, such limiting constraints should be prepared very carefully, using as much knowledge of the modeled system as possible. This is another place where expert systems might come in handy.

Third, even if exhaustive tests cannot always be completed in reasonable amounts of time, it would be wise to have them run in the background, perhaps at night or on weekends, for as long as we can afford. There is nothing wrong with routinely submitting large system models to powerful supercomputers for exhaustive testing, even non-exhaustively. Since the tool can be set up to report on phenomena as they are discovered, the more time we observe such tests running without surprises the more confidence we have in the integrity of our model.

Watchdogs and temporal verification. Often, we are interested in establishing properties of the model that are of a global nature but are more involved than reachability or freedom from deadlock. Suppose we want to make sure that a certain party in a communication protocol never sends two consecutive messages unless a special item, say, an acknowledgement, is sent in the interim.

Although seemingly more complicated, this query can be cast in the form of a reachability test in the following way. First, construct a small special-purpose "piece" of behavioral specification that is carefully set up to enter a special state if and when the offending situation occurs. Next, attach this *watchdog*, as it is called, to the original model as a concurrent behavioral component and run a reachability test on the extended model to find out whether the special state can ever be entered. Since the watchdog runs in parallel with the rest of the model, the effect will be as desired.

Watchdogs can be used to verify the model against a wide variety of properties. *Temporal logic* [6], one of the most useful and well-known media for specifying global constraints on the behavior of a system, nicely complements modeling approaches that specify behavior in a more local, operational fashion. Under certain technical conditions, any temporal logic formula can be systematically translated into a watchdog, reducing the problem of verifying the complicated formula to that of establishing a much simpler property, such as reachability. The watchdog is then attached to the high-level controlling activity of the original model, resulting in a modified model, and an appropriate exhaustive test is run.

Actually, such verification need not be based solely on exhaustive executions. Research into the theory and technology of automatic verification of very large (but finite-state) systems against properties in temporal logic is already showing promising results. The techniques being developed in this area are far more subtle and efficient than brute-force exhaustive executions, and I believe that they will eventually find their way into system analysis tools. This direction of work might very well bring true system verification into the living room, so to speak.

Code generation. Even in its most advanced forms, executability is analogous to running conventional programs using *interpretation*. Complex systems are also amenable to the analog of *compilation* – that is, translating a model into a runnable code in a lower level language. We call this ability *code generation*, although the term is often used to denote the more humble ability to recast an unadorned functional description as a template of code that contains empty-body procedures for the controllers and the bottom-level activities. However, since the behavioral view does not exist (or is not covered) in such cases, the resulting code is but a scaffold that has to be enriched by handwritten code for the most crucial parts – notably, those that depict the dynamics. It is thus like an automobile without an engine. The notion we have in mind here is far stronger. (Indeed, new terms, such as *codifier* and *codification*, might be more appropriate than *code generator* and *code generation*.)

Using the vanilla approach terminology discussed earlier, we are talking about the translation of an entire conceptual model, that is, an activity hierarchy with all of its add-ons, including the controlling statecharts, into a programming language such as C, Modula 2, or Ada.

If the model contains bottom-level activities that were left unspecified, but have library routines or specially prepared code supplied by the user, this code can be linked to the code generator's output, thus completing the picture. Since the behavioral aspects are an integral part of the conceptual model, they too are included in the translation. Hence, the resulting code can be run as is and, in terms of its dynamic semantics, is equivalent to the model itself. Needless to say, as in model execution, code generation can be carried out on any syntactically legal portion of the model and at any stage of its development.

Generated code is sometimes referred to as *prototype code*, since it reflects only the design decisions made in the process of preparing the conceptual model, and not decisions driven by implementation concerns. In many real-time applications, this code is not as efficient as the required real-time code. Nevertheless, it runs much faster than executions of the raw model itself, just as compiled code usually runs faster than an interpreted program.

Using generated code. One of the main uses of code-generator output is in observing the system performing under close-to-real world circumstances. For example, the code can be ported to, and executed in, the actual target environment or, as is often the case in earlier stages, in a simulated version of the target environment.

The code can be linked to "soft" panels – graphical mock-ups of control boards, complete with images of display screens, switches, dials, and gauges – that represent the actual user interface of the final system. These panels appear on the screen and can be manipulated with mouse and keyboard.

In the past few years, a number of companies have used this approach in design reviews involving customers and contractors, and it has proved to be extremely helpful – much more so than the typical documentation that accompanies such reviews.

It's important to point out that these system interface panels are not driven by hastily written code prepared especially for prototype purposes, but by code that was generated automatically from a model that is typically thoroughly tested and analyzed before being subjected to code generation. Moreover, when parts of the real target environment are available, they too can be linked to the code, and the runs become even more realistic.

Code generation is thus to be used for goals that go beyond the development team, in that code-driven mock-ups can be used as part of the standard communication between customer and contractor or contractor and subcontractor. It is not unreasonable that such a running version of the system model be a required deliverable in certain development stages.

A good code-generation facility would also have a debugging mechanism, with which the user can trace the executing parts of the code back up to the system model. Breakpoints can be inserted to stop the run when specified events occur, at which point the model's status can be examined and elements can be modified on-the-fly before resuming the run.

If substantial problems arise, changes can be made in the original model, which is then recompiled down into code and rerun. As in executions, trace files can be requested, recording crucial information for future inspection. Carrying the analogy between compilation and code generation a step further, this ability is tantamount to source-level debugging.

In addition to compiling, or codifying, the model itself, we can automatically produce code from specially prepared segments of behavior, such as watchdogs or test suites that are not part of the model but are used to execute and analyze it. For these, of course, the code generator output is actually final code.

An interesting variation calls for replacing high-level programming languages as the target medium for generated code by hardware description languages. A particular example is VHDL (which stands for VHSIC hardware description language, with VHSIC the abbreviation for very high-speed integrated circuit). In this way, hardware designers can also benefit from the virtues of the modeling and analysis techniques discussed above, and then translate their models into VHDL code, which can be subjected to silicon compilation or other appropriate procedures.

Verifying consistency between levels. Recall the process of preparing tiers, or strata, of conceptual models according to the physical model of the system. How can we establish the consistency of one level with the next?

There are a number of ways in which model-analysis techniques can help. The basic idea is to redirect the efforts from the task of inspecting and debugging a single model to the task of comparing two models. This applies to all manner of analysis and verification: interactive, programmed, and exhaustive execution; watchdogs and temporal verification; and code generation.

For example, we may execute the conceptual model prepared for a subsystem under the same conditions used to execute the original model of the entire system, and compare the results. One way to do this involves preparing scenarios for executing the new model directly from trace files of executions run on the original model. Clearly, this is not as simple as it sounds, and much research on this topic is still needed.

As far as code generation goes, we can often replace parts of the code generated from the original model by code generated from the newly designed subsystem models. If the final system is to be implemented in software, this has the effect of gradually bringing the original prototype code down toward a real implementation.

As subsystems are remodeled, their generated code is incorporated into the code that was generated one level higher. As more and more of the code becomes final production code, the entire system comes closer to its final form.

It is not out of the question that this process will also become amenable to computerization. We can envision a user making restructuring decisions in the design states (perhaps aided by an expert system) and the tool taking over from there, reorganizing the generated code in new, more efficient ways that reflect those decisions.

Combined with optimization procedures, which are badly needed and will hopefully be developed in the future, code generation has a chance to go far beyond prototyping, further justifying its role as the true complex system analog of conventional compilation.

The vanilla framework for system modeling outlined above is far from being universally accepted. Many of is facets are rooted in well-established and familiar ideas, but others are more recent and immature and require further work and experience.

On some issues, there is little agreement among researchers and practitioners, such as how to best approach the specification of behavior. I believe that the general framework is a good one and that there are also adequate proposals for behavioral specification. However, even the overall mold could easily turn out to be inadequate.

If it does not become the accepted analog of good old vanilla programming, then some other approach will. The precise form the winning effort takes on will be secondary, though I am fully convinced that reactive behavior will be one of its most crucial and delicate components, rigorous semantics included, and that visuality will play center stage. From this basic framework will evolve more specialized and exotic ones, for which appropriate modeling languages will be designed and implemented and methods and guidelines conceived and mastered.

Things are far clearer in the analysis realm, where most of the abilities we have discussed are, to some extent, independent of the idiosyncrasies of the particular modeling approach. I believe that system development tools that lack powerful execution and code-generation capabilities will all but disappear.

Whichever approach people ultimately use to conceptualize and model their systems, the ability to thoroughly execute the resulting models and to compile them down into conventional high-level code will become indispensable. In a way, this too is vanilla. I believe that in time more exotic kinds of executability features will emerge, such as ones tailored to carry out timing and performance analysis, gather statistics, or compare the behavioral aspects of separate models.

A number of research directions present themselves, and in some there is already a promising body of work. Among the most important are

(1) improving the techniques for generating high-quality code from conceptual models, and providing (semi)automated help to make design decisions in the process, and
(2) enabling truly useful computerized verification of conceptual models against global constraints.

One of the crucial ingredients for success in these areas is extensive cooperation and collaboration of researchers in software and systems engineering with those in compilers, optimization, and heuristics for item (1) and in logic, semantics, and verification for item (2).

The current situation and the prospects for significant improvement indicate that we are at the start of a new and exciting era.

Acknowledgements. Discussions over the years with Amir Pnueli, Michal Politi, Rivi Sherman, and Moshe Cohen were extremely beneficial in helping me form the opinions voiced in this article. I am indebted to Derek J. Hatley, C.A.R. Hoare, Daniel Jackson, Ray Moritz, David L. Parnas, and the anonymous referees for commenting on a preliminary version of this material. This research was supported in part by grants from the Gutwirth Foundation and the Yeda Foundation for Applied Research.

References

1. F.P. Brooks, Jr., "No Silver Bullet: Essence and Accidents of Software Engineering," *Computer*, Vol. 20, No. 4, Apr. 1987, pp. 10–19. Also appeared in *Information Processing 86*, H.-J. Kugler, ed., Elsevier Science Publishers B.V., North-Holland, 1986, pp. 1,069–1,076.
2. D.L. Parnas, "Software Aspects of Strategic Defense Systems," *Comm. ACM*, Vol. 28, No. 12, 1985, 1,326–1,335. Also in *Am. Scientist*, Vol. 73, No. 5, 1985, pp. 432–440.
3. P. Ward and S. Mellor, *Structured Development for Real-Time Systems*, Vols. 1–3, Yourdon Press, New York, 1985.
4. D.J. Hatley and I. Pirbhai, *Strategies for Real-Time System Specification*, Dorset House, New York, 1987.
5. D. Harel et al., "Statemate: A Working Environment for the Development of Complex Reactive Systems," *IEEE Trans. Software Eng.*, Vol. 16, No. 4, Apr. 1990, pp. 403–414. Preliminary version in *Proc. 10th Int'l Conf. Software Eng.*, IEEE CS Press, Los Alamitos, Calif., Order No. 849 (microfiche only), 1988, pp. 396–406.
6. A. Pnueli, "Applications of Temporal Logic to the Specification and Verification of Reactive Systems: A Survey of Current Trends," *Current Trends in Concurrency*, de Bakker et al., eds., Lecture Notes in Computer Science, Vol. 224, Springer-Verlag, Berlin, 1986, pp. 510–584.
7. D.L. Parnas, "On the Criteria to be Used in Decomposing Systems," *Comm. ACM*, Vol. 15, No. 5, 1972, pp. 1,053–1,058.
8. T. DeMarco, *Structured Analysis and System Specification*, Yourdon Press, New York, 1978.
9. L.L. Constantine and E. Yourdon, *Structured Design*, Prentice Hall, Englewood Cliffs, N.J., 1979.

10. G. Berry and G. Gonthier, "The Esterel Synchronous Programming Language: Design, Semantics, Implementation," to appear in *Science of Computer Programming*, North Holland. Also in INRIA Research Report 842, 1988.
11. D. Harel, "Statecharts: A Visual Formalism for Complex Systems," *Science of Computer Programming*, North-Holland, Vol. 8, No. 3, 1987, pp. 231–274. Preliminary version appeared as Tech. Report CS84-05, Weizmann Inst. of Science Rehovot, Israel, 1984.
12. D. Harel, "On Visual Formalisms," *Comm. ACM*, Vol. 31, No. 5, 1988, pp. 514–530.

2. Structured Methods

In the early 1960s, as it became obvious that computer systems would be developed by teams of professionals rather than by individual programmers, and that as the functionality required would push available resources to the limit, more appropriate specification and design methods (as discussed in the previous Part) were needed.

Various notations and techniques that had evolved for use by programmers, such as structured text, pseudo-code and flow-charts were useful for individual programs, but insufficient for use in large scale *system* development. For this reason, a number of new notations and techniques evolved during the 1960s and '70s to aid in the description, specification and design of computer systems.

These techniques were generally referred to as *structured techniques* or (when applied at the analysis phase of system development) *structured analysis techniques* because they based the design of the system on structural decomposition and emphasized structured programming [142]. As more and more notations evolved, proposals were made to combine them in various ways to provide complete descriptions of a system, and a *structured method* of development.

2.1 Structured Notations

Development methods such as Yourdon [262], Structured Design [261] and the Structured Systems Analysis and Design Methodology (SSADM) [56] are in fact unifying approaches, drawing together various structured notations, together with Hierarchy Charts, Decision Tables, Data Dictionaries, Structured English, etc., in an attempt to devise a coherent methodology.

Such methodologies vary in the notations that they see as essential, and in the emphasis they place on different techniques; there are also minor syntactic differences in their representation of various constructs.

Methodology: the Experts Speak (reprinted here) is a unique paper in that it provides an overview of various methodologies and notations, with the descriptions being written by the actual originators of the methodologies [199].

Ken Orr differentiates between a *method* and a *methodology*, which is strictly speaking the study of methods. He gives a detailed account of the history of the development of what has become known as the Warner-Orr method (more correctly named *Data-Structured Systems Development*, or DSSD), and how it relates to various other techniques and approaches. The name itself emphasizes the application of the approach to information systems and the reliance on the description of a system according to the structure of its data. As such, *Entity diagrams* describing relationships between entities (objects of concern in the system) play a major rôle, with *Assembly-line diagrams* describing logical flows through the system.

Chris Gane describes the approach co-developed with Trish Sarson, which emphasizes the use of Entity-Relationship Diagrams (ERDs) and Data-Flow Diagrams (DFDs). The ERD (described in more detail by Peter Chen) describes the logical relationships between entities and their attributes (data) in a representation-independent manner, but focusing on the structure of the data to be stored. The DFD, as the name suggests, focuses on the flow of data through a system, delimiting the system by considering only the relevant data flows. DFDs are written at various levels of abstraction, with the top level, or context diagram, defining the scope of the system. More and more detailed levels are derived, with a 'bubble' representing a process, and arrows representing the flow of data. Each process can be broken down into a more detailed DFD showing its structure and the flow of data within it. This process continues, in a *top-down* fashion, until the process is at a level at which it can be described in pseudo-code or structured text.

Edward Yourdon describes partitioning a system in terms of DFDs, and the rôle of DFDs in the Yourdon method, while Larry Constantine describes the Structured-Design Approach, which emphasizes the use of models (design methods), measures of system cohesion and complexity, and methods of development. He describes the need for tool support and automation in the application of structured methods, and overviews the rôle of CASE (Computer-Aided Software Engineering) technology, which is described in more detail in Part 9.

Most of the structured methods in popular usage have evolved to meet the needs of information systems (one of the primary applications of computers in the 1960s), although most have been extended to meet the needs of concurrent and real-time systems, with the addition of State-Transition Diagrams (STDs) and other notations to address changes in state, causality, etc. One method however, Jackson System Development (JSD), was developed with concurrency and the requirements of control systems specifically in mind.

2.2 The Jackson Approach

With the introduction of JSP (Jackson Structured Programming) [142], Michael Jackson greatly simplified the task of program design. The success of his approach lies in its intuitiveness and the simple graphical notation that facilitates the design of programs which obey the laws of structured programming – that use only the simple constructs of sequence, selection and iteration, and avoid the 'harmful' goto statement [69] or its equivalent.

Eight years later, with the evident need to address *system design* rather than merely program design, Jackson introduced JSD, or Jackson System Development (often erroneously, but still appropriately, referred to as Jackson Structured Design), which has had a major influence on many subsequent development methods, in particular on both structured and formal methods intended for use in the development of concurrent systems.

In his paper *An Overview of JSD* (reprinted here), John Cameron describes the method, with many examples illustrating its application from analysis through to implementation [55].

The method incorporates JSP itself, in that JSP descriptions of each program or *process* in the system are combined by placing such processes running in parallel and in communication over various types of buffered communication channels. As such, the description of a system is at two levels – each process is described in terms of JSP, while the entire system is described as a network of such processes, executing independently. A process becomes suspended when it requires a particular input, and resumes again when that input is available to it.

As the method does not address process scheduling, clearly a certain degree of non-determinism is inherent [137]. Although it is considered inappropriate in conventional programming languages, non-determinism can be advantageous in system design. JSD also supports high levels of abstraction in that there are generally more processes in the network than available processors in the implementation environment. In the implementation phase of JSD, the number of processes in the network is reduced, often just to a single process (for execution in a single processor environment).

Methodology: The Experts Speak

Ken Orr, Chris Gane, Edward Yourdon, Peter P. Chen and Larry L. Constantine

Summary.

Five prominent software engineers discuss the methodologies for which they are famous.

1. The Warnier/Orr Approach

Ken Orr

It's more or less impossible to write about the Warnier/Orr methodology because, in fact, there is no such thing. While there are Warnier/Orr diagrams, Warnier's methodology (i.e., logical data structure, logical construction of systems, and logical construction of programs), and Orr's methodology (data-structured systems development), there is not, strictly speaking, a Warnier/Orr methodology.

Many software engineers confuse diagrams with methodologies. Perhaps this is natural, since the diagrams are the most visible part of most methodologies; but it's unfortunate, for methodologies are much more than just a set of diagrams and syntax rules.

Within the context of software engineering, a *method* is a procedure or technique for performing some significant portion of the software life cycle. Over the years, techniques have been developed for requirements definition, database design, program design, test-case development, and so on. A *methodology*, in software engineering terms, is a collection of methods based on a common philosophy that fit together in a framework called the systems development *life cycle*.

© April 1989, by Byte, Jericho, NY 11753. Reprinted by permission.
Reprinted from *BYTE*, 14(4):221–233, April 1989.

Methods often use a variety of tools: diagrams, forms and text for documenting and communicating. Not surprisingly, these diagrams and forms often take on a life of their own. Diagrams, like words, can be used out of context, without understanding the purpose for which they were intended. While the results can be confusing, new possibilities and uses often arise that are quite fortuitous.

People who develop software engineering methods and methodologies attempt to solve problems, observe what others do, and derive, or abstract, patterns from all this. Those patterns ultimately turn into methodologies.

In my experience, my colleagues and I always know *what* works long before we know *why* it works. Software engineering methodologists are skilled at working with experts, such as analysts, programmers, database administrators, and so forth, finding out how these experts do what they do, and putting these findings down in such a way that other can follow them.

The correct name for what many people call the Warnier/Orr methodology is data-structured systems development. DSSD, like most methodologies, is actually the result of many people's efforts, in addition to my own, including my co-workers at Optima, colleagues, and clients. Much of the methodology has come about by taking various component technologies, such as structured programming and relational-database design, and putting them together into a coherent framework.

A little history

In 1972, Terry Baker's article "Chief Programmer Team Operations" in the *IBM Systems Journal* had a major impact on the field. It brought together several ideas: structured programming, top-down design and implementation, the chief programmer, the chief-programmer team, and the documentation librarian. If there was a shot that started the "structured revolution" in the U.S., Baker's article was it.

In the early 1970s, I became interested in structured programming and in structured design. In applying the principles of top-down design, I discovered that many of my best, most intelligible solutions were those in which the hierarchical structure of the program mirrored the hierarchical structure of the data the program was processing.

Shortly after this discovery, I stumbled across the work of Jean Warnier and realized that he had not only made the same discovery with regard to data-structured programming but had already built a systematic methodology around it. I also followed Michael Jackson's work, another form of data-structured design.

I already believed that you could and should construct programs hierarchically using only a few basic logical structures. Moreover, I believed that if you were going to build very large things, you should build them in systematic ways based on simple structures. This coincided with design and construction techniques used in fields such as electrical engineering. Structured programming represented a base on which to build; therefore, using the data structure as the framework for building the program structure seemed like the next natural step.

Data-structured programming meant that you could create predictably correct solutions for a wide class of programming problems – problems in which the structures of the input and the output were the same or very similar. But beyond that, Warnier, Jackson, and those of us involved in developing DSSD were able to extend data-structured techniques to arbitrarily complex programs.

To solve these more complex problems, you must recognize that the nature of the problem of complexity is, on one level at least, fundamentally mathematical in nature – that is, complex problems are fundamentally $n : n$ (many-to-many) mappings from input to output. To deal with this complexity systematically, you must break the problems down into a series of less complex mappings.

This is what mathematicians have been doing for thousands of years – breaking large troublesome problems into smaller ones for which there are clear precise answers. In the case of data-structured design, this meant developing a scheme in which the physical inputs were mapped into logical inputs; the logical inputs were then mapped into the logical outputs; and finally, the logical outputs were mapped into the physical outputs.

With this overall program-design framework comes a goal-oriented design strategy – an approach that starts with the structure of the output and works backward, first to the logical, or ideal, input, and then to the physical input.

The data-structured approach to program design has proven to be successful on a wide variety of problems, but is clearly no panacea. What it does represent is a systematic approach to attacking complex programs (simple problems have a way of taking care of themselves, or, alternatively, becoming complex).

Programming in the large

At some point in developing techniques for building systems, you realize that the most significant problems in software occur not at the programming level but at the systems level. How do you design entire suites of programs so that they work effectively together? How do you get the right requirements? Where does planning fit into the scheme of things?

Little by little, DSSD moved from a program-design methodology to a systems-design methodology. Over a period of years, the methodology was expanded to deal with database design, requirements definition, and finally systems planning and architecture.

At a conceptual level, DSSD still retains features that characterized it at the programming level. For example, it still focuses (in its design phase) on working backward from outputs. But at the systems level, instead of working backward to the ideal inputs, as it does in the programming methodology, DSSD works backward to the logical database and then to the inputs (see Figure 1.1). The logical database turns out, not surprisingly, to be a normalized relational database.

While a complete definition of the results (outputs plus algorithms) is an excellent point at which to begin the design process, it is not the proper place to start requirements definition. So, over the years, DSSD has been extended to cover first the context, then the functions, and finally the results of the system in question.

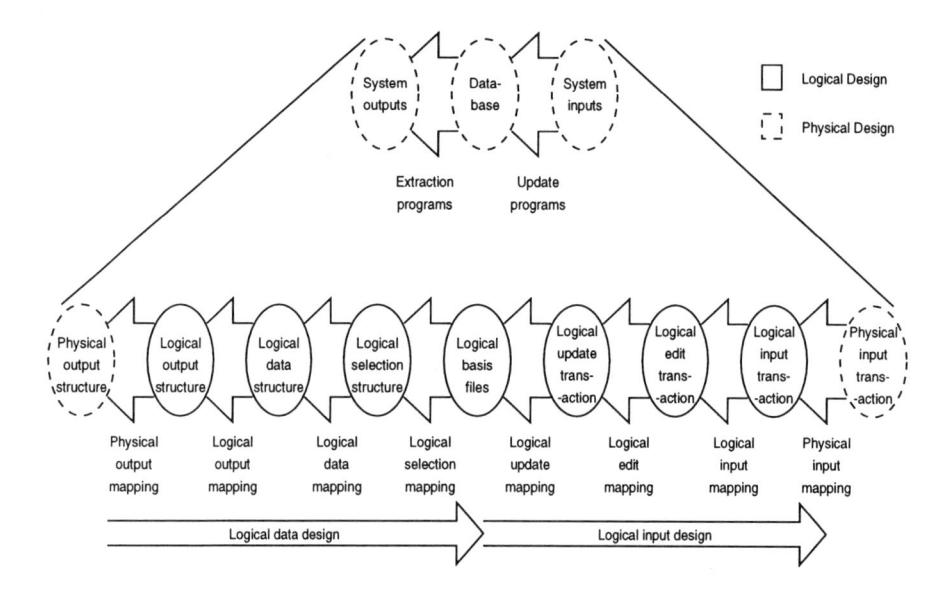

Figure 1.1: **At the systems level, instead of working backwards to the ideal inputs, DSSD works backward to the logical database and then to the inputs.**

Thus, a number of tools were needed to facilitate this process. *Entity diagrams* help you define the systems context, and *assembly-line diagrams* (a modified form of Warnier/Orr diagrams) help you define the functional flow of the system.

Data-structured methodologies have, I believe, a leg up on more process-oriented methodologies, since they are more rigorous and hence provide a better basis for true integration throughout the systems life cycle. DSSD has been used successfully on a range of software systems, from commercial on-line systems to real-time control systems. Thousands of people have been trained and thousands of systems have been built using it.

DSSD is a software engineering approach that has provided a stable framework for incorporating new technologies as they come along. For example, we have incorporated prototyping, on-line, and real-time design into DSSD without sacrificing the rigor or completeness. But there is a catch: To use DSSD successfully, you must invest time in training, use, and automation. In software engineering, as in life, there is no free lunch.

Bibliography

Hansen, Kirk. *Data Structured Program Design*, 2d ed. Englewood Cliffs, NJ: Prentice-Hall, 1986.

Higgins, David A. *Designing Structured Programs*. Englewood Cliffs, NJ: Prentice-Hall, 1983.

Jackson, Michael A. *Principles of Program Design.* New York: Academic Press, 1975.
Orr, Kenneth T. *Structured Systems Development.* New York: Yourdon Press, 1977.
—. *Structured Requirements Definition.* Topeka, KS: Ken Orr & Associates, 1980.
Warnier, Jean-Dominique. *Logical Construction of Programs.* New York: Van Nostrand Reinhold, 1976.
—. *Program Modification.* Boston: Martinus Nijhoff, 1978.
—. *Logical Construction of Systems.* New York: Van Nostrand Reinhold, 1981.

2. The Gane/Sarson Approach

Chris Gane

When we think about an information system that doesn't exist yet, our ideas are usually pretty vague and general. This is not an accusation; it's a fact of human psychology.

The purpose of logical modeling is to take these necessarily vague ideas about requirements and convert them into precise definitions as fast as possible. Part of the speed comes from having graphical techniques that enable you to put down the essence of a system without going through the trouble of actually physically implementing it, as you might do, for example, in a prototype.

Several approaches to logical modeling have been proposed. The one outlined here is the current version of the approach set out in a book I wrote with Trish Sarson (see reference 1). It has become generally known as the Gane/Sarson methodology.

Logical modeling

You can think of logical modeling as a seven-step process. Suppose the users say "We need a system that integrates sales, inventory control, and purchasing." What exactly does that mean?

• *Step 1.* Develop a system-wide dataflow diagram (DFD) describing the underlying nature of what occurs in the sales, inventory control, and purchasing areas of the business. The simplicity of the DFD comes from the use of only four symbols to produce a picture of the underlying logical nature of any information system, at any desired level of detail.

Figure 2.1 shows CUSTOMERS (an external entity, something outside the system) sending in a stream of sales orders along the data-flow arrow. Process 1, process sales, handles those orders using product information from the data store called D1: PRODUCTS and puts information about sales into the data store named D3: SALES.

This figure also shows the whole of the business area, depicted using only the four symbols. For each sale, process 1 updates the INVENTORY data store, D2, with

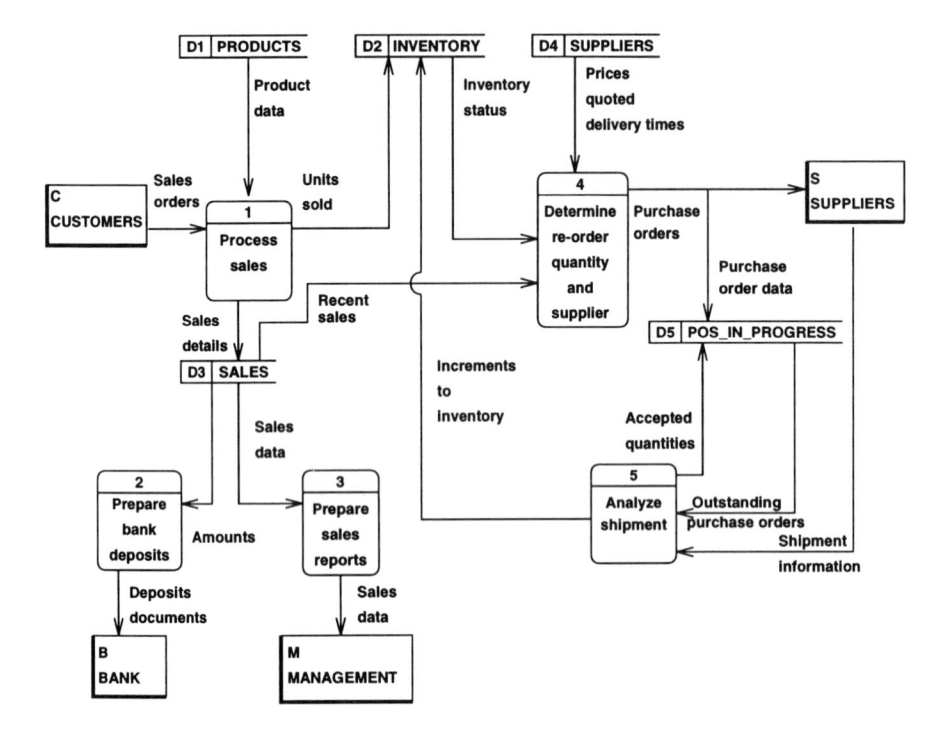

Figure 2.1: A DFD for the whole of the business area. Note the box for external entities, the open rectangles for data stores, the rounded box for the process, and the data-flow arrow, which shows the direction of data movement. Notice also that time is not shown on a DFD.

the units sold. The data stored in D3 is used by processes 2 and 3 to prepare bank deposit documents and send them to the bank, and to prepare sales reports and send them to management.

At some appropriate time – notice that time is not shown on the DFD – process 4 extracts information about the inventory status of various products from D2 and combines it with information from D3 concerning their past sales, to determine whether a product needs to be reordered. If so, based on information in D4, which describes the prices and delivery times quoted by suppliers, process 4 chooses the best supplier to order from.

Process 4 sends purchase orders to the external entity SUPPLIERS and stores information about each purchase order in D5: POS_IN_PROGRESS. When a shipment is received from a supplier, process 5 analyzes it, extracting data from POS_IN_PROGRESS to determine whether what has been received is what was ordered, incrementing the INVENTORY, D2, with the accepted amount, and storing the accepted quantities in POS_IN_PROGRESS.

This DFD achieves three things. First, it sets a boundary to the area of the system and of the business covered by the system. Things represented by the external-entity symbol (i.e., customers, the bank, management, and suppliers) are, by definition, outside the system. Processes not shown are not part of the project. For example, the diagram shows receiving shipments from suppliers but not handling the invoices received from them, implying that accounts payable is outside the scope of the project as well.

Second, it is nontechnical. Nothing is shown on a DFD that is not easily understandable to people familiar with the business area depicted, whether or not they know anything about computers.

Third, it shows both the data stored in the system and the processes that transform that data. It shows the relationships between the data and the processes in the system.

- *Step 2.* Derive a first-cut data model – that is, a list of the data elements to be stored in each data store, as defined on the DFD. You should draw up this list from your own knowledge and from the knowledge of users about what information you need to describe a product, a supplier, a sale, and so on.

You can refine the list by looking as each system input, such as sales orders or shipments in Figure 2.1, determining what data elements each input represents, looking at each output in the same way, and then working from the outputs back to the data stores or from the inputs forward to the data stores.

- *Step 3.* See what entity-relationship analysis can tell you about the structure of the data to be stored in the system. First, you ask, "What are the entities of interest about which I may need to store data?" For this business, the answer might be CUSTOMERS, PRODUCTS, INVENTORY, SUPPLIERS, SALES and PURCHASE_ORDERS. Then, you create a diagram with a block for each entity you have identified. (It is conventional in this diagram to state the entities as singular nouns – for example, CUSTOMER instead of CUSTOMERS.)

Next, looking at each pair of entities on the diagram, you ask, "What, if any, relationships exist between them?" For example, you know that one customer may be associated with many sales, but each sale can be for only one customer. This is conventionally shown by a line with an arrowhead against the "many" block and a plain line at the "one" block.

Take, for instance, PRODUCT and SALE: One product may be associated with many sales, and one sale may be for many products – at least one, and possibly more. This relationship is shown by a line with an arrowhead on both ends. On the other hand, each product has only one inventory record, and each inventory record refers to only one product. Consequently, they are joined by a simple line. Adding in all the identifiable relationships creates a diagram like Figure 2.2.

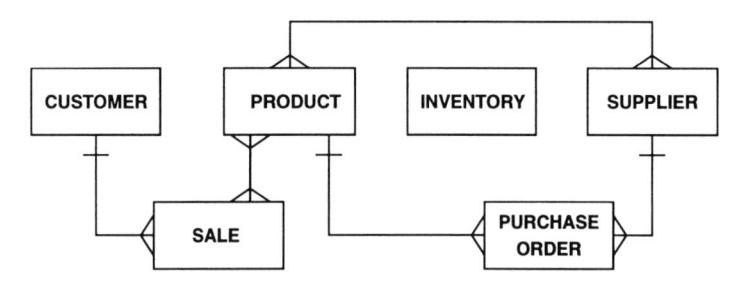

Figure 2.2: All the identifiable realtionships between entities. For each pair of entities on the diagram that has a relationship between its elements, the relationship may be one-to-one, many-to-one, or many-to-many. This diagram provides a lot of information about the system in showing all the relationships that exist between the entities involved.

- *Step 4.* Use all the information you have about the data so far to describe the data model as one made of linked, two-dimensional tables. These tables should be *normalized* (i.e., made as simple as possible). One way to summarize the rules of normalization is to say that in a properly simplified table, in which a column or combination of columns uniquely identifies each row (the key), each non-key column should depend only on the key.

- *Step 5.* Redraft the DFD to reflect a more precise view of the system data as a result of entity-relationship analysis and normalization.

- *Step 6.* Partition this logical model of process and data into *procedure units* – that is, chunks of automated and manual procedures that can be executed (and therefore developed) as units. To do this, you consider each input and output and ask the following questions for each one:

  1. When does it happen?
  2. How large an area of the DFD is involved in handling or producing it?
  3. Can that area be implemented as a single unit? If not, why not?

- *Step 7.* Specify the details of each procedure unit that will be required to implement the system. A procedure-unit specification may involve

  1. an extract from the system DFD showing where this procedure unit fits into the rest of the system;
  2. details of the tables accessed by the procedure unit;
  3. layouts for any screens and reports involved in the procedure unit; and
  4. details of the logic and procedures to be implemented, written in structured English or some other unambiguous form.

With the nature of the procedure unit defined, you can decide whether it should be prototyped or implemented directly in the target language. You can develop the screen and report layouts by prototyping.

Steps 6 and 7 in this sequence are not, strictly speaking, logical modeling, since they deal with converting the logical model into a physical model. They are included, however, because they form part of the natural flow of thought processes beginning with defining the system and ending in its physical design.

Editor's note: *Chris Gane extracted this article form Chapter 1 of his book* Rapid System Development, *published by Prentice-Hall in December 1988.*

References

1. Gane, Chris, and Trish Sarson. *Structured Systems Analysis.* Englewood Cliffs, NJ: Prentice-Hall, 1979.

3. The Yourdon Approach

Edward Yourdon

The Yourdon method is a generic, ecumenical collection of software engineering ideas developed over the past 20 years by a variety of people who have worked at Yourdon, Inc. Taken together, these ideas are often referred to as *structured techniques:* structured programming, structured design, and structured analysis.

Because of the continuing influx of new ideas from new people, the Yourdon method is constantly evolving. The method that thousands read about in Tom DeMarco's book in 1978 (see reference 1) has changed considerably in the past 10 years. And the Yourdon method of 1989 is evolving to incorporate the best ideas of object-oriented design and analysis.

But what *is* the "Yourdon method" today? It consists of two things: tools and techniques. The tools are a variety of graphical diagrams used to model the requirements and the architecture of an information system. The most familiar of these

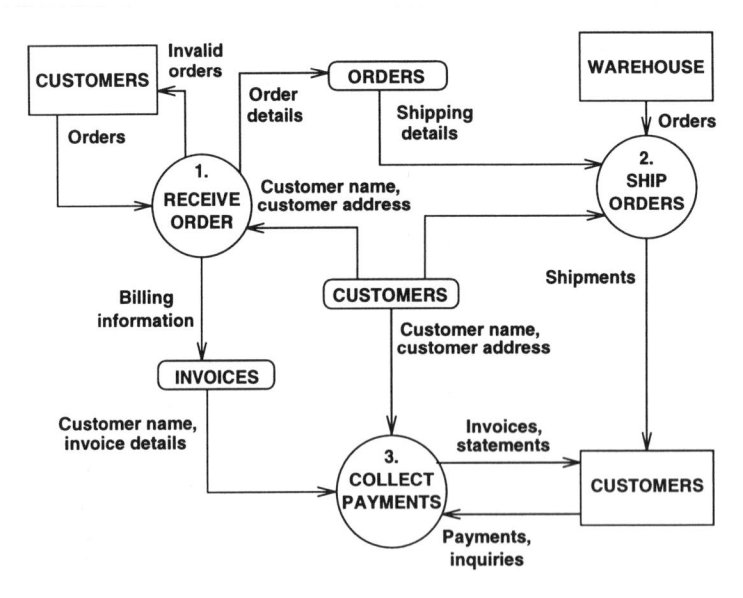

Figure 3.1: A data-flow diagram. The DFD models the functions that a system must perform.

tools is the data-flow diagram (DFD) (see Figure 3.1). The original DFD notation was extended a few years ago to support real-time systems; a real-time DFD includes control flows and control processes. For a detailed description of real-time DFDs, see reference 2.

While the DFD is an excellent tool for modeling the *functions* that a system must carry out, it says little or nothing about data relationships and time-dependent behavior. Thus, the current Yourdon method also includes entity-relationship diagrams (ERDs) and state-transition diagrams (STDs) (see reference 3).

After you have finished describing the system requirements, you can use a structure chart to illustrate the organization of modules that will implement those requirements. A number of guidelines exist that the systems analyst can follow to ensure that each diagram is complete and logically consistent.

While the graphical diagrams provide an effective way of communicating information about different aspects of a system, they don't tell the whole story. For a complete system description, you need additional textual support: a data dictionary, which describes the composition of each data element, and a set of process specifications that describe the required behavior of each bottom-level "bubble" in the DFD.

The techniques

The techniques of the Yourdon method consist of some "cookbook" guidelines that help you go from a blank sheet of paper, or a blank screen, to a well-organized system model. Originally, these guidelines were based on the simple concept of top-down partitioning of system functions (e.g., draw a single bubble or box to represent the entire system, then draw lower-level bubbles or boxes to represent subsystems, and so forth).

Today, the Yourdon method uses a technique known as *event partitioning* (see reference 4). This approach begins by drawing a top-level *context diagram* to identify the system boundary and to define the interfaces between the system and external sources and sinks. Then, after interviewing the user, you can write a list of the *events* that occur in the external environment and to which the system must respond. (Events are often input transactions.)

The event-partitioning approach provides a simple guideline to help you compose a first-cut crude DFD: For each event, draw one bubble whose function is to provide the required response to the event. (In most cases, the response involves generating an output, but it may also involve storing some information in a data store to be used by some subsequent event.)

For a system with 100 events, the DFD would have 100 bubbles. This is too complex to work with, so the event-partitioning technique provides guidelines to help you partition *upward* – that is, to gather several of the DFD bubbles together and represent them by a single bubble in a higher-level DFD. The strategy for deciding which bubbles should be grouped together is to look for bubbles that deal with common data (e.g., a common data store). In this sense, event partitioning is very similar to the object-oriented design approach.

There are various additional guidelines and techniques to help you compose well-formed models of both system requirements and system architecture. (One book that discusses both the analysis area and the design area – as well as the "twilight zone" that separates the two – is given in reference 5.)

The Yourdon philosophy

Throughout all of the Yourdon method – regardless of variant or dialect, whether you draw circles or ovals in your DFD, or where you hear about it – you will see the following philosophies.

• *Modeling is good.* Developing a model of a system before you build it is almost always a useful, educational activity. For this to work, however, the model has to be inexpensive and easy to build: If it costs as much to develop the model as to develop the system, it's obviously a waste of time. The model also has to be accurate – it should not mislead you or lie to you. And it should be easy to understand. It should highlight those aspects of the system that are important, and it should deemphasize or hide those aspects that are unimportant or uninteresting.

Since most systems are complex in three different dimensions – functions, data, and timing and control – it is useful to have three different types of models, DFDs, ERDs, and STDs, each of which illustrates a single perspective of the system. The Yourdon method is based on abstract, pictorial models – either on paper or on a computer screen.

Another approach is to develop a prototype of the system as a model – a living, breathing model instead of a passive collection of diagrams. When prototyping was first introduced in the early 1980s, it was considered an alternative to paper based modeling approaches – the systems analyst was often told to make a binary choice between prototyping and drawing DFDs.

Today, we know that the two approaches are complementary: You can draw diagrams as a permanent record of system requirements and use prototyping to experiment with such key issues as the user interface (input screens, report layouts, and so on). For a good discussion of the marriage of prototyping and "classical" structured analysis, see reference 6.

- *Iteration is good.* As fallible humans with limited intelligence, we rarely, if ever, develop a perfect solution to a complex problem on the first attempt. At best, we can hope for a crude beginning that, through iteration, we can gradually refine and improve. To practice iteration, we must have models that are easy to create and easy to revise. In the past, we grappled with the finality of pen and ink; with the word processors of today, most of us take iteration for granted in composing reports and memos.

In systems development, we tried to make iteration of system models easier by insisting on partitioning the overall system model into a number of separable submodels. Thus, if one aspect of a system changes, ideally only one page of a diagram has to be modified. As a practical matter, though, most systems analysts in the 1970s and early 1980s drew DFDs only once – on paper. This is one reason why today's microcomputer-based computer-aided software engineering products are so important: They make iteration a practical reality.

- *Partitioning is good.* When we first learned how to write computer programs, we were given simple problems that we could finish in a day or two, keeping every aspect of the problem in our heads at once. With real-world programming problems, however, the only way we can successfully build systems that, today, typically involve more than a million lines of code is by partitioning the system into smaller and smaller pieces.

There are great debates about whether the partitioning should be based on functional decomposition or data decomposition. But either approach, followed rigorously, is better than no partitioning, or sloppy partitioning that leads to subsystems with subtle, pathological interconnections.

Acknowledgements. The author gratefully acknowledges the contributions of the following people to the Yourdon method: Tom DeMarco, Larry Constantine, Chris Gane, Trish Sarson, Steve McMenamin, Tim Lister, John Palmer, Paul Ward, Steve Mellor, Meilir Page-Jones, Bob Block, Al Brill, Tim Wells, and Matt Flavin.

References

1. DeMarco, Tom. *Structured Analysis and System Specification.* New York: Yourdon Press, 1978.

2. Ward, Paul, and Steve Mellor. *Structured Techniques for Real-Time Systems.* New York: Yourdon Press/Prentice-Hall, 1985.
3. Yourdon, Edward. *Modern Structured Analysis.* New York: Yourdon Press / Prentice-Hall, 1989.
4. —. *Essential Systems Analysis.* New York: Yourdon Press/Prentice-Hall, 1984.
5. Page-Jones, Meilir. *The Practical Guide to Structured Systems Design.* 2d ed. New York: Yourdon Press/Prentice-Hall, 1988.
6. Connell, John, and Linda Schafer. *Rapid Prototyping.* New York: Yourdon Press / Prentice-Hall, 1989.

4. The Entity-Relationship Approach

Peter P. Chen

One of the major problems in software engineering today is the piecemeal approach to systems design. This approach makes the integration of different application systems difficult, if not impossible. We try to design the data structures and formats to fit current processing needs and then later run into problems of data conversion and integration.

An integrated database is a solution to these problems. However, acquiring a DBMS does not make them go away. What is needed is a structured methodology that can systematically convert user requirements into well-designed databases. The entity-relationship (ER) approach is such a methodology.

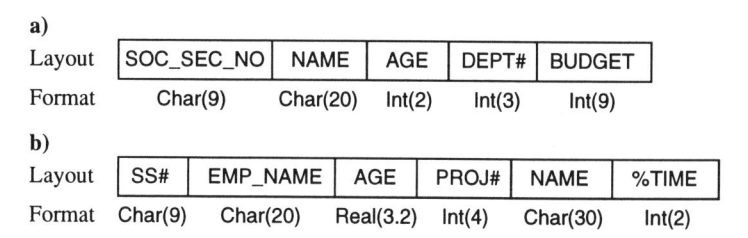

a)
Layout	SOC_SEC_NO	NAME	AGE	DEPT#	BUDGET
Format	Char(9)	Char(20)	Int(2)	Int(3)	Int(9)

b)
Layout	SS#	EMP_NAME	AGE	PROJ#	NAME	%TIME
Format	Char(9)	Char(20)	Real(3.2)	Int(4)	Char(30)	Int(2)

Figure 4.1:
(a) File format for the program to list employees in each department.
(b) File format for the program to list projects for each employee.

Let's start with an example. Say you need a program to keep track of the list of employees working for each department in your company. This program needs to accept data on the screen, store it on disk, and print out the report on demand. The programmer/analyst comes up with a file format (see Figure 4.1a).

In the meantime, another group in the company implements a program to keep track of employee information for each project; the file format in this program turns out a little different from the other (see Figure 4.1b). Each program satisfies the needs of the group that requested it. However, one day the company president wants to know which departments have employees working on project X. Then everyone scrambles around trying to convert the data in one file to the format of the other file. Let's look deeply into these two file formats to see what kinds of problems they had.

- Synonym (the same data element has different names): For example, SOC_SEC_NO in Figure 4.1a is the same data element as SS# in Figure 4.1b.
- The same name for different data elements: For example, NAME in Figure 4.1a refers to the name of an employee, while NAME in Figure 4.1b is the name of a project.
- Incompatibility of data formats: For example, the data-type format of AGE in Figure 4.1a is Int(2), while the data format of AGE in Figure 4.1b is Real(3.2).
- Duplication of data: For example, the project data (PROJ#, NAME) is duplicated for each employee associated with the project in Figure 4.1b, and the BUDGET data of each department in Figure 4.1a is repeated for each employee.
- Update anomalies: For example, changing any of an employee's data-element values in one file but not in the other will result in inconsistent data.

If the above file designs are not good, what would be a good design? How many record types (or relations in the case of relational databases) should there be? Should there be one huge record type consisting of all data elements, or the other extreme – many small records, each consisting of a pair of data elements? Furthermore, what is the primary key for each record (relation) type? The main question is: Do we have a methodology for file and database design? The answer is yes, and the leading methodology is the ER approach.

Six years ago, a survey of Fortune 500 companies (published in ACM SIGMOD proceedings, 1983) conducted by two Ohio professors showed that ER methodology ranked as the most popular methodology in data modeling and database design. Why? Because it is simple, easy to understand by noncomputer people, and theoretically sound. To illustrate, here are the major steps of the ER approach using the above example:

• *Develop an entity-relationship diagram (ERD)*. This step identifies ER types and associated attributes and also the primary keys for each entity type.

An *entity* is a thing (e.g., a person or an automobile), a concept, an organization, or an event of interest to the organization doing the modeling. An *entity type* is a classification of entities satisfying certain criteria. A *relationship* is an interaction between entities. A *relationship type* is a classification of relationships based on certain criteria. Usually, nouns in English correspond to entities, while verbs correspond to relationships.

In the example in Figures 4.1a and 4.1b, you can identify three entity types: DEPT, EMP, and PROJ. You can also identify two relationship types: HAS and WORK_FOR (note that relationship-type names are verbs). Figure 4.2 depicts an

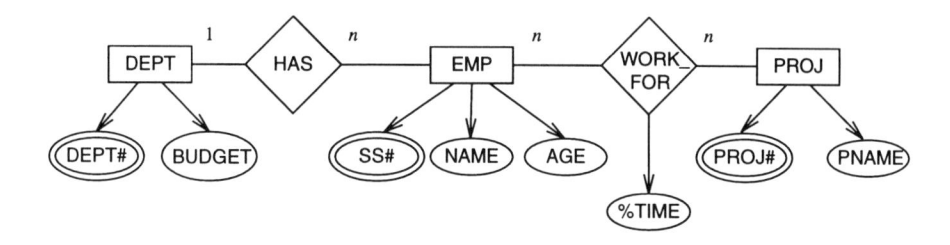

Figure 4.2: Entity-relationship diagram (ERD) for a database based on Figure 4.1.

ERD in which rectangular boxes represent entity types and diamond-shaped boxes represent relationship types.

The next step is to identify the *cardinality* of the relationship types. The cardinality of HAS (between DEPT and EMP) is $1:n$ (one-to-many); that means a department can have many employees, but each belongs to at most one department. The cardinality of WORK_FOR (between EMP and PROJ) is $n:n$ (many-to-many). You then identify the properties (attributes) of each ER and express them graphically as circles (or ellipses). For example, each DEPT has attributes DEPT# and BUDGET. The primary key is indicated by a double circle. Note that there is an attribute called % TIME for relationship WORK_FOR.

• *Convert the ERD into conventional file and database structures.* There are rules for doing this. For example, you can convert the ERD in Figure 4.2 into the relational structure with all the primary keys underlined.

DEPT (<u>DEPT#</u>, BUDGET)
EMP (<u>SS#</u>, NAME, AGE, DEPT#)
PROJECT (<u>PROJ#</u>, PNAME)
WORK_FOR (<u>SS#</u>, <u>PROJ#</u>, % TIME)

Simply speaking, each entity type is converted into a relation, and a relationship type is converted into a stand-alone relation or consolidated with another relation, depending on the cardinality of the relationship.

If you are familiar with relational normalization theory, you can prove that these relations are in Third Normal Form. As you can see, all the primary keys of the relations are derived automatically, and DEPT# in EMP relation is a *foreign* key (i.e., the primary key of another relation – DEPT).

• *Develop application programs based on the file and database structures.* If you are using a relational DBMS, you can now write a System Query Language (SQL) program to express the question, Which departments have employees working on project X?

SELECT EMP.DEPT#
FROM EMP, WORK_FOR

```
WHERE (WORK_FOR.PROJ# = X)
AND (WORK_FOR.SS# = EMP.SS#)
```

This article shows how to design a relational database based on the ER approach. Similarly, you can design file structures and various other databases – from microcomputer-based DBMSes, such as dBASE, to mainframe-based DBMSes, such as DB2 and IMS – based on the ER approach.

Future trends

You have seen how to design a database and an application program based on the ER approach. The resultant database is sound and avoids such problems as data duplication and update anomalies. Commercial tools are available today to automate the ER approach.

The ER model can be used not only as a design tool but also as the underlying model for a DBMS. In the microcomputer and minicomputer range, Zanthe (Ottawa) has a product called ZIM. In the mainframe area, several computer vendors have ER-like DBMSes ready for marketing. For example, Software AG has ADABAS/Entire, and Unisys has SIM as part of its InfoExec offering.

On another front, ANSI recently approved an Information Resource Dictionary Systems standard based on the ER model. In the near future, we'll see a flood of IRDS products as well as computer-aided software engineering tools based on the ER model.

Bibliography

ANSI. *Standards on Information Resource Dictionary Systems*, 1988.
Chen, Peter P. "Entity-Relationship Model: Toward a Unified View of Data." *ACM Transactions on Database Systems*, vol. 1, no. 1, pages 9–36, March 1976.
Davis, C. G., S. Jajodia, P. Ng, and R. Yeh, eds. *Entity-Relationship Approach to Software Engineering*. New York: North-Holland, 1983.
March, Sal, ed. *Entity-Relationship Approach*. New York: North-Holland, 1988.
Teorey, Toby, and James Fry. "An Extended Entity-Relationship Approach to Logical Database Design." *ACM Survey*, 1986.

5. The Structured-Design Approach

Larry L. Constantine

The computer field likes big words. Why call something an *instance* when *instantiation* works just as well, even if it isn't in the dictionary? A software design *method* sounds like the sort of generic-brand thinking that anyone could work out over a long weekend. But a software design *methodology* sounds like an elaborate and well-thought-out concept, perhaps worth attending a seminar on by a major software guru, and certainly worth the price of a book. However, *methodology* actually means the study of methods, and *software methodology* is an ungrammatical use of the word.

Structured design is both a generic term for various systematic approaches to designing program structure and also a kind of brand name for one particular approach. The structured design world is a competitive arena. Varying principles or specialized diagrams reflect some real technical differences. But, more than anything else, competing approaches are based on product differentiation, personal ego, and the territorial imperative. These methods, their associated tools, and the names of the principals are widely recognized.

The school with the longest legitimate claim to the banner of structured design is the Constantine-Myers-Stevens-Yourdon (in alphabetical order, of course) approach that I originated in the late 1960s. It begins with a data-flow diagram (DFD) (often called a "bubble chart") showing the transformational structure of an information-processing problem; then it derives a model of the modular structure of software that will solve that problem.

Models

Much is made of design methods, but structured design is really powered by a *troika* consisting of models, methods, and measures (see Figure 5.1). The models make it possible to picture and play with the modular structure of software systems without actually having to program them first.

System-structure modeling, now accepted as essential to software engineering, was a novel and suspect notion when I first introduced it. The models used in structured design are graphical tools, annotated to represent the structure of problems and programs. For example, the structure chart, an elaboration of the older hierarchy chart, shows all the modules in a system and their essential inter-relationships in one compact model. It allows you to see the "shape of things to come" and to explore alternative ways to organize software.

Measures

Structured design, unlike some other structured techniques and software engineering "methodologies", is grounded in a body of underlying theory about what makes

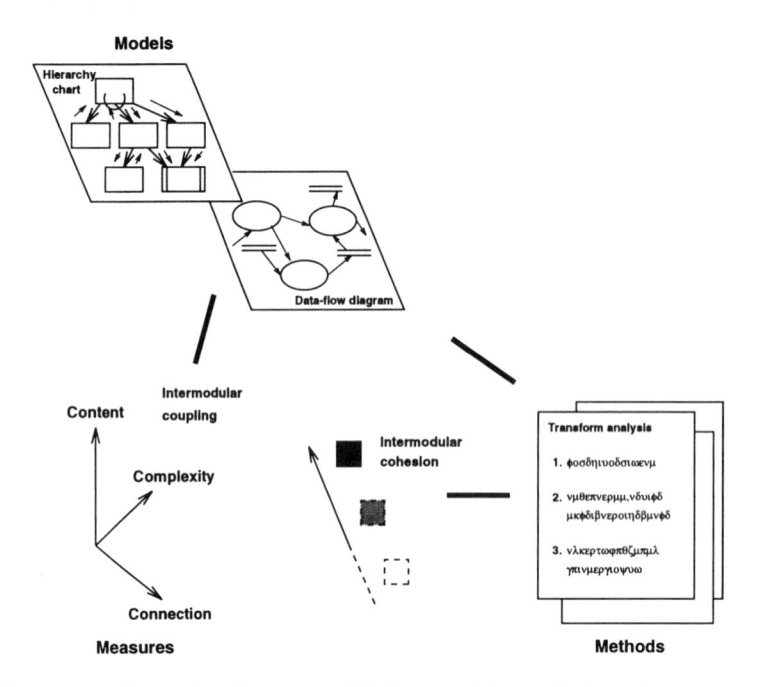

Figure 5.1: The troika of structured design: models, methods, and measures.

programs complicated to build right in the first place and difficult to change in the second. The practical embodiment of this theory takes the form of two measures – coupling and cohesion – that index the relative complexity or difficulty of various designs.

Simple programs are, simply put, made out of little pieces, each of which is easily thought of as a unit or a whole that is mostly independent of other pieces. Module cohesion is a measure of module "wholeness," and coupling measures interdependence. In other word, good designs that are easy to build and change are based on a bunch of modules, each of which is "cohesive," or well-glued together, and only loosely "coupled" to other modules.

Designing in this way, you can program very large systems by writing only small, separate pieces of code. This theory is proving to be the most durable element of the troika. A decade of research has demonstrated the soundness of the basic assumptions about coupling and cohesion and has refined our understanding of how they affect programming and maintenance costs, fault rates, and ease of modification. Quantitative metrics based on the theory now make it possible to automate design evaluation and even parts of the design process.

Object-oriented methods are emerging as major factors in software engineering, but even with these powerful new techniques, the cohesion of actual modules that implement object classes and their coupling with other modules turn out to be important for building simple systems with truly reusable components. As a consequence, the original measures of coupling and cohesion have now been extended and adapted to evaluate the quality of so-called object class modules and abstract data types.

Methods

Methods is the weak third member of the structured design team, but the one that gets much of the attention. The methods of structured design include a loose collection of rules and some moderately systematic strategies for the step-by-step design of software. These strategies are based on specific kinds of software organization that have proved effective in practice. Among the most durable are the balanced system structure known as *transform-centered* organization and the event-oriented organization called *transaction-centered*. Distinct design methods are aimed at producing each variation on system organization.

You might outline an overall structured design method as follows:

1. Develop a nonprocedural (method-independent) statement of the system requirements, usually centered around a DFD.
2. Based on the structure of the problem, choose an appropriate software organizational model or combination.
3. Guided by the data flow and the chosen organizational model, decompose overall functions into subfunctions and compose primitive functions into higher-level functions until the complete requirements are satisfied.
4. Using various design rules and measures of coupling and cohesion, refine the design for increased modularity, extensibility, and likely reusability of modules.
5. Complete detailed designs as necessary for all modules.

The problem, of course, is that actually carrying out the modeling, evaluation, and refinement involved in structured design takes discipline and time, uses a lot of paper, and can wear out the erasers on every pencil in the office. Unaided by computer tools, many developers who use structured design have used it informally and unsystematically, while others have used its concepts to shape their thinking without ever applying the formal models, measures, and methods.

Automating methods

Computer-aided software engineering is not a replacement or substitute for systematic methods; it's the key that unlocks their full potential. With CASE tools, real structured design on problems of interesting size becomes truly practical for the first time. The diagram editors of CASE systems assist in developing and refining complex graphical models. CASE tools with built-in knowledge of the models' meaning can check them for consistency and conformance with the established rules of structured design.

With intelligence about good designs incorporated into CASE tools, the computer can evaluate the quality of actual structured designs or even sketch out a rough initial design. At present, the most advanced CASE workbenches provide powerful support for existing software engineering methods; in the future, new structured methods are likely to be developed based on the use of quasi-intelligent CASE tools.

CASE systems can also reinforce or impose standards for software architectures and the diagrams that document them, but CASE vendors have yet to take on much responsibility for standardization. Most of the available tools and workbenches are methodology-independent – meaning you can use them to do any brand of design, structured or unstructured, that you may choose.

This may be an acceptable level of flexibility, given the state of the science in "computer science," but some of these tools have arbitrarily departed from what few standards and conventions do exist. It doesn't make sense for a system to use its own peculiar icon for an included module any more than to allow a CAD/CAM system for electrical engineers to use just any old shape to represent a transistor.

If we use computer-aided software engineering tools, and we call ourselves software engineers, perhaps it's time we acted more like engineers.

Bibliography

Stevens, W. P., G. J. Myers, and L. L. Constantine. "Structured Design." *IBM Systems Journal*, vol. 13, no. 2, 1974.

Yourdon, Edward, and Larry L. Constantine. *Structured Design*. Englewood Cliffs, NJ: Yourdon Press/Prentice-Hall, 1979.

An Overview of JSD

John R. Cameron

Summary.

The Jackson System Development (JSD) method addresses most of the software lifecycle. JSD specifications consist mainly of a distributed network of processes that communicate by message-passing and by read-only inspection of each other's data. A JSD specification is therefore directly executable, at least in principle. Specifications are developed middle-out from an initial set of "model" processes. The model processes define a set of events, which limit the scope of the system, define its semantics, and form the basis for defining data and outputs. Implementation often involves reconfiguring or transforming the network to run on a smaller number of real or virtual processors. The main phases of JSD are introduced and illustrated by a small example system. The rationale for the approach is also discussed.

Keywords: Design methodology, system design, systems analysis.

I. Introduction

The Jackson System Development (JSD) approach aims to address most of the software lifecycle either directly or by providing a framework into which more specialized techniques can fit. JSD can be used from the stage in a project when there is only a general statement of requirements right through to the finished system and its subsequent maintenance. Many projects that have used JSD actually started slightly later in the lifecycle, doing the first steps largely from existing documents rather than directly with the users.

A JSD specification consists (mainly) of a distributed network of sequential processes. Each process can contain its own local data. The processes communicate by reading and writing messages and by read-only access to one another's data. The specification is developed middle-out starting with a particular set of "model" processes. Most of the data in the system belongs to these model processes. New processes are added to the specification by connecting them to the model. Usually the only direct connections in a network are between model and nonmodel processes

---

© 1986 IEEE. Reprinted by permission.
Reprinted from *IEEE Transactions on Software Engineering*, 12(2):222–240, February 1986.

and between nonmodel processes and the outside. Thus one model process is not directly connected to another or to the network boundary, and nonmodel processes only interact via the model processes. The exceptions to the general rule are discussed in Section V-B.

Direct implementations of this executable network are possible in principle and sometimes also in practice. Often, however, the network is reconfigured during the implementation phase by mapping the specification processes on to a smaller number (perhaps one) of the implementation processes. The reconfiguration involves fixing some of the scheduling that was left relatively unconstrained in the specification network. The other major concern in the implementation phase is the choice of storage structures (physical database design in an information system) to hold the data owned by the processes. The storage structures must also support the read-only access requirements of the other processes.

There are three main phases in the JSD method, the Model phase in which the model processes are selected and defined, the Network phase in which the rest of the specification is developed, and the Implementation phase in which the processes and their data are fitted on to the available processors and memory.

Sections II, III, and IV of this paper are concerned with, respectively, the model, network, and implementation phases. Section V contains the following five topics:

- A comparison of the JSD modeling approach to a more functional view of systems.
- A discussion of composition and of decomposition as general development strategies.
- A discussion of the variety of ways that the JSD steps can be mapped into the managerial framework of a project plan.
- A brief description of projects that are using or have used JSD.
- A brief description of available support tools.

II. The Modeling Phase

A. A model with only one process type

The modeling phase is concerned first with "actions" (or "events") about which the system has to produce displays, reports, signals, and other outputs. For most systems these events are mainly to be found in the world external to the system being built. They are selected and defined along with their associated attributes, and their mutual orderings described by a number of sequential processes.

Fig. 1, for example, is a list of eight actions taken from a simplified library system. By choosing these actions, and only these, we are defining a first scoping of the system. By "scoping" we mean a (indirect) definition of the range of functionality of the system. Later in the development a detailed choice will be made from this range.

Action	Definition and Attributes
ACQUIRE	The library acquires the book. id, date, title, author, ISBN, price
CLASSIFY	The book is classified and catalogued. id, date
LEND	Someone borrows the book. id, date, borrower
RENEW	The borrower renews the loan. id, date
RETURN	The borrower returns the book to the library. id, date
SELL	The book is sold. id, date, vendor, price
OUTCIRC	The book is taken out of circulation as part of the inter-library swop scheme. id, date, destination
DELIVER	The book is delivered to the other library. id, date

Figure 1

We may imagine a pair of spectacles through which only the selected actions can be observed. The system to be built is like a person wearing these spectacles; its outputs can only be based on what has been observed of the world.

The diagram in Fig. 2 describes for one book the order in which the actions can happen. The diagram is a tree structure; the leaves are the actions; all the other components describe sequential relationships between actions or between groups of actions. Excepting the leaves there are three types of component – sequence, iteration, and selection. BOOK is a sequence of ACQUIRE, CLASSIFY, LOANPART, and ENDPART. That means that BOOK consists of one ACQUIRE, followed by one CLASSIFY, followed by one LOANSET, followed by one ENDPART. Similarly LOAN is a sequence of one LEND, then one OUTONLOAN, and then one RETURN.

LOANPART is an iteration of LOAN. That means LOANPART consists of zero or more LOANs, one after the other. (An iteration is a generalization of a sequence.) Similarly, OUTONLOAN consists of zero or more RENEWs.

ENDPART is a selection component. That means ENDPART consists of either exactly one SELL or exactly one SWOPSCHEME. Sequences and selections can be of two or more parts; iterations can only be of one. Iterations and selections are denoted, respectively, by the "*" and "o" in the top right corner of their constituent components. (Logically, but somehow not to the eye, the identifying symbol is in the wrong box.)

We are, of course, using a diagrammatic notation for regular expressions. We also use recursion within the diagrams, where appropriate.

Fig. 2 describes a set of sequences of actions. The following are two members of the set, two possible life histories for a book.

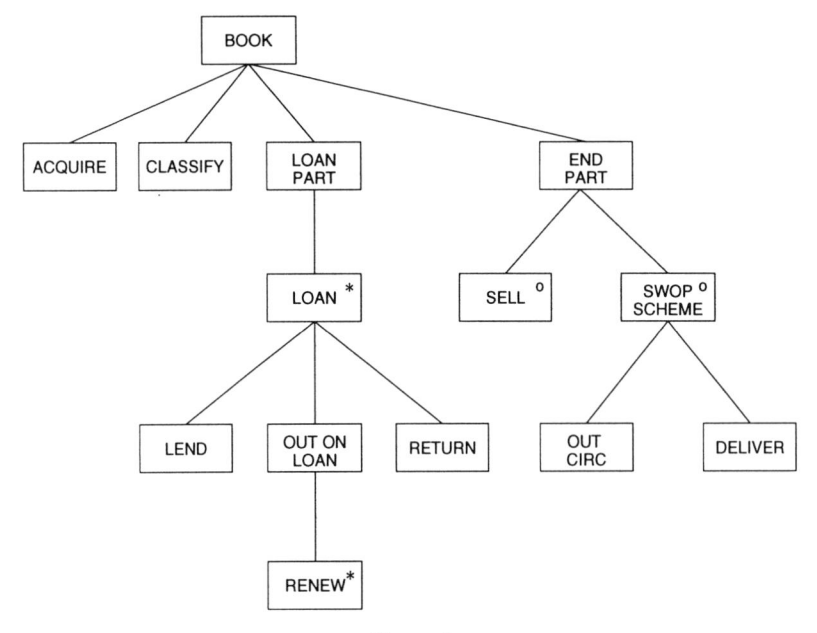

```
                              BOOK
          ┌──────┬────────┬────┴─────────────┐
       ACQUIRE CLASSIFY  LOAN              END
                         PART              PART
                          │              ┌───┴────┐
                         LOAN*         SELL°    SWOP°
                    ┌─────┼─────┐              SCHEME
                   LEND  OUT ON RETURN        ┌───┴────┐
                         LOAN                OUT     DELIVER
                          │                  CIRC
                        RENEW*
```

Figure 2

ACQUIRE, CLASSIFY, LEND, RETURN, LEND, RENEW, RETURN, SELL.
ACQUIRE, CLASSIFY, LEND, RENEW, RENEW, RETURN, OUTCIRC, DELIVER.

The complement of the set of sequences describes, by implication, what cannot happen. A LEND cannot immediately follow an ACQUIRE; a SELL cannot immediately follow a LEND. Later this information will be used to build some of the error-handling parts of the system.

If an input suggests that a book has been SOLD immediately after a LEND, we know that there has been some error on input because in accepting this diagram we are agreeing that a SELL cannot follow a LEND without an intervening RETURN.

The diagram describes orderings but it says nothing about how much time elapses between successive actions.

Each diagram describes the actions of one book. To describe the many books in the library we must have many instances of the diagram.

So far the diagram describes the library itself. Now we are also going to use the same diagram to describe a process type within our specification. The name of the process type is BOOK; there will be one instance for each book in the library; the purpose of a BOOK process is to model or mimic what is happening to the real book outside; to this end the process reads inputs, one for each action; the purpose of the input is to inform the BOOK model of what has happened so that the model can coordinate itself with the reality. A textual form of the process is shown in Fig. 3. This pseudocode is simply a transcription of the diagram with conditions added

```
BOOK seq
    read next input;
    ACQUIRE seq
        read next input;
    ACQUIRE end
    CLASSIFY seq
        read next input;
    CLASSIFY end
    LOANPART iter while (input = LEND)
        LOAN seq
            LEND seq
                read next input;
            LEND end
            OUT-ON-LOAN iter while (input = RENEW)
                RENEW seq
                    read next input;
                RENEW end
            OUT-ON-LOAN end
            RETURN seq
                read next input;
            RETURN end
        LOAN end
    LOANPART end
    ENDPART select (input = SELL)
        SELL seq
        SELL end
    ENDPART alt (input = OUTCIRC)
        SWOPSCHEME seq
            read next input;
        SWOPSCHEME end
        DELIVER seq
        DELIVER end
    ENDPART end
BOOK end
```

Figure 3

and reads inserted according to a read-ahead scheme. Note that one instance of this process will take as long to execute as the corresponding book is in the library. If we were able to observe the state of the partially executed process we would know something, but not much, about the state of the corresponding book.

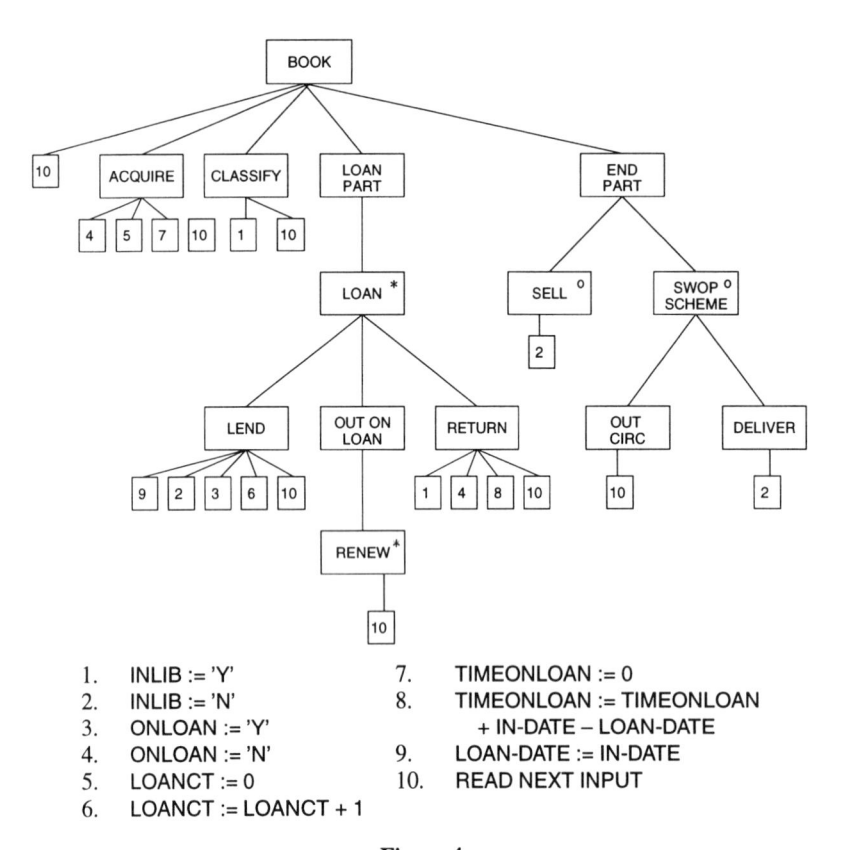

```
                              BOOK
        ┌───────────┬─────────┼─────────────┐
       [10]                                 
     ACQUIRE    CLASSIFY    LOAN          END
                            PART          PART
     ┌─┬─┐       ┌─┐       ┌─┐      ┌─────┼─────┐
    [4][5][7]  [10][1]    [10]    LOAN*  SELL°  SWOP°
                                                SCHEME
                                                  [2]
                          ┌────────┼────────┐
                        LEND    OUT ON   RETURN    OUT    DELIVER
                                LOAN               CIRC
                      ┌──┬──┬──┐          ┌──┬──┐  [10]    [2]
                     [9][2][3][6][10]    [1][4][8][10]
                                  │
                               RENEW*
                                 │
                                [10]
```

1.	INLIB := 'Y'	7.	TIMEONLOAN := 0
2.	INLIB := 'N'	8.	TIMEONLOAN := TIMEONLOAN
3.	ONLOAN := 'Y'		+ IN-DATE – LOAN-DATE
4.	ONLOAN := 'N'	9.	LOAN-DATE := IN-DATE
5.	LOANCT := 0	10.	READ NEXT INPUT
6.	LOANCT := LOANCT + 1		

Figure 4

Having described what happens in the library, and built a process model that keeps track of what happens, we are in a position to define data. The diagrams and equivalent text in Figs. 4 and 5 define some example data items: INLIB, ONLOAN, LOANCT, TIMEONLOAN, and LOANDATE. Ignoring some of the technical details, the important points are as follows: the original model process is used as a framework for defining the data to be stored for one book; the meaning of the data is formally tied to the meaning of the actions and their attributes; a data item is local to a process instance; the mechanism for updating the data is part of its definition, not something separate; the definition is in terms of event histories; as the model process executes to keep in step with the reality the data is also kept up to date; for this reason we have avoided problems of data integrity.

```
BOOK seq
   read next input;
   ACQUIRE seq
      ONLOAN := 'N';  LOANCT := 0;  TIMEONLOAN := 0;
      read next input;
   ACQUIRE end
   CLASSIFY seq
      INLIB := 'Y';
      read next input;
   CLASSIFY end
   LOANPART iter while (input = LEND)
      LOAN seq
         LEND seq
            LOAN-DATE := IN-DATE;  ONLOAN := 'Y';
            INLIB := 'N';
            read next input;
         LEND end
         OUT-ON-LOAN iter while (input = RENEW)
            RENEW seq
               read next input;
            RENEW end
         OUT-ON-LOAN end
         RETURN seq
            INLIB := 'Y';  ONLOAN := 'N';
            TIMEONLOAN := TIMEONLOAN – IN-DATE + LOAN-DATE;
            read next input;
         RETURN end
      LOAN end
   LOANPART end
   ENDPART select (input = SELL)
      SELL seq
         INLIB := 'N';
      SELL end
   ENDPART alt (input = OUTCIRC)
      SWOPSCHEME seq
         .
         .
         .
         .
```

Figure 5

84   High-Integrity System Specification and Design

Defining these data begins a second, more restrictive scoping of the specification. The actions define what happens, the data define what is to be remembered about what has happened. The system can only use historical data in its outputs or in the conditions for producing outputs if that data has been stored. This also applies to simple items like ACQUIRE-DATE, ISBN, and TITLE which are attributes of the ACQUIRE action and therefore are part of the ACQUIRE input transaction. Simple operations are needed in the BOOK process to store these data items, if they are required. (So far we have only shown how to define data in model processes; other processes may contain data; for example, we may introduce a process to hold the total numbers and values of books acquired in each of the last five weeks, or a process for each author to accumulate the number of LENDs in successive periods. These extra data are also part of the second scoping. Nevertheless, unless we remember every attribute of every action, the second scoping will be more restrictive than the first.)

For obvious reasons, we sometimes describe processes like the BOOK process as long-running processes. Only in some environments can such processes be executed directly. In others, an explicit suspend-and-resume mechanism has to be introduced. It could work as follows. When the process reaches a read it suspends itself; when a record becomes available, possibly several months later, the process resumes where it left off, executes as far as the next read, and suspends itself again. Between suspension and resumption, the values of any local variables and the resume point in the program (collectively called its "state vector") must be stored explicitly on some file or database. From the JSD point of view, the files or database of a system are simply the state vectors of the partially executed long-running processes that make up the specification.

A possible suspend-and-resume mechanism is illustrated in Fig. 6. Some details are omitted. For example, QS must be initialized before the first call, either by declaration or perhaps by the calling program. This mechanism converts the BOOK process into a BOOK subroutine. If several processes are similarly converted into subroutines of the same main program, then the several specification processes will have been combined into a single implementation process.

The diagrams used in the first instance simply to describe and analyze the library later become part of the code of the final system. Model processes can be turned into update subroutines for the database, files, or other stored data.

We have digressed into a discussion of some issues to do with the implementation of model processes. We now return to the modeling phase and consider some more complicated models.

B. More complicated models

Fig. 7 introduces five new actions to the library system and discriminates between two cases of an existing action. There can be several copies of the same book, so a RESERVE refers to a title not to an individual book. Fig. 8 shows two more structures that describe the orderings of the actions, making three structures in all.

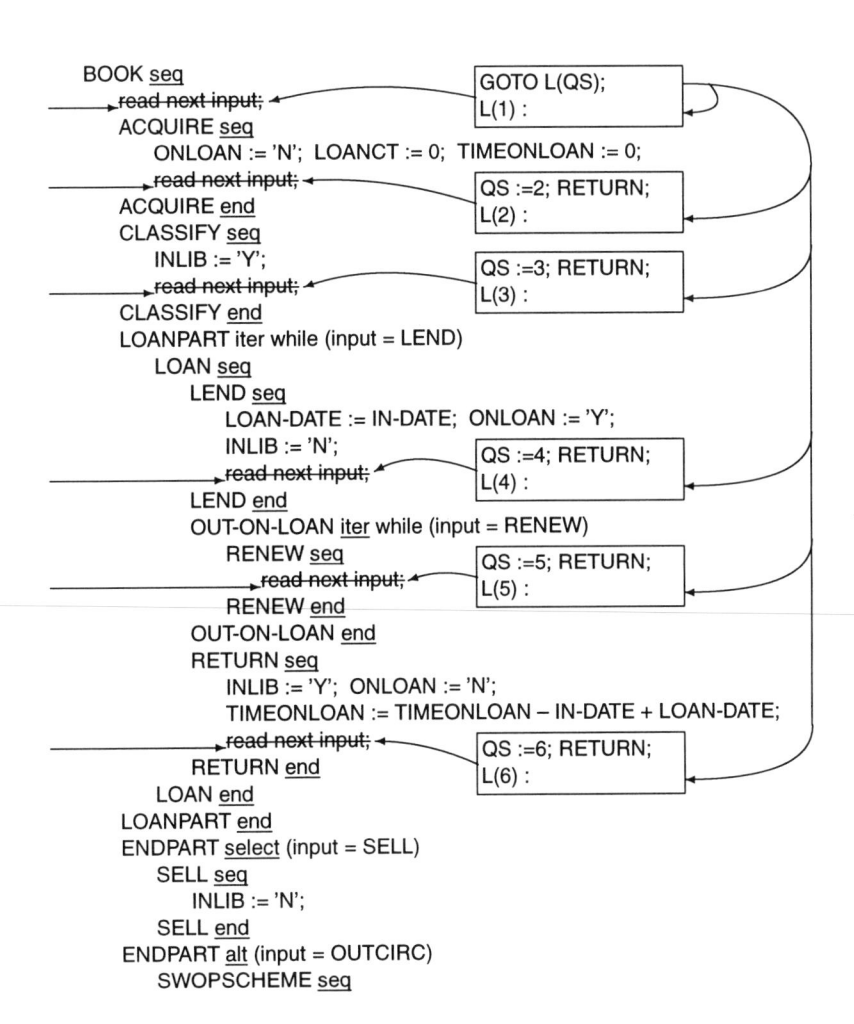

```
BOOK seq                                    ┌─────────────────────┐
   read next input;  ◄───────────────────── │ GOTO L(QS);         │◄──┐
   ACQUIRE seq                              │ L(1) :              │   │
      ONLOAN := 'N';  LOANCT := 0;  TIMEONLOAN := 0;
      read next input; ◄─────────────────── │ QS :=2; RETURN;     │
   ACQUIRE end                              │ L(2) :              │◄──┤
   CLASSIFY seq                             └─────────────────────┘   │
      INLIB := 'Y';                         ┌─────────────────────┐   │
      read next input; ◄─────────────────── │ QS :=3; RETURN;     │   │
   CLASSIFY end                             │ L(3) :              │◄──┤
   LOANPART iter while (input = LEND)       └─────────────────────┘   │
      LOAN seq                                                        │
         LEND seq                                                     │
            LOAN-DATE := IN-DATE;  ONLOAN := 'Y';                     │
            INLIB := 'N';                   ┌─────────────────────┐   │
            read next input; ◄───────────── │ QS :=4; RETURN;     │   │
         LEND end                           │ L(4) :              │◄──┤
         OUT-ON-LOAN iter while (input = RENEW)                       │
            RENEW seq                       ┌─────────────────────┐   │
               read next input; ◄────────── │ QS :=5; RETURN;     │   │
            RENEW end                       │ L(5) :              │◄──┤
         OUT-ON-LOAN end                    └─────────────────────┘   │
         RETURN seq                                                   │
            INLIB := 'Y';  ONLOAN := 'N';                             │
            TIMEONLOAN := TIMEONLOAN – IN-DATE + LOAN-DATE;           │
            read next input; ◄───────────── │ QS :=6; RETURN;     │   │
         RETURN end                         │ L(6) :              │◄──┘
      LOAN end
   LOANPART end
   ENDPART select (input = SELL)
      SELL seq
         INLIB := 'N';
      SELL end
   ENDPART alt (input = OUTCIRC)
      SWOPSCHEME seq
```

Figure 6

A More Complicated Model for the Library

More Actions

Action	Definition and Attributes
JOIN	A new member joins the library member-id, name, address, lend-limit, date.
LEAVE	A member leaves the library, or through inactivity is deemed to have left. member-id, date.
CHANGE-DETAILS	A member's address, lend-limit or reserve-limit is changed. member-id, address, lend-limit, reserve-limit
RESERVE	A member reserves a title that isn't available member-id, title
CANCEL	A reservation is no longer wanted. member-id, title

In addition we have sometimes to distinguish two kinds of LEND action:

LEND-RESERVE	The LEND is the result of a reservation
LEND-NORMAL	The LEND is not the result of a reservation

Figure 7

Several of the actions belong to more than one of the structures. The different structures describe intersecting subsets of actions; each structure describes a set of ordering constraints on its own actions. Thus we can view the same events in the same reality from different points of view. The constraints on any one action are the sum of the constraints imposed by the structures to which it belongs. The library only LENDs a BOOK to a MEMBER if the member has JOINED but not yet LEFT and if the BOOK has just been CLASSIFIED or RETURNED. Looking ahead to the error handling, a LEND input has to be checked against both relevant BOOK process and the relevant MEMBER process.

There is an implied CSP-like [1] parallel composition between processes (i.e., structures) that have actions in common, at least in as much as the processes describe the library itself.

The problem of data integrity is the problem of ensuring that several data items cannot take mutually inconsistent values. For the data items within one process integrity is ensured by the process itself, which defines an appropriate update mechanism. When an action happens that is common to two processes, both must execute to keep in step with the external reality. Common actions therefore ensure integrity among data items that belong to different processes.

Interestingly, many systems deliberately allow their data to reach inconsistent states over controlled periods. For example, we may choose to run the BOOK and MEMBER processes as part of various on-line update transactions and the RESERVATION processes as part of a daily batch run; in this case the LEND-RESERVE in RESERVATION is not synchronized with the same action in BOOK and MEMBER.

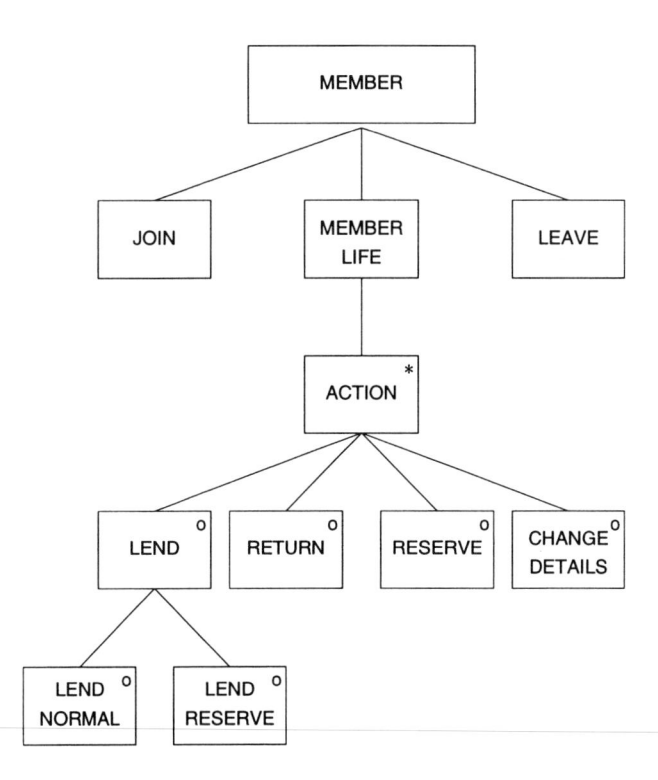

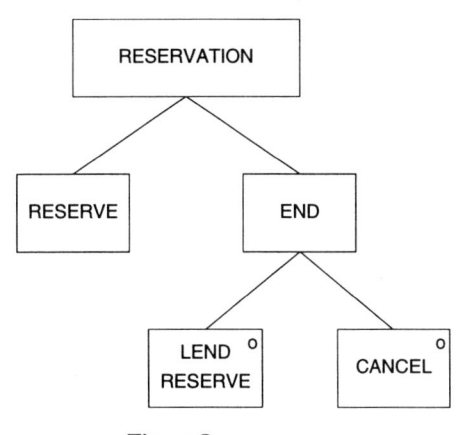

Figure 8

Interfacing with existing systems also often leads to processes with common actions being left unsynchronized. For example, the BOOK processes may be part of an existing system to which a MEMBER and RESERVATION subsystem has to be added. The existing system already has a means of collecting an input for the LEND action. If the only convenient interface with the existing system is to extract periodically a file of LENDs then the BOOK and MEMBER processes cannot be synchronized.

Obviously, we want to avoid the kind of over-specification that excludes perfectly reasonable implementations. In the JSD specification, therefore, the processes that model BOOKs, MEMBERs, and RESERVATIONs are not initially synchronized at their common actions. Synchronization can be added later if it is needed.

Allowing the same action in several processes improves the power of the notation, but still not enough to handle all circumstances conveniently. Suppose that no member is allowed to have more than some number, "lend-limit," of books on loan at one time. Lend-limit is defined from the JOIN and CHANGE DETAILS actions. To describe this constraint we fall back on an informal technique. We introduce a variable to the MEMBER process, set it to zero at the JOIN, increment it at a LEND, and decrement it at a RETURN (that is rigorous enough). Then we informally note the constraint ($N \leq$ lend-limit) beside the structure. We are here describing a library in which exceeding the limit is impossible, not just undesirable. So we are happy for subsequently defined error checking routines to reject a LEND if it would break the limit. If not, the constraint should not be added to the model. In practice this kind of constraint is only sensible if a member cannot take the book without the check being run.

Now consider the following description, in which the relevant actions/events are underlined.

> "Film stars often marry but their marriages always end in divorce. They are frequently hired to work on a film but they are always fired for breaking one or other of the terms of their contract."

Fig. 9 describes one possible interpretation of this description and illustrates how there can be more than one structure or process for the same entity. There are no ordering constraints between the events in a film star's married life and the events in his or her working life. The two aspects proceed in parallel. We call different structures that share the same identifier, different roles of the entity.

Any structure with more than one instance has to have an identifier, or some equivalent means of associating action inputs with their appropriate model instances. For example, a RETURN input has to be directed to the appropriate BOOK process. Thus, every action has to have among its attributes the identifiers of the structures to which it belongs. And if an action does not have a particular attribute, then it cannot belong to that structure; for example, RESERVE cannot be action of BOOK.

Fig. 9 reflects the assumptions that a film star can only have one spouse at a time and one contract at a time. A typical sequence of actions for a single film star is

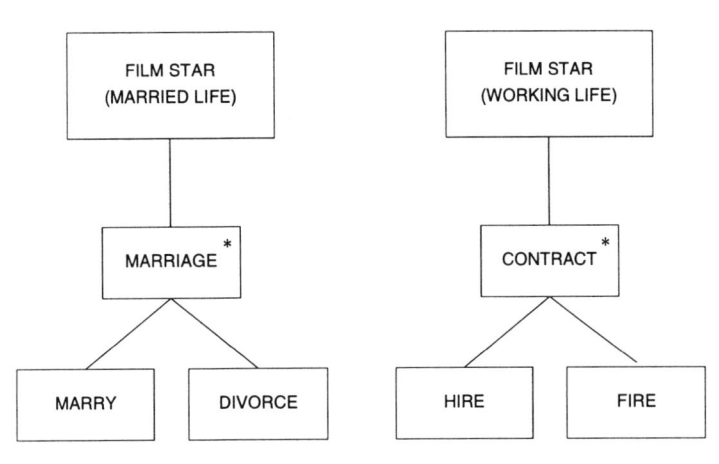

[Figure 9: Two tree diagrams. Left tree: FILM STAR (MARRIED LIFE) → MARRIAGE* → MARRY, DIVORCE. Right tree: FILM STAR (WORKING LIFE) → CONTRACT* → HIRE, FIRE.]

Figure 9

$$M, H, D, M, D, M, F, H, F, D.$$

Fig. 10 relaxes the second of these restrictions. A typical sequence of actions for a single film star is

$$M, H_1, H_2, F_2, D, M, H_3, F_1, D, F_3$$

where the index on H and F is a contract-id.

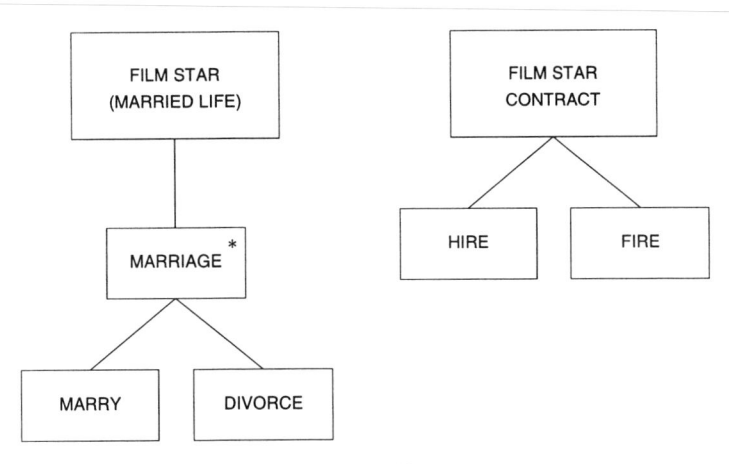

[Figure 10: Left tree: FILM STAR (MARRIED LIFE) → MARRIAGE* → MARRY, DIVORCE. Right tree: FILM STAR CONTRACT → HIRE, FIRE.]

Figure 10

More parallelism implies more and smaller structures. Drawing these structures is as much about parallelism as about ordering. A sequence of actions for many film stars is any interleaving of the sequences for individual film stars. (A qualification must be added if film stars can marry each other. MARRY and DIVORCE are then common actions of different instances of the same structure thus placing a constraint on their possible interleavings.)

An entity is defined in terms of its actions. It is simply the suitable name in the top box of a structure, the object on whose instances the ordering constraints apply. BOOK is not defined as a thing with lots of printed pages but as something which is ACQUIRED, CLASSIFIED, LENT, etc. Book would not be a good name if the library also had music cassettes which were ACQUIRED, CLASSIFIED, LENT, and so on according to the same ordering rules as apply to things with printed pages. In practice a developer works with actions and entities together (best of all with phrases like "the member returns the book"). In theory, though, the actions come slightly first.

C. Event models and data models

Database oriented approaches to the development of business systems start by building a data model of the enterprise (interpreting that term widely). Proponents argue, quite rightly, that the users' detailed requirements change very fast; that the stored data from which the requirements are calculated is much more stable; that therefore the key to robust systems is to get the database right; and the way to get the database right is to base it, via the stepping stone of a data model, on a description of the enterprise.

For data-processing systems, JSD can be viewed as a generalization of this approach, a generalization that includes the time dimension in the model of the enterprise. The state of a database (or equivalent files) does not reflect the state of the enterprise. However, the way the database changes also reflects the way the enterprise evolves. We argue that it is just as important to capture the dynamics of the enterprise in the description which forms the basis of the system as it is to capture its static properties. In JSD we describe the dynamics first (what happens? in what order?) and then we define the states of the enterprise (the data) in terms of these dynamics (what is stored or remembered about what has happened?). Not only is this more powerful for almost all the problems to which the database approach does apply, but it also extends the applicability of the approach to real-time and other systems in which the data are not of central importance.

In making this generalization, we are also offering some clarification of some of the conceptual difficulties at the heart of data modeling. In his book *Data and Reality* [2], William Kent shows by a series of examples that the terms entity, attribute, and relationship, as commonly used, are very difficult to define and in particular very difficult to distinguish. He also argues that any record oriented description (let alone particular hierarchical, network, or relational descriptions) has important limitations and that these limitations are only difficult to see because our habits of thought are conditioned by available implementation techniques.

Events are the basic medium of JSD modeling, not n-tuples of data items. Events have the immediate advantage that they are usually directly visible in the enterprise. Many data items are not (TIMEONLOAN, ACQUIREDATE, LOANCT, etc.), even though the data model is supposed to describe the enterprise. The concept of an event is fairly easy to define. The important point, apart from relevance to the system to be built, is that we must be prepared to regard the event as atomic, happening at a single instant of time. We are building a discrete simulation whether or not the enterprise evolves continuously or discretely or both. The choice of actions determines the resolution of our simulation. Actions correspond to the smallest updates that can be made to the database or its equivalent.

An event can have any number of attributes, which simply further describe the event. (For example, in a system to support the use of JSD a single event "AMEND STRUCTURE DIAGRAM OF ENTITY," which was constructed by a whole session with a front-end editor, had the attributes developer-id, time, entity-id, version-id, and the whole of the new structure.)

We have defined the term "entity" as a process (or set of processes sharing the same identifier) that describes constraints on the orderings of the events. Data are defined for an entity by adding variables to its process. The variables can be declared in any way we choose. We can also introduce other processes to hold extra data that do not fit any entity process. For example, we may introduce AUTHOR processes to keep count of the number of LENDs of books by each author in successive periods of time.

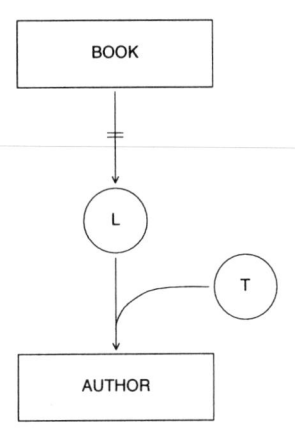

Figure 11

(Fig. 11 shows an appropriate fragment of network. The BOOK processes output LEND messages to the appropriate AUTHOR process. The T messages define the end of the periods. Author is an attribute of ACQUIRE and not of LEND and so has to be stored within BOOK so the message can be sent to the right destination. These networks are described in Section III. Extra processes that hold data always feed off the basic entity processes in this way.)

Relationships: Relationships are, according to Kent [2], "the very stuff of which data models are made." Although relationships are not a fundamental concept in

JSD, they can nevertheless be defined in terms of a JSD model in order to derive a data model of the desired flavor. Deriving a data model is useful if we are heading for a database implementation because most existing techniques of physical database design use some kind of "logical" data model as their starting point.

We would further argue a JSD model clarifies the definition of most relationships. For example, BOOK X "is-now-lent-to" MEMBER Y if LEND $(X, Y, \cdots)$ but not yet the corresponding RETURN. The relationship is many–one because in the BOOK structure two LENDs must have an intervening RETURN whereas in the MEMBER structure there is no such constraint. BOOK X "has-been-lent-to" MEMBER Y if there has ever been a LEND $(X, Y, \cdots)$.

Existence rules are also best expressed by considering the time dimension. The rule "A Y cannot exist unless an X exists" is described by a process in which the CREATE of a Y can only happen between the CREATE and the DELETE of the X.

The following rules will derive a data model from the JSD model.

1) Define relationships between entities where
   a) the identifier of one entity is part of the identifier of another (for example, MEMBER to RESERVATION if the identifier of RESERVATION is member.title);
   b) the identifier of one entity is part of the state vector of another (for example, MEMBER to BOOK if the borrower is stored in the BOOK process);
   c) part of the identifier of an entity is part of the state vector of another (for example, RESERVATION to BOOK where title is the relevant attribute).
2) Normalize any state vectors that are not already n-tuples, adding the obvious relationships between the separated parts. (For example, we could define within the BOOK process a list of all the MEMBERs who had ever borrowed the book. Normalization produces a new data modeling entity but not a new JSD entity.)

The JSD approach breaks down for data and relationships that cannot reasonably be defined in terms of histories of events, for example, for a database describing chemical compounds and their relationships. Except for correcting errors, such data are never changed. Data only need to be changed when something has happened (i.e., an event) that makes the current version inaccurate. The restriction to systems whose databases (or equivalent) evolve is not severe. Still, some static portions of an otherwise evolving database may not be amenable to the JSD approach.

Let us summarize some of the points in Section II. JSD models are defined in terms of events (or, synonymously, actions), their attributes, and a set of processes that describe their time orderings, and by implication possible parallelism. Processes are described by structure diagrams – tree structures whose leaves are the actions. The same action can appear in more than one structure. Usually the description requires multiple instances of a process type, in which case all the actions of a process must share an identifying attribute or attributes. Several processes can share the same identifier; each process is called a role of that entity. Data are defined directly in terms of the model either directly by adding variables to the existing processes or by adding new processes and adding variables to these; in either case data are defined in terms of event histories. The processes, called model processes, are the basis for the specification network.

Actions correspond to the transactions that cause database updates (or their equivalent in a real-time system). Model processes will be converted into database update subroutines. Stored data in the implemented system appears in the specification as the variables of long running processes, mainly of long running model processes.

III. The Network Phase

A. Elaboration of the model into a specification

The JSD model consists of actions, attributes of actions, and a set of disconnected sequential processes that describe the time orderings of the actions. These sequential processes are the start of the network that will eventually comprise the specification. Development proceeds incrementally, by adding new processes to the network and by elaborating processes that are already there. Three issues must be addressed when a new process is added.

1) How is the new process connected to the rest of the network?
2) What elaboration is necessary to the existing processes to which it is connected? (For example, a new data item may have to be added to a model process, as described above.)
3) The internal workings of the new process must be defined. Unless there is a good reason to the contrary, the internal structure is expressed using the same sequence, selection, and iteration notation used for the model processes.

Processes are added for three main reasons. Data collection and error handling processes fit between the reality and the model. Their purpose is to collect information about the actions and make sure, so far as possible, that only error-free data are passed on to the model. Output processes extract information from the model, perform calculations and summaries, and produce the system outputs. Interactive functions are like output functions, except that instead of producing outputs they feed back into the model. They handle those cases, represented in the extreme by simulations, where the system can create or substitute for what would otherwise have been external events. Oversimplifying somewhat, the model processes hold the main data for the system along with its update rules. The other processes contain the algorithms that calculate and format outputs, and drive the model either by collecting and checking inputs or by generating new actions.

Some examples of output and interactive functions are described below. We omit examples of input collection processes. For business and for real-time systems, typical examples are on-line data-collection programs and device drivers, respectively. The details of error handling are also omitted. (One technique is to add "guard" processes to filter inputs that look good but which do not fit the current state of the

[Figure 12: JSD network diagram showing Real World at top connecting to Model Processes, with Diagnostics and Error Handling on the left, Output Function Processes leading to Outputs, and Interactive Function Processes on the right.]

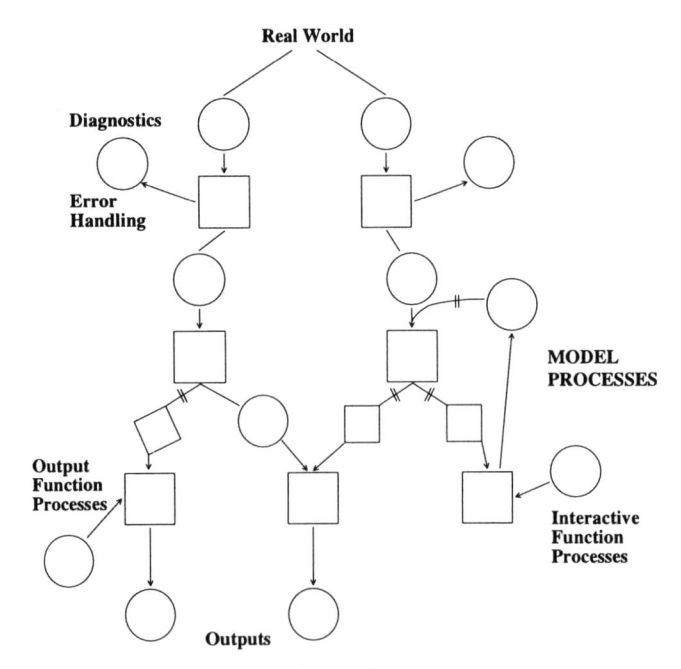

Figure 12

model. Before each read in a model process a write operation is inserted to send a message to its guard describing what the model is prepared to accept next.)

Fig. 12 shows how the four kinds of process in a JSD specification fit together. The network phase can be divided into three parallel subphases corresponding to the three kinds of process added to the network.

In a JSD network diagram the rectangles represent sequential process types and the circles and diamonds the two basic means of process communication, data stream and state vector communication, respectively. Data stream communication is by messages written by one process and read by another. The writes and corresponding reads are not synchronized; the messages can build up in a FIFO queue. In the specification, we assume that the queue is big enough for processes never to be blocked on a write; however, a process is blocked on a read if no message is available. (The BOOK processes spend most of their time blocked waiting for an input.)

The state vector of a process consists of all its local variables including its text pointer. State vector inspection is a form of shared variable communication; one process is allowed read-only access to the other's state vector. We will see below how enquiries about the state of a particular book are answered by a process that examines the state vector of the corresponding BOOK model process.

The double bars in the network diagrams indicate relative multiplicity in the way process instances communicate – the double bars are on the side of the many.

(Remember that communication is between process instances, but the rectangles represent process types.) Thus, Fig. 14 indicates that many instances of BOOK write messages to the same NEW BOOKS LISTER and that each process F_j, over its lifetime, examines many instances of the BOOK state vectors.

The merging of the input lines on two or more data streams indicates that the streams are merged before they are read. To the reading process they appear as one stream. The merging algorithm must not starve any stream, must preserve the ordering of messages from one stream, but is otherwise unspecified. This "rough-merging" introduces some indeterminacy into the specification, an indeterminacy that is limited by the kind of overall timing constraints discussed in Section III-C below. Section III-C also contains a discussion of the choice of data streams and state vector inspections as communication primitives.

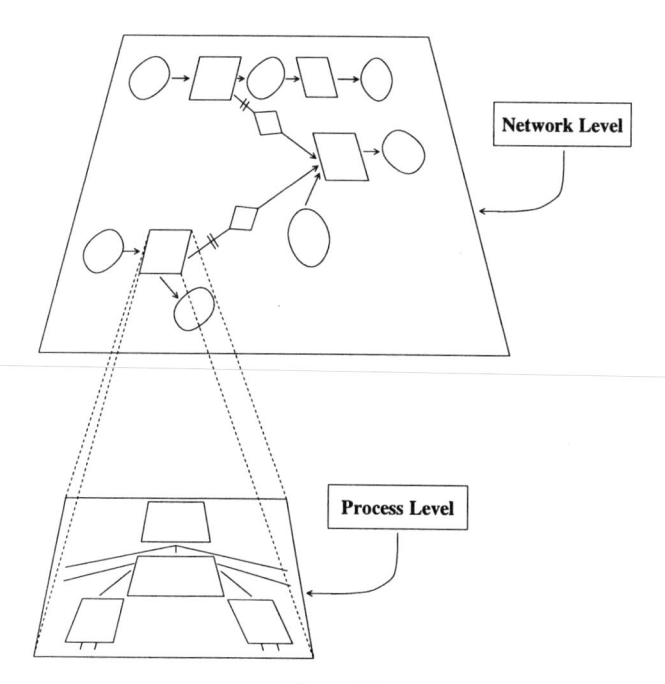

Figure 13

Fig. 13 summarizes the nature of a JSD specification: there is a network of a large number of sequential processes; each process is, in general, long-running; each process has its own internal structure consisting of sequences, selections, and iterations; the processes communicate by writing and reading messages and by a one-writer–many-readers form of shared variable communication; the state vectors of the processes, particularly the model processes, make up the files, databases, and other storage structures of typical implementations.

The network and the details of the processes are not quite the whole specification. We also need the definition of the actions to describe the way the network has to be embedded into the reality. These definitions fix the specification boundaries for most of the inputs. There must also be an equivalent agreed interpretation for the outputs from the specification. We need to know whether an output circle on the boundary describes a voltage difference, a screen display, or an invoice printed on gold-embossed paper.

We also need information about the desired speed of execution of the processes – this is not part of the definition of the network. Indeed, we are careful to ensure that correct operation of the network does not depend on some particular relative speed of the processes. Nevertheless, the system will be useless if it executes too slowly and we must complete the specification by describing, albeit informally, the required and desired limits on the speed of the processes.

B. Some examples

First, we will add the following output functions, which can be based on the BOOK model process alone.

1) On input of a given book-id, output the whereabouts of the particular book.
2) On input of a given author, output the titles of the books of that author with counts of the number of books and the total number of loans for each title.
3) On input of a given title, output whether or not any books of that title are in the library and available for loan.
4) Periodically list the overdue books, grouped by borrower.

These functions are specified by the processes $F1$, $F2$, $F3$, and $F4$ in Fig. 14. Each F_j accesses the state vectors of the BOOK processes. Each F_j uses a particular ideal access path through the state vectors. These access paths are the raw material for the file design part of the implementation step. They are part of the definition of the state vector inspection.

For the above four functions the ideal access paths are as follows.

1) Direct access by book-id.
2) For a given author, grouped by title.
3) For a given title, books with INLIB = "*Y*".
4) Books grouped by borrower, with ONLOAN = "*Y*" and LENDDATE LT LIMIT.

In the implementation phase, some kind of file design will be chosen to hold the BOOK state vectors. A sophisticated design will support these access paths directly. A simple design will mean that extra components must be added in front of each F_j to extract from the state vectors actually accessed the ones F_j actually needs. In extreme cases sorting is also needed. The main point is that the network and the details of the F_j's are specified without any commitment to the file design or data storage structures that are to be used.

Fig. 15 describes the internal structure of $F4$.

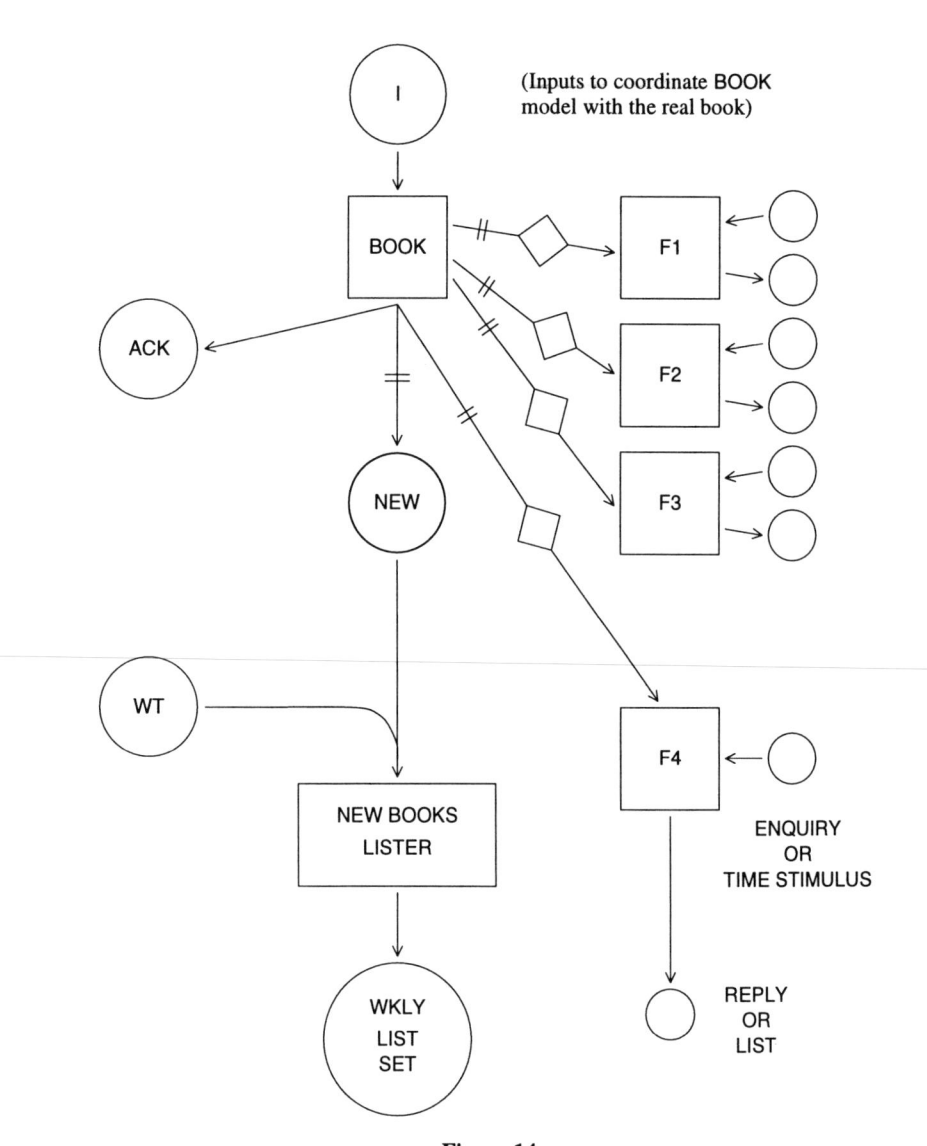

Figure 14

```
            ┌────┐
            │ F4 │
            └────┘
           ╱   │
        ┌─┐   │
        │1│   │
        └─┘   │
      ┌───────────────┐
      │  REQUEST    * │
      │   /LIST       │
      └───────────────┘
       ╱  │       │  ╲
     ┌─┐┌─┐     ┌─┐┌─┐
     │2││3│     │4││1│
     └─┘└─┘     └─┘└─┘
        ┌──────────────┐
        │  BORROWER  * │
        └──────────────┘
              │  ╲
            ┌─┐
            │5│
            └─┘
           ┌──────────────┐
           │ O'DUE BOOK * │
           └──────────────┘
              ╱      ╲
            ┌─┐     ┌─┐
            │6│     │2│
            └─┘     └─┘
```

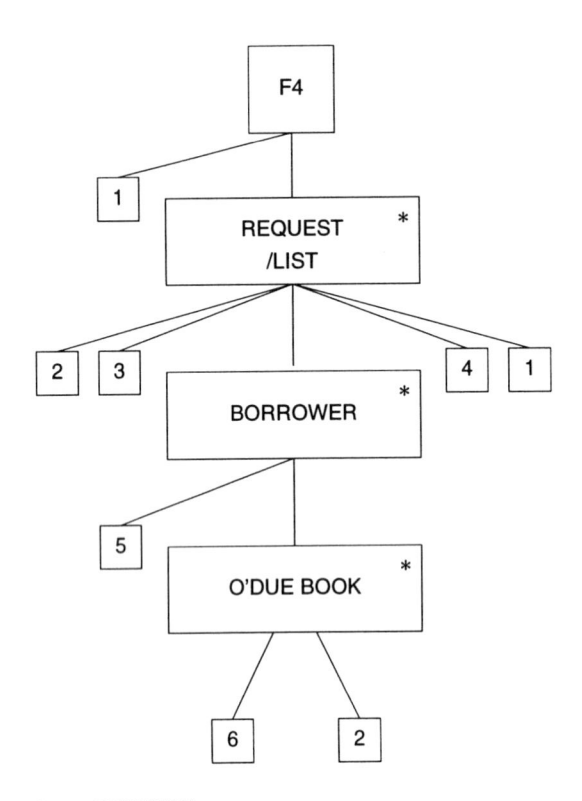

1. read next REQUEST
2. read next BOOK SV   (overdue books only, sorted by borrower)
3. write LIST-HDR
4. write LIST-TRLR
5. write BORROWER-HDR
6. write BOOK-LINE

Figure 15

The following two functions require data stream outputs from the model for their formal specification, as shown in Fig. 14.

1) Output an acknowledgement slip when a book is returned.
2) Output a periodic list of new books acquired since the last report. Include the cost of each book, the total value of books acquired in this period, and the brought forward and carried forward totals for the year.

Data streams are used when the model process has the initiative for the communication. The model sends a message to kick the other process into doing something, or at least because it is aware of the messages that need summarizing or further processing to produce the desired output.

State vector inspections are used when the initiative is with the function process. The communication takes place because the F_j's are triggered by enquiries or timing inputs to examine the state of the model.

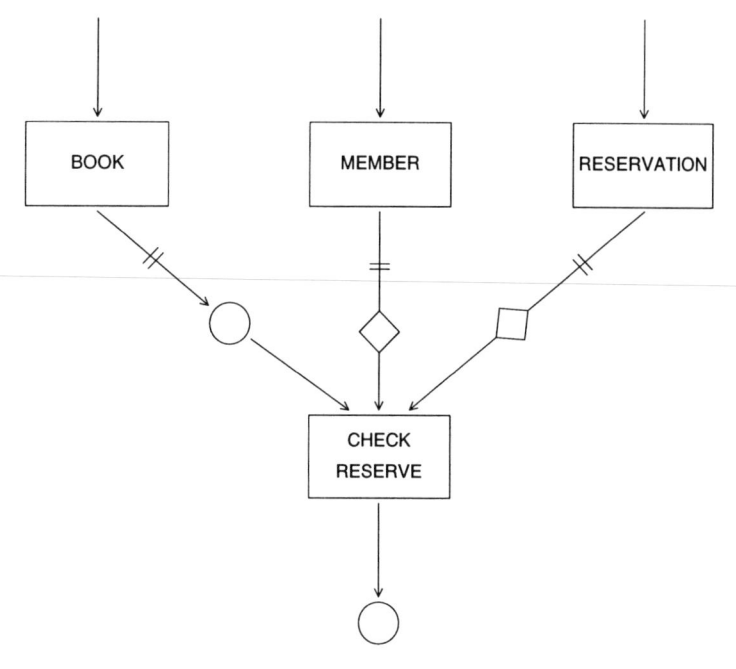

Figure 16

Figs 16 and 17 show the network part of the specification for two more complicated functions.

1) When a book is returned check if there are any reservations outstanding for that title and output the name and address of the member who has been waiting longest.

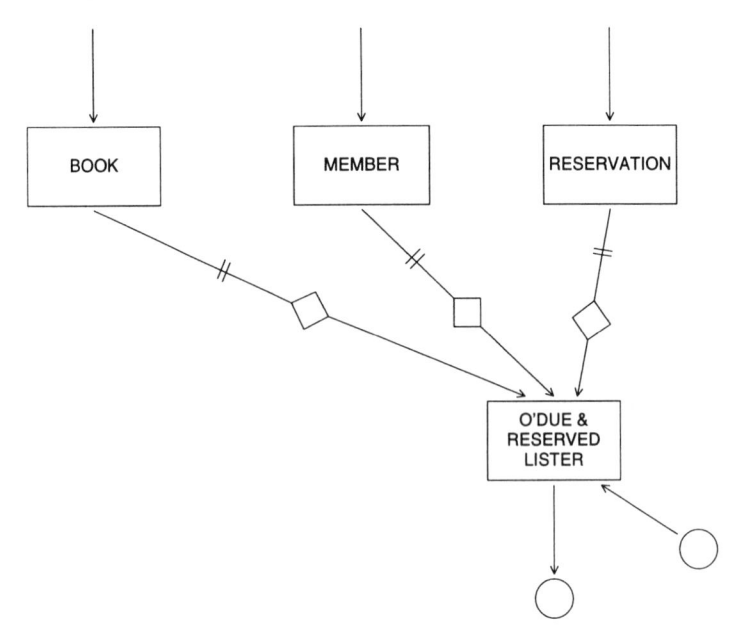

Figure 17

2) On request, produce a list of overdue books (grouped by title) whose titles are reserved and also the name and address of the member who has borrowed them.

In the first function the BOOK process sends a message to CHECK RESERVE when the book is RETURNed; CHECK RESERVE then examines the state vectors of the RESERVATIONS, and if necessary the MEMBER, in order to output the result. The second function just needs state vector inspections.

The new processes do not communicate directly with each other. We only need to understand their connections with the model. That is why we only need to draw fragments of the network at a time and why each fragment contains some of the model processes.

In each case we have only considered the network part of the specification. We also have to consider the model processes we are connecting to. For each data stream we have to add appropriate write operations; for each state vector inspection we have to check that the data we expect to find has in fact been defined. These details have been omitted, as have the internal structures of the new processes. The JSP programming method [4]–[7] can be used to design these processes.

Fig. 18 shows the network part of the specification for two more functions.

1) When a member leaves, output a list of any outstanding reservations he or she may have.
2) On request output a list of members who have been inactive for at least a year.

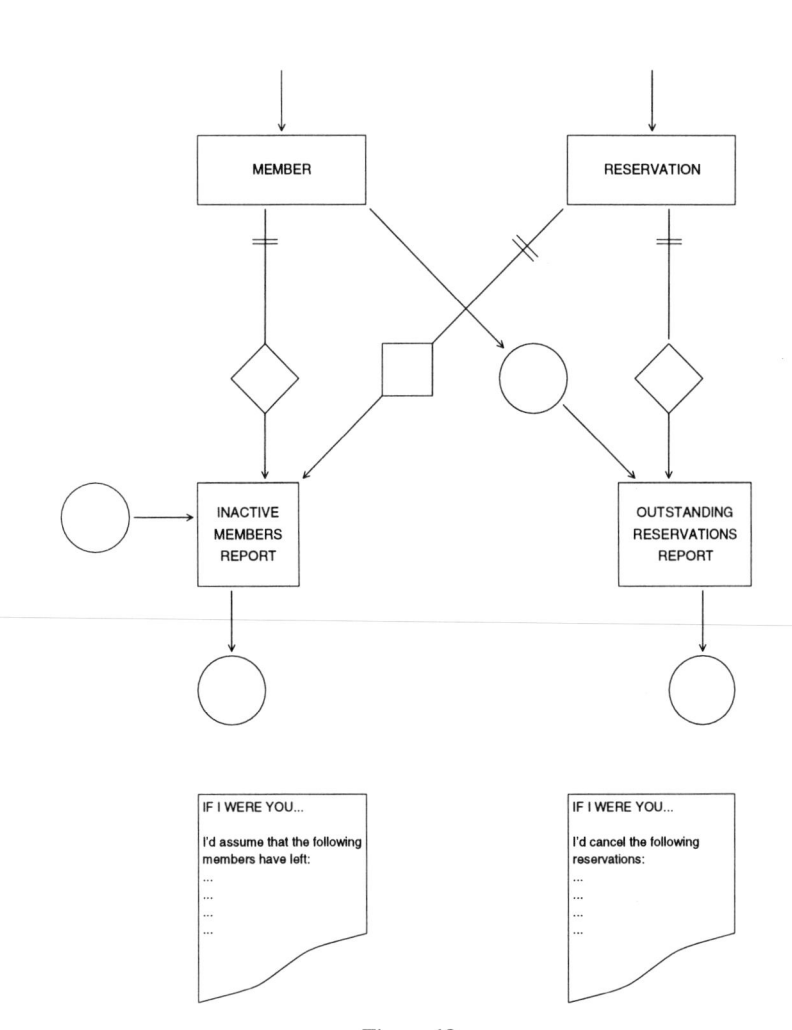

Figure 18

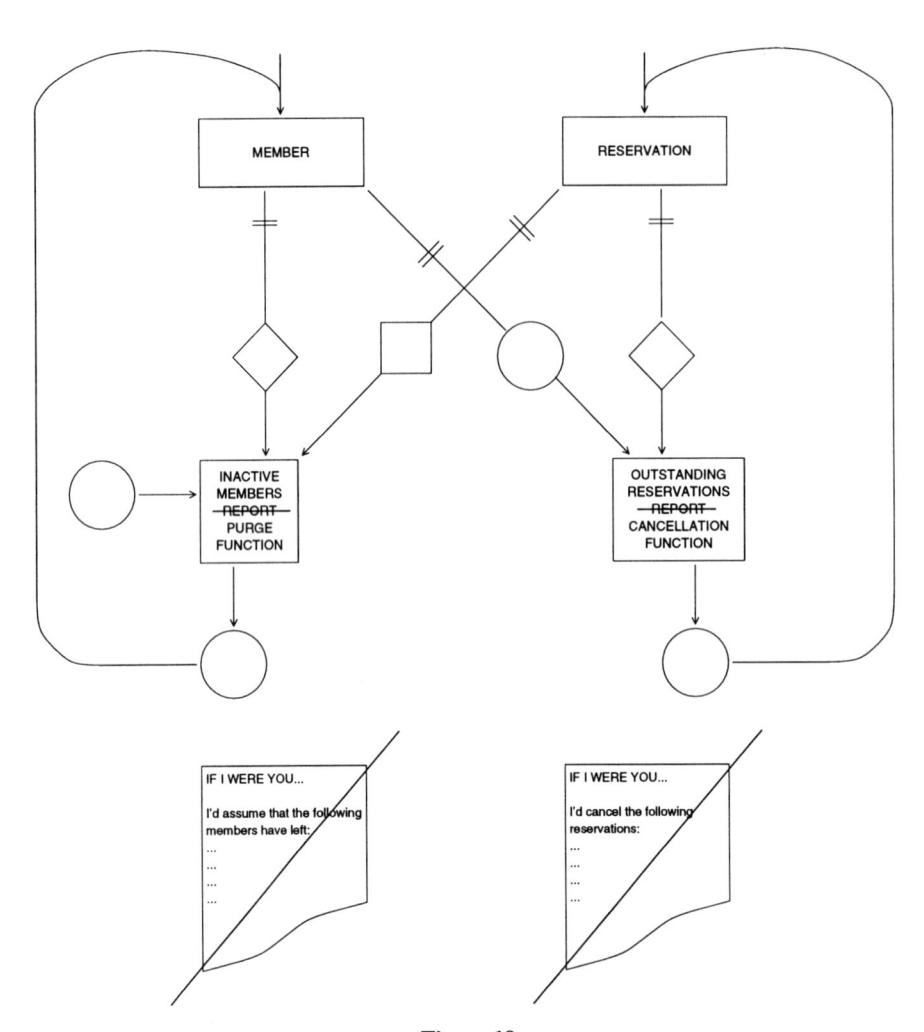

Figure 19

Fig. 19 shows a modified specification. The output functions of Fig. 18 have been replaced by similar interactive functions. Now the system automatically cancels reservations when a member leaves, the system automatically makes inactive members leave (the library leaves the member), whether they like it or not.

The system is now generating actions that previously were happening only outside. In a simulation most or all of the actions are generated by interactive functions in this way. The exceptions, for example in a training simulation, are the actions that are still happening externally and for which inputs have to be collected in the usual way. The model processes describe the reality that is to be simulated. The choice of actions and attributes determines the scope and resolution of the simulation. The interactive functions describe the rules by which the actions are deemed to have happened.

Our example also shows that we cannot just look to the external reality to find the initial set of actions.

C. The choice of communication primitives

1) Asynchronous Writing and Reading: The tiny specification in Fig. 20 describes a set of BOOK processes each reading F's and writing G's. The processes are directly executable but the required speed of execution has not yet been specified. Of course the overall speed cannot be very fast – the whole point of these long-running processes is that they can be blocked for months at a read. However, there will be some execution speed of the operations between the reads which is so slow that the results appear on G too late to be useful. The specification has to include some description of required speeds. In the present state of JSD such constraints are specified informally by statements such as, "the BOOK's data must not be more than a day out-of-date" and, "any responses on G should occur within 5 seconds of the input of the triggering F record." Perhaps this informality is a weakness. However, we are reluctant to introduce a more formal notation because there is no means of embodying these timing constraints directly in an implementation in the way that BOOK processes can be converted into subroutines and embodied in the implementation. The extra precision would not really help the implementor.

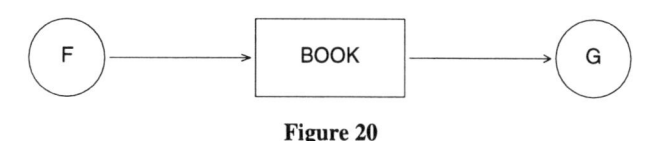

Figure 20

In the specification in Fig. 21, there would be no point in using synchronous writing and reading on G. It would be unnecessarily restrictive. Any acceptable response time between an F and an H record could be met by making P and Q very fast and using up the time in the delay between writing and reading. Nor would synchronous communication save us if P or Q was too slow. The general reason

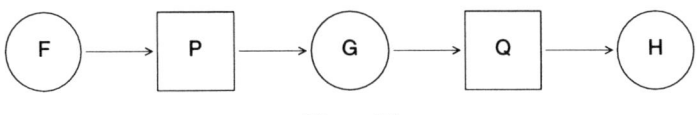

Figure 21

for rejecting synchronous message-passing as our specification primitive is that it often leads to overspecification, that is, to specifications that unnecessarily exclude reasonable implementations.

That is not to say that we will not often choose to implement asynchronous writing and reading by a synchronous message passing mechanism. That is part of our implementation freedom. (In languages that do not support concurrency the easiest way is to implement the messages as parameters passed across a subroutine interface, for example, by introducing into Q a suspend-and-resume mechanism such as was described in Section II-A.) It is also part of our implementation freedom to buffer the G records or whatever period is consistent with the response constraints. For networks like Fig. 21 and many others, this implementation freedom is worth plenty and costs nothing.

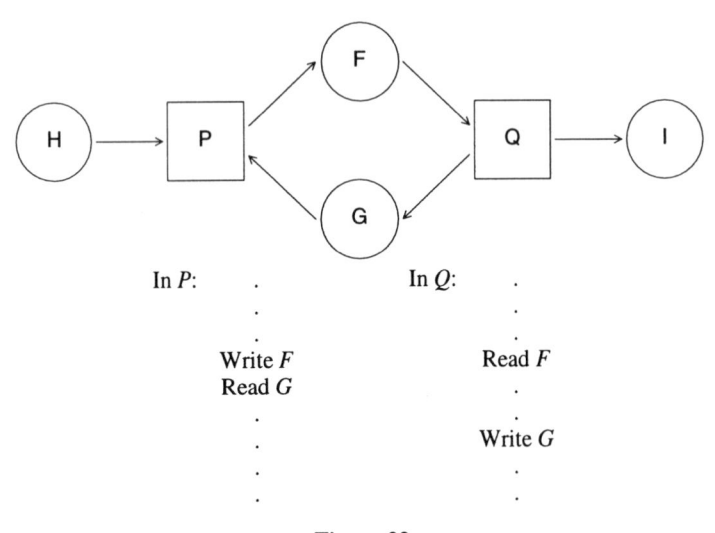

In P:
.
.
.
Write F
Read G
.
.
.

In Q:
.
.
.
Read F
.
.
Write G
.
.
.

Figure 22

Sometimes we do have to synchronize processes more tightly in the specification. For example, Fig. 22 shows P and Q more tightly synchronized. Process Q is held up at the "read F" until P reaches the "write F." P is also held up at the "read G" (effectively the same place as the "write F") until Q not only reaches "read G" but also the "write G". This is the data stream equivalent of an Ada rendezvous.

2) State Vector Inspection: State vector inspection can be defined in terms of data streams, so it is not strictly necessary to have another communication primitive. However it is very attractive to be able to specify directly inspections of, for example, the data in the BOOK processes. In implemented systems generally there are very many components that have read-only access to stored data, so the extra complication of another primitive seems well worthwhile.

An informal description of state vector inspection uses such phrases as "only coherent states returned," "communication invisible to inspected process" and "a 'get SV of P' operation returns P's state vector without any operations being executed in P." These statements are correct but they skate around the mutual exclusion problem. A particular inspection may be invisible to P, but P still has to do enough to ensure that the results of inspections correspond only to particular coherent states, for example, to the states of P just before the execution of a read operation.

The mutual exclusion can be handled either on the state vector of P itself, or on a copy. The two cases correspond to slightly different definitions of state vector inspection. In the first P cannot be executing and being inspected at the same time; if P is not at one of the approved states the inspection must be delayed. In the second P writes a copy of each coherent state; the copy can be inspected while P is executing and the result of an inspection may now be out-of-date. Of course, the mutual exclusion problem does not disappear in the second case. An inspection must still be prevented while the copy is being updated.

At first sight surprisingly, we have chosen a definition that fits the second looser description. The reasons are similar to those for choosing asynchronous rather than synchronous message passing: we gain implementation freedom at little extra cost. Moreover, we are certainly not excluded from implementing the loose definition by using only one physical copy of the data.

The differences between the two possible definitions are clarified by considering their data stream equivalences. Fig. 23(b) is the equivalent of the first, tighter definition, and (c) is the equivalent of our chosen, looser definition. In both $Q1$ and $Q2$ the "get SV of P" operation has been replaced by a "write enquiry on E; read reply from $S(2)$" pair of operations. P1 is the process P elaborated to answer the enquiries; it answers by writing a copy of its state on S. The ordinary inputs F and the stream of enquiries E are merged; P1 reads the single stream $F \& E$; since P1 is a sequential process, it cannot be processing an E and an F record at the same time.

P2 outputs its state on $S1$. P2STATE is very simple; it reads the merged stream $E \& S1$; it stores the latest state from an $S1$ record; it answers enquiries from E by outputting this latest state. P2STATE executes concurrently with P2. The state stored in P2STATE may lag behind the real state of P2.

State vector inspection could be defined by Fig. 23(c) (plus the details of the internals of the processes), or more abstractly along the following lines.

> Let $S_1, S_2, \ldots, S_m$ be the chosen coherent states reached during an execution of P. Let $G_1, G_2, \ldots, G_n$ be the "get SV of P" operations executed during an execution of Q. Then the result of each G_i is one of the S_k and:
> if G_i results in S_k and G_j results in S_l, then

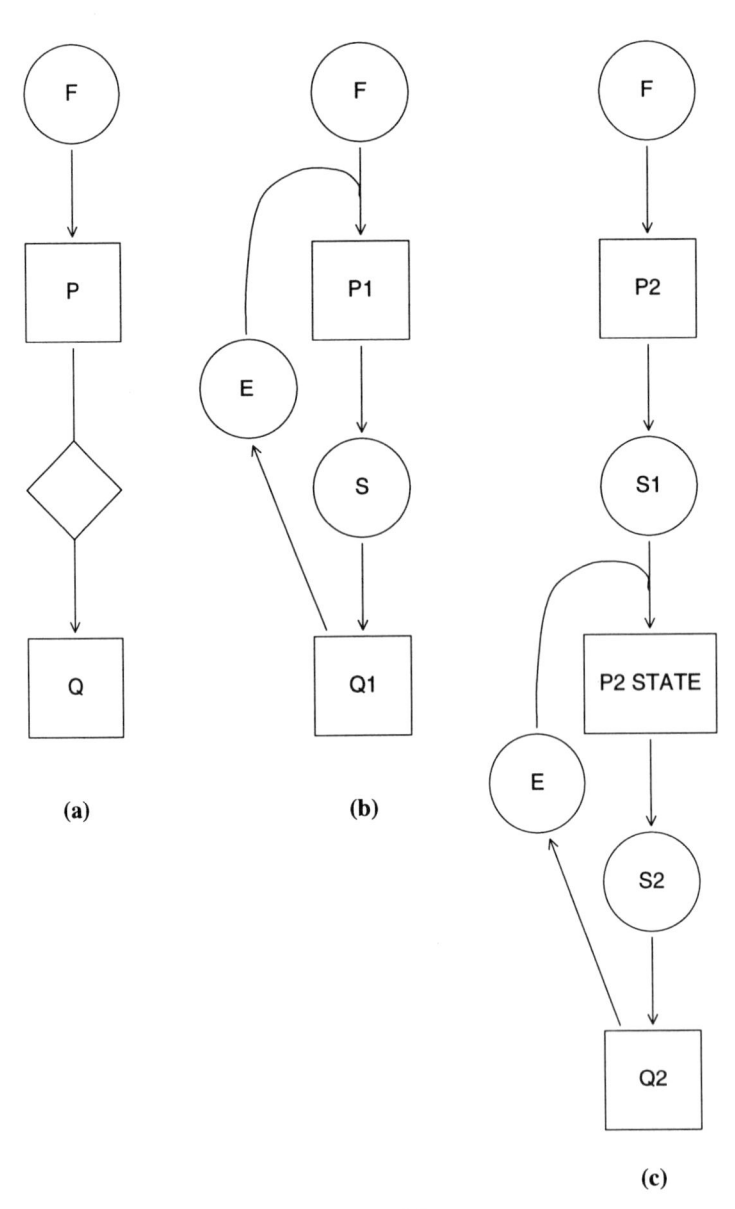

Figure 23

$i > j \Rightarrow k \geq l.$

Let us now return to more practical matters. We have gained the freedom to implement state vector inspection using a second copy of the state vector. This freedom is particularly important in the following cases.

- In distributed implementations, local enquiries are answered by accessing a local copy of the data. The local copy is not necessarily exactly in step with the main copy.
- There is a trend in data processing towards having an operational database which is updated on-line and a decision support database which is periodically updated with an extract from the operational database. (IBM's new database system DB2 may mainly be used for this decision support role.)
- In real-time applications where virtual processors access the same global memory, second copies can reduce the problems of mutual exclusion and interrupt masking.

In our network the BOOK model already lags behind the real BOOK by some indeterminate amount, so there is no extra indeterminacy if the *SV* copy we access lags behind the real BOOK state vector. Descriptions of overall constraints on processor execution speeds like "for this enquiry the data accessed must be no more than 5 seconds (or 24 hours) behind the reality" limit the sum of the indeterminacies.

With the JSD style of distributed specification, we have to ensure that the problem really is solved in the specification. Because we often fix the relative scheduling of processes in the implementation phase, it is sometimes tempting to build a network that only "works" given particular relative processor speeds, in other words to anticipate the implementation. Certainly, it is unacceptable if some of the processes in the network execute too slowly; that would violate the extra, informally expressed timing constraints. But if a given set of processor speeds does meet all the constraints, then we should not be able to produce unacceptable results by making some of the processes run faster. The (small) price to pay for the implementation freedom we gain by using asynchronous message passing and the looser form of state vector inspection is occasionally some extra care in constructing the specification network.

IV. The Implementation Phase

There are two main issues in the implementation phase: how to run the processes that comprise the specification, and how to store the data that they contain. The first turns out to be particularly concerned with the data streams in the specification, the second with the state vector inspections.

Of course, there may be no work at all in the implementation phase. We only need to find a machine that will execute our executable network of processes. If we can, and if we meet the timing constraints that is fine. We are not looking for extra work.

The problem, though, is the number of (instances of) processes in our specifications and the length of time it takes for their input to accumulate. In our library, books last for up to 20 years and we have over 100,000 of them. Will our operating systems and concurrent languages allow us to run 100,000 processes concurrently for 20 years? We often have to combine and package the specification processes into a more familiar arrangement of "short-running" jobs and transaction-handling modules. Admittedly, our library example is fairly extreme. Many real-time environments do support some number of long-running processes, but probably still not as many as in our specifications.

A basic technique has already been introduced in Section II-A. A process can be converted into a subroutine by inserting a suspend-and-resume mechanism at its read statements and by passing the input records as parameters of the call. Every time the subroutine is called it executes part of the long-running program. It is passed an input record and returns control when it is ready to read another.

(The coding details of this suspend-and resume mechanism can be found in [3]–[7]. The technique can be generalized to allow suspend points at the reads and writes on several or all of the data streams in the program.)

A. Data design

After we have converted processes into subroutines, we can also easily separate the data (that is the state vector) from the subroutine text so that many instances of a process can be implemented by one copy of the subroutine and many copies of the data. For example, the state vector can be made a parameter of the subroutine. When the subroutine is called it is passed the input record and a state vector; this allows it temporarily to assume the identity of a particular instance; the subroutine executes and passes back the updated state vector when it returns; the calling program is responsible for storing and retrieving the state vectors. Alternatively, the extra parameter may only be the instance-id; the subroutine itself accesses the state vector by retrieval from a file or perhaps by using the id as a pointer into an array.

Once the data are separated, questions of storage and access can be considered. We deal with them here only briefly, not because they are unimportant, but because there is nothing new or special about the way physical data design is handled in JSD. From the specification we have a definition of the state vectors, that is of the data to be stored, and from the state vector inspections we have the definition of how the data are to be accessed. If we wanted we could also map the JSD model on to a data model of any desired flavor. We know the desired response times, the likely volumes, and we can add security and backup information as required. These are the essential inputs from the specification into database design or into the design of storage structures in main memory.

B. Combining processes

First we show how an abstract network of programs can be combined into a main program and a hierarchy of subroutines. Then we apply the technique to the library example.

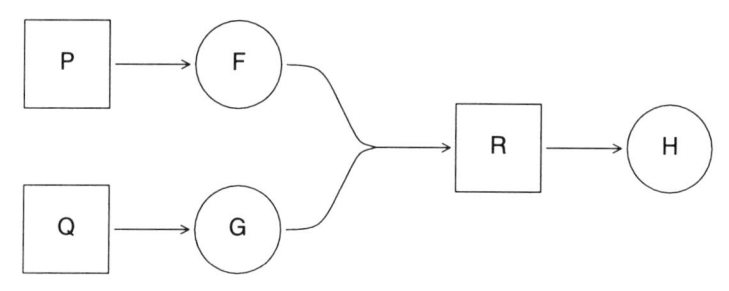

Figure 24

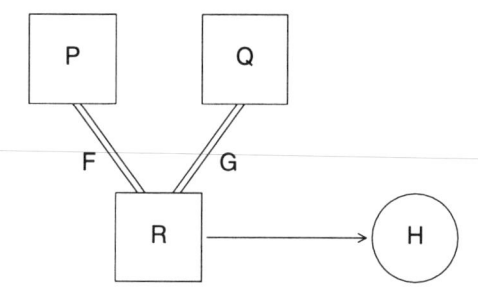

Figure 25

Two or more rough merged data streams can be implemented by making the reading process a common subroutine of the several writing processes. In Fig. 24 P writes F, Q writes G, R reads the merged $F\&G$ as one stream. Fig. 25 is a subroutine hierarchy diagram in which P calls R passing F records as parameters, and in which Q calls R passing G records as parameters.

Now we will combine the four processes P, Q, R, and S in Fig. 26 so that they run as subroutines of a single main program. The technique works as follows. Imagine taking a knitting needle and threading it through all the external input streams, in this case A, B, and C. Pick up the needle and hold it horizontally. The programs will hang in the correct subroutine hierarchy, in this case as shown in Fig. 27. Each program is called by the supplier(s) of its input, all the programs return control upwards when they want to read a new input; the MAIN program is very simple – it

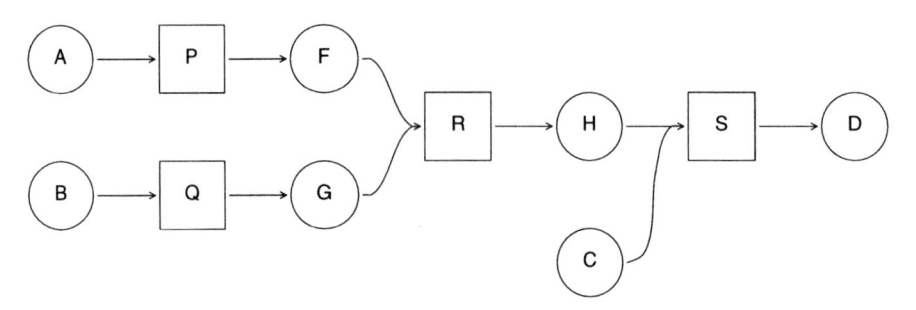

Figure 26

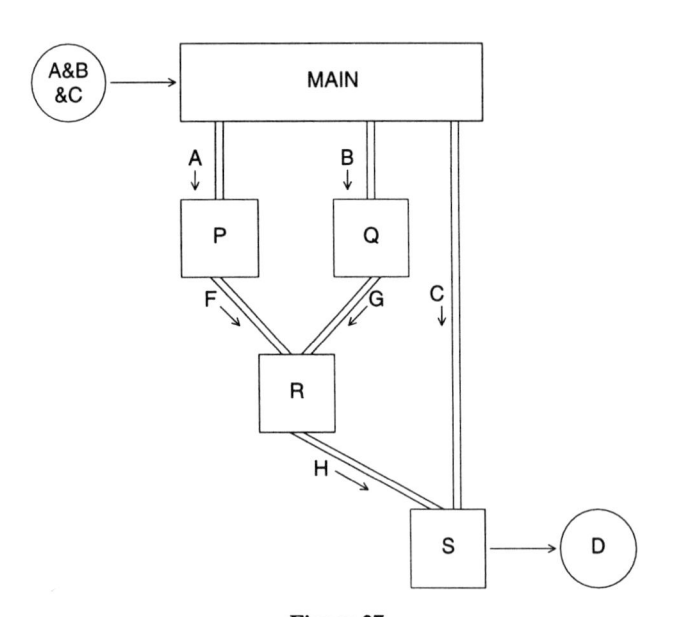

Figure 27

reads *A&B&C* and calls *P*, *Q*, and *S* with, respectively, the *A*, *B*, and *C* records as parameters.

This technique works provided every program only reads one input stream (the one stream may be the result of merging several) and provided there are no loops in the network. Loops are dealt with below. The treatment of programs with several input streams is omitted: the common special cases are easy; otherwise a more complex suspend-and-resume mechanism is needed.

State vector inspections in the network can simply be ignored. The subroutine will naturally access only a coherent version because the processes only give up control at read or write operations.

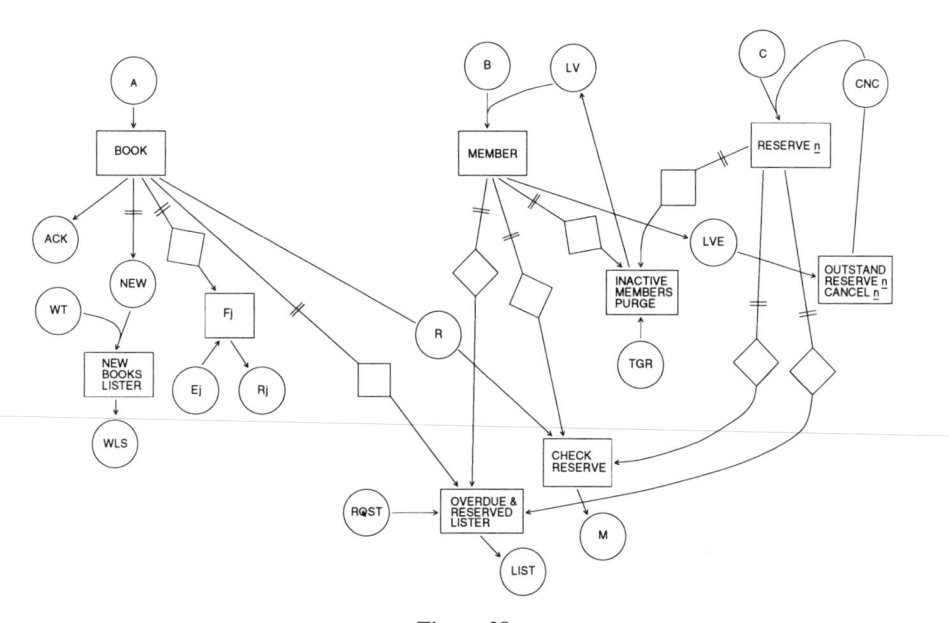

Figure 28

Fig. 28 shows the network for the library example. (We did not have to consider the whole of the network during the specification.) Fig. 29 shows the same network rearranged and with the state vector inspections removed. Fig. 30 shows the whole network implemented as a hierarchy of subroutines. A probable internal structure of MAIN is shown in Fig. 31. This style of implementation has no buffering on any of the internal data streams. It corresponds to a transaction oriented implementation in which one input and all its consequences are completely dealt with before the next. MAIN has only been introduced as part of the implementation. It is a scheduling program; it controls the sequential interleaving of the processes in the network.

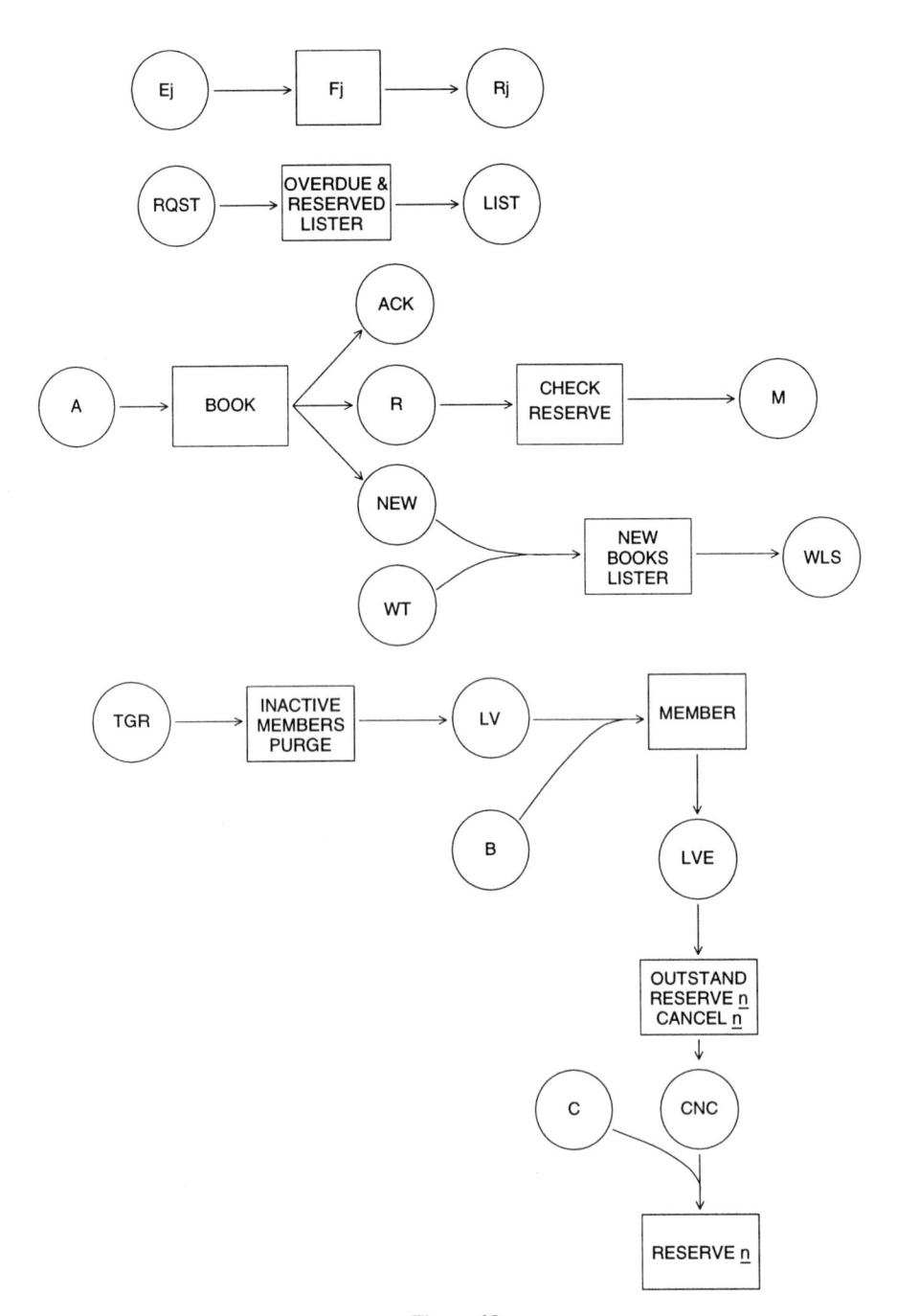

112   High-Integrity System Specification and Design

Figure 29

Cameron An Overview of JSD 113

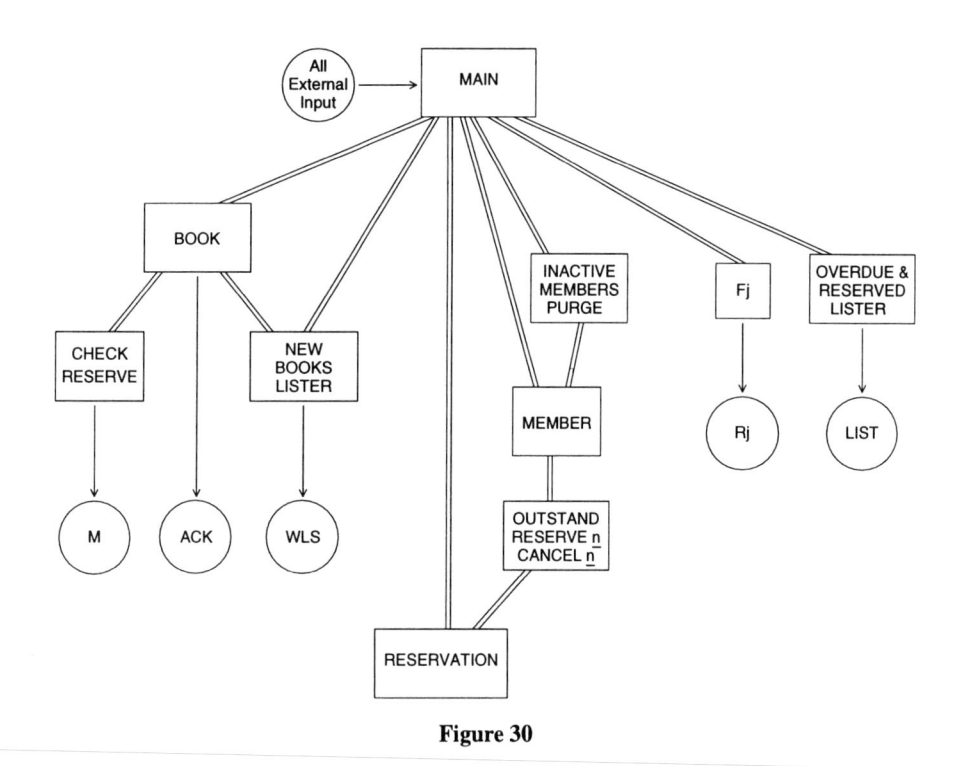

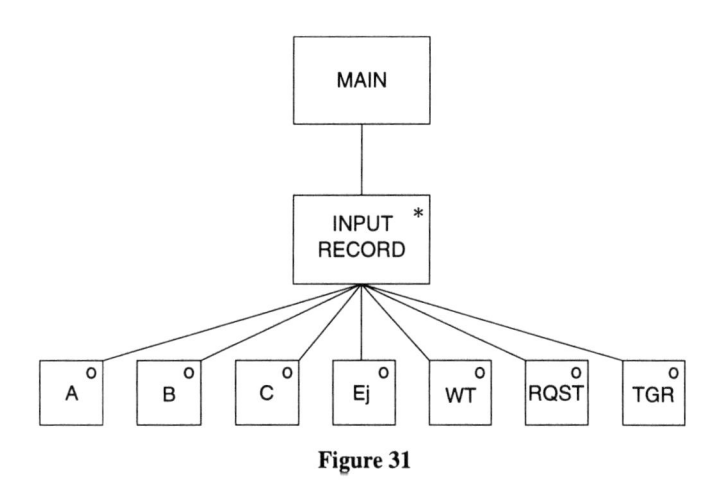

Figure 30

Figure 31

C. Internal buffering

Fig. 32 is the same as Fig. 26, except for the extra data stream E from S to P, which introduces a loop into the network. There has to be some buffering on at least one of the data streams in the loop, on either F, H, or E. By cutting the network at F, H, or E and introducing an explicit buffer, the same knitting needle technique can be used to combine the processes into one. The buffer is written by one of the subroutines and read back through the main program. Cutting at E would leave the hierarchy the same as in Fig. 27. S would write an EBUFFER which is read back through MAIN. Fig. 33 shows the hierarchy with the cut made at H. HBUFFER is shown as an oval because it is not a true data stream; MAIN can examine HBUFFER without reading from it.

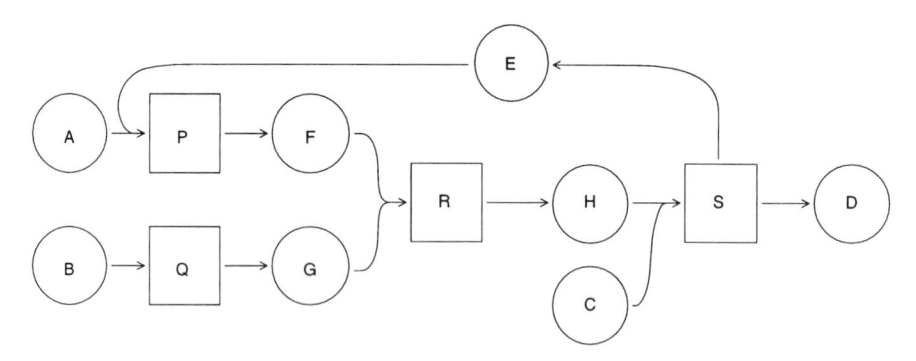

Figure 32

MAIN now has to make some scheduling decisions; whether to favor $A\&B\&C$ or HBUFFER. Fig. 34 shows a MAIN that empties HBUFFER after every A, B, or C record.

Buffering is necessary to deal with loops, but it can optionally and often quite reasonably be introduced for any internal data stream. In general, the more the buffering the more work the main program has to do. Fig. 35 describes an implementation of the network in Fig. 32 in which G, H, and E have been buffered but not F. Notice how different buffering decisions and different algorithms in MAIN lead to different mergings of the pairs of streams A and E, F and G, H, and C.

Fig. 36 shows the structure of a typical MAIN program for the kind of batch implementation that makes extensive use of buffering. Many long-running processes have been combined into one long-running program, which can be implemented by a combination of JCL and operator instructions. The bottom line is that if you do not have a long-running computer then you need a long-running operator.

Cameron An Overview of JSD 115

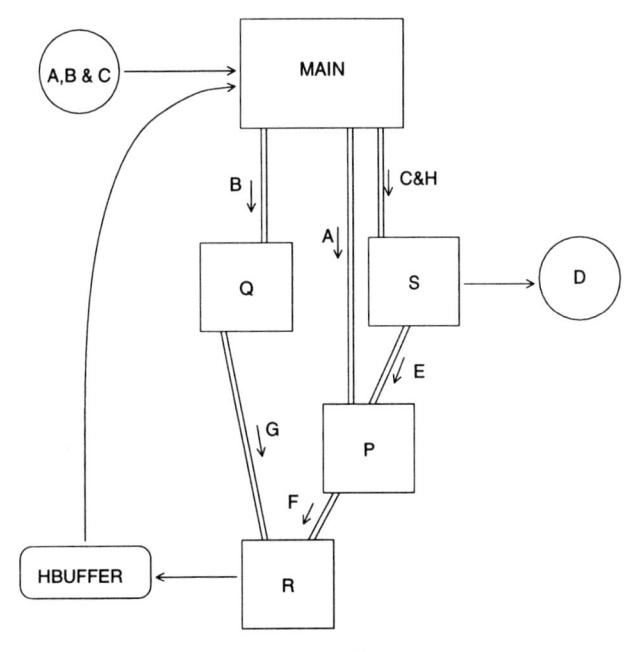

Figure 33

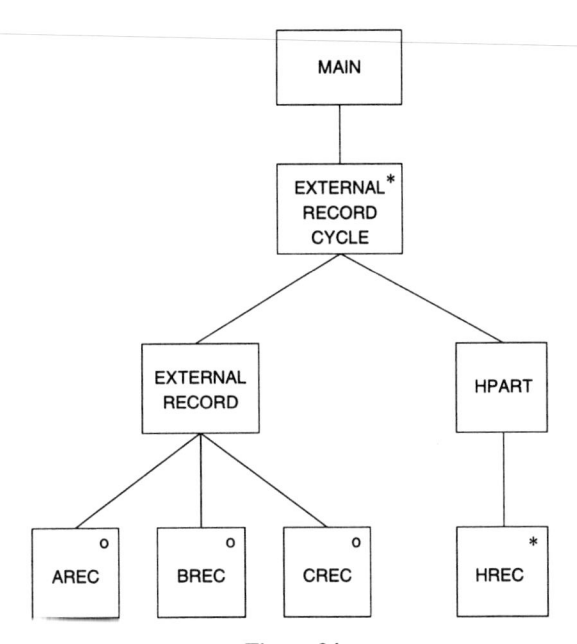

Figure 34

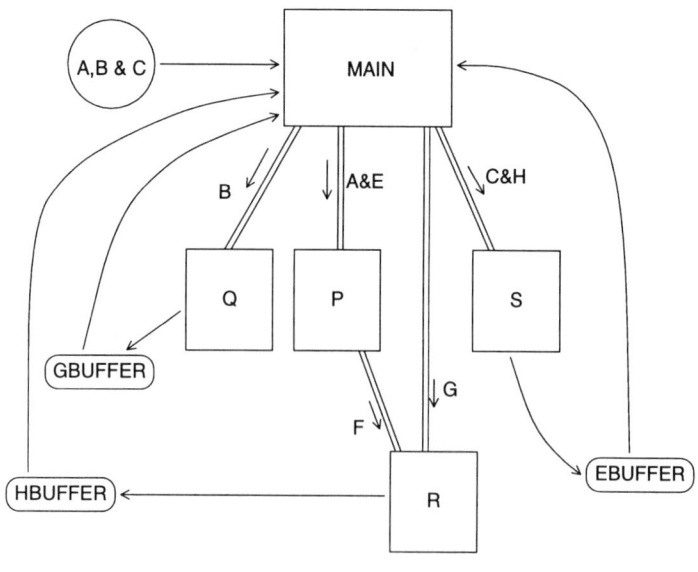

Figure 35

D. Implementations with several processors

The above techniques combine a network into a single program with or without buffering. Often it is neither necessary nor appropriate to combine all the processes into one. Then the problem is to allocate all the processes to available processors, either real or virtual; to use the above techniques where there is more than one process on the same processor; and to implement the data streams and state vector inspections that pass between the processors.

Between virtual processors communicating via shared memory the state vectors can be put in the shared memory and the data streams implemented by, for example, a circular buffer. Care must be taken in both cases over mutual exclusion. Between real processors data streams will probably be simple messages. State vector inspection can be implemented either by an enquiry and reply pair of messages or by downloading and storing locally a copy of the state vector either periodically or on each update.

Alternatively and preferably we might be able to use directly the facilities of an operating system or of a language such as Ada that supports concurrency.

From among these many implementation possibilities we have to choose the simplest that meets the informally laid down timing constraints. The plethora of possibilities is not a disadvantage, but a sign of success in separating specification from implementation.

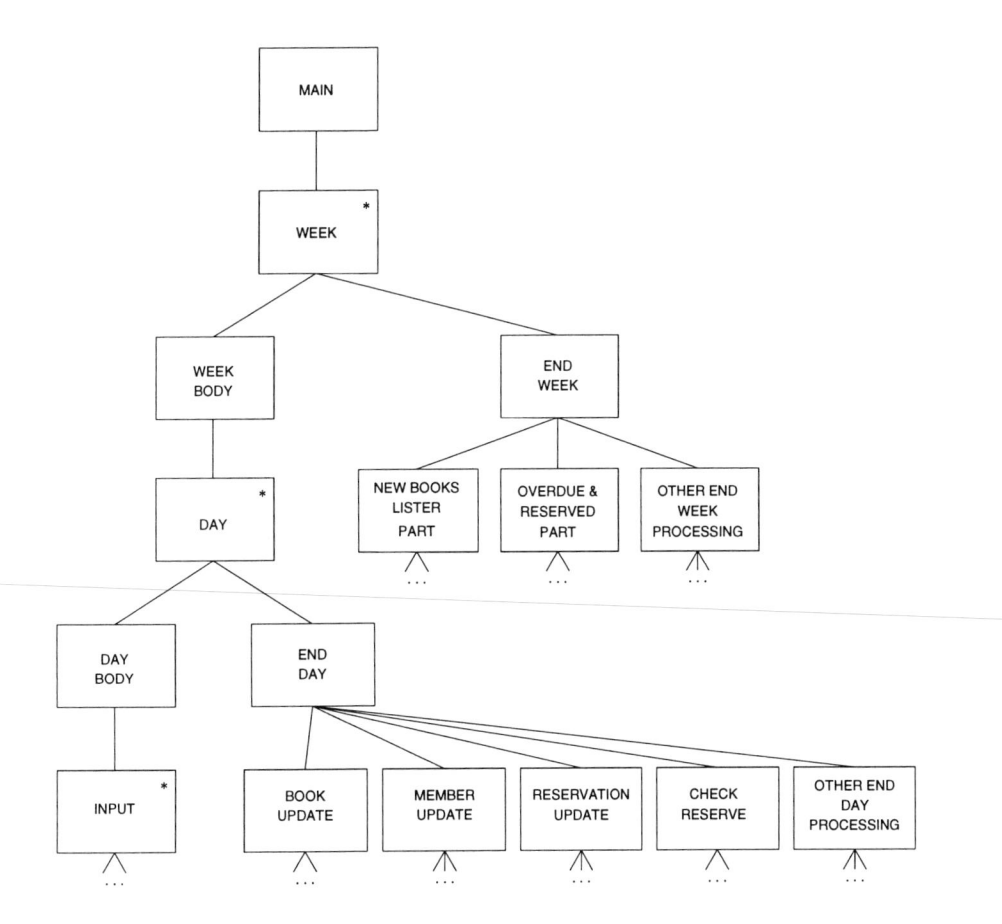

(In a Pure Batch System **DAYBODY** simply stores Records for later processing.)

Figure 36

V. Discussion

A. Why modeling first?

The Meaning of System Outputs: Suppose that the librarian says at an early stage in the development of his system that he would like an output of the form

    Number of books in the library   =   5921

    Average loan period   =   12.3 days

What does this output mean? The librarian understands it by reference to the world he knows about. We, as developers, therefore have to understand the world of the library at least well enough to understand what the librarian is asking for. One major purpose of the modeling phase is to establish a basis for understanding and discussing the outputs of the system. That basis consists of the events in the JSD model, their attributes, and their orderings, and it is used not just to define the system outputs but also the data stored by the system and all the terms used in discussions with the users.

If you doubt the importance of establishing this basis, consider what the phrase "in the library" might mean. Is a book to be considered "in the library" if it has been ACQUIRED but not yet CLASSIFIED, or if it has been taken OUT of CIRCulation but not yet DELIVERED? Is the book in the library if it is really out of the library, that is, if it has been LENT but not yet RETURNed? There are many opportunities here for programming the wrong system. A specification document that is signed off, but which lacks a satisfactory model as a basis, is no guarantee of avoiding them.

Comparison to Physics: In any application of mathematics there is a bridge (a mapping) between the reality of the application domain and the formalism of the mathematics. The idea is that the mapping should capture in mathematical form some structure from the application domain. In physics, for example, we might define certain symbols as representing the charge of the electron, the speed of light, and so on; we manipulate the symbols according to some mathematical formalism; we then interpret the results back into the reality via the original definitions. In a similar way the definition of the events is the bridge between the reality of the library and the formal specification (and via the specification to the implementation) of the library system. The manipulations within the specification produce outputs which can be interpreted back into the world of the library via the definitions of events. In this sense building a library system is an application of mathematics to a library.

The bridge between the reality and the formalism can never be completely formal because the reality is not completely formal. Thus, the definitions of the actions are informal dictionary-type definitions whereas the data, for example, can be defined quite formally in terms of the actions.

One of the fundamental ideas in JSD is that the structure of the application domain should be directly reflected in the structure of the specification. The secondary assumption is that for a very wide class of information systems, real-time control and embedded systems and others, the important structure is sequential and should therefore be captured by sequential processes.

Contrast with the Functional View of Specifications: These arguments conflict directly with the widely supported functional view of specifications. According to this, view systems are functions mapping their inputs to their outputs; a specification should define the external behavior of the system, the behavior of the system as if it were a black box; internal structure is dealt with later in a design phase; no internal structure should be part of the specification.

With this view the output "number of books in the library = 5921" is explained in terms of the system inputs. This is, to say the least, uncomfortable for the librarian. Avoiding internal structure is supposed to avoid premature implementations commitments. We argue, however, that the sequential structure of BOOK, MEMBER, and RESERVATION is part of the problem statement and not an artifact of a particular implementation.

Maintenance: The second major purpose of JSD modeling is to clarify the problem of maintenance. The model is defined first and limits the scope of the system. A given model can support a whole family of outputs. The detailed functional requirements change much more quickly than the model on which they are based. Maintenance is easier because we can move relatively easily within the family of functions and, secondly, because we can explain up-front to a user what the family of functions is and therefore what the consequences are of choosing one or another model.

By including ideas of scoping (actually two scopings were discussed in Section II-A) and therefore of families of outputs, we can begin a serious discussion of maintenance. Maintenance is only comprehensible through some concept of families of functional requirements, through some idea of persistence of certain entities and structures through a number of changed specifications. The lack of such concepts is a serious weakness of the functional view. Extreme proponents sometimes argue that there is no such thing as maintenance, that a changed problem is a new problem. However, that is surely bending the facts to fit the theory.

Other Modeling Approaches: At least two other approaches similarly defer consideration of functionality and of outputs. Builders of simulation systems focus first on an abstraction of the reality to be simulated and defer consideration of reports and other outputs.

Database-oriented approaches use data models. We have argued in Section II-C that using events as the basic modeling tool is superior because it extends the modeling to include the time dimension as an integral part of the model and in so doing clarifies the semantics of data and of relationships, both of which are defined in terms of histories of events.

B. Composition and decomposition

JSD cannot reasonably be called a top-down method (nor for that matter a bottom-up method).

- The network is not built by successive explosions of a process into a subnetwork of processes but middle-out from an initial set of model processes. The complexity of the network is not controlled by hierarchical description but by limitations on the interaction of nonmodel processes.
- The specification consists of an upper-level network and lower-level tree descriptions of the processes in the network. The whole of the first phase is concerned with the lower level, that is with the definition of the model processes. Then the network is developed middle-out. For each nonmodel process the lower level description is added. Development starts at the lower level of the specification and proceeds up, across and down.
- Even the development of the tree structures in the modeling phase is not indisputably top-down. Consider the film star example from Section II-B. We started with the actions, the bottom level of the trees. We did not know at the outset whether there should be one top box or two, or even what the top boxes would be.
- Top-down development is characterized by the successive refinement of a single system structure. Using JSD the specification structure is (usually) repackaged into a completely different implementation structure. Figs. 33 and 35 (or 31 and 36) describe two different implementations; each has a different structure from that of the specification from which they were derived; the top levels of each did not even appear in the specification.
- The JSP programming method, used to develop the internals of nonmodel processes, starts with a number of data structure diagrams, composes them into a control structure of the program and then fleshes out the control structure. The data structure diagrams (and also the program structure) are abstractions of the whole program, not a description of its top levels.

Sometimes we do explode a process into a network of processes. Fig. 37 shows the output function process P decomposed into processes A and B and the interactive function process Q decomposed into processes C and D. In the Introduction we stated that nonmodel processes did not usually communicate with each other directly, that they interacted only via the model. That is true of P and Q, but obviously not of A and B or of C and D. The statement is true of the larger-scale structure of the network, that is, if the phrase "nonmodel process" is replaced by "nonmodel process or small subnetwork."

Even here we are just as likely to develop P incrementally by working outwards from the model. We might first add process A which does the basic calculations to produce the output G and only later add process B to do some device dependent formatting of the final output H.

The Weakness of Development by Decomposition: The idea of top-down decomposition (or stepwise refinement) is to develop software by successive decomposition. We start with single box marked "system". If the system is not trivially simple it is decomposed into parts; the connections between the parts are defined; each part is then considered independently; any part which is not trivially simple is further decomposed.

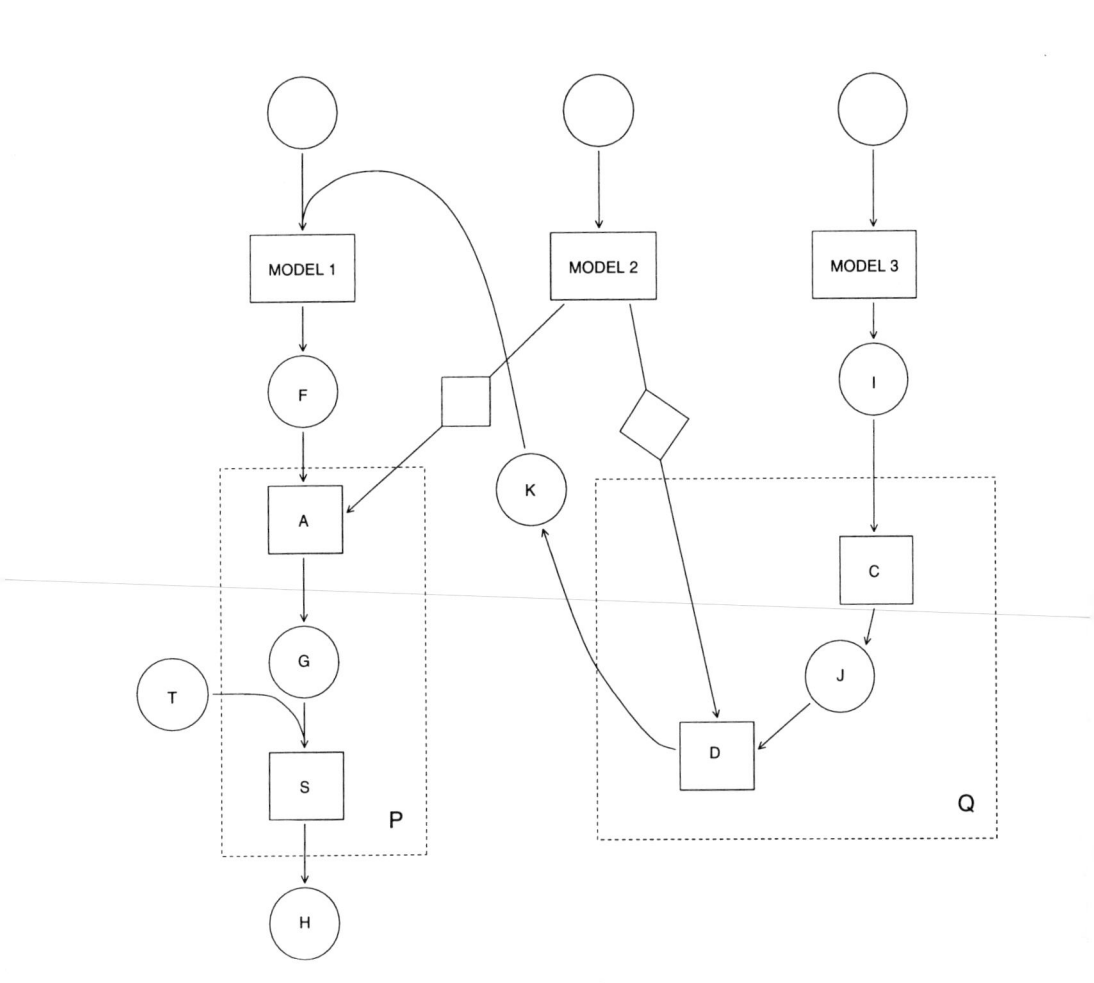

Figure 37

The motivation is clear: small programs are easier than large programs; large programs are easier than small systems; small systems are easier than large systems. The idea is eminently saleable, especially to management. However, except in a very dilute form the idea is naive. If it were really possible for most developers to make good decompositions, the software problem would have been solved long ago.

The difficulty is this. That first box marked "system" is largely unknown, yet the first decomposition is a commitment to a system structure; the commitment has to be made from a position of ignorance. This dilemma is repeated at successive levels; the designer's ignorance decreases only as the decisions become less critical.

The same argument can be restated as follows. Each decision about the decomposition of a subsystem depends on the decisions that have led to that particular subsystem. This hierarchical decision structure makes the early decisions very critical. A bad early decision may not be discovered until very late. The designer must exercise tremendous foresight to make good decompositions.

We argue that decomposition or stepwise refinement only really works when a designer is effectively writing down a solution he already knows and understands. But then, he is using decomposition as a method of description, not of development. The distinction between the description of something known and thoroughly understood and the development of something largely unknown is often blurred, for example when a developer presents his design to a manager, or when the writer of a textbook presents a solution.

Proponents argue that most software development is on problems that are well understood. This view would be more convincing if most software projects met their deadlines.

If decomposition does not work, or does not work well for problems above a certain size, what is the alternative?

Development by Composition: The alternative is to develop software by composition. Instead of starting with a single box marked "system" we start with a blank piece of paper. Each increment added is precisely defined; an increment is any abstraction of the whole, not necessarily just a component of the whole; part of the system may have to be restructured, repackaged, or transformed in order to compose it with another part; at intermediate stages there is a well-defined incomplete system rather than an ill-defined complete system. JSD shows that such an approach is at least possible.

Finally, while it is a very appealing idea to make multiple descriptions of the same system, in effect to be allowed to view the same system from different perspectives, the idea does not really become useful unless there is some way to put the different descriptions together.

C. Technical substance and managerial framework

Sensible managers of software projects always produce a plan dividing the project into phases. The manager is concerned with the deliverables at the end of each phase, the user signoff points, the usage of staff, the detection of slippage in time estimates, the political and organizational framework within which the project fits, and other similar issues. The managerial perspective is quite different from that of the technical staff doing the "real" work.

JSD is about the technical substance of a project. The technical substance of a project can be mapped on to a project plan in different ways. This flexibility is necessary because, even among technically similar projects, the managerial and organizational characteristics may vary widely.

For example, since a system may be needed quickly and for competitive or legal reasons, there is no possibility of not going ahead. The main uncertainty is over what and how much can be delivered in the first of several releases. A second system may have a much less certain cost justification, so that throughout the early stages the users only want to be committed to small increments of work, and they want the option of stopping the project as the end of each increment. The project plan, the phasing, and the phase-end deliverables ought not to be the same for these two projects even though they may be technically similar.

Some methodologies concentrate on the management framework rather than on its technical substance. The danger is that the development team gets locked into a framework that is totally inappropriate for their project. That is why many developers do not like methodologies and think them a waste of time. They are forced to produce documents which, in their circumstances, have little value. Their only option is to leave out some steps, which they are told, means they are not using the methodology properly.

Obviously there are fairly standard mappings of the technical substance of JSD on to project plans. However, flexibility in choosing the mapping includes at least the following:

- considering the most critical implementation issues well before the specification is complete;
- doing a little of each of the model, network, and implementation phases as part of a feasibility or estimating study;
- iterating over the model, network, and implementation phases on a planned series of releases;
- building a low-volume prototype, amending the specification, and reimplementing to produce a high-volume production system.

We can summarize as follows. In JSD specification is strictly separated from implementation and, within the specification, model is strictly separated from the rest. But the ordering of model, network, and implementation is a local, not a global ordering. We need the BOOK model process before the output "Number of books in the library = 5921" can be formally added to the specification, but we do not need MEMBER or RESERVATION. We need part of the model but not all. Similarly, we need some knowledge of the specification to make implementation decisions, but we do not need a complete specification. A project plan fixes the ordering of the work more strictly than is implied by JSD alone; therefore JSD can be mapped in various ways on to a project plan.

D. Tools

Three JSD support tools are currently available, all from Michael Jackson Systems Ltd., 22 Little Portland St., London, W1.

- PDF is a graphics editor for tree diagrams and lists of operations (as in Fig. 4) and a code generator from these diagrams into a variety of commonly used languages. The idea of the package is that the diagrams become the source of the program. PDF runs on the IBM PC, VAX VMS with VT100 type terminals and under Unix.
- SPEEDBUILDER is planned to be a series of JSD support products. So far only Unit One has been released. Unit One is a database for holding a JSD specification, a user-friendly editor for the database and a document maker that allows subsets of the database to be printed in a user-defined format. SPEEDBUILDER runs on the IBM PC.
- JSP-Cobol is a Cobol preprocessor that automates the insertion of suspend-and-resume mechanisms like the one described in Sections II-A and II-C, and provides a variety of testing aids. JSP-Cobol runs on a wide variety of mini and mainframe computers.

E. Projects

About 30 JSD or substantially JSD projects have been completed and perhaps as many again are underway. Most, but not all, are data-processing applications. The following are some brief notes about a sample.

- A Fleet Personnel system for a multinational oil company had a ship and employee as its main entities and kept track of people's careers, which ships they were on, where they could join a ship , etc. The system had 120 screen types, about 300,000 lines of procedural Cobol, had interfaces with an existing payroll system, and was implemented under IMS DB/DC.
- A Time Stamp project kept track of employees arriving for and leaving work. They work flexitime around core periods. Different shifts have different core periods, some employees work part-time, some employees are sick or on holiday. The implementation was distributed between IBM Series/1 and System 38 computers. Recovery problems were handled by running the on-line system under a batch scheduler.
- A Fingerprint Checking system restricts entry to a building by scanning in real-time the finger of the person trying to get in. Obviously, response times are critical. Implementation was in Fortran under the operating system RSX-11M.

Projects that are underway include the following:

- the redesign of a substantial part of the on-board software for a torpedo;
- the application software for a communications system to support air defense on the battlefield;

– a set of systems to support the merchandising function of a retail chain, the development of which will take several hundred man-years.

The experience from these projects deserves a more substantial treatment. Suffice here to report that the results have been generally favorable, although for no real project has JSD worked as cleanly or as clearly as it does on the Library example.

Acknowledgements. JSD has been developed (and is developing) within Michael Jackson Systems, Ltd. mainly by M. Jackson and the author, but also with contributions from A. McNeile, J. Kathirasoo, and T. Debling. M. Jackson and I. Smith both suggested a number of improvements to this paper.

References

1. C.A.R. Hoare, "Communicating sequential processes," *Commun. ACM*, Dec. 1978.
2. W. Kent, *Data and Reality*. Amsterdam, The Netherlands: North-Holland, 1978.
3. M.A. Jackson, *System Development*. Englewood Cliffs, NJ: Prentice-Hall, 1982.
4. —, *Principles of Program Design*. New York: Academic, 1975.
5. J.R. Cameron, *JSP and JSD: The Jackson Approach to Software Development*. IEEE Comput. Soc., 1983.
6. L. Ingevaldsson, *JSP: A Practical Method of Program Design* (in Swedish). Studentlitteratur, 1977; (in English). Chartwell-Bratt, 1979.
7. H. Jansen, *JSP-Jackson Struktureel Programmeren* (in Dutch). Academic Service, 1984.

3. Formal Methods

Although they are widely cited as one of those techniques that can result in high-integrity systems [31], and are being mandated more and more in certain applications (see Part 6), formal methods remain one of the most controversial areas of current software engineering practice [119].

They are unfortunately the subject of extreme hyperbole by self-styled 'experts' who fail to understand exactly what formal methods are; and, of deep criticism and subjective evaluation by proponents of other techniques who see them as merely an opportunity for academics to exercise their intellects using mathematical hieroglyphics. Notwithstanding, the level of application of formal techniques in the specification and design of complex systems has grown phenomenally, and there have been a significant number of industrial success stories [125, 106, 160].

Whether one accepts the need for formal methods or not, one must acknowledge that a certain degree of formality is required as a basis for all system development. Conventional programming languages are themselves, after all, formal languages. They have a well-defined formal semantics, but unfortunately as we have already seen, deal with particular implementations rather than a range of possible implementations.

The formal nature of programming languages enables analysis of programs, and offers a means of determining definitively the expected behavior of a program (in the case of closed systems; with open systems the situation is complicated by environmental factors). In a similar fashion, formality at earlier stages enables us to rigorously examine and manipulate requirements specifications and system designs, to check for errors and miscomprehensions. A formal notation makes omissions obvious, removes ambiguities, facilitates tool support and automation, and makes reasoning about specifications and designs an exact procedure (e.g., using a formal verification environment [13]), rather than 'hand-waving'. Systems can be formally verified at various levels of abstraction, and these can be formally linked [36, 155], but normally the higher levels (e.g., requirements [64] and specification) are the most cost effective.

3.1 What are Formal Methods?

The term 'formal methods' is rather a misleading one; it originates in formal logic, but nowadays is used in computing to cover a much broader spectrum of activities based upon mathematical ideas [133].

So-called formal methods are not so much 'methods' as formal systems. While they also support design principles such as decomposition and stepwise refinement [187], which are found in the more traditional structured design methods, the two primary components of formal methods are a notation and some form of deductive apparatus (or proof system).

3.2 Formal Specification Languages

The notation used in a formal method is called a formal specification language or 'notation' to emphasize its potential non-executability. The language is 'formal' in that it has a formal semantics and consequently can be used to express specifications in a clear and unambiguous manner.

Programming languages are formal languages, but are not considered appropriate for use in formal specifications for a number of reasons:

- Firstly, very few programming languages have been given a complete formal semantics (Ada and Modula-2 are exceptions), which makes it difficult to prove programs correct and to reason about them.
- Secondly, when programming languages (particularly imperative languages) are used for specifications, there is a tendency to over-specify the ordering of operations. Too much detail at an early stage in the development can lead to a *bias* towards a particular implementation, and can result in a system that does not meet the original requirements.
- Thirdly, programming languages are inherently executable, even if they are declarative in nature. This forces executability issues to the fore, which may be inappropriate at the early stages of development, where the 'what' rather than the 'how' should be considered.

The key to the success of formal specification is that we *abstract* away from details and consider only the essential relationships of the data. We need to move away from the concrete, which has an indeterminate semantics, and use a formal language so that we can specify the task at hand in a manner that is clear and concise. In this way, abstraction both shortens and clarifies the specification.

Mathematics are used as the basis for specification languages, and formal methods in general. This is because mathematics offer an unchanging notation with which computer professionals should be familiar; in addition the use of mathematics allows us to be very precise and to provide convincing arguments to justify our solutions. This allows us to *prove* that an implementation satisfies the mathematical specification. More importantly, however, mathematics allows us to generalize a problem so that it can apply to an unlimited number of different cases (in this way, there is no *bias* towards a particular implementation), and it is possible to model even the most complex systems using relatively simple mathematical objects, such as sets, relations and functions [41, 206].

3.3 Deductive Apparatus

The deductive apparatus is an equally important component of a formal method. This enables us to propose and verify properties of the specified system, sometimes leading people to believe erroneously that formal methods will eliminate the need for testing.

Using the deductive apparatus (proof system) of a formal method, it is possible to prove the correctness of an implemented system *with respect to its specification*. Unfortunately, the media, and many computer science authors too, tend to forget to mention the specification when writing about *proof of correctness*; this is a serious oversight, and is what has led some people to believe that formal methods are something almost 'magical'. A proof of correctness demonstrates that a mathematical model of an implementation 'refines', with respect to some improvement ordering, a mathematical specification, not that the actual real-world implementation meets the specification.

We cannot speak of absolute correctness when verifying a system, and to suggest that the proof system enables us to definitively prove the correctness of an implementation is absurd, but the production of 'correct' programs is still a subject of debate [253]. Mathematical proof has essentially been a social process historically and accelerating this process using tool support in a software engineering context is difficult to achieve [178]. What a proof system does do, however, is to let us prove rigorously that the system we have implemented satisfies the requirements determined at the outset. If these requirements were not what we really intended, then the implementation will not function as we intended, but may still be correct with respect to those particular requirements.

The deductive apparatus does however let us *validate* these original requirements; we may propose properties and using a rigorous mathematical argument demonstrate that they hold. While natural language is notorious for introducing contradictory requirements which are often only discovered during implementation, using formal methods we may demonstrate that requirements are contradictory (or otherwise) *before* implementation.

Similarly, natural language requirements tend to result in ambiguity and incomplete specifications. Often when reading systems requirements we have to ask ourselves questions such as 'But what happens if ... ?', and have no way of determining the answer. With formal methods, however, we can *infer* the consequences based on the requirements that have been specified.

Validation of requirements and *verification* of the matching implementation against those requirements are both useful complementary techniques in aiding the reduction of errors and formal methods can help in both this areas [74].

3.4 Myths of Formal Methods

The computer industry is slow to adopt formal methods in system development. There is a belief that formal methods are difficult to use and require a great deal of mathematical ability. Certainly some of the symbols look daunting to the uninitiated, but it's really just a matter of learning the notation [47]. For complete formal development including proofs and refinement (a process whereby a formal specification is translated systematically into a lower-level implementation, often in a conventional programming language), a strong mathematical background is required, but to write and understand specifications requires only a relatively basic knowledge of mathematics.

There is also a misconception that formal methods are expensive. Experience has now shown that they do not necessarily increase development costs; while costs are increased in the initial stages of development, coding and maintenance costs are reduced significantly, and overall development costs can be lower [123].

It has been suggested that formal methods could result in error-free software and the end of testing. But will they? In a word, no; but they are certainly a step in the right direction to reduce the amount of testing necessary. Indeed, the test phase may become a certification phase, as in the Cleanroom approach [73, 183, 184, 215], if the number of errors are reduced sufficiently. Formal methods and testing are both complementary and worthwhile techniques that are useful in attempting to construct 'correct' software [62]. Formal methods aim to avoid the inclusion of errors in the first place whereas testing aims to detect and remove errors if they have been introduced.

Formal methods enable us to rigorously check for contradictory requirements and to reason about the effects of those requirements. That unfortunately does not mean that we will eliminate requirements errors completely. Proofs are still performed by humans, and are thus still prone to error. Many automated proof assistants are now available which check proof justifications and some can even generate proof obligations as a guide to the construction of a proof. But as we all well know, computer-based tools may themselves contain errors. As research in this area progresses, we can anticipate simplified proofs in the future.

Unfortunately refinement and proof techniques are not exploited as much as they might be [132]. Most developers using formal methods tend to use them at the requirements specification and system specification stages of development [81]. This is still worthwhile, and is indeed where the greatest pay-offs from the use of formal methods have been highlighted, since most errors are actually introduced at the requirements stage rather than during coding. But, as specifications are not refined to executable code, coding is still open to human error. Refinement *is* difficult, and certainly does not guarantee error-free code, as mistakes can still be made during the refinement process. Forthcoming refinement tools should simplify the refinement process and help to eliminate errors. There is disagreement as to how much refinement can be automated, but in any case these tools should help us to eliminate the scourge of computer programming – the ubiquitous 'bug'.

After over a quarter of a century of use, one would have hoped that misconceptions and 'myths' regarding the nature of formal methods, and the benefits that they can bring, would have been eliminated, or at least diminished. Unfortunately, this is not the case; many developers still believe that formal methods are very much a 'toy' for those with strong mathematical backgrounds, and that formal methods are expensive and just deal with proving programs correct. We must attempt to learn lessons from the experience of applying formal methods in practice [68].

In a seminal article *Seven Myths of Formal Methods* (reprinted in this Part), Anthony Hall attempts to dispel many 'myths' held by developers and the public at large [105]. By reference to a single case study, he cites seven major 'myths' and provides an argument against these viewpoints.

While Hall deals with myths held by non-specialists, the authors, writing five years later, identify yet more myths of formal methods. What is disconcerting is that these myths, described in *Seven More Myths of Formal Methods* (reprinted here) are myths accepted to be valid by specialist developers [39]. By reference to several highly successful applications of formal methods, all of which are described in greater detail in [125], we aim to dispel many of these misconceptions and to highlight the fact that formal methods projects can indeed come in on-time, within budget, produce correct software (and hardware), that is well-structured, maintainable, and which has involved system procurers and satisfied their requirements. There is still debate on how formal specification can actually be in practice [163].

3.5 Which Formal Method?

Formal methods are not as new as the media would have us believe. One of the more commonly-used formal methods, the Vienna Development Method (VDM) [17, 146, 141], first appeared in 1971, Hoare first proposed his language of Communicating Sequential Processes (CSP) [128, 129, 127] in 1978, and the Z notation [28, 145, 236, 268] has been under development since the late 1970s. In fact the first specification language, Backus-Naur Form (BNF), appeared as long ago as 1959. It has been widely accepted that *syntax* can be formally specified for quite some time, but there has been more resistance to the formal specification of *semantics*.

Over the last twenty years, these formal methods and formal languages have all changed quite considerably, and various extensions have been developed to deal with, for example, object-orientation and temporal (timing) aspects in real-time systems. But which is the best one to use?

This is very subjective; in fact, it is not really a question of 'which is best' but 'which is most appropriate'. Each of the commonly used formal methods have their own advantages, and for particular classes of system some are more appropriate than others. Another consideration is the audience for which the specification is intended. Some people argue that VDM is easier to understand than Z because it is more like a programming language; others argue that this causes novices to introduce too much detail. Really it is a matter of taste, and often it depends on the 'variety' of Z or

VDM you are using. Both of these methods have been undergoing standardization by the International Standards Organization (ISO) [141, 268], and VDM is now an accepted ISO standard. Newer formal methods such as the B-Method (pehaps one of the more successful tool-supported formal developments methods, with a good range of supporting books [2, 15, 115, 156, 230, 260]) and RAISE [218] tend to have increasing tool support, but depend on a critical mass of users to ensure successful transfer into genuine industrial application [100].

Another consideration is the extent to which the formal specification language is executable (see Part 8 for a discussion of the relative merits and demerits of executable specification languages). OBJ [94], for example, has an executable functional programming subset, and CSP is almost executable in the parallel programming language Occam [139].

We can divide specification languages into essentially three classes:

- Model-oriented
- Property-oriented
- Process algebras

Model-oriented approaches, as exemplified by Z and VDM, involve the explicit specification of a state model of the system's desired behavior in terms of abstract mathematical objects such as sets, relations, functions, and sequences (lists).

Property-oriented approaches can be further subdivided into *axiomatic methods* and *algebraic methods*. Axiomatic methods (e.g., Larch [103]) use first-order predicate logic to express preconditions and postconditions of operations over abstract data types, while algebraic methods (e.g., Act One, Clear and varieties of OBJ) are based on multi- and order-sorted algebras and relate properties of the system to equations over the entities of the algebra.

While both model-oriented and property-oriented approaches have been developed to deal with the specification of sequential systems, process algebras have been developed to meet the needs of concurrent systems. The best known theories in this class are Hoare's Communicating Sequential Processes (CSP) [128, 129] and Milner's Calculus of Communicating Systems (CCS) [185], both of which describe the behavior of concurrent systems by describing their algebras of communicating processes.

It is often difficult to classify specification language, and these categories merely act as guidelines; they are certainly not definitive – some languages are based on a combination of different classes of specification language in an attempt to exploit the advantages of each. The protocol specification language LOTOS [140, 247], for example, is based on a combination of Act One and CCS; while it can be classed as an algebraic method, it certainly exhibits many properties of a process algebra also, and has been successfully used in the specification of concurrent and distributed systems. Similarly, in some ways CSP may be considered to be a process *model* since the algebraic laws of CSP can (and indeed should, for peace of mind) be proven correct with respect to an explicit model [131].

An advantage of reasoning using formal methods is that unlike software testing in general, they can be used effectively on systems with large or infinite states.

Sometimes however, a system may have a sufficiently small state space for an alternative approach to be used. Model checking [179] (with tool support such as SPIN [136] allows exhaustive analysis of a finite system, normally with tool support, for certain types of problem, including requirements [16]. Where this approach can be applied (e.g., for hardware and protocols), it may be deemed the preferred option because of the increased confidence provided by the use of a mechanical tool without the necessity of a large amount of intervention and guidance by the engineer that most more general purpose proof tools require.

In general, model-based formal methods [41] are considered easier to use and to understand; proofs of correctness and refinement, it has been said, are equally difficult for each class. But in some cases, algebraic methods are more appropriate and elegant. In fact, using a library of algebraic laws may help to split the proof task and make some of the proofs reusable. For the future, it is hoped that greater unification of the various approaches will be achieved [134].

In her article *A Specifier's Introduction to Formal Methods* (reprinted here), Jeannette Wing gives an excellent overview of formal methods, and more in-depth detail on the various issues raised above [255]. She describes the differences between the different classes of formal methods and provides some very simple examples to illustrate the differences between different formal methods; the article also includes an excellent classified bibliography.

We saw in Part 1, however, how each specification is in fact a lower level implementation of some other specification. The program itself is also a specification, again written in a formal language. While formal languages of the sort that have been described thus far in this Part are concerned with clarity and simplicity, programs must consider efficiency and the correct implementation of requirements.

As such, while 'broad-spectrum' notations such as Z and VDM can be used at all stages in the development, at the final stages of development, there is a considerable 'jump' from neat mathematical notations to the complex details of optimizing programs. To overcome this, we often require to use different specification languages at different levels of abstraction and at different stages of development. C.A.R. Hoare in *An Overview of Some Formal Methods for Program Design* (reprinted here) describes how a variety of formal methods and notations may be used in the design of a single system, and highlights how functional programming can aid in reducing the size of this 'jump' [130]. A goal is to unify the various programming paradigms [134].

In the article *Ten Commandments of Formal Methods* (reprinted here), the authors discuss a number of maxims which, if followed, may help to avoid some of the common pitfalls that could be encountered in the practical application of formal methods [38]. The future of formal methods is still unsure, but the potential benefits are large if the techniques are incorporated into the design process in a sensible manner [58, 173]. We will discuss how method integration and executable specifications can also help in Parts 7 and 8, respectively.

Seven Myths of Formal Methods

Anthony Hall

Summary.

Formal methods are difficult, expensive, and not widely useful, detractors say. Using a case study and other real-world examples, this article challenges such common myths.

Formal methods are controversial. Their advocates claim they can revolutionize development. Their detractors think they are impossibly difficult. Meanwhile, for most people, formal methods are so unfamiliar that it is difficult to judge the competing claims. There is not much published evidence to support one side or the other, and a lot of what is said about formal methods is based on assertions, not on facts. Thus, some of the beliefs about formal methods have been exaggerated and have acquired almost the status of myths.

Praxis is a software-engineering company where we use formal methods for real projects: We write real specifications, not just exercises, and we develop real software from them. As a result of this experience, many of us are enthusiasts for formal methods. We have found that they offer real benefits; at the same time, we have found that many things that people believe about formal methods are not true.

This article takes a practical look at formal methods, presents some of the myths – favorable and unfavorable – and explains what we have found to be the truth behind them. As an example throughout this article of the use of formal methods, I draw particularly from our experience on a CASE project, which is described in the box on p. 137.

The CASE project was certainly not the kind of project that most people associate with the use of formal methods, and we did not do a completely formal development involving proofs and program verification. Nevertheless, we found that we gained enormous benefit from using the Z specification notation [1], which is one of

© 1990 IEEE. Reprinted by permission.
Reprinted from *IEEE Software*, 7(5):11–19, September 1990.

several formal-methods notations. The seven most prevalent formal-methods myths are variants of the following:

1. *Formal methods can guarantee that software is perfect.* The most important myth is that formal methods are somehow all-powerful – if only we mortals could apply them. This is a pernicious myth, because it leads to both unrealistic expectations and the idea that formal methods are somehow all-or-nothing. The reality is that no such guarantee can be given – but the usefulness of formal methods does not depend on such absolute perfection.

2. *They work by proving that programs are correct.* In the US, a lot of the work in formal methods has concentrated on program verification. This has made formal methods seem very hard and not very relevant to real life. However, you can achieve a lot without any formal proofs at all.

3. *Only highly critical systems benefit from their use.* This belief is based on the perceived difficulty of using formal methods. The truth is that critical systems do demand the most thorough use of formal methods, but any system benefits generally from using at least some formal techniques.

4. *They involve complex mathematics.* Formal methods are based on mathematics, and many people believe that this makes them too difficult for practicing software engineers. This myth is in turn based on a view that mathematics is intrinsically difficult. At Praxis, we have found that the mathematics of specification, at least, is easily learned and used.

5. *They increase the cost of development.* It used to be said that, although the use of formal methods was very expensive, it was worthwhile because of the lower maintenance costs for the resulting software. But this is a difficult argument to sell to hard-pressed project managers, whose budget is for development, not maintenance. In fact, we have some evidence that *development* can be cheaper when you use formal specification.

6. *They are incomprehensible to clients.* A formal specification is full of mathematical symbols, which render it incomprehensible to anyone unfamiliar with the terminology. Therefore, it is supposed, a formal specification is useless for nonmathematical clients. However, mathematics is not the only part of a formal specification – it supports many other ways of expressing the specification that give the client a better understanding early on in the project.

7. *Nobody uses them for real projects.* Formal methods are often associated with academic departments and research organizations. It is thought that only such organizations have the expertise necessary to use them and that they are only suitable for the idealized applications that such groups would carry out. But our experience in the CASE project, and the experience of other industrial users, is turning this point of view into a myth – or at least into history.

The CASE project

The CASE project we applied formal specifications to is a software-engineering tool set to support project teams using SSADM, a structured systems-analysis and -design method. Each team member has a workstation, and the workstations are networked to a central project machine. The infrastructure of the CASE project provides

- a multiuser distributed project-management and configuration-management system controlling all development information and tasks and

- a set of basic classes (like diagram, table, and matrix) from which tools for structured analysis can be developed by specialization.

The infrastructure is implemented on top of Sun Unix. It is coded in Objective C.

The specification is a document of about 340 pages written in Z with English comments. It contains about 550 schemas defining about 280 operations.

Development from this specification proceeded by

- writing a concrete specification of the interfaces in Objective C,

- writing, for some parts of the system, informal design documents,

- coding other parts directly from the Z specification,

- writing some Z specifications of lower level modules, and

- coding from the informal designs or lower level specifications.

We did no proof or mathematical program construction. We used our normal company standards for project planning, integration and testing, configuration management, and so on.

We coded about 58,000 lines of Objective C, of which about 37,000 lines were deliverable software.

The project lasted nearly 90 weeks and used about 450 man-weeks of effort, of which about 90 were devoted to the system specification.

Myth 1

- *Formal methods can guarantee that software is perfect.*
The fact is that formal methods are fallible.

It ought to be too obvious to need saying, but nothing can achieve perfection. Unfortunately, it sometimes seems that proponents of formal methods claim they offer an absolute guarantee that cannot be achieved any other way. If you take this position then any problem with formally developed software is a refutation of formal methods' usefulness. Formal methods have been strongly criticized precisely on this absolutist basis.

It is important to understand formal methods' intrinsic limitations. Their fallibility is the most fundamental limitation, and it arises from two facts: Some things can never be proved and we can make mistakes in the proofs of those things we can prove.

Limits on proofs. A proof is a demonstration that one formal statement follows from another. The real world is not a formal system. A proof, therefore, does not show that, in the real world, things will happen as you expect. So you can never be sure that your specifications are "correct," however much you prove about them.

This should not deter you. All engineering is concerned with making models of the real world and using those models to design artifacts. Models based on mathematics are ideal because you can establish the models' properties by reasoning and because you can manipulate the models during design. The designer of a crane, for example, abstracts the real crane into a structure of idealized components with known properties like mass and load-bearing capacity. He uses this model to design and predict the properties of the real crane. There is no way he can prove that the real crane will behave as he predicted.

But, on the whole, the correspondence between the mathematical models used in structural engineering and the real world is well enough understood that we trust such mathematical models. The more mature the engineering discipline, the more likely we are to trust the models it uses. There have certainly been enough engineering disasters to convince anyone that the correspondence is not perfect, but nobody would suggest that crane builders should abandon mathematics.

In software, the limits of our modeling techniques are also reasonably well understood. First, models cover only some aspects of a program's behavior. Second, the correspondence between the formal description and the real world is limited.

There are good mathematical models for the behavior of sequential programs. Models for concurrent behavior are also available but less easy to use. Some people say we cannot model timing constraints formally; this is not strictly true, but it is true that we do not know how to use such models to help us develop software that meets the constraints. Finally, we cannot yet model nonfunctional properties like performance, reliability, maintainability, and availability.

The correspondence between our formal models of programs and the actual behavior of real systems is limited by three factors: the behavior of the programming language, the operating system, and the underlying hardware. For safety-critical systems, these limitations are crucially important and we cannot assume that a program is correct just because it has been proved.

Mistakes may be made. Even within our formalism, we can make mistakes in doing proofs, just as we can make mistakes in writing programs. Indeed, published formal specifications have errors in them.

In spite of these apparent problems, formal methods *do* work. There are two reasons. One is that there are some ways in which formal methods offer qualitatively different and better guarantees than any other method. The other is that even though formal methods still let you make mistakes, they are much better at exposing these mistakes.

Demonstrating correctness. There is an often quoted remark that "Program testing can be used to show the presence of bugs, but never to show their absence!" [2] This seems to imply that something else – proving – can show the absence of bugs. There are two senses in which this is true (although in both cases the possibility of errors in the reasoning process means that the demonstration is not absolutely infallible):

– Some properties can be established *only* by formal reasoning. Many requirements are couched as universal statements, like "The program will always log user actions" and "The system will never lose a message." Such statements can in principle not be established by testing or simulation, but they can be established by reasoning about the specification.

– Some steps *can* be demonstrably correct. For example, the relation between a program and its specification is a formal one and can be proved to be correct. So you can nearly guarantee that a program meets a specification, even though this does not mean that the program is perfect. (The guarantee is only "near" because of the limits of the mathematical model in capturing the real world; even if the guarantee were absolute, it would not mean the program was perfect because the specification might be wrong.)

Finding errors. Although they eliminate only certain classes of errors – and then not with absolute certainty – formal methods do make it much easier to find all sorts of errors. In an informal specification, it is hard to tell what is an error, because it is not clear what is being said. When challenged, people try to defend their informal specification by reinterpreting it to meet the criticism. With a formal specification, we have found that errors are much more easily found – and, once they are found, everyone is more ready to agree that they are errors.

In this sense, formal methods are a scientific approach to development, since they offer specifications that can be refuted. (In informal software development, the specification is usually only refuted by testing. By this stage, it has of course been made formal – by translation into a programming language – but it is no longer easily comprehended by people.)

In the CASE and other projects using formal methods at Praxis, we have found that the ability to expose errors is one of these methods' key benefits. Even though we have undertaken very few proofs or completely formal development steps, we have found that inspections of formal specifications reveal more errors than those of informal specifications, and it is more effective to inspect designs or programs against formal specifications than against other kinds of design documentation. IBM has reported similar experiences [3].

Myth 2

- *Formal methods are all about program proving.*
  The fact is that formal methods are all about specifications.

  I use the term formal methods to cover the use of mathematics in software development. The main activities I include are

- writing a formal specification,
- proving properties about the specification,
- constructing a program by mathematically manipulating the specification, and
- verifying a program by mathematical argument.

Thus, program verification is only one aspect of formal methods. In many ways, it is the most difficult. For non-safety-critical projects, program verification is far from the most important aspect of a formal development. Since the cost of removing errors increases dramatically as a project progresses, it is more important to pay thorough attention to the early phases.

System specification. From an economic point of view, therefore, the most important part of a formal development is the *system specification.* For many projects, this is the only part of the development that is formal. In any case, a formal specification of what a program is to do is a prerequisite for verifying that the program is correct.

A formal specification is a precise definition of what the software is intended to do. You can give any piece of software, from a single module to a whole system, a formal specification. On the CASE project, we used Z to write the formal specification of the whole system. Such system specifications are the most practical and valuable ways of using formal methods.

A formal system specification is comparable in scope to a conventional requirements analysis using dataflow or entity-relationship diagrams. It differs from conventional design specifications in that it is concerned only with the function of the system and makes no commitments to its structure.

To illustrate the notion of a formal specification, the box below shows an example that is a simplification of part of the CASE specification. It is written in Z. A Z specification is a mathematical model of the system to be built. It consists of two parts: a definition of the state of the system and a collection of definitions of operations on the system.

A specification is abstract in three senses:

- It uses data types, like sets and relations, that can model applications directly, rather than computer-oriented types like arrays. In the example, I use sets to represent the collections of tasks and documents in the system and a function to represent the relationship between them. These representations capture the essence of what is required better than the corresponding implementation structures.

- It specifies *what* is to be done rather than *how* it is to be done. The definition of the operation *RemoveDocument*[1], for example, simply says that, after the operation, the relevant document has been removed. It needs to say nothing about how the removal is done, nor how any related task is found and removed.

- It specifies only whatever level of detail is necessary; you can simply leave unsaid things that are not important. In the example, we did not say what *TASK* and *DOC* actually were. This too is an implementation detail of no interest to the specifier or client.

This abstraction represents a proper separation of concerns between what the users want to define and what they are content to leave to the implementers. Such separation of concerns is important in controlling the development process, whatever life-cycle model you use. For example, in a development that uses prototyping to explore user requirements, it is important to separate the essential behavior of the prototypes from incidental details of the prototype implementation.

You remove the incompleteness of the specification in two ways. First, you record in other documents like statements of nonfunctional requirements those things that you would like to say at the specification stage but cannot because of your mathematical models' limitations. Second, you supply during the subsequent design and implementation steps the information that has been deliberately omitted.

Occasionally, these subsequent steps reveal problems with the specification that had been hidden by the abstraction. For example, it is possible to write specifications that cannot be implemented efficiently. In that case, you must revise the specification itself at the design stage.

A specification is central to a project in three ways:

- The actual process of constructing the specification is as important as its existence.

- Proofs of the specification's properties are at least as useful as proofs of correct implementation.

- You can construct implementations from the specification so they are correct.

Benefits. We found that writing the CASE specification helped us to clarify the requirements, discover latent errors and ambiguities, and make decisions about functionality at the right stages.

For example, we started off with elaborate requirements for documents to have different status values with complex transitions between them. A formalization of this let us simplify the model into a few distinct concepts. For example, we modeled the extent of machine-checking a document separately from how far it had been through a formal approval process. This made it easy to understand and verify with the user that our rules governing these status values were correct. Such clarification of requirements can lead to smaller and simpler systems – and to less rework in system test [4].

---

[1] See page 152.

It is hard to fudge a decision when writing formal specifications, so if there are errors or ambiguities in your thinking, they will be mercilessly revealed: You will find you cannot write a coherent specification or that, when you present the specification to the users, they will quickly tell you that you have got it wrong. Better now than when all the programming money has been spent!

Several times during the development of the CASE project, we discovered unexpected consequences of the specification. For example, early on we wrote a specification that allowed documents, but not tasks, to have versions. We rapidly discovered that we could not express this model formally. To get over this, we introduced the concept of a task version, which represented the running of a task with a particular collection of document versions. This concept turned out to represent a real-world object that was central to the way that the CASE tool set would be used, but we had not been able to see this usage clearly in an informal description of the system.

Formal specifications let you say whatever you think is important at the specification stage. At the same time, if you really are prepared to leave decisions until a later stage, you can do that, too.

Our example has a typical instance of such a decision. We defined, in the specification, precisely what happens when the last output of a task is removed: The task is removed as well. It is likely that an informal specification would not have made this clear, and the coder would have had to make a decision. But this clearly is a specification matter, since the effect is visible to the user. Omitting it from the formal specification, whether accidentally or deliberately, would be very obvious – there would be a component of the state whose value was undefined.

Specifications and proofs. Once you have a formal specification, you can prove things about the specification itself, as well as proving that a program satisfies it. These other properties may have to do with consistency of the specification or completeness of operation definitions. They may also be proofs that the specification (and thus the developed software) will meet certain key requirements. For safety and security, these may be certain kinds of integrity or other important requirements. In any case, because errors at this stage are more costly than implementation errors, proofs of these properties are correspondingly more important than proofs of implementations. Jim Woodcock [5] has shown reasoning applied to a practical specification (the CICS storage manager).

Implementing from formal specifications. When you do come to implement specifications formally, you do not do it by writing a program and then trying to prove that it meets the specification. This is infeasible for any but the smallest programs. Instead, you construct a correct program in small steps. Each step takes the specification and produces something a little nearer to the final program. Each step is small enough that you can see exactly what needs to be proved to show that the step is correct – and, if you doubt the correctness, you can actually carry out the proof. This style of development is described in a textbook on the Vienna Development Method [6] and a book on constructing correct algorithms [7]. It has been used, for example, to implement hardware from a formal specification in Z [8].

Each design step in such a development adds some detail that was omitted from the formal specification or makes some decision that was postponed. The implementers must

- provide efficient implementation structures to represent the application concepts,
- know or develop algorithms to carry out the required operations, and
- fill in details where these have deliberately been left to their judgement.

In the CASE project, we used formality only in writing the specification. We did not try any program proving at all. The kinds of design steps we made on the CASE project were to:

- Decide on a concrete language interface for the operations.

- Decide on a concrete data structure to represent some abstract structure in the specification; for example, an object class to represent the function *outputTask*[2]. The designer was free to choose any suitable representation that had the required properties.

- Decide on some lower level operations needed to implement the top level operations. For example, we identified a component called the kernel that provided low-level storage and distribution functions. We specified this component formally and implemented it from its Z specification.

Of course, these design steps required creativity: The specification did not overconstrain the designers, but it also did not do their job for them. We found that making such design decisions was in practice relatively straightforward and that, most important, it was easy to see if any proposed design met the specification.

A specification is a kind of contract between specifiers and implementers, and if the specification is formal, it is easy to interpret the contract and to decide if it has been satisfied.

Myth 3

• *Formal methods are only useful for safety-critical systems.*

The fact is that formal specifications help with *any* system.

Probably the largest practical applications of formal methods have been in noncritical projects. Our CASE project, for example, was not at all safety- or security-critical. Formal methods should be used wherever the cost of failure is high. Systems whose cost of failure is high include those that are

- critical in some way,
- replicated many times,
- fixed into hardware, or
- dependent on quality for commercial reasons.

---

[2] See page 151.

Almost any serious piece of software qualifies for at least one of these reasons. Our CASE project, for example, had to be a high quality product to satisfy the client and its users.

Applying formal methods can benefit many areas, including fitness for purpose, maintainability, ease of construction, and better visibility.

Formality offers ways to ensure the right software is built. You can discuss the specification with the user and, in some cases, build prototypes on the basis of the specification to demonstrate just what is proposed. You can use formal reasoning to demonstrate some of the specification's consequences, giving you something on which to have a discussion with the user.

One of the main problems in maintaining software is knowing what it is supposed to do. Another is knowing what each part is supposed to do, and thus what must be preserved as the software is changed. Formal specifications are ideal for this purpose.

Our experience shows that it is easier to build a system from a formal specification than by using other methods. Even when we have not done development rigorously, we have found coding from a formal specification to be straightforward.

The application of formal methods can also make you more confident in the development process because at each stage it is clearer what has and has not been done. Monitoring is more reliable and thus development is less risky.

Starting from a formal specification, the development process can be very rigorous, if it is done in small steps with each step formally expressed and justified. It can also be less rigorous, if the steps are larger and justified only informally. You choose the degree of rigor to suit the application. If the system is critical, it must of course be developed completely formally.

However, many benefits of formal methods come from the specification stage. Thus, on a noncritical system, even if none of the rest of the development is formal, just writing a formal specification is a big improvement over other informal methods.

Myth 4

- *Formal methods require highly trained mathematicians.*
The fact is that the mathematics for specification is easy.

Once it is recognized that the practice of formal methods is most concerned with writing specifications, the mathematical difficulties become much less significant. You can develop specifications themselves with very straightforward mathematics that any practicing engineer should know.

For example, in Z, the only branches of mathematics you need to write specifications are set theory and logic. The elements of both these are easily understood and nowadays are taught to teenagers.

Of course, before engineers can use formal methods, they must be trained – in this respect, formal methods are no different from other methods. Our experience is that such training is not difficult and that people with only high-school math training can write excellent formal specifications. Certainly anyone who can learn a programming language can learn a specification notation like Z.

The specification of a problem is shorter and much easier to understand than its expression in a programming language. Consider the operation *RemoveDocument* in the example on p. 152: A definition of this operation in, say, pseudocode would be far longer and less comprehensible.

People have a fear of new symbols. But mathematical symbols are introduced to make mathematics easier, not more difficult. People quickly become familiar with the new symbols. The difficulty in learning logic is not the symbols, any more than the difficulty in learning Russian is learning the Cyrillic alphabet.

Difficulties. This does not mean that everything about writing specifications is easy. When the notation has been learned, there are still difficulties. Some people are better at it than others, just as some people are better at programming than others.

The main difficulty is making the right connections between the real world and the mathematical formalism. It can be hard to choose the right things in the real world to model – to get the right level of abstraction. Some programmers put too much detail into their specifications and make them too complicated. You can also make the opposite error: writing specifications that are too abstract.

However, these are problems of any kind of specification, not problems introduced by formality. Many programmers find it difficult to write specifications in any notation, because it is difficult for them to get away from programming-language detail. When using formal specifications, studying good published case studies and getting advice from an experienced person can help you avoid these problems.

Training hints. We have found that there are three stages of training needed:

- Training in discrete mathematics, which needs to cover elementary set theory and formal logic. For those who have a mathematical background but are unfamiliar with these topics, a single day suffices to introduce the ideas. Even for the innumerate, less than a week's training is needed. There are many good textbooks on discrete mathematics.

- Training in the particular formal notation. A Z or VDM course typically takes one or two weeks, assuming that the participants have the necessary mathematical background. Textbooks are available for VDM [6] and Z [1].

- Tutoring and consultation in real projects. After training, students can use formal methods, but they will still encounter difficulties. To get over these, we recommend workshops where you can tackle problems with the help of a tutor. It is also essential that every project using formal methods have access to at least one person with experience using the method. If necessary, you can ensure this by hiring some consultants during the early stages of the project: 10 man-days of effort, used wisely, may suffice.

A much higher level of mathematical skill is needed if you intend to go beyond formal specification and carry out a fully formal development that includes proofs. It is unrealistic to expect the majority of software engineers to be able to do proofs easily. Nor is it likely that machine assistance will be any help. Proof tools are still in a very primitive state – and, in any event, there are fundamental difficulties with machine assistance for proof. Therefore, competent people who can cope with the necessary mathematical manipulations are the ones who must carry out safety-critical projects. Of course, the same is true of bridge building.

Myth 5

- *Formal methods increase the cost of development.*
The fact is that writing a formal specification *decreases* the cost of development.

A completely formal development that includes proving each development step is very expensive – probably infeasibly so for all but the most critical applications. But because many benefits come just from writing formal specifications, it is important to know if this too is costly.

Lower development costs. It is notoriously difficult to compare the costs of developing software under different methods. There are no figures for the development costs for the same piece of software using both a well-established formal method and a comparable informal method. However, experience on the cost of projects that use formal specification is beginning to accumulate. None of this evidence supports the idea that development costs are higher if you use formal specifications; if anything, it suggests that they are *lower*.

Our own experience on the CASE project showed a productivity (measured in lines of code per day) measured from start of specification to acceptance that was much higher than our normal estimating figure. Because we implemented the CASE project in a productive language (Objective C), the productivity ratio in terms of useful function implemented per day would probably be even higher.

Rolls-Royce and Associates has reported [4] that on a safety-critical project where it used formal specification and planned testing, it achieved better productivity figures than when it did neither. (At first, the productivity was lower, but this was attributed to learning to use various non-user-friendly tools and was not connected with the formal method itself.) The cost of learning to use the formal method was not a significant problem, although IBM has highlighted this learning as an important one-time cost [3]. Rolls Royce reported that the 7 percent of the time spent on specification avoided large costs at the back end of the project.

Life-cycle changes. Although using formal specification on a project does not cost more, it does change the shape of the project. More time is spent on the specification phase – in the CASE project, about 30 percent of the effort was spent before implementation started. Why? Because more of the work is being done at this stage than typical. But the implementation, integration, and testing phases are shorter.

The longer specification phase does cause a problem: It can be difficult to manage the specification process, because it is harder to see what progress is being made. Especially at the beginning, it can be hard to believe that any progress is being made at all, since all sorts of ideas are being tried and thrown away-which is as it should

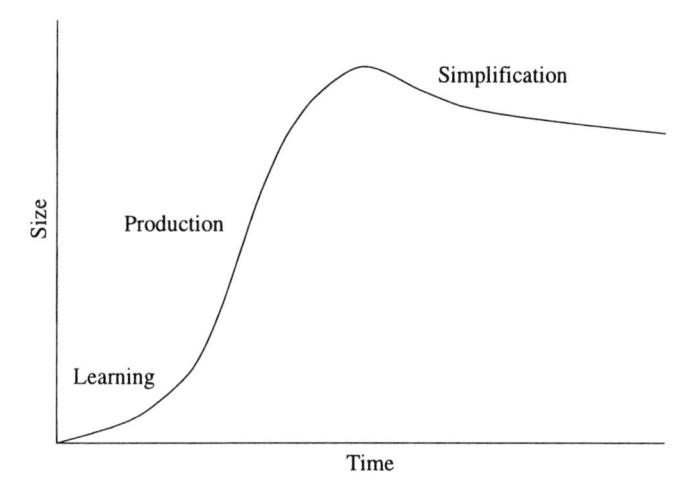

Figure 1. The life history of a specification.

be. Our experience of how the size of a specification grows is shown in Figure 1. (For the actual size of a real specification and the corresponding code, see p. 151.)

At first, very little seems to happen. But after a time, people begin to understand the problem, and rapid progress is made. Then the growth slows down and, if things are going well, the specification starts to get smaller. This is the where the problem is really understood and where regularities and similarities are recognized, which leads to the specification's structure being tightened and improved. This polishing process can continue indefinitely, and a good project manager must know when to stop. He certainly should not stop while the specification is still growing – at that point, the problem is still not fully cracked.

It is important to record the plausible specifications that were tried and rejected, as well as the reasons for their rejection, not just the final specification. These records will help guide future projects, prevent the repetition of unfruitful work, and guide the maintainers.

It is also imperative to recognize that specifications are never perfect. When it comes to the implementation stage, you will find deficiencies in the specification. When this happens, you must modify the specification – under change control, of course. There is a strong temptation to correct the implementation but not the specification – this leads to rapidly increasing divergence between the specification and the actual software and means that the specification becomes useless for maintenance. The two must be kept in step. If you do this, the specification continues to be a valuable document throughout the software's life. Clearly, there is a cost in doing this, but it is not large: On the CASE project, it was less than 5 percent of the implementation phase's effort.

Myth 6

- *Formal methods are unacceptable to users.*

The fact is that formal specifications help users understand what they are getting.

How? The specification captures what the user wants *before* it is built. But to realize this benefit, you must make the specification comprehensible to the user. There are three ways to do this:

– Paraphrase the specification in natural language.
– Demonstrate consequences of the specification.
– Animate the specification.

The first way is always essential. A mathematical specification must be accompanied by a natural-language description that explains what the specification means in real-world terms and why the specification says what it does.

You must allocate time and resources for the effort to write this accompanying text. This effort is worthwhile, since our experience has shown that documents produced from a formal specification can be more comprehensible, more accurate, shorter, and more useful than informal specifications.

A well-produced formal specification can have the mathematics taken out of it entirely – the result is a natural-language document that is a much better specification of the system than a conventional informal specification. You can also use formal specifications with diagrammatic notation – there is nothing to prevent the use of any notation that helps explain the system.

One way that formal specifications are more useful than any other method is that they may let you demonstrate by formal reasoning to the user that the specifications meet certain requirements. You can do this only if the requirements can themselves be expressed formally, but many properties like safety and security can be partially expressed formally. Even if there are no formally expressed requirements, you can draw out certain consequences of the specification and present them to the user. In the CASE project, for example, we deduced (although we did not formally prove) properties like "No version stored on the project machine is ever changed."

Formal specifications are sometimes thought of as antithetical to techniques like animation and prototyping. In fact, the approaches are complementary, and both have the goal of establishing user requirements more reliably. One way to use them together is to build prototypes to explore requirements issues and then to record the results in a formal specification as the basis of subsequent development. Sometimes, you can use prototypes to define areas that are not well expressed in formal specifications. On the CASE project, we used prototyping to explore details of the user interface and formal specifications for the system's actual functions.

You can animate some formal notations, giving you an immediate prototyping capability. However, the more powerful specification languages cannot be executed this way, and so a separate step, like implementation in Prolog, is required to animate the specification.

Myth 7

- *Formal methods are not used on real, large-scale software.*
  The fact is that formal methods are used daily on industrial projects.

Several organizations, not just Praxis, are using formal methods on industrial-scale projects. Many people know of applications in the security area, but the scope of formal methods is far wider. Examples of the kinds of project that are using formal methods include the following:

- Transaction processing. IBM's CICS is a large, 20-year-old transaction-processing system. It contains more than a half million lines of code. IBM is using Z to respecify key CICS interfaces to improve its maintainability. So far, Z specifications have been written for more than 100,000 lines of new or changed code [3].
- Hardware. The use of formal methods is not confined to software. There are at least three examples of the notation Z being used to specify hardware. One is the Secure Multiprocessing of Information by Type Environment secure computer architecture. SMITE's order code has been specified in Z by the British company Plessey. The floating-point unit for the transputer was specified in Z, incidentally revealing errors in many other floating-point implementations [8]. Tektronix has been using Z to specify the functionality of oscilloscope families[3].
- Compilers. The Danish Datamatik Center has for many years been developing industrial compilers using formal methods.
- Software tools. Our CASE project system is only one, although the most complete, example of the use of formal specification in software tools. Other examples are the interface to the Portable Common Tools Environment [9], a European standard for software engineering, and the specifications of database-based software-engineering environments [10].
- Reactor control. Rolls-Royce and Associates used a combination of English and formal specification to specify nuclear-reactor control software [4]. It used animation to explore the specification with the responsible engineer.

Clearly, these projects represent a tiny fraction of all software development. However, they are real industrial-scale applications, and they report positive benefits from the use of formal methods.

Our own experience on the CASE project has been that formal methods can be very effective. But they are only one part of a project: The CASE project used formal specification in the framework of normal quality-assurance and project-management controls and with other good design, implementation, and testing techniques.

Formal methods offer no magic guarantees: Our CASE project was an ordinary project with its share of problems. But the project team believes that the formality of the specification was a major benefit throughout the project.

---

[3] See: Norman Delisle and David Garlan, "A Formal Specification of an Oscilloscope," *IEEE Software*, 7(5):29–36, September 1990.

As a result of our experiences, we believe that formal methods must be better understood by developers at large. They are powerful tools, although by no means a panacea. The reasons for their effectiveness are not necessarily the reasons for which they were originally developed. Nor are the difficulties in their use the obvious ones of notation and mathematical sophistication.

Instead of perpetuating the seven myths, I offer seven facts to replace them:

1. Formal methods are very helpful at finding errors early on and can nearly eliminate certain classes of error.
2. They work largely by making you think very hard about the system you propose to build.
3. They are useful for almost any application.
4. They are based on mathematical specifications, which are much easier to understand than programs.
5. They can decrease the cost of development.
6. They can help clients understand what they are buying.
7. They are being used successfully on practical projects in industry.

References

1. J.M. Spivey, *The Z Notation: A Reference Manual*, Prentice-Hall, Englewood Cliffs, NJ., 1989.
2. O.-J. Dahl, E.W. Dijkstra, and C.A.R. Hoare, *Structured Programming*, Academic Press, Orlando, Fla., 1972, p. 6.
3. C.J. Nix and B.P. Collins, "The Use of Software Engineering, Including the Z Notation, in the Development of CICS," *Quality Assurance*, September 1988, pp. 103–110.
4. J.V. Hill, P. Robinson, and P.A. Stokes, "Safety-Critical Software in Control Systems," in *Computers and Safety*, Inst. Electrical Eng., Stevenage, Herts, England, UK, 1990, pp. 92–96.
5. J.C.P. Woodcock, "Calculating Properties of Z Specifications," *ACM SIGSoft Software Eng. Notes*, July 1989, pp. 43–54.
6. C.B. Jones, *Systematic Software Development Using VDM*, Prentice-Hall, Englewood Cliffs, NJ., 1986.
7. D. Gries, *The Science of Programming*, Springer-Verlag, New York, 1981.
8. G. Barrett, "Formal Methods Applied to a Floating-Point Number System," *IEEE Trans. Software Eng.*, May 1989, pp. 611–621.
9. C.A. Middleburg, "VVSL. A Language for Structured VDM Specifications," *Formal Aspects of Computing*, Jan.–March 1989, pp. 115–135.
10. A.N. Earl et al., "Specifying a Semantic Model for Use in an Integrated Project Support Environment," in *Software-Engineering Environments*, I. Sommerville, ed., Peregrinus, London, 1986, pp. 202–219.

Appendix: Example Formal Specification

The CASE project system contains a collection of documents and a collection of tasks. Each document is produced by a task; tasks may produce more than one document; all tasks produce at least one document.

To describe this in Z, we built a mathematical model. We did not say what "tasks" and "documents" are, so we just let these be represented by the names *TASK* and *DOC* at this stage. In Z notation, the text in the first part of a schema is the declaration, which describes the model's *components*; the text in the second part of the schema is the predicate, which describes the model's *properties*. Schemas are split by horizontal rules.

Defining tasks and documents. This part of the model is called *TasksAndDocuments*. The specification is

$$
\begin{array}{|l}
\hline
\textit{TasksAndDocuments} \\
\hline
\textit{documents} : \mathbb{P}\,\textit{DOC} \\
\textit{tasks} : \mathbb{P}\,\textit{TASK} \\
\textit{outputTask} : \textit{DOC} \rightarrowtail \textit{TASK} \\
\hline
\mathrm{dom}\,\textit{outputTask} = \textit{documents} \\
\mathrm{ran}\,\textit{outputTask} = \textit{tasks} \\
\hline
\end{array}
$$

In Z, the symbol for a set of things is $\mathbb{P}$, which you can pronounce "set of." The first two lines of our model define the components *documents*, which is a set of *DOC*s, and *tasks*, which is a set of *TASK*s. This expresses the fact that "the system contains a collection of documents and a collection of tasks."

Next, you must say that "each document is produced by a task." We did this in two parts. First, we set up an association between documents and the tasks that produce them, which we called outputTask. This association is written as a function, for which the Z symbol is $\rightarrowtail$, that tells us that a document can only be the output of one task.

Then you must say that each document is produced this way, so you say that the action associates all the documents you know about with tasks: That is done in the statement "dom *outputTask* = *documents*," because the expression "dom *outputTask*" means "all the documents that are associated with tasks by the function *outputTask*."

Similarly, the Z expression "ran *outputTask*" means "all the tasks that are associated with documents by the function *outputTask*." To express the requirement that all tasks produce at least one document, we said "ran *outputTask* = *tasks*."

The final part of our English specification is that "tasks may produce more than one document"; there is no need to say anything special about this in the mathematics, since the specification as it stands allows it. In formal specifications, anything not forbidden is allowed; if we had wanted to say that "tasks may not produce more than one document," we could easily have done so.

Removing documents. We then specified the operation to remove a document. A document can be removed only if it is known to the system. When it is removed, the document is no longer recorded as a task's output. If this causes a task to have no remaining outputs, the task is also removed. The specification is

―― *RemoveDocument* ――――――――――――――――
$\Delta TasksAndDocuments$
$oldDoc? : DOC$
――
$oldDoc? \in documents$
$outputTask' = \{oldDoc?\} \vartriangleleft outputTask$
―――――――――――――――――――――――――――

To say this in Z, you first say that you are defining an operation that changes the part of the state called *TasksAndDocuments*; that is the meaning of the line "$\Delta TasksAndDocuments$."

Next, you declare that the operation has an input parameter, *oldDoc?*, of type *DOC*, which is the document to be removed.

Now you have to say what the operation actually does. First, for it to do anything, the document you are trying to get rid of must be one of the known documents. In Z, you say it must be a member of the set of known documents: "$oldDoc? \in documents$."

Finally, you define the effect. You can do this very simply: All you do is remove the document from the function *outputTask*. The way to do this in Z is to give an equation that tells you what the new value of *outputTask*, called *outputTask'*, will be. The symbol for removing elements from the domain of a function is $\vartriangleleft$, so the equation you want is "$outputTask' = \{oldDoc?\} \vartriangleleft outputTask$."

You can rely on the other properties of the state to ensure that, when you do this, the document will also disappear from the documents set, since you defined the documents set to be identical to the domain of *outputTask*. Furthermore, if this leaves a task with no outputs, that task too will disappear, since all tasks are defined to produce at least one document. If you want, you can prove that these changes will happen.

Seven More Myths of Formal Methods

Jonathan P. Bowen and Michael G. Hinchey

Summary.

New myths about formal methods are gaining tacit acceptance both outside and inside the system-development community. The authors address and dispel these myths based on their observations of industrial projects.

Mathematicians first used the sign $\sqrt{-1}$ without in the least knowing what it could mean, because it shortened work and led to correct results. People naturally tried to find out why this happened and what $\sqrt{-1}$ really meant. After two hundred years they succeeded.
— W. W. Sawyer, Mathematician's Delight, 1943.

In 1990, Anthony Hall published a seminal article that listed and dispelled seven myths about the nature and application of formal methods [1]. Today – five years and many successful applications later – formal methods remain one of the most contentious areas of software-engineering practice.

In essence, a formal method is a mathematically based technique for describing a system. Using formal methods, people can systematically specify, develop, and verify a system. However, as we show in the box on page 154, basic definitions of formal methods and related terms are somewhat confused.

What *is* clear is that despite 25 years of use, few people understand exactly what formal methods are or how they are applied [2]. Many nonformalists seem to believe that formal methods are merely an academic exercise – a form of mental masturbation that has no relation to real-world problems. The media's portrayal of formal methods does little to help the situation. In many "popular press" science

© 1994 IEEE. Reprinted by permission.
Reprinted from *IEEE Software*, 12(4):34–41, July 1995.

journals, formal methods are subjected to either deep criticism or, worse, extreme hyperbole.

Many of Hall's myths were – and we believe to a certain extent still are – propagated by the media. Fortunately, today these myths are held more by the public and the computer-science community at large than by system developers. It is our concern, however, that new myths are being propagated, and more alarmingly, are receiving a certain tacit acceptance from the system-development community. We reexamine Hall's myths in the box on page 155, and, following his lead, we address and dispel seven new myths about formal methods.

Defining Formal Methods

Highly publicized accounts of formal-methods application to a number of well-known systems, such as the Sizewell-B nuclear power plant in the UK, IBM's CICS system, and the most recent Airbus aircraft, have helped bring the industrial application of formal methods to a wider audience.

However, even basic terms such as "formal specification" are still likely to be confusing. For example, the following alternative definitions are given in a glossary issued by the IEEE:

1. A specification written and approved in accordance with established standards.
2. A specification written in a formal notation, often for use in proof of correctness.

Although the latter is accepted in the formal-methods community, the former may have more widespread acceptance in industrial circles. A search of the abbreviation CSP in an online acronym database cited "Commercial Subroutine Package," "CompuCom Speed Protocol," and "Control Switching Point," but not "Communicating Sequential Processes" – which would be the likely choice of people working with formal methods. Finally, a search for VDM did reveal the term Vienna Development Method, but also "Virtual DOS Machine" and "Virtual Device Metafile" which may or may not be desirable bedfellows!

Besides ambiguity in the basic terminology, the formal notations themselves can be confusing to practitioners not trained in their use, and as a result the uninitiated might find it easier to ignore them than to investigate further.

Myth 8

- *Formal methods delay the development process.*

Several formal-methods projects have run notoriously over schedule. However, to assume this is a problem inherent in formal methods is irrational. These projects were delayed not because formal-methods specialists lacked ability, but because they lacked experience in determining how long development should take.

Hall's myths revisited

In 1990, Hall articulated and dispelled the following myths about formal methods,

- Myth 1: *Formal methods can guarantee that software is perfect.*
- Myth 2: *Formal methods are all about program proving.*
- Myth 3: *Formal methods are only useful for safety-critical systems.*
- Myth 4: *Formal methods require highly trained mathematicians.*
- Myth 5: *Formal methods increase the cost of development.*
- Myth 6: *Formal methods are unacceptable to users.*
- Myth 7: *Formal methods are not used on real, large-scale software.*

Myths that formal methods can guarantee perfect software and eliminate the need for testing (Myth 1) are not only ludicrous, but can have serious ramifications in system development if naive users of formal methods take them seriously.

Although claims that formal methods are all about proving programs correct (Myth 2) and are only useful in safety-critical systems (Myth 3) are untrue, they are not quite so detrimental. A number of successful applications in non-safety-critical domains have helped to clarify these points.

The derivation of many simple formal specifications of complex problems, and the successful development of several formal-methods projects under budget have served to dispel the myths that the application of formal methods requires highly trained mathematicians (Myth 4) and increases development costs (Myth 5). The successful participation of end users and other nonspecialists in system development with formal methods has ruled out the myth that formal methods are unacceptable to users (Myth 6). The successful application of formal methods to several large-scale, complex systems – many of which have received much media attention – should put an end to beliefs that formal methods are not used on real large-scale systems (Myth 7).

Estimating project cost is a major headache for any development team. If you follow the old adage, "estimate the cost and then double it," you're still likely to underestimate. Determining development time is equally difficult (in fact, the two are inevitably intertwined). A number of models have been developed to cover cost- and development-time estimation. Perhaps the most famous is Barry Boehm's Cocomo model [3], which weights various factors according to the organization's history of system development. Herein is the crux of the problem.

Any successful model of cost- and development-time estimation must be based on historical information and details such as levels of experience and familiarity with the problem. Even with traditional development methods, this information is not always available. Historical information about projects that used formal development techniques is likely to be even more scarce, because we have not yet applied formal methods to a sufficient number of projects. Surveys of formal development [4,5] and highlights of successes, failures, hindrances, and so on, will eventually provide us with the information we require.

Many of the much-publicized formal-methods projects have been in very specialized domains, producing data that is of limited use. Future work with more conventional developments and applications in domains such as process control will likely provide more useful data.

Despite these difficulties, there have been some very successful formal-methods projects in which development time was significantly reduced. The Inmos T800 floating-point unit chip, produced using Z and the Occam Transformation System, was finished 12 months ahead of schedule, and the application of Z (and more recently B) to IBM's CICS system resulted in a 9 percent savings in development costs.

Myth 9

- *Formal methods lack tools.*

Just as in the late 1970s and early 1980s, when CASE and computer-aided structured-programming tools were seen as a way to increase programmer productivity and reduce "bugs," tool support is now seen as a way to increase productivity and accuracy in formal development. Many projects place great emphasis on tool support [5].

This is by no means coincidental, but rather follows a trend that we expect will result in integrated workbenches to support formal specification, just as CASE workbenches support system development using more traditional structured methods.

Several formal methods incorporate tool support within the method itself. In this category are specification languages with executable subsets (such as OBJ) and formal methods that incorporate theorem provers as a key component, such as Larch (with the Larch Prover), Nqthm (successor to the Boyer-Moore prover), and higher order logic (supported by HOL and more recently, the PVS Prototype Verification System).

Many basic tools are widely available today. For example, Z is supported by ZTC, a PC- and Sun-based type-checking system available via anonymous file transfer protocol for noncommercial purposes, and by Fuzz, a commercial type-checker that also runs under Unix and DOS. More integrated packages that support typesetting and specification integrity checking include Logica Cambridge's Formaliser (for Microsoft Windows), Imperial Software Technology's Zola (which also incorporates a tactical proof system), and York Software Engineering's CADiZ (a tool suite for Z that now supports the refinement to Ada code). The Mural system, developed at University of Manchester, supports the construction of VDM specifications and refinements; using the proof assistant, users can generate proof obligations to verify the internal consistency of specifications. FDR, from Formal Systems Europe, is a model- and refinement-checker for CSP (communicating sequential processes). CRI (Computer Resources International) produces an associated toolset for the Raise development method (Rigorous Approach to Industrial Software Engineering), which is a more comprehensive successor to VDM. Finally, ICL's ProofPower uses higher order logic to support specification and verification in Z.

Perhaps motivated by the ProofPower approach, much attention has been focused on tailoring various "generic" theorem provers for use with model-based specification languages like Z. Although an implementation in OBJ seems to be too slow, success has been reported with HOL and EVES, a toolset based on Zermelo-Fraenkel set theory.

In the future, we expect more emphasis to be placed on integrated formal-development support environments, which are intended to support most formal-development stages, from initial functional specifications through design specifications and refinement. These environments will also support specification animation, proof of properties, and proofs of correctness. Such toolkits will be integrated so that, like integrated programming-support environments, they will support both version control and configuration management and development by larger teams. They will also facilitate more harmonious development by addressing all of the development-process activities. Such environments do not as yet exist, but several toolkits represent steps in the right direction.

IFAD's VDM-SL Toolbox supports formal development in VDM-SL and includes, as you might expect, standard type checkers and static semantics checkers. Developers enter VDM-SL specifications in ASCII. An interpreter supports all of the executable constructs of VDM-SL, allowing a form of animation and specification "testing." The executed specifications can be debugged using an integrated debugger, and testing information is automatically generated. Finally, a pretty-printer uses the ASCII input to generate VDM-SL specifications in LaTeX format.

The B-Toolkit, from B-Core, is a set of integrated tools that augment Abrial's B-Method and the associated B-Tool for formal software development by addressing industrial needs in the development process. Many believe that B and the B-Method represent the next generation of formal methods; if this is true, then B and similar toolkits will certainly form the basis of future formal-development environments.

Myth 10

- *Formal methods replace traditional engineering design methods.*

One of the major criticisms of formal methods is that they are not so much "methods" as formal systems. Although they provide support for a formal notation (formal specification language), and some form of deductive apparatus (proof system), they fail to support many of the methodological aspects of the more traditional structured-development methods.

In the context of an engineering discipline, a *method* describes how a process is to be conducted. In the context of system engineering, a method consists of an underlying development model; a language or languages; defined, ordered steps; and guidance for applying these in a coherent manner [6].

Many so-called formal methods do not address all of these issues. Although they support some of the design principles of more traditional methods – such as top-down design and stepwise refinement – they place little emphasis on the underlying development model and provide little guidance as to how development should proceed. Structured-development methods, using a model such as Boehm's spiral model, on the other hand, generally support all stages of the system life-cycle from requirements elicitation through post-implementation maintenance. In general, these underlying models recognize the iterative nature of system development. However, many formal development methods assume that specification is followed by design and then by implementation, in strict sequence. This is an unrealistic view of development – every developer of complex systems must revisit both the requirements and the specification at much later stages in development.

Although Hall disputes the myths that formal methods are unacceptable to users and require significant mathematical ability, more traditional design methods excel at requirements elicitation and interaction with users. They offer notations that can be understood by nonspecialists and serve as the basis for a contract.

Traditional structured methods are severely limited because they offer few ways to reason about the validity of a specification or whether certain requirements are mutually exclusive. The former is often only discovered after implementation; the latter, during implementation. Formal methods, of course, allow the possibility of reasoning about requirements, their completeness, and their interactions.

Indeed, instead of formal methods replacing traditional engineering-design methods, a major area for research is the *integration* of structured and formal methods. Such an integration leads to a "true" development method that fully supports the software life-cycle and allows developers to use more formal techniques in the specification and design phases, supporting refinement to executable code and proof of properties. The result is that two views of the system are presented, letting developers concentrate on aspects that interest them.

Some people suggest that this integrated approach lets structured design serve as a basis for insights into the formal specification. This idea is clearly controversial. Opponents argue that an approach that allows a structured design to guide formal-specification development severely restricts levels of abstraction and goes against many principles of formal-specification techniques. Proponents of integration argue that the approach is easier for users unskilled in formal-specification techniques, that it aids in size and complexity management, and that it provides a way to structure specifications [7].

Approaches to method integration vary from running structured and formal methods in parallel, to formally specifying transformations from structured-method notations to formal-specification languages.

Much success has been reported using the former technique. The problem, however, is that because the two methods are being addressed by different personnel, the likelihood that benefits will be highlighted is low. In many cases, the two development teams do not adequately interact. For example, there is a project underway at British Aerospace using traditional and formal development methods in parallel. The two development teams are not permitted to communicate, and the formal approach will be subject to the same standards reviews, which are certified against ISO 9000. The project's aim is to investigate how formal methods might better fit into current development practices.

More integrated approaches to integration include the translation of SSADM (Structured Systems Analysis and Design Methodology) into Z as part of the SAZ project; the integration of Yourdon Modern Structured Analysis and Z in a more formalized manner, and the integration of various structured notations with VDM and CSP. Although these approaches may have great potential, unlike the parallel approach they have yet to be applied to realistic systems.

Myth 11

- *Formal methods only apply to software.*

Formal methods can be applied equally well to hardware design and software development. Indeed, this is one of the motivations of the HOL theorem prover that was used to verify parts of the Viper microprocessor. Other theorem-proving systems that have been applied to hardware verification include the Boyer-Moore, Esterel, Nuprl, 2OBJ, Occam Transformation System, and Veritas proof tools. Model checking is also important in checking hardware designs if the state space is small enough (and techniques like Binary Decision Diagrams handle an impressive number of states). Perhaps the most convincing and complete hardware-verification exercise is Computational Logic's FM9001 microprocessor, which has been verified down to a gate-level netlist representation using the Boyer-Moore theorem prover. (A netlist is a list of component gates and their interactions.)

Inmos provides two examples of real-world industrial use. The T800 transputer floating-point unit has been verified by starting with a formalized Z specification of the IEEE floating-point standard. The Occam Transformation System was then used to transform a high-level program to the low-level microcode by means of proven algebraic laws. More recently, parts of the new T9000 transputer pipeline architecture have been formalized using CSP and checked for correctness. (A collection of papers by experts in the field covers these applications in more detail [8].)

A more recent approach to hardware development is *hardware compilation*. This allows a high-level program to be compiled directly into a netlist of simple components and their interconnections. If required, Field Programmable Gate Arrays allow this to be done entirely as a software process, since these devices let the circuit be configured according to the static RAM contents within the chip (this route is particularly useful for rapid prototyping).

It is also possible to prove that the compilation process itself is correct. In this case, the burden of proof is reduced considerably because there is no need to prove the hardware correct with each separate compilation. For example, a microprocessor could be compiled into hardware by describing the microprocessor as an interpreter written in a high-level language. Additions and changes to the instruction set can be made easily by editing the interpreter and recompiling the hardware with no additional proof-of-correctness required.

In the future, such an approach could make provably correct hardware/software codesign possible. A unified proof framework would facilitate the exploration of design trade-offs and interactions between hardware and software in a formal manner.

Myth 12

- *Formal methods are unnecessary.*

At some point or another, most of us have heard the argument that formal methods are not required. This is untrue. Although there are occasions in which formal methods are in a sense "overkill," in other situations they are very desirable. In fact, the use of formal methods is recommended in any system where correctness is of concern. This clearly applies to safety- and security-critical systems, but it also applies to systems in which you need (or want) to ensure that the system will avoid the catastrophic consequences of a failure.

Sometimes formal methods are not only desirable, but required. Many standards bodies have not only used formal specification languages in making their own standards unambiguous, but have mandated or strongly recommended the use of formal methods in certain classes of applications [9,10].

The International Electrotechnical Commission specifically mentions temporal logic and several formal methods (CCS, CSP, HOL, LOTOS, OBJ, VDM, and Z) in the development of safety-critical systems. The European Space Agency suggests that VDM or Z, augmented with natural-language descriptions, should be used to specify safety-critical system requirements. It also advocates proof-of-correctness, a review process, and the use of a formal proof before testing. The UK Ministry of Defence draft Interim Defence Standards 00-55 and 00-56 mandate the extensive use of formal methods. The draft standard 00-55 sets forth guidelines and requirements that include the use of a formal notation in the specification of safety-critical components and an analysis of such components for consistency and completeness. All safety-critical software must also be validated and verified; this includes formal proofs and rigorous (but informal) correctness proofs, as well as more conventional static and dynamic analysis. The draft standard 00-56 deals with the classification and hazard analysis of the software and electronic components of defense equipment, and also mandates the use of formal methods.

Canada's Atomic Energy Control Board has commissioned, in conjunction with David Parnas at McMaster University, a proposed standard for software in the safety systems of nuclear-power stations. Ontario-Hydro has developed a number of standards and procedures within the framework set by AECB, and more procedures are under development. Standards and procedures developed by Canadian licensees mandate the use of formal methods and, together with 00-55, are among the farthest reaching at the moment.

Whether or not you believe that formal methods are necessary in system development, you cannot deny that they are indeed *required* in certain classes of applications and are likely to be required more often in the future [9].

Myth 13

- *Formal methods are not supported.*

Once upon a time (as all good stories start) formal development might have been a solitary activity, a lone struggle. Today, however, support for formal methods is indisputable. If media attention is anything to go by, interest in formal methods has grown phenomenally, albeit from a small base. Along with object orientation, formal methods have quickly become great buzzwords in the computer industry. Long gone are the days when lone researchers worked on developing appropriate notations and calculi. The development of more popular formal methods owes much to the contributions of many people beyond the method originators. In many cases, researchers and practitioners extended the languages to support their particular needs, adding useful (though sometimes unsound) operators and data structures and extending the languages with module structures and object-oriented concepts.

There is a certain trade-off between the expressiveness of a language and the levels of abstraction that it supports. Making a language more expressive facilitates briefer and more elegant specifications, but it can also make reasoning more difficult. LOTOS was standardized in 1989, and the International Organization for Standardization proposed draft standards for both Z and VDM [9].

These standards set forth sound constructs and their associated formal semantics, making it easier to read other people's specifications (assuming, of course, that they conform to the standards).

Obviously, a standard is pointless if it does not reflect the opinions of active users and the developments that have evolved in formal methods. There are now several outlets for practitioners to discuss draft standards and to seek advice and solutions to problems and difficulties from other practitioners. Chief among these outlets are various distribution lists, books, periodicals, and conferences. We list some examples of each in the appendix on page 164.

Formal methods (in particular Z, VDM, CSP, and CCS) are taught in most UK undergraduate computer-science courses. Although still quite uncommon in the US, a recent NSF-sponsored workshop sought to establish a curriculum for teaching formal methods in US undergraduate programs. We hope this will become a regular event, and will help to establish formal methods as a regular component of US university curricula. A number of industrially based courses are also available, and in general can be tailored to the client organization's needs.

Myth 14

- *Formal-methods people always use formal methods.*

There is widespread belief that proponents of formal methods apply them in all aspects of system development. This could not be further from the truth. Even the most fervent supporters of formal methods recognize that other approaches are sometimes better.

In user-interface design, for example, it is very difficult for the developer to determine, and thus formalize, the exact requirements of human-computer interaction at the outset of a project. In many cases, the user interface must be configurable, with various color combinations highlighting certain conditions (such as red to denote an undesirable situation). The great difficulty, however, is in determining how the user interface should look and feel. The appropriateness of a particular interface is a subjective matter and not really amenable to formal investigation. Although there have been several (somewhat successful) approaches to formal specification in user interfaces [11], in general conformance testing here falls in the domain of informal reasoning.

There are many other areas in which, although possible, formalization is impractical because of resources, time, or money. Most successful formal-methods projects involve the application of formal methods to critical portions of system development. Only rarely are formal methods alone applied to all aspects of system development. Even within IBM's CICS project – which is often cited as a major successful application of formal methods – only about one-tenth of the entire system was actually subjected to formal techniques (although this still involved hundreds of thousands of lines of code and thousands of pages of specifications). Clearly (with appropriate apologies to Einstein), *system development should be as formal as necessary, but not more formal.*

Formal methods have been used to develop a number of support tools for conventional development methods, such as the SSADM CASE tool described by Hall. Formal methods have also been used to help redevelop a reverse engineering and analysis toolset for Cobol at Lloyd's Register. Both of these projects used Z, which was also used in defining reusable software architectures and greatly simplified the decomposition of function into components and the protocols of interaction between components.

To the best of our knowledge, however, formal methods have not been used extensively to develop the formal-methods support tools described in Myth 9. Exceptions to this are the VDM-SL Toolbox and the addition of a formally developed proof checker to HOL.

How can the technology-transfer process from formal-methods research to practice be facilitated? To start with, more *real* links between industry and academia are required, and the successful use of formal methods must be better publicized. We have edited a forthcoming collection of papers [5] that will play its part by describing the use of formal methods at an industrially useful scale.

More research is required to further develop the use of formal methods. For example, ProCoS, the Esprit basic research project on provably correct systems, is investigating theoretical underpinnings and techniques to allow the formal development of systems in a unified framework – from requirements to specification, program, and hardware. In addition, a ProCoS Working Group of 24 industrial and academic partners has been established. Joint meetings between the project and working groups over the next three years allows a free flow of ideas. The hope is that some of these ideas will be used in a more industrially oriented collaborative project in the future.

Formal methods are not a panacea, but one approach among many that can help to improve system reliability. However, to quote from a BBC radio interview with Bev Littlewood of the Centre for Software Reliability at City University in London,

> "... if you want to build systems with ultra-high reliability which provide very complex functionality and you want a guarantee that they are going to work with this very high reliability...
>
> ... you can't do it!"

Acknowledgements. We thank Anthony Hall for inspiring this article by authoring the "Seven Myths of Formal Methods." Jonathan Bowen is funded by UK Engineering and Physical Sciences Research Council (EPSRC) grant GR/J15186. Mike Hinchey is funded by ICL.

References

1. J.A. Hall, "Seven Myths of Formal Methods," *IEEE Software*, Sept. 1990, pp. 11–19.
2. W.W. Gibbs, "Software's Chronic Crisis," *Scientific American*, Sept. 1994, pp. 86–95.
3. B.W. Boehm, *Software Engineering Economics*, Prentice-Hall, Englewood Cliffs, N.J., 1981.
4. S.L. Gerhart, D. Craigen, and T. Ralston, "Experience with Formal Methods in Critical Systems," *IEEE Software*, Jan. 1994, pp. 21–28.
5. *Applications of Formal Methods*, M.G. Hinchey and J.P. Bowen, eds., 1995, Prentice-Hall, Hemel Hempstead, UK.
   http://www.comlab.ox.ac.uk./archive/formal-methods/afm book.html.
6. *Method Integration: Concepts and Case Studies*, K. Kronlf, ed., John Wiley & Sons, New York, 1993.

7. L.T. Semmens, R.B. France, and T.W.G. Docker, "Integrating Structured Analysis and Formal Specification Techniques," *The Computer J.*, Dec. 1992, pp. 600–610.
8. *Mechanized Reasoning and Hardware Design*, C.A.R. Hoare and M.J.C. Gordon, eds., Prentice-Hall, Englewood Cliffs, N.J., 1992.
9. J.P. Bowen, "Formal Methods in Safety-Critical Standards," *Proc. 1993 Software Engineering Standards Symp.*, IEEE CS Press, Los Alamitos, Calif., 1993, pp. 168–177.
10. J.P. Bowen, and V. Stavridou, "Safety-Critical Systems, Formal Methods and Standards," *Software Engineering J.*, July 1993, pp. 189–209.
11. A. Dix, *Formal Methods for Interactive Systems*, Academic Press, San Diego, Calif., 1991.

Appendix. Formal Methods Resources

There are several electronic distribution lists on formal methods and related topics, including

- Z Forum (*zforum-request@comlab.ox.ac.uk*),
- VDM Forum (*vdm-forum-request@mailbase.ac.uk*),
- Larch Interest Group (*larch-interest-request@src.dec.com*), and
- OBJ Forum (*objforum-request@comlab.ox.ac.uk*).

Z Forum has spawned *comp.specification.z*, an electronic newsgroup that is read regularly by about 30,000 people worldwide. A newsgroup devoted to specification in general, *comp.specification.misc*, regularly generates discussions on formal methods, as well as the more traditional structured methods, object-oriented design, and so on, as does the *comp.software-eng* newsgroup.

A recently established mailing list at University of Idaho (*formal-methods-request@cs.uidaho.edu*) addresses formal methods in general, rather than any specific notation, and a new mailing list run by the Z User Group addresses educational issues (*zugeis-request@comlab.ox.ac.uk*). In addition, the newsletter of the IEEE Technical Segment Committee on the Engineering of Complex Computer Systems (*ieee-tsc-eccs-request@cl.cam.ac.uk*) addresses issues related to formal methods and formal-methods education.

There are also anonymous FTP archives for Z (including an online and regularly revised comprehensive bibliography). The global World Wide Web electronic hypertext system, which is rapidly becoming very popular, also provides support for formal methods. A useful starting point is *http://www.comlab.ox.ac.uk/archive/formal-methods.html* which provides pointers to other electronic archives concerned with formal methods and lets you download tools such as HOL and PVS.

Periodicals. The proceedings of the Formal Methods Europe symposiums (and their predecessors, the VDM symposiums) are available in Springer-Verlag's *Lecture Notes in Computer Science* series, while the proceedings of the Refinement Workshops and the last five Z User Meetings have been published in Springer-Verlag's *Workshops in Computing*[1] Both of these series contain the proceedings of many other interesting colloquiums, workshops, and conferences on formal methods.

Although papers on formal methods are becoming well-established at a number of US conferences, there is as yet no regular conference in the US devoted to formal methods. The Workshop on Industrial-Strength Formal Specification Techniques may represent a step in that direction. Although formal methods are gaining momentum in the US, the main journals and publications devoted to formal methods are based in Europe – and in the UK, specifically.

These include *Formal Aspects of Computing, Formal Methods in System Design* and the *FACS Europe* newsletter run by Formal Methods Europe and the British Computer Society's Special Interest Group on Formal Aspects of Computing Science, among others. *The Computer Journal, Software Engineering Journal*[2], and *Information and Software Technology* regularly publish articles on or related to formal methods, and have run or plan to run special issues on the subject.

As far as we know, there are no US journals devoted specifically to formal methods, although some of the highly respected journals, such as *IEEE Transactions on Software Engineering* and *Journal of the ACM*, and popular periodicals, such as *Computer, IEEE Software*, and *Communications of the ACM*, regularly publish relevant articles. *IEEE TSE, Computer*, and *IEEE Software* coordinated successful special issues on formal methods in 1990. In January 1994, an *IEEE Software* special issue on safety-critical systems devoted considerable attention to formal methods, as has a newly launched journal, *High Integrity Systems*[3].

Courses. Popular Z courses are run by Logica Cambridge, Praxis, Formal Systems (Europe), and Oxford University Computing Laboratory. About 70 percent of all industrially based formal-methods courses focus on the Z notation. Formal Systems also runs a CSP course and a CSP with Z course, both of which have been given in the US as well as the UK. IFAD in Denmark offers an industrially based formal-methods course using VDM and VDM++.

---

[1] The Springer-Verlag *Workshops in Computing* series has been available on-line as the *Electronic Workshops in Computing* (eWiC) series under *http://ewic.springer.co.uk/* since late 1995.

[2] The IEE/BCS *Software Engineering Journal* was relaunched in January 1997 as the *IEE Proceedings – Software*.

[3] The *High Integrity Systems* journal was published by Oxford University Press. Volume 1, numbers 1–6, appeared 1994–1996.

A Specifier's Introduction to Formal Methods

Jeannette M. Wing

Summary.

Applied to computer systems development, formal methods provide mathematically based techniques that descript system properties. As such, they present a framework for systematically specifying, developing, and verifying systems.

Formal methods used in developing computer systems are mathematically based techniques for describing system properties. Such formal methods provide frameworks within which people can specify, develop, and verify systems in a systematic, rather than ad hoc, manner.

A method is formal if it has a sound mathematical basis, typically given by a formal specification language. This basis provides the means of precisely defining notions like consistency and completeness, and more relevantly, specification, implementation, and correctness. It provides the means of proving that a specification is realizable, proving that a system has been implemented correctly, and proving properties of a system without necessarily running it to determine its behavior.

A formal method also addresses a number of pragmatic considerations: who uses it, what it is used for, when it is used, and how it is used. Most commonly, system designers use formal methods to specify a system's desired behavioral and structural properties.

However, anyone involved in any stage of system development can make use of formal methods. They can be used in the initial statement of a customer's requirements, through system design, implementation, testing, debugging, maintenance, verification and evaluation.

Formal methods are used to reveal ambiguities, incompleteness, and inconsistency in a system. When used early in the system development process, they can reveal design flaws that otherwise might be discovered only during costly testing

© 1990 IEEE. Reprinted by permission.
Reprinted from *IEEE Computer*, 23(9):8–24, September 1990.

168   High-Integrity System Specification and Design

and debugging phases. When used later, they can help determine the correctness of a system implementation and the equivalence of different implementations.

For a method to be formal, it must have a well-defined mathematical basis. It need not address any pragmatic considerations, but lacking such considerations would render it useless. Hence, a formal method should come with a set of guidelines, or "style sheet" that tells the user under what circumstances the method can and should be applied as well as how it can be applied most effectively.

One tangible product of applying a formal method is a formal specification. A specification serves as a contract, a valuable piece of documentation, and a means of communication between client, specifier, and implementer. Because of their mathematical basis, formal specifications are more precise, and usually more concise, than informal ones.

Since a formal method is a method and not just a computer program or language, it may or may not have tool support. If the syntax of a formal method's specification language is made explicit, providing standard syntax analysis tools for formal specifications would be appropriate. If the language's semantics are sufficiently restricted, varying degrees of semantic analysis can be performed with machine aids as well. Thus, formal specifications have the additional advantage over informal ones of being amenable to machine analysis and manipulation.

For more on the benefits of formal specification, see Meyer [10]. For more on the distinction between a method and a language, and what specifying a computer system means, see Lamport [9].

What is a Specification Language?

A formal specification language provides a formal method's mathematical basis. I borrowed the terms and definitions from Guttag et al [1]. Burstall and Goguen have used the term "language" and more recently the term "institution" for the notion of a formal specification language.

>   Definition: A formal specification language is a triple, $< Syn, Sem, Sat >$, where Syn and Sem are sets and $Sat \subseteq Syn \times Sem$ is a relation between them. Syn is called the language's syntactic domain; Sem, its semantic domain; Sat, its satisfies relation.

>   Definition: Given a specification language, $< Syn, Sem, Sat >$, if $Sat(syn, sem)$, then syn is a specification of sem, and sem is a specificand of syn.

>   Definition: Given a specification language, $< Syn, Sem, Sat >$, the specificand set of a specification syn in Syn is the set of all specificands sem in Sem such that $Sat(syn, sem)$.

Less formally, a formal specification language provides a notation (its syntactic domain), a universe of objects (its semantic domain), and a precise rule defining which objects satisfy each specification. A specification is a sentence written in terms of the elements of the syntactic domain. It denotes a specificand set, a subset of the semantic domain. A specificand is an object satisfying a specification. The satisfies relation provides the meaning, or interpretation, for the syntactic elements.

Backus-Naur form is an example of a simple formal specification language, with a set of grammars as its syntactic domain and a set of strings as its semantic domain. Every string is a specificand of each grammar that generates it. Every specificand set is a formal language.

In principle, a formal method is based on some well-defined formal specification language. In practice, however, this language may not have been explicitly given. The more explicit the specification language's definition, the more well-defined the formal method.

Formal methods differ because their specification languages have different syntactic and/or semantic domains. Even if they have identical syntactic and semantic domains, they may have different satisfies relations.

Syntactic domains. We usually define a specification language's syntactic domain in terms of a set of symbols (for example, constants, variables, and logical connectives) and a set of grammatical rules for combining these symbols into well-formed sentences. For example, using standard notation for universal quantification ($\forall$) and logical implication ($\Rightarrow$), let x be a logical variable and P and Q be predicate symbols. Then this sentence, $\forall x. P(x) \Rightarrow Q(x)$, would be well-formed in predicate logic, but this one, $\forall x. \Rightarrow P(x) \Rightarrow Q(x)$, would not because $\Rightarrow$ is a binary logical connective.

A syntactic domain need not be restricted to text; graphical elements such as boxes, circles, lines, arrows, and icons can be given a formal semantics just as precisely as textual ones. A well-formedness condition on such a visual specification might be that all arrows start and stop at boxes.

Semantic domains. Specification languages differ most in their choice of semantic domain. The following are some examples:

- Abstract-data-type specification languages are used to specify algebras, theories, and programs. Though specifications written in these languages range over different semantic domains, they often look syntactically similar.
- Concurrent and distributed systems specification languages are used to specify state sequences, event sequences, state and transition sequences, streams, synchronization trees, partial orders, and state machines.
- Programming languages are used to specify functions from input to output, computations, predicate transformers, relations, and machine instructions.

Each programming language (with a well-defined formal semantics) is a specification language, but the reverse is not true because specifications in general do not have to be executable on some machine whereas programs do. By using a more abstract specification language, we gain the advantage of not being restricted to expressing only computable functions. It is perfectly reasonable in a specification to express notions like "For all x in set A, there exists a y in set B such that property P holds of x and y," where A and B might be infinite sets.

Programs, however, are formal objects, susceptible to formal manipulation (for example, compilation and execution). Thus, programmers cannot escape from formal methods. The question is whether they work with informal requirements and (formal) programs, or whether they use additional formalism to assist them during requirements specification.

When a specification language's semantic domain is over programs or systems of programs, the term *implements* is used for the satisfies relation, and the term *implementation* is used for a specificand in *Sem*. An implementation *prog* is correct with respect to a given specification *spec* if *prog* satisfies *spec*. More formally,

> Definition: Given a specification language, $< Syn, Sem, Sat >$, an implementation *prog* in *Sem* is correct with respect to a given specification *spec* in *Syn* if and only if $Sat(spec, prog)$.

Satisfies relation. We often would like to specify different aspects of a single specificand, perhaps using different specification languages. For example, you might want to specify the functional behavior of a collection of program modules as the composition of the functional behaviors of the individual modules. You might additionally want to specify a structural relationship between the modules such as what set of modules each module directly invokes.

To accommodate these different views of a specificand, we first associate with each specification language a semantic abstraction function, which partitions specificands into equivalence classes.

> Definition: Given a semantic domain, *Sem*, a semantic abstraction function is a homomorphism, $A : Sem \to 2^{Sem}$, that maps elements of the semantic domain into equivalence classes.

For a given specification language, we choose a semantic abstraction function to induce an *abstract satisfies relation* between specifications and equivalence classes of specificands. This relation defines a view on specificands.

> Definition: Given a specification language, $< Syn, Sem, Sat >$, and a semantic abstraction function, A, defined on *Sem*, an abstract satisfies relation, $ASat : Syn \to 2^{Sem}$, is the induced relation such that
>
> $$\forall spec \in Syn, prog \in Sem \bullet [Sat(spec, prog) = ASat(spec, A(prog))]$$

Different semantic abstraction functions make it possible to describe multiple views of the same equivalence class of systems, or similarly, impose different kinds of constraints on these systems. Having several specification languages with different semantic abstraction functions for a single semantic domain can be useful. This encourages and supports complementary specifications of different aspects of a system.

For example, in Figure 1, a single semantic domain, *Sem*, is on the right. One semantic abstraction function partitions specificands in *Sem* into a set of equivalence classes, three of which are drawn as blobs in solid lines. Another partitions specificands into a different set of equivalence classes, two of which are drawn as blobs in dashed lines. Via the abstract satisfies relation *ASat*1, specification *A* of syntactic domain *Syn*1 maps to one equivalence class of specificands (denoted by a solid-lined blob), and via *ASat*2, specification *B* of syntactic domain *Syn*2 maps to a different equivalence class of specificands (denoted by a dashed-line blob). Note the overlap between the solid-lined and dashed-lined blobs.

To be concrete, suppose *Sem* is a library of Ada program modules. Imagine that *A* specifies (perhaps through a predicate in first-order logic) all procedures that sort arrays, and *B* specifies (perhaps through a call graph) all procedures that call functions on a user-defined enumeration type *E*. Then, a procedure that sorted arrays of *E*'s might be in the intersection of *ASat*1(*A*) and *ASat*2(*B*).

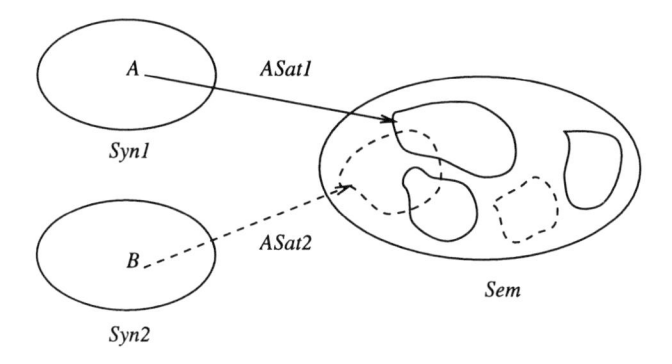

Figure 1. Abstract satisfies relations.

Two broad classes of semantic abstraction functions are those that abstract preserving each system's behavior and those that abstract preserving each system's structure. In the example above, *A* specifies a behavioral aspect of the Ada program modules, but *B* describes a structural aspect.

Behavioral specifications. Behavioral specifications describe only constraints on the observable behavior of specificands. The behavioral constraint that most formal methods address is a system's required functionality (that is, mapping from inputs to outputs). Current research in formal methods addresses other behavioral aspects, such as fault tolerance, safety, security, response time and space efficiency.

Often some of these behavioral aspects, such as security, are included as part of, rather than separate from, a system's functionality. If the overall correctness of a system is defined so that it must satisfy more than one behavioral constraint, a system that satisfies one but not another would be incorrect. For example, if functionality and response time were the constraints of interest, a system producing correct answers past deadlines would be just as unacceptable as a system producing incorrect answers on time.

Structural specifications. Structural specifications describe constraints on the internal composition of specificands. Example structural specification languages are module interconnection languages. Structural specifications capture various kinds of hierarchical and uses relations such as those represented by procedure-call graphs, data-dependency diagrams, and definition-use chains. Systems that satisfy the same structural constraints do not necessarily satisfy the same behavioral constraints. Moreover, the structure of a specification need not bear any direct relationship to the structure of its specificands.

Properties of specifications. Each specification language should be defined so each well-formed specification is unambiguous.

> Definition: Given a specification language, $< Syn, Sem, Sat >$, a specification *syn* in *Syn* is unambiguous if and only if *Sat* maps *syn* to exactly one specificand set.

Informally, a specification is unambiguous if and only if it has exactly one meaning. This key property of formal specifications means that any specification language based on or incorporating a natural language (like English) is not formal since natural languages are inherently ambiguous. It also means that a visual specification language that permits multiple interpretations of a box and/or arrow is ill-defined, and hence not formal.

Another desirable property of specifications is consistency.

> Definition: Given a specification language, $< Syn, Sem, Sat >$, a specification *syn* in *Syn* is consistent (or satisfiable) if and only if *Sat* maps *syn* to a non-empty specificand set.

Informally, a specification is consistent if and only if its specificand set is non-empty. In terms of programs, consistency is important because it means there is some implementation that will satisfy the specification. If you view a specification as a set of facts, consistency implies that you cannot derive anything contradictory from the specification.

Were you to pose a question based on a consistent specification, you would not get mutually exclusive answers. Obviously we want consistent specifications. An inconsistent specification, which negates on one occasion what it asserts on another, means you have no knowledge at all.

Specifications need not be complete in the sense used in mathematical logic, though certain relative-completeness properties might be desirable (for example, sufficient completeness of an algebraic specification [3]).

In practice, you must usually deal with incomplete specifications. Why? Specifiers may intentionally leave some things unspecified, giving the implementer some freedom to choose among different data structures and algorithms. Also, specifiers cannot realistically anticipate all possible scenarios in which a system will be run and thus, perhaps unwittingly, have left some things unspecified. Finally, specifiers develop specifications gradually and iteratively, perhaps in response to changing customer requirements, and hence work more often with unfinished products than finished ones.

A delicate balance exists between saying just enough and saying too much in a specification. Specifiers want to say enough so that implementers do not choose unacceptable implementations. Specifiers are responsible for not making oversights; any incompleteness in the specification should be an intentional incompleteness. On the other hand, saying too much may leave little design freedom for the implementer. A specification that overspecifies is guilty of implementation bias [5].

Informally, a specification has implementation bias if it specifies externally unobservable properties of its specificands; it places unnecessary constraints on its specificands. For example, a set specification that keeps track of the insertion order of its elements has implementation bias toward an ordered-list representation and against a hash table representation.

Proving properties of specificands. Most formal methods are defined in terms of a specification language that has a well-defined logical inference system. A logical inference system defines a consequence relation, typically given in terms of a set of inference rules, mapping a set of well-formed sentences in the specification language to a set of well-formed sentences.

We use this inference system to prove properties from the specification about specificands. Again taking a specification as a set of facts, we derive new facts through the application of the inference rules.

When you prove a statement inferable from these facts, you prove a property that a specificand satisfying the specification will have, a property not explicitly stated in the specification. An inference system gives users of formal methods a way to predict a system's behavior without having to execute or even build it. It gives users a way to state questions, in the form of conjectures, about a system cast in terms of just the specification itself. Users can then answer these questions in terms of a formal proof constructed through a formal derivation process.

The inference system increases confidence in the specification's validity. If users are able to prove a surprising result from the specification, then perhaps the specification is wrong.

A formal method with an explicitly defined inference system usually has the further advantage that this system can be completely mechanized (for example, if it has a finite set of finite rules). Theorem provers and proof checkers are example tools that assist users with the tedium of deriving and managing formal proofs.

Pragmatics

Certain pragmatic concerns exist about formal methods, their users, their uses, and their characteristics.

Users. Some users of formal methods are actually going to produce something tangible: formal specifications. However, most people need only read specifications,

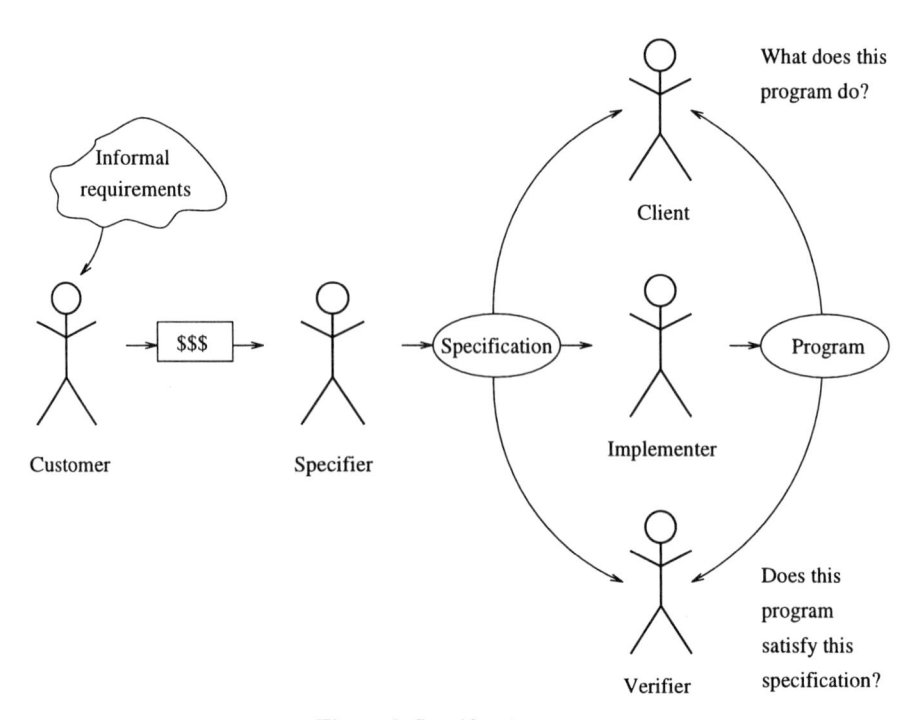

Figure 2. Specification users.

not develop their own from scratch. Besides specification writers, there are several kinds of specification readers.

In Figure 2 each stick figure represents a different role in the system development process. A person playing any of these roles is a potential specification user. In practice, one person may play multiple roles, and some role may not be played at all.

Specifiers write, evaluate, analyze, and refine specifications. They prove that their refinements preserve certain properties and prove properties of specificands through specifications. Specification readers, besides specifiers, are *customers*, those people who may have hired the specifiers; *implementers*, those people who realize a specification; *clients*, those people who use a specified system, usually without knowledge of how it is implemented; and *verifiers*, those people who prove the correctness of implementations. All these people can benefit from the assistance of machine tools (another kind of specification reader), some of which might blindly manipulate specifications without regard to their meaning.

One point of tension in many formal methods is that their languages may be more suitable to one type of specification user than to others. Most language designers will target their language for at least two types of users (for example, clients and specifiers, or specifiers and implementers). Some specification languages contain a lot of syntactic sugar to make specifications more readable by customers. Some contain a minimal amount because the intent of the method is to do formal proofs by machines or because the meaning of a rich set of cryptic mathematical notation is assumed.

An advocate of a particular formal method should tell potential users the method's domain of applicability. For example, a formal method might be applicable for describing sequential programs but not parallel ones, or for describing message-passing distributed systems, but not transaction-based distributed databases. Without knowing the proper domain of applicability, a user may inappropriately apply a formal method to an inapplicable domain.

A formal method's set of guidelines should identify different types of users the method is targeted for and the capabilities each should have. To apply some methods properly, users might need to know modern algebra, set theory, and/or predicate logic. To apply some domain-specific methods, users might need to know additional mathematical theories – for example, digital logic, if specifying hardware, or probability and statistics, if specifying system reliability.

Uses. You can apply formal methods in all phases of system development. Such applications shouldn't be considered a separate activity, but rather an integral one. The greatest benefit in applying a formal method often comes from the process of formalizing rather than from the end result. Gaining a deeper understanding of the specificand by forcing yourself to be abstract yet precise about desired system properties can be more rewarding than having the specification document alone.

Consider, for each system development phase, some uses of formal specifications and the formal methods that support them. (See *"Further Reading"*[1] for specific citations.)

Requirements analysis. Applying a formal method helps clarify a customer's set of informally stated requirements. A specification helps crystallize the customer's vague ideas and reveals contradictions, ambiguities, and incompleteness in the requirements. A specifier has a better chance of asking pertinent questions and evaluating customer responses through the use of a formal, rather than an informal, specification. Both the customer and specifier can pose and answer questions based on the specification to see whether it reflects the customer's intuition and whether the specificand set has the desired set of properties. Systems such as Kate and the Requirements Apprentice address the problem of transforming informal requirements into formal specifications; the Gist explainer addresses the converse problem of translating a formal specification into a restricted subset of English.

System design. Two of the most important activities during design are decomposition and refinement. The Vienna Development Method (VDM), Z, Larch, and Lamport's transition axiom method are formal methods that are especially suitable for system design.

Decomposition is the process of partitioning a system into smaller modules. Specifiers can write specifications to capture precisely the interfaces between these modules. Each interface specification provides the module's client the information needed to use the module without knowledge of its implementation. At the same time, it provides the module's implementer the information needed to implement the module without knowledge of its clients.

Thus, as long as the interface remains the same, the implementation of the module can be replaced, perhaps by a more efficient one, at some later time without affecting its clients. The interface provides a place for recording design decisions; moreover, any intentional incompleteness can be captured succinctly as a parameter in the interface.

Refinement involves working at different levels of abstraction, perhaps refining a single module at one level to be a collection of modules at a lower level, or choosing a representation type for an abstract data type. Each refinement step requires showing that a specification (or program) at one level satisfies a higher-level specification.

Proving satisfaction often generates additional assumptions, called proof obligations, that must be discharged for the proof to be valid. A formal method provides the language to state these proof obligations precisely and the framework to carry out the proof.

Program refinement dates back to Dijkstra's work on stepwise refinement and predicate transformers and Hoare's work on data representation and abstraction functions. Related work on program transformation, program synthesis, and inferential programming has spawned the design of languages like Refine and Ex-

---

[1] Pages 194–199.

tended ML, and programming environments like CIP-S and the Ergo Support System. These refinement approaches are based on classical mathematical logic. An alternative approach to program development based on constructive logic gave rise to proof development environments like NuPRL in which programs are proofs and vice versa.

System verification. Verification is the process of showing a system satisfies its specification. Formal verification is impossible without a formal specification. Although you may never completely verify an entire system, you can certainly verify smaller, critical pieces. The trickiest part is in explicitly stating the assumptions about the environment in which each critical piece is placed. (I elaborate on this point in the *"Bounds of Formal Methods"* section[2].) Systems such as Gypsy, the Hierarchical Development Method (HDM), the Formal Development Method (FDM), and m-EVES (Environment for Verifying and Evaluating Software) evolved as a result of a primary focus on program verification. Higher Order Logic (HOL) was originally developed for hardware verification.

System validation. Formal methods can aid in system testing and debugging. Specifications alone can be used to generate test cases for black-box testing. Specifications that explicitly state assumptions on a module's use identify test cases for boundary conditions.

Specifications along with implementations can be used for other kinds of testing analysis such as path testing, unit testing, and integration testing. Testing based solely on an analysis of the implementation is not sufficient; the specification must be taken into account. For example, a test set may be complete for doing a path analysis, but may not reveal missing paths that the specification would otherwise suggest. The success of unit and integration testing depends on the precision of the specifications of the individual modules.

Only a few formal methods have been developed explicitly for testing. Three examples are: the Data Abstraction, Implementation, Specification and Testing System, used to test implementations of abstract data types; Kemmerer's symbolic execution tool, used to generate and execute test cases from Ina Jo specifications; and the Task Sequencing Language Runtime System, used to automatically check the execution of Ada tasking statements against TSL specifications.

System documentation. A specification is a description alternative to system implementation. It serves as a communication medium between a client and a specifier, between a specifier and an implementer, and among members of an implementation team. In reply to the question "What does it do?" no answer is more exasperating than "Run it and see." One of the primary intended uses of formal methods is to capture the "what" in a formal specification rather than the "how." A client can then simply read the specification rather than read the implementation or worse, execute the system, to find out the system's behavior.

---

[2] Pages 189–192.

System analysis and evaluation. To learn from the experience of building a system, developers should do a critical analysis of its functionality and performance once it has been built and tested. Does the system do what the customer wants? Does it do it fast enough? If formal methods were used in its development, they can help system developers formulate and answer these questions. The specification serves as a reference point. If the customer is unhappy, but the system meets the specification, the specification can be changed and the system changed accordingly.

Indeed much recent work in the application of formal methods to nontrivial examples has been in specifying a system already built, running, and used. Some of these exercises revealed bugs in published algorithms and circuit designs, serious bugs that had gone undiscovered for years. As expected, most revealed unstated assumptions, inconsistencies, and unintentional incompleteness in the system.

Medium-sized systems that have been specified formally include VLSI circuits, microprocessors, oscilloscopes, operating systems kernels, distributed databases, and secure systems. Most formal methods have not yet been applied to specifying large-scale software or hardware systems; most are still inadequate to specify many important behavioral constraints beyond functionality, for example, fault-tolerance and real-time performance.

This problem of scale exists in two, often confused, dimensions: size of the specification and complexity of the specificands. Tools can help address specification size, since managing large specifications is just like managing other large documents (such as programs, proofs, and test suites) and their structural interrelationships.

The problem of dealing with a specificand's inherent complexity remains. System complexity results from internal complexity and/or interface complexity. For example, an optimizing compiler is internally more complex than a nonoptimizing one for the same language, yet, in principle, they would both provide the same simple interface to their clients (for example, "compile *program_name*"). By providing a systematic way to think and reason about specificands, formal methods can help people grapple with both kinds of system complexity.

Characteristics. A formal method's characteristics, such as whether its language is graphical or whether its underlying logic is first-order, influence the style in which a user applies it. This article is not intended to give a complete taxonomy of all possible characteristics of a method nor to classify exhaustively all methods according to these characteristics. Instead, I give a partial listing of characteristics, noting that a method typically reflects a combination of many different ones. (See *"Further Reading"*[3] for citations of the methods mentioned.)

Model- versus property-oriented. Two broad classes of formal methods are called model-oriented and property-oriented. Using a model-oriented method, a specifier defines a system's behavior directly by constructing a model of the system in terms of mathematical structures such as tuples, relations, functions, sets, and sequences.

---

[3] Pages 194–199.

Using a property-oriented method, a specifier defines the system's behavior indirectly by stating a set of properties, usually in the form of a set of axioms, that the system must satisfy.

A specifier following a property-oriented method tries to state no more than the necessary minimal constraints on the system's behavior. The fewer the properties specified, the more the possible implementations that will satisfy the specification.

Model-oriented methods for specifying the behavior of sequential programs and abstract data types include Parnas's state-machines, Robinson and Roubine's extensions to them with V-, O-, and OV-functions, VDM and Z. Methods for specifying the behavior of concurrent and distributed systems include Petri nets, Milner's Calculus of Communicating Systems, Hoare's Communicating Sequential Processes, Unity, I/O automata, and TSL. The Raise Project represents more recent work on combining VDM and CSP.

Property-oriented methods can be broken into two categories, sometimes referred to as axiomatic and algebraic. Axiomatic methods stem from Hoare's work on proofs of correctness of implementations of abstract data types, where first-order predicate logic preconditions and postconditions are used for the specification of each operation of the type. Iota, OBJ, Anna, and Larch are example specification languages that support an axiomatic method.

In an algebraic method, data types and processes are defined to be heterogeneous algebras. This approach uses axioms to specify properties of systems, but the axioms are restricted to equations. Much work has been done on the algebraic specification of abstract data types, including the handling of error values, nondeterminism, and parameterization. The more widely known specification languages that have evolved from this work are Clear and Act One (Algebraic Specification Techniques for Correct and Trusty Software Systems).

Property-oriented methods for specifying the behavior of concurrent and distributed systems include extensions to the Hoare-axiom method, temporal logic, and Lamport's transition axiom method. The Language of Temporal Ordering of Specifications (LOTOS) specification language represents more recent work on the combination of Act One and CCS (with some CSP influence).

Visual languages. Visual methods include any whose language contains graphical elements in their syntactic domain. The most prominent visual method is Petri nets, and its many variations, used most typically to specify the behavior of concurrent systems.

More recent visual language work includes Harel's statecharts based on higraphs, used to specify state transitions in reactive systems. Figure 3 gives a simple example of a statechart that describes the behavior of a one-slot buffer. Rounded rectangles ("roundtangles") represent states in a state machine and arrows represent state transitions. Initially, the one-slot buffer is empty. If a message arrives and is put in the buffer, the buffer becomes full; when the message has been serviced and removed from the buffer, its state changes back to being empty.

The example shows one of the more notable features of statecharts that distinguish them from "flat" state-transition diagrams: A roundtangle can represent a hierarchy of states (and in general, an arrow can represent a set of state transitions), thereby letting users zoom in and zoom out of a system and its subsystems.

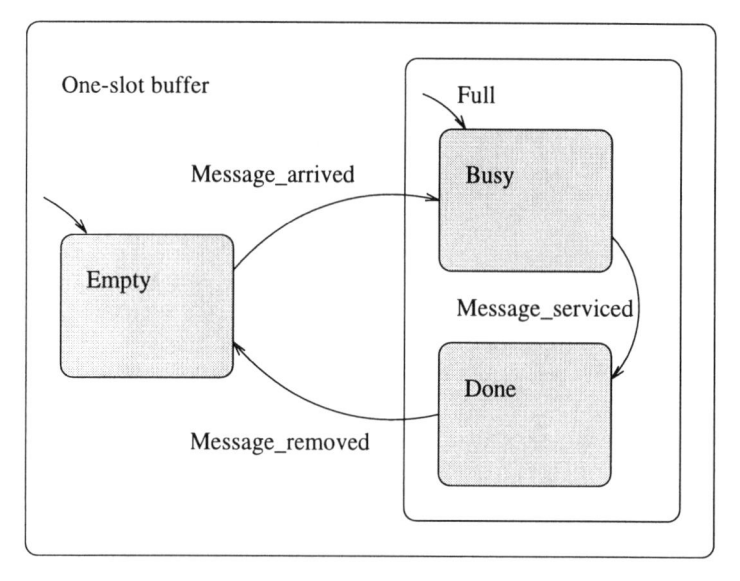

Figure 3. Statechart specification of a one-slot buffer.

Harel's higraph notation inspired the design of the Miró visual languages, which specify security constraints. Like statecharts, the Miró languages have a formally defined semantics and tool support.

Many informal methods use visual notations. These methods allow the construction of ambiguous specifications, perhaps because English text is attached to the graphical elements or because multiple interpretations of a graphical element (usually different meanings for an arrow) are possible. Many popular software and system design methods such as Jackson's method, Hierarchy-Input-Processing-Output (HIPO), Structured Design, and Software Requirements Engineering Methodology are examples of semi-formal methods that use pictures.

Executable. Some formal methods support executable specifications, specifications that can be run on a computer. An executable specification language is by definition more restricted in expressive power than a non-executable language because its functions must be computable and defined over domains with finite representations. As long as users realize that the specification may suffer from implementation bias, executable specifications can play an important role in the system development process. Specifiers can use them to gain immediate feedback about the specification itself, to do rapid prototyping (the specification serves as a prototype of the system), and to test a specificand through symbolic execution of the specification. For example, the Statemate tool lets users run simulations through the state transition diagram represented by a statechart.

Besides statecharts, executable specification languages include OBJ; Prolog, a logic programming language that when used in a property-oriented style lets specifiers state logical relations on objects; and Paisley, a model-oriented language, based on a model of event sequences and used to specify functional and timing behavioral constraints for asynchronous parallel processes.

Tool-supported. Some formal methods evolved from the semantic-analysis tools that were built to manipulate specifications and programs. Model-checking tools let users construct a finite-state model of the system and then show a property holds of each state or state transition of the system. Tools such as Extended Model Checker (EMC) are especially useful for specifying and verifying properties of VLSI circuits.

Proof-checking tools that let users treat algebraic specifications as rewrite rules include Affirm, Reve, the Rewrite Rule Laboratory, and the Larch Prover. Tools (and their associated specification language) that handle subsets of first-order logic include the Boyer-Moore Theorem Prover (and the Gypsy specification language), FDM (Ina Jo), HDM (Special), and m-EVES (m-Verdi). Finally, tools that handle subsets of higher-order logics include HOL, LCF, and OBJ.

Some Examples

This section illustrates six well-known or commonly used formal methods, half applied to one simple example and the other half applied to another example. All six methods have been used to specify much more complex systems.

Sometimes, when specifying the same problem using different methods, the resulting specifications look remarkably similar (as in the first three examples), and sometimes they don't (as in the last three). The similarity or difference is sometimes attributable to the nature or simplicity of the specificand and sometimes to the methods themselves.

The choice of a method is likely to affect what a specification says and how it is said. A method's guidelines may encourage the specifier to be explicit about some system behaviors (for example, state changes) and not others (for example, error handling). Syntactic conventions (such as indentation style), special notation (vertical and horizontal lines), and keywords affect a specification's physical appearance and its readability.

Most proponents of methods used primarily to specify behavioral properties of concurrent and distributed systems have carefully defined the satisfies relation for a given semantic domain. Many of their methods lack the niceties – the syntactic sugar and software support tools – that formal methods for sequential systems provide. For some theories or models of concurrent and distributed systems more user-friendly specification languages (LOTOS and Raise) are beginning to appear.

Abstract data types: Z, VDM, Larch. Z, a formal method based on set theory, can be used in both model-oriented and property-oriented styles. Figure 4 gives a model-oriented specification of a symbol table, following the Z notation of Spivey [12]. The state of the table is modeled by a partial mapping from keys to values ($X \nrightarrow Y$ denotes a set of partial mappings from set X to set Y; a partial mapping relates each member of X to at most one member of Y.) By convention, unprimed variables in Z stand for the state before an operation is performed and primed variables for the state afterwards. I will use the same convention in the VDM and Larch specifications.

The table contains four operations: *INIT*, *INSERT*, *LOOKUP*, and *DELETE*. *INIT* initializes the symbol table to be empty. *INSERT* modifies the table by adding a new binding to *st*, in the case the key k is not already in the domain of *st*. *LOOKUP* requires that the key k be in the domain of the mapping, returns the value to which k is mapped, and does not change the state of the symbol table ($st' = st$). *DELETE* also requires that the key k be in the domain of the mapping, and modifies the table by deleting the binding associated with k from st ($\triangleleft$ is a domain subtraction operator). The proof checker B has been used for proving theorems based on Z specifications.

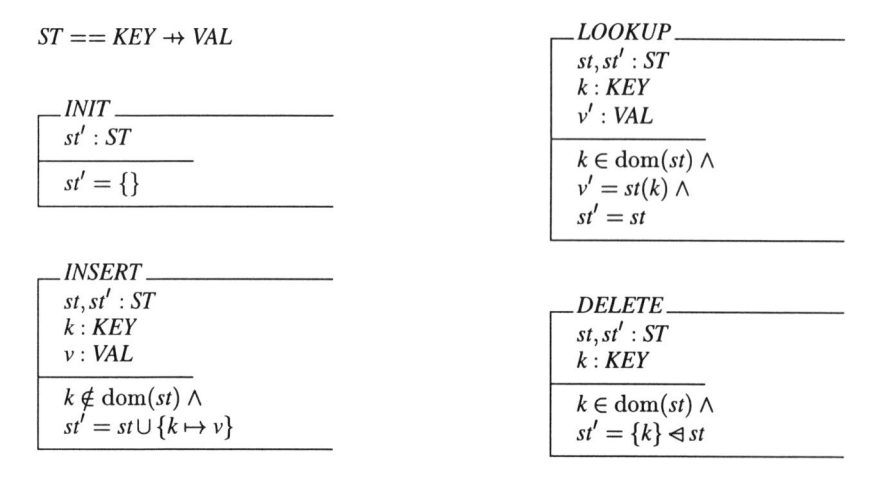

$ST == KEY \nrightarrow VAL$

―― *INIT* ――――――――――
$st' : ST$
―――――――――――――
$st' = \{\}$

―― *INSERT* ―――――――――
$st, st' : ST$
$k : KEY$
$v : VAL$
―――――――――――――
$k \notin \text{dom}(st) \land$
$st' = st \cup \{k \mapsto v\}$

―― *LOOKUP* ―――――――――
$st, st' : ST$
$k : KEY$
$v' : VAL$
―――――――――――――
$k \in \text{dom}(st) \land$
$v' = st(k) \land$
$st' = st$

―― *DELETE* ―――――――――
$st, st' : ST$
$k : KEY$
―――――――――――――
$k \in \text{dom}(st) \land$
$st' = \{k\} \triangleleft st$

Figure 4. Z specification of a symbol table.

VDM supports a model-oriented specification style and defines a set of built-in data types (such as sets, lists, and mappings), which specifiers use to define other types.

The VDM specification in Figure 5 defines a symbol table also in terms of a **map**ping from keys to values. I follow the VDM notation given in Jones [6]. The behavior of the INIT, INSERT, LOOKUP and DELETE operations are the same as specified in the Z specification. However, the preconditions specified in **pre** clauses are made explicit and separate from the postconditions, specified in **post** clauses.

A precondition on an operation is a predicate that must hold in the state on each invocation of the operation; if it does not hold, the operation's behavior is unspecified. A postcondition is a predicate that holds in the state upon return. An operation's clients are responsible for satisfying preconditions, and its implementer is responsible for guaranteeing the postcondition.

The fact that LOOKUP does not modify the symbol table (hence $st' = st$) but INSERT and DELETE do is specified by using **rd** (for read-only access) instead of **wr** (for write-and-read access) in the declaration of the **ext**ernal state variables accessed by each operation.

$ST = $ **map** *Key* **to** *Val*

INIT( )
ext   **wr** *st* : *ST*
post $st' = \{\}$

INSERT(k : *Key*, v : *Val*)
ext   **wr** *st* : *ST*
pre $k \notin \textbf{dom } st$
post $st' = st \cup \{k \mapsto v\}$

LOOKUP(k : *Key*) v : *Val*
ext   **rd** *st* : *ST*
pre $k \in \textbf{dom } st$
post $v' = st(k)$

DELETE(k : *Key*)
ext   **wr** *st* : *ST*
pre $k \in \textbf{dom } st$
post $st' = \{k\} \triangleleft st$

Figure 5. VDM specification of a symbol table.

Larch is a property-oriented method that combines both axiomatic and algebraic specifications into a two-tiered specification [2]. The axiomatic component specifies state-dependent behavior (for example, side effects and exceptional termination) of programs. The algebraic component specifies state-independent properties of data accessed by programs. Figure 6 gives a Larch specification of the symbol table example. I follow the Larch notation given in Guttag et al [3].

The first piece of the Larch specification, called an interface specification, looks similar to the Z and VDM specifications. For each operation, the **requires** and **ensures** clauses specify its pre- and postconditions. The **modifies** clause lists those objects whose value may possibly change as a result of executing the operation. Hence, LOOKUP is not allowed to change the state of its symbol table argument, but INSERT and DELETE are.

One difference (not shown in the example) between Larch and VDM (and Larch and Z), is that, if the target programming language supports exception handling, the interfaces would specify whether and under what conditions an operation signals exceptions. For example, we could remove INSERT's **requires** clause and instead use a special **signals** clause in its postcondition to specify that a signal should be raised in the case that the key k is already in the symbol table.

The second piece of the Larch specification, called a trait, looks like an algebraic specification. It contains a set of function symbol declarations and a set of equations that define the meaning of the function symbols. The equations determine an equiv-

symbol_table **is data type based on** S **from** SymTab
    init = **proc** ( ) **returns** (s: symbol_table)
        ensures s' = emp ∧ **new** (s)
    insert = **proc** (s: symbol_table, k: key, v: val)
        requires ∼ isin(s, k)
        modifies (s)
        ensures s' = add(s, k, v)
    lookup = **proc** (s: symbol_table, k: key) **returns** (v: val)
        requires isin(s, k)
        ensures v' = find(s, k)
    delete = **proc** (s: symbol_table, k: key)
        requires isin(s, k)
        modifies (s)
        ensures s' = rem(s, k)
    end symbol_table

SymTab: **trait**
    introduces
        emp: → S
        add: S, K, V → S
        rem: S, K → S
        find: S, K → V
        isin: S, K → Bool
    asserts
    S **generated by** (emp, add)
    S **partitioned by** (find, isin)
    for all (s: S, k, k1: K, v: V)
        rem(add(s, k, v), k1) == **if** k = k1 **then** s **else** add(rem(s, k1), k, v)
        find(add(s, k, v), k1) == **if** k = k1 **then** v **else** find(s, k1)
        isin(emp, k) == **false**
        isin(add(s, k, v), k1) == (k = k1) ∨ isin(s, k1)
    implies
        converts (rem, find, isin) **exempting** (rem(emp), find(emp))
    end SymTab

Figure 6. Larch specification of a symbol table.

alence relation on sorted terms. Objects of the symbol_table data type specified in the interface specification range over values denoted by the terms of sort S.

The **generated by** clause states that all symbol table values can be represented by terms composed solely of the two function symbols, emp and add. This clause defines an inductive rule of inference and is useful for proving properties about all symbol table values.

The **partitioned by** clause adds more equivalences between terms. Intuitively it states that two terms are equal if they cannot be distinguished by any of the functions listed in the clause. In the example, we could use this property to show that order of insertion of distinct key-value pairs in the symbol table does not matter, that is, insertion is commutative.

The **exempting** clause documents the absence of right sides of equations for rem(emp) and find(emp); the **requires** and **signals** clauses in the interface specification deal with these "error values." The **converts** and **exempting** clauses together provide a way to state that this algebraic specification is sufficiently complete.

Syntax analyzers exist for Larch traits and interfaces. The Larch Prover has been used to perform semantic analysis on Larch traits.

The user-defined function symbols in a Larch trait are exactly those used in the pre- and postconditions of the interface specification; they serve the same role as the built-in symbols like $\cup$ and $\triangleleft$ used in the Z and VDM specifications.

Unlike Z and VDM, Larch does not come with any special built-in notation nor with any built-in types. The advantage is that the user does not have to learn any special vocabulary for those concepts and is free to introduce whatever symbols he or she desires, giving them the exact meaning suitable for the specificand set. Exactly those properties of a data type being specified need to be stated explicitly and satisfied by an implementation.

The disadvantage is that the user may often need to provide a large set of user-defined symbols, as well as the equations that define their meaning. Since I modeled symbol tables in Z and VDM in terms of finite mappings, I did not need to state explicitly that insertion is commutative. This is a property of mappings – the commutative property came for free. The Larch handbook [3] serves as a compromise between the two extremes in that it provides a library of traits that define many general and commonly used concepts (for example, properties of finite mappings, partial orders, sets, and sequences).

Concurrency: Temporal logic, CSP, transition axioms. As mentioned before, many formal methods for specifying the behavior of concurrent and distributed systems differ because of their choice in semantic domain. Some focus on just the states, some on just the events, and some on both. To be more concrete here, I will model a system's behavior as a set of linear sequences of states and associated events. An alternative approach, used by CCS and EMC, is to model a system's behavior as a set of trees of states and associated events. When a specification is interpreted with respect to sets of sequences, separating properties of concurrent and distributed systems into two general categories, safety and liveness, is common.

Safety properties ("nothing bad ever happens") include functional correctness and liveness properties ("something good eventually happens") include termination.

Temporal logic is a property-oriented method for specifying properties of concurrent and distributed systems. For a given temporal logic inference system, special modal operators concisely state assertions about system behavior. Specifiers use these operators to refer to past, current, and future states (or events).

There is no one standard temporal logic inference system nor one standard set of operators. Modal operators commonly used are □, ◇, and ◯. Informally, when interpreted with respect to a sequence of states, □P says that in all future states, the state predicate P holds; ◇P says that in some future state P will hold; and ◯P says that in the next state P will hold. For example, $P \Rightarrow \Diamond Q$ says that if P holds in the current state, Q will eventually hold. Temporal logic notation tends to be terse, and a temporal logic specification is simply an unstructured set of predicates, all of which must be satisfied by a given implementation.

Figure 7 presents a temporal logic specification of the behavior of an unbounded buffer in an asynchronous environment. The example is adapted from Koymans et al., [7], using the temporal logic system in Pneuli [11], which has twelve different modal operators. The formula are interpreted with respect to sequences of events. A buffer has a *left* input channel and a *right* output channel. The expression $\langle c!m \rangle$ denotes the event of placing message m on channel c. The first predicate,

$$\langle right!m \rangle \Rightarrow \Diamond \langle left!m \rangle$$

states that any message transmitted to the right channel ($\langle right!m \rangle$) must have been previously placed on the left channel ($\Diamond \langle left!m \rangle$). The second predicate,

$$(\langle right!m \rangle \wedge \ominus \Diamond \langle right!m' \rangle) \Rightarrow \Diamond (\langle left!m \rangle \wedge \ominus \Diamond \langle left!m' \rangle)$$

states that messages are transmitted first in, first out. If a message m placed on the output channel is preceded by some other message m' also on the output channel ($\ominus \Diamond \langle right!m' \rangle$), there must have been a preceding (the second $\Diamond$) event of placing m on the input channel ($\langle left!m \rangle$) and, moreover, an even earlier event that placed m' on the input channel ahead of m ($\ominus \Diamond \langle left!m' \rangle$). The third predicate,

$$(\langle left!m \rangle \wedge \ominus \Diamond \langle left!m' \rangle) \Rightarrow (m \neq m')$$

states that all messages are unique. For each message m currently placed on the input channel and for each previously placed message m' ($\ominus \Diamond \langle left!m' \rangle$), m and m' are not equal. This property is not a property of the buffer, but an assumption of the environment. This assumption is essential to the validity of the specification. Without it, a buffer that outputs duplicate copies of its input would be considered correct.

Whereas the first three predicates state safety properties of the system (and its environment), the fourth predicate,

$$(\langle left!m \rangle) \Rightarrow \Diamond (\langle right!m \rangle)$$

$$\langle right!m \rangle \Rightarrow \Diamond \langle left!m \rangle \tag{1}$$
$$(\langle right!m \rangle \wedge \ominus \Diamond \langle right!m' \rangle) \Rightarrow \Diamond (\langle left!m \rangle \wedge \ominus \Diamond \langle left!m' \rangle) \tag{2}$$
$$(\langle left!m \rangle \wedge \ominus \Diamond \langle left!m' \rangle) \Rightarrow (m \neq m') \tag{3}$$
$$(\langle left!m \rangle) \Rightarrow \Diamond (\langle right!m \rangle) \tag{4}$$

Figure 7. Temporal logic specification of an unbounded buffer.

states a liveness property: Each incoming message will eventually be transmitted.

CSP uses a model-oriented method for specifying concurrent processes and a property-oriented method for stating and proving properties about the model. CSP is based on model of *traces*, or event sequences, and assumes that processes communicate by sending messages across channels. Processes synchronize on events so that the event of sending output message m on a named channel c is synchronized with the event of simultaneously receiving an input message on c. Figure 8 gives a CSP specification of an unbounded buffer (adapted from Hoare [4]). *BUFFER* itself is specified to be a process P that acts as an unbounded buffer. The recursive definition of P is divided into two clauses to handle the empty and non-empty cases. The first clause,

$$P_{<>} = left?m \rightarrow P_{<m>}$$

says that if the buffer is empty, in the event that there is a message m on the *left* channel (*left?m*), it will input it. In CSP, if x is an event and P is a process, the notation $x \rightarrow P$ denotes a process that first engages in the event x and then behaves exactly as described by P. The second clause,

$$P_{<m>\hat{\ }s} = (left?n \rightarrow P_{<m>\hat{\ }s<n>} \mid right!m \rightarrow P_s)$$

says that if the buffer is non-empty, then either the buffer will input another message n from the *left* channel, appending it to the end of the buffer, or output the first message in the buffer to the *right* channel. CSP uses $s\hat{\ }t$ to denote the concatenation of sequence s to sequence t. It uses | to denote choice: If x and y are distinct events, $x \rightarrow P \mid y \rightarrow Q$ describes a process that initially engages in either x or y. After this first event, subsequent behavior is described by P, if the first event was x, and by Q, if the first event was y.

In CSP's formalism, *BUFFER* is a CSP program; you can state and prove properties about the traces it denotes. Using algebraic laws on traces you can formally verify that a given CSP program satisfies a specification on traces. The last line in Figure 8 states that *BUFFER* describes a set of traces, each of which satisfies the predicate given on the right-hand side of **sat**. The predicate's first conjunct says that the sequence of (output) messages on the right channel is a prefix of the sequence of (input) messages on the left channel. CSP uses the notation $s \leq t$ to denote that the sequence *s* is a prefix of sequence *t*. The prefix property of sequences guarantees that only messages sent from the left will be delivered to the right, only once, and in the same order. The second conjunct says that the process never stops: it cannot *ref*use to communicate on either the right or left channel. This implies that input messages will eventually be delivered, which is the same property as stated in the temporal logic specification's fourth predicate.

$$BUFFER = P_{<>}$$
$$\text{where } P_{<>} = left?m \to P_{<m>}$$
$$\text{and } P_{<m>\hat{\ }s} = (left?n \to P_{<m>\hat{\ }s<n>} \mid right!m \to P_s)$$

$BUFFER$ **sat** $(right \leq left) \wedge (\textbf{if } right = left \textbf{ then } left \notin ref \textbf{ else } right \notin ref)$

Figure 8. CSP program and specification of an unbounded buffer.

B, previously mentioned for proving theorems from Z specifications, has also been used to prove properties of CSP specifications. Occam is a programming language derivative of CSP that has been implemented and used on Transputers.

Lamport's transition axiom method combines an axiomatic method for describing the behavior of individual operations with temporal logic assertions for specifying safety and liveness properties. In the buffer example of Figure 9 (adapted from Lamport [8]) I use his original notation, although Lamport introduced two other notations in a more recent description of his method [9].

In the example, the functions *buffer*, *parg*, and *gval* define the state of the buffer, which has two operations, PUT and GET, and an initial size of 0. For this example, we assume that invocations of different operations can be active concurrently, but at most one invocation of a given operation can be active at once.

The predicates $at(OP), in(OP)$, and $after(OP)$ state whether control is at the point of calling the operation OP, within the execution of OP, or at the point of return from OP.

The first pair of safety properties states that the value of the state function *parg* is equal to the input parameter to PUT at the time of call and equal to *NULL* upon return.

The second pair states similar properties for GET. The third pair of properties indicates how the state functions change as a result of executing PUT and GET: If control is in PUT, *buffer* gets updated by appending the non-*NULL* message to its end; if control is in GET and the buffer is non-empty, *buffer* gets updated by removing its first message, which is GET's return value *gval*. (The ∗ denotes appending an element to a sequence.)

The fourth and fifth properties are liveness properties requiring that PUT return whenever there are fewer than *min* messages in the buffer and that GET return whenever the buffer is non-empty. (The temporal logic operator ↝ stands for "leads to.") These requirements ensure that progress is made, that once control is within the

module BUFFER **with subroutines** PUT, GET
state functions:
   buffer : **sequence of** *message*
   parg : *message* **or** *NULL*
   gval : *message* **or** *NULL*
initial conditions:
   | *buffer* | = 0
safety properties
   1. (a) $at(\text{PUT}) \Rightarrow parg = \text{PUT.PAR}$
     (b) $after(\text{PUT}) \Rightarrow parg = NULL$
   2. (a) $at(\text{GET}) \Rightarrow gval = NULL$
     (b) $after(\text{GET}) \Rightarrow \text{GET.PAR} = gval$
   3. **allowed changes to** *buffer*
                 parg **when** *in*(PUT)
                 gval **when** *in*(GET)
     (a) $\alpha[\text{BUFFER}]:in(\text{PUT}) \wedge parg \neq NULL \rightarrow$
                     $parg' = NULL \wedge buffer' = buffer * parg$
     (b) $\alpha[\text{BUFFER}]:in(\text{GET}) \wedge gval = NULL \wedge |\,buffer\,| > 0 \rightarrow$
                     $gval' \neq NULL \wedge buffer = gval' * buffer'$
liveness properties
   4. $in(\text{PUT}) \wedge |\,buffer\,| < min \rightsquigarrow after(\text{PUT})$
   5. $in(\text{GET}) \wedge |\,buffer\,| > 0 \rightsquigarrow after(\text{GET})$

Figure 9. Transition axiom specification of an unbounded buffer.

PUT (or GET) operation, control will reach its corresponding return point. The fifth implies that messages received (through PUT) are eventually transmitted (through GET) since, if control is in GET, it must eventually return.

Unlike the temporal logic and CSP examples – but like the Z, VDM, and Larch examples – the last example uses keywords and distinct clauses for highlighting a model of state (**state functions**), state initialization (**initial conditions**), and state changes (**allowed changes to**). Again, unlike the temporal logic and CSP examples, it uses similar notational conveniences to highlight synchronization conditions (the enabling predicates to the left-hand side of →) and safety and liveness constraints on the processes' behaviors. Hence, this last example shows a combination of linguistic features borrowed from formal methods used to specify sequential programs and others used to specify concurrent ones.

Bounds of Formal Methods

Between the ideal and the real worlds. Formal methods are based on mathematics but are not entirely mathematical. Formal methods users must acknowledge the two important boundaries between the mathematical world and the real world.

Users cross the first boundary in codifying the customer's informally stated requirements. Figure 10 illustrates this mapping, where the cloud symbolizes the customer's informal requirements and the oval symbolizes a formal specification of them.

This mapping from informal to formal is typically achieved through an iterative process not subject to proof. A specifier might write an initial specification, discuss its implications with the customer, and revise it as a result of the customer's feedback.

At all times the formal specification is only a mathematical representation of the customer's requirements. On one hand, any inconsistencies in the requirements would be faithfully preserved in the specifier's mapping. On the other, the specifier might incorrectly interpret the requirements and formally characterize the misinterpretation. For these reasons, it is important that specifiers and customers interact.

Specifiers can help customers clarify their fuzzy, perhaps contradictory, notions; customers can help specifiers debug their specifications. The existence of this boundary should not be surprising because people use formal methods.

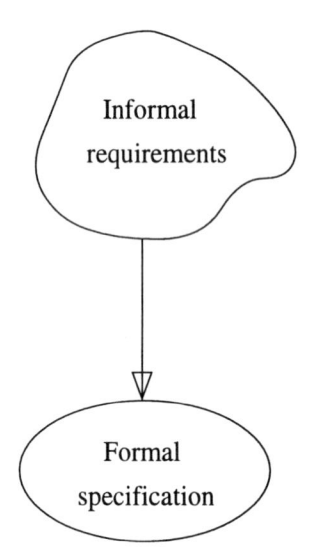

Figure 10. Mapping informal requirements to a formal specification.

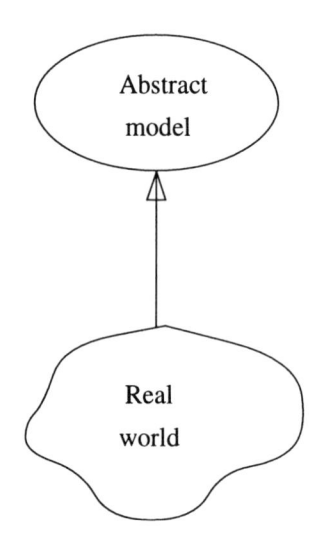

Figure 11. Mapping the real world to an abstract model.

The second boundary is crossed in the mapping from the real world to some abstract representation of it. Figure 11 illustrates this mapping where the cloud symbolizes the real world and the oval symbolizes an abstract model of it.

The formal specification language encodes this abstraction. For example, a formal specification might describe properties of real arithmetic, abstracting away from the fact that not all real numbers can be represented in a computer. The formal specification is only a mathematical approximation of the real world. This boundary is not unique to formal methods, or computer science in general; it is ubiquitous in all fields of engineering and applied mathematics.

Assumptions about the environment. Another kind of boundary is often neglected by even experienced specifiers. It's the boundary between a real system and its environment. A system does not run in isolation; its behavior is affected by input from the external world, which in turn consumes the system's output.

Given that you can formally model the system (in terms of a specification language's semantic domain), then, if you can formally model the environment, you can formally characterize the interface between a system and its environment. Most formal methods leave the environment's specification (formal or otherwise) outside of the specification of the system. An exception is the Gist language used to specify closed systems. In theory, a complete Gist specification includes not only a description of the system's behavior, but also of its clients and other environmental factors like hardware.

A system's behavior as captured in its specification is conditional on the environment's behavior:

Environment $\Rightarrow$ *System*

This implication says that if the environment satisfies some precondition, *Environment*, then the system will behave as specified in *System*. If the environment fails to satisfy the precondition, then the system is free to behave in any way.

Environment is a set of assumptions. Whereas a system specifier places constraints on the system's behavior, the specifier cannot place constraints on the environment, but can only make assumptions about its behavior. For example, in the temporal logic specification of the unbounded buffer, the assumption that messages are unique is an obligation the environment is expected to satisfy, not a property the buffer is expected to satisfy nor a constraint that the system specifier can place on the environment.

A specifier often makes implicit assumptions about a system's environment when specifying something like a procedure in a programming language because the environment is usually fixed or at least well-defined.

A procedure's environment is defined in terms of the programming language's invocation protocol. A procedure's specification will typically omit explicit mention of the language's parameter passing mechanism, or, for a compile-time type-checked language, that the argument types are correct. The specifier presumably knows the details of the programming language's parameter-passing mechanism, and assumes the programmer will compile the procedure, thereby doing the appropriate type checking.

However, when specifying a large, complex, software or hardware system, the specifier should take special care to make explicit as many assumptions about the environment as possible. Unfortunately, when specifying a large system, specifiers too often forget to state explicitly the circumstances under which the system is expected to behave properly.

In reality, it is impossible to formally model many environmental aspects such as unpredictable or unanticipated events, human error, and natural catastrophes (lightning, hurricanes, earthquakes). Hazard analysis, as a complementary technique to formal methods, can identify a system's safety-critical components. Formal methods can then be used to describe and reason about these components, where reasoning holds only for those system input parameters that are made explicit.

In a strict mathematical sense, formal methods differ greatly from one another. Not only does notation vary, but the choice of the semantic domain and definition of the satisfies relation both make a tremendous difference between what a specifier can easily and concisely express in one method versus another. An idiom in one language might translate into a long list of unstructured statements in another or might not even have a counterpart.

But, in a more practical sense, formal methods do not differ radically from one another. Within some well-defined mathematical framework, they let system developers couch their ideas precisely. The more rigor applied in system development, the more likely developers are to state requirements correctly and to get the design right and, of course, the more precisely they can argue the correctness of the implementation.

In conclusion, existing formal methods can be used to

- identify many, though not all, deficiencies in a set of informally stated requirements, to discover discrepancies between a specification and an implementation, and find errors in existing programs and systems;
- specify medium-sized and non-trivial problems, especially the functional behavior of sequential programs, abstract data types, and hardware; and
- provide a deeper understanding of the behavior of large, complex systems.

Many challenges remain. In an effort to push against some of the current pragmatic bounds (in contrast to the two theoretical bounds covered in the previous section), the formal methods community is actively pursuing the following goals:

- specifying non-functional behavior such as reliability, safety, real-time, performance, and human factors;
- combining different methods, such as a domain-specific one with a more general one, or an informal one with a formal one;
- building more usable and more robust tools, in particular tools to manage large specifications and tools to perform more complicated semantic analysis of specifications more efficiently, perhaps by exploiting parallel architectures and parallel algorithms;
- building specification libraries so that systems and their components can be reused based on information captured in their specification (general libraries, like the Larch Handbook [3] and the Z mathematical toolkit [12], and domain-specific ones like that for oscilloscopes are recent examples);

- integrating formal methods with the entire system development effort, for example, to provide a formal way to record design rationale in the system development process;
- demonstrating that existing techniques scale up to handle real-world problems and to scale up the techniques themselves; and
- educating and training more people in the use of formal methods.

Acknowledgements. I thank several people, including John Guttag and Jim Horning, who introduced me to formal specifications. They have been instrumental in shaping my opinions about the role formal methods can and should play in system development. I am grateful to Susan Gerhart for affording me this opportunity to express my thoughts about formal methods. I especially credit Jim Horning for suggesting this article's title, a subject of much controversy, and Joseph Goguen who has suggested that formal methods can be given a formal characterization in terms of institutions where semantic abstraction functions are institution morphisms. I also thank all those who attended Formal Methods '89 in Halifax, Nova Scotia, Canada, for helpful feedback and discussion. Finally, I thank Mark Ardis, Dan Craigen, Susan Gerhart, Joseph Goguen, Bob Harper, Jim Horning, Leslie Lamport, and David Parnas for their critical comments on an earlier draft of this article.

References

1. J.V. Guttag, J.J. Horning, and J.M. Wing. Some remarks on putting formal specifications to productive use. *Science of Computer Programming*, North-Holland, 2(1), October 1982.
2. J.V. Guttag, J.J. Horning, and J.M. Wing. The Larch family of specification languages. *IEEE Software*, 2(5):24–36, September 1985.
3. J.V. Guttag, J.J. Horning, and J.M. Wing. Larch in five easy pieces. Technical Report 5, DEC Systems Research Center, July 1985.
4. C.A.R. Hoare. *Communicating Sequential Processes*. Prentice-Hall International, 1985.
5. C.B. Jones. *Software Development: A Rigorous Approach*. Prentice-Hall International, 1980.
6. C.B. Jones. *Systematic Software Development Using VDM*. Prentice-Hall International, 1986.
7. R. Koymans, J Vytopil, and W.P. de Roever. Real time programming and asynchronous message passing. In *Proceedings of the 2nd ACM Symposium on Principles of Distributed Programming*, pages 187–197, 1983.
8. L. Lamport. Specifying concurrent program modules. *ACM Trans. Programming Languages and Systems (TOPLAS)*, 5(2):190–222, April 1983.
9. L. Lamport. A simple approach to specifying concurrent systems. *CACM*, 32(1):32–45, January 1989.
10. B. Meyer. On formalism in specifications. *IEEE Software*, pages 6–26, January 1985.
11. A. Pnueli. Applications of temporal logic to the specification and verification of reactive systems: A survey of current trends. In W.-P. de Roever and G. Rozenberg, editors, *Current Trends in Concurrency: Overviews and Tutorials*, pages 510–584. Springer-Verlag, 1986. *Lecture Notes in Computer Science* 224.
12. J.M. Spivey. *Introducing Z: a Specification Language and its Formal Semantics*. Cambridge University Press, 1988.

Further Reading

Specifying sequential programs and data abstractions. Two key ideas to good program design are modularity and abstraction. In addition to VDM, Z, and Larch, the methods presented in five of the papers below (Futatsugi et al.; Lukham and von Henke; Nakajima et al.; Robinson and Roubine; and Wing) focus on specifying modules (for example, functions, procedures, and packages, of sequential programs). Besides procedural abstraction, data abstraction can greatly enhance a program's design. The use of data abstraction for structuring programs motivated much work in the late 70s and early 80s on algebraic specification techniques, the focus of the remaining papers in this section.

- R.M. Burstall and J.A. Goguen. The semantics of Clear, a specification language. In *Proceedings of the 1979 Copenhagen Winter School on Abstract Software Specification*, pages 292–332. Springer-Verlag, 1980. *Lecture Notes in Computer Science* 86.
- H.-D. Ehrich. Extensions and implementations of abstract data type specifications. In *Mathematical Foundations of Computer Science 1978 Proceedings*, pages 155–164. Springer-Verlag, Poland, 1978. *Lecture Notes in Computer Science* 64.
- H. Ehrig and B. Mahr. *Fundamentals of Algebraic Specification 1*. Springer-Verlag, Berlin, 1985.
- K. Futatsugi, J.A. Goguen, J.-P. Jouannaud, and J. Meseguer. Principles of OBJ2. In *Proceedings of ACM Principles of Programming Languages (POPL)*, pages 52–66, 1985.
- J.A. Goguen, J.W. Thatcher, E.G. Wagner, and J.B. Wright. Abstract data types as initial algebras and correctness of data representations. In *Proceedings of the Conference of Computer Graphics, Pattern Recognition and Data Structures*, pages 89–93. ACM, May 1975.
- J.V. Guttag. *The Specification and Application to Programming of Abstract Data Types*. PhD thesis, University of Toronto, Toronto, Canada, September 1975.
- S. Kamin. Final data types and their specification. *ACM Trans. Programming Languages and Systems (TOPLAS)*, 5(1):97–121, January 1983.
- D.C. Luckham and F.W. von Henke. An overview of Anna, a specification language for Ada. *IEEE Software*, 2(2):9–23, March 1985.
- R. Nakajima, M. Honda, and H. Nakahara. Hierarchical program specification and verification – a many-sorted logical approach. *Acta Informatica*, 14:135–155, 1980.
- L. Robinson and O. Roubine. Special – a specification and assertion language. Technical Report CSL-46, Stanford Research Institute, Menlo Park, CA, January 1977.
- M. Wand. Final algebra semantics and data type extensions. *Journal of Computer and System Sciences*, 19(1):27–44, August 1979.
- J.M. Wing. Writing Larch interface language specifications. *ACM Trans. Programming Languages and Systems (TOPLAS)*, pages 1–24, January 1987.

- S.N. Zilles. Abstract specifications for data types. IBM Research Laboratory, San Jose, CA, 1975.

Program refinement, transformation, and verification. Two complementary techniques for developing provably correct programs are refinement and verification. Refinement is a process of adding more and more implementation details (for example, choosing a particular algorithm or data representation) until an acceptably efficient implementation is achieved. Often these refinement steps are a result of applying transformations that are guaranteed to preserve the program's correctness from one level to the next. Verification is the process of proving that a given program satisfies a given specification.

- R. Balzer. Transformational implementation: An example. *IEEE Trans. Software Eng.*, 7(1):3–14, January 1981.
- F.L. Bauer et al. *The Munich Project CIP, Volume 1: The Wide Spectrum Language CIP-L, Lecture Notes in Computer Science* 183. Springer-Verlag, 1985.
- R.M. Burstall and J. Darlington. A transformation system for developing recursive programs. *Journal of the ACM*, 24(1):44–67, January 1977.
- R. Constable et al. *Implementing Mathematics with the NuPRL Proof Development Environment*. Prentice-Hall, 1986.
- E.W. Dijkstra. *A Discipline of Programming*. Prentice-Hall, 1976.
- A. T. Goldberg. Knowledge-based programming: A survey of program design and construction techniques. *IEEE Trans. Software Eng.*, 12(7):752–768, 1986.
- C.A.R. Hoare. *Notes on Data Structuring*, pages 83–174. Academic Press, 1972.
- C.A.R. Hoare. Proof of correctness of data representations. *Acta Informatica*, 1(1):271–281, 1972.
- P. Lee, F. Pfenning, G. Rollins, and W. Scherlis. The Ergo Support System: An integrated set of tools for prototyping integrated environments. In *Proceedings of the Third ACM SIGSOFT Symposium on Software Development Environments*, Boston, MA, pages 25–34, November 1988.
- Z. Manna and R. Waldinger. A deductive approach to program synthesis. *ACM Trans. Programming Languages and Systems (TOPLAS)*, 2(1):90–121, January 1980.
- P. Martin-Löf. Constructive mathematics and computer programming. In *Sixth International Congress for Logic, Methodology, and Philosophy of Science*, pages 153–175. North-Holland, Amsterdam, 1973.
- D. Sannella and A. Tarlecki. Program specification and development in Standard ML. In *Proceedings of the Symposium on Principles of Programming Languages*, pages 67–77, 1985.
- W.L. Scherlis and D. Scott. First steps toward inferential programming. In *Proceedings of IFIPS '83*, Paris, pages 199–212, 1983.

Models and logics for specifying concurrent and distributed systems. Unlike the situation for sequential programs and data abstractions for which there is some consensus on underlying formal models, little consensus exists today on general models of concurrent and distributed systems or logics for reasoning about their properties. The references below present a wide range of approaches to supplement the CSP, temporal logic, and Lamport's state transition approaches used in this article. Not surprisingly, the particular choice of model or logic can greatly affect the ease in expressing and/or proving some property of a given system.

- K.R. Apt, N. Francez, and W.P. de Roever. A proof system for Communicating Sequential Processes. *ACM Trans. Programming Languages and Systems (TOPLAS)*, 2(3):359–385, July 1980.
- M. Broy. A fixed point to applicative multiprogramming. In M. Broy and G. Schmidt, editors, *Theoretical Foundations of Programming Methodology*, pages 565–623. Reidel Publishing Company, 1982.
- K.M. Chandy and J. Misra. *Parallel Program Design*. Addison-Wesley, 1988.
- M. Feather. Language support for the specification and development of composite systems. *ACM Trans. on Prog. Lang.*, 9(2):198–234, April 1987.
- D. Harel. On visual formalisms. *CACM*, 31(5):514–530, 1988.
- Information systems processing – open systems interconnection – LOTOS. Technical Report, International Standards Organization, 1987.
- N. Lynch and M. Tuttle. Hierarchical correctness proofs for distributed algorithms. Technical Report, MIT Laboratory for Computer Science, Cambridge, MA, April 1987.
- Z. Manna and A. Pnueli. Verification of concurrent programs, part 1: The temporal framework. Technical Report STAN-CS-81-836, Dept. of Computer Science, Stanford University, CA, June 1981.
- A.J.R.G. Milner. *A Calculus of Communicating Systems, Lecture Notes in Computer Science 92*. Springer-Verlag, 1980.
- M. Nielsen, K. Havelund, K.R. Wagner, and C. George. The RAISE language, method, and tools. *Formal Aspects of Computing*, 1:85–114, 1989.
- S. Owicki and D. Gries. Verifying properties of parallel programs: An axiomatic approach. *CACM*, 19(5):279–285, May 1976.
- S. Owicki and L. Lamport. Proving liveness properties of concurrent programs. *ACM Trans. Programming Languages and Systems (TOPLAS)*, 4(3):455–495, July 1982.
- J.L. Peterson. Petri nets. *Computing Surveys*, 9(3), September 1977.
- V. Pratt. Modeling concurrency with partial orders. *International Journal of Parallel Programming*, 15(1):33–71, February 1986.
- P. Zave. An operational approach to requirements specification for embedded systems. *IEEE Trans. Software Eng.*, 8(3):250–269, May 1972.

Specification, verification, and testing tools. Many formal methods provide semantic analysis tools because the underlying semantics of their languages is sufficiently restricted so that reasoning in terms of specifications becomes tractable. As specifications grow in length and complexity, such tools become invaluable to the specifier. Many of the theorem-proving or proof-checking tools described in the papers below deal with some subset or small extension of first-order logic. The model checking, simulation, and testing tools typically deal with a finite or bounded state space, and hence can also be used as effective semantic analyzers.

- J.-R. Abrial. B user manual. Technical Report, Programming Research Group, Oxford University, 1988.
- R. S. Boyer and J S. Moore. *A Computational Logic.* Academic Press, New York, 1979. ACM monograph series.
- E.M. Clarke, E.A. Emerson, and A.P. Sistla. Automatic verification of finite-state concurrent systems using temporal logic specifications. *ACM Trans. Programming Languages and Systems (TOPLAS)*, 8(2):244–263, 1986.
- D. Craigen, S. Kromodimoeljo, I. Meisels, A. Neilson, B. Pase, and M. Saaltink. m-EVES: A tool for verifying software. In *Proceedings of the 10th IEEE International Conference on Software Engineering*, Singapore, April 1988. IEEE CS Press, Los Alamitos, CA, pages 324–333.
- S.J. Garland and J.V. Guttag. An overview of LP, the Larch Prover. In *Proceedings of the 3rd International Conference on Rewriting Techniques and Applications*, Chapel-Hill, NC, pages 137–151, 1989.
- J.A. Goguen. OBJ as a theorem prover with applications to hardware verification. Technical Report SRI-CSL-88-4R2, Stanford Research Institute, Menlo Park, CA, August 1988.
- D.I. Good, R.L. London, and W.W. Bledsoe. An interactive program verification system. *IEEE Trans. Software Eng.*, 1(1):59–67, 1979.
- M. Gordon. HOL: A proof-generating system for higher-order logic. In *VLSI Specification, Verification and Synthesis*. Kluwer, 1987.
- M. J. Gordon, A. J. Milner, and C. P. Wadsworth. *Edinburgh LCF, Lecture Notes in Computer Science 78.* Springer-Verlag, 1979.
- D. Harel, H. Lachover, A. Naamad, A. Pnueli, M. Politi, R. Sherman, and A. Shtul-Trauring. Statemate: A working environment for the development of complex reactive systems. In *Proceedings of the 10th IEEE International Conference on Software Engineering*, Singapore, April 1988. IEEE CS Press, Los Alamitos, CA.
- D. Kapur and D. Musser. Proof by consistency. *Artificial Intelligence*, 31:125–157, 1987.
- R.A. Kemmerer and S.T. Eckmann. A user's manual for the unisex system. Technical Report, Dept. of Computer Science, Univ. Calif., Santa Barbara, CA, December 1983.
- P. Lescanne. Computer experiments with the REVE term rewriting system generator. In *Proceedings of the 10th Symposium on Principles of Programming Languages*, pages 99–108, Austin, Texas, January 1983.
- K.N. Levitt, L. Robinson, and B.A. Silverberg. The HDM handbook. Technical Report Volumes 1–3, SRI International, Menlo Park, CA, 1979.
- R. Locasso, J. Scheid, D.V. Schorre, and P.R. Eggert. The Ina Jo reference manual. Technical Report TM-(L)-6021/001/000, System Development Corporation, Santa Monica, CA, 1980.
- P.R. McMullin and J.D. Gannon. Combining testing with formal specifications: A case study. *IEEE Trans. on Software Eng.*, 9(3), May 1983.

- D.S. Rosenblum and D.C. Luckham. Testing the correctness of tasking supervisors with TSL specifications. In *Proceedings of the ACM SIGSOFT '89 3rd Symposium on Software Testing, Analysis, and Verification (TAV-3)*, pages 187–196, Key West, FL, 1989.

Examples. All the work referenced below is cited at the end of the *"Uses"* section[4]. Many draw upon the hardware domain. See Clarke and Grumberg's paper for a survey of even more hardware examples.

- W.R. Bevier. A verified operating system kernel. Technical Report 11, Computational Logic, Inc., March 1987.
- M.C. Browne, E.M. Clarke, and D. Dill. Checking the correctness of sequential circuits. In *Proceedings of the IEEE International Conference on Computer Design*, pages 545–548, 1985.
- M. Burrows, M. Abadi, and R. Needham. A logic of authentication. In *Proceedings of the Symposium on Operating Systems*, 1989.
- E.M. Clarke and O. Grumberg. Research on automatic verification of finite-state concurrent systems. *Ann. Rev. Comput. Sci.*, 2:269–290, 1987.
- B.P. Collins, J.E. Nicholls, and I.H. Sorensen. Introducing formal methods: the CICS experience with Z. Technical Report TR 12.260, IBM, United Kingdom Laboratories, Hursley, 1987.
- W.J. Cullyer. Implementing safety-critical systems: The Viper microprocessor. In *VLSI Specification, Verification and Synthesis*. Kluwer, 1987.
- N. Delisle and D. Garlan. Formally specifying electronic instruments. In *Proceedings of the Fifth International Workshop on Software Specification and Design*, pages 242–248, Pittsburgh, 1989.
- S.J. Garland, J.V. Guttag, and J. Staunstrup. Verification of VLSI circuits using LP. In *Proceedings of the IFIP WG 10.2, The Fusion of Hardware Design and Verification*. North-Holland, 1988.
- A. Heydon, M. Maimone, J.D. Tygar, J.M. Wing, and A. Moormann Zaremski. Constraining pictures with pictures. In *Proceedings of IFIPS '89*, San Francisco, August 1989.
- W.A. Hunt. The mechanical verification of a microprocessor design. Technical Report 6, Computational Logic, Inc., 1987.
- A.P. Moore. Investigating formal specification and verification techniques for COMSEC software security. In *Proceedings of the 1988 National Computer Security Conference*, October 1988.
- P. Narendran and J. Stillman. Formal verification of the sobel image processing chip. In G. Birtwistle and P.A. Subrahmanyam, editors, *Current Trends in Hardware Verification and Automated Theorem Proving*, pages 92–127. Springer-Verlag, 1989.
- J.C.P. Woodcock. Transaction processing primitives and CSP. *IBM Journal of Research and Development*, 31(5):535–45, 1987.

---

[4] Pages 175–177.

Informal and semi-formal methods. Less formal methods can play an important role in software development too. Some of the papers below present traditional design methods that are gaining popularity in industry today. Some describe ways to deal with system complexity through hierarchical structuring techniques. Some borrow ideas from the area of artificial intelligence. In addition, I include below a reference to Leveson's work on hazard analysis.

- M. Alford. SREM at the age of eight: The distributed computing design system. *Computer*, 18(4):36–46, April 1985.
- F. DeRemer and H.H. Kron. Programming-in-the-large versus programming-in-the-small. *IEEE Trans. on Software Eng.*, June 1976.
- S. Fickas. Automating the analysis process: An example. In *Proceedings of the Fourth International Workshop on Software Specification and Design*, pages 79–86, April 1987.
- M.A. Jackson. *Principles of Program Design*. Academic Press, London, 1975.
- H. Katzan. *Systems Design and Documentation: An Introduction to the HIPO Method*. Van Nostrand Reinhold, New York, 1976.
- N.G. Leveson. Software safety: What, why, and how. *ACM Computing Surveys*, 18(2):125–163, June 1986.
- D.L. Parnas. A technique for software module specification with examples. *CACM*, 15(5):330–336, May 1972.
- C. Rich, R.C. Waters, and H.B. Reubenstein. Toward a requirements apprentice. In *Proceedings of the Fourth International Workshop on Software Specification and Design*, pages 79–86, April 1987.
- W. Swartout. The Gist behavior explainer. In *Proceedings of the American Association Artificial Intelligence Conference*, pages 402–407, August 1983.
- E. Yourdon and L.L. Constantine. *Structured Design: Fundamentals of a Discipline of Computer Programs and Systems Design*. Yourdon Press, New York, 1978.

An Overview of Some Formal Methods for Program Design

C.A.R. Hoare

Summary.

The design of a small program, like that of a large system, requires a variety of formal methods and notations, related by mathematical reasoning.

The code of a computer program is a formal text, describing precisely the actions of a computer executing that program. As in other branches of engineering, the progress of its implementation as well as its eventual quality can be promoted by additional design documents, formalized before starting to write the final code. These preliminary documents may be expressed in a variety of notations suitable for different purposes at different stages of a project, from capture of requirements through design and implementation, to delivery and long-term maintenance. These notations are derived from mathematics, and include algebra, logic, functions, and procedures. The connection between the notations is provided by mathematical calculation and proof.

This article introduces and illustrates a selection of formal methods by means of a single recurring example, the design of a program to compute the greatest common divisor of two positive numbers. It is hoped that some of the conclusions drawn from analysis of this simple example will apply with even greater force to software engineering projects on a more realistic scale.

Requirements

Imagine that a software engineer is called upon to construct a mechanism or subroutine to compute the greatest common divisor z of two positive integers x and y.

© 1987 IEEE. Reprinted by permission.
Reprinted from *IEEE Computer*, 20(9):85–91, September 1987.

By an even greater feat of imagination, assume no prior knowledge of the concept of greatest common divisor, or of how to compute it. So the first task is to ensure that the engineer and client have the same understanding of what is required. Let us suppose first that they agree to confine attention to positive whole numbers (excluding zero). The required relationship between the parameters (x, y) and the result (z) may be formalized as follows:

D1.1 z divides x

D1.2 z divides y

D1.3 z is the greatest of the set of numbers satisfying both these conditions

D1.4   "p divides q" means "there exists a positive whole number w such that $pw = q$"

D1.5   "p is the greatest member of a set S" means "p is in S, and no member of S is strictly greater than p"

It is essential that the notations used for formalization of requirements should be mathematically meaningful, but it would be unwise to place any other restriction upon them. Even in this simple example we have used logic, arithmetic, and set theory. An engineer should take advantage of this early notational freedom to ensure that the formalization of requirements is simple and well-structured so that, together with its informal explanation, it obviously describes what is really wanted, and not something else. There can never be any formal method of checking this vital correspondence, because there should not be any more obviously correct description to check it against. Clarity is our only defense against the embarrassment felt on completion of a large project when it is discovered that the wrong problem has been solved.

The most important mathematical notations needed in requirements specification are also the simplest – for example, the familiar Boolean connectives AND, OR, and NOT. The connective AND (known as *conjunction*) is needed to put together the separate requirements imposed upon a product. In the example above, we want the answer z to be a divisor of x and we want it to be a divisor of y. Sometimes we need universal quantification ("for all x"), which is a generalization of AND. The connective OR (known as *disjunction*) is needed to achieve simplicity and symmetry by maintaining a high level of abstraction. Sometimes we need *existential quantification* ("there exists"), which is a generalization of OR. For example, in clause D1.4 above, we want there to exist a w exactly dividing x, but we don't care if there is more than one, and if so we don't care which one is chosen. And we certainly don't want to describe in gory detail how a computer is to find one. Finally, it is often easier and clearer to say what we want the product not to do. For example, there must be no divisor of x and y greater than z. In the formulation of requirements, we certainly need the simple Boolean connectives AND and OR, and especially NOT.

By using such a powerful specification language, we run the risk of writing a falsehood, inconsistency, or other absurdity which could never be implemented. This risk can be eliminated by an early consistency check. In our example, what we need to check is that for every pair of positive numbers x and y there exists a number z with the properties specified in D1.3. A proof of this has three steps:

P1.1   The number one is a divisor of every number. So it is a common divisor of every pair of numbers. This shows that the set of common divisors of two numbers is non-empty.

P1.2   Each number is its own greatest divisor, so every set of divisors is finite. The common subset of any two finite sets is also finite. So the set of common divisors of two numbers is both finite and non-empty.

P1.3   Every finite non-empty set of integers has a greatest member. So the maximum used to define the greatest common divisor always exists.

At the end of requirements analysis, we aim to have a mathematically precise, complete, consistent, and above all obviously appropriate mathematical description of the result we want. It would be very nice to input this description into some suitably programmed computer, and get the computer to translate it automatically into a subroutine. On each call of the subroutine, it would return the greatest common divisor of any pair of numbers supplied as arguments. If we are willing to overlook the problem of efficiency, there is an easy way of doing this, known as the British Museum algorithm. A computer can be programmed to start with some standard set of axioms of mathematics, and to use them to generate at random all provable mathematical theorems. It will therefore eventually generate such startling theorems as

One is the greatest of all numbers which divide both two and three.

So if we want to know the greatest common divisor of two and three, all we need to do is to program another computer to recognize when the British Museum computer has produced a result of this form. Then we just wait for it to do so. We may have to wait a very long time – under reasonable assumptions, all the particles in the universe will decay to photons before our fastest computers can carry out even the most trivial calculations. And if the theorem-generator attempts a strategy much better than random generation, it is difficult to avoid the risk that some true theorem will never be generated. In mathematics, the question of efficiency is rightly considered irrelevant, but in using computers to do mathematics, efficiency cannot forever be ignored – or else it will really be forever. Efficiency is therefore the main driving force in the development of an acceptable program to meet its mathematical specification, as shown in the following sections.

Logic Program

A solution to the unavoidable problem of efficiency is to recast the specification of requirements into some notational framework less powerful and less general than the whole of mathematics. This restricted notation is so designed that its use will be rewarded by more efficient execution on a computer. One of the concepts of mathematics that is most difficult to implement effectively is negation of specification. For example, if you want a program that does not trigger a holocaust, you cannot hope to write a program that does trigger a holocaust and just negate it before submitting it to the computer. For this reason, even the highest level logic programming languages prohibit or severely restrict the use of negation, requiring the programmer to implement it whenever needed.

Here is an idealized logic program to compute the greatest common divisor of two positive integers. To help in checking its correctness, it has been designed to preserve as far as possible the structure and clarity of the original requirements. We assume that "isproduct" and "differsfrom" are available as built-in predicates on positive integers.

L2.1 isdivisor(x, z) if there exists a w not greater than x such that isproduct(z, w, x)

L2.2 iscommondiv(x, y, z) is isdivisor(x, z) and isdivisor(y, z)

L2.3 isgcd(x, y, z) if iscommondiv(x, y, z) and for all w from z to x isnotcommondiv(x, y, z)

L2.4 isnotcommondiv(x, y, z) if isnotdiv(x, z) or isnotdiv(y, z)

L2.5 isnotdiv(x, z) if for all w from 1 to x isnotproduct(z, w, x)

L2.6 isnotproduct(z, w, x) if isproduct(z, w, y) and differsfrom(y, x)

This program is a great deal more complicated than the requirements specification in the previous section. The obvious reason is that the absence of negation in the programming language requires explicit programming of a search through all possibilities before a negative answer is given. In order to ensure termination, a finite range for each search has to be specified, and setting this limit requires knowledge of the application domain. For example, in L2.3 we rely on the fact that the common divisor of two numbers cannot exceed either number.

Note that in the best known programming language, Prolog, it would be permitted to replace L2.3 to L2.6 by the single clause

L2.3′ isgcd(x, y, z) if iscommondiv(x, y, z) and not(iscommondiv(x, y, w) and isgreater(w, z))

This restores the brevity of the specification of requirements, but when submitted to a standard implementation of Prolog, this program may turn out to be slightly worse than the British Museum algorithm because it does not terminate at all. The trouble is that the "not" of Prolog does not mean the same as the NOT of mathematics, logic, or even normal technical discourse, and its meaning cannot be fully understood except in terms of the way that Prolog programs are executed. In fact, in Prolog the "and" and the "or" also have peculiar meanings, as a result of which they are not even symmetric. The motive for this was to achieve greater efficiency of execution, particularly on traditional sequential computers.

In spite of considerable ingenuity of implementation, logic programs are inherently inefficient, particularly if the specification takes proper advantage of the power of the available combination of conjunction and disjunction. The reason is that in principle all combinations of possibilities described by each disjunction have to be explored, in order to be sure of finding one that is consistent with the rest of the specification. Consider the conjunction of (A or B) with (C or D). This gives rise to four alternatives, (A and C) or (A and D) or (B and C) or (B and D), all of which may have to be tried. An existential quantifier multiplies the number of cases by a larger factor, and if recursion is involved, the number of cases to be explored increases exponentially. All but one of these cases will eventually be discarded.

Algebra

A possible way of improving efficiency is by restricting yet further the power of the language, for example by avoiding disjunction as well as negation. This is the major restriction imposed when formulating a specification in the algebraic style. In an algebraic specification, fresh names (such as "*gcd*") must be introduced for each function to be specified. The specification is formalized as a set of algebraic equations, each of which must be true of all values of the variables they contain. These equations are connected implicitly by AND. Only this form of conjunction is allowed – no negation and no disjunction. As a result, it is even more difficult or even impossible to write a program which preserves the clause structure or content of the original requirements. Instead, the algebraic equations have to be derived as needed by mathematical reasoning from the whole of the original specification. This is illustrated in the case of the greatest common divisor:

L3.1   The greatest divisor of x is x. So the greatest common divisor of x and x is also x:
$$x = gcd(x,x) \qquad \text{for all } x$$

L3.2   If z divides x and y, it also divides $x+y$. So every common divisor of x and y is also a common divisor of $x+y$ and y. Similarly, every common divisor of $x+y$ and y is also a common divisor of x and y. So the greatest of these identical sets of common divisors are the same:
$$gcd(x,y) = gcd(x+y,y) \qquad \text{for all } x, y$$

L3.3   Every common divisor of x and y is also a common divisor of y and x:
$$gcd(x,y) = gcd(y,x) \qquad \text{for all } x, y$$

The three laws given above can serve as an algebraic specification of the *gcd* function. The *consistency* of the specification has been guaranteed by proof, which shows that the laws follow from a set of requirements already known to be consistent. But the question remains, are the laws a *complete* specification, in the sense that there is only one function satisfying them? Or do we need to look for more laws? A proof of completeness has to show that for any given positive numerals p and q there is a numeral r such that the equation

$$r = gcd(p,q)$$

can be proved solely from the algebraic specification and the previously known laws of arithmetic.

This can be shown by mathematical induction: We assume the result for all p and q strictly less than N, and prove it for all p and q less than or equal to N. For such numbers, four cases can be distinguished:

(1) Both p and q are strictly less than N. In this case, what we have to prove is the same as the induction hypothesis, which may be assumed without proof.

(2) Both p and q are equal to N. Then the result

$$N = gcd(p,q)$$

is proved immediately by law L3.1.

(3) $p = N$ and $q < N$. It follows that $p - q$ is positive and less than N. By the induction hypothesis, there is an r such that

$$r = gcd(p-q, q)$$

is deducible from the algebraic laws. One application of L3.2 then gives

$$r = gcd(p-q)+q, q)$$

which by the laws of arithmetic leads to the required conclusion:

$$r = gcd(p,q)$$

(4) $p < N$ and $q = N$. Then there is an r such that

$$r = gcd(q, p)$$

is provable in the same way as in case (3) described above. One application of L3.3 then gives

$$r = gcd(p,q)$$

That concludes the proof that the algebraic specification is complete.

Clearly there is no structural correspondence between the three clauses of the algebraic specification and the five clauses expressing the original requirement. As a result, some mathematical ingenuity and labour has been needed to prove that the two orthogonal specifications describe (and completely describe) the same function. This labor could be avoided by simply leaving out the original formalization of requirements in the general notations of mathematics, and by starting instead within the more restricted equational framework of algebra.

But this would be a mistake. In the example we have been considering, the mistake can be explained as follows. The purpose of the specification is to tell the user of a subroutine the properties of the result it produces, and to do so in a manner conducive to the wider objectives of the program as a whole. Clearly, the user of a subroutine to compute the greatest common divisor will be very directly interested in the fact that the result of every subroutine call divides each of its two arguments exactly. But the algebraic law tells us only that the same result would have been obtained if the two arguments had been permuted (L3.3) or added together (L3.2) before the call. These facts by themselves seem a lot less directly useful.

It would also be a mistake to regard the different specifications, the abstract one and the algebraic one, as rivals or even as alternatives. They are both needed; they are essentially complementary, and they can be used for different purposes at different stages in the progress of a software project. Algebraic laws are relevant in the design of an efficient algorithm; they are useful even at an earlier stage, because they help to decide how a program should deal with extreme or exceptional cases. For example, if one of the arguments of the *gcd* subroutine is zero or negative, the result should obey the same laws as the greatest common divisor of positive numbers, as far as mathematically possible.

For specifications of the highest quality and importance I would recommend complete formalization of requirements in two entirely different styles, together with a proof that they are consistent or even equivalent to each other. For example, a programming language can be defined axiomatically, by giving methods of proving correctness of programs expressed in the language. A language can also be defined algebraically, by giving algebraic laws from which equivalence of programs can be proved. A language for which two consistent and complementary definitions are provided may be confidently taken as a secure basis for software engineering.

Like the original software requirements specification, a set of algebraic laws can be input to the British Museum computer, which will add these laws to the previously known axioms of mathematics and then start deriving theorems from them. Provided that the laws are complete (as we have proved our laws for *gcd* to be), the computer will eventually discover any fact that we want, for example, that the greatest common divisor of three and two is one. Furthermore, the amount of time we have to wait for this earth-shattering result will be millions of times less than the original British Museum algorithm applied to the original requirements. But we would still have to wait too long – on reasonable assumptions, the whole universe will reach a uniform temperature around four degrees Kelvin long before any interesting calculation is complete.

Functional Program

Again an enormous increase in efficiency is required. And again, it can be obtained by restricting yet further the set of notations in which the mathematical equations are expressed. These restrictions are designed to prevent the pursuit of deductions irrelevant to the required result. That is achieved by use of an applicative or functional programming language.

Here is the functional program to compute the greatest common divisor of positive integers:

F4.1	$gcd(x,y) = x$	if $x = y$
F4.2	$gcd(x,y) = gcd(x-y,y)$	if $x > y$
F4.3	$gcd(x,y) = gcd(y,x)$	if $x < y$

In structure and content, this is very similar to the algebraic laws, but it conforms to the restriction imposed by a functional programming language. A typical restriction is that the left-hand side of each equation must consist of a single application of the operator being defined (gcd) to distinct simple parameters (x and y). There is no such restriction on the right-hand side, which may even contain occurrences of the operator being defined. In the evaluation of an expression, a computer treats each equation of the program as a substitution rule. At each application of the rule, a call of the function is replaced by a copy of the right-hand side of the definition, with appropriate substitution of arguments for parameters.

For example, here is a sequence of substitutions which calculates the greatest common divisor of 10 and 6:

$$
\begin{aligned}
gcd(10,6) &= gcd(4,6) && \text{by F4.2} \\
&= gcd(6,4) && \text{by F4.3} \\
&= gcd(2,4) && \text{by F4.2} \\
&= gcd(4,2) && \text{by F4.3} \\
&= gcd(2,2) && \text{by F4.2} \\
&= 2 && \text{by F4.1}
\end{aligned}
$$

This trace of execution of a functional program is nothing but a proof of the fact that $gcd(10,6) = 2$. It is the same proof as would eventually be discovered by the British Museum algorithm. But the British Museum algorithm starts from the axioms and generates vast numbers of hopelessly irrelevant truths. The implementation of a functional programming language starts from the left-hand side of the theorem to be proved, and every intermediate step should lead directly towards the goal. However, the responsibility for controlling this goal-directed behavior is placed upon the programmer, who has to prove that there is no infinite chain of substitutions. For example, as an algebraic formula,

$$gcd(x,y) = gcd(y,x)$$

is quite correct, but if this is executed as part of a functional program, it leads to an infinite chain of substitutions. In the program shown above, this cycle is broken by ensuring that the dangerous substitution is made only when y is strictly greater than x.

Proof of termination of a functional program is very similar to proof of completeness of algebraic equations. It requires knowledge of the domain of application, and it may also require knowledge of the strategy used by the language implementor for selecting between substitutions when more than one is possible. A simple strategy (of lazy evaluation), which is also the one that most often succeeds, is not generally the most efficient one.

Let us now consider how long the program will take to terminate. In the calculation of $gcd(N,1)$, the number 1 will be subtracted from N until it reaches 1, and this will be done $N-1$ times. On a typical 32-bit microprocessor, N is limited to about 10^{10}, so the calculation will take a few hours, which might be acceptable for a program or prototype intended to be used only once. On our largest and fastest supercomputers, numbers range up to about 10^{20}, and we might have to wait around a million years or so for an answer. It seems we are still left with a problem of efficiency, and we need to look for an improvement of at least twenty orders of magnitude.

Optimization

Use of a more restricted and more efficient programming language might gain us one or two orders of magnitude in efficiency which is hardly worthwhile. What we need is a method of calculation inherently faster than the one we have first stumbled upon; for example, one requiring a number of steps proportional only to the logarithm of the arguments to which it is applied. For this, we need to go back to the earlier stage of analyzing the algebra, and take advantage of our knowledge of the nature of the mechanism used to execute the algorithm. On modern computers, division and multiplication by two are extremely fast, and it is equally fast to test whether a number is odd or even. We are therefore led to derive algebraic laws involving these operations.

Three new laws will be sufficient:

L5.1 If z divides x, then $2z$ divides $2x$. So if z is the greatest common divisor of x and y, then $2z$ is a common divisor of $2x$ and $2y$. It is therefore not greater than their greatest common divisor:

$$2gcd(x,y) \leq gcd(2x,2y)$$

Conversely, if z is the greatest common divisor of $2x$ and $2y$, then z is even and $z/2$ is a common divisor of x and y:

$$gcd(2x,2y)/2 \leq gcd(x,y)$$

From these two inequations it follows that

$$2gcd(x,y) = gcd(2x,2y)$$

L5.2   All divisors of an odd number are odd, and if an odd number divides $2x$ it also divides x. If y is odd, the greatest common divisor of $2x$ and y is odd, so it is also a common divisor of x and y:

$$gcd(2x,y) \leq gcd(x,y) \qquad \text{if } y \text{ is odd}$$

Conversely, every divisor of x divides $2x$:

$$gcd(x,y) \leq gcd(2x,y)$$

From these two inequations it follows that

$$gcd(2x,y) = gcd(x,y) \qquad \text{if } y \text{ is odd}$$

L5.3   If both x and y are odd, and x is greater than y, it follows that $x - y$ is positive and even. So under these conditions,

$$gcd(x,y) = gcd((x-y)/2,y)$$

Similarly, if x and y are odd and y is larger,

$$gcd(x,y) = gcd((y-x)/2,x)$$

When these equations are coded as a functional program, it becomes clear that the number of operations required when the argument is of size 2^N has been reduced to about N. The question arises whether this is the very best that can be done, or whether it might be worth trying to find a better algorithm. This is the kind of question studied by complexity theory. But experts in complexity theory tell me that they do not know whether a better algorithm for *gcd* exists, so we shall have to do the best we can with this one.

Procedural Program

Pursuit of the very highest efficiency yet again requires adoption of a restricted notation in which conjunction is disallowed. Such a restriction is imposed by a procedural programming language like Fortran or Pascal. The component parts (P and Q) of a procedural program are joined not by any propositional connective, but rather by sequential composition, usually denoted by a semicolon:

$P; Q$

which instructs a computer to execute P first, and to continue with Q only when P terminates.

Sequential composition is the secret of the efficiency of procedural programs. All of the computing resources, storage, and communication capacity which have been used by the earlier component P become available immediately, without overhead of reclamation and reallocation, for reuse by the later component Q. However, the responsibility for planning the use and reuse of resources is placed on the programmer, and much opportunity is offered for subtle errors. Perhaps the main attraction of functional and logic programming is that the claiming of new resources and the reclaiming of unused resources are automatics, once the overhead of garbage collection is accepted.

The replacement of conjunction by composition means that the sequential structure of a program will in general be radically different from the conjunctive structure of a specification, and the necessary correspondence between them must be established by mathematical calculation or proof. Fortunately, these calculations can be carried out stepwise during the early stages of the design of a program, and each design decision can be proved correct before embarking on the next. Each design step transforms the structure of the specification to correspond more closely to the structure of the eventual program. After this, work on the component parts of the structure can proceed concurrently and independently, because each of them has been fully specified, with the same precision as the whole of the original requirements. When the implementations of the parts are delivered, they can be assembled together with reasonable confidence that the system as a whole will work. This confidence is obtained not by laborious integration testing when the code is delivered, but rather by proof that was conducted before a word of code was written. Reliable assembly of prespecified parts is an essential mark of maturity in any engineering discipline.

A procedural program or subprogram can be specified by a pair of assertions, a precondition and a postcondition. A precondition describes properties of the program variables which may be assumed to hold when the program starts. For example, let the lowercase letters x and y stand for the values of the arguments supplied on entry to the *gcd* subroutine. The precondition states that these are positive:

P6.1 $x > 0 \wedge y > 0$

In fact, the program will not change the values of x and y, so this assertion remains true throughout execution.

A postcondition describes properties of the program variables that must be true when the program terminates. For example, let Z be the program variable introduced to hold the result of the subroutine. Then the postcondition is

P6.2 $Z = gcd(x, y)$

The first step in the design of a sequential program $(P; Q)$ is to formalize separate specifications of P and of Q and to prove that the combination of these separate specifications will meet the original specification of the whole program. This is easily achieved if

(1) the precondition of P is the same as the precondition of the whole program (or is implied by it);
(2) the postcondition of Q is the same as the postcondition of the whole program (or implies it); and

(3) the postcondition of P is the same as the precondition of Q (or implies it).

So the design of a sequential program involves only the discovery of an appropriate intermediate assertion which will be true when control passes the semicolon which separates the parts of the program. The intermediate assertion may contain new program variables local to the subroutine, which are introduced to assist in the calculation; we will denote these by capital letters, for example, X, Y, and N. In general, the discovery of a suitable intermediate assertion requires all the skill and judgement of the program designer. Though there are a number of useful heuristics, this is not the right place to explain them; so without further ado, here is an intermediate assertion for the example program to compute the greatest common divisor:

P6.3 $\quad 2^N gcd(X,Y) = gcd(x,y)$

Now the two parts of the program may be considered independently. The task of the first part is to make P6.3 true on termination. That is easily accomplished by just one multiple assignment:

$N, X, Y := 0, x, y$

If proof is needed, it may be obtained by substituting the final values for the assigned variables in the postcondition, and observing that

$(2^0) gcd(x,y) = gcd(x,y)$

The second task is harder, and will again be split into two parts by the intermediate assertion

P6.4 $\quad 2^N Z = gcd(x,y)$

The second of the new subtasks would already be accomplished if N were zero. If N is non-zero, it can be made closer to zero by subtracting one. But that would make P6.4 false, and therefore useless. Fortunately, the truth of P6.4 can easily be restored if every subtraction of one from N is accompanied by a doubling of Z. This can be checked if it is felt necessary by proving that

$n > 0 \wedge 2^N Z = gcd(x,y) \Rightarrow 2^{N-1}(2Z) = gcd(x,y)$

Since termination is obvious, we have proved the correctness of the loop

while $N > 0$ **do** $N, Z := N - 1, 2Z$

On termination of this loop, the value of N is zero, and P6.4 is still true. Consequently, the postcondition of the whole program has been established.

Having completed the first and last of the three tasks, the time has come to confess that the middle task is the most difficult. Its precondition is P6.3 and its postcondition is P6.4. I suggest that the task be split yet again into four subtasks, in accordance with the following series of intermediate assertions:

P6.3 ∧ (X odd ∨ Y odd)
P6.3 ∧ (Y odd)
P6.3 ∧ (Y odd) ∧ X = Y

The coding of these parts can be derived almost entirely from the algebraic laws, and is left as an exercise.

When this coding has been done, we will have a complete program expressed in some mathematically meaningful programming notation such as Pascal. In suitable circumstances, a reliable automatic translator will be available to translate the program into binary machine code of an available computer, and this will be fast enough for most general purposes. If still higher speed is required, it may be necessary to carry out yet another stage of formal design, optimization and verification. For example, the Pascal program may be converted into the even lower level language of a horizontal microcode, or other hardware description for custom-built VLSI. In this context, the cost of design errors is extremely high, and the competent hardware engineer will warmly welcome the extra confidence that can be gained by the formal manipulations and proofs conducted at earlier stages in the design.

In a software project, the process of formal design may also have a beneficial influence on delivery dates and on reliability of the finished product. This will be important in safety-critical applications. But as in other branches of engineering, the full benefit of documentation will be most clearly felt in the long years of maintenance following first delivery of a large program. Apart from easing the removal of any remaining errors, a well documented program can be more readily and confidently improved or altered to meet changing requirements. As in other branches of engineering, the documentation should be kept up-to-date. This is likely to become more and more difficult as the changes accumulate, and when it becomes impossible, this should be the signal that the time has come to rewrite or replace the whole program.

In selection of formal notations for the various phases of a software engineering project, the following criteria are relevant:

(1) For original capture of requirements, only clarity and precision are of importance.
(2) In intermediate documentation used by the implementor, we have the related objectives of clarity and correctness.
(3) In finally delivered code, we require correctness and also seek efficiency of execution.

The final code of the program must, of course, be expressed in a formal notation that can be automatically translated and executed by computer. But there is no need for any of the preceding documents to be executed, or even input to a computer.

Their main purpose is clarity and convenience for communication, calculation, and proof. A premature insistence on execution (on a less that cosmological timescale) may stand in the way of these more important objectives.

It is obviously sensible to use for final coding a language which is as close as possible to that of the original specification, so that the number of steps in the design process is kept small. But the programming language must not be so inefficient that clever and complicated coding tricks are needed to compensate. This seems to be a major problem with logic programming. My view is that a modern functional programming language can provide a nice compromise between the abstract logic of a requirements specification and the detailed resource management provided by procedural programming.

Such a high-level language may also be used for rapid implementation (partial or total) of the original requirements, and so provide a rapid check of the adequacy and completeness of the specification of requirements. A similar role is played by wooden models and perspective drawings in architecture or car design. But it is advisable to plan to throw away such models after use. The overriding need for rapid implementation gives scope for the talents of an experienced hacker rather than the formal precision of an engineer, and it is unlikely that the model can be taken as the basis or framework for subsequent development of the delivered product.

The example which I have used to illustrate these conclusions is one which has been used over and over again in textbooks on computing science. Because it is such a small and familiar example, it does not complicate the explanation of more general and more important ideas. For this reason, it has also revealed (all too clearly) the full weight of the notations and complexity of the mathematical proofs involved in formalization of the process of program design. The reader may well be discouraged from applying these methods to problems of a scale more typical of software engineering. And there are many other serious concerns which are not addressed directly by formalization, for example, cost estimation, project management, quality control, testing, maintenance, and enhancement of the program after delivery.

Nevertheless, I conjecture that such pessimism would be premature, and that a more formal understanding of the decisions involved in program design will provide a more secure framework within which solutions to the other problems can be fitted. The reason for my optimism is that formal methods find their most effective application in splitting large and complex projects into shorter phases, and in splitting large and complex products into small components, which may then be designed and implemented independently. This splitting may be repeated as often as necessary, until each subtask is no larger and no more complex than the simple example treated above.

And maybe this was not such a simple example after all. The reader who finds it too simple is invited to improve the program so that it accepts and deals sensibly with negative numbers and zero. There are two ways of doing this:

(1) The traditional method of program maintenance is to re-test the final program on the new range of arguments, change the program as little as possible, and describe the resulting program behavior in the user manual.

(2) The method which I recommend is to re-examine the specifications and proofs presented above, to see where they have relied on the assumption that the arguments are positive; these are the places where the design and the program must be altered. This method is in accordance with sound engineering principles, and is therefore more likely to deliver a product of high quality.

The main purpose of this article has been to show the all-pervasive role of mathematical reasoning throughout all stages of a product life-cycle, and to show the need for an appropriate range of mathematical notations to communicate design decisions with other people, with a computer, and even with oneself.

Acknowledgements. To Richard Karp for advice on computational complexity, and to all seven referees of this article.

Bibliography

This brief overview of formal methods for program design has necessarily omitted some important topics, for example, data refinement. No mention has been made of concurrent or distributed programming, for which some kind of formal development method is almost essential. No adequate instruction has been provided to enable the reader to put into practice the methods described. And finally, no acknowledgement has been made to the brilliant researchers who have contributed to progress in the field. I hope the reader may remedy some of these deficiencies by consulting some of the books listed in this personally selected bibliography.

1. **Requirements**
   Specification Case Studies, Ian Hayes, ed., Prentice-Hall International, U.K., 1987.

2. **Logic programming**
   R. Kowalski, *Logic for Problem Solving*, North Holland, Amsterdam, 1979.
   K. L. Clark and F. G. McCabe, *micro Prolog: Programming in Logic*, Prentice-Hall International, U.K., 1984.

3. **Algebra**
   J. J. Martin, *Data Types and Data Structures*, Prentice-Hall International, U.K., 1986.

4. **Functional programming**
   P. Henderson, *Functional Programming: Application and Implementation*, Prentice-Hall International, U.K., 1980.
   H. Abelson and G. J. Sussman, *Structure and Interpretation of Computer Programs*, MIT Press, Cambridge, Mass., 1985.

5. **Procedural programming**
   D. Gries, *The Science of Programming*, Springer-Verlag, New York, 1981.
   R. C. Backhouse, *Program Construction and Verification*, Prentice-Hall International, U.K., 1987.

6. **Data refinement**
   C. B. Jones, *Systematic Software Development Using VDM*, Prentice-Hall International, U.K., 1986.

7. **Parallel programming**
   C. A. R. Hoare, *Communicating Sequential Processes*, Prentice-Hall International, U.K., 1985.
   K. M. Chandy and J. Misra, *Parallel Program Design: a Foundation*, Addison-Wesley, Reading, Mass., 1988.

8. **Computational complexity**
   A. V. Aho, J. E. Hopcroft, and J. D. Ullman, *The Design and Analysis of Computer Algorithms*, Addison-Wesley, Reading, Mass., 1974.

9. **General**
   Programming Methodology, D. Gries, ed., Springer-Verlag, New York, 1978.

Ten Commandments
of Formal Methods

Jonathan P. Bowen and Michael G. Hinchey

Summary.

Formal methods permit more precise specifications and earlier error detection. Software developers who want to benefit from formal methods would be wise to heed these ten guidelines.

Why does this magnificent applied science which saves work and makes life easier bring us so little happiness? The simple answer runs: because we have not yet learned to make sensible use of it.
— Albert Einstein

Producing correct, reliable software in systems of ever increasing complexity is a problem with no immediate end in sight. The software industry suffers from a plague of bugs on a near-biblical scale. One promising technique in alleviating this problem is the application of formal methods that provide a rigorous mathematical basis to software development. When correctly applied, formal methods produce systems of the highest integrity and thus are especially recommended for security- and safety-critical systems [1–3]. Unfortunately, although projects based on formal methods are proliferating, the use of these methods is still more the exception than the rule [4], which results from many misconceptions regarding their costs, difficulties, and payoffs [5,6].

Surveys of formal methods applied to large problems [7–9] in industry help dispel these misconceptions and show that formal methods projects can be completed on schedule and within budget. Moreover, these surveys show that formal methods

---

© 1995 IEEE. Reprinted by permission.
Reprinted from *IEEE Computer*, 28(4):56–63, April 1995.

projects produce correct software (and hardware) that is well structured, maintainable, and satisfies customer requirements. Representative case studies explain this in detail [10].

The subjective question "What makes a formal methods project successful?" cannot be definitively answered. However, through observations of many recently completed and in-progress projects – successful and otherwise – we've come up with ten "commandments" that, if adhered to, will greatly increase a project's chances for success.

I THOU SHALT CHOOSE AN APPROPRIATE NOTATION.

The specification language is the specifier's primary tool during the initial stages of system development. To be consistent with the principles of formal methods, the notation should have a well-defined formal semantics.

Choosing the most appropriate notation is a significant task. Each of the myriad specification languages available claims superiority, and many of these claims are valid. Different specification languages excel when used with particular system classes.

There's always a trade-off between the expressiveness of a specification language and the levels of abstraction it supports. Certain languages may have wider "vocabularies" and more constructs to support the specific situations we want to deal with, but they also force us toward specific implementations. Although these languages will shorten the specification, they also reduce its abstraction.

Languages with small vocabularies, on the other hand, generally result in longer specifications, offering high levels of abstraction and little implementation bias. For example, consider Hoare's language, Communicating Sequential Processes. CSP's only first-class entities are processes (or pipes and buffers, which are particular process types). CSP specifications can thus become lengthy, but they're easier to understand due to the small number of constructs. Likewise, there's no bias toward implementing communication primitives – CSP channels may be implemented as physical wires, buses, mailboxes, or even shared variables.

Vocabulary is not the only consideration. Some specification languages just aren't as good as others when used with particular system classes. Trying to specify a concurrent system in a model-based specification language, such as Z or VDM, is like using a hammer to insert a screw. A process algebra, such as CSP or Milner's Calculus of Communicating Systems, is much more appropriate; however, the drawback is an inattention to system state aspects. The situation has prompted research to integrate process algebras with model-based specification languages and to extend these languages to handle concurrency and temporal aspects.

To achieve commercial success, a notation should be well established with a solid user base. Typically, a formal notation developed for industrial use takes at least a decade, from conception to application. It takes this long for the notation to be developed, taught, promulgated, documented, and marketed. And building the requisite user community has many tasks associated with it: writing textbooks, developing courses, fostering industrial-academic liaisons, and developing and marketing support tools. The technology transfer of formal notations, as with many new developments, involves many potentially troublesome hurdles.

An international standard increases the likelihood that a notation will win general acceptance among project developers. This is a chicken-and-egg situation, since developers want the standard but not the expense and time associated with producing it. However, a standard is essential to ensure support-tool uniformity and compatibility. Then, too, conforming to a specification notation standard is more difficult than conforming to a programming language standard because a notation is inherently nonexecutable.

> *By relieving the mind of all unnecessary work, a good notation sets it free to concentrate on more advanced problems, and in effect increases the mental power of the race.*
> — Alfred North Whitehead

II THOU SHALT FORMALIZE BUT NOT OVERFORMALIZE.

Just as many companies needlessly converted systems to object-oriented implementations, companies may unnecessarily adopt formal methods, either to satisfy corporate whim or peer pressure. First, determine that formal methods are really needed – whether to increase system confidence, to satisfy a customer-imposed standard, or to reduce complexity, for example.

Even the most fervent formal methods advocates must admit that, occasionally, formal methods fall short of more conventional methods. For example, although some user-interface designs have successfully incorporated formal specification techniques, it's generally accepted that user-interface design conformance resides in the domain of informal reasoning.

Applying formal methods to all system aspects is both unnecessary and costly. During development of the Customer Information Control System (CICS), a joint Oxford University Computing Laboratory/IBM effort, scarcely one tenth of the system underwent formal development. The project generated over 100,000 lines of code and thousands of specification pages. The project, having saved nine percent over costs using conventional methods (confirmed by independent audit), is often cited as a major, successful application of formal methods.

When it's been determined that formal methods are required, an appropriate notation should be selected and system components identified that will benefit from a formal treatment. Then, the level to which formal methods will be employed must be considered.

We identify three such levels.

Formal specification

Formal specification techniques are generally beneficial because a formal language makes specifications more concise and explicit. These techniques help us acquire greater insights into the system design, dispel ambiguities, maintain abstraction levels, and determine both our approach to the problem as well as its implementation.

Such techniques have proved useful in developing, for example, a software architecture for a product line of oscilloscopes. They've also been beneficial in specifying the algorithm in a single-transferable voting system, describing document structure, and highlighting inconsistencies in the World Wide Web design.

Formal development/verification

To date, full formal development is rarely attempted. It involves formally specifying the system, proving that certain properties are maintained while others are avoided or overcome, and applying a refinement calculus to translate the abstract specification into progressively more efficient, concrete representations. The final representation, of course, is executable code.

The proofs involved at this level can be formal, or they can be informal but rigorous. Applications using different levels of rigorous proofs are discussed elsewhere [10].

Machine-checked proofs

Support tools, particularly theorem provers or theorem checkers, have allowed machine-checked proofs for consistency and integrity. Mechanical proof checking is especially important for safety- and security-critical systems; in fact, numerous standards bodies are officially advocating this technique. The European Space Agency, for example, advocates formal proof in advance of testing wherever feasible. The agency also suggests that proofs be checked independently to reduce possible human error [3]; increasingly, this is likely to involve mechanical proof checking.

Several formal methods incorporate theorem provers (for example, HOL, Larch, Nqthm, OBJ, and PVS). There are also a number of theorem provers and support environments that incorporate theorem provers for methods such as B, CSP, FDR, RAISE, VDM, and Z. Lately, there's been interest in tailoring theorem provers to specific methods. For example, theorem provers for Z have been developed in EVES, HOL, and OBJ.

Each level is useful in itself. Full formal development and machine-checked proofs, however, cost additional time, effort, manpower, and tool support. Such an investment might be *required*, however, for high-integrity systems where failure could cause loss of life, great financial loss, or massive property destruction.

There are two ways of constructing a software design. One way is to make it so simple that there are obviously no deficiencies. And the other way is to make it so complicated that there are no obvious deficiencies.

— C.A.R. Hoare

III THOU SHALT ESTIMATE COSTS.

There's a steep learning curve in becoming an accomplished user, and introducing formal methods into a development environment typically requires significant investment in training, consultancy, and support tools. Set-up costs aside, however, there is considerable evidence that formal methods projects can run at least as cheaply as projects developed with conventional methods.

Savings achieved with formal methods was evidenced a couple of years ago by two formal methods projects in the UK that received the Queen's Award for Technological Achievement. In the first project, test time was reduced by an estimated 12 months for the T800 Transputer's Inmos floating-point unit through formally developed microcode using machine-supported algebraic techniques. In the second, an estimated nine percent of development costs was saved for part of the earlier mentioned IBM CICS system's development by respecifying the software with the Z notation. This also reduced errors and improved code quality. In both cases, formal methods resulted in saving millions of dollars.

The fact that many formal methods projects have exceeded their budgets proves not that the methods are more expensive but that cost estimation techniques need improvement [6].

Project-cost and development-time estimation models have been produced based on conventional structured, rather than formal, development methods. These models typically base costs on a measure of the number of lines of executable code produced in the final implementation, a subjective measure at best. Although several approaches to obtain metrics from formal specifications have been suggested, these have not yet been extended to usable models for cost estimation.

For now, we must rely on models predating formal methods. Perhaps the most famous of these is Boehm's Constructive Cost Model (Cocomo), which weights various factors according to historical results. The intermediate model augments the basic one with 15 cost-contributing factors categorized as computer, personnel, or project attributes.

These attributes will significantly affect the cost of formally developed systems. When formal methods are applied to complex systems or subsystems requiring the highest integrity and reliability, the weightings for two computer attributes – RELY (required software reliability) and CPLX (product complexity) – are likely to be very high. As formal methods are increasingly employed in real-time systems, TIME (execution time constraints) will significantly influence costs.

Boehm's other computer attributes, like most of his personnel attributes, probably will not significantly affect cost. In fact, additional new personnel attributes can be expected, such as SEXP (specification language experience), MCAP (mathematical capability), FMEX (formal methods experience) and DEXP (domain experience).

Of Boehm's project attributes, MODP (modern programming practices) is likely to be constant, while the development of more useful tools and support environments [6] should enhance the TOOL (software tools) attribute. Again, new attributes are likely to be required, such as DFOR (percentage of the system that has been subjected to formal specification techniques and formal analysis), and PROF (degree of rigorous and formal proof required).

One might expect that formal methods would greatly increase attribute weightings and, by extension, system cost. However, it's not the methods but the systems where they are used that are expensive: High-integrity systems are intrinsically expensive, especially if high confidence levels and a fail-safe operation are required.

Determining the values of these attributes is problematic. The Cocomo model requires that we determine them from historical data derived from other projects, both similar and dissimilar. Such information is difficult enough to obtain; it will be even more difficult with formal methods, due to the relatively few projects that have used them. Moreover, many formal methods projects aren't representative because they're very highly specialized. Technology transfer and formal development surveys [7–9] will eventually supply the needed detail. We have, in fact, already begun to consolidate this information [10].

For high-integrity systems, the investment in costly formal methods is warranted and will be justified by the anticipated returns, as long as development lead times and development costs are correctly estimated. Entirely new cost models may be required; for now, extensions to existing models are a useful starting point, provided that we allow for significant margins of error.

The advantages of implicit definition over construction are roughly those of theft over honest toil.

— Bertrand Russell

IV THOU SHALT HAVE A FORMAL METHODS GURU ON CALL.

Most successful formal methods projects have relied on at least one consultant with formal techniques expertise. Such outside expertise appears almost indispensable, as evidenced by the IBM CICS project and the Inmos T800 Transputer project.

In IBM's case, formal methods experts extensively trained employees to become self-sufficient in formal techniques. A different approach was adopted at Inmos, where consultants and project engineers worked in tandem but communicated constantly to ensure success. Inmos also hired people with the relevant mathematical experience to formally produce and check critical designs and consulted with outside experts.

Both approaches have proved successful – a company must choose an approach that reflects its organizational style as well as its long-term goals.

Progress will only be achieved in programming if we are willing to temporarily fully ignore the interconnection between our programs (in textual form) and their implementation as executable code ... In short: for the effective understanding of programs, we must learn to abstract from the existence of computers.

— Edsger W. Dijkstra

V THOU SHALT NOT ABANDON THY TRADITIONAL DEVELOPMENT METHODS.

There's been considerable investment expended on existing software development techniques, so it would be foolhardy to replace them entirely with formal methods. A better approach would be to cost-effectively integrate formal methods into existing design processes, an example of which is known as the SAZ method, which combines SSADM (Structured Systems Analysis and Design Method) and Z. Ideally, any combination of structured and formal methods would meld the best of each. For example, formal methods enable more precise specifications, whereas structured methods are more presentable to a nonexpert.

An alternative is to have a design team, using traditional development methods, obtain feedback from another team that formally analyzes the specification early in the design process. This effectively catches many errors while it still makes economic sense to correct them. Z has been applied successfully and cost-effectively with this approach.

The Cleanroom approach could easily incorporate existing formal notations to produce highly reliable software through nonexecution-based program development. This technique has a successful track record of significant error reduction in both safety-critical and noncritical applications. The programs are developed separately using informal proofs before they are certified, rather than tested. If too many errors are found, the process (not the program) must be changed. Realistically, most programs are too large to be formally proven, so they should be written correctly in the first place. The possibility of combining Cleanroom techniques and formal methods has been investigated, but applying even semiformal development on an industrial scale is difficult without machine assistance.

Sometimes different formal methods can be effectively combined. For example, HOL has provided tool support for Z, which gives the more readable Z notation the benefit of mechanical proof checking, thus increasing development confidence.

The managers of formal methods projects must be more technically cognizant than usual because, with formal approaches, the specification stage requires far more effort than is customary; consequently, code is produced much later in the design cycle. More errors are thus removed prior to coding, but early progress might not be as obvious as in a more conventional project. One way to assure feedback, particularly for a customer, might be to produce a rapid prototype from the specification.

But two permissible and correct models of the same external objects may yet differ in respect of appropriateness.
— Heinrich Hertz

VI THOU SHALT DOCUMENT SUFFICIENTLY.

Documentation is important to the design process, particularly if changes will later be required. Formalizing the documentation reduces both ambiguity and errors. With safety-critical systems, for example, documenting timing issues is especially important.

Formal methods are a powerful documentation aid because they can precisely record the system's functionality, both expected and delivered. Normally, the system documentation features the requirements and corresponding specification in a suitable formal notation, accompanied with natural language narrative, where appropriate. Natural language is particularly important for conveying information that has not otherwise been formally specified.

It's highly recommended that an informal specification be produced to explain a formal project description. This reinforces and clarifies the reader's understanding of the formal text. If there is any discrepancy, the formal specification takes precedence because it is the more explicit of the two descriptions.

Formal documentation could also facilitate software maintenance. Eventually, it may be possible to maintain the formal description rather than the executable code directly, with corresponding changes made to those parts of the code affected by the modifications, rather than changing the code directly so that it becomes out of step with the documentation.

You should not put too much trust in any unproved conjecture, even if it has been propounded by a great authority, even if it has been propounded by yourself. You should try to prove it or disprove it ...

— George Polya

VII THOU SHALT NOT COMPROMISE THY QUALITY STANDARDS.

To date, there have been few standards concerned specifically with software where formal methods are particularly applicable, as they are with safety-critical systems. Software quality standards, such as the ISO 9000 series, have been applied instead because these were the nearest relevant guidelines. Now many standards that address formal methods have recently been, or soon will be, issued [1,3]. Although some of these recommend or even mandate formal methods, these standards are not the only ones to consider.

There is a clear danger that developers will regard formal methods as a means of developing *correct* software. On the contrary, they are merely a means of achieving higher system integrity *when applied appropriately.*

Formal methods alone won't suffice; an organization must continue to satisfy its quality standards. This includes ensuring appropriate feedback between development teams and management; ensuring continuity of software inspection and walkthroughs; developing, expanding and maintaining testing policies; and ensuring that system documentation meets the quality standards that were set for conventional development methods.

Have nothing in your houses that you do not know to be useful or believe to be beautiful.

— William Morris

VIII. THOU SHALT NOT BE DOGMATIC.

Formal methods are just one of many techniques that, when applied correctly, have demonstrably resulted in systems of the highest integrity. Other methods should not be simply dismissed, however, because formal methods cannot guarantee correctness; they are applied by humans, who are obviously error prone. Support tools – such as specification editors, type checkers, consistency checkers, and proof checkers – might reduce the likelihood of human error but will not eliminate it. System development is a human activity and will always be prone to human whim, indecision, the ambiguity of natural language, and simple carelessness.

Absolute correctness is, simply, impossible to achieve. Ongoing debates in *Communications of the ACM* and other forums have been criticized because of a mismatch between the mathematical model and reality. No proponent of formal methods however would claim definitive correctness. In fact, one should speak not of correctness but of correctness *with respect to the specification*. And if an implementation was correct with respect to the specification but the specification was not what the customers intended, then the customers' (albeit subjective) view will be that the system is incorrect.

Communication between developers and customers is essential because system development is not straightforward. In fact, Royce's waterfall model was abandoned precisely because it viewed system development simplistically. System development is iterative and nonlinear, as exemplified by Boehm's spiral model; indeed, some requirements may not be determined even at post-implementation.

The developer must anticipate the need to modify the specification to meet the customer's requirements. Every developer has had to revisit requirements and rework the specification periodically – in the best traditions of Roland H. Macy, "the customer is always right." And, even if the requirements have been fully satisfied, there are still opportunities for error – until, and including, post-implementation execution.

The developer must also consider the right level of abstraction for the specification, which is a matter of experience. Too much abstraction makes it difficult to find omissions and to determine what the system is meant to do; too little causes bias toward particular implementations.

Similarly, no proof should be considered definitive. Manual proofs are notoriously error-prone and illogical. Even a proof checker doesn't guarantee a proof's correctness, but it does highlight unsubstantiated jumps and avoidable errors.

Errors are not in the art but in the artificers.

— Sir Isaac Newton

IX THOU SHALT TEST, TEST, AND TEST AGAIN.

Dijkstra has pinpointed a major limitation of testing: It can demonstrate the presence of bugs but not their absence. Just because a system has passed unit and system testing, it does not follow that the system will be bug-free.

In testing high-integrity systems, formal methods offer considerable advantages. For example, they let us demonstrate that proposed system properties actually exist. They let us examine system behavior and convince ourselves that all possibilities have been anticipated. Finally, they let us prove that an implementation conforms to its specification.

For all this, unfortunately, formal methods still cannot guarantee correctness, contrary to the hyperbolic claims made by many so-called experts. Formal methods can increase confidence in both a system's integrity and its expected performance, but bugs are still found, even after implementation.

A formal specification abstractly represents reality, and it has an infinite number of potential implementations. In considering a conventional implementation, however, there are very few programming languages that support the required structures, either explicitly or efficiently. Therefore, determine the most appropriate data structures to implement the higher level entities (this is called data refinement) and translate the operations already defined to operate on pointers, arrays, and records, for example. If a computer program were to choose the eventual implementation structures, assuming that it could be relied on to do so appropriately, it would cause a bias toward particular implementations. Bias should be avoided to give the implementor maximum design freedom. Refinement will always require a certain degree of human input, along with possibilities of human error.

Testing is necessary, even when formal methods are used in design, to isolate any errors that either escaped earlier detection or were caused during refinement. For example, in the case of the T800 Transputer's floating-point unit, one error *was* found by testing. The error resulted from an "obviously correct" change to the microcode after the formal development had begun. Conclusion: Never underestimate human fallibility – testing will always be a useful check.

Testing might be conducted in a traditional manner, using techniques such as McCabe's Complexity Measure to first determine the required amount of testing. Alternatively, testing might employ simulation, using executable specification languages or some form of specification animation.

With formal methods, specification-based testing is yet another alternative to determine functional tests to be run. The specification's abstraction can be exploited to concentrate on key functionality aspects, an approach that offers structured testing, which simplifies regression testing and helps isolate errors.

The specification can also be used to derive expected test results and to identify tests to be run in parallel with design and implementation, which enables earlier unit testing and which should reduce system maintenance costs.

"Look at this mathematician," said the logician. "He observes that the first ninety-nine numbers are less than a hundred and infers hence, by what he

calls induction, that all numbers are less than a hundred."

"A physicist believes," said the mathematician, "that 60 is divisible by all numbers. He observes that 60 is divisible by 1, 2, 3, 4, 5 and 6. He examines a few more cases, such as 10, 20 and 30, taken at random as he says. Since 60 is divisible also by these, he considers the experimental evidence sufficient."

"Yes, but look at the engineer," said the physicist. "An engineer suspected that all odd numbers are prime numbers. At any rate, 1 can be considered as a prime number, he argued. Then there comes 3, 5 and 7, all indubitably primes. Then there comes 9; an awkward case, it does not seem to be a prime number, yet 11 and 13 are certainly primes. "Coming back to 9," he said, "I conclude that 9 must be an experimental error."

— George Polya

X THOU SHALT REUSE.

Programming is outweighed by system maintenance when it comes to system development costs. Rising software development costs can be significantly offset by exploiting software reuse, including code, specifications, designs, and documentation. This applies to formal as well as more conventional development methods; theoretically, reuse can offset some set-up costs such as tools, training, and education.

Studies quoted by Capers Jones [11] claim that in 1983 only 15 percent of all new code was unique and application specific. The remaining 85 percent, it was claimed, was common, generic, and in fact could have been rewritten from reusable components.

Four major factors conspire against software reuse:

1. *The very large-scale reuse problem.* The VLSR problem is the prohibitive cost of developing an architectural superstructure to support component composition when compared to the potential savings to be gained from reuse.
2. *Generality versus specialization.* In terms of applicability, smaller components are more general, whereas larger units are more specialized and therefore less likely to be reused. But the larger the component, the greater the payoff, and a seemingly endless dichotomy exists.
3. *Cost of library population.* Determining suitable program components for inclusion in a library is time-consuming, yet essential for reuse. Having propagated a library of reusable components, a developer is still faced with the question of how suitable components can be identified for future reuse.
4. *The not-invented-here syndrome.* The NIH syndrome holds that components reused from previous development projects cannot be relied upon to work as anticipated, to satisfy the organization's quality control, or to be sufficiently understood in new systems.

The use of formal methods in system development can help overcome these problems and promote software reuse.

Formal specification languages clearly state the system requirements, which makes it easy to identify those components that also meet the requirements of a new system's specification. Components that have thus been formally specified and sufficiently well documented can be identified, reused, and combined in a new system. Library population costs are substantially reduced, though not eliminated, and confidence in component integrity is greatly increased.

It's important to focus on the reuse of formally developed specifications as well as formally developed code, as such reuse can ameliorate the generality-versus-specialization trade-off. Formal specifications are written at a high level of abstraction with, ideally, no bias toward particular implementations. During the refinement process abstract specifications are translated into ever more concrete representations, resulting in a representation that can be executed in a programming language. Reusing specifications rather than source code makes possible many different implementations in many different environments, with the most appropriate implementation chosen for the environment in question. In this way, even large components, which offer greater payoffs, can be made very general and reusable.

What's more, code that was previously written via informal development methods can be reused without compromising the formal development itself. Techniques featuring interactive tools have evolved for reverse-engineering legacy programs (mainly Cobol) in accordance with formal specifications and have, in fact, been successfully applied to programs tens of thousands of lines long. These old programs are then redeveloped for better structure and comprehension. After initially applying this process, it is possible to maintain both the formal specification and the program code, so that the two may be correlated.

> ... A method was devised of what was technically designated backing the cards in certain groups according to certain laws. The object of this extension is to secure the possibility of bringing any particular card or set of cards into use any number of times successively in the solution of one problem...
> — Augusta Ada Lovelace

These guidelines will help ensure that formal methods can be successfully applied in an industrial context.

It is important for the developer to have up-to-date information about best practice and industrial usage when selecting from the many notations and methods available. (The number of those actually used in an industrial setting is, to date, quite small.) The notation must then be carefully integrated with existing development processes, while retaining existing guidelines and procedures as much as possible.

A few last caveats: Always remember that software engineering is a human activity and that formal methods will not – cannot – guarantee correctness; and if we're willing to learn from our mistakes and those of others; if we're willing to exploit existing best practice and to check our work, through appropriate testing and tools, then we can successfully use formal methods to develop high-integrity systems.

For more information

Readers with access to the World Wide Web may find the following WWW Uniform Resource Locator (URL) of interest:

http://www.comlab.ox.ac.uk/archive/formal-methods.html

This provides hyperlinks to many on-line repositories of information relevant to formal methods, including some freely available tools, around the world.

Acknowledgements. The authors are grateful to John Fitzgerald, Robert France, Larry Paulson, and Phil Stocks for helpful comments on an earlier draft of this article.

Jonathan Bowen is funded by the UK Engineering and Physical Sciences Research Council under grant No. GR/J15186. Mike Hinchey is funded by ICL.

References

1. J.P. Bowen, "Formal Methods in Safety-Critical Standards," *Proc. SESS 93, Software Eng. Standards Symp.*, IEEE CS Press, Los Alamitos, Calif., Order No. 4240, 1993, pp. 168–177.
2. J.P. Bowen, and V. Stavridou, "Safety-Critical Systems, Formal Methods, and Standards," *IEE/BCS Software Eng. J.*, Vol. 8, No. 4, July 1993, pp. 189–209.
3. J.P. Bowen, and M.G. Hinchey, "Formal Methods and Safety-Critical Standards," *Computer*, Vol. 27, No. 8, Aug. 1994, pp. 68–71.
4. J.P. Bowen, and V. Stavridou, "The Industrial Take-up of Formal Methods in Safety-Critical and Other Areas: A Perspective," *Proc. FME 93, First Formal Methods Europe Symp.*, in *Lecture Notes in Computer Science*, J.C.P. Woodcock and P.G. Larsen, eds., Vol. 670, Springer-Verlag, Berlin and London, pp. 183–195.
5. J.A. Hall, "Seven Myths of Formal Methods," *IEEE Software*, Vol. 7, No. 5, Sept. 1990, pp. 11–19.
6. J.P. Bowen, and M.G. Hinchey, "Seven More Myths of Formal Methods," IEEE Software, Tech. Report 357, University of Cambridge Computer Laboratory, Cambridge, UK, Dec. 1994; also published in *IEEE Software*, Vol. 12, No. 4, July 1995, pp. 34–41 and in a shortened format as "Seven More Myths of Formal Methods: Dispelling Industrial Prejudice," in *Proc. FME 94, Second*

Formal Methods Europe Symp., T. Denvir, M. Naftalin, and M. Bertran, eds., *Lecture Notes in Computer Science*, Springer-Verlag, Berlin and London, Vol. 873, 1994, pp. 105–117.

7. D. Craigen, S. Gerhart, and T. Ralston, *An International Survey of Industrial Applications of Formal Methods*, Atomic Energy Control Board of Canada, US National Institute of Standards and Technology, and US Naval Research Laboratories, NIST GCR 93/626, National Technical Information Service, 5285 Port Royal Road, Springfield, VA 22161, USA, 1993.
8. D. Craigen, S. Gerhart, and T. Ralston, "Formal Methods Technology Transfer: Impediments and Innovation," *Applications of Formal Methods*, in Prentice Hall Int'l Series in Computer Science, M.G. Hinchey and J.P. Bowen, eds., Prentice Hall, Hemel Hempstead, UK, 1995.
9. J.P. Bowen, and M.G. Hinchey, "Ten Commandments of Formal Methods," Tech. Report No. 350, Sept. 1994, Computer Laboratory, Univ. of Cambridge, Cambridge, UK.
10. M.G. Hinchey, and J.P. Bowen, eds., *Applications of Formal Methods*, Prentice Hall Int'l Series in Computer Science, Prentice Hall, Hemel Hempstead, UK, 1995.
11. T.C. Jones, "Reusability in Programming: A Survey of the State of the Art," *IEEE Trans. Software Eng.*, Vol. 10, No. 5, Sept. 1984, pp. 488–494.

4. Object-Orientation

Although object-oriented programming languages appeared in the late 1960s with the advent of Simula-67, it was not until the late 1980s that the object paradigm became popular. Over the last decade we have seen the emergence of many object-oriented programming languages, and extensions to existing languages to support object-oriented programming (e.g., C++, Object Pascal).

The object paradigm offers many distinct advantages both at implementation, and also at earlier phases in the life-cycle. Before we consider these, first let us consider what we mean by Object-Orientation.

4.1 The Object Paradigm

Object-orientation, or the object paradigm, considers the Universe of Discourse to be composed of a number of independent entities (or *objects*). An object provides a *behavior*, which is a set of operations that the object can be requested to carry out on its data. An object's actions are carried out by internal computation, and by requesting other objects to carry out operations. Each object is responsible for its own data (or state), and only the object that owns particular data can modify it. Objects can only effect changes to data owned by another object by sending a message requesting the change.

Thus, an object can be defined as the encapsulation of a set of operations or *methods* which can be invoked externally, and of a state which remembers the effect of the methods.

Object-oriented design [60] bases the modular decomposition [203] of a software system on the classes of objects that the system manipulates, not on the function the system performs. Abstract Data Types (ADTs) are essential to the object-oriented approach, as object-oriented design is essentially the construction of software systems as structured collections of ADT implementations. We call the implementation of an Abstract Data Type a *module*.

The object-oriented approach supports the principle of data abstraction, which encompasses two concepts:

1. Modularization, and
2. Information Hiding.

4.2 Modularization

Modularization is the principle whereby a complex system is sub-divided into a number of self-contained entities or modules, as described above. All information relating to a particular entity within the system is then contained within the module. This means that a module contains all the data structures and algorithms required to implement that part of the system that it represents.

Clearly then, if errors are detected or changes are required to a system, modularization makes it easy to identify where the changes are required, simply by identifying the entity that will be affected. Similarly for reuse, if we can identify entities in existing systems that are to be replicated (perhaps with minor alterations) in a new system, then we can identify potentially reusable code, routines, etc., by finding the module that implements the particular entity. Since the module is self-contained, it can be transported in its entirety to the new system, save for checking that any requests it makes of other modules can be satisfied.

4.3 Information Hiding

The term *Information Hiding* refers to keeping implementation details 'hidden' from the user. The user only accesses an object through a protected interface. This interface consists of a number of operations which collectively define the behavior of the entity. By strictly controlling the entry points to a program, it is not possible for other modules or other programs to perform unexpected operations on data. In addition, other modules are not dependent on any particular implementation of the data structure.

This makes it possible to replace one implementation with another equivalent implementation, and (more importantly) to reuse a module in another system without needing to know how the data structures are actually implemented. We also know that the state of the data is not dependent on any spurious updates from other modules.

The generic term for those techniques that realize data abstraction is *encapsulation*. By encapsulating both the data and the operations on that data in a single, manageable Module (as in Modula-2 and Modula-3), Package (as in Ada) or Unit (as in Object Pascal), we facilitate their transportation and reuse in other systems.

4.4 Classes

Object-oriented systems generally support one or more techniques for the classification of objects with similar behaviors. The concept of a *class* originated in Simula-67, the purpose being to allow groups of objects which share identical behavior to be created.

This is done by providing a number of templates (i.e., classes) for the creation of objects within a system. The class template provides a complete description of a class in terms of its external interface and internal algorithms and data structures. The primary advantage of this approach is that the implementation of a class need only be carried out once. Descriptions of classes may then be reused in other systems, and with specialization may even be reused in the implementation of new classes.

Specialization is the process whereby one creates a new class from an existing class, and is thereby effectively moving a step nearer the requirements of the application domain. A new system can take advantage of classes as they have been defined in other systems, and also specialize these further to suit the requirements.

Specialization can take one of four forms:

1. adding new behavior;
2. changing behavior;
3. deleting behavior;
4. a combination of 1 to 3 above.

Object-oriented languages and systems vary in their support for the different forms of specialization. Most support the addition and changing of behavior, while only a few support the deletion of behavior. Those languages and systems that only allow for the addition of behavior are said to exhibit *strict inheritance*, while those that also support the deletion and changing of behavior are said to exhibit *non-strict inheritance*. From the point of view of software reuse, while support for any form of class inheritance is of great use, languages exhibiting non-strict inheritance offer the greatest possibilities.

4.5 Genericity and Polymorphism

Both Ada and CLU support the use of generic program units (and). This means that instead of writing separate routines to perform the same operation on different types (e.g., sorting an array of integers, sorting an array of reals), only one 'template' routine needs to be written, which can then be *instantiated* with the required type. That is, an instance of the generic subprogram or package is created with the actual type replacing the generic type. The instantiation is achieved by passing the required type as a parameter to the generic program unit.

While genericity enables the reuse of a generic 'template', and avoids having to write separate routines for each type to be operated on, it does not reduce the number of routines in the system. That is, a separate instance of the instantiated template exists for each type that is to be handled by the system; one routine does not accommodate more than one type.

One routine accommodating more than one type is termed *polymorphism*. In terms of object-oriented computing it may be defined as the ability of behavior to have an interpretation over more than one class. For example, it is common for the method print to be defined over most of the classes in an object-oriented system. Polymorphism can be achieved in two ways – through sub-classing, and through overloading. As such, it is supported by most object-oriented languages and systems.

Overloading, with which we can achieve polymorphism, is evident in most programming languages. Overloading the meaning of a term occurs when it is possible to use the same name to mean different things. For example, in almost all programming languages, we would expect to be able to use the plus-sign (+) to mean the addition of both fixed-point and floating-point numbers. Many programming languages also interpret the plus-sign as disjunction (logical OR). In this way, we can reuse the code written to perform the addition of two integers A and B, to mean the addition of two real numbers A and B, or the disjunction of A and B (i.e., $A \vee B$), etc.

4.6 Object-Oriented Design

Object-oriented programming languages clearly offer benefits in that they permit a more intuitive implementation of a system based on the real-life interaction of entities, and offer much support for software reuse, avoiding 're-inventing the wheel'.

The object paradigm also offers benefits at earlier stages in the life-cycle, however, facilitating greater savings through the reuse of specification and design components as well as code, and a more intuitive approach to modeling the real-world application.

In his paper *Object-Oriented Development* (reprinted in this Part), which has become perhaps the most widely-referenced paper in the field, Grady Booch describes the motivation for an object-oriented approach to system design, and outlines his own approach to object-oriented development [22]. This approach has become known as the 'Booch approach' or simply *Object-Oriented Design* [23]. The development process is clearly simplified with the use of an object-oriented programming language (such as Ada) for the final implementation, although implementation in languages not supporting the object paradigm is also possible.

Booch is careful to point out that object-oriented design is a partial life-cycle method, that must be extended with appropriate requirements and specification methods. To this end, a large number of object-oriented analysis and design methodologies (e.g., see [263]) have evolved, many based firmly on the various structured methods discussed in Part 2.

These approaches differ greatly, some being minor extensions to existing methods, others being entirely new approaches. In *Object-Oriented and Conventional Analysis and Design Methodologies: Comparison and Critique* (reprinted here), Fichman and Kemerer review approaches to object-oriented analysis and design, comparing various approaches and the notations and techniques that they use, and concluding that the object-oriented approach represents a radical change from more conventional methods [78].

The formal methods community too have been quick to realize the benefits of object-orientation, and how it can smooth the transition from requirements, through specification, design and finally into implementation in an object-oriented programming language [157]. The object paradigm also greatly facilitates the reuse of formal specifications and of system maintenance at the specification level rather than merely at the level of executable code [30]. A large number of differing approaches to object-orientation in Z and VDM have emerged, with none as yet being taken as definitive. Readers are directed to [159] for overviews of the various approaches.

A number of other object-oriented development approaches exist, such as the Fusion method used at Hewlett-Packard [61]. More recently, Booch *et al.*'s Unified Modeling Language (UML) has been very successful [25, 226]. Although it has been developed by Rational, Inc., it is non-proprietory and is being adopted widely [76]. This language is formalizable [158] and thus may be used as a formal modelling notation [80] although further work in this area would be worthwhile. There are possibilities of combining UML with other formal notations [83]. Project management issues are also very important [24, 224]. Further developments and use of object-oriented approaches look likely for the future.

Object-Oriented Development

Grady Booch

Summary.

Object-oriented development is a partial-lifecycle software development method in which the decomposition of a system is based upon the concept of an object. This method is fundamentally different from traditional functional approaches to design and serves to help manage the complexity of massive software-intensive systems. The paper examines the process of object-oriented development as well as the influences upon this approach from advances in abstraction mechanisms, programming languages, and hardware. The concept of an object is central to object-oriented development and so the properties of an object are discussed in detail. The paper concludes with an examination of the mapping of object-oriented techniques to Ada® using a design case study.

Keywords: Abstract data type, Ada, object, object-oriented development, software development method.

1. Introduction

Rentsch predicts that "object-oriented programming will be in the 1980's what structured programming was in the 1970's" [1]. Simply stated, *object-oriented development* is an approach to software design in which the decomposition of a system is based upon the concept of an object. An *object* is an entity whose behavior is characterized by the actions that is suffers and that it requires of other objects.

Object-oriented development is fundamentally different from traditional functional methods, for which the primary criteria for decomposition is that each module in the system represents a major step in the overall process. The differences between these approaches becomes clear if we consider the class of languages for which they are best suited.

© 1986 IEEE. Reprinted by permission.
Reprinted from *IEEE Transactions on Software Engineering*, 12(2):211–221, February 1986.
® Ada is a registered trademark of the U.S. Department of Defense (Ada Joint Program Office).

The proper use of languages like Ada and Smalltalk requires a different approach to design than the approach one typically takes with languages such as Fortran, Cobol, C, and even Pascal. Well-structured systems developed with these older languages tend to consist of collections of subprograms (or their equivalent), mainly because that is structurally the only major building block available. Thus, these languages are best suited to functional decomposition techniques, which concentrate upon the algorithmic abstractions. But as Guttag observes, "unfortunately, the nature of the abstractions that may be conveniently achieved through the use of subroutines is limited. Subroutines, while well suited to the description of abstract events (operations), are not particularly well suited to the description of abstract objects. This is a serious drawback" [2].

Languages like Ada also provide the subprogram as an elementary building block. However, Ada additionally offers the package and task as major structural elements. The package gives us a facility for extending the language by creating new objects and classes of objects, and the task gives us a means to naturally express concurrent objects and activities. We can further extend the expressive power of both subprograms and packages by making them generic. Together, these facilities help us to better build abstractions of the problem space by permitting a more balanced treatment between the nouns (objects) and verbs (operations) that exist in our model of reality.

Of course, one can certainly develop Ada systems with the same methods as for these more traditional languages, but that approach neither exploits the power of Ada nor helps to manage the complexity of the problem space.

In general, functional development methods suffer from several fundamental limitations. Such methods

- do not effectively address data abstraction and information hiding;
- are generally inadequate for problem domains with natural concurrency;
- are often not responsive to changes in the problem space.

With an object-oriented approach, we strive to mitigate these problems.

Before we get too detailed, let us consider alternate designs for a simple real-time system using functional and object-oriented techniques.

A cruise-control system exists to maintain the speed of a car, even over varying terrain [3]. In Figure 1 we see the block diagram of the hardware for such a system. There are several inputs:

– System on/off	If on, denotes that the cruise-control system should maintain the car speed.
– Engine on/off	If on, denotes that the car engine is turned on; the cruise-control system is only active if the engine is on.
– Pulses from wheel	A pulse is sent for every revolution of the wheel.
– Accelerator	Indication of how far the accelerator has been pressed.

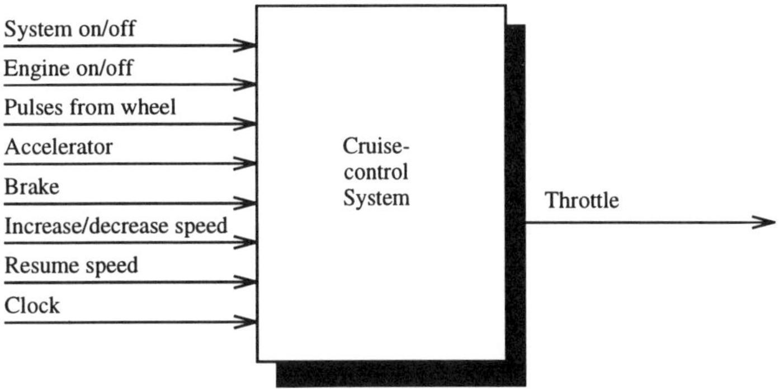

Figure 1. Cruise-control system hardware block diagram.

- Brake
On when the brake is pressed; the cruise-control system temporarily reverts to manual control if the brake is pressed.

- Increase/Decrease Speed
Increase or decrease the maintained speed; only applicable if the cruise-control system is on.

- Resume
Resume the last maintained speed; only applicable if the cruise-control system is on.

- Clock
Timing pulse every millisecond.

There is one output from the system:

- Throttle
Digital value for the engine throttle setting.

How might we approach the design of the software for the cruise control system? Using either functional or object-oriented approaches, we might start by creating a data flow diagram of the system, to capture our model of the problem space. In Figure 2, we have provided such a diagram, using the notation by Gane and Sarson [4].

With a functional method, we would continue our design by creating a structure chart. In Figure 3, we have used the techniques of Yourdon and Constantine [5] to decompose the system into modules that denote the major functions in the overall process.

With an object-oriented approach, we proceed in an entirely different manner. Rather than factoring our system into modules that denote operations, we instead structure our system around the objects that exist in our model of reality. By extracting the objects from the data flow diagram, we generate the structure seen in Figure 4. We will more fully explain the process and the meaning of the symbols used in the figure later. For the moment, simply recognize that the amorphous blobs denote objects and the directed lines denote dependencies among the objects.

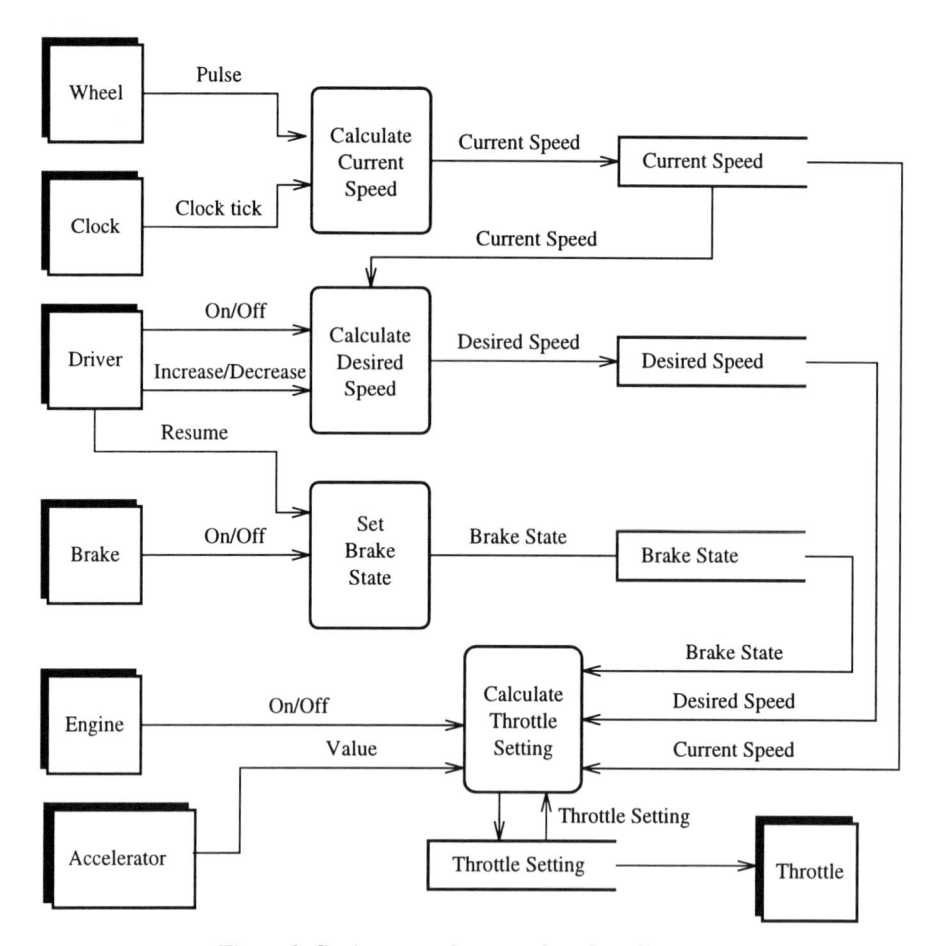

240   High-Integrity System Specification and Design

Figure 2. Cruise-control system data flow diagram.

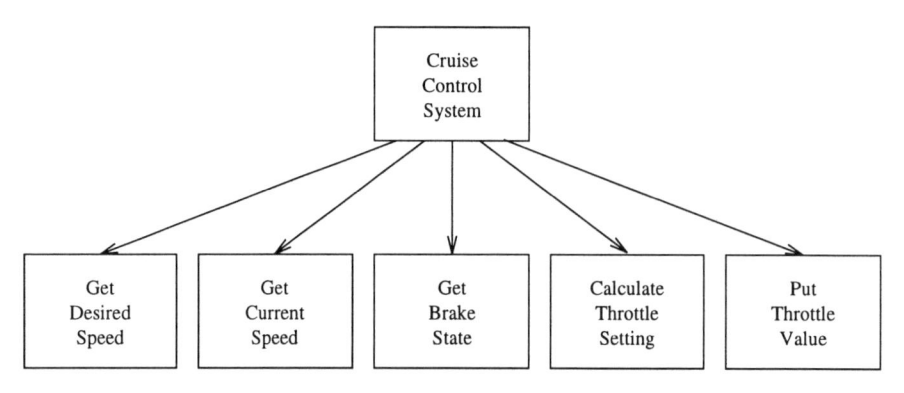

Figure 3. Functional decomposition.

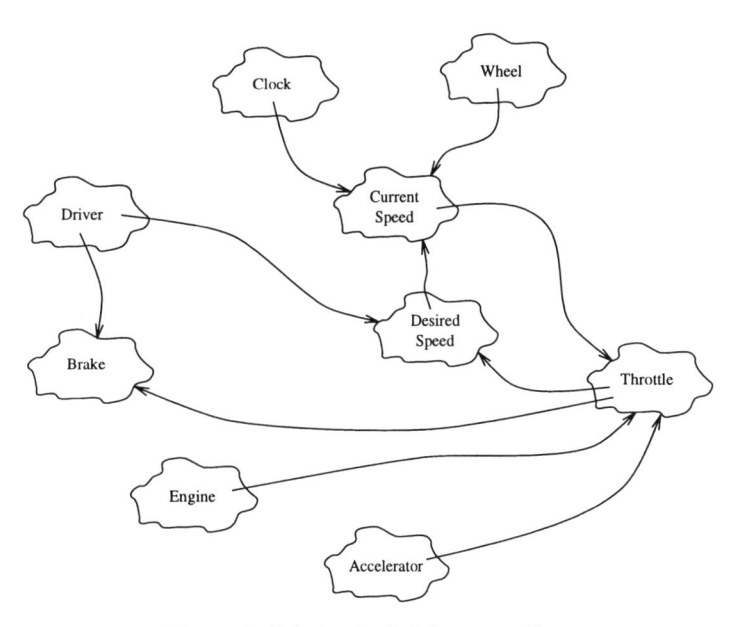

Figure 4. Object-oriented decomposition.

Immediately, we can see that the object-oriented decomposition closely matches our model of reality. On the other hand, the functional decomposition is only achieved through a transformation of the problem space. This latter design is heavily influenced by the nature of the subprogram and so emphasizes only the algorithmic abstractions that exist. Hence, we can conclude that a functional decomposition is imperative in nature: it concentrates upon the major actions of a system and is silent on the issue of the agents that perform or suffer these actions.

The advantages of the object-oriented decomposition are also evident when we consider the effect of change (and change will happen to any useful piece of software). One side-effect of the functional decomposition is that all interesting data end up being global to the entire system, so that any change in representation tends to affect all subordinate modules. Alternately, in the object-oriented approach, the effect of changing the representation of an object tends to be much more localized. For example, suppose that we originally chose to represent car speed as an integer value denoting the number of wheel revolutions per some time unit (which would not be an unreasonable design decision). Suppose that we are now told to add a digital display that indicates the current speed in miles per hour. In the functional decomposition, we might be forced to modify every part of the system that deals with the representation of speed, as well as to add another major module at the highest level of the system to manage the display. However, in the object-oriented decomposition, such a change directly affects only two objects (current speed and desired speed) and would require the addition of one more object (the display) that directly parallels our modification of reality.

Regarding an even more fundamental change, suppose that we chose to implement our cruise-control system using two microcomputers, one for managing the current and desired speeds and the second to manage the throttle. To map the functional decomposition to this target architecture requires that we split the system design at the highest level. For the object-oriented approach, we need make no modification at this level of the design to take advantage of the physical concurrency.

2. Object-Oriented Development

Let us examine the process of object-oriented development more closely. Since we are dealing with a philosophy of design, we should first recognize the fundamental criteria for decomposing a system using object-oriented techniques:

> *Each module in the system denotes an object or class of objects from the problem space.*

Abstraction and information hiding form the foundation of all object-oriented development [6], [7]. As Shaw reports, "an abstraction is a simplified description, or specification, of a system that emphasizes some of the system's details or properties while suppressing others" [8]. Information hiding, as first promoted by Parnas, goes on to suggest that we should decompose systems based upon the principle of hiding design decisions about our abstractions [9].

Abstraction and information hiding are actually quite natural activities. We employ abstraction daily and tend to develop models of reality by identifying the objects and operations that exist at each level of interaction. Thus, when driving a car, we consider the accelerator, gauges, steering wheel, and brake (among other objects) as well as the operations we can perform upon them and the effect of those operations. When repairing an automobile engine, we consider objects at a lower level of abstraction, such as the fuel pump, carburetor, and distributor.

Similarly, a program that implements a model of reality (as all of them should) may be viewed as a set of objects that interact with one another. We will study the precise nature of objects in the following section, but next, let us examine how object-oriented development proceeds. The major steps in this method are as follows:

- Identify the objects and their attributes.
- Identify the operations suffered by and required of each object.
- Establish the visibility of each object in relation to other objects.
- Establish the interface of each object.
- Implement each object.

These steps are evolved from an approach first proposed by Abbott [10].

The first step, *identify the objects and their attributes,* involves the recognition of the major actors, agents, and servers in the problem space plus their role in our model of reality. In the cruise-control system, we identified concrete objects such as the accelerator, throttle, and engine and abstract objects such as speed. Typically, the objects we identify in this step derive from the nouns we use in describing the problem space. We may also find that there are several objects of interest that are similar. In such a situation, we should establish a class of objects of which there are many instances. For example, in a multiple-window user interface, we may identify distinct windows (such as a help window, message window, and command window) that share similar characteristics; each object may be considered an instance of some window class.

The next step, *identify the operations suffered by and required of each object*, serves to characterize the behavior of each object or class of objects. Here, we establish the static semantics of the object by determining the operations that may be meaningfully performed on the object or by the object. It is also at this time that we establish the dynamic behavior of each object by identifying the constraints upon time or space that must be observed. For example, we might specify that there is a time ordering of operations that must be followed. In the case of the multiple-window system, we should permit the operations of open, close, move, and size upon a window object and require that the window be open before any other operation be performed. Similarly, we may constrain the maximum and minimum size of a particular window.

Clearly, the operations suffered by an object define the activity of an object when acted upon by other objects. Why must we also concern ourselves with the operations required of an object? The answer is that identifying such operations lets us decouple objects from one another. For example, in the multiple-window system we might assume the existence of some terminal object and require the operations of Move_Cursor and Put. As we will see later, languages such as Ada provide a generic mechanism that can express these requirements. The result is that we can derive objects that are inherently reusable because they are not dependent upon any specific objects, but rather depend only upon other classes of objects.

In the third step, to *establish visibility of each object in relation to other objects*, we identify the static dependencies among objects and classes of objects (in other words, what objects see and are seen by a given object). The purpose of this step is to capture the topology of objects from our model of reality.

Next, to *establish the interface of each object*, we produce a module specification, using some suitable notation (in our case, Ada). This captures the static semantics of each object or class of objects that we established in a previous step. This specification also serves as a contract between the clients of an object and the object itself. Put another way, the interface forms the boundary between the outside view and the inside view of an object.

The fifth and final step, *implement each object*, involves choosing a suitable representation for each object or class of objects and implementing the interface from the previous step. This may involve either decomposition or composition. Occasionally an object will be found to consist of several subordinate objects and in this case we repeat our method to further decompose the object. More often, an object will be implemented by composition; the object is implemented by building on top of existing lower-level objects or classes of objects. As a system is prototyped, the developer may chose to defer the implementation of all objects until some later time and just rely upon the specification of the objects (with suitably stubbed implementations) to experiment with the architecture and behavior of a system. Similarly, the developer may chose to try several alternate representations over the life of the object, in order to experiment with the behavior of various implementations.

We must point out that object-oriented development is a partial-lifecycle method; it focuses upon the design and implementation stages of software development. As Abbott observes, "although the steps we follow in formalizing the strategy may appear mechanical, it is not an automatic procedure... [it] requires a great deal of real world knowledge and intuitive understanding of the problem" [11]. It is therefore necessary to couple object-oriented development with appropriate requirements and analysis methods in order to help create our model of reality. We have found Jackson Structured Development (JSD) to be a promising match [12] and recently, there has been interest in mapping requirements analysis techniques such as SREM to object-oriented development [13].

Systems designed in an object-oriented manner tend to exhibit characteristics quite different than those designed with more traditional functional approaches. As Figure 5 illustrates, large object-oriented systems tend to be built in layers of abstraction, where each layer denotes a collection of objects and classes of objects with restricted visibility to other layers; we call such a collection of objects a *subsystem*. Furthermore, the components that form a subsystem tend to be structurally flat (like we saw in Figure 4) rather than being strictly hierarchical and deeply nested.

It is also the case that the global flow of control in an object-oriented system is quite different from that of a functionally decomposed system. In the latter case, there tends to be a single thread of control that follows the hierarchical lines of decomposition. In the case of an object-oriented system, because objects may be independent and autonomous, we typically cannot identify a central thread of control. Rather, there may be many threads active simultaneously throughout a system. This model is actually not a bad one, for it more often reflects our abstraction of reality. We should add that the subprogram call profile of an object-oriented system typically exhibits deeply nested calls; the implementation of an object operation most often involves invoking operations under other objects.

There are many benefits to be derived from an object oriented approach. As Buzzard notes, "there are two major goals in developing object-based software. The first is to reduce the total life-cycle software cost by increasing programmer productivity and reducing maintenance costs. The second goal is to implement software systems that resist both accidental and malicious corruption attempts" [14]. Giving empirical evidence that supports these points, a study by Boehm-Davis notes that "the completeness complexity, and design time data would seem to suggest that there is an advantage to generating program solutions using... object-oriented methods" [15]. Regarding the maintainability of object-oriented systems, Meyer observes that "apart from its elegance, such modular, object-oriented programming yields software products on which modifications and extensions are much easier to perform

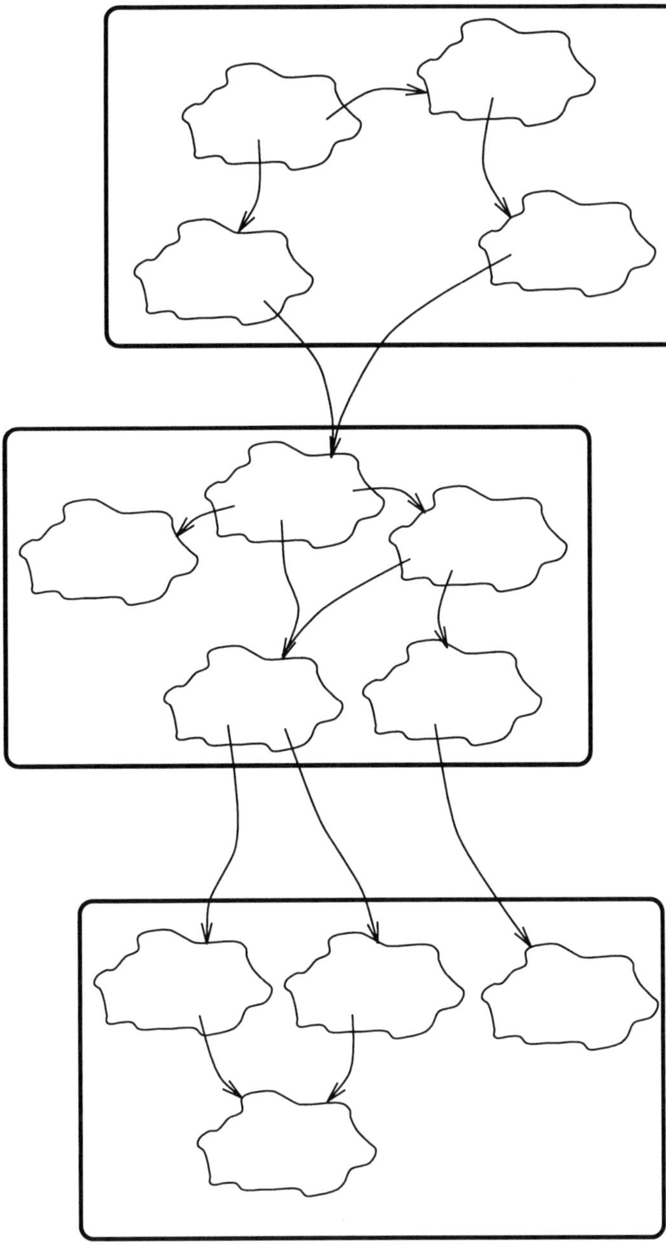

Figure 5. Canonical structure of large object-oriented systems.

than with programs structured in a more conventional, procedure-oriented fashion" [16]. In general, understandability and maintainability are enhanced due to the fact that objects and their related operations are localized.

Perhaps the most important benefit of developing systems using object-oriented techniques is that this approach gives us a mechanism to formalize our model of reality. As Borgida notes, "the chief advantage of object-oriented frameworks is that they make possible a direct and natural correspondence between the world and its model" [17]. This even applies to problems containing natural concurrency, for as the Boehm-Davis study reports, "the object-oriented method seemed to produce better solutions for [a problem] which involved real-time processing" [18].

3. The Properties of an Object

The notion of an object plays the central role in object-oriented systems, but actually, the concept is not a new one. Indeed, as MacLenna reports, "programming is object-oriented mathematics" [19]. Lately, we have observed a confluence of object-oriented work from many elements of computer science. Levy suggests that the following events have influenced object-oriented development [20]:

- advances in computer architecture, including capability systems and hardware support for operating systems concepts;
- advances in programming languages, as demonstrated in Simula, Pascal, Smalltalk, CLU, and Ada;
- advances in programming method, including modularization and information hiding and monitors.

We would add to this list the work on abstraction mechanisms by various researchers.

Perhaps the first person to formally identify the importance of composing systems in levels of abstraction was Dijkstra [21]. Parnas later introduced the concept of information hiding [9] which, as we will discuss later, is central to the nature of an object. In the 1970's, a number of researchers, most notably Liskov, Guttag, and Shaw, pioneered the development of abstract data type mechanisms [22] – [24]. The late 1970's and early 1980's also saw the application of a number of software development methods (such as JSD) that were declarative rather than imperative in nature.

The greatest influence upon object-oriented development derives from a small number of programming languages. SIMULA 67 first introduced the class as a language mechanism for encapsulating data, but, as Rentsch reports, "the Smalltalk programming system carried the object-oriented paradigm to a smoother model." Indeed, "the explicit awareness of the idea, including the term object-oriented, came from the Smalltalk effort" [1]. Other object-oriented languages such as Ada and Clascal followed the more traditional path of SIMULA, but in the early 1980's we also saw a number of languages merge the concepts of Lisp and Smalltalk; thus evolved languages such as Flavors and LOOPS. It is also clear that Lisp alone may be effectively used to apply object-oriented techniques [25]. More recently, there has been work to add Smalltalk constructs to C, resulting in a language named Objective-C [26]. Languages such as Smalltalk have collectively been called actor languages, since they emphasize the role of entities as actors, agents, and servers in the structures of the real world [27].

Interestingly, the concept of an object has precedence in hardware. Work with tagged architectures and capability-based systems has led to a number of implementations that we can classify as object-oriented. For example, Myers reports on two object-oriented architectures, SWARD and the Intel 432 [28]. The IBM System 38 is also regarded as an object-oriented architecture [29].

Every source we have introduced presents a slightly different view of object-oriented systems, but from this background we can extract the common properties of the concept. Thus, we may define an object as an entity that:

- has state;
- is characterized by the actions that it suffers and that it requires of other objects;
- is an instance of some (possibly anonymous) class;
- is denoted by a name;
- has restricted visibility of and by other objects;
- may be viewed either by its specification or by its implementation.

The first and second points are the most important: an object is something that exists in time and space and may be affected by the activity of other objects. The state of an object denotes its value plus the objects denoted by this value. For example, thinking back to the multiple-window system we discussed in the first section, the state of a window might include its size as well as the image displayed in the window (which is also an object). Because of the existence of state, objects are not input/output mappings as are procedures or functions. For this reason, we distinguish objects from mere processes, which are input/output mappings.

From Smalltalk, we get the notion of a method, which denotes the response by an object to a message from another object. The activity of one method may pass messages that invoke the methods of other objects. Abstract data types deal with operations is a related way. Liskov suggests that such operations be divided "into two groups: those which do not cause a state change but allow some processes. Whereas an aspect of the state to be observed... and those which cause a change of state" [30]. In practice, we have encountered one other useful class of operations, the iterator, which permits us to visit all subcomponents of an object. The concept of an iterator was formalized in the language Alphard [31]. For example, given an instance of a terminal screen, we may wish to visit all the windows visible on the screen.

Together, we may classify these operations as follows:

- *Constructor:* An operation that alters the state of an object.
- *Selector:* An operation that evaluates the current object state.
- *Iterator:* An operation that permits all parts of an object to be visited.

To enhance the reusability of an object or class of objects, these operations should be primitive. A primitive operation is one that may be implemented efficiently only if it has access to the underlying representation of the object. In this sense, the specification of an object or class of objects should define "the object, the whole object, and nothing but the object."

We may classify an object as an actor, agent, or server, depending on how it relates to surrounding objects. An actor object is one that suffers no operations but only operates upon other objects. At the other extreme, a server is one that only suffers operations but may not operate upon other objects. An agent is an object that serves to perform some operation on the behalf of another object and in turn may operate upon another object.

Another important characteristic of objects is that each object is a unique instance of some class. Put another way, a class denotes a set of similar but unique objects. A class serves to factor the common properties of a set of objects and specify the behavior of all instances. For example, we may have a class named Window from which we create several instances, or objects. It is important to distinguish between an object and its class: operations are defined for the class, but operations only have an effect upon the object.

Of course, and this gets a little complicated, one can treat a class as an object (forming a *metaclass*), with operations such as creating an instance of the class. This strange loop in the definition is not only academically interesting, but also permits some very elegant programs.

The term *class* comes from SIMULA 67 and Smalltalk; in other languages, we speak of the *type* of an object. Also from Smalltalk, we get the concept of inheritance, which permits hierarchy of classes. In this sense, all objects are an instance of a class, which is a subclass of another class (and so on). For example, given an object, its class may be Text_Window, which is in turn a subclass of the more general class Window. An object is said to inherit the methods of this chain of classes. Thus, all objects of the class Text_Window have the same operations as defined by the class Window (and we may also add operations, modify existing operations, and hide operations from the superclass).

Now, and this is an area of much emotional debate, we suggest that inheritance is an important, but not necessary, concept. On a continuum, of "object-orientedness," development without inheritance still constitutes object-oriented development. On the other hand, object-oriented development is more than just programming with abstract data types, although abstract data types certainly serve as an important influence: indeed, we can characterize the behavior of most objects using the mechanisms of abstract data types. Whereas development with abstract data types tends to deal with passive objects (that is, *agents* and *servers*), object-oriented development also concerns itself with objects that act without stimulus from other objects (we call such objects *actors*). Another difference between programming with abstract data types and object-oriented development is that, in both cases, we concern ourselves with the operations suffered by an object, but in the latter case, we also concern ourselves with the operations that an object requires of other objects. As we have mentioned, the purpose of this view is to decouple the dependencies of objects, especially when coupled with a language mechanism such as Ada generic units.

Another way to view the relationship between object-oriented development and programming with abstract data types is that object-oriented development builds on the concepts of the latter, but also serves as a method that exposes the interesting objects and classes of objects from our abstraction of reality.

In some cases, the class of an object may be anonymous. Here, the object does have a class but its class is not visible. The implication is that there may be only one object of the class (since there is no class name from which instances may be declared). Practically, we implement such objects as abstract state machines instead of instances of a class.

Another important consideration of any object-oriented system is the treatment of names. The rule is simple: objects are unique instances of a class, and names only serve to denote objects. As Liskov observes, "variables are just the names used in a program to refer to objects" [32]. Thus, an object may be denoted by one name (the typical case) or by several names. In the latter situation, we have an alias such that operation upon an object through one name has the side-effect of altering the object denoted by all the aliases. For example, we may have several variables in our window system that denote the same window object; operating upon an object through one name (such as destroying the window) has the effect of altering the object denoted by all other names. This one object/many name paradigm is a natural consequence of the notion of an object, but depending upon the manner of support offered by the underlying language, is the source of many logical errors. The key concept to remember is that supplying a name to a constructor does not necessarily alter the value of the name, but instead alters the object denoted by the name.

The names of objects should have a restricted scope. Thus, in designing a system, we concern ourselves with what objects see and are seen by another object or class of objects. This in fact is the purpose of one of the steps in our method, that of establishing the visibility among objects. In the worst case, all objects can see one another and so there is the potential of unrestricted action. It is better that we restrict the visibility among objects, so as to limit the number of objects we must deal with to understand any part of the system and also to limit the scope of change.

Finally, every object has two parts, and so may be viewed from two different ways: there is an outside view and an inside view. Whereas the outside view of an object serves to capture the abstract behavior of the object, the inside view indicates how that behavior is implemented. Thus, by seeing only the outside view, one object can interact with another without knowing how the other is represented or implemented. When designing a system, we first concern ourselves with the outside view.

The outside view of an object or class of objects is its specification. The specification captures all of the static and (as much as possible) dynamic semantics of the object. In the specification of a class of objects, we export a number of things to the rest of the system, including the name of the class and the operations defined for objects of the class. Ideally, our implementation language enforces this specification, and prevents us from violating the properties of the specification.

Whereas the outside view of an object is that which is visible to other objects, the inside view is the implementation and so is hidden from the outside. In the body of an object or object class, we must chose one of many possible representations that implements the behavior of the specification. Again, if the language permits it, we may replace the implementation of an object or class of objects without any other part of the system being affected. The benefits of this facility should be clear: not only does this enforce our abstractions and hence help manage the complexity of the problem space, but by localizing the design decisions made about an object, we reduce the scope of change upon the system.

4. Ada and Object-Oriented Development

Clearly, some languages are better suited than others to the application of object-oriented development; the major issue is how well a particular language can embody and enforce the properties of an object. Smalltalk and its immediate relatives provide the best match with these concepts, but it is also the case that languages such as Ada may be applied in an object-oriented fashion. Specifically, in Ada:

- Classes of objects are denoted by packages that export private or limited private types.
- Objects are denoted by instances of private or limited private types or as packages that serve as abstract state machines.
- Object state resides either with a declared object (for instances of private or limited private types) or in the body of a package (in the case of an abstract state machine).
- Operations are implemented as subprograms exported from a package specification; generic formal subprogram parameters serve to specify the operations required by an object.
- Variables serve as names of objects; aliases are permitted for an object.
- Visibility is statically defined through unit context clauses.
- Separate compilation of package specification and body support the two views of an object.
- Tasks and task types may be used to denote actor objects and classes of objects.

Figure 6. illustrates the interaction of these points.

It is also the case that we can provide a form of inheritance using derived types. Thus, we could define a class of objects in a package that exports a nonprivate type, and then build on top of this class by deriving from the first type. The derivation inherits all the operations from the parent type. Because we have used an unencapsulated type (a type that is not private or limited private), we may add new operations, replace existing operations, and hide operations from the parent class. However, we must realize that there is a trade-off between safety and flexibility. By using an unencapsulated type, we avoid much of the protection offered by Ada's strong typing

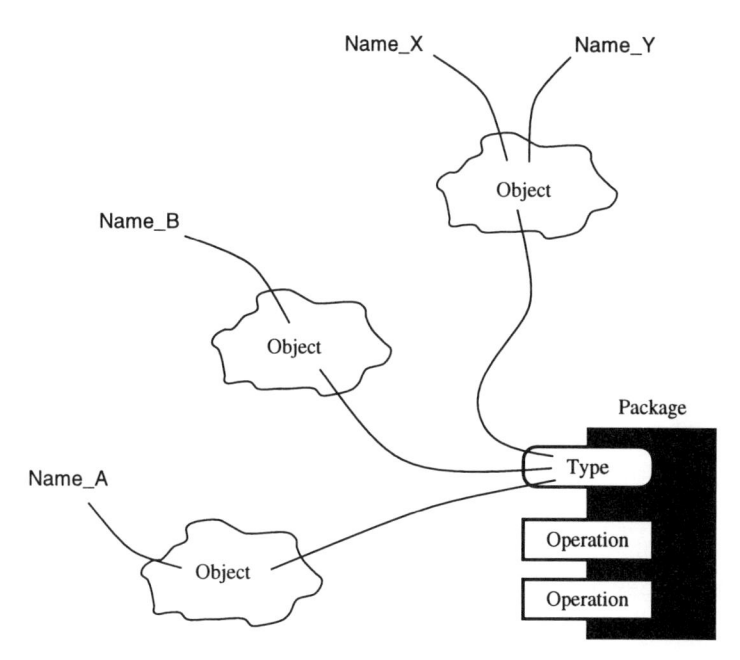

Figure 6. Names, objects, and classes.

mechanism. Smalltalk favors the side of flexibility; we prefer the safety offered by Ada, especially when applied to massive software-intensive systems.

Earlier, we used a few simple symbols to represent the design of the cruise-control system. It should come as no surprise that some people can grasp the essence of a design just by reading package specifications, while others are more effective if they are first given a graphical representation of the system architecture: we fall into the latter category. Since neither structure charts nor data flow diagrams capture the interesting properties of an object, we offer the set of symbols in Figure 7, evolved from our earlier work [33]. We have found them to be an effective design notation that also serve to directly map from data flow diagrams to Ada implementations.

As Figure 7 represents, these symbols are connected by directed lines. If we draw a line from object A to object B, this denotes that A depends upon the resources of B in some way. In the case of Ada units, we must make a distinction regarding the parts of a unit that exhibit these dependencies. For example, if the specification of package X depends upon Y, we start the directed line from the colorless part of the symbol for X; if the body of X depends upon Y, we start the directed line from the shaded part of X.

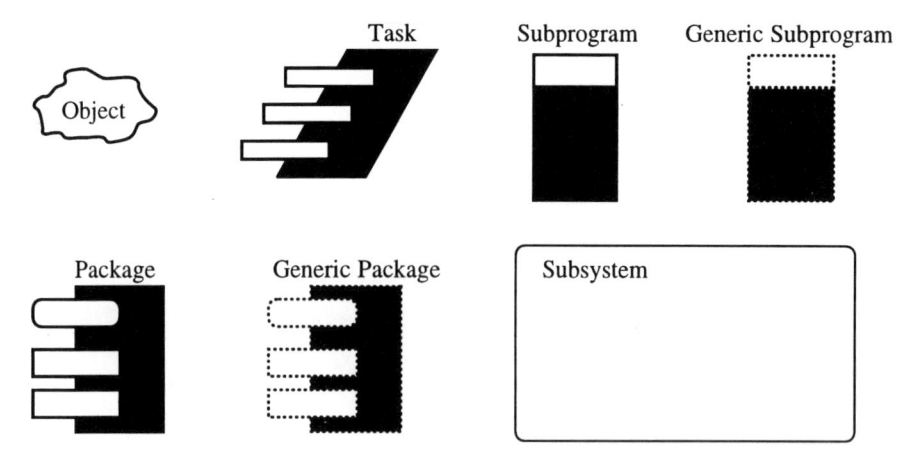

Figure 7. Symbols for object-oriented design.

5. Design Case Study

Let us apply the object-oriented method to one more problem, adapted from the study of Boehm-Davis [15].

There exists a collection of free-floating buoys that provide navigation and weather data to air and ship traffic at sea. The buoys collect air and water temperature, wind speed, and location data through a variety of sensors. Each buoy may have a different number of wind and temperature sensors and may be modified to support other types of sensors in the future. Each buoy is also equipped with a radio transmitter (to broadcast weather and location information as well as an SOS message) and a radio receiver (to receive requests from passing vessels). Some buoys are equipped with a red light, which may be activated by a passing vessel during sea-search operations. If a sailor is able to reach the buoy, he or she may flip a switch on the side of the buoy to initiate an SOS broadcast. Software for each buoy must:

- maintain current wind, temperature, and location information; wind speed readings are taken every 30 seconds, temperature readings every 10 seconds and location every 10 seconds; wind and temperature values are kept as a running average.
- broadcast current wind, temperature, and location information every 60 seconds.
- broadcast wind, temperature, and location information from the past 24 hours in response to requests from passing vessels; this takes priority over the periodic broadcast.
- activate or deactivate the red light based upon a request from a passing vessel.
- continuously broadcast an SOS signal after a sailor engages the emergency switch; this signal takes priority over all other broadcasts and continues until reset by a passing vessel.

To formalize our model of reality, we begin by devising a data flow diagram for this system, as illustrated in Figure 8. The design proceeds by first identifying

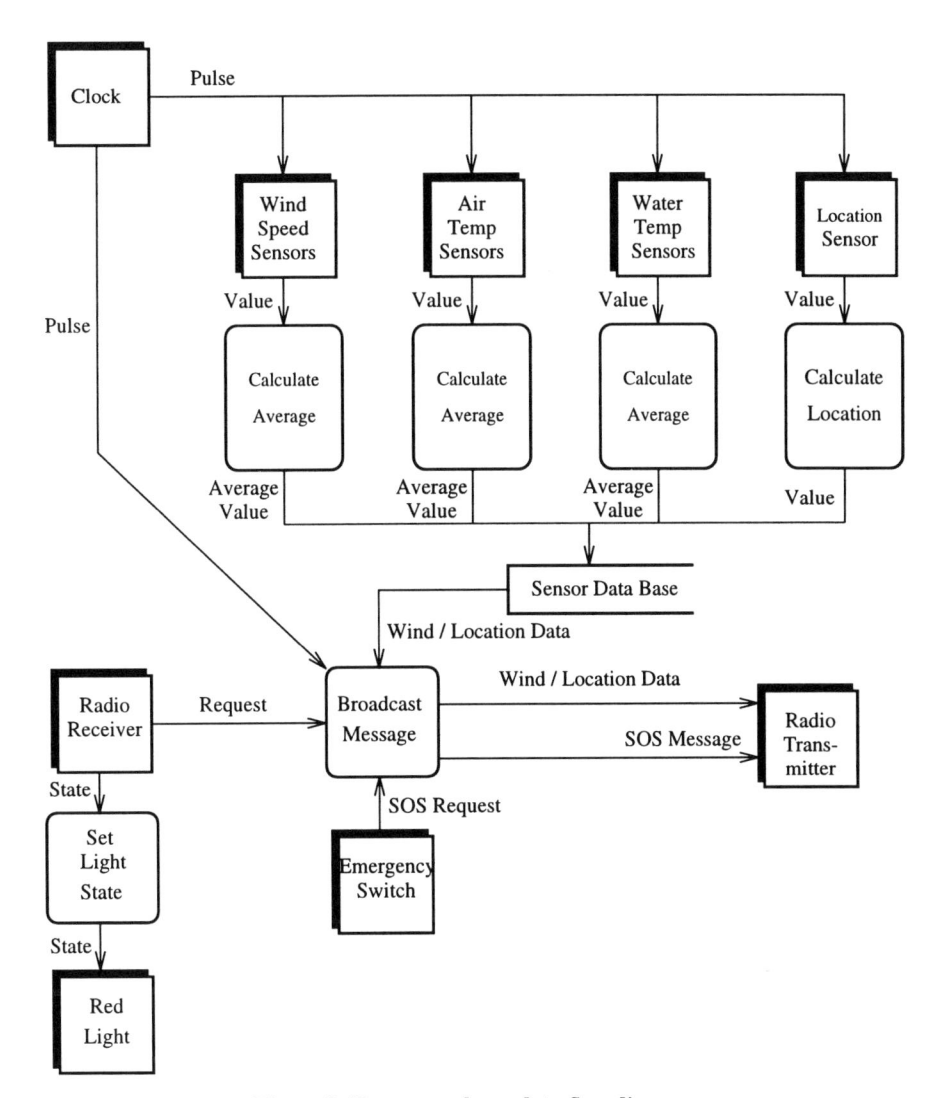

Figure 8. Host at sea buoy data flow diagram.

the object and their attributes. Drawing from this level of the data flow diagram, we include all sources and destinations of data as well as all data stores. In general, data flows have a transitory state; we will typically not treat them as objects, but rather just as instances of a simple type. Additionally, wherever there is a major process that transforms a data flow, we will allocate that process to an object that serves as the agent for that action. Thus, our objects of interest at this level of decomposition include the following:

– Clock	Provides the stimulus for periodic actions.
– Wind Speed Sensors	Maintains a running average of wind speed.
– Air Temperature Sensors	Maintains a running average of air temperature.
– Water Temperature Sensors	Maintains a running average of water temperature.
– Location Sensor	Maintains the current buoy location.
– Sensor Database	Serves to store weather and location history.
– Radio Receiver	Provides a channel for requests from passing vessels.
– Radio Transmitter	Provides a channel for broadcast of weather and location reports as well as SOS messages.
– Emergency Switch	Provides the stimulus for the SOS signal.
– Red Light	Controls the activity of the emergency light.
– Message Switch	Serves to generate and arbitrate various broadcast messages.

Next, we consider the operations suffered by and required of each object. We will take a first cut by simply listing the operations that characterize fundamental behavior. First, we identify the operations suffered by each object from within the system; these operations roughly parallel the state change caused by a data flow into an object:

– Clock	None
– Wind Speed Sensors	Take Sample
– Air Temperature Sensors	Take Sample
– Water Temperature Sensors	Take Sample
– Location Sensor	Take Sample
– Sensor Database	Put Value Get Value
– Radio Receiver	None

– Radio Transmitter	Broadcast Weather/ Location Report
	Broadcast SOS
– Emergency Switch	None
– Red Light	Set State
– Message Switch	Request History Report
	Request Periodic Report
	Request SOS

Notice that for the Sensor Database, we have the operation Get Value which seems to go against the data flow implied by all other operations. In practice, we will encounter some objects that are passive in nature, especially those that denote data stores. Whereas Get Value does not change the state of the object, it returns a value of the state of the object. Since a passive object such as the Sensor Database cannot know when a value is needed, we must supply this operation to permit the state to be retrieved by another object.

Second, we must identify the operations required of each object; these operations roughly parallel the action of a data flow from an object:

– Clock	Force Sample
	Force Periodic Report
– Wind Speed Sensors	Put Value
– Air Temperature Sensors	Put Value
– Water Temperature Sensors	Put Value
– Location Sensor	Put Value
– Sensor Database	None
– Radio Receiver	Force History Report
	Set Light State
– Radio Transmitter	None
– Emergency Switch	Force SOS
– Red Light	None
– Message Switch	Send Weather/Location Report
	Send SOS

Notice that we have a balance between the operations suffered by and required of all objects. For each operation suffered by an object, we have some other object or set of objects that requires that action.

This analysis leads us directly to the next two steps, establishing the visibility of each object in relation to other objects and its interface. Using the symbols we introduced earlier, we may start by indicating the dependencies among objects, as

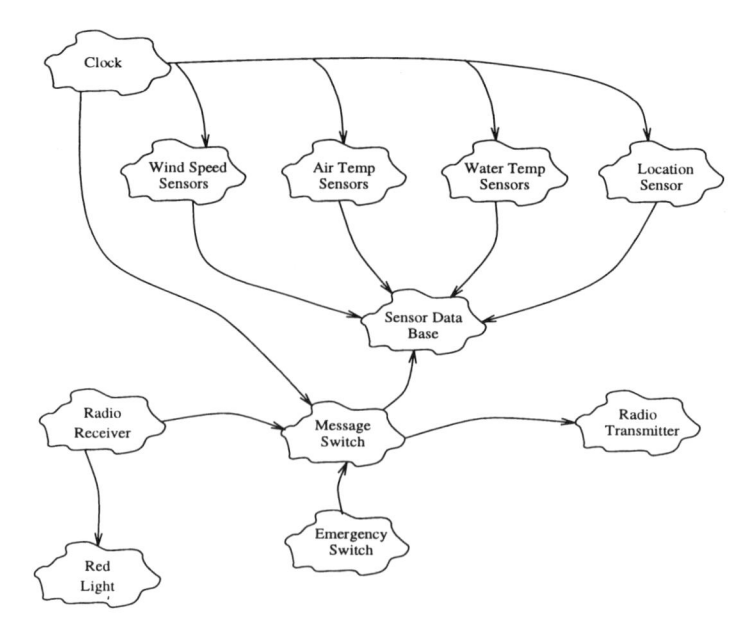

Figure 9. Host at sea buoy objects.

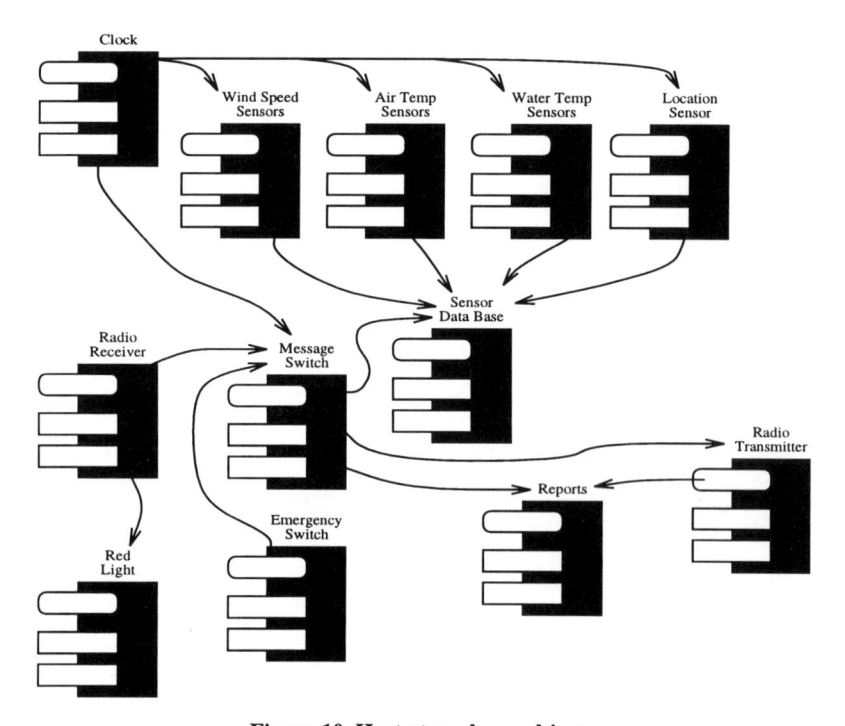

Figure 10. Host at sea buoy objects.

denoted in Figure 9. In general, the dependencies follow the direction of the operations required of each object.

In the previous section, we noted the correspondence between Ada units and objects. Hence, we may transform the design in Figure 9 to an Ada representation. This transformation is simple: we denote each object or class of objects as a package, and for all but the most primitive data flows, we also provide a package that exports the type of the data flow, made visible to both the source and the destination of the flow. Figure 10 illustrates this design after the transformation. Notice that there is a one-to-one correspondence between the objects in Figure 9 with the packages in Figure 10. We have only introduced one new package, Reports, which provides types that denote messages broadcast from the system.

Continuing our object-oriented development, we would next write the Ada specification for every package and then implement each unit. For example, we might write the specification of the Air Temperature Sensors as:

generic
type Value **is digits** < >;
with procedure Put_Value (The_Value: **in** Value);
package Air_Temperature_Sensors **is**

type Sensor **is limited private**;

procedure Take_Sample (The_Sensor: **in out** Sensor);

private
type Sensor **is** ...
end Air_Temperature_Sensors;

In this package, we export a limited private type (so as to provide a class of sensors) as well as one operation (Take_Sample). We also import one operation (Put_Value), that each sensor requires of the Sensor Database.

There are some interesting generalities we can draw from the design in Figure 10. Notice that each package that denotes a sensor has the same set of dependencies and roughly the same set of operations that characterize its behavior. Therefore, it would be possible for us to factor out the similarities among these objects, produce one generic Sensor package and then treat each sensor object as an instance of this component. Furthermore, if we already have a simple data base package, we might adapt it to provide the Sensor Database instead of creating a new one for this application. Finally, if we are careful, we could write the Radio Transmitter and the Radio Receiver packages such that they could be applied in other problems that use similar equipment.

In all these cases, we have identified the need for a reusable software component. Indeed, we find that there is a basic relationship between reusable software components and object-oriented development:

Reusable software components tend to be objects or classes of objects.

Given a rich set of reusable software components, our implementation would thus proceed via *composition* of these parts, rather than further *decomposition*.

6. Conclusion

We must remember that object-oriented development requires certain facilities of the implementation language. In particular, we must have some mechanism to build new classes of objects (and ideally, a typing mechanism that serves to enforce our abstractions). It is also the case that object-oriented development is only a partial-lifecycle method and so must be coupled with compatible requirements and specification methods. We believe that object-oriented development is amenable to automated support; further research is necessary to consider the nature of such tools.

Perhaps the greatest strength of an object-oriented approach to development is that it offers a mechanism that captures a model of the real world. This leads to improved maintainability and understandability of systems whose complexity exceeds the intellectual capacity of a single developer or a team of developers.

References

1. T. Rentsch, "Object-oriented programming." *SIGPLAN Notices*, vol. 17, no. 9, p. 51, Sept. 1982.
2. J. Guttag, E, Horowitz, and D. Musser, *The Design of Data Type Specification* (Current Trends in Programming Methodology, Vol. 4). Englewood Cliffs, NJ: Prentice Hall, 1978, p. 200.
3. Adapted from an exercise provided by P. Ward at the Rocky Mountain Institute for Software Engineering, Aspen, CO, 1984.
4. C. Gane and T. Sarson, *Structured Systems Analysis: Tools and Techniques*. Englewood Cliffs, NJ: Prentice Hall, 1979.
5. E. Yourdon and L. Constantine, *Structured Design*. Englewood Cliffs, NJ: Prentice Hall, 1979.
6. H. Levy, *Capability-Based Computer Systems*, Badford, MA: Digital Press, 1984, p. 13.
7. G. Curry and R. Ayers, "Experience with traits in the Xerox Star workstation," in *Proc. Workshop Reusability in Program.*, ITT Programming, Stratford, CT, 1983, p. 83.
8. M. Shaw, "Abstraction techniques in modern programming languages," *IEEE Software*, vol. 1, no. 4, p. 10, Oct. 1984.
9. D. L. Parnas, "On the criteria to be used in decomposing systems into modules," *Commun. ACM*, Dec. 1972.
10. R. Abbott, "Report on teaching Ada," Science Applications, Inc., Rep. SAI-81-312WA, Dec. 1980.
11. —, "Program design by informal English descriptions," *Commun. ACM*, vol. 26, no. 11, p. 884, Nov. 1983.
12. M. Jackson, *System Development*. Englewood Cliffs, NJ: Prentice Hall, 1983.
13. M. Alford, "SREM at the age of eight: The distributed computing design system," *Computer*, vol. 18, no. 4, Apr. 1985.

14. G. Buzzard and T. Mudge, "Object-based computing and the Ada programming language," *Computer*, vol. 18, no. 3, p. 12, 1985.
15. D. Boehm-Davis and L. Ross, "Approaches to structuring the software development process," General Elec. Co., Rep. GEC/DIS/TR84-B1V-1, Oct. 1984, p. 13.
16. B. Meyer, "Towards a two-dimensional programming environment," in *Readings in Artificial Intelligence*. Palo Alto, CA: Tioga, 1981, p. 178.
17. A. Borgida, S. Greenspan and J. Mylopoulos, "Knowledge representation as the basis for requirements specification," *Computer*, vol. 18, no. 4, p. 85, Apr. 1985.
18. D. Boehm-Davis and L. Ross, "Approaches to structuring the software development process," General Elec. Co., Rep. GEC/DIS/TR-84-B1V-1, Oct. 1984, p. 14.
19. B. MacLennan, "Values and objects in programming languages," *SIGPLAN Notices*, vol. 17, no. 12, p. 75, Dec. 1982.
20. H. Levy, *Capability-Based Computer Systems*. Bedford, MA: Digital Press, 1984, p. 13.
21. B. Liskov, "A design method for reliable software systems," in *Proc. Fall Joint Comput. Conf.*, AFIPS, 1972, p. 67.
22. B. Liskov, and S. Zilles, "Specification techniques for data abstractions," *IEEE Trans. Software Eng.*, vol. SE-1, Mar. 1975.
23. J. Guttage, E. Horowitz, and D. Musser, *The Design of Data Type Specification* (Current Trends in Programming Methodology, Vol. 4). Englewood Cliffs, NJ: Prentice Hall, 1978.
24. M. Shaw, "Abstraction techniques in modern programming languages," *IEEE Software*, vol. 1, no. 4, Oct. 1984.
25. A. Abelson, G. Sussman, and J. Sussman, *Structure and Interpretation of Computer Programs*. Cambridge, MA: M.I.T. Press, 1985.
26. B. Cox, "Message/object programming: An evolutionary change in programming technology," *IEEE Software*, vol. 1, no. 1, Jan. 1984.
27. "A symposium on actor languages," *Creative Comput.*, Oct. 1980.
28. G. Myers, *Advances in Computer Architecture*. New York: Wiley, 1982.
29. H. Deitel, *An Introduction to Operating Systems*. Reading, MA: Addison-Wesley, 1983, p. 456.
30. B. Liskov and S. Zilles, *An Introduction to Formal Specifications of Data Abstractions* (Current Trends in Programming Methodology, Vol. 1). Englewood Cliffs, NJ: Prentice Hall, 1977, p. 19.
31. M. Shaw, W. Wulf, and R. London, "Abstraction and verification in Alphard: Iteration and generators," in *Alphard: Form and Content*. New York: Springer-Verlag, 1981.
32. B. Liskov, R. Atkinson, T. Bloom, E. Moss, J. Schaffert, R. Schiefler, and A. Snyder, *CLU Reference Manual*. New York: Springer-Verlag, 1981, p. 8.
33. E. G. Booch, "Describing software design in Ada," *SIGPLAN Notices*, Sept. 1981.

Object-Oriented and Conventional Analysis and Design Methodologies

Comparison and Critique

Robert G. Fichman and Chris F. Kemerer

Summary.

The question of whether emerging object-oriented analysis and design methodologies require incremental or radical changes on the part of prospective adopters is being vigorously debated.

Although the concepts underlying object-orientation as a programming discipline go back two decades, it's only in the last few years that object-oriented analysis (OOA) and object-oriented design (OOD) methodologies have begun to emerge. Object orientation certainly encompasses many novel concepts, and some have called it a new paradigm for software development. Yet, the question of whether object-oriented methodologies represents a radical change over such conventional methodologies as structured analysis remains a subject of much debate.

Yourdon has divided various object-oriented methodologists into two camps, *revolutionaries and synthesists* [1]. Revolutionaries believe that object orientation is a radical change that renders conventional methodologies and ways of thinking about design obsolete. Synthesists, by contrast, see object orientation as simply an accumulation of sound software engineering principles that adopters can graft onto their existing methodologies with relative ease. On the side of the revolutionaries, Booch [2] states

Let there be no doubt that object-oriented design is fundamentally different from traditional structured design approaches: it requires a different way of thinking about decomposition, and it produces software architectures that are largely outside the realm of the structured design culture.

Coad and Yourdon [3] add

We have no doubt that one could arrive at the same results [as Coad and Yourdon's OOA methodology produces] using different methods; but it has also been our experience that the thinking process, the discovery process, and the communication between user and analyst are fundamentally different with OOA than with structured analysis.

On the side of the synthesists, Wasserman, Pircher, and Muller [4] take the position that their object-oriented structured design (OOSD) methodology is essentially an elaboration of structured design. They state that the "foundation of OOSD is structured design" and that structured design "includes most of the necessary concepts and notations" for OOSD. Page-Jones and Weiss [5] take a similar position in stating that

The problem is that object orientation has been widely touted as a revolutionary approach, a complete break with the past. This would be fascinating if it were true, but it isn't. Like most engineering developments, the object-oriented approach is a refinement of some of the best software engineering ideas of the past.

Factors to consider. One of the most important assessments a company must make in considering the adoption of a technical innovation is where the innovation falls on the incremental-radical continuum in relation to its own current practice. Incremental innovations introduce relatively minor changes to an existing process or product and reinforce the established competencies of adopting firms. Radical innovations are based on a different set of engineering and scientific principles, and draw on new technical and problem-solving skills.

If object-oriented analysis and design comes to be regarded as a radical change by most organizations, then a strong, negative impact on the ultimate rate of adoption of the technology can be expected. Compared with incremental change, implementation of radical change involves greater expense and risk, and requires different management strategies. Many development groups have already invested considerable resources in conventional methodologies like structured analysis/structured design or information engineering. These investments can take many forms, including training in the specifics of the methodology, acquisition of automated tools to support the methodology, and repositories of analysis and design models accumulated over the course of employing the methodology.

On an industry-wide level, vendors have been actively developing more powerful tools to support conventional methodologies, and a growing pool of expertise now exists in the use of these tools. To the extent that object orientation is a radical change, investments in conventional methodologies will be lost: Staff will have to be retrained, new tools will have to be purchased, and a likely expensive conversion process will be necessary.

Implementation of radically new technologies also involves a much greater element of risk because the full range of impacts is typically unknown. Moreover, the implementation of a radically new methodology requires different strategies to manage this risk and to overcome other implementation barriers (such as resistance to change).

The radical-versus-incremental debate is crucial to assessing the future of object orientation and formulating a transition strategy, but unfortunately no comprehensive analyses have been performed comparing leading object-oriented methodologies with conventional methodologies. Two surveys of object-oriented methodologies have been compiled, but these only cover either analysis [6] or design [7], and neither draws specific comparisons with conventional methodologies. Loy [8] provides an insightful commentary on the issue of conventional versus object-oriented methodologies, although no specific methodologies are compared.

The current research fills the gap left by other surveys by analyzing several leading conventional and object-oriented analysis and design methodologies, including a detailed point-by-point comparison of the kinds of modeling tools provided by each. A review (described below in greater detail) was performed that resulted in the selection of six analysis methodologies and five design methodologies. The analysis methodologies were

- DeMarco structured analysis,
- Yourdon modern structured analysis,
- Martin information engineering analysis,
- Bailin object-oriented requirements specification,
- Coad and Yourdon object-oriented analysis, and
- Shlaer and Mellor object-oriented analysis.

The design methodologies were

- Yourdon and Constantine structured design,
- Martin information engineering design,
- Wasserman et al. object-oriented structured design,
- Booch object-oriented design, and
- Wirfs-Brock et al. responsibility-driven design.

Incremental or radical? We conclude that the object-oriented analysis methodologies reviewed here represent a radical change over process-oriented methodologies such as DeMarco structured analysis but only an incremental change over data-oriented methodologies such as Martin information engineering. Process-oriented methodologies focus attention away from the inherent properties of objects during the modeling process and lead to a model of the problem domain that is orthogonal to the three essential principles of object orientation: encapsulation, classification of objects, and inheritance.

By contrast, data-oriented methodologies rely heavily on the same basic technique – information modeling – as each of the three OOA methodologies. The main differences between OOA and data-oriented conventional methodologies arise from the principle of encapsulation of data and behavior: OOA methodologies require that all operations be encapsulated within objects, while conventional methodologies permit operations to exist as subcomponents of disembodied processes. At the level of detail required during analysis, however, we conclude that expert information modelers will be able to learn and apply the principle of encapsulation without great difficulty.

Regarding design methodologies, we conclude that object-oriented design is a radical change from *both* process-oriented and data-oriented methodologies. The OOD methodologies we review here collectively model several important dimensions of a target system not addressed by conventional methodologies. These dimensions relate to the *detailed* definition of classes and inheritance, class and object relationships, encapsulated operations, and message connections. The need for adopters to acquire new competencies related to these dimensions, combined with Booch's uncontested observation that OOD uses a completely different structuring principle (based on object-oriented rather than function-oriented decomposition of system components), renders OOD as a radical change.

Conventional Methodologies

A systems development methodology combines tools and techniques to guide the process of developing large-scale information systems. The evolution of modern methodologies began in the late 1960s with the development of the concept of a systems development life cycle (SDLC). Dramatic increases in hardware performance and the adoption of high-level languages had enabled much larger and more complicated systems to be built. The SDLC attempted to bring order to the development process, which had outgrown the ad hoc project control methods of the day, by decomposing the process into discrete project phases with "frozen" deliverables – formal documents – that served as the input to the next phase.

Structured methodologies. The systems development life cycle concept gave developers a measure of control, but provided little help in improving the productivity and quality of analysis and design per se. Beginning in the 1970s, structured methodologies were developed to promote more effective analysis and more stable and maintainable designs. Early structured methodologies were largely *process-oriented*, with only a minor emphasis on modeling of entities and data. This emphasis on processes seemed natural, given the procedural programming languages and batch, file-based applications commonplace at the time. Although many authors contributed to the so-called structured revolution, our review concentrates on the critical contributions of Yourdon and Constantine [9], DeMarco [10], and Ward and Mellor [11].

Yourdon and Constantine structured design provided a method for developing a system architecture that conformed to the software engineering principles of modularity, loosely coupled modules, and module cohesion. The structure chart (see the box, "Tools for structured methodologies") was the primary tool for modeling a system design. (Although the emphasis of structured design was on creating a module architecture, the methodology also suggested dataflow diagrams for modeling processes and hierarchy diagrams for defining data structure.)

Tools for structured methodologies

Dataflow diagram (DFD) – Depicts processes (shown as bubbles) and the flow of data between them (shown as directed arcs). DFDs are usually organized into a hierarchy of nested diagrams, where a bubble on one diagram maps to an entire diagram at the next lower level of detail. Does not depict conditional logic or flow of control between modules.

Data-dictionary – A repository of definitions for data elements, files, and processes. A precursor to the more comprehensive "encyclopedias."

Entity-relationship diagram (ERD) – Depicts real-world entities (people, places, things, concepts) and the relationships between them. Various notations are used, but usually entities are portrayed as boxes and relationships as arcs, with different terminating symbols on the arcs to depict cardinality and whether the relationship is mandatory or optional.

Hierarchy diagram – A simple diagram that shows a top-to-bottom hierarchical decomposition of data files and data items (enclosed within boxes) connected by undirected arcs.

Mini-spec – A structured-English specification of the detailed procedural logic within a process; performs the same function as the traditional flow chart. A mini-spec is developed for each process at the lowest level of nesting in a set of DFDs.

State-transition diagram – Depicts the different possible states of a system or system component, and the events or messages that cause transitions between the states.

Structure chart – Depicts the architecture of a system as a hierarchy of functions (boxes) arranged in a tree-like structure. Identifies interconnections between functions, and input and output parameters. Does not depict control structures like condition, sequence, iteration, or selection.

DeMarco's seminal work enlarged the structured approach to encompass analysis. DeMarco prescribed a series of steps for performing structured analysis, flowing from modeling of existing systems (using dataflow diagrams) to modeling of the system to be developed (using dataflow diagrams, mini-specifications, and a data dictionary). Although modeling of data was not ignored, the emphasis was on modeling processes. The ultimate goal of structured analysis and design was to create a top-down decomposition of the functions to be performed by the target system.

Continuing in the structured tradition, Ward and Mellor recommended significant extensions to structured analysis to better support modeling of real-time systems. Their methodology added entity-relationship diagrams and state-transition diagrams to the structured analysis toolset. Entity-relationship diagrams illustrate the structure of entities and their interrelationships, while state-transition diagrams focus on system and subsystem states and the events that caused transitions between states.

In recognition of the evolution of systems, languages, and tools over the past two decades, Yourdon [12] updated structured analysis under the name *modern structured analysis*. Modern structured analysis differs from DeMarco's original work in several respects: It no longer recommends modeling of current implemented systems; it adds a preliminary phase to develop an "essential model" of the system; it substitutes a technique known as "event partitioning" for top-down functional decomposition as the preferred technique for constructing dataflow diagrams; it places more emphasis on information modeling (via entity-relationship diagrams) and behavior modeling (via state-transition diagrams); and it encourages prototyping.

These updates have served to blur somewhat the one-time clear distinctions between structured methods and the data-oriented methods that we describe next.

Information engineering. In the late 1970s and early 1980s, planning and modeling of data began to take on a more central role in systems development, culminating in the development of data-oriented methodologies such as information engineering. The conceptual roots of data-oriented methodologies go back to the 1970s with the invention of the relational database model and entity-relationship modeling, although it took several years for mature data-oriented methodologies to emerge.

The data-oriented approach has two central assumptions:

(1) Organizational data provides a more stable foundation for a system design than organizational procedures.
(2) Data should be viewed as an organizational resource independent of the systems that (currently) process the data.

One outgrowth of the data-oriented approach was the creation of a new information systems subfunction, data administration, to help analyze, define, store, and control organizational data.

Martin [13] information engineering is a comprehensive methodology that extends the data-oriented approach across the entire development life cycle. While structured methods evolved backwards through the life cycle from programming, information engineering evolved forward through the life cycle from planning and analysis. Martin defines information engineering as consisting of four phases:

(1) Information strategy planning,
(2) Business area analysis,
(3) System design, and

(4) Construction.

Information engineering distinguishes activities that are performed on the level of a business unit (planning and analysis) from those that are project-specific (design and construction). Compared with structured methods, information engineering recommends a much broader range of analysis techniques and modeling tools, including enterprise modeling, critical-success-factors analysis, data modeling, process modeling, joint-requirements planning, joint-applications design, time-box methodology, and prototyping (see the box, "Tools for Martin information engineering").

Information engineering describes planning as an organization-wide activity that develops an enterprise model and a high-level data architecture. Business area analysis attempts to capture a more detailed understanding of business activities and their interdependencies, using such tools as data-model diagrams, decomposition diagrams, process-dependency diagrams, and entity process matrices. The design phase builds on the results of prior phases and produces a detailed model of a target system consisting of process-decomposition diagrams, process-dependency diagrams, dataflow diagrams action diagrams, and data-structure diagrams. System construction, the last phase of information engineering, consists of translating the models from the design phase to an operational system – ideally using a code generator.

Object-Oriented Analysis Methodologies

As with traditional analysis, the primary goal of object-oriented analysis is the development of an accurate and complete representation of the problem domain. We conducted a literature search to identify, well-documented, broadly representative OOA methodologies first published in book form or as detailed articles in refereed journals from 1980 to 1990. This search resulted in the selection of three methodologies from Coad and Yourdon [3], Bailin [14], and Shlaer and Mellor [15,16]. Numerous OOA methodologies have emerged in recent years. Since no more than a few methodologies could be compared in depth, two criteria – maturity (first published prior to 1990) and form of publication (book or refereed journal) – were used to select among them. Several methodologies were identified that did not meet these criteria (see Fichman and Kemerer 17) although this should not be taken to mean they are inferior to those that did. Object-oriented analysis is, of course, quite young; it is much too early to predict which (if any) of the current methodologies will come to be recognized as standard works in the field. The goal here is to provide a detailed comparison of representative methodologies at a single point in time, not a comprehensive review.

The three methodologies are presented in the order of their similarity to conventional methodologies. Bailin's methodology is viewed as most similar, followed by Coad and Yourdon's, and then Shlaer and Mellor's.

Tools for Martin information engineering

Action diagram – Used to depict detailed procedural logic at a given level of detail (for example, at a system level or within individual modules). Similar to structured English, except graphical constructs are used to highlight various control structures (condition, sequence, iteration, and selection).

Bubble chart – A low-level diagram used as an aide to normalization of relational tables. Shows attributes (depicted as bubbles) and the functional dependencies between them (depicted as directed arcs).

Dataflow diagram (DFD) – Conforms to the conventional notation and usage for dataflow diagrams (see the box, "Tools for structured methodologies").

Data-model diagram – Depicts data entities (boxes) and their relational connections (lines). Shows cardinality and whether the connections are optional or mandatory. Similar to the entity-relationship diagram.

Data-structure diagram – Shows data structures in a format appropriate to the database management system to be used for implementation.

Encyclopedia – A more comprehensive version of the data dictionary that serves as an integrated repository for modeling information from all development phases, including the enterprise model; organizational goals, critical success factors, strategies, and rules; data models and data definitions; process models and process definitions; and other design-related information. Automated support is assumed.

Enterprise model – A model that defines, at a high level, the functional areas of an organization and the relationships between them. It consists of text descriptions of functions (usually an identifiable business unit such as a department) and processes (a repetitive, well-defined set of tasks that support a function).

Entity-process matrix – Cross-references entities to the processes that use them.

Process-decomposition diagram – A hierarchical chart that shows the breakdown of processes into progressively increasing detail. Similar to the conventional tree diagram, except a particularly compact notation is used to fit many levels on one page.

Process-dependency diagram – A diagram consisting of processes (depicted by bubbles) and labeled arcs. It shows how each process depends on the prior execution of other processes. Similar to a dataflow diagram, except conditional logic and flow of control is also depicted.

State-transition diagram – Conforms to the conventional notation and usage for state-transition diagrams (see the box, "Tools for structured methodologies").

Bailin object-oriented requirements specification. Bailin developed object-oriented requirements specification (OOS) in response to a perceived incompatibility between conventional structured analysis and object-oriented design. Outwardly, the method resembles structured analysis in that a system decomposition is performed using a dataflow diagram-like notation. Yet, there is an important difference: Structured analysis specifies that functions should be grouped together only if they are "constituent steps in the execution of a higher level function," while OOS groups functions together only if they "operate on the same data abstraction" [14]. In other words, functions cannot exist as part of disembodied processes, but must be subordinated to a single entity. (Bailin uses the term entity rather than object for stylistic reasons only; the terms are assumed to be interchangeable.) This restriction is used to promote encapsulation of functions and data.

Two distinctions are central to OOS. First, Bailin distinguishes between *entities*, which possess underlying states that can persist across repeated execution cycles, and *functions*, which exist solely to transform inputs to outputs and thus have no underlying states remembered between cycles. Entities can be further decomposed into subentities or functions, but functions can only be decomposed into subfunctions.

Second, Bailin distinguishes between two classes of entities, *active* and *passive*. Active entities perform operations (on themselves or other entities) important enough to be considered in detail during the analysis phase, while passive entities are of lesser importance and can therefore be treated as a "black box" until the design phase. These distinctions are important because, as we show below, active entities, passive entities, and functions are each modeled differently during the analysis process.

The OOS methodology consists of a seven-step procedure:

(1) *Identify key problem domain entities.* Draw dataflow diagrams and then designate objects that appear in process names as candidate entities.
(2) *Distinguish between active and passive entities.* Distinguish between entities whose operations are significant in terms of describing system requirements (active entities) versus those whose detailed operations can be deferred until design (passive). Construct an entity-relationship diagram (ERD).
(3) *Establish dataflows between active entities.* Construct the top-level (level 0) entity-dataflow diagram (EDFD). Designate each active entity as a process node and each passive entity as a dataflow or data store.
(4) *Decompose entities (or functions) into subentities and/or functions.* This step is performed iteratively together with steps 5 and 6. Consider each active entity in the top-level EDFD and determine whether it is composed of lower level entities. Also consider what each entity does and designate these operations as functions. For each of the subentities identified, create a new EDFD and continue the decomposition process.
(5) *Check for new entities.* At each stage of decomposition, consider whether any new entities are implied by the new functions that have been introduced and add them to the appropriate EDFD, reorganizing EDFDs as necessary.

(6) *Group functions under new entities.* Identify all the functions performed by or on new entities. Change passive to active entities if necessary and reorganize EDFDs as appropriate.
(7) *Assign entities to appropriate domains.* Assign each entity to some application domain, and create a set of ERDs, one for each domain.

The end result of OOS is an entity relationship diagram, together with a hierarchy of entity-dataflow diagrams (see the box "Tools for Bailin object-oriented requirements specification"). Bailin's methodology conforms to the essential principals of object orientation, although explicit object-oriented terminology is not used. (Loy [8] lists three principles that distinguish object orientation from other approaches: encapsulation of attributes, operations, and services within objects; classification of object abstractions; and inheritance of common attributes between classes.) The entity-relationship diagrams capture a classification of objects as well as opportunities for inheritance, and Bailin's functions map to the object-oriented concept of encapsulated services.

Coad and Yourdon object-oriented analysis. Coad and Yourdon [3] view their OOA methodology as building "upon the best concepts from information modeling, object-oriented programming languages, and knowledge-based systems." OOA results in a five-layer model of the problem domain, where each layer builds on the previous layers. The layered model is constructed using a five-step procedure:

(1) *Define objects and classes.* Look for structures, other systems, devices, events, roles, operational procedures, sites, and organizational units.
(2) *Define structures.* Look for relationships between classes and represent them as either general-to-specific structures (for example, employee-to-sales manager) or whole-to-part structures (for example, car-to-engine).
(3) *Define subject areas.* Examine top level objects within whole-to-part hierarchies and mark these as candidate subject areas. Refine subject areas to minimize interdependencies between subjects.
(4) *Define attributes.* Identify the atomic characteristics of objects as attributes of the object. Also look for associative relationships between objects and determine the cardinality of those relationships.
(5) *Define services.* For each class and object, identify all the services it performs, either on its own behalf or for the benefit of other classes and objects.

The primary tools for Coad and Yourdon OOA are class and object diagrams and service charts (see the box, "Tools for Coad and Yourdon object-oriented analysis"). The class and object diagram has five levels, which are built incrementally during each of the five analysis steps outlined above. Service charts, which are "much like a [traditional] flow chart," are used during the service definition phase to represent the internal logic of services." In addition, service charts portray state-dependent behavior such as preconditions and triggers (operations that are activated by the occurrence of a predefined event).

Coad and Yourdon explicitly support each of the essential principles of object orientation. The class and objects diagram (levels 1, 2, and 4) provides an object classification and identifies potential inheritance relationships. In addition, encapsulation of objects is modeled through the concept of exclusive services. Coad and Yourdon OOA is similar to modern structured analysis (MSA) and information engineering in its emphasis on information modeling, but differs in providing constructs for modeling exclusive services and message connections.

Tools for Bailin object-oriented requirements specification

Entity-relationship diagram – Conforms to the conventional notation and usage for entity-relationship diagrams (see the box "Tools for structured methodologies").

Entity-dataflow diagram (EDFD) – A variant on the conventional dataflow diagram wherein each process node contains either an active entity or some function related to an active entity, rather than disembodied processes. Active entities and functions are enclosed within bubbles. Bubbles are connected to each other and to data stores by labeled arcs containing dataflows. Dataflows and data stores are passive entities.

Entity dictionary – A repository of entity names and descriptions, analogous to the data dictionary of DeMarco structured analysis.

Shlaer and Mellor object-oriented analysis. Shlaer and Mellor developed their object-oriented analysis methodology over the course of several years of consulting practice in information modeling. Although information modeling forms the foundation of the method, two other views of the target system are prescribed as well: a state model and a process model. This three-way view of the system, contained in interrelated information, state, and process models, is proposed as a complete description of the problem domain. Shlaer and Mellor advocate a six-step procedure:

(1) *Develop an information model.* This model consists of objects, attributes, relationships, and multiple-object constructions (based on is-a, is-part-of, and associative relationships). (The term object, as used by Shlaer and Mellor, is equivalent to the conventional notion of an entity, that is, a person, place, thing, or event that exists in the real world.)

(2) *Define object life cycles.* The focus here is on analyzing the life cycle of each object (from creation through destruction) and formalizing the life cycle into a collection of states (some predefined condition of an object), events (signals that cause transitions from state to state), transition rules (which specify the allowable transitions between states), and actions (activities or operations that must be done by an object upon arrival in a state). This step also defines *timers*, mechanisms used by actions to generate a future event. The primary tool during this step is the state model (See the box, "Tools for Shlaer and Mellor object-oriented analysis.")

> **Tools for Coad and Yourdon object-oriented analysis**
>
> *Class and object diagram* – A complex diagram consisting of five layers, each adding a level of detail. The layers are (1) class and object layer, which shows classes and objects enclosed within boxes with rounded corners, (2) structures layer, which connects classes and objects with arcs to show generalization-specialization and whole-part inheritance relationships, (3) subjects layer, which adds a border around closely related classes, (4) attributes layer, which adds a list of attributes inside the class and object boxes and identifies associative relationships between objects, and (5) service layer, which adds a list of services inside the class and object boxes and provides arcs showing message connections between boxes.
>
> *Object-state diagram* – A simple diagram that shows all the possible states of an object and the allowed transitions between states. States are enclosed within boxes and transitions are represented as directed, unlabeled arcs between states.
>
> *Service chart* – A flowchart-like diagram that depicts the detailed logic within an individual service, including object-state changes that trigger or result from the service.

(3) *Define the dynamics of relationships.* This step develops a state model for those relationships between objects that evolve over time (dynamic relationships). For each dynamic relationship, an associative object is defined in the information model. Special assigner state models are defined for relationships in which there may be contention between object instances for resources of another object instance.

(4) *Define system dynamics.* This step produces a model of time and control at the system level. An object-communication model (OCM) is developed to show asynchronous control (akin to simple message passing). An object-access model is developed to show synchronous control (instances where one object accesses the instance data of another through an accessor process). Shlaer and Mellor also describe a procedure for tracing threads of control at a high level (by following events on the OCM) and at a more detailed level (by creating a thread-of-control chart for individual actions).

(5) *Develop process models.* For each action, an action-dataflow diagram is created that shows all of the processes for that action, and the data flows among the processes and data stores. (Standard DeMarco notation for DFDs is used, except additional notations are provided to show control flows and to show conditionality in the execution of dataflows and control flows.) OOA defines four types of processes (accessors, event generators, transformations, and tests) and provides guidelines for decomposing actions into these constituent processes.

(6) *Define domains and subsystems.* For large problems, it can be useful to decompose the subject matter into conceptually distinct domains. Four types of domains are identified: application, service, architectural. and implementation.

Tools for Shlaer and Mellor object-oriented analysis

Action-dataflow diagram (ADFD) – Similar to DFDs, except ADFDs are used to model elementary "action" processes rather than to create a topdown functional decomposition of the entire system. Standard DeMarco notation is used, except additional notations are provided to show control flows and to show conditionality in the execution of dataflows and control flows.

Domain chart – A simple diagram that illustrates all domains relevant to the implementation of an OOA model. Domains are enclosed within bubbles and are connected by directed arcs. These arcs represent bridges between domains. Four types of domains are identified: application, service, architectural and implementation.

Information structure diagram – A variant on the entity-relationship diagram that shows objects (boxes) connected by relationships (labeled arcs). Attributes are listed within object boxes. Relationship conditionality and multiplicity are also shown.

Object and attribute description – A text description of an object, including object name, object description, object identifier, a list of attributes, and descriptions of each attribute.

Object-access model – Shows the synchronous interactions between state models at the global system level. Synchronous interactions occur when one state model accesses the instance data of another object via an accessor process. State models (enclosed in ovals) are connected to each other by directed arcs labeled with the accessor process.

Object-communication model – Shows the asynchronous interactions between state models and external entities at the global system level. State models (enclosed in ovals) are connected to each other and to external entities (enclosed in boxes) by directed arcs labeled with communicating events.

Process description – A narrative description of a process. A process description is needed for every process appearing on an action-dataflow diagram.

Relationship specification – A text description of each relationship, including the name of the relationship (from the point of view of each object), conditionality (required or optional), multiplicity (one-to-one, one-to-many, many-to-many), a general description of the relationship, and identification of the attributes (foreign keys) through which the relationship is formalized.

State model – State models conform to the conventional notation for state-transition diagrams (see the box, "Tools for structured methodologies.), except they are used to model the states of problem domain entities. (Traditional STDs, by contrast, model the states of a system, system component, or process.)

Subsystem access model – Shows synchronous interactions between object-access models (one OAM exists for each subsystem). Directed, labeled arcs represent synchronous processes flowing between OAMs (enclosed in boxes).

Subsystem communication model – Shows asynchronous interactions between object-communication models (one OCM exists for each subsystem). Directed, labeled arcs represent asynchronous events flowing between OAMs (enclosed in boxes).

Subsystem relationship model – Shows relationships between information models (where each subsystem has exactly one information model). Information models (enclosed in boxes) are connected by undirected arcs (labeled with relationships).

In addition, it is sometimes useful to decompose the application domain into multiple subsystems.

Shlaer and Mellor provide implicit, rather than explicit, support for the three essential principles of object orientation – classification, inheritance, and encapsulation. The objects and relationships contained in the information structure diagram, while not identical to object-oriented concepts of classification and inheritance, can easily be mapped to these concepts during design. (Regular entities and parent entities engaged in is-a style relationships correspond to classes and superclasses, respectively, and identify candidate inheritance relationships. The is-part-of style relationships correspond to whole-to-part class relationships.) The requirement that each action process (and associated dataflow diagram) be associated with exactly one object preserves encapsulation of those operations.

Comparison of Analysis Methodologies

The conventional and OOA methodologies reviewed here can be compared along 11 modeling dimensions; these dimensions represent the superset of dimensions supported by the individual methodologies (see Table 1). Since the various methodologists tend to use widely divergent terminology and notations for similar concepts, Table 1 presents the dimensions at a level that captures essential similarities and differences between the methodologies. We examined the concepts and notations advocated by each methodology in detail to determine those that were variants on the same basic idea. (For example, Coad and Yourdon's concept of a generalization-specialization relationship between objects is viewed as essentially the same as the is-a style or subtype/supertype entity relationships described in the other analysis methodologies. When used as part of an OOA methodology, generalization-specialization and is-a relationships are both intended to identify candidate opportunities for inheritance.)

Object-oriented versus conventional analysis. As Table 1 shows, object-oriented analysis covers many of the same dimensions as Yourdon MSA and Martin information engineering, although there is a marked contrast between OOA and DeMarco structured analysis. MSA, information engineering, and all of the object-oriented methodologies provide a variety of tools for modeling entities. These include tools for defining entity relationships and attributes (see Table 1, rows 1 through 4) and partitioning large models by grouping naturally related entities (row 5). MSA, Coad and Yourdon OOA, and Shlaer and Mellor OOA support modeling of states (row 6), although within MSA states are modeled at the level of a system or system component, while in the OOA methodologies states are modeled at the level of problem domain entities (objects). DeMarco structured analysis, MSA, Coad and Yourdon OOA, and Shlaer and Mellor OOA provide tools for defining the detailed logic within functions or services (row 7).

	Component	DeMarco Structured Analysis	Yourdon Modern Structured Analysis	Martin Information Engineering	Bailin Object-Oriented Requirements Specification	Coad and Yourdon Object-Oriented Analysis	Shlaer and Mellor Object-Oriented Analysis
1.	Indentification/ classification of entities*	Not supported	Entity-relationship diagram	Data-model diagram	Entity-relationship diagram	Class and objects diagram layer 1	Information-structure diagram
2.	General-to-specific and whole-to-part entity-relationships	Not supported	Entity-relationship diagram	Data-model diagram	Entity-relationship diagram	Class and objects diagram layer 2	Information-structure diagram
3.	Other entity-relationship (creates, uses, etc.)	Not supported	Entity-relationship diagram	Data-model diagram	Entity-relationship diagram	Class and objects diagram layer 4	Information-structure diagram
4.	Attributes of entities	Data dictionary	Data dictionary	Bubble chart	Not supported	Class and objects diagram layer 4	Information-structure diagram
5.	Large-scale model partitioning	Dataflow diagram	Event-partitioned dataflow diagram	Subject databases	Domain-partitioned entity-relationship diagrams	Class and objects diagram layer 3	Domain chart; subsystem communication access, and relationship models
6.	States and transitions**	Not supported	State-transition diagram	Not supported	Not supported	Object-state diagram: service chart	State model
7.	Detailed logic for functions/services	Mini-specification	Mini-specification	Not supported	Not supported	Service chart	Action data-flow diagram; process descriptions
8.	Top-down decomposition of functions***	Dataflow diagram	Dataflow diagram	Process-decomposition diagram	Not supported	Not supported	Not supported
9.	End-to-end processing sequences	Dataflow diagram	Dataflow diagram	Process-dependency diagram	Not supported	Not supported	Not supported
10.	Identification of exclusive services	Not supported	Not supported	Not supported	Entity-dataflow diagram	Class and objects diagram layer 5	State model, action-data-flow diagram
11.	Entity communication (via messages or events)	Not supported	Not supported	Not supported	Entity-dataflow diagram	Class and objects diagram layer 5	Object communication model; object-access model

* For stylistic reasons, the term entity, when it appears in this column, is intended to encompass the terms entity (as used in conventional methodologies and by Bailin), object (as used by Shlaer and Mellor), and class (as used by Coad and Yourdon).
** Conventional STDs as used in Yourdon's MSA describe the states of a system or system component, whereas Shlaer and Mellor's state model and Coad and Yourdon's object-state diagram describe the states of problem domain entities. STDs are not an integral part of information engineering because they are thought to be too detailed for the analysis phase, although Martin allows that they may be used occasionally.
*** Bailin does provide some support for decomposition of functions via entity-dataflow diagrams, but functions are decomposed only at the lowest levels of the diagram rather than at all levels.

Table 1. Comparison of analysis methodologies.

The most important differences between object-oriented and conventional analysis methodologies ultimately stem from the object-oriented requirement of encapsulated operations. Conventional methodologies provide tools to create a functional decomposition of operations (row 8) and to model end-to-end processing sequences (row 9). A functional decomposition of systems violates encapsulation because operations can directly access a multitude of different entities and are not subordinated to any one entity; so it is appropriate that no object-oriented methodology provides support here. It is less clear why none of the OOA methodologies as reviewed here provide an explicit model of end-to-end processing sequences, since there is no inherent incompatibility between this view of a system and object orientation. This issue is discussed further in the concluding section.

All the OOA methodologists recognize a need to develop some sort of model of system operations, albeit in a way that preserves encapsulation. As a result, each methodology provides new tools, or variants on conventional tools, for modeling operations as exclusive services of objects (row 10). Row 11 illustrates a further distinction between object-oriented and conventional analysis that arises from the need in object orientation for active communication between entities. (Entities communicate explicitly in an object-oriented system, whereas in a conventional system, entities are passive data stores manipulated by active, independent procedures.)

OOA methodology similarities. The three OOA methodologies illustrated in Table 1 overlap significantly, although different notations and terminology are used for essentially the same concepts. These stylistic differences obscure the fact that, in each of the three methodologies, entities (objects) and relationships establish a foundation for later stages of analysis. Bailin uses a standard ERD notation, which includes the idea of subtype/supertype relationships, as well as any number of user-defined relationships. Shlaer and Mellor's information structure diagrams are similar in terms of content to ERDs. While neither of these methodologies specifically mentions such object-oriented notions as inheritance and object classification, ERDs do, in fact, capture candidate instances of these sorts of relationships using subtype/supertype constructs.

Dynamic entity connections and using-style relationships are also captured in ERDs through such relationship types as creates, destroys, uses, and modifies. Unlike the other two methodologies, Coad and Yourdon refer explicitly to object-oriented concepts such as inheritance and object decomposition. Nonetheless, layers 1, 2, and 4 of the class and objects diagram can easily be mapped to an ERD notation, and these three layers serve essentially the same purpose as an ERD. (The objects and classes identified in level 1 map to the ERD concept of an entity. The generalization-specialization relationships defined in level 2 correspond to subtype/supertype relationships in an ERD. The whole part structures defined in level 2 and the associative relationships identified in layer 4 correspond to general relationships in an ERD.)

OOA methodology differences. The clearest differences between the methodologies occur in three areas:

(1) depiction of entity states,

(2) definition of exclusive services, and
(3) attention to attribute modeling.

Shlaer and Mellor place the most emphasis on modeling entity states and devote an entire phase of their methodology to defining entity life cycles and depicting them in state models. Coad and Yourdon also model entity states, although this does not appear to be a significant component of the methodology. (Coed and Yourdon's service chart contains much of the same information as Shlaer and Mellor's state model, although it also contains procedural logic unrelated to entity states and transitions. Coad and Yourdon recommend the use of an object-state diagram where helpful, but this diagram does not explicitly name the events that trigger transitions. The object-state model is referred to only sparingly, and does not appear to be a significant component of the final system model.) Bailin has no formal means of depicting entity states and transitions, although he notes that state-transition diagrams are being considered as one possible extension of the method.

Coad and Yourdon and Shlaer and Mellor provide the most detailed representations of exclusive services. In Coad and Yourdon, exclusive services are assigned to objects in layer 5 of the class and objects diagram, and the procedural logic contained in each service is defined in detail in an associated service chart. Shlaer and Mellor also identify exclusive services, which they term *actions*. Actions are identified on state models (object specific) and are defined in detail in the action-dataflow diagram (ADFD) and corresponding process descriptions. The primary tool for modeling Bailin's functions – the entity-dataflow diagram – contains much less detail than Coad and Yourdon's service chart or Shlaer and Mellor's ADFD with process descriptions.

The methodologies differ substantially in their level of attention to attribute modeling. Bailin places a very low emphasis on defining attributes of entities; in fact, he makes no mention of attribute modeling at all. Coad and Yourdon devote a phase to identifying attributes, although not to the extent of ensuring that attributes are normalized within entities. Shlaer and Mellor provide the most emphasis on attribute modeling of the three methodologies, including extensive guidance for describing and normalizing attributes.

Finally, Shlaer and Mellor support some concepts not addressed by Coad and Yourdon or Bailin. These include

(1) a distinction between asynchronous and synchronous control,
(2) the use of timers to generate future events. and
(3) the concept of a dynamic relationship and its role in handling contention between concurrent processes.

OOA: Incremental versus radical change.. With regard to the incremental versus radical debate, object-oriented analysis does represent a radical departure from older process-oriented methodologies such as DeMarco structured analysis, but is only an incremental change from data-oriented methodologies like Martin information engineering. Table 1 shows that OOA methodologies typically model six dimensions of the problem domain not contained in a structured analysis model (see rows 1–3, 6, 10–11) and do not model two process-oriented dimensions (rows 8–9) that form the foundation of a DeMarco structured analysis model. OOA decomposes the problem domain based on a classification of entities (objects) and their relationships, while structured analysis provides a decomposition based on processes. Developers schooled in DeMarco structured analysis will find the competencies they developed in the construction of hierarchies of DFDs to be, for the most part, irrelevant. Meanwhile, a whole new set of competencies relating to the classification and modeling of entities will have to be developed. The revolutionaries quoted in the introduction rightly observe that object orientation is fundamentally at odds with the process-oriented view of systems favored by structured methodologies during the 1970s. However, they ignore important changes in these same methodologies over the course of the 1980s towards a more balanced view of data and processes. OOA methodologies only model two dimensions of the problem domain not modeled by Yourdon MSA or Martin information engineering (see Table 1, rows 10–11).

All the OOA methodologies reviewed here contain a heavy information modeling component, and potential adopters with a strong information modeling background should require only limited exposure to absorb the notational differences between conventional information modeling diagrams and the variants developed by OOA methodologists. The idea of shifting from disembodied processes (modeled in dataflow diagrams) to encapsulated services will be more challenging. However, at the level of detail required for analysis, this conceptual shift can probably be absorbed without great difficulty. Shlaer and Mellor OOA, with its emphasis on modeling object life cycles, appears to represent the most significant change of the three OOA methodologies.

Object-Oriented Design Methodologies

Design is the process of mapping system requirements defined during analysis to an abstract representation of a specific system-based implementation, meeting cost and performance constraints. As was done with OOA methodologies, we conducted a literature search to identify broadly representative OOD methodologies first published in book form or as detailed articles in refereed journals from 1980 to 1990. This resulted in the selection of three methodologies from Booch [2], Wasserman et al. [4], and Wirfs-Brock et al. [18]. Implementation-specific methodologies, such as those targeted at real-time systems using the Ada language, were excluded from consideration.

We present the methodologies in an order based on their similarities to conventional methodologies. Wasserman et al. draws most heavily on structured design and is presented first, followed by Booch, and Wirfs-Brock et al.

Wasserman et al. object-oriented structured design. Object-oriented structured design (OOSD) was developed by Wasserman, Pircher, and Muller. The methodology provides a detailed notation for describing an *architectural design*, which they define as a high-level design that identifies individual modules but not their detailed internal representation. Wasserman et al. state that the overall goal of OOSD is to provide a standard design notation that can support every software design, including both object-oriented and conventional approaches. OOSD offers a hybrid notation that incorporates concepts from previous work from several areas, including structure charts from structured design; Booch's notation for Ada packages and tasks; hierarchy and inheritance from object orientation; and the concept of monitors from concurrent programming. However, as Wasserman et al. observe, OOSD does not provide a detailed procedure for developing the design itself.

Tools for Wasserman et al. object-oriented structured design

Object-oriented structure chart – An updated version of the classical structure chart that adds notations for objects and classes ("information clusters"), methods, visibility, instantiation, exception handling, hidden operations, generic definitions (abstract classes), inheritance, and concurrency. The charts can also be used to show multiple inheritance, message passing, polymorphism, dynamic binding, and asynchronous processes.

The primary tool for OOSD is the object-oriented structure chart (see the box, "Tools for Wasserman et al. object-oriented structured design"). This chart takes the symbols and notations from conventional structure charts, including modules, data parameters, and control parameters, and adds notations for such object-oriented constructs as objects and classes (called "information clusters" by the authors), methods, instantiation, exception handling, generic definitions (similar to abstract classes), inheritance, and concurrency. Object-oriented structure charts can be used to show multiple inheritance, message passing, polymorphism, and dynamic binding. OOSD also supports the concept of a monitor, which is useful in depicting the asynchronous processes typically found in real-time systems.

Although OOSD is intended primarily for architectural design, the authors state that OOSD provides a foundation for representing design decisions associated with the physical design. The authors recommend that annotations be used to reflect the idiosyncrasies of individual implementation languages, while preserving the generic character of basic symbols. For example, OOSD includes optional Ada language-specific annotations to provide for packages, sequencing, and selective activation.

Booch object-oriented design. Booch pioneered the field of object-oriented design. As originally defined in the early 1980s, Booch's methodology was Ada language specific, but it has been significantly expanded and generalized since then. Booch views his methodology as an alternative to, rather than an extension of, structured design.

Although Booch describes a host of techniques and tools to assist design, ranging from informal lists to formal diagrams and templates, he is reluctant to prescribe a fixed ordering of phases for object-oriented design. Rather, he recommends that analysts work iteratively and incrementally, augmenting formal diagrams with informal techniques as appropriate to the problem at hand. Nevertheless, Booch does delineate four major steps that must be performed during the course of OOD:

(1) *Identify classes and objects.* Identify key abstractions in the problem space and label them as candidate classes and objects.
(2) *Identify the semantics of classes and objects.* Establish the meaning of the classes and objects identified in the previous step using a variety of techniques, including creating "scripts" that define the life cycles of each object from creation to destruction.
(3) *Identify relationships between classes and objects.* Establish class and object interactions, such as patterns of inheritance among classes and patterns of cooperation among objects. This step also captures visibility decisions among classes and objects.
(4) *Implement classes and objects.* Construct detailed internal views of classes and objects, including definitions of their various behaviors (services). Also, allocate objects and classes to modules (as defined in the target language environment) and allocate programs to processors (where the target environment supports multiple processors).

The primary tools used during OOD are

– class diagrams and class templates (which emphasize class definitions and inheritance relationships);
– object diagrams and timing diagrams (which stress message definitions, visibility, and threads of control);
– state-transition diagrams (to model object states and transitions);
– operation templates (to capture definitions of services);
– module diagrams and templates (to capture physical design decisions about the assignment of objects and classes to modules); and
– process diagrams and templates (to assign modules to processors in situations where a multiprocessor configuration will be used).

(See the box, "Tools for Booch object-oriented design.")

Booch OOD provides the widest variety of modeling tools of the OOD methodologies reviewed here. Although he does not prescribe a fixed sequence of design steps, Booch does provide a wealth of guidance on the design process by describing in detail the types of activities that must be performed and by working through the design of five hypothetical systems from different problem domains.

Wirfs-Brock et al. responsibility-driven design. Wirfs-Brock, Wilkerson, and Wiener developed their responsibility-driven design (RDD) methodology during several years of internal software development experience in various corporate settings. RDD is based on a client-server model of computing in which systems are seen as being composed of collections of *servers* that hold private responsibilities and also render services to *clients* based on contracts that define the nature and scope of valid client-server interactions.

To map these terms to more conventional object-oriented terminology, clients and servers are different kinds of objects, while services and responsibilities correspond to methods. Contracts and collaborations are metaphors for the idea that, to preserve encapsulation, some objects must be willing to perform certain tasks (such as modifying the values of their own internal variables) for the benefit of other objects, and that some kinds of services require several objects to work together to achieve the desired result.

Their methodology is responsibility-driven because the focus of attention during design is on contracts between clients and server objects. These contracts spell out what actions each object is responsible for performing and what information each object is responsible for sharing. Wirfs-Brock et al. contrast their approach with what they term data-driven object-oriented design methodologies (they cite no specific authors), which are said to emphasize the design of data structures internal to objects and inheritance relationships based on common attributes. In contrast, the responsibility-driven approach is intended to maximize the level of encapsulation in the resulting design. Data-driven design is said to focus more on classes and inheritance, while responsibility-driven design focuses more on object interactions and encapsulation.

Like Booch, Wirfs-Brock et al. recommend an incremental/iterative approach to design, as opposed to rigid phases with fixed deliverables. RDD provides for a six-step procedure spread across two phases. An exploration phase finds candidate classes, responsibilities, and collaborations. A second analysis phase builds hierarchies, defines subsystems, and defines protocols. The steps are

(1) *Find classes.* Extract noun phrases from the requirements specification and build a list of candidate classes by looking for nouns that refer to physical objects, conceptual entities, categories of objects, and external interfaces. Attributes of objects and candidate superclasses are also identified.

(2) *Find responsibilities and assign to classes.* Consider the purpose of each class and examine the specification for action phrases to find candidate responsibilities. Assign responsibilities to classes such that system intelligence is evenly distributed, behaviors reside with related information, and responsibilities are shared among related classes.

(3) *Find collaborations.* Examine responsibilities associated with each class and consider which other classes are needed for collaboration to fulfill each responsibility.

(4) *Define hierarchies.* Construct class hierarchies for kind-of inheritance relationships such that common responsibilities are factored as high as possible and abstract classes do not inherit from concrete classes. Construct contracts by grouping together responsibilities used by the same clients.

(5) *Define subsystems.* Draw a collaborations graph for the complete system. Look for frequent and complex collaborations and identify these as candidate subsys-

tems. Classes within a subsystem should support a small and strongly cohesive set of responsibilities and should be strongly interdependent.

(6) *Define protocols.* Develop design detail by writing design specifications for classes, subsystems, and contracts. Construct the protocols for each class (the signatures for the messages to which each class responds).

Tools used throughout the design process include

- Class cards (steps 1, 2 and 3);
- Hierarchy diagrams (step 4);
- Venn diagrams (step 4);
- Collaborations graphs (steps 4 and 5);
- Subsystem cards (step 5);
- Class specifications (step 6); and
- Subsystem specifications (step 6).

(See the box, "Tools for Wirfs-Brock et al. responsibility-driven design.")

In advocating an approach that emphasizes the dynamic behavior and responsibilities of objects rather than their static class relationships, RDD provides a significant contrast to Booch OOD and to the OOA methodologies reviewed earlier. Unlike these other methodologies, the initial steps of RDD do not focus on establishing a hierarchy of classes, but rather attempt to construct a close simulation of object behaviors and interactions.

Comparison of Design Methodologies

Object-oriented design versus conventional design. The distinctions between conventional and object-oriented development, some of which were identified in the discussion of analysis methodologies, are amplified during design due to the growing importance of implementation-specific issues (see Table 2). None of the conventional methodologies support the definition of classes, inheritance, methods, or message protocols, and while it may not be necessary to consider these constructs explicitly during object-oriented analysis, they form the foundation of an object-oriented design (Table 2, rows 6 through 10). In addition, while conventional and object-oriented methodologies both provide tools that define a hierarchy of modules (row 1), a completely different method of decomposition is employed, and the very definition of the term module is different.

In conventional systems, modules – such as programs, subroutines, and functions – only contain procedural code. In object-oriented systems, the object – a bundling of procedures and data – is the primary unit of modularity. Structured design and information engineering both use function-oriented decomposition rules, resulting in a set of procedure-oriented program modules. OOD methodologies, by contrast, employ an object-oriented decomposition resulting in collections of methods encapsulated within objects.

Tools for Booch object-oriented design

Class diagram/template – Shows the existence of classes (enclosed in dotted-line "clouds") and their relationships (depicted by various kinds of directed and undirected arcs) in the logical design of a system. Relationships supported include uses, instantiates, inherits, metaclass, and undefined.

Module diagram/template – Documents the allocation of objects and classes to modules in the physical design of a system. Only needed for languages (such as Ada) that support the idea of a module as distinct from objects and classes.

Object diagram/template – Used to model some of dynamics of objects. Each object (enclosed in solid line "clouds") represents an arbitrary instance of a class. Objects are connected by directed arcs that define object visibility and message connections. Does not show flow of control or ordering of events.

Operation template – Structured text that provides detailed design documentation for operations.

Process diagram/template – Used to show the allocation of processes to processors in the physical design of a system. Only for implementations in multiprocessor environments.

State-transition diagram – Shows the states (depicted by circles) of a class, the events (directed arcs) that cause transitions from one state to another, and the actions that result from a state change.

Timing diagram – A companion diagram to the object diagram, shows the flow of control and ordering of events among a group of collaborating objects.

Tools for Wirfs-Brock et al. responsibility-driven design

Class cards – A physical card used to record text describing classes, including name, superclasses, subclasses, responsibilities, and collaborations.

Class specification – An expanded version of the class card. Identifies superclasses, subclasses, hierarchy graphs, collaborations graphs. Also includes a general description of the class, and documents all of its contracts and methods.

Collaborations graph – A diagram showing the classes, subsystems, and contracts within a system and the paths of collaboration between them. Classes are drawn as boxes. Subsystems are drawn as rounded-corner boxes enclosing multiple classes. Collaborations are directed arcs from one class to the contract of another class.

Hierarchy diagram – A simple diagram that shows inheritance relationships in a lattice-like structure. Classes (enclosed within boxes) are connected by undirected arcs that represent an inheritance relationship. Superclasses appear above subclasses.

Subsystem card – A physical card used to record text describing subsystems, including name and a list of contracts.

Subsystem specification – Contains the same information as a class specification, only at the level of a subsystem.

Venn diagram – Used to show the overlap of responsibilities between classes to help identify opportunities to create abstract superclasses. Classes are depicted as intersecting ellipses.

	Component	Yourdon and Constantine Structured Design	Martin Information Engineering	Wasserman et al. Object-Oriented Structured Design	Booch Object-Oriented Design	Wirfs-Brock et al. Responsibility-Driven Design
1.	Hierarchy of modules (physical design)	Structure chart	Process-decomposition diagram	Object-oriented structure chart	Module diagram	*Not supported*
2.	Data definitions	Hierarchy diagram	Data-model diagram; data-structure diagram	Object-oriented structure chart	Class diagram	Class specification
3.	Procedural logic	*Not supported*	Action diagram	*Not supported*	Operation template	Class specification
4.	End-to-end processing sequences	Dataflow diagram	Dataflow diagram; process-dependency diagram	*Not supported*	Timing diagrams	*Not supported*
5.	Object states and transitions	*Not supported*	*Not supported*	*Not supported*	State-transition diagram	*Not supported*
6.	Definition of classes and inheritance	*Not supported*	*Not supported*	Object-oriented structure chart	Class diagram	Hierarchy diagram
7.	Other class relationships (instantiates, uses, etc.)	*Not supported*	*Not supported*	Object-oriented structure chart	Class diagram	Class specification
8.	Assignment of operations/services to classes	*Not supported*	*Not supported*	Object-oriented structure chart	Class diagram	Collaborations graph; class specification
9.	Detailed definition of operations/services	*Not supported*	*Not supported*	*Not supported*	Operations template	Class specification
10.	Message connections	*Not supported*	*Not supported*	Object-oriented structure chart	Object diagram and template	Collaborations graph

Table 2. Comparison of design methodologies.

The greatest overlap between conventional and object-oriented design methodologies is between Booch OOD and information engineering. Both methodologies provide a tool for defining end-to-end processing sequences (row 4), although Booch's timing diagram contains much less detail than information engineering's data-dependency diagram. Both methodologies provide for a detailed definition of procedural logic.

Booch recommends the use of a generic program definition language (PDL) or structured English, while information engineering recommends the use of a graphical action diagram for this purpose. Finally, for information-intensive applications, Booch recommends that a normalization procedure be used for designing data. This normalization procedure is very similar to the one employed by information engineering.

OOD methodology differences. The most notable differences among the three OOD methodologies have to do with

(1) data design,
(2) level of detail in describing the process of OOD, and
(3) level of detail provided by diagram notations.

Booch, as mentioned above, employs a detailed procedure (where appropriate) for designing the data encapsulated within objects. In fact, Booch [2] sees many parallels between database design and OOD:

> In a process not unlike object-oriented design, database designers bounce between logical and physical design throughout the development of the database ... The ways in which we describe the elements of a database are very similar to the ways in which we describe the key abstractions in an application using object-oriented design.

Wasserman et al. and Wirfs-Brock et al., by contrast, say little on the issue of data design or normalization.

Wirfs-Brock et al. provide a very thorough description of the design process, which they break into 26 identifiable design activities spread across six steps. Booch offers less in the way of explicit, step-wise design procedures, although he does provide a wealth of implicit guidance, using a detailed description of five hypothetical design projects. Wasserman et al., by contrast, assume that the particulars of an implementation environment will dictate what kinds of procedures and quality metrics are best; they do not offer a procedural description of OOSD.

Wasserman et al. and Booch both provide a comprehensive and rigorous set of notations for representing an object-oriented design. Wirfs-Brock et al. provide a less detailed notation in their RDD methodology, and do not address such concepts as persistence, object instantiation, and concurrent execution. The authors claim that RDD is appropriate for object-oriented and conventional development projects alike; this may explain the lack of attention to implementation issues that are more closely associated with object orientation.

OOD: Incremental versus radical change. Regarding the incremental-versus-radical debate, object-oriented design is clearly a radical change from both process-oriented methodologies and data-oriented methodologies (Yourdon and Constantine structured design and Martin information engineering, respectively). Table 2 shows that the number of modeling dimensions on which conventional and object-oriented methodologies overlap ranges from a maximum of four out of 10 (information engineering and Booch OOD) to as few as one out of 10 (structured design and Wirfs-Brock OOD). Although conventional methodologies such as information engineering support a data-oriented view in modeling the problem domain during analysis, they use a function-oriented view in establishing the architecture of program modules during design. As a result, not only is the primary structuring principle for program code different – functions versus objects – but at least half of the specific dimensions of the target system model are different.

Object-oriented design requires a new set of competencies associated with constructing detailed definitions of classes and inheritance, class and object relationships, and object operations and message connections. The design trade-offs between maximizing encapsulation (by emphasizing object responsibilities) versus maximizing inheritance (by emphasizing commonalities among classes) are subtle ones. Designing classes that are independent of the context in which they are used is required to maximize reuse, and here again, very subtle design decisions must be made [19]. As mentioned in the introduction, the important point is not whether object-oriented concepts are radically new in some absolute sense, but rather whether they are radically new to the population of potential adopters. The idea of building systems devoid of global-calling programs, where everything literally is defined as an object, will certainly be a radical concept to designers schooled in conventional design methodologies.

Transition from Analysis to Design

Analysis is usually defined as a process of extracting and codifying user requirements and establishing an accurate model of the problem domain. Design, by contrast, is the process of mapping requirements to a system implementation that conforms to desired cost, performance, and quality parameters. While these two activities are conceptually distinct, in practice the line between analysis and design is frequently blurred. Many of the components of an analysis model have direct counterparts in a design model. In addition, the process of design usually leads to a better understanding of requirements, and can uncover areas where a change in requirements must be negotiated to support desired performance and cost constraints. In recognition of these realities, most current methodologies recommend that analysis and design be performed iteratively, if not concurrently.

One of the frequently cited advantages of object orientation is that it provides a smoother translation between analysis and design models than do structured methodologies. It is true that no direct and obvious mapping exists between structured analysis and structured design:

Anyone involved with [structured design] knows that the transition from the analysis model to the design model can be tricky. For example, in moving from a dataflow diagram view of the system to creating design-structure charts the modeler is forced to make a significant shift in perspective, There are strategies to assist in the matter (transform analysis, transaction analysis, etc.), but it remains a difficult task because the mapping is not truly isomorphic [6].

With object orientation, the mapping from analysis to design does appear to be potentially more isomorphic, as a comparison of Tables 1 and 2 reveals. Every analysis model component supported by at least one OOA methodology can be mapped to a similar (albeit usually more detailed) component supported by at least one design methodology. Rows 1–3, 4, 5, 6, 7, 10, and 11 in Table 1 correspond to rows 6–7, 2,1, 5, 9, 8 and 10 in Table 2, respectively.

Only two object-oriented methodologists provided detailed procedures encompassing both analysis and design (Coad and Yourdon [20] and Rumbaugh et al. [21]). Shlaer and Mellor also briefly describe a procedure for translating OOA into OOD. Development groups that do not elect to adopt a single methodology spanning analysis and design will face the problem of matching up incompatible terminology and notations from different methodologists. The blurring between analysis and design is a particularly acute issue because the somewhat arbitrary line between analysis and design is drawn in different places by different methodologists. Of the OOA methodologies, Coad and Yourdon's and Shlaer and Mellor's seem to encroach the most on design. Coad and Yourdon explicitly identify inheritance relationships (usually considered a design activity) and provide for a formal and detailed specification of the logic within services. Shlaer and Mellor provide for complete normalization of attributes and advocate detailed modeling of entity life cycles. Of the design methodologies reviewed here, Wirfs-Brock et al. RDD appears to encroach the most on analysis in that it assumes that only an English-language specification (rather than a full-analysis model) is the input to the methodology.

Overall Critique

Object-oriented methodologies are less mature than conventional methodologies, and may be expected to undergo a period of expansion and refinement as project experience uncovers gaps in modeling capabilities or misplaced assumptions. Three areas currently stand out as candidates for further development work. To begin with, a rigorous mechanism is needed for decomposing very large systems into components, such that each component can be developed separately and subsequently integrated. Second, tools for modeling end-to-end processing sequences that involve multiple objects are either cumbersome or wholly lacking. Third, in the area of reuse, much is made of designing in reuse ("sowing" reuse), but no more than passing mention is made of techniques or procedures for finding and exploiting existing models, domain knowledge, or components ("harvesting" reuse). The first two areas are ones where object-oriented methodologies lack functionality provided by conventional methodologies, while the third area lacks support in both object-oriented and conventional methodologies.

System partitioning/object clustering. Traditional methodologies, such as structured analysis and information engineering, provide mechanisms for creating a natural, coarse-grained decomposition of systems (nested processes in the case of structured analysis, and subject databases in the case of information engineering). This decomposition is essential because many projects are too large to be developed by a single team within the desired time frame and, hence, must be divided into components and assigned to multiple teams working in parallel. To be most beneficial, the decomposition must be performed early in the development process, which also suggests it must be created in top-down fashion rather than bottom-up. In addition, the decomposition must create natural divisions between components and allow for a rigorously defined process of subsequent reintegration of the components.

The most coarse-grained, formally defined entities in object orientation are objects and classes. While objects and classes certainly provide a powerful mechanism for aggregating system functionality, they are usually defined in a bottom-up fashion as common characteristics get factored to ever higher levels in an inheritance structure. In addition, very large systems, even after this factoring process has been completed, may still consist of hundreds of top-level classes. De Champeaux [22] notes

> While the analysis of a toy example like the popular car cruise control system yields only a "flat" set of objects [classes], the analysis of... an airline system or a bank will yield "objects" [classes] at different abstraction levels.

The objects and classes, even at the highest level, are too fine-grained and defined too late in the development process to provide a basis for partitioning large development projects. This limitation has apparently been recognized by several methodologists; they have responded by inventing high-level constructs for clustering related object classes. These constructs include subject areas [3], domains [16], systems [16,18], and ensembles [22].

Two of these constructs – Coad and Yourdon's subject areas and the Wirfs-Brock et al. subsystems – appear to be very similar conceptually and provide a starting point for partitioning object-oriented models. Yet they are quite informally defined, and they provide little indication of how individually developed system components might interact. Shlaer and Mellor's concepts of domains and subsystems are better developed, and four of the methodology's diagrams are devoted to modeling the interactions between domains and between application domain subsystems (domain chart, subsystem relationship model, subsystem communication model, and subsystem access model).

De Champeaux's *ensembles* and *ensemble classes* [22] are the most rigorously defined of the clustering mechanisms. Ensembles are analogous to conventional objects, while ensemble classes are analogous to conventional classes. An ensemble is a flat grouping of objects (or other ensembles) that naturally go together – usually because they participate in whole-to-part relationships. An automobile, for example, is an ensemble consisting of an engine, doors, wheels, etc. Ensembles have many of the same characteristics as conventional objects, including attributes, states and transitions, and the capability of interacting with other objects and ensembles.

De Champeaux distinguishes ensembles from objects on this basis: Ensembles can have *internal parallelism* while objects cannot. That is, ensembles may consist of subordinate objects or ensembles that each exhibit behaviors in parallel during system execution. Objects, by contrast, are assumed to exhibit only sequential behaviors (for example, as modeled in a finite-state machine.)

De Champeaux distinguishes ensembles from other clustering mechanisms (such as, the Wirfs-Brock et al. subsystems) in that they are more than just conceptual entities; they exist during system execution and may have persistent attributes. It is less clear how ensembles differ from the conventional notion of a compound or composite object [2], except that ensembles seem to be a more general concept than composite objects. That is, an ensemble might refer to a cluster of related entities, such as a fleet of ships that would not ordinarily be viewed as a composite object in the real world.

Yet, in terms of how they behave, ensembles and composite objects appear to be quite similar. De Champeaux notes that the constituents of an ensemble only interact directly with each other or with the encompassing ensemble. An ensemble hides the details of constituents that are irrelevant outside of the ensemble, and acts as a gateway that forwards messages or triggers to external objects and ensembles. Likewise, Booch recommends that when using composite objects, the encapsulating object should hide the details of the constituent objects and mediate between constituent objects and external objects [2].

Although De Champeaux's use of ensembles seems promising on a conceptual level, actual project experiences will tell whether or not ensembles provide a practical basis for partitioning large projects. An interesting question for language designers is whether ensembles, or some similar construct, should be explicitly supported, for example, through mechanisms that limit the allowable patterns of interaction between ensembles, their constituents, and external objects to just those envisioned by de Champeaux.

End-to-end process modeling. Many problem domains contain global processes that impact many objects and involve the serial or parallel execution of numerous intermediary steps between initiation and conclusion. Examples of such processes include the ordering process for a manufacturer, daily account reconciliation in a bank, and monthly invoice processing by a long-distance telecommunications carrier. Conventional methodologies provide well established tools such as dataflow diagrams (see the "Tools for structured methodology" box) and process-dependency diagrams (see the box, "Tools for Martin information engineering") for modeling these sorts of processes.

None of the object-oriented methodologies reviewed here provide a specific model for describing global processes end to end, although individual parts of the process are modeled piecemeal using such concepts as operations [2,4], services [3], actions and processes [16], and responsibilities [18]. (Shlaer and Mellor describe a procedure for following threads of control, but this procedure spans several different diagrams and seems rather cumbersome. In any case, no distinct view of end-to-end processing – devoid of extraneous information – is provided.)

Bailin supports the idea of using dataflow diagrams (and presumably, global process modeling as well) during analysis, but only to help achieve a better understanding of objects. The resulting diagrams serve only as an intermediate representation and are not part of the object-oriented specification [14].

Booch's timing diagram (see the box, "Tools for Booch object-oriented design") is the closest that any of the methodologies come to supporting a distinct view of end-to-end process modeling. Yet this diagram contains very little expressive power compared with, for example, information engineering's process-dependency diagram. A timing diagram only shows flow of control information, whereas a process-dependency diagram shows flow of control, flow of data, and conditional execution. Bailin also recognizes the need for end-to-end process modeling and has listed composition graphs (similar to timing diagrams in terms of expressive power) as a possible extension of his methodology. (Note that the most recent Bailin methodology refers to compositions graphs as "stimulus-response diagrams.")

This lack of support for global processes is not surprising since the concept of a global process, not subordinated to any individual object, seems to be at odds with the spirit of object orientation. In fact, Booch [2] and de Champeaux [22] both warn against the use of even throw-away dataflow models, for fear that it will irrevocably bias subsequent object modeling towards a "function" orientation.

Still, there is no reason to believe that complicated business processes and the system components that automate them will no longer exist simply because one adopts object orientation. Nor is elimination of end-to-end processes listed by any methodologist as a precondition for adopting object orientation. Thus, it would seem that a separate tool is needed to arrange the mosaic of encapsulated services into a model that illustrates sequencing, conditional execution, and related ideas for certain key global processes.

Harvesting reuse. One of the most persistently claimed advantages of object orientation is that it enables pervasive levels of software reuse. If properly applied, object-oriented mechanisms such as encapsulation, inheritance, polymorphism, and dynamic binding certainly obviate many technical barriers to reuse of program code. In addition, it has been claimed that object orientation opens the way to reuse of design models, or frameworks [7], and even analysis models from relevant problem domains [6]. At the level of analysis and design, reuse can take two basic forms: reuse of components from previously developed analysis and design models, and reuse of abstractions of previously implemented program components.

Even within an object-oriented implementation environment, achieving high levels of reuse is by no means automatic; virtually all object-oriented methodologists emphasize that reuse must be designed into an application from the start. This emphasis on sowing reuse is not surprising; however, it is curious how little attention object-oriented methodologists pay to harvesting reuse during analysis and design. Analysis and design consume more resources than programming, and perhaps more importantly, development budgets and management decisions – both of which should be strongly influenced by anticipated levels of reuse – are set early in the development process.

Of the methodologies described here, only two address the issue of harvesting reuse from beyond the confines of the project at hand. Coad and Yourdon refer to the need to examine previous analysis models for reusable components and also provide a procedure for merging existing design or program components with new applications [20]. Like Coad and Yourdon, Booch emphasizes the importance of seeking reusable software components from existing class libraries during design. Yet, neither author provides specific guidance on how to find or evaluate existing components.

De Champeaux and Faure [6] and Caldiera and Basili [19] discuss the issue of harvesting reuse at the level of analysis and design. De Champeaux and Faure recommend a repository-based approach to managing reuse. They suggest that the software development process can be seen as a process of creating and modifying three cross-referenced repositories with analysis, design, and implementation components. In this view, the analysis components serve as annotations to the design and implementation components and may point to alternative realizations of the same requirements (for example, with different performance parameters). They further suggest that these annotations could be the basis for a smart library transversal mechanism. This mechanism could assist in identifying candidate reusable components.

Caldiera and Basili provide a much more thorough examination of the issue of harvesting reuse, especially in the areas of identifying and qualifying software components. They suggest a model for project organization where application developers are segregated from "reuse specialists." Reuse specialists work in a "component factory" and are responsible for the development and maintenance of a repository of reusable components. The component factory is responsible for identifying, qualifying, and tailoring reusable components for subsequent integration – by application developers – into ongoing applications development projects.

Object-oriented analysis and design methodologies are rapidly evolving, but the field is by no means fully mature. None of the methodologies reviewed here (with the possible exception of Booch OOD) has – as of this writing – achieved the status of a widely recognized standard on the order of the conventional methodologies of Yourdon and Constantine or DeMarco. Object-oriented methodologies will continue to evolve, as did conventional methodologies before them, as subtler issues emerge from their use in a wide array of problem domains and project environments. As discussed above, three areas – system partitioning, end-to-end process modeling, and harvesting reuse – appear to be especially strong candidates for further development work. In the meantime, adopters of current object-oriented methodologies may need to develop their own extensions to contend with these issues, or alternatively, limit application of the methodologies to problem domains where these issues are of lesser importance.

Compared with object-oriented methodologies, conventional methodologies fall at different places along the incremental-radical continuum. Developers schooled only in structured analysis circa 1978 can be expected to have great difficulty making the transition to OOA, while those with an information modeling background will find much of OOA to be based on familiar concepts.

During design, all conventional methodologies revert to a process-oriented view in establishing the architecture of program modules and as a result, object orientation will likely be viewed as radical change by developers schooled in any of the conventional design methods reviewed here. Since organizations will have to adopt object-oriented design methodologies to end up with object-oriented implementations, a move to an object-oriented environment in general may be seen predominantly as a radical change.

Object orientation is founded on a collection of powerful ideas – modularity, abstraction, encapsulation, reuse – that have firm theoretical foundations. In addition, trends in computing towards complex data types and complex new forms of integrated systems seem to favor the object model over conventional approaches.

Although little empirical evidence exists to support many of the specific claims made in favor of object orientation, the weight of informed opinion among many leading-edge practitioners and academics favors object orientation as a "better idea" for software development than conventional approaches. Organizations that are able to absorb this radical change may well find themselves in a significantly stronger competitive position vis-a-vis those incapable of making the transition.

References

1. E. Yourdon, "Object-Oriented Observations," *Am. Programmer*, Vol. 2, No. 7–8, Summer 1989, pp. 3–7.
2. G. Booch "What Is and What Isn't Object-Oriented Design?" *Am. Programmer*, Vol. 2, No. 7–8, Summer 1989, pp. 14–21.
3. P. Coad and E. Yourdon, *Object-Oriented Analysis*, 2nd edition, Prentice Hall, Englewood Cliffs, N.J., 1991.
4. A.I. Wasserman, P.A. Pircher, and R.J. Muller, "An Object-Oriented Structured Design Method for Code Generation," *Software Eng. Notes*, Vol. 14, No. 1, Jan. 1989, pp. 32–55.
5. M. Page-Jones and S. Weiss, "Synthesis: An Object-Oriented Analysis and Design Method," *Am. Programmer*, Vol. 2, No. 7–8, Summer 1989, pp. 64–67.
6. D. De Champeaux and P. Faure, "A Comparative Study of Object-Oriented Analysis Methods," *J. Object-Oriented Programming*, Vol. 5, No. 1, 1992, pp. 21–33.
7. R.J. Wirfs-Brock and R.E. Johnson, "Surveying Current Research in Object-Oriented Design," *Comm. ACM*, Vol. 33, No. 9, Sept. 1990, pp. 104–124.

8. P.H. Loy, "A Comparison of Object-Oriented and Structured Development Methodologies," *ACM SIGSoft Software Eng. Notes*, Vol. 15, No. 1, Jan. 1990, pp. 44–48.
9. E. Yourdon and L. Constantine, *Structured Design: Fundamentals of a Discipline of Computer Programming and Design*, 2nd edition, Prentice Hall, New York, 1979.
10. T. DeMarco, *Structured Analysis and System Specification*, Yourdon Inc., New York, 1978.
11. P.T. Ward and S.J. Mellor, *Structured Development of Real-Time Systems*, Yourdon Press, Englewood Cliffs, N.J., 1985.
12. E. Yourdon, *Modern Structured Analysis*, Yourdon Press, Englewood Cliffs, N.J, 1989.
13. J. Martin, *Information Eng., Books I, II, and III*, Prentice Hall, Englewood Cliffs, N.J., 1990.
14. S.C. Bailin, "An Object-Oriented Requirements Specification Method," *Comm. ACM*, Vol. 32, No. 5, May 1989, pp. 608–623.
15. S. Shlaer and S.J. Mellor, *Object-Oriented Analysis: Modeling the World in Data*, Yourdon Press, Englewood Cliffs. N.J., 1988.
16. S. Shlaer and S.J. Mellor, *Object Life Cycles: Modeling the World in States*, Yourdon Press, Englewood Cliffs, N.J., 1992.
17. R.G. Fichman and C.F. Kemerer, "Object-Oriented Analysis and Design Methodologies: Comparison and Critique," MIT Sloan School of Management, Center for Information Systems Research Working Paper No. 230, Nov. 1991.
18. R. Wirts-Brock, B. Wilkerson, and L. Wiener, *Designing Object-Oriented Software*, Prentice Hall, Englewood Cliffs, N.J., 1990.
19. G. Caldiera and V. Basili, "Identifying and Qualifying Reusable Software Components," *Computer*, Vol. 24, No. 2, Feb. 1991, pp. 61–70.
20. P. Coad and E. Yourdon, *Object-Oriented Design*, Prentice Hall, Englewood Cliffs, N.J., 1991.
21. J. Rumbaugh et al., *Object-Oriented Modeling and Design*, Prentice Hall, Englewood Cliffs, N.J., 1991.
22. D. De Champeaux, "Object-Oriented Analysis and Top-Down Software Development," *Proc. European Conf. Object-Oriented Programming*, Lecture Notes in Computer Science, P. America, ed., Springer-Verlag, Geneva, 1991, pp. 360–376.

5. Concurrent and Distributed Systems

In a concurrent system, two or more activities (e.g., processes or programs) progress in some manner in parallel with each other. A distributed system consists of a number of independent computer systems connected together so that they can cooperate with each other in some manner. Inevitably these two concepts are intertwined.

The last decade and more has seen a rapid expansion of the field of distributed computing systems. The two major forces behind the rapid adoption of distributed systems are *technical* and *social* ones, and it seems likely that the pressure from both will continue for some time yet.

Technical reasons: The two major technical forces are *communication* and *computation*. Long haul, relatively slow communication paths between computers have existed for a long time, but more recently the technology for fast, cheap and reliable *local area networks* (LANs) has emerged and dominated the field of cooperative computing. These LANs allow the connection of large numbers of computing elements with a high degree of information sharing. They typically run at 10–100 Mbits per second (for example, the ubiquitous Ethernet) and have become relatively cheap and plentiful with the advances of microelectronics and microprocessor technology. In response, the *wide area networks* (WANs) are becoming faster and more reliable. Speeds are set to increase dramatically with the use of fiber optics and the introduction of ATM (Asynchronous Transfer Mode) networks.

Social reasons: Many enterprises are cooperative in nature – e.g., offices, multinational companies, university campuses etc. – requiring sharing of resources and information. Distributed systems can provide this either by integrating pre-existing systems, or building new systems which inherently reflect sharing patterns in their structure. A further, and somewhat contrary, motivation is the desire for autonomy of resources seen by individuals in an enterprise. The great popularity and ease of use of distributed information systems such as the World Wide Web (WWW) distributed hypermedia system on the Internet [14] are transforming the way in which information is made available for the future.

Distributed systems can offer greater *adaptability* than localized ones. Their nature forces them to be designed in a modular way and this can be used to advantage to allow incremental (and possibly dynamic) changes in performance and functionality by the addition or removal of elements.

The *performance* of distributed systems can be made much better than that of centralized systems and with the fall in the price of microprocessors can also be very much cheaper. However, this performance gain is usually manifested in the form of greater *capacity* rather than *response*. Increasing the latter is limited by the ability to make use of parallelism, which is mainly a software problem, and will probably see most progress in the area of *tightly coupled systems*. These are multiprocessor systems with very fast communications, such as is provided by shared memory systems and Transputer systems. This is in contrast to the *loosely coupled systems*, typified by asynchronous, autonomous computers on a LAN.

Availability can be increased because the adaptability of distributed systems allows for the easy addition of redundant elements. This is a potential benefit which has only been realized in a few systems. In many, the system as a whole becomes less available because it is made dependent on the availability of all of (the large number of) its components. This again is largely a software problem.

5.1 Concurrent Systems

The advent of concurrent systems has complicated the task of system specification and design somewhat. Concurrent systems are inherently more complex, offering the possibility of parallel and distributed computation, and the increased processing power that this obviously facilitates.

Standard methods of specifying and reasoning about computer systems are not sufficient for use with concurrent systems. They do not allow for side-effects, the occurrence of multiple events simultaneously, nor for the synchronization required between processes to ensure data integrity, etc. A specialized environment will normally be required for effective design [188].

A major approach to the handling of concurrency in a formal manner has been the use of process algebras and models. Hoare's CSP (Communicating Sequential Processes) [129, 220] and Milner's CCS (Calculus of Communicating Systems) [185] are perhaps the two foremost and widely accepted examples of such an approach. C.A.R. Hoare's original paper on CSP [128], *Communicating Sequential Processes* is reprinted in this Part since it was seminal to this field. Subsequently the approach has been given a more formal footing [52], and also expanded in several directions to handle real-time, probability, etc. [127, 220].

A more recent paper by Leslie Lamport, *A Simple Approach to Specifying Concurrent Systems*, is also reprinted here, and provides a more current view of the field [152]. Lamport provides an approach to the specification of concurrent systems with a formal underpinning, using a number of examples. The *transition axiom* method described provides a logical and conceptual foundation for the description of concurrency. Safety and liveness properties are separated for methodological rather than formal reasons.

The method described in this paper has been refined using the formal logic TLA (the Temporal Logic of Actions) [153]. The major advance has been to write this style of specification as a TLA formula, providing a more elegant framework that permits a simple formalization of all the reasoning.

Since the two included papers with this Part are mainly on *concurrent* issues, the rest of this Part redresses the balance by discussing *distributed* systems in more depth. [4] is a major survey which, while quite old, gives a good and authoritative grounding in the concepts behind the programming of concurrent systems for those who wish to follow this area up further.

The future for concurrent systems looks very active [59]. In particular the boundaries of hardware and software are becoming blurred as programmable hardware such as Field Programmable Gate Arrays (FPGA) becomes more prevalent. Hardware is parallel by its very nature, and dramatic speed-ups in naturally parallel algorithms can be achieved by using a hardware/software co-design approach [196].

5.2 Distributed Systems

To consider the issues and problems in designing distributed systems we need to define their fundamental properties. For this we can use the analysis of LeLann [164] who lists the following characteristics:

1. They contain an arbitrary number of processes.
2. They have a modular architecture and possibly dynamic composition.
3. The basic method of communication is message passing between processes.
4. There is some system-wide control.
5. There are variable (non-zero) message delays.

The existence of the last item means that centralized control techniques cannot be used, because there may never be a globally consistent state to observe and from which decisions can be made. Distributed systems carry over most of the problems of centralized systems, but it is this last problem which gives them their unique characteristics.

5.3 Models of Computation

Two popular models for distributed systems are the 'object–action' model and the 'process–message' model. In the former, a system consists of a set of objects (e.g. files) on which a number of operations (e.g. read and write) are defined; these operations can be invoked by users to change the state of the objects to get work done. In the latter model, a system is a set of processes (e.g. clients and file severs) prepared to exchange messages (e.g. read file request, write file request); receipt of messages causes processes to change state and thus get work done.

The terminology in this area can be confusing, but 'object–action' systems roughly correspond to 'monitor-based' and 'abstract data type' systems while 'process–message' systems correspond to 'client–server' systems. Lauer and Needham [161] have shown these models to be duals of each other. Most systems can be placed in one of these categories.

This characterization should not be applied too zealously. Both models essentially provide a way of performing computations and it is relatively straightforward to transform one type of system to the other. As already mentioned, because of the nature of the hardware, the basic method of communication in distributed systems is message passing between processes but in many cases the two models can be found at different layers within a system.

5.4 Naming Considerations

Objects and processes have to be named so that they can be accessed and manipulated. Since there are many sorts of objects in a system it is tempting to adopt many sorts of names. This must be tempered by a desire for conceptual simplicity. An important property of names is their scope of applicability; e.g., some may only be unique within a particular machine. Examples of such contexts are names of different sorts of objects which reside in a WAN, on a single LAN, in a service, on a server or somewhere in the memory of a particular machine.

Transforming names from one form to another is a very important function, even in centralized systems. One example is transforming a string name for a UNIX file to an *inode* number. Because distributed systems are so much more dynamic it is even more important to delay the binding of 'logical' and 'physical' names. Some sort of *mapping* or *name service* is required. Since this is such an important function, availability and reliability are vital. The domains and ranges of the mapping are often wide but sparse so in many systems names are structured to allow more efficient searches for entries.

5.5 Inter-Process Communication

The exchange of messages between processes – Inter-Process Communication (IPC) – is the basic form of communication in distributed systems, but note that it is easy to build the actions of object–action systems on top of this mechanism. For these, the idea of *remote procedure call* (RPC) forms a useful extension from the world of single machine local procedure calls. How transparent these should be from issues of location and errors is a matter of some debate. Whether RPCs or messages are used, the destination has to be located, using the mapping facilities already sketched. The use of RPCs has become popular because they represent an easy to use, familiar communication concept. They do not, however, solve all problems, as discussed in [242].

The structure of units of activity is very important. Work in recent years (in centralized as well as distributed systems) has led to the realization that a single kind of activity is inadequate in system design. Many have adopted a two level structuring. The outer level, called *heavy-weight processes* (HWPs), representing complete address spaces, are relatively well protected and accounted for, but switching between them is slow because of the large amount of state involved. Distribution is performed at the level of HWPs. They are typified by UNIX processes.

Within an HWP, a number of *light-weight processes* (LWPs) operate; these have much less state associated with them, are unprotected, share the address space of the containing HWP but it is possible to switch between these relatively rapidly. For example, there may be a number of HWPs on each node. One of these may represent a server. The server may be structured as a number of LWPs, one dedicated to the service of each client request.

5.6 Consistency Issues

The abnormal (e.g., crashes) and normal (e.g., concurrent sharing) activity of a system may threaten its consistency. The problem of concurrency control is well-known in multiprocessing systems. This problem and its solutions becomes harder when the degree of sharing and the amount of concurrency increase in distributed systems. In particular, the lack of global state first of all makes the solutions more difficult and also introduces the need for replication which causes more consistency problems.

Maintaining consistency requires the imposition of some ordering of the events within a system. The substantial insight of Lamport [151] is that the events in a distributed system only define a *partial order* rather than a *total order*. Required orderings can be achieved by extending existing centralized mechanisms, such as *locking*, or using *time-stamp* based algorithms.

Making systems resilient to faults in order to increase their reliability is an often quoted, rarely achieved feature of distributed systems. Both of these issues have been tackled with the notion of *atomic actions*. Their semantics are a conceptually simple 'all or nothing', but their implementation is rather harder, requiring essentially images of 'before' states should things prove sufficiently difficult that the only option is to roll back. This gets much harder when many objects are involved. Much work from the database world, particularly the notions of *transactions* and *two-phase commit* protocols have been adapted and extended to a distributed world. Atomic actions match quite well to RPC systems that provide 'at-most-once' semantics.

Another source of problems for consistency is dynamic reconfiguration of the system itself, adding or perhaps removing elements for maintenance while the system is still running.

5.7 Heterogeneity and Transparency

Heterogeneity must often be handled by operating systems (OSs) and particularly by distributed operating systems. Examples of possible heterogeneity occur in network hardware, communication mechanisms, processor architectures (including multiprocessors), data representations, location etc. In order that such disparate resources should not increase system complexity too much, they need to be accommodated in a coherent way. The key issue of such systems is *transparency*. How much of the heterogeneity is made visible to the user and how much is hidden depends very much on the nature of the heterogeneity. Other factors apart from heterogeneity can be made transparent to users, such as plurality of homogeneous processors in, for example, a processor pool.

The choice to be made is generally one of providing users with conceptually simpler interfaces, or more complicated ones which allow for the possibility of higher performance. For example, if location of processes is not transparent and can be manipulated, users can co-locate frequently communicating elements of their applications. If location is transparent the system will have to infer patterns of communication before it can consider migrating processes.

Issues of transparency cut across many other issues (e.g. naming, IPC and security) and need to be considered along with them.

5.8 Security and Protection

A *security policy* governs who may obtain, and how they may modify, information. A *protection mechanism* is used to reliably enforce a chosen security policy. The need to identify users and resources thus arises.

The distribution of a system into disjoint components increases the independence of those components and eases some security problems. On the other hand, a network connecting these components is open to attack, allowing information to be tapped or altered (whether maliciously or accidentally), thus subverting the *privacy* and *integrity* of their communication. In such a situation each component must assume much more responsibility for its own security.

Claims about identity must be *authenticated*, either using a local mechanism or with some external agency, to prevent impersonation. The total security of a system cannot rely on all the kernels being secure since there may be many types of these (for all the different processors) and a variable number of instances of them. It would be easy to subvert an existing instance or to insert a new one. Thus authentication functions should be moved out of kernels.

Access control is a particular security model. There exists a conceptual matrix which identifies the *rights* that *subjects* (e.g. users, processes, process groups) have over all *objects* (e.g. data, peripherals, processes). Two popular realizations of this are *access control lists* (ACLs) and *capabilities*. In the former, an ACL is associated with each object, listing the subjects and their rights over it. In the latter, each subject possesses a set of capabilities each of which identifies an object and the rights that the subject has over it. Each realization has its own merits and drawbacks, but capability based distributed systems seem to be more numerous.

Capabilities must identify objects and rights, so it is natural to extend a naming scheme to incorporate this mechanism. They must also be difficult to forge, which is harder to achieve without a trusted kernel. Drawing them from a sparse space and validating them before use allows them to be employed in distributed systems.

Cryptographic techniques can be used to tackle a number of these problems including ensuring privacy and integrity of communications, authentication of parties and digital signatures as proof of origins [190]. VLSI technology is likely to make their use, at least at network interfaces, standard, though they can be used at different levels in the communications hierarchy for different purposes.

Many of these techniques depend on the knowledge that parties have about encryption *keys* and thus *key distribution* becomes a new problem which needs to be solved. Use of *public key* systems can ease this, but many systems rely on some (more or less) trusted registry of keys, or an authentication server. The parallels with name servers again show the interdependence of naming and security.

5.9 Language Support

The trend has been for generally useful concepts to find themselves expressed in programming languages, and the features of distributed systems are no exception. There are many languages that incorporate the notions of processes and messages, or light-weight processes and RPCs.

Other languages are object-oriented and can be used for dealing with objects in a distributed environment and in others still the notion of atomic actions is supported. A choice must be made between the shared variable paradigm and the use of communication channels, as adopted by Occam [139] for example. The latter seems to be more tractable for formal reasoning and thus may be the safest and most tractable approach in the long run.

The problem of separately compiled, linked and executed cooperating programs are to some extent a superset of those already found in programs with separately compiled modules in centralized systems. The notion of a server managing a set of objects of a particular abstract data type and its implementation as a module allows module interfaces to be used as the unit of binding before services are used.

5.10 Distributed Operating Systems

Distributed Operating Systems (DOSs) have been the subject of much research activity in the field of distributed systems. Operating systems (OSs) control the bare resources of a computing system to provide users with a more convenient abstraction for computation. Thus the user's view of a system is mostly determined by the OS. A DOS is an OS built on distributed resources. There is much argument over what abstraction for computation a DOS should provide for its users.

The term *network operating system* (NOS) has faded in its usage, but requires some mention in the history of the development of distributed systems. Like many terms it means different things to different people. For many, a NOS is a 'guest level extension' applied to a number of existing centralized operating systems which are then interconnected via a network. These systems are characterized by the high degree of autonomy of the nodes, the lack of system-wide control and the non-transparency of the network.

On the other hand, DOSs are normally systems designed from scratch to be integrated and exercise much system-wide control. Others distinguish the two not on the lines of implementation but on the lines of the view of computation provided to users: in a DOS it is generally transparent while in a NOS it is not; special utilities are needed to use network facilities. See [34] for some examples of distributed operating systems. Further information on distributed systems in general may be found in [189], and [267] contains large bibliographies on the subject.

Communicating Sequential Processes

C.A.R. Hoare

Summary.

This paper suggests that input and output are basic primitives of programming and that parallel composition of communicating sequential processes is a fundamental program structuring method. When combined with a development of Dijkstra's guarded command, these concepts are surprisingly versatile. Their use is illustrated by sample solutions of a variety of familiar programming exercises.

Keywords: programming, programming languages, programming primitives, program structures, parallel programming, concurrency, input, output, guarded commands, nondeterminacy, coroutines, procedures, multiple entries, multiple exits, classes, data representations, recursion, conditional critical regions, monitors, iterative arrays.

1. Introduction

Among the primitive concepts of computer programming, and of the high level languages in which programs are expressed, the action of assignment is familiar and well understood. In fact, any change of the internal state of a machine executing a program can be modeled as an assignment of a new value to some variable part of that machine. However, the operations of input and output, which affect the external environment of a machine, are not nearly so well understood. They are often added to a programming language only as an afterthought.

Among the structuring methods for computer programs, three basic constructs have received widespread recognition and use: A repetitive construct (e.g. the while loop) an alternative construct (e.g. the conditional **if**...**then**...**else**), and normal sequential program composition (often denoted by a semicolon). Less agreement has

ⓒ 1978 Association for Computing Machinery, Inc. Reprinted by permission.
Reprinted from *Communications of the ACM*, 21(8):666–677, August 1978.

been reached about the design of other important program structures, and many suggestions have been made: Subroutines (Fortran), procedures (Algol 60 [15]), entries (PL/I), coroutines (UNIX [17]), classes (SIMULA 67 [5]), processes and monitors (Concurrent Pascal [2]), clusters (CLU [13]), forms (ALPHARD [19]), actors (Hewitt [1]).

The traditional stored program digital computer has been designed primarily for deterministic execution of a single sequential program. Where the desire for greater speed has led to the introduction of parallelism, every attempt has been made to disguise this fact from the programmer, either by hardware itself (as in the multiple function units of the CDC 600) or by the software (as in an I/O control package, or a multiprogrammed operating system). However, developments of processor technology suggest that a multiprocessor machine, constructed from a number of similar self-contained processors (each with its own store), may become more powerful, capacious, reliable, and economical than a machine which is disguised as a monoprocessor.

In order to use such a machine effectively on a single task, the component processors must be able to communicate and to synchronize with each other. Many methods of achieving this have been proposed. A widely adopted method of communication is by inspection and updating of a common store (as in Algol 68 [18], PL/I, and many machine codes). However, this can create severe problems in the construction of correct programs and it may lead to expense (e.g. crossbar switches) and unreliability (e.g. glitches) in some technologies of hardware implementation. A greater variety of methods has been proposed for synchronization: semaphores [6], events (PL/I), conditional critical regions [10], monitors and queues (Concurrent Pascal [2]), and path expressions [3]. Most of these are demonstrably adequate for their purpose, but there is no widely recognized criterion for choosing between them.

This paper makes an ambitious attempt to find a single simple solution to all these problems. The essential proposals are:

(1) Dijkstra's guarded commands [8] are adopted (with a slight change of notation) as sequential control structures, and as the sole means of introducing and controlling nondeterminism.
(2) A parallel command, based on Dijkstra's *parbegin* [6], specifies concurrent execution of its constituent sequential commands (processes). All the processes start simultaneously, and the parallel command ends only when they are all finished. They may not communicate with each other by updating global variables.
(3) Simple forms of input and output command are introduced. They are used for communication between concurrent processes.
(4) Such communication occurs when one process names another as destination for output *and* the second process names the first as source for input. In this case, the value to be output is copied from the first process to the second. There is *no* automatic buffering: In general, an input or output is delayed until the other process is ready with the corresponding output or input. Such delay is invisible to the delayed process.

(5) Input commands may appear in guards. A guarded command with an input guard is selected for execution only if and when the source named in the input command is ready to execute the corresponding output command. If several input guards of a set of alternatives have ready destinations, only one is selected and the others have *no* effect; but the choice between them is arbitrary. In an efficient implementation, an output command which has been ready for a long time should be favoured; but the definition of a language cannot specify this since the relative speed of execution of the processes is undefined.

(6) A repetitive command may have input guards. If all the sources named by them have terminated, then the repetitive command also terminates.

(7) A simple pattern-matching feature, similar to that of [16], is used to discriminate the structure of an input message, and to access its components in a secure fashion. This feature is used to inhibit input of messages that do not match the specified patterns.

The programs expressed in the proposed language are intended to be implementable both by a conventional machine with a single main store, and by a fixed network of processors connected by input/output channels (although very different optimizations are appropriate in the different cases). It is consequently a rather static language: The text of a program determines a fixed upper bound on the number of processes operating concurrently; there is no recursion and no facility for process-valued variables. In other respects also, the language has been stripped to the barest minimum necessary for explanation of its more novel features.

The concept of a communicating sequential process is shown in Sections 3–5 to provide a method of expressing solutions to many simple programming exercises which have previously been employed to illustrate the use of various proposed programming language features. This suggests that the process may constitute a synthesis of a number of familiar and new programming ideas. The reader is invited to skip the examples which do not interest him.

However, this paper also ignores many serious problems. The most serious is that it fails to suggest any proof method to assist in the development and verification of correct programs. Secondly, it pays no attention to the problems of efficient implementation, which may be particularly serious on a traditional sequential computer. It is probable that a solution to these problems will require (1) imposition of restrictions in the use of the proposed features; (2) reintroduction of distinctive notations for the most common and useful special cases; (3) development of automatic optimization techniques; and (4) the design of appropriate hardware.

Thus the concepts and notations introduced in this paper (although described in the next section in the form of a programming language fragment) should not be regarded as suitable for use as a programming language, either for abstract or for concrete programming. They are at best only a partial solution to the problems tackled. Further discussion of these and other points will be found in Section 7.

2. Concepts and Notations

The style of the following description is borrowed from Algol 60 [15]. Types, declarations, and expressions have not been treated; in the examples, a Pascal-like notation [20] has usually been adopted. The curly braces { } have been introduced into BNF to denote none or more repetitions of the enclosed material. (Sentences in parenthesis refer to an implementation: they are not strictly part of a language definition.)

```
<command> ::= <simple command>|<structured command>
<simple command> ::= <null command>|<assignment command>
    |<input command>|<output command>
<structured command> ::= <alternative command>
    |<repetitive command>|<parallel command>
<null command> ::= skip
<command list> ::= {<declaration>;|<command>;} <command>
```

A command specifies the behavior of a device executing the command. It may succeed or fail. Execution of a simple command, if successful, may have an effect on the internal state of the executing device (in the case of assignment), or on its external environment (in the case of output), or on both (in the case of input). Execution of a structured command involves execution of some or all of its constituent commands, and if any of these fail, so does the structured command. (In this case, whenever possible, an implementation should provide some kind of comprehensible error diagnostic message.)

A null command has no effect and never fails.

A command list specifies sequential execution of its constituent commands in the order written. Each declaration introduces a fresh variable with a scope which extends from its declaration to the end of the command list.

2.1 Parallel commands

```
<parallel command> ::= [<process>{||<process>}]
<process> ::= <process label> <command list>
<process label> ::= <empty>|<identifier> ::
    |<identifier>(<label subscript>{,<label subscript>}) ::
<label subscript> ::= <integer constant>|<range>
<integer constant> ::= <numeral>|<bound variable>
<bound variable> ::= <identifier>
<range> ::= <bound variable>:<lower bound>..<upper bound>
<lower bound> ::= <integer constant>
<upper bound> ::= <integer constant>
```

Each process of a parallel command must be *disjoint* from every other process of the command, in the sense that it does not mention any variable which occurs as a target variable (see Sections 2.2 and 2.3) in any other process.

A process label without subscripts, or one whose label subscripts are all integer constants, serves as a name for the command list to which it is prefixed; its scope extends over the whole of the parallel command. A process whose label subscripts include one or more ranges stands for a series of processes, each with the same label and command list, except that each has a different combination of values substituted for the bound variables. These values range between the lower bound and the upper bound inclusive. For example, $X(i:1..n) :: CL$ stands for

$$X(1) :: CL_1 || X(2) :: CL_2 || \ldots || X(n) :: CL_n$$

where each CL_j is formed from CL by replacing every occurrence of the bound variable i by the numeral j. After all such expansions, each process label in a parallel command must occur only once and the processes much be well formed and disjoint.

A parallel command specifies concurrent execution of its constituent processes. They all start simultaneously and the parallel command terminates successfully only if and when they have all successfully terminated. The relative speed with which they are executed is arbitrary.

Examples:

(1) [cardreader?cardimage|||lineprinter!lineimage]

Performs the two constituent commands in parallel, and terminates only when both operations are complete. The time taken may be as low as the longer of the times taken by each constituent process, i.e. the sum of its computing, waiting, and transfer times.

(2) [west :: DISASSEMBLE||X :: SQUASH||east :: ASSEMBLE]

The three processes have the names "west," "X", and "east." The capitalized words stand for command lists which will be defined in later examples.

(3) [room :: ROOM||fork(i:0..4) :: FORK||phil(i:0..4) :: PHIL]

There are eleven processes. The behavior of "room" is specified by the command list ROOM. The behavior of the five processes fork(0), fork(1), fork(2), fork(3), fork(4), is specified by the command list FORK, within which the bound variable I indicates the identity of the particular fork. Similar remarks apply to the five processes PHIL.

2.2 Assignment commands

<assignment command> ::= <target variable> := <expression>
<expression> ::= <simple expression>|<structured expression>
<structured expression> ::= <constructor>(<expression list>)
<constructor> ::= <identifier>|<empty>
<expression list> ::= <empty>|<expression>{,<expression>}
<target variable> ::= <simple variable>|<structured target>
<structured target> ::= <constructor>(<target variable list>)
<target variable list> ::= <empty>|<target variable>
    {,<target variable>}

An expression denotes a value which is computed by an executing device by application of its constituent operators to the specified operands. The value of an expression is undefined if any of these operations are undefined. The value denoted by a simple expression may be simple or structured; its constructor is that of the expression, and its components are the list of values denoted by the constituent expressions of the expression list.

An assignment command specifies evaluation of its expression, and assignment of the denoted value to the target variable. A simple target variable may have assigned to it a simple or a structured value. A structured target variable may have assigned to it a structured value, with the same constructor. The effect of such assignment is to assign to each constituent simpler variable of the structured target the value of the corresponding component of the structured value. Consequently, the value denoted by the target variable, if evaluated *after* a successful assignment, is the same as the value denoted by the expression, as evaluated *before* the assignment.

An assignment fails if the value of its expression is undefined, or if that value does not *match* the target variable, in the following sense: A *simple* target variable matches any value of its type. A *structured* target variable matches a structured value, provided that: (1) they have the same constructor, (2) the target variable list is the same length as the list of components of the value, (3) each target variable of the list matches the corresponding component of the value list. A structured value with no components is known as a "signal."

Examples:

(1) $x := x + 1$	the value of x after the assignment is the same as the value of $x + 1$ before.
(2) $(x, y) := (y, x)$	exchanges the values of x and y.
(3) $x := \text{cons}(\text{left}, \text{right})$	constructs a structured value and assigns it to x.
(4) $\text{cons}(\text{left}, \text{right}) := x$	fails if x does not have the form $\text{cons}(y, z)$; but if it does, then y is assigned to left, and z is assigned to right.
(5) $\text{insert}(n) := \text{insert}(2*x + 1)$	equivalent to $n := 2*x + 1$.
(6) $c := P()$	assigns to c a "signal" with constructor P, and no components.
(7) $P() := c$	fails if the value of c is not $P()$; otherwise has no effect.
(8) $\text{insert}(n) := \text{has}(n)$	fails, due to mismatch.

Note: Successful execution of both (3) and (4) ensures the truth of the postcondition $x = \text{cons}(\text{left}, \text{right})$; but (3) does so by changing x and (4) does so by changing left and right. Example (4) will fail if there is *no* value of left and right which satisfies the postcondition.

2.3 Input and output commands

<input command> ::= <source>?<target variable>
<output command> ::= <destination>!<expression>
<source> ::= <process name>
<destination> ::= <process name>
<process name> ::= <identifier>|<identifier>(<subscripts>)
<subscripts> ::= <integer expression>{,<integer expression>}

Input and output commands specify communication between two concurrently operating sequential processes. Such a process may be implemented in hardware as a special-purpose device (e.g. cardreader or lineprinter), or its behaviour may be specified by one of the constituent processes of a parallel command. Communication occurs between two processes of a parallel command whenever (1) an input command in one process specifies at its source the process name of the other process; (2) an output command in the other process specifies as its destination the process name of the first process; and (3) the target variable of the input command matches the value denoted by the expression of the output command. On these conditions, the input and output commands are said to *correspond*. Commands which correspond are executed simultaneously, and their combined effect is to assign the value of the expression of the output command to the target variable of the input command.

An input command fails if its source is terminated. An output command fails if its destination is terminated or if its expression is undefined.

(The requirement of synchronization of input and output commands means that an implementation will have to delay whichever of the two commands happens to be ready first. They delay is ended when the corresponding command in the other process is also ready, or when the other process terminates. In the latter case the first command fails. It is also possible that the delay will never be ended, for example, if a group of processes are attempting communication but none of their input and output commands correspond with each other. This form of failure is known as a deadlock.)

Examples:

(1) cardreader?cardimage   from cardreader, read a card and assign its value (an array of characters) to the variable cardimage.

(2) lineprinter!lineimage   to lineprinter, send the value of lineimage for printing.

(3) $X?(x, y)$ from process named X, input a pair of values and assign them to x and y.

(4) DIV!$(3{*}a + b, 13)$ to process DIV, output the two specified values.

Note: If a process named DIV issues command (3), and a process named X issues command (4), these are executed simultaneously, and have the same effect as the assignment: $(x, y) := (3{*}a + b, 13)$ ($\equiv x := 3{*}a + b; y := 13$).

(5) console(i)?c   from the ith element of an array of consoles, input a value and assign it to c.

(6) console(j − 1)!"A"   to the $(j − 1)$th console, output character "A".

(7) X(i)?V()   from the ith of an array of processes X, input a signal V(); refuse to input any other signal.

(8) sem!P()   to sem ouput a signal P().

2.4 Alternative and repetitive commands

```
<repetitive command> ::= *<alternative command>
<alternative command> ::= [<guarded command>
    {[]<guarded command>}]
<guarded command> ::= <guard> → <command list>
    |(<range>{,<range>})<guard> → <command list>
<guard> ::= <guard list>|<guard list>;<input command>
    |<input command>
<guard list> ::= <guard element>{;<guard element>}
<guard element> ::= <boolean expression>|<declaration>
```

A guarded command with one or more ranges stands for a series of guard commands, each with the same guard and command list, except that each has a different combination of values substituted for the bound variables. The values range between the lower bounds and upper bound inclusive. For example, $(i{:}1..n)G \to CL$ stands for

$$G_1 \to CL_1 [] G_2 \to CL_2 [] \ldots [] G_n \to CL_n$$

where each $G_j \to CL_j$ is formed from $G \to CL$ by replacing every occurrence of the bound variable i by the numeral j.

A guarded command is executed only if and when the execution of its guard does not fail. First its guard is executed and then its command list. A guard is executed by execution of its constituent elements from left to right. A Boolean expression is evaluated: If it denotes false, the guard fails; but an expression that denotes true has no effect. A declaration introduces a fresh variable with a scope that extends from the declaration to the end of the guarded command. An input command at the end of a guard is executed only if and when a corresponding output command is executed. (An implementation may test whether a guard fails simply by trying to execute it, and discontinuing execution if and when it fails. This is valid because such a discontinued execution has no effect on the state of the executing device.)

An alternative command specifies execution of exactly one of its constituent guarded commands. Consequently, if all guards fail, the alternative command fails. Otherwise an arbitrary one with successfully executable guard is selected and executed. (An implementation should take advantage of its freedom of selection to ensure efficient execution and good response. For example, when input commands appear as guards, the command which corresponds to the earliest ready and matching output command should in general be preferred; and certainly, no executable and ready output command should be passed over unreasonably often.)

A repetitive command specifies as many iterations as possible of its constituent alternative command. Consequently, when all guards fail, the repetitive command terminates with no effect. Otherwise, the alternative command is executed once and then the whole repetitive command is executed again. (Consider a repetitive command when all its true guard lists end in an input guard. Such a command may have to be delayed until either (1) an output command corresponding to one of the input guards becomes ready, or (2) all the sources named by the input guards have terminated. In case (2), the repetitive command terminates. It neither event ever occurs, the process fails (in deadlock).

Examples:

(1) $[x \geq y \to m := x [\!] y \geq x \to m := y]$

If $x \geq y$, assign x to m; if $y \geq x$ assign y to m; if both $x \geq y$ and $y \geq x$, either assignment can be executed.

(2) $i := 0; *[i <$ size; content$(i) \neq n \to i := i + 1]$

The repetitive command scans the elements content(i), for $i = 0, 1, \ldots$, until either $i \geq$ size, or a value equal to n is found.

(3) $*[c$:character; west$?c \to$ east$!c]$

This reads all the characters output by west, and outputs them one by one to east. The repetition terminates when the process west terminates.

(4) $*[(i$:1..10)continue(i); console$(i)?c \to X!(i, c)$; console(i)!ack();
    continue$(i) := (c \neq$ sign off$)]$

This command inputs repeatedly from any of ten consoles, provided that the corresponding element of the Boolean array continue is true. The bound variable i identifies the originating console. Its value, together with the character just input, is output to X, and an acknowledgement signal is sent back to the originating console. If the character indicated "sign off," continue(i) is set false, to prevent further input from that console. The repetitive command terminates when all ten elements of continue are false. (An implementation should ensure that no console which is ready to provide input will be ignored unreasonably often.)

(5) $*[n$:integer; X?insert$(n) \to$ INSERT
    $[\!] n$:integer; X?has$(n) \to$ SEARCH; $X!(i <$ size$)$
    ]

(Here, and elsewhere, capitalized words INSERT and SEARCH stand as abbreviations for program text defined separately.)

On each iteration this command accepts from X *either* (a) a request to "insert(n)," (followed by INSERT) *or* (b) a question "has(n)," to which it outputs an answer back to X. The choice between (a) and (b) is made by the next output command in X. The repetitive command terminates when X does. If X sends a nonmatching message, deadlock will result.

(6) $*[X?V() \to \text{val} := \text{val} + 1$
    $\llbracket \text{val} > 0; Y?P() \to \text{val} := \text{val} - 1$
    ]

On each iteration, accept *either* a V() signal from X and increment val, *or* a P() signal from Y, and decrement val. But the second alternative cannot be selected unless val is positive (after which val will remain invariantly nonnegative). (When val > 0, the choice depends on the relative speeds of X and Y, and is not determined.) The repetitive command will terminate when both X and Y are terminated, or when X is terminated and val $\leq$ 0.

3. Coroutines

In parallel programming coroutines appear as a more fundamental program structure than subroutines, which can be regarded as a special case (treated in the next section).

3.1 COPY

Problem: Write a process X to copy characters output by process west to process east.

Solution:

$X :: *[c:\text{character}; \text{west}?c \to \text{east}!c]$

Notes: (1) When west terminates, the input "west?c" will fail, causing termination of the repetitive command, and of process X. Any subsequent input command from east will fail. (2) Process X acts as a single-character buffer between west and east. It permits west to work on production of the next character, before east is ready to input the previous one.

3.2 SQUASH

Problem: Adapt the previous program to replace every pair of consecutive asterisks "**" by an upward arrow "↑". Assume that the final character input is not an asterisk.

Solution:

```
X :: *[c:character; west?c →
      [c ≠ asterisk → east!c
      ▯c = asterisk → west?c;
            [c ≠ asterisk → east!asterisk; east!c
            ▯c = asterisk → east!upward arrow
            ]
      ]
     ]
```

Notes: (1) Since west does not end with asterisk, the second "west?c" will not fail. (2) As an exercise, adapt this process to deal sensibly will input which ends with an odd number of asterisks.

3.3 DISASSEMBLE

Problem: to read cards from a cardfile and output to process X the stream of characters they contain. An extra space should be inserted at the end of each card.

Solution:

```
*[cardimage:(1..80)character; cardfile?cardimage →
     i:integer; i := 1;
     *[i ≤ 80 → X!cardimage(i); i := i + 1];
     X!space
]
```

Notes: (1) "(1..80)character" declares an array of 80 characters, with subscripts ranging between 1 and 80. (2) The repetitive command terminates when the cardfile process terminates.

3.4 ASSEMBLE

Problem: To read a stream of characters from process X and print them in lines of 125 characters on a lineprinter. The last line should be completed with spaces if necessary.

Solution:

```
lineimage:(1..125)character;
i:integer; i := 1;
*[c:character; X?c →
     lineimage(i) := c;
     [i ≤ 124 → i := i + 1
     ▯i = 125 → lineprinter!lineimage; i := 1
     ]
];
[i = 1 → skip
```

    〚i > 1 → *[i ≤ 125 → lineimage(i) := space; i := i + 1];
        lineprinter!lineimage
    ]

Note: (1) When X terminates, so will the first repetitive command of this process. The last line will then be printed, if it has any characters.

3.5 Reformat

Problem: Read a sequence of cards of 80 characters each, and print the characters on a lineprinter at 125 characters per line. Every card should be followed by an extra space, and the last line should be completed with spaces if necessary.

Solution:

   [west::DISASSEMBLE||X::COPY||east::ASSEMBLE]

Notes: (1) The capitalized names stand for program text defined in previous sections. (2) The parallel command is designed to terminate after the cardfile has terminated. (3) This elementary problem is difficult to solve elegantly without coroutines.

3.6 Conway's problem [4]

Problem: Adapt the above program to replace every pair of consecutive asterisks by an upward arrow.

Solution:

   [west::DISASSEMBLE||X::SQUASH||east::ASSEMBLE]

4. Subroutines and Data Representations

A conventional nonrecursive subroutine can be readily implemented as a coroutine, provided that (1) its parameters are called "by value" and "by result," and (2) it is disjoint from its calling program. Like a Fortran subroutine, a coroutine may retain the values of local variables (*own* variables, in Algol terms) and it may use input commands to achieve the effect of "multiple entry points" in a safer way than PL/I. Thus a coroutine can be used like a SIMULA class instance as a concrete representation for abstract data.

A coroutine acting as a subroutine is a process operating concurrently with its user process in a parallel command: [subr::SUBROUTINE||X::USER]. The SUBROUTINE will contain (or consist of) a repetitive command: *[X?(value params) → ... ; X!(result params)], where ... computes the results from the values input. The subroutine will terminate when its user does. The USER will call the subroutine by a pair of commands: subr!(arguments); ... ; subr?(results). Any commands between these two will be executed concurrently with the subroutine.

A multiple-entry subroutine, acting as a representation for data [11], will also contain a repetitive command which represents each entry by an alternative input to a structured target with the entry name as constructor. For example,

*[X?entry1(value params) → ...
⫿X?entry2(value params) → ...
]

The calling process X will determine which of the alternatives is activated on each repetition. When X terminates, so does this repetitive command. A similar technique in the user program can achieve the effect of multiple exits.

A recursive subroutine can be simulated by an array of processes, one for each level of recursion. The user process is level zero. Each activation communicates its parameters and results with its predecessor and calls its successor if necessary:

[recsub(0)::USER‖recsub(i:1..reclimit)::RECSUB] .

The user will call the first element of

recsub: recsub(1)!(arguments); ... ; recsub(1)?(results); .

The imposition of a fixed upper bound on recursion depth is necessitated by the "static" design of the language.

This clumsy simulation of recursion would be even more clumsy for a mutually recursive algorithm. It would not be recommended for conventional programming; it may be more suitable for an array of microprocessors for which the fixed upper bound is also realistic.

In this section, we assume each subroutine is used only by a *single* user process (which may, or course, itself contain parallel commands).

4.1 Function: division with remainder

Problem: Construct a process to represent a function-type subroutine, which accepts a positive dividend and divisor, and returns their integer quotient and remainder. Efficiency is of no concern.

Solution:

[DIV::*[x,y:integer;$X?(x, y)$ →
    quot,rem:integer; quot := 0; rem := x;
    *[rem $\geq y$ → rem := rem − y; quot := quot + 1];
    X!(quot, rem)
    ]
‖X::USER
]

4.2 Recursion: factorial

Problem: Compute a factorial by the recursive method, to a given limit.

Solution:

```
[fac(i:1..limit)::
*[n:integer;fac(i − 1)?n →
    [n = 0 → fac(i − 1)!1
    []n > 0 → fac(i + 1)!n − 1;
        r:integer; fac(i + 1)?r; fac(i − 1)!(n * r)
    ]
]
||fac(0)::USER
]
```

Note: This unrealistic example introduces the technique of the "iterative array" which will be used to a better effect in later examples.

4.3 Data representation: small set of integers [11]

Problem: To represent a set of not more that 100 integers as a process, S, which accepts two kinds of instruction from its calling process X: (1) S!insert(n), insert the integer n in the set, and (2) S!has(n); ... ; S?b, b is set true if n is in the set, and false otherwise. The initial value of the set is empty.

Solution:

```
S::
content:(0..99)integer; size:integer; size := 0;
*[n:integer; X?has(n) → SEARCH; X!(i < size)
[]n:integer; X?insert(n) → SEARCH;
    [i < size → skip
    []i = size; size < 100 →
        content(size) := n; size := size + 1
    ]
]
```

where SEARCH is an abbreviation for:

```
i:integer; i := 0;
*[i < size; content(i) ≠ n → i := i + 1]
```

Notes: (1) The alternative command with guard "size < 100" will fail if an attempt is made to insert more than 100 elements. (2) The activity of insertion will in general take place concurrently with the calling process. However, any subsequent instruction to S will be delayed until the previous insertion is complete.

4.4 Scanning a set

Problem: Extend the solution to 4.3 by providing a fast method for scanning all members of the set without changing the value of the set. The user program will contain a repetitive command of the form:

    S!scan( ); more:boolean; more := true;
    ∗[more; x:integer; S?next(x) → ... deal with x ...
    []more; S?noneleft( ) → more := false
    ]

where S!scan( ) sets the representation into a scanning mode. The repetitive command serves as a **for** statement, inputting the successive members of x from the set and inspecting them until finally the representation sends a signal that there are no members left. The body of the repetitive command is *not* permitted to communicate with S in any way.

Solution: Add a third guarded command to the outer repetitive command of S:

    ... []X?scan( ) →
        i:integer; i := 0;
        ∗[i < size → X!next(content(i)); i := i + 1];
        X!noneleft( )

4.5 Recursive data representation: small set of integers

Problem: Same as above, but an array of processes is to be used to achieve a high degree of parallelism. Each process should contain at most one number. When it contains no number, it should answer "false" to all inquiries about membership. On the first insertion, it changes to a second phase of behavior, in which it deals with instructions from its predecessor, passing some of them onto its successor. The calling process will be named S(0). For efficiency, the set should be sorted, i.e. the ith process should contain the ith largest number.

Solution:

    S(i:1..100)::
    ∗[n:integer; S(i − 1)?has(n) → S(0)!false
    []n:integer; S(i − 1)?insert(n) →
        ∗[m:integer; S(i − 1)?has(m) →
            [$m \leq n$ → S(0)!($m = n$)
            []$m > n$ → S(i + 1)!has(m)
            ]
        []m:integer; S(i − 1)?insert(m) →
            [$m < n$ → S(i + 1)!insert(n); n := m
            []$m = n$ → skip
            []$m > n$ → S(i + 1)!insert(m)   ]
        ]
    ]

Notes: (1) the user process S(0) inquires whether n is a member by the commands S(1)!has(n); ... ; [(i:1..100)S(i)?b → skip]. The appropriate process will respond to the input command by the output command in line 2 or line 5. This trick avoids passing the answer back "up the chain." (2) Many insertion operations can proceed in parallel, yet any subsequent "has" operation will be performed correctly. (3) All repetitive commands and all processes of the array will terminate after the user process S(0) terminates.

4.6 Multiple exits: remove the least member

Exercise: Extend the above solution to respond to a command to yield the least member of the set and to remove it from the set. The user program will invoke the facility by a pair of commands:

S(1)!least( );
 [x:integer;S(1)?x → ... deal with x ...
 []S(1)?noneleft( ) → ...
 ]

or, if he wishes to scan and empty the set, he may write:

S(1)!least( );
 more:boolean; more := true;
 *[more; x:integer; S(1)?x → ... deal with x ... ; S(1)!least( )
 []more; S(1)?noneleft( ) → more := false
 ]

Hint: Introduce a Boolean variable, b, initialized to true, and prefix this to all the guards of the inner loop. After responding to a !least( ) command from its predecessor, each process returns its contained value n, asks its successor for its least, and stores the response in n. But if the successor returns "noneleft( )," b is the set false and the inner loop terminates. The process therefore returns to its initial state. (Solution due to David Gries.)

5. Monitors and Scheduling

This section shows how a monitor can be regarded as a single process which communicates with more than one user process. However, each user process must have a different name (e.g. producer, consumer) or a different subscript (e.g. X(i)) and each communication with a user must identify its source or destination uniquely.

 Consequently, when a monitor is prepared to communicate with *any* of its user processes (i.e. whichever of them calls first) it will use a guarded command with a range. For example: *[(i:1..100)X(i)?(value parameters) → ... ; X(i)!(results)]. Here, the bound variable i is used to send the results back to the calling process. If the monitor is not prepared to accept input from some particular user (e.g. X(j)

on a given occasion, the input command may be preceded by a Boolean guard. For example, two successive inputs from the same process are inhibited by $j = 0$; $*[(i:1..100) i \neq j; X(i)?(\text{values}) \rightarrow \ldots ; j := i]$. Any attempted output from $X(j)$ will be delayed until a subsequent iteration, after the output of some other process $X(i)$ has been accepted and dealt with.

Similarly, conditions can be used to delay acceptance of inputs which would violate scheduling constraints – postponing them until some later occasion when some other process has brought the monitor into a state in which the input can validly be accepted. This technique is similar to a conditional critical region [10] and it obviates the need for special synchronizing variables such as events, queues, or conditions. However, the absence of these special facilities certainly makes it more difficult or less efficient to solve problems involving priorities – for example, the scheduling of head movement on a disk.

5.1 Bounded buffer

Problem: Construct a buffering process X to smooth variations in the speed of output of portions by a producer process and input by a consumer process. The consumer contains pairs of commands X!more(); X?p, and the producer contains commands of the form X!p. The buffer should contain up to ten portions.

Solution:

```
X::
buffer:(0..9) portion;
in,out:integer; in := 0; out := 0;
comment 0 ≤ out ≤ in ≤ out + 10;
    *[in < out + 10; producer?buffer(in mod 10) → in := in + 1
    []out < in; consumer?more( ) → consumer!buffer(out mod 10);
        out := out + 1
    ]
```

Notes: (1) When out < in < out + 10, the selection of the alternative in the repetitive command will depend on whether the producer produces before the consumer consumes, or vice versa. (2) When out = in, the buffer is empty and the second alternative cannot be selected even if the consumer is ready with its command X!more( ). However, after the producer has produced its next portion, the consumer's request can be granted on the next iteration. (3) Similar remarks apply to the producer, when in = out + 10. (4) X is designed to terminate when out = in and the producer has terminated.

5.2 Integer semaphore

Problem: To implement an integer semaphore, S, shared among an array $X(i:1..100)$ of client processes. Each process may increment the semaphore by S!V( ) or decrement it by S!P( ), but the latter command must be delayed if the value of the semaphore is not positive.

Solution:

```
S::val:integer; val := 0;
    *[(i:1..100)X(i)?V( ) → val := val + 1
    [](i:1..100)val > 0; X(i)?P( ) → val := val - 1
    ]
```

Notes: (1) In this process, no use is made of knowledge of the subscript i of the calling process. (2) The semaphore terminates only when all hundred processes of the process array X have terminated.

5.3 Dining philosophers (Problem due to E. W. Dijkstra)

Problem: Five philosophers spend their lives thinking and eating. The philosophers share a common dining room where there is a circular table surrounded by five chairs, each belonging to one philosopher. In the center of the table there is a large bowl of spaghetti, and the table is laid with five forks (see Figure 1). On feeling hungry, a philosopher enters the dining room, sits in his own chair, and picks up the fork on the left of his place. Unfortunately, the spaghetti is so tangled that he needs to pick up and use the fork on his right as well. When he has finished, he puts down both forks, and leaves the room. The room should keep a count of the number of philosophers in it.

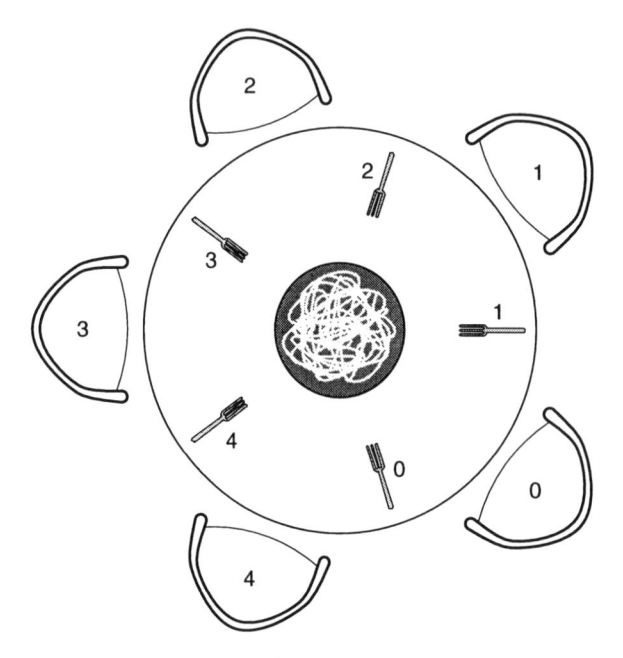

Figure 1.

Solution: The behavior of the *i*th philosopher may be described as follows:

```
PHIL =
   *[... during ith lifetime ... →
   THINK;
   room!enter( );
   fork(i)!pickup( ); fork((i + 1) mod 5)!pickup( );
   EAT;
   fork(i)!putdown( ); fork((i + 1) mod 5)!putdown( );
   room!exit( )
   ]
```

The fate of the *i*th fork is to be picked up and put down by a philosopher sitting on either side of it.

```
FORK =
   *[phil(i)?pickup( ) → phil(i)?putdown( )
   []phil((i -1)mod 5)?pickup( ) → phil((i - 1) mod 5)?putdown( )
   ]
```

The story of the room may be simply told:

```
ROOM = occupancy:integer; occupancy := 0;
   *[(i:0..4)phil(i)?enter( ) → occupancy := occupancy + 1
   [](i:0..4)phil(i)?exit( ) → occupancy := occupancy − 1
   ]
```

All these components operate in parallel:

   [room::ROOM||fork(i:0..4)::FORK||phil(i:0..4)::PHIL] .

Notes: (1) The solution given above does not prevent all five philosophers from entering the room, each picking up his left fork, and starving to death because he cannot pick up his right fork. (2) Exercise: Adapt the above program to avert this sad possibility. Hint: Prevent more than four philosophers from entering the room. (Solution due to E. W. Dijkstra.)

6. Miscellaneous

This section contains further examples of the use of communicating sequential processes for the solution of some less familiar problems; a parallel version of the sieve of Eratosthenes, and the design of an iterative array. The proposed solutions are even more speculative than those of the previous sections, and in the second example, even the question of termination is ignored.

6.1 Prime numbers: the sieve of Eratosthenes [14]

Problem: To print in ascending order all primes less than 10000. Use an array of processes, SIEVE, in which each process inputs a prime from its predecessor and prints it. The process then inputs an ascending stream of numbers from its predecessor and passes them on to its successor, suppressing any that are multiples of the original prime.

Solution:

```
[SIEVE(i:1..100)::
    p,mp:integer;
    SIEVE(i − 1)?p;
    print!p;
    mp := p; comment mp is a multiple of p;
    *[m:integer; SIEVE(i − 1)?m →
        *[m > mp → mp := mp + p];
        [m = mp → skip
        []m < mp → SIEVE(i + 1)!m
        ]
    ]
||SIEVE(0)::print!2; n:integer; n := 3;
    *[n < 10000 → SIEVE(1)!n; n := n + 2]
||SIEVE(101)::*[n:integer;SIEVE(100)?n → print!n]
||print::*[(i:0..101)n:integer; SIEVE(i)?n → ...]
]
```

Note: (1) This beautiful solution was contributed by David Gries. (2) It is algorithmically similar to the program developed in [7, pp. 27–32].

6.2 An iterative array: matrix multiplication

Problem: A square matrix A of order 3 is given. Three streams are to be input, each stream representing a column of an array M. Three streams are to be output, each representing a column of the product matrix $M \times A$. After the initial delay, the results are to be produced at the same rate as the input is consumed. Consequently, a high degree of parallelism is required. The solution should take the form shown in Figure 2. Each of the nine nonborder nodes inputs a vector component from the west and a partial sum from the north. Each node outputs the vector component to its east, and an updated partial sum to the south. The input data is produced by the west border nodes, and the desired results are consumed by south border nodes. The north border is a constant source of zeros and the east border is just a sink. No provision need be made for termination nor for changing the values of the array A.

Solution: There are twenty-one nodes, in five groups, comprising the central square and the four borders:

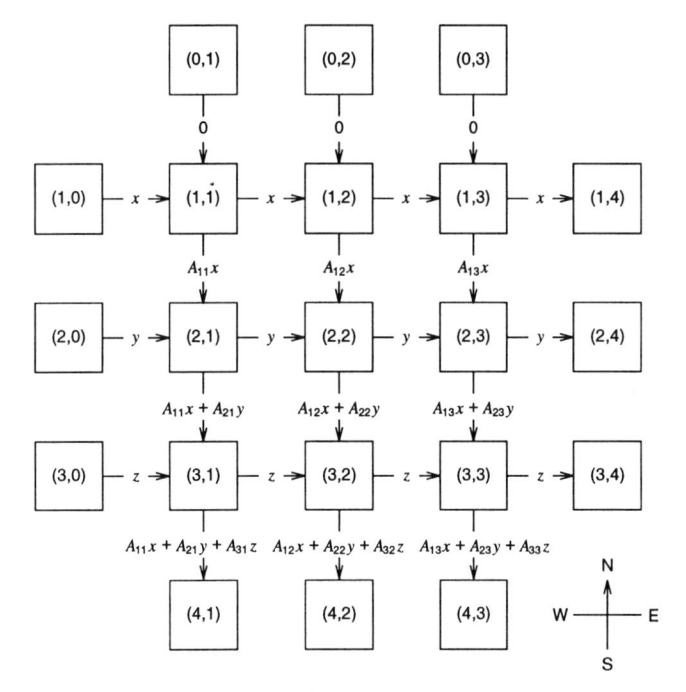

Figure 2.

```
[M(i:1..3,0)::WEST
||M(0,j:1..3)::NORTH
||M(i:1..3,4)::EAST
||M(4,j:1..3)::SOUTH
||M(i:1..3,j:1..3)::CENTER
]
```

The WEST and SOUTH borders are processes of the user program; the remaining processes are:

```
NORTH = *[true → M(1,j)!0]
EAST  = *[x:real; M(i,3)?x → skip]
CENTER = *[x:real; M(i,j − 1)?x →
         M(i,j + 1)!x; sum:real;
         M(i − 1,j)?sum; M(i + 1,j)!(A(i,j)*x + sum)
       ]
```

7. Discussion

A design for a programming language must necessarily involve a number of decisions which seen to be fairly arbitrary. The discussion of this section is intended to explain some of the underlying motivation and to mention some unresolved questions.

7.1 Notations

I have chosen single-character notations (e.g. !,?) to express the primitive concepts, rather than the more traditional boldface or underlined English words. As a result, the examples have an APL-like brevity, which some readers find distasteful. My excuse is that (in contrast to APL) there are only a very few primitive concepts and that is standard practice of mathematics (and also good coding practice) to denote common primitive concepts by brief notations (e.g. +,×). When read aloud, these are replaced by words (e.g. plus, times).

Some readers have suggested the use of assignment notation for input and output:

<target variable> := <source>
<destination> := <expression>

I find this suggestion misleading: it is better to regard input and output as distinct primitives, justifying distinct notations.

I have used the same pair of brackets ([...]) to bracket all program structures, instead of the more familiar variety of brackets (**if...fi, begin...end, case...esac**, etc.). In this I follow normal mathematical practice, but I must also confess to a distaste for the pronunciation of words like **fi, od**, or **esac**.

I am dissatisfied with the fact that my notation gives the same syntax for a structured expression and a subscripted variable. Perhaps tags should be distinguished from other identifiers by a special symbol (say #).

I was tempted to introduce an abbreviation for combined declaration and input, e.g. $X?(n:\text{integer})$ for $n:\text{integer}; X?n$.

7.2 Explicit naming

My design insists that every input or output command must name its source or destination explicitly. This makes it inconvenient to write a library of processes which can be included in subsequent programs, independent of the process names used in that program. A partial solution to this problem is to allow one process (the *main* process) of a parallel command to have an empty label, and to allow the other processes in the command to use the empty process name as source or destination of input or output.

For construction of large programs, some more general technique will also be necessary. This should at least permit substitution of program text for names defined elsewhere – a technique which has been used informally throughout this paper. The Cobol COPY verb also permits a substitution for formal parameters within the copied text. But whatever facility is introduced, I would recommend the following principle: Every program, after assembly with its library routines, should be printable as a text expressed wholly in the language, and it is this printed text which should describe the execution of the program, independent of which parts were drawn from a library.

Since I did not intend to design a complete language, I have ignored the problem of libraries in order to concentrate on the essential semantic concepts of the program which is actually executed.

7.3 Port names

An alternative to explicit naming of source and destination would be to name a *port* through which communication is to take place. The port names would be local to the processes, and the manner in which pairs of ports are to be connected by channels could be declared in the head of a parallel command.

This is an attractive alternative which could be designed to introduce a useful degree of syntactically checkable redundancy. But it is semantically equivalent to the present proposal, provided that each port is connected to exactly one other port in another process. In this case each channel can be identified with a tag, together with the name of the process at the other end. Since I wish to concentrate on semantics, I preferred in this paper to use the simplest and most direct notation, and to avoid raising questions about the possibility of connecting more than two ports by a single channel.

7.4 Automatic buffering

As an alternative to synchronization of input and output, it is often proposed that an outputting process should be allowed to proceed even when the inputting process is not yet ready to accept the output. An implementation would be expected automatically to interpose a chain of buffers to hold output messages that have not yet been input.

I have deliberately rejected this alternative, for two reasons: (1) It is less realistic to implement in multiple disjoint processors, and (2) when buffering is required on a particular channel, it can readily be specified using the given primitives. Of course, it could be argued equally well that synchronization can be specified when required by using a pair of buffered input and output commands.

7.5 Unbounded process activation

The notation for an array of processes permits the same program text (like an Algol recursive procedure) to have many simultaneous "activations"; however, the exact number must be specified in advance. In a conventional single-processor implementation, this can lead to inconvenience and wastefulness, similar to the fixed-length array of Fortran. In would therefore be attractive to allow a process array with no a priori bound on the number of elements; and so specify that the exact number of elements required for a particular execution of the program should be determined dynamically, like the maximum depth of recursion of an Algol procedure or the number of iterations of a repetitive command.

However, it is a good principle that every actual run of a program with unbounded arrays should be identical to the run of some program with all its arrays bounded in advance. Thus the unbounded program should be defined as the "limit" (in some sense) of a series of bounded programs with increasing bounds. I have chosen to concentrate on the semantics of the bounded case – which is necessary anyway and which is more realistic for implementation on multiple microprocessors.

7.6 Fairness

Consider the parallel command:

[X::Y!stop( )||Y::continue:boolean; continue := true;
  *[continue; X?stop( ) → continue := false
  []continue → n := n + 1
  ]
].

If the implementation always prefers the second alternative in the repetitive command of Y, it is said to be *unfair*, because although the output command in X could have been executed on an infinite number of occasions, it is in fact always passed over.

The question arises: Should a programming language definition specify that an implementation must be *fair*? Here I am fairly sure that the answer is NO. Otherwise, the implementation would be obliged to successfully complete the example program shown above, in spite of the fact that its nondeterminism is unbounded. I would therefore suggest that it is the programmer's responsibility to prove that his program terminates correctly – without relying on the assumption of fairness in the implementation. Thus the program shown above is incorrect, since its termination cannot be proved.

Nevertheless, I suggest that an efficient implementation should try to be reasonably fair and should ensure that an output command is not delayed unreasonably often after it first becomes executable. But a proof of correctness must not rely on this property of an efficient implementation. Consider the following analogy with a sequential program: An efficient implementation of an alternative command will tend to favor the alternative which can be most efficiently executed, but the programmer must ensure that the logical correctness of his program does not depend on this property of his implementation.

This method of avoiding the problem of fairness does not apply to programs such as operating systems which are intended to run forever because in this case termination proofs are not relevant. But I wonder whether it is ever advisable to write or to execute such programs. Even an operating system should be designed to bring itself to an orderly conclusion reasonably soon after it inputs a message instructing it to do so. Otherwise, the *only* way to stop it is to "crash" it.

7.7 Functional coroutines

It is interesting to compare the processes described here with those proposed in [12]; the differences are most striking. There, coroutines are strictly deterministic: No choice is given between alternative sources of input. The output commands are automatically buffered to any required degree. The output of one process can be automatically fanned out to any number of processes (including itself!) which can consume it at differing rates. Finally, the processes there are designed to run forever, whereas my proposed parallel command is normally intended to terminate. The design in [12] is based on an elegant theory which permits proof of the properties of programs. These differences are not accidental – they seem to be natural consequences of the difference between the more abstract applicative (or functional) approach to programming and the more machine-oriented imperative (or procedural) approach, which is taken by communicating sequential processes.

7.8 Output guards

Since output commands may appear in guards, it seems more sympathetic to permit output commands as well. This would allow an obvious and useful simplification in some of the example programs, for example, in the bounded buffer (5.1). Perhaps a more convincing reason would be to ensure that the externally visible effect and behaviour of every parallel command can be modeled by some sequential command. In order to model the parallel command

$Z :: [X!2 || Y!3]$

we need to be able to write the sequential alternative command:

$Z :: [X!2 \rightarrow Y!3 \,[]\, Y!3 \rightarrow X!2]$

Note that this *cannot* be done by the command

$Z :: [\text{true} \rightarrow X!2; Y!3 \,[]\, \text{true} \rightarrow Y!3; X!2]$

which can fail if the process Z happens to choose the first alternative, but the processes Y and X are synchronized with each other in such a way that Y must input from Z before X does, e.g.

$Y :: Z?y; X!\text{go}(\ )$
$||X :: Y?\text{go}(\ ); Z?x$

7.9 Restriction: repetitive command with input guard

In proposing an unfamiliar programming language feature, it seems wiser at first to specify a highly restrictive version rather than to propose extensions – especially when the language feature claims to be primitive. For example, it is clear that the multidimensional process array is not primitive, since it can readily be constructed in a language which permits only single-dimensional arrays. But I have a rather more serious misgiving about the repetitive command with input guards.

The automatic termination of a repetitive command on termination of the sources of all its input guards is an extremely powerful and convenient feature but it also involves some subtlety of specification to ensure that it is implementable, and it is certainly not primitive since the required effect can be achieved (with considerable inconvenience) by explicit exchange of "end( )" signals. For example, the subroutine DIV (4.1) could be rewritten:

[DIV :: continue:boolean; continue := true;
    *[continue; X?end( ) → continue := false
    []continue; x,y:integer; X?(x,y) → ... ; X!(quot,rem)
    ]
||X :: USER PROG; DIV!end( )
]

Other examples would be even more inconvenient.

But the dangers of convenient facilities are notorious. For example, the repetitive commands with input guards may tempt the programmer to write them without making adequate plans for their termination; and if it turns out that the automatic termination is unsatisfactory, reprogramming for explicit termination will involve severe changes, affecting even the interfaces between the processes.

8. Conclusion

This paper has suggested that input, output, and concurrency should be regarded as primitives of programming, which underlie many familiar and less familiar programming concepts. However, it would be unjustified to conclude that these primitives can wholly replace the other concepts in a programming language. Where a more elaborate construction (such as a procedure or a monitor) is frequently useful, has properties which are more simply provable, and can also be implemented more efficiently than the general case, there is a strong reason for including in a programming language a special notation for that construction. The fact that the construction can be defined in terms of similar underlying primitives is a useful guarantee that its inclusion is logically consistent with the remainder of the language.

Acknowledgements. The research reported in this paper has been encouraged and supported by a Senior Fellowship of the Science Research Council of Great Britain. The technical inspiration was due to Edsger W. Dijkstra [9], and the paper has been improved in presentation and content by valuable and painstaking advice from D. Gries, D. Q. M. Fay, Edsger W. Dijkstra, N. Wirth, Robert Milne, M. K. Harper, and its referees. The role of IFIP W.G.2.3 as a forum for presentation and discussion is acknowledged with pleasure and gratitude.

References

1. Atkinson, R., and Hewitt, C. Sychronisation in actor systems. Working Paper 83, M.I.T., Cambridge, Mass., Nov. 1976.
2. Brinch Hansen, P. The programming language Concurrent Pascal. *IEEE Trans. Software Eng. 1*, 2 (June 1975), 199-207.
3. Campbell, R.H., and Habermann, A.N. The specification of process synchronisation by path expressions. *Lecture Notes in Computer Science 16*, Springer, 1974, pp. 80-102.
4. Conway, M.E. Design of a separable transition-diagram compiler. *Comm. ACM 6*, 7 (July 1963), 396-408.
5. Dahl, O-J., et al. SIMULA 67, common base language. Norwegian Computing Centre, Forskningveien, Oslo, 1967.
6. Dijkstra, E.W. Co-operating sequential processes. In *Programming Languages*, F. Genuys, Ed., Academic Press, New York, 1968, pp. 43-112.
7. Dijkstra, E.W. Notes on structured programming. In *Structured Programming*, Academic Press, New York 1972, pp. 1-82.
8. Dijkstra, E.W. Guarded commands, nondeterminacy, and formal derivation of programs. *Comm. ACM 18*, 8 (Aug. 1975), 453-457.
9. Dijkstra, E.W. Verbal communication, Marktoberdorf, Aug. 1975.
10. Hoare, C.A.R. Towards a theory of parallel programming. In *Operating Systems Techniques*, Academic Press, New York, 1972, pp. 61-71.
11. Hoare, C.A.R. Proof of correctness of data representations. *Acta Informatica 1*, 4 (1972), 271-281.
12. Kahn, G. The semantics of a simple language for parallel programming. In *Proc. IFIP Congress 74*, North Holland, 1974.
13. Liskov, B.H. A note on CLU. Computation Structures Group Memo. 112, M.I.T., Cambridge, Mass., 1974.
14. McIlroy, M.D. Coroutines. Bell Laboratories, Murray Hill, N.J., 1968.
15. Naur, P., Ed. Report on the algorithmic language ALGOL 60. *Comm. ACM 3*, 5 (May 1960), 299-314.
16. Reynolds, J.C. COGENT. ANL-7022, Argonne Nat. Lab., Argonne, Ill., 1965.
17. Thompson, K. The UNIX command language. In *Structured Programming*, Infotech, Nicholson House, Maidenhead, England, 1976, pp. 375-384.
18. van Wijngaarden, A. Ed. Report on the algorithmic language ALGOL 68. *Numer. Math. 14* (1969), 79-218.
19. Wulf, W.A., London, R.L., and Shaw, M. Abstraction and verification in ALPHARD. Dept. of Comptr. Sci., Carnegie Mellon U., Pittsburgh, Pa., June 1976.
20. Wirth, N. The programming language PASCAL. *Acta Informatica 1*, 1 (1971), 35-63.

A Simple Approach to Specifying Concurrent Systems

Leslie Lamport

Summary.

In the transition axiom method, safety properties of a concurrent system can be specified by programs; liveness properties are specified by assertions in a simple temporal logic. The method is described with some simple examples, and its logical foundation is informally explored through a careful examination of what it means to implement a specification. Language issues and other practical details are largely ignored.

Over the past few years, I have developed an approach to the formal specification of concurrent systems that I now call the *transition axiom* method. The basic formalism has already been described in [12] and [1], but the formal details tend to obscure the important concepts. Here, I attempt to explain these concepts without discussing the details of the underlying formalism.

Concurrent systems are not easy to specify. Even a simple system can be subtle, and it is often hard to find the appropriate abstractions that make it understandable. Specifying a complex system is a formidable engineering task. We can understand complex structures only if they are composed of simple parts, so a method for specifying complex systems must have a simple conceptual basis. I will try to demonstrate that the transition axiom method provides such a basis. However, I will not address the engineering problems associated with specifying real systems. Instead, the concepts will be illustrated with a series of toy examples that are not meant to be taken seriously as real specifications.

Are you proposing a specification language?

© 1989 Association for Computing Machinery, Inc. Reprinted by permission.
Reprinted from *Communications of the ACM*, 32(1):32–45, January 1989.

No. The transition axiom method provides a conceptual and logical foundation for writing formal specifications; it is not a specification language. The method determines *what* a specification must say; a language determines in detail *how* it is said.

What do you mean by a formal specification?
I find it helpful to view a specification as a contract between the user of a system and its implementer. The contract should tell the user everything he must know to use the system, and it should tell the implementer everything he must know about the system to implement it. In principle, once this contract has been agreed upon, the user and the implementer have no need for further communication. (This view describes the *function* of the specification; it is not meant as a paradigm for how systems should be built.)

For a specification to be formal, the question of whether an implementation satisfies the specification must be reducible to the question of whether an assertion is provable in some mathematical system. To demonstrate that he has met the terms of the contract, the implementer should resort to logic rather than contract law. This does not mean that an implementation must be accompanied by a mathematical proof. It does mean that it should be possible, in principle though not necessarily in practice, to provide such a proof for a correct implementation. The existence of a formal basis for the specification method is the only way I know to guarantee that specifications are unambiguous.

Ultimately, the systems we specify are physical objects, and mathematics cannot prove physical properties. We can prove properties only of a mathematical model of the system; whether or not the system correctly implements the model must remain a question of law and not of mathematics.

Just what is a system?
By "system", I mean anything that interacts with its environment in a discrete (digital) fashion across a well-defined boundary. An airline reservation system is such a system, where the boundary might be drawn between the agents using the system, who are part of the environment, and the terminals, which are part of the system. A Pascal procedure is a system whose environment is the rest of the program, with which it interacts by responding to procedure calls and accessing global variables. Thus, the system being specified may be just one component of a larger system.

The solar system is not a system in this sense, both because it is not discrete and because there is no well-defined notion of an environment with which it interacts.

A real system has many properties, ranging from its response time to the color of the cabinet. No formal method can specify all of these properties. Which ones can be specified with the transition axiom method?
The transition axiom method specifies the behavior of a system – that is, the sequence of observable actions it performs when interacting with the environment. More precisely, it specifies two classes of behavioral properties: safety and liveness

properties. Safety properties assert what the system is allowed to do, or equivalently, what it may not do. Partial correctness is an example of a safety property, asserting that a program may not generate an incorrect answer. Liveness properties assert what the system must do. Termination is an example of a liveness property, asserting that a program must eventually generate an answer. (Alpern and Schneider [2] have formally defined these two classes of properties.) In the transition axiom method, safety and liveness properties are specified separately.

There are important behavioral properties that cannot be specified by the transition axiom method; these include average response time and probability of failure. A transition axiom specification can provide a formal model with which to analyze such properties,[1] but it cannot formally specify them.

There are also important nonbehavioral properties of systems that one might want to specify, such as storage requirements and the color of the cabinet. These lie completely outside the realm of the method.

Why specify safety and liveness properties separately?
There is a single formalism that underlies a transition axiom specification, so there is no formal separation between the specification of safety and liveness properties. However, experience indicates that different methods are used to reason about the two kinds of properties and it is convenient in practice to separate them. I consider the ability to decompose a specification into liveness and safety properties to be one of the advantages of the method. (One must prove safety properties in order to verify liveness properties, but this is a process of decomposing the proof into smaller lemmas.)

Can the method specify real-time behavior?
Worst-case behavior can be specified, since the requirement that the system must respond within a certain length of time can be expressed as a safety property – namely, that the clock is not allowed to reach a certain value without the system having responded. Average response time cannot be expressed as a safety or liveness property.

The transition axiom method can assert that some action either must occur (liveness) or must not occur (safety). Can it also assert that it is possible for the action to occur?
No. A specification serves as a contractual constraint on the behavior of the system. An assertion that the system may or may not do something provides no constraint and therefore serves no function as part of the formal specification. Specification methods that include such assertions generally use them as poor substitutes for liveness properties. Some methods cannot specify that a certain input *must* result in a certain response, specifying instead that it is possible for the input to be followed by the response. Every specification I have encountered that used such assertions was

---

[1] See [20] for an example of failure analysis applied to a specification.

improved by replacing the possibility assertions with liveness properties that more accurately expressed the system's informal requirements.

Imprecise wording can make it appear that a specification contains a possibility assertion when it really doesn't. For example, one sometimes states that it must be possible for a transmission line to lose messages. However, the specification does not require that the loss of messages be possible, since this would prohibit an implementation that guaranteed no messages were lost. The specification might require that something happens (a liveness property) or doesn't happen (a safety property) despite the loss of messages. Or, the statement that messages may be lost might simply be a comment about the specification, observing that it does not require that all messages be delivered, and not part of the actual specification.

If a safety property asserts that some action cannot happen, doesn't its negation assert that the action is possible?
In a formal system, one must distinguish the logical formula A from the assertion $\vdash A$, which means that A is provable in the logic; $\vdash A$ is not a formula of the logic itself. In the logic underlying the transition axiom method, if A represents a safety property asserting that some action is impossible, then the negation of A, which is the formula $\neg A$, asserts that the action must occur. The action's possibility is expressed by the negation of $\vdash A$, which is a metaformula and not a formula within the logic. See [10] for more details.

Safety Properties

A soda machine

We begin with a system consisting of a soda machine, in which the user deposits either a half dollar or two quarters and the machine in return dispenses a can of soda.[2] Figure 1, together with the initial condition that the machine starts in state I, provides a simple specification of the safety properties of this machine.

Figure 1 specifies that, when the machine is in state I, either a *deposit quarter* action can occur that takes the machine to state II or a *deposit half dollar* action can occur that takes it to state III. From state II, only a *deposit quarter* action taking the machine to state III can occur. From state III, only a *dispense soda* action taking the machine to state I can occur. This is a safety specification, so it asserts that these are the only actions that are allowed to occur; it does not assert that any actions must occur.

What happens if the user deposits first a quarter then a half dollar?

---

[2] For the reader unfamiliar with colloquial American English and United States currency: *soda* is a carbonated soft drink, a *quarter* is a coin worth $0.25, and a *half dollar* coin is worth $0.50.

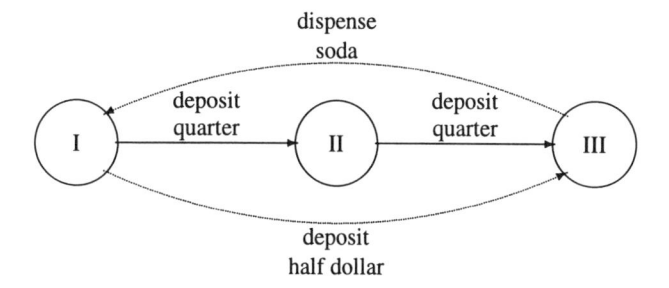

Lamport   A Simple Approach to Specifying Concurrent Systems   335

Figure 1. Specification of a soda machine

The specification disallows this behavior. (Remember that the examples are not supposed to be realistic specifications.) There are two ways to view this aspect of the specification:

– The specification constrains the behavior of the user, forbidding him to deposit a half dollar after he has deposited a quarter.
– The specification does not state what the soda machine is supposed to do if the user deposits a quarter then a half dollar; the implementer is free to build the machine so it does anything he wants if the user exhibits this kind of "incorrect" behavior.

Which view we take makes no difference to how we write and reason about specifications.

Figure 1 is supposed to specify the soda machine's behavior; why does it also specify the user's behavior?
It is impossible to implement a system that functions properly in the presence of arbitrary behavior by the environment. A more realistic specification would allow the user to deposit an arbitrary sequence of coins, perhaps returning them if an inappropriate sequence had been deposited; it would not allow the user to attack the machine with a sledgehammer. (We shall see later how the sledgehammer is disallowed.) The specification of a program procedure usually includes a precondition that constrains the environment by forbidding calls whose arguments do not satisfy the precondition; the specification of a circuit includes timing constraints that restrict when the environment can change the input levels [16].

Figure 1 is a simple state-transition diagram. Such diagrams work well for very simple examples, but don't they become too complicated when specifying real systems?
Yes; these diagrams do not scale well to larger problems. State-transition diagrams represent just one particular language that can be used with the transition axiom method. The shortcomings of these diagrams are limitations of the language, not of the transition axiom method. Other languages are needed for writing transition axiom specifications of larger systems; I will have more to say about languages later.

What is the fundamental, language-independent concept that is expressed by the state-transition diagram of Figure 1?

Allowed state transitions. In the transition axiom method, one specifies safety properties by describing a set of states and all transitions between states that are allowed to occur. There are many different languages with which one can describe states and transitions.

The concept of state transitions, as illustrated by the diagram of Figure 1, has been used for years. Is there anything different about the transition axiom method?

What is new in the transition axiom method is not the diagram, but its interpretation as a formal specification. This new interpretation is needed because conventional state-transition methods do not adequately address the fundamental question of what it means for an implementation to meet such a specification. One of the advantages of the transition axiom method is that specifications of safety properties can be written in friendly, familiar notations such as state-transition diagrams. The specifications look old; the meaning we assign to them is new.[3]

What is different about the interpretation of Figure 1 in the transition axiom method?

The naive interpretation of Figure 1 is that it specifies a three-state machine. In more sophisticated approaches, such as the one described by Jones [8], the diagram is interpreted to mean that there exists some state function, let's call it f, that assumes the values I, II, and III; the diagram specifies how f can change. More precisely, the soda machine is assumed to have some unspecified set of states, let's call it S; the machine's behavior is described by the sequence of states $s_0, s_1, s_2, \ldots$ it passes through. The state function f is a mapping from S to the set of values $\{I, II, III\}$. The diagram of Figure 1 specifies that for each state transition $s_i \rightarrow s_{i+1}$ in this sequence, the change of value from $f(s_i)$ to $f(s_{i+1})$ is one of the following:

- $f(s_i) = I, f(s_{i+1}) = II$, and the change is caused by a *deposit quarter* action.
- $f(s_i) = I, f(s_{i+1}) = III$, and the change is caused by a *deposit half dollar* action.
- $f(s_i) = II, f(s_{i+1}) = III$, and the change is caused by a *deposit quarter* action.
- $f(s_i) = III, f(s_{i+1}) = I$, and the change is caused by a *dispense soda* action.

With this interpretation, the entire interaction of the user depositing a half dollar and the machine dispensing a soda is performed as two actions. In the transition axiom method's interpretation, we allow the additional possibility that $f(s_i) = f(s_{i+1})$ (even if $s_i \neq s_{i+1}$). The interaction of buying a soda with a half-dollar coin could involve dozens or hundreds of state transitions, only two of which change the value of f.

What is gained by this new interpretation?

In a real soda machine, dispensing a soda could involve hundreds of separate state transitions. If a specification asserts that this is just a single action, then one has to say what it means for a machine operation with hundreds of state transitions to

---
[3] More precisely, I believe that this meaning was new when it was proposed in [12] and [13]; it has since appeared in [9] and elsewhere.

satisfy a specification asserting that it is a single action. In the transition axiom method's interpretation, this is not a problem because the specification asserts that there is a state function that changes only once during the dispensing of the soda; it says nothing about how many separate state transitions occur. The advantages of this interpretation are discussed later.

A formal specification should provide all the necessary information to determine if an implementation is correct. However, from Figure 1, there is no way to determine if the implementation is supposed to consist of: (1) the entire soda machine, including the coin box and the soda rack, (2) a control circuit inside the machine, or (3) a program for the soda machine's microprocessor. The choice of labels on the arcs may provide some clue, but surely this choice can have no formal significance. Can a soda machine, a circuit, and a computer program all be correct implementations of the same formal specification?

A specification must be incomplete if it does not distinguish between a mechanical device, a circuit, and a program. What is missing from Figure 1 is a specification of the *interface* – the mechanism by which the system communicates with the environment. The specification must state whether communication is by depositing coins and dispensing cans, by raising and lowering voltages on wires, or by calling and returning from program procedures. The interface specification stipulates that the *deposit quarter* action may not be performed with a sledgehammer. The difference between depositing a quarter and wielding a sledgehammer, or between raising a 5 volt signal and raising a 5000 volt signal, can be described only in terms of implementation details. The interface must therefore be specified at the implementation level.

How is the interface specified?

The environment and the system communicate by changing the values of state functions. For example, if we are specifying a circuit, then communication between the circuit and its environment is achieved by changing the values of state functions that represent the voltages on wires.[4] To each wire w there might correspond a state function f_w that represents the voltage on the wire. The specification might permit the environment to communicate with the circuit by changing the value of f_w to 4.5 ± 1.2 (the voltage on the wire having some fixed value between 3.3 and 5.7 volts) when the value of $f_{w'}$ for some other wire w' equals 0 ± 1.2. (Despite the continuous range of voltages, this can still be considered a discrete system because the voltage changes are assumed to be instantaneous.)

To specify the interface, we must specify how such interface state functions change. This can be done by the same method used to specify changes to internal state functions, such as the function f of the soda machine specification. Thus, no

---

[4] What we are really specifying is not a circuit but a mathematical model of the circuit. The state functions are the mathematical objects within the model that represent the voltages on the wires of the real circuit.

extra machinery need be added to the transition axiom method to specify the interface.

In practice, we usually don't bother specifying the interface in this way. Instead, we specify the interface in the implementation language, making it trivial to check that the interface is implemented correctly. For example, the wires connecting a circuit with its environment would be specified directly in the hardware design language used to implement the circuit. Instead of specifying how the actual voltages on a wire w change, we would describe those changes with the hardware design language's primitives, such as a $w := true$. The actual voltages would not be described.

How are program interfaces specified?
The exact nature of the interface specification depends upon the programming language. For a Pascal procedure, the interface is specified by giving the name of the procedure, the types of its arguments, and the names and types of any global variables accessed by the procedure. For a Modula-2 package, the interface is specified by the definition module [21].

This implies that we cannot specify a procedure independently of the language in which it is implemented. Shouldn't we be able to write a single specification of, say, a square root function that is independent of the language in which it is implemented?
We are not specifying the language in which the procedure is implemented; we are just specifying the implementation of the interface. A system whose interface is specified as a Pascal procedure could be implemented in assembly language; it need only obey the same calling conventions as a Pascal procedure.

While the specifications of a square root function for different programming languages may be similar, they will not be identical. For example, how errors are handled will depend upon whether or not the language provides an exception-handling mechanism. Separating the specification of a square root function into a common part and an interface-dependent part is a specification-language design issue that is addressed by Guttag, Horning, and Wing in Larch [6].

The influence of the interface on the rest of the specification is especially important in concurrent systems. It is shown in [14] that the specification of even so basic a property as first-come-first-served priority cannot be independent of the interface's implementation details.

You are saying that, even for the highest-level specification, the interface must be specified at the implementation level. Can't one hide these low-level implementation details in the high-level specification?
The interface is specified by describing how interface state functions can change. We shall see below how the changes to internal state functions can be specified hierarchically; the same approach can be applied to the interface state functions. However, the high level specification is not complete until the interface is completely specified down to the implementation level. A complete specification should eliminate

the need for any communication between the user of the system and its implementor. For example, the specification of a control circuit for a soda machine should contain all the information about that circuit's behavior needed by the person designing the rest of the machine, which means that it must specify the actual voltages on the wires.

While a hierarchical decomposition of the interface may be quite useful, it is logically just a method of organizing the high level specification. I will therefore not consider such a decomposition of the interface.

Can interfaces be specified solely in terms of state functions?
In addition to interface state functions, we need to introduce the notion of who is responsible for changing the values of these state functions. A specification of the soda machine interface must state that the environment (the user) performs the *deposit quarter* and *deposit half dollar* actions and the system (the machine) performs the *dispense soda* action. The specification of a procedure interface must state that the environment (the rest of the program) performs the procedure call and the system (the procedure) performs the return.

Usually, actions are performed either by the environment or by the system. However, it is sometimes useful to assert which part of the environment performs an action. For example, to specify a process that interacts with its environment through both shared variables and CSP-style operations [7], it may be useful to distinguish actions performed by a communication channel ("!" and "?" operations) from ones performed by other processes (setting shared variables).[5]

Why is it necessary to state who performs an interface action?
Consider a Modula-2 package that implements a queue by providing *put* and *get* procedures. If we failed to specify that only the environment can call these procedures, then the specification would be satisfied by an implementation that calls the *put* procedure itself to cause random elements to appear in the queue.

What is the general form of a safety specification in the transition axiom method?
A safety specification consists of:

- A set of state functions, partitioned into interface and internal state functions.
- A specification of the initial value of every state function.
- A set of actions, partitioned into interface and internal actions.
- For each interface action, a specification of who performs the action. (Internal actions are always performed by the system.)
- A set of rules, called transition axioms, that describe how each action changes the state functions. An interface state function may be changed only by an interface action.

---

[5] Although one often thinks of a CSP communication as an action performed jointly by the sender and the receiver, thinking of it as an action of the channel makes it unnecessary to introduce the concept of joint actions.

In the soda machine example, there is a single internal state function f whose initial value is I; the interface state functions have been left unspecified. There are three actions, all of which are interface actions: *deposit quarter* and *deposit half dollar*, performed by the environment, and *dispense soda*, performed by the system. The effect of the *deposit quarter* action is described by a transition axiom asserting that the action can occur only when f equals I, in which case it changes the value of f to II, or when f equals II, in which case it changes the value of f to III. The rules for the *deposit half dollar* and *dispense soda* actions are similar, but a bit simpler. A complete soda machine specification would also have to describe how these three actions change the interface state functions.

Precisely what is the meaning of such a specification?
The formal meaning of a transition axiom specification is a formula of temporal logic. To give a rigorous definition of that meaning, one must define the formal semantics of temporal logic and provide an algorithm for translating a specification into a temporal logic formula. This is done in [12]. Instead of taking such a formal approach here, I will try to provide an intuitive understanding of what a transition axiom specification means through careful consideration of what it means to implement the specification.

In developing an intuitive understanding of transition axiom specifications, it is useful to know the general shape of the formula underlying a specification. I will ignore the part of the specification having to do with who performs the actions. Let $f_1, \ldots, f_n$ be the internal state functions and $g_1, \ldots, g_m$ be the interface state functions of the specification. The formal meaning of the specification is a temporal logic formula of the form[6]

$$\exists f_1, \ldots, f_n \text{ s.t. } X$$

where X is a formula describing how the f_i and g_i are allowed to change. More precisely, X is a formula that constrains the sequence of states the system assumes by constraining the values of the state functions f_i and g_i on this sequence of states.

Why is there quantification only over internal state functions and not over interface state functions?
The absence of quantification over the interface state functions is the formal expression of the observation that the interface must be specified at the implementation level. The existential quantification over the internal state functions allows complete freedom in how these state functions are implemented. Because the interface state functions are free (not quantified over) in the specification, those same state functions must appear in the implementation. All this should become clearer with the next example, which will serve to address the question of what it means for an implementation to be correct.

---

[6] Note that the interface state functions g_i are free variables in the formula; the significance of this is discussed below.

Another specification of a soda machine

Figure 2 is a soda machine specification written in an *ad hoc* language that resembles an ordinary declarative programming language. The **interface procedures**

> **interface procedures** *deposit_coin* ... ;
> *dispense_soda* ... ;
> **var** x: $\{0, 25, 50\}$;
> y: $\{25, 50\}$;
> **begin loop** α: $\langle x := 0 \rangle$;
> β: **while** $\langle x < 50 \rangle$
> **do** γ: $\langle y := deposit\_coin$ **only if** $x + y_{\text{new}} \leq 50 \rangle$;
> δ: $\langle x := x + y \rangle$
> **od**;
> ϵ: $\langle dispense\_soda \rangle$
> **end loop**

Figure 2. Another specification of a soda machine.

declarations provide the interface specification, which is omitted; the **var** declarations determine the range of values that can be assumed by x and y. Angle brackets denote that the operation they surround is a single (atomic) action. Statement γ performs an action consisting of a *deposit_coin* interface action plus the action of setting the value of y to the value of the deposited coin, the **only if** clause (a notation invented just for this statement) meaning that the action can take place only if the value of $x + y$ after the assignment is at most 50. Thus, the **only if** clause disallows the possibility of depositing a half dollar after a quarter is deposited.

Figure 2 looks like a program. How is it interpreted as a transition axiom specification?

To interpret Figure 2 as a transition axiom specification, we must describe the state functions, actions, etc. that it defines. The internal state functions are the variables x and y and an additional state function, let us call it pc, that describes the program control state; the interface state functions are presumably specified (perhaps implicitly) in the omitted part of the **interface procedures**. The state function x can assume the values 0, 25, and 50; the state function y can assume the values 25 and 50; and the state function pc can assume the values α, β, γ, δ, and ϵ. The initial values of x and y are unspecified; the initial value of pc is α, indicating that control is initially at statement α. There are five actions, one for each pair of angle brackets, that are labeled $\alpha \ldots \epsilon$. Actions γ and ϵ are interface actions, the former performed by the environment and the latter by the system; the rest are internal actions. The transition axioms for these actions specify the following allowed changes to the state functions.

α: This action can occur only when pc has the value α. It changes the value of x to 0, it changes the value of pc to β, and it leaves the value of y unchanged.

β: Can occur only when $pc = \beta$. If $x < 50$ then it changes the value of pc to γ, otherwise it changes the value of pc to ϵ. It leaves the values of x and y unchanged.

γ: Represents the user action of depositing a coin. It sets the value of y equal to the value of the coin deposited, which must be either a quarter or a half dollar (because y can equal only 25 or 50); it leaves the value of x unchanged. This action can occur only when $pc = \gamma$ and the new value of y will satisfy $x + y \leq 50$.

δ: Can occur only when $pc = \delta$. It sets the value of x equal to its old value plus the old value of y, it leaves the value of y unchanged, and it sets the value of pc to β.

ϵ: Can occur only when $pc = \epsilon$. It sets pc to α and leaves the values of x and y unchanged. This action represents the dispensing of a can of soda.

In this specification, x and y look like ordinary program variables, but pc seems strange. Isn't there a fundamental difference between the state function pc and the state functions x and y?

No. To describe the execution of a program written in a declarative programming language, we must describe how the program control position changes as well as how the values of variables change. The programmer cannot explicitly refer to the "program counter", but its value is just as much part of the program state as is the value of an ordinary variable. A programmer often has the choice of whether to use an extra variable or a more complicated control structure to represent the state of a computation.

Is every program a specification?

Yes. A program written in any programming language can be interpreted as a transition axiom specification. A major task in writing a compiler from a source language to a target language is to represent, in the target language, the state functions specified by the program, including ones like pc and the procedure-calling stack that are not explicitly declared. A program written in a higher-level language is a specification of the object code produced by the compiler. The only difference between a program and a higher-level specification is that the program is implemented by the compiler without human intervention.

If any program is a specification, why not write specifications in an ordinary programming language instead of devising specification languages?

This can be done. However, programming languages are constrained by the requirement that programs must be compiled into reasonably efficient code. Because specifications do not have to be compiled, specification languages can permit simpler specifications than can be written in programming languages. Also, programming languages tend to encourage overly restrictive specifications. For example, in most programming languages it is easy to state that one action must follow another but hard to state that two actions can be performed in either order. Such languages encourage specifications that unnecessarily constrain the order in which actions must be performed.

What kind of constructs can specification languages use that programming languages cannot?

The primary programming language construct for indicating explicit state changes is the assignment statement. In a specification language, the assignment statement can be extended to allow an arbitrary relation between the old and new values of state functions. For example, statement γ of Figure 2 can be described as the following relation between the old and new values of the variables:

$$(y_{\text{new}} = deposit\_coin) \wedge (x_{\text{new}} = x_{\text{old}}) \wedge (y_{\text{new}} + x_{\text{old}} \leq 50) \qquad (1)$$

where *deposit_coin* is some expression involving old and new values of interface state functions that is presumably defined by the omitted interface specification.

An ordinary assignment statement is a specific form of relation in which the new value of a variable equals an expression involving only the old values of variables. However, one can have more general relations, such as

$$a_{\text{old}} = \sin^2 b_{\text{new}} + 3 \cos b_{\text{new}}$$

which expresses a relation between the new value of the variable b and the old value of the variable a. Such a relation cannot be expressed in a programming language because it cannot be compiled into efficient code, but there is no reason not to allow it in a specification language.

A transition axiom for an action, which determines the changes to state functions allowed by the action, is just such a relation between old and new values of state functions. For example, the transition axiom for statement γ is obtained by conjoining relation (1), which asserts how x and y may change, with

$$(pc_{\text{old}} = \gamma) \wedge (pc_{\text{new}} = \delta)$$

The latter relation asserts how pc may change and includes the requirement that the action can be performed only when the initial value of pc equals γ. The program of Figure 2 can be replaced by a set of five transition axioms of this form. However, the specification is easier to follow if we use ordinary programming language constructs like ";" and **while** to describe implicitly how the value of pc may change instead of explicitly writing the relations between its old and new values.

Figures 1 and 2 are two different specifications of the soda machine. How are they related?

They are equivalent – assuming that they are completed with the proper interface specifications. In other words, each one is a correct implementation of the other. I will show that Figure 2 correctly implements Figure 1. Demonstrating the converse requires some concepts that will be introduced with another example.

The interpretation of Figure 1 as a transition axiom specification asserts the existence of a state function f with certain properties. To prove that Figure 2 satisfies this specification, we must demonstrate the existence of f. This is done by defining f in terms of the state functions x, y, and pc, whose existence is asserted by the interpretation of Figure 2 as a transition axiom specification. We first observe that $x < 50$ when $pc = \gamma$ and $x + y \le 50$ when $pc = \delta$. (This is proved by showing that these two assertions are true initially and are left true by every action.) The value of f is defined by the expression in Figure 3, written using Dijkstra's **if** construct.[7]

$$\begin{aligned}
&\textbf{if } pc = \alpha && \to f = \text{I} \;\square\\
&\phantom{\textbf{if }} pc = \beta \text{ or } pc = \gamma \to \textbf{if } x = 0 &&\to f = \text{I} \;\square\\
&&& x = 25 \to f = \text{II} \;\square\\
&&& x = 50 \to f = \text{III (impossible if } pc = \gamma)\\
&&& \textbf{fi} \;\square\\
&\phantom{\textbf{if }} pc = \delta && \to \textbf{if } x+y = 25 \to f = \text{II} \;\square\\
&&& \phantom{\to \textbf{if }} x+y = 50 \to f = \text{III} \;\square\\
&&& \phantom{\to \textbf{if }} x+y = 75 \to \text{impossible}\\
&&& \textbf{fi} \;\square\\
&\phantom{\textbf{if }} pc = \epsilon && \to f = \text{III}\\
&\textbf{fi}
\end{aligned}$$

Figure 3. Definition of f in terms of x, y, and pc.

Finally, we show that, with this definition of f, every action allowed by the specification of Figure 2 either leaves f unchanged or corresponds to an action (a change of f) allowed by the specification of Figure 1. The reader can check that actions α, β, and δ do not change f. For example, α can be executed only when $pc = \alpha$, in which case $f = \text{I}$, and its execution sets $pc = \beta$ and $x = 0$, which leaves f equal to I. The reader can also check that execution of γ corresponds either to a *deposit quarter* or a *deposit half dollar* action allowed by Figure 1. For example, suppose γ is executed starting in a state with $x = 25$. Since it can only be executed when $pc = \gamma$, this implies that initially $f = \text{II}$. The specification of the γ action implies that, starting with $x = 25$, it can change the values of x, y, and pc only by setting y to 25 and pc to δ, which makes $f = \text{III}$. This change of the value of f from II to III is permitted by the *deposit quarter* action of Figure 1. The reader can check that executing γ starting with $x = 0$, the only other possibility, also yields a change of f allowed by the *deposit quarter* or *deposit half dollar* action of Figure 1, and that executing ϵ changes f as allowed by the *dispense soda* action of Figure 1.

Is this all there is to the proof?
We have not proved that Figure 2 correctly implements the interface of Figure 1. This requires showing that *deposit_coin* and *dispense_soda* are correct implementations of the corresponding actions of Figure 1, which we cannot do because neither they nor the interface of Figure 1 have been specified.

How can we formalize the informal reasoning used in the proof?

---

[7] Note that Figure 3 is not a program; it is just an ordinary mathematical definition of f as a function of x, y, and pc written with Dijkstra's notation.

Let a *state vector* for the specification of Figure 2 be a triple of possible values of x, y, and pc, and let a state vector for the specification of Figure 1 be a possible value of f (either I, II, or III). To define f in terms of x, y, and pc, we defined a mapping F from state vectors of Figure 2 to state vectors of Figure 1. For example, $F(0, 25, \delta) = \text{II}$ means that $f = \text{II}$ when $x = 0$, $y = 25$, and $pc = \delta$.

For any action ξ, let A_ξ denote the transition axiom for ξ. This is a relation between old and new values – in other words, a set of pairs of state vectors. For example, the pair $((0, 50, \gamma), (0, 25, \delta))$ is in A_γ because it is possible to execute γ starting with $x = 0$, $y = 50$, and $pc = \gamma$ and ending with $x = 0$, $y = 25$, and $pc = \delta$.

Let $\mathbf{A_1}$ and $\mathbf{A_2}$ denote the set of actions of Figures 1 and 2, respectively. Formally, we proved the theorem

$$\forall \xi \in \mathbf{A_2}\ \forall (v, w) \in A_\xi\ \exists \eta \in \mathbf{A_1}\ \text{s.t.}\ (F(v), F(w)) \in A_\eta$$

This formula has the following English translation, where bracketed expressions indicate the correspondence with the formula: for every action [ξ] of Figure 2 [in $\mathbf{A_2}$] and every change to the values of x, y, and pc [from v to w] allowed by this action [(v, w) in A_ξ], there exists an action [η] of Figure 1 [in $\mathbf{A_1}$] such that the corresponding change to the value of f [from $F(v)$ to $F(w)$] is allowed by that action [$(F(v), F(w))$ is in A_η].

Exactly what does this prove?

The formal meaning of the specification of Figure 1 is a formula $\exists f$ s.t. X_1, where X_1 is a formula describing how the value of f is allowed to change; the meaning of Figure 2 is a formula $\exists x, y, pc$ s.t. X_2, where X_2 describes how the values of x, y, and pc are allowed to change. We proved the formula

$$(\exists x, y, pc\ \text{s.t.}\ X_2) \supset (\exists f\ \text{s.t.}\ X_1)$$

Thus, correctness of an implementation means simple logical implication: the specification is implied by the (specification of the) implementation. This implication was proved by proving $X_2 \supset \overline{X_1}$, where $\overline{X_1}$ is the formula obtained by substituting for f in X_1 its expression in terms of x, y, and pc defined in Figure 3. In other words, assuming the existence of the state functions x, y, and pc satisfying X_2, we proved the existence of a state function f satisfying X_1 by explicitly constructing the required f in terms of x, y, and pc.

In a complete specification, X_1 and X_2 would also describe the allowed changes to the interface state functions. However, because there is no quantification over interface state functions, this type of argument can work only if X_1 and X_2 contain the same interface state functions, and the behavior of those interface state functions asserted by X_1 is implied by the assertions about their behavior made by X_2. This is the formal statement of the observation that the interface must be specified (in X_1) at the implementation level (using the same state functions and interface actions as in X_2).

The proof that Figure 2 correctly implements Figure 1 can be reduced to logical implication because both specifications are expressed by formulas in the same logical system. This in turn is possible only because we interpret the state-transition diagram of Figure 1 in terms of the state function f. If Figure 1 were interpreted as specifying the behavior of a three-state machine while Figure 2 specified the behavior of a 30-state machine, then they would express formulas in different logical systems and it would not be clear what correctness of an implementation meant. Traditional definitions of correctness of an implementation, involving mappings on behaviors, have ignored problems that arise in specifying the interface. See [13] for further discussion of this issue.

A database

Let us now consider a toy specification of a database concurrency control mechanism. Clients of the database issue operations by calling an *exec* procedure with arguments indicating the operation to be performed. There are two arguments: *op*, indicating the change to the database and *res*, indicating the value to be returned. (I assume that, as in Modula-2, procedures may return values.) These arguments are described formally as functions. Although the *exec* procedure may be called concurrently by multiple clients, the operations are to be performed as if they occur in a serial order. In other words, the database operations are to be performed as if they were atomic.[8]

The specification is given in Figure 4, using programming language notation.

>   **type** dbase : ... ;
>   value : ... ;
>   op_fcn : dbase → dbase;
>   res_fcn : dbase → value;
>   **internal state function** *data* : dbase;
>   **procedure** *exec*(*op*: op_fcn; *res*: res_fcn) : value
>   **begin** α: $\langle data_{\text{new}} = op(data_{\text{old}}) \land exec_{\text{new}} = res(data_{\text{old}}) \rangle$
>   **end**

Figure 4. A database specification.

The internal state function *data* represents the state of the database. The interface is specified as a procedure call. There is a single internal action α. In this action, *op* and *res* denote the arguments of the procedure call, and *exec* is the value that is returned by the procedure. The procedure call and return are interface actions that are not explicitly specified.

How is Figure 4 interpreted as a transition axiom specification?

---

[8] In database circles, atomicity often means that a failure cannot result in a partially completed operation. The possibility of failure is not considered in this example.

The interface specification must contain state functions whose values indicate the set of processes currently executing the *exec* procedure – that is, the set of processes that executed a call that has not yet returned. There must also be state functions that indicate the following information for each such process:

- The values of *op* and *res*.
- The program control location, indicating whether the process is executing the call, is at control point α, or is executing the return.
- The value of *exec* (the value to be returned), if the process has executed action α.

Figure 4 seems to specify that the entire database operation must be done as a single atomic action; doesn't this rule out concurrency?

The specification asserts the existence of a state function *data* that changes atomically; it does not assert that changes to the database must actually be performed atomically. Figure 2 implements Figure 1 even though the operations of depositing a half dollar and dispensing a can of soda consist of two atomic actions in Figure 1 and six atomic actions in Figure 2. The implementation was proved correct by defining f in such a way that only two of those six actions change f, doing so as allowed by Figure 1; the other four actions leave f unchanged.

In the same way, the change to the database, which is represented by executing the single atomic action α in Figure 4, can be implemented as a sequence of thousands of atomic actions. Correctness of the implementation means that the state function *data* can be defined as a function of the implementation state functions in such a way that only one of those thousands of atomic actions changes its value, doing so as indicated by Figure 4.

The state function must be defined so that a single atomic action causes the entire database operation, which could be arbitrarily complex, suddenly to be performed – even though each atomic action makes only a small change to the actual database. How is this possible?

The only way to understand how it is done is by working out an example. One such example is the specification and implementation of a FIFO queue in [12], where the specification asserts that the operations of adding and removing an element from the queue are atomic, but an implementation that adds and removes elements one bit at a time is proved correct.

The proof method is a generalization of assertional methods for proving safety properties of concurrent programs [18]. In these assertional methods, one constructs an invariant, which is a boolean state function whose value never changes; in the transition axiom method, one constructs state functions whose values change only in the manner prescribed by the transition axioms.

Another database specification

The concurrency control mechanism specified by Figure 4 is called serialization [5] because database operations are executed as if they occurred in some serial order.

However, Figure 4 is not the most general specification of serialization because it requires that the actual reading and writing of the database occurs between the call of *exec* and the subsequent return, which implies that if one call to *exec* returns before another call is initiated, then the operation performed by the first call precedes the operation performed by the second in the serialization order. Some concurrency control algorithms that are considered to be serializable do not have this property. So, let us now consider the more general specification of a serializable database given in Figure 5.

> **type** dbase : ... ;
>   value : ... ;
>   op_fcn : dbase → dbase;
>   res_fcn : dbase → value;
> **internal state function**
>   *gdata* : dbase;
>   *saved_ops* : **bag of** (op_fcn, res_fcn, value);
> **procedure** *exec*(*op*: op_fcn; *res*: res_fcn) : value
>   **begin** β: $\langle \exists v$ s.t. $exec_{new} = v \land$
> $saved\_ops_{new} = saved\_ops_{old} \cup \{(op, res, v)\}\rangle$
> **end**
> **internal process**
>   **begin loop** γ: $\langle \exists (o, r, v) \in saved\_ops_{old}$ s.t.
> $gdata_{new} = o(gdata_{old}) \land$
> $v = r(gdata_{old}) \land$
> $saved\_ops_{new} = saved\_ops_{old} - \{(o, r, v)\}\rangle$
>   **endloop**
> **end**

Figure 5. A more general database specification.

The interface of the new specification is the same as that of Figure 4: a procedure named *exec* with two arguments that specify the operation. However, instead of performing the operation immediately, action β chooses a completely arbitrary value to return (the value v) and saves that value together with the arguments of the procedure call in *saved_ops*, a bag of operations to be performed later.[9] A separate, asynchronous action γ at some later time will perform the operation. The **internal process** keyword denotes that its actions are performed by the system independently of actions performed through calls to the *exec* procedure. The clause $v = r(gdata_{old})$ in the specification of action γ means that the action is performed only if the database state is such that the result that was already chosen (by the β execution that put the triple (o, r, v) in the bag *saved_ops*) was the correct one.

Since this is a safety specification, it does not assert that γ will ever do anything; it simply asserts that γ cannot perform a database operation unless the result agrees

---
[9] A bag, also called a *multiset*, is a set in which the same element can appear more than once.

with the one that the β action had already decided to return. We must also require the liveness property that every operation saved in *saved_ops* is eventually performed. The "Liveness Properties" section (pages 350–353) indicates how this property is specified.

This specification is completely bizarre; it requires that the exec procedure guess what the correct result of the database operation will be before actually executing it. How can one possibly implement such a specification?

Figure 5 is bizarre only if viewed as a description of *how* the *exec* procedure is to be implemented. A program describes how something is to be done, while a specification describes only *what* is to be done. Figure 5 describes the observable behavior of the database system; it makes no formal assertion about how that behavior is to be implemented.

It is important to realize that even though a transition axiom specification may look superficially like a program, apparently describing how the system is to be implemented, it really specifies only the externally visible behavior – that is, how the interface state functions may change. Internal state functions such as *saved_ops* need not appear in any obvious form in the implementation's data structures. Indeed, as I will explain below, they need not appear at all.

If Figure 5 is a more general specification than Figure 4, then Figure 4 should implement Figure 5. However, the implementation executes fewer actions than the specification, a single α action performing the database operation that the specification asserts is done by a β action (to put the operation in saved_ops) and a γ action (to change the database). How do we prove that this is a correct implementation?

As in the proof for the soda machine example, we must define the specification state functions *gdata* and *saved_ops* in terms of the implementation state function *data*. We let *gdata* equal *data* and define *saved_ops* always to equal the empty bag. Again we must show that every action of the implementation changes the values of the specification state functions as allowed by the specification actions. However, we drop the requirement that each implementation action corresponds to at most a single specification action and allow it to correspond to a sequence of specification actions. There is only one internal action in Figure 4: the action α. Executing action α produces the same changes to *gdata* and *saved_ops* as an execution of a β action followed by an execution of a γ action. The γ action immediately executes the operation that the β action puts in *saved_ops*, the total effect being to leave *saved_ops* empty and to produce the required change to *gdata*.

Is one always allowed to implement a sequence of specification actions with a single implementation action?

Two conditions must be satisfied for a sequence of specification actions to be implementable by a single implementation action:

– At most one of the specification actions can be an interface action.

– All the actions (the specification actions and the implementation action) must be performed by the same agent – either the system or the environment.

These two conditions rule out pathological implementations.

The case of several specification actions implemented with a single action arises only when demonstrating that one specification is at least as general as another. (I just demonstrated that Figure 5 is at least as general as Figure 4.) In real implementations, a single specification action is usually implemented with dozens or even thousands of separate actions.

What is the formal justification for the correctness of implementing several specification actions with a single action?
Recall that the formula represented by a transition axiom specification is of the form $\exists f_1, \ldots, f_n$ s.t. X, where the f_i are the internal state functions. The reason we are allowed to implement several actions with a single one lies in the formal meaning, given in [4], of existential quantification of a state function. In proving that the formula represented by the implementation implies the formula represented by the specification, the existential quantification over the internal state functions allows one to consider the execution obtained by splitting one action into several successive actions to be equivalent to the original execution if the extra actions change only the internal state functions. However, an explanation of why this is so involves subtle points of temporal logic that are beyond the scope of this paper.

Is this all there is to the proof that Figure 4 correctly implements Figure 5?
Yes. The two systems have identical interfaces, so it is obvious that the interface actions of Figure 4 – the ones that perform the procedure call and the return – correctly implement the interface actions of Figure 4; they are the same actions. Therefore, we just have to show that the internal state functions of Figure 5 are correctly implemented by Figure 4, which we did.

Liveness Properties

Liveness properties assert that something must happen. In a transition axiom specification, the things that happen are changes to values of state functions; what must happen is expressed by explicit axioms about how these values must eventually change.

Axioms to specify liveness are written in *temporal logic*, obtained by extending ordinary logic with the temporal operators □ (read *henceforth*) and ◇ (read *eventually*). The formula □P asserts that P is true now and at all future times, and the formula ◇P asserts that P is true now or at some future time. Since P is eventually true if and only if it is not always false, ◇P is equivalent to ¬□¬P. (See [10] for a discussion of this equivalence.) It is convenient to define the operator ↝ (read *leads to*) by letting $P \leadsto Q$ equal $\Box(P \supset \Diamond Q)$, which asserts that whenever P becomes true, Q will be true then or at some later time. A more detailed exposition of our temporal logic can be found in [19].

In the soda machine specification of Figure 1, we might require that, after the user has deposited enough money, the machine must eventually dispense the soda. This is expressed by the formula $(f = \text{III}) \leadsto (f = \text{I})$, which asserts that if $f = \text{III}$ then f must eventually equal I.

The soda machine specification should probably have no other liveness axioms, since we don't require that the user must deposit money. However, we might require that if he deposits one quarter then he must deposit another, which is asserted by the axiom $(f = \text{II}) \leadsto (f = \text{III})$.

In the soda machine specification of Figure 2, we require that the next action must eventually be performed, except if it is a γ action, which the user need never perform. If the next action is an α action, this is asserted by the axiom $(pc = \alpha) \leadsto (pc = \beta)$. However, we could instead make only the weaker assertion that $(pc = \alpha) \leadsto (pc \neq \alpha)$, since Figure 2 implies that if $pc = \alpha$, then the only way the value of pc can change is for it to become equal to β. The complete liveness specification for this example is

$$\forall \xi \neq \gamma : (pc = \xi) \leadsto (pc \neq \xi) \qquad (2)$$

These liveness axioms are obvious from looking at Figures 1 and 2. Can't we just make the liveness axioms implicit in the language instead of having to write them separately?

One might want to make certain liveness axioms implicit in the language. However, the liveness conditions that appear in specifications are too varied to be expressed only implicitly by any reasonable collection of language constructs.

The informal liveness requirement for the database specification of Figure 5 is that any operation saved in saved_ops *is eventually executed. How is this expressed formally?*

Our first attempt at specifying this might be the axiom

$$\forall (o,r,v) : (o,r,v) \in \textit{saved\_ops} \leadsto (o,r,v) \notin \textit{saved\_ops}$$

which asserts that if a triple (o,r,v) is in the bag *saved_ops*, then eventually it will not be in that bag. The rest of the specification implies that the only way a triple can be removed from the bag is by performing the appropriate database operation with a γ action.

This axiom would express the desired requirement if *saved_ops* could never contain two copies of one triple. However, if the same triple (o,r,v) were continually inserted by different calls to the *exec* procedure, then *saved_ops* might always contain a copy of (o,r,v), so the axiom would not be satisfied. All we can assert is that, if some triple (o,r,v) is in *saved_ops*, then eventually at least one copy of it is removed – that is, eventually there is a γ action that removes (o,r,v).[10] Our

---

[10] Note that identical triples are indistinguishable, so it makes no sense to ask which copy of a triple is removed.

formulas mention states, not actions; we assert that a γ action occurs by a temporal formula asserting that, at some time, the bag contains k copies of the triple and, at a later time, it contains fewer copies. The desired liveness condition is expressed by the following axiom, where $e \sharp B$ denotes the number of copies of element e in bag B:

$$\forall (o,r,v) : [(o,r,v) \in saved\_ops] \rightsquigarrow$$
$$[\exists k \text{ s.t. } ((o,r,v) \sharp saved\_ops = k) \land \Diamond((o,r,v) \sharp saved\_ops < k)]$$

One can introduce notations that make it easier to assert that a certain action eventually occurs, allowing this axiom to be written more or less as

$$[(o,r,v) \in saved\_ops] \rightsquigarrow \gamma(o,r,v)$$

However, explaining these notations would lead us into language design issues that I do not wish to discuss here.

Are $\Box$ and $\Diamond$ (and operators like $\rightsquigarrow$ defined in terms of them) all one needs for specifying liveness properties?
Yes.

How does one verify that an implementation satisfies the liveness properties of a specification?
One must verify each liveness axiom. Consider the liveness axiom

$$(f = \text{III}) \rightsquigarrow (f = \text{I}) \tag{3}$$

for the specification of Figure 1. To prove that Figure 2 implements this specification, we defined f in terms of the implementation state functions x, y, and pc, the definition appearing in Figure 3. Substituting this expression for f in (3) yields

$$[(pc = \beta \land x = 50) \lor (pc = \delta \land x + y = 50) \lor (pc = \epsilon)] \rightsquigarrow [(pc = \alpha) \lor \ldots] \tag{4}$$

To verify that the implementation satisfies axiom (3), we must prove that the liveness axioms and the safety properties of the specification of Figure 2 imply (4). (This makes sense because (4) is an expression about the implementation state functions.)
    From the liveness axiom (2) and the safety properties, we can establish the following chain of $\rightsquigarrow$ relations:[11]

$$(pc = \delta \land x + y = 50) \rightsquigarrow (pc = \beta \land x = 50) \rightsquigarrow (pc = \epsilon) \rightsquigarrow (pc = \alpha)$$

For example, to verify $(pc = \beta \land x = 50) \rightsquigarrow (pc = \epsilon)$, observe that (2) implies that eventually $pc \neq \beta$, and the transition axioms imply that if $pc = \beta$ and $x = 50$, then the value of pc can change only to ϵ. (Note that the proof uses both safety and liveness properties of the implementation.)

---
[11] The formula $A \rightsquigarrow B \rightsquigarrow C$ is an abbreviation for $(A \rightsquigarrow B) \land (B \rightsquigarrow C)$.

We leave it to the reader to check that this chain of $\leadsto$ relations intuitively implies (4). The formal method underlying all of this informal reasoning is described in [19].

What is the general method behind this example?
Recall that formally, a specification is a formula $\exists f_1 \ldots f_n$ s.t. X, where the f_i are the internal state functions and X is a formula specifying how the values of the internal and interface state functions change. Similarly, the implementation is represented by a formula $\exists h_1 \ldots h_m$ s.t. Y, where the h_i are the implementation's internal state functions and Y is a formula involving the h_i and the interface state functions. Correctness of the implementation is expressed by the formula

$$(\exists h_1 \ldots h_m \text{ s.t. } Y) \supset (\exists f_1 \ldots f_n \text{ s.t. } X)$$

This formula is proved by expressing the specification state functions f_i in terms of the implementation state functions h_i and proving $Y \supset \overline{X}$, where $\overline{X}$ is the formula obtained from X by substituting for the f_i their expressions in terms of the h_i.

Splitting the specification into its safety and liveness requirements means writing $X = X_s \wedge X_l$, where X_s are the safety axioms and X_l are the liveness axioms, and similarly writing $Y = Y_s \wedge Y_l$. When we prove that the safety properties of the specification are satisfied, which we do by showing that every implementation action that changes the specification state functions does so as allowed by some specification action, we are proving $Y_s \supset X_s$. To prove that the liveness properties of the specification are satisfied, we prove $(Y_s \wedge Y_l) \supset X_l$; in other words, we use both safety and liveness properties of the implementation to prove the liveness properties of the specification.

Further Questions

A specification should specify only the externally observable behavior of a system, yet the transition axiom method introduces internal state functions and internal transitions. Doesn't this produce overly restrictive specifications?
To specify externally observable behavior, one must describe all permitted sequences of interface actions. Most conventional methods for specifying sequences of actions use implicit internal states. For example, a context-free grammar is equivalent to an automaton, whose states are implicit in the grammar. Milner's CCS [17] can be viewed as a single automaton whose states are the set of CCS formulas. It would be easy to use context-free grammars or CCS as the language in which to express transition axioms. Using explicit rather than implicit internal state functions does not make the specifications any more restrictive.

Temporal logic and other axiomatic methods have been used to write specifications that do not mention internal states. Aren't these specifications more general than transition axiom specifications?

Let us call a specification *purely temporal* if it does not mention internal states. The work of Alpern and Schneider [3] shows that purely temporal specifications are no more general than transition axiom specifications. They defined a logic that is at least as powerful as most of the logics used for purely temporal specifications and showed that any formula in their logic is equivalent to an assertion about an automaton constructed from the formula. This automaton can be interpreted as a transition axiom specification that is equivalent to the purely temporal specification represented by the original formula.

Even if purely temporal specifications are logically no more general than transition axiom specifications, doesn't their avoidance of explicit internal state functions mean that, in practice, they are less likely to overly constrain the implementation?
The transition axiom method does make it easier than purely temporal methods to describe a particular implementation instead of specifying only the desired interface behavior. However, eliminating internal state functions requires the use of complicated temporal formulas. The reader can appreciate the extra complexity needed to specify behavior with purely temporal methods by writing two informal prose specifications of a memory register: one that uses the value of the register (which is an internal state function) and a purely temporal one that talks only about read and write operations without mentioning the register's value.

I have found that purely temporal specifications are hard to understand. While they are less likely to overspecify the system, they are much more likely to underspecify it by omitting important constraints. In practice, purely temporal methods are hard to use because they don't tell one where to start (what properties should be specified explicitly and what properties should be consequences of other properties?) or when to stop (do all desired properties follow from the specification?). In contrast, the transition axiom method provides a well structured approach to writing specifications: first choose the state functions, then specify how they are allowed to change (the transition axioms), and finally specify when they must change (the liveness axioms).

Proving the correctness of an implementation requires defining the specification state functions in terms of the implementation state functions. Aren't there cases when this is impossible because some specification state functions are unnecessary and are not actually implemented?
Yes. One example is a program, viewed as a specification of its compiled version, in which an optimizing compiler eliminates a local variable that it discovers is set but never read. Moreover, the unimplemented state function need not be unnecessary. Imagine a specification that begins by letting the system decide if it is to act as a soda machine or a database, and thereafter acts exactly like the single system chosen. This absurd specification describes the state functions for both the soda machine and the database. However, the specification can be met by implementing either a soda machine or a database, without implementing the state functions of the other.

How is the correctness of an implementation proved if it does not implement the specified state functions?
In proving the correctness of the implementation, one is allowed to add *auxiliary state functions* to the implementation. An auxiliary state function is similar to an auxiliary variable added to prove the correctness of a concurrent program [18]. It is an internal state function that is added in such a way that it does not alter the specification of how the "real" state functions are allowed to change. The existing transition axioms are modified to indicate how they change the auxiliary state functions.

By adding auxiliary state functions, isn't one proving the correctness of a new implementation – one with extra state functions – rather than the original implementation?
No. To understand why not, one must again examine the formal meaning of existential quantification over state functions. Intuitively, the formula $\exists h$ s.t. A asserts the existence of h not in the "real world", in which the only state functions that exist are the ones described by the implementation, but in a "mythical world" in which every possible state function is assumed to exist. The auxiliary state functions do not change the implementation; they serve as constructive proofs of the existence of certain possible state functions. One could rewrite the correctness proof to eliminate the auxiliary state functions, but the resulting proof would be harder to understand.

The situation in which a specification state function is not expressible in terms of implementation state functions is atypical. Just as a good program does not compute values that are never used, a good specification does not include state functions that are not needed. Specifications that give the implementer the choice of which state functions to implement are rare; in practice, one does not specify a system that can choose to act as either a soda machine or a database system. Auxiliary state functions are therefore seldom needed. I advise against introducing them just to make it easier to express the specification state functions, since one learns a great deal about an implementation by expressing the specification state functions in terms of the "real" implementation state functions.

The transition axiom method is supposed to specify concurrent systems, yet the system's behavior is described as a sequence of actions. Where's the concurrency?
Underlying almost all formal methods in computer science is the assumption that the behavior of a system can be described as a collection of discrete atomic actions. The most general approach is to assume that the temporal ordering among these atomic actions is a partial order. However, a partial order is equivalent to the set of all total orders that are consistent with it. It turns out that as long as one is concerned only with safety and liveness properties, no information is lost by replacing a partially ordered set of events by the set of all sequences obtained by extending the partial order to a total order. Thus, we can consider a behavior to be a sequence of actions. Concurrency appears as nondeterminism – if two actions are concurrent, then the

set of possible behaviors contains sequences in which they are performed in either order.

A formalism based upon sequences may be inadequate for discussing other properties of the system's behavior, such as whether two actions occur concurrently. While such properties may be of interest when analyzing a given system, I have not found them to be relevant to the system's specification.

The transition axiom method specifies the atomic actions comprising each operation. Can one specify an operation without stating what the atomic actions are?
The transition axiom method can be extended to allow the specification of nonatomic operations – that is, operations composed of an unspecified number of atomic actions. Writing such a specification is easy; for example, we can just remove the angle brackets from Figure 2. However, it is not so easy to say precisely what such a specification means and how one verifies the correctness of an implementation. The transition axiom method can be extended to handle nonatomic operations by introducing the formal concepts described in [11] and [15].

Can one hierarchically decompose transition axiom specifications?
There are two kinds of hierarchical decomposition: (1) decomposition within a single level of abstraction, and (2) representation of a higher-level system as a composition of lower-level ones. The second kind of decomposition involves a change in the grain of atomicity – usually a single atomic action is decomposed as a set of lower-level actions; the first does not.

Decomposition within a single level involves organizing the information contained in a single specification to make it easier to understand. For example, one can decompose a transition axiom by writing it as a conjunction of several relations, where each conjunct is described separately. This type of decomposition is a language design issue that raises no basic logical questions.

Representing a higher-level system as the composition of lower-level systems means implementing the higher-level system with the lower-level composite system. The implementation of one system with a lower-level one has already been discussed here at considerable length.

How are specifications of individual components combined to specify a single system?
Formally, to say that a system M is the composition of two systems M_1 and M_2 means that the specification of M, which is a temporal logic formula, is the conjunction of the specifications of M_1 and M_2. In the transition axiom method, the specification of M is obtained by simply combining the specifications of M_1 and M_2. The state functions in the specification of M consist of the state functions from the specifications of both M_1 and M_2, and the set of actions of M is the union of the sets of actions of M_1 and M_2.

Combining specifications may necessitate some renaming. Internal state functions and actions may have to be renamed to avoid conflicts, since an internal state function of M_1 represents a different state function from any internal state function of M_2. Also, the act of combining M_1 and M_2 may imply a renaming or identification of interface state functions. Suppose M_1 is a circuit with an interface state function named *output* that represents the voltage on its output wire and M_2 is a circuit with an interface state function named *input* the represents the voltage on its input wire. Connecting the output wire of M_1 to the input wire of M_2 implies that *input* and *output* become two names for the same state function.

Acknowledgements. I wish to thank Amir Pnueli for teaching me what existential quantification over state functions means, Jim Horning and John Guttag for numerous helpful discussions, and the following for their comments on earlier versions of this paper: Jim Gray, Brent Hailpern, Luigi Logrippo, Jay Misra, Susan Owicki, Willem-Paul de Roever, Fred Schneider, Fritz Vogt, Jeanette Wing, and Pamela Zave.

References

1. Alford, M.W. et al. *Distributed systems: methods and tools for specification.* Lecture Notes in Computer Science, 190. Springer-Verlag, New York, 1985, 270–285.
2. Alpern, B., and Schneider, F.B. Defining liveness. *Inf. Process. Lett. 21*, 4 (Oct. 1985), 181–185.
3. Alpern, B., and Schneider, F.B. *Verifying temporal properties without using temporal logic.* Tech. Rep. TR85-723, Dept. of Computer Science, Cornell Univ., Dec. 1985.
4. Barringer, H., Kuiper, R., and Pnueli, A. A really abstract concurrent model and its temporal logic. In *13th Annual ACM Symposium on Principles of Programming Languages* (St. Petersburg Beach, Fla., Jan. 13–15) ACM, New York, 1986, pp. 173–183.
5. Bernstein, P.A., and Goodman, N. Concurrency control in distributed database systems. *Comput. Surv. 13*, 2 (June 1981), pp. 185–222.
6. Guttag, J.V., Horning, J.J., and Wing, J.M. *Larch in five easy pieces.* Tech. Rep. 5, Digital Equipment Corporation, Systems Research Center, 1985.
7. Hoare, C. A.R. Communicating sequential processes. *Commun. ACM 21*, 8 (Aug. 1978), pp. 666–677.
8. Jones, C.B. *Systematic Software Development Using VDM.* Prentice-Hall, Englewood Cliffs, N.J., 1986.
9. Lam, S.S., and Shankar, A.U. Protocol verification via projections. *IEEE Trans. Softw. Eng. SE-10*, 4 (July 1984), pp. 325–342.
10. Lamport, L. "Sometime" is sometimes "not never": A tutorial on the temporal logic of programs. In *Proceedings of the 7th Annual Symposium on Principles of Programming Languages* (Las Vegas, Nev., Jan. 28–30), ACM, New York, 1980, pp. 174–185.
11. Lamport, L. Reasoning about nonatomic operations. In *Proceedings of the 10th Annual Symposium on Principles of Programming Languages* (Austin, Texas, Jan. 24–26), ACM, New York, 1983, pp. 28–37.
12. Lamport, L. Specifying concurrent program modules. *ACM Trans. Program. Lang. Syst. 5*, 2 (Apr. 1983), pp. 190–222.
13. Lamport, L. What good is temporal logic? In *Information Processing 83: Proceedings of the IFIP 9th World Congress* R.E.A. Mason, Ed., IFIP, North-Holland, Paris, September 1983, 657–668.

14. Lamport, L. What it means for a concurrent program to satisfy a specification: why no one has specified priority. In *Proceedings of the 12th ACM Symposium on Principles of Programming Languages* (New Orleans, La., Jan. 14–16), ACM, New York, 1985, pp. 78–83.
15. Lamport, L. Win *and* sin: *predicate transformers for concurrency.* Res. Rep. 17, Digital Equipment Corporation, Systems Research Center, 1987. (Also *ACM Trans. Program. Lang. Syst. 12*, 3 (July 1990), 396–428.)
16. Mead, C., and Conway, L. In *Introduction to VLSI Systems.* Addison-Wesley, Reading, Mass., 1980, 218–262.
17. Milner, R. *A Calculus of Communicating Systems*, Springer-Verlag, Berlin, 1980.
18. Owicki, S., and Gries, D. An axiomatic proof technique for parallel programs. *Acta Informatica 6*, 4, 1976, 319–340.
19. Owicki, S., and Lamport, L. Proving liveness properties of concurrent programs. *ACM Trans. Program. Lang. Syst. 4*, 3 (July 1982), 455–495.
20. Wensley, J. et al. SIFT: Design and analysis of a fault-tolerant computer for aircraft control. *Proc. IEEE 66*, 10 (Oct. 1978), 1240–1254.
21. Wirth, N. *Programming in Modula-2*, 3rd ed. Springer-Verlag, Berlin, 1985.

6. Real-Time and Safety-Critical Systems

A system is one in which the timing of the output is significant [195]. Such a system accepts inputs from the 'real world' and must respond with outputs in a timely manner (typically within milliseconds – a response time of the same order of magnitude as the time of computation – otherwise, for example, a payroll system could be considered 'real-time' since employees expect to be paid at the end of each month). Many real-time systems are *embedded* systems, where the fact that a computer is involved may not be immediately obvious (e.g., a washing machine). Real-time software often needs to be of high integrity [10].

The term *safety-critical system* has been coined more recently as a result of the increase in concern and awareness about the use of computers in situations where human lives could be at risk if an error occurs. Such systems are normally real-time embedded systems. The use of software in safety-critical systems has increased by around an order of magnitude in the last decade and the trend sees no sign of abating, despite continuing worries about the reliability of software [172, 92].

The software used in computers has become progressively more complex as the size and performance of computers has increased and their price has decreased [216]. Unfortunately software development techniques have not kept pace with the rate of software production and improvements in hardware. Errors in software are renowned and software manufacturers have in general issued their products with outrageous disclaimers that would not be acceptable in any other more established industrial engineering sector. Some have attempted to use a 'safe' subset of languages known to have problematic features [8, 113]. In any case, when developing safety-critical systems, a *safety case* should be made to help ensure the avoidance of dangerous failures [254].

6.1 Real-Time Systems

Real-time systems may be classified into two broad types. *Hard real-time* systems are required to meet explicit timing constraints, such as responding to an input within a certain number of milliseconds. The temporal requirements are an essential part of the required behavior, not just a desirable property. *Soft real-time* systems relax this requirement somewhat in that, while they have to run and respond in real-time, missing a real-time deadline occasionally only causes degradation of the system, not catastrophic failure.

In the first paper in this Part [200], Jonathan Ostroff considers the specification, design and verification of real-time systems, particularly with regard to *formal methods*, with mathematical foundation. He addresses the application of various formal methods that are suitable for use in the development of such systems, including the difficulties encountered in adopting a formal approach.

As well as the formal correctness of a real-time system [120, 147], there are other issues to consider. Predicting the behavior of a real-time system can be problematic, especially if interrupts are involved. The best approach is to ensure predictability by constructing such systems in a disciplined manner [104]. Often real-time systems incorporate more than one computer and thus all the difficulties of a parallel system must also be considered as well, while still trying to ensure system safety, etc. [238].

Hybrid systems [102] generalize on the concept of real-time systems. In the latter, real-time is a special continuous variable that must be considered by the controlling computer. In a hybrid system, other continuous variables are modeled in a similar manner, introducing the possibility of differential equations, etc. Control engineers may need to interact effectively with software engineers to produce a satisfactory system design. The software engineer involved with such systems will need a much broader education than that of many others in computing.

6.2 Safety-Critical Systems

The distinguishing feature of safety-critical software is its ability to put human lives at risk. Neumann has cataloged a large number of accidents caused by systems controlled by computers, many as a result of software problems [192] and software failures are an issue of continuing debate [114]. One of the most infamous accidents where software was involved is the Therac-25 radiotherapy machine which killed several people [169]. There was no hardware interlock to prevent overdosing of patients and in certain rare circumstances, the software allowed such a situation to occur.

The approaches used in safety-critical system development depends on the level of risk involved, which may be categorized depending on what is acceptable (both politically and financially) [12]. The analysis, perception and management of risk is an important topic in its own right, as one of the issues to be addressed when considering safety-critical systems [221].

The techniques that are suitable for application in the development of safety-critical systems are a subject of much debate. The following extract from the BBC television program *Arena* broadcast in the UK during October 1990 (quoted in [45]) illustrates the publicly demonstrated gap between various parts of the computing industry, in the context of the application of formal methods to safety-critical systems:

Narrator: '... *this concentration on a relatively immature science has been criticized as impractical.*'

Phil Bennett, IEE: '*Well we do face the problem today that we are putting in ever increasing numbers of these systems which we need to assess. The engineers have to use what tools are available to them today and tools which they understand. Unfortunately the mathematical base of formal methods is such that most engineers that are in safety-critical systems do not have the familiarity to make full benefit of them.*'

Martyn Thomas, Chairman, Praxis: '*If you can't write down a mathematical description of the behavior of the system you are designing then you don't understand it. If the mathematics is not advanced enough to support your ability to write it down, what it actually means is that there is no mechanism whereby you can write down precisely that behavior. If that is the case, what are you doing entrusting people's lives to that system because by definition you don't understand how it's going to behave under all circumstances? ... The fact that we can build over-complex safety-critical systems is no excuse for doing so.*'

This sort of exchange is typical of the debate between the various software engineering factions involved with safety-critical systems [209, 211, 212]. As indicated above, some suggest that formal methods, based on mathematical techniques, are a possible solution to help reduce errors in software, especially in safety-critical systems ehere correctness is of prime importance [9]. Sceptics claim that the methods are infeasible for any realistically sized problem. Sensible proponents recommend that they should be applied selectively where they can be used to advantage. In any case, assessment of approaches to software development, as well as safety-critical software itself [213], is required to determine the most appropriate techniques for use in the production of future software for high-integrity systems [166, 174].

6.3 Formal Methods for Safety-Critical Systems

As has previously been mentioned, the take up of formal methods is not yet great in industry, but their use has often been successful when they have been applied appropriately [243]. Some companies have managed to specialize in providing formal methods expertise (e.g., CLInc in the US, ORA in Canada and Praxis in the UK), although such examples are exceptional. A recent international investigation of the use of formal methods in industry [63] provides a snapshot view of the situation by comparing some significant projects which have made serious use of such techniques. Some sections of industry are applying formal methods effectively and satisfactorily to safety-critical systems (e.g., see [66, 123, 225]). Medical applications are an example sector where formal methods are being considered and used (see for example, [144, 149]).

[46], included in this Part, provides a survey of selected projects and companies that have used formal methods in the design of safety-critical systems, as well as

a number of safety-related standards. In critical systems, reliability and safety are paramount, although software reliability is difficult to assess [54]. Extra cost involved in the use of formal methods is acceptable, and the use of mechanization for formal proofs may be worthwhile for critical sections of the software, and at various levels of abstraction [27, 118]. In other cases, the total cost and time to market is of highest importance. For such projects, formal methods should be used more selectively, perhaps only using rigorous proofs or just specification alone. Formal documentation of key components may provide significant benefits to the development of many industrial software-based systems.

The *human-computer interface* (HCI) [71] is an increasingly important component of most software-based systems, including safety-critical systems. Errors often occur due to misunderstandings caused by poorly constructed interfaces [162]. It is suspected that the 'glass cockpit' interface of fly-by-wire aircraft may be a contributing factor in some crashes, although absolute proof of this is difficult to obtain.

Formalizing an HCI in a realistic and useful manner is a difficult task, but progress is being made in categorizing features of interfaces that may help to ensure their reliability in the future [202]. There seems to be considerable scope for further research in this area, which also spans many other disparate disciplines, particularly with application to safety-critical systems where human errors can easily cause death and injury [112].

6.4 Standards

Until the last decade, there have been few standards concerned specifically with software for safety-critical systems. Now a plethora are in the process of being or have recently been introduced or revised [250], as well as even more that are applicable to the field of software engineering in general [180].

An important trigger for the exploitation of research into new techniques such as formal methods could be the interest of regulatory bodies or standardization committees (e.g., the *International Electrotechnical Commission*). A significant number of emerging safety-related standards are now explicitly mentioning formal methods as a possible approach for use on systems of the highest integrity levels [26, 37]. Many are strongly recommending the use of formal methods, requiring specific explanation if they are not used.

A major impetus has already been provided in the UK by promulgation of the proposed MoD Interim Defence Standard 00-55 [186], the draft of which mandates the use of formal methods, languages with sound formal semantics and at least a *rigorous argument* to justify software designs. The related Interim Defence Standard 00-56 has itself been subjected to formal analysis [258].

It is important that standards should not be prescriptive, or that parts that are prescriptive should be clearly separated and marked as such. Goals should be set and the onus placed on the software supplier to demonstrate that their methods achieve the required level of confidence. If particular methods are recommended or mandated, it is possible for the supplier to assume that the method will produce the desired results and blame the standards body if it does not. This reduces the responsibility and accountability of the supplier. Some guidance is worthwhile, but is likely to date quickly. As a result, it may be best to include it as a separate document or appendix so that it can be updated more frequently to reflect the latest available techniques and best practice. For example, 00-55 includes a separate guidance section.

6.5 Legislation

Governmental legislation is likely to provide increasing motivation to apply appropriate techniques in the development of safety-critical systems. For example, the Machine Safety Directive, legislation issued by the European Commission, has been effective from January 1993. This encompasses software and if there is an error in the machine's logic that results in injury then a claim can be made under civil law against the supplier. If negligence can be proved during the product's design or manufacture then criminal proceedings may be taken against the director or manager in charge. A maximum penalty of three months imprisonment or a large fine are possible. Suppliers will have to demonstrate that they are using best working practice to avoid conviction.

However, care should be taken in not overstating the effectiveness of a particular technique. For example, the term *formal proof* has been used quite loosely sometimes, and this has even led to litigation in the law courts over the VIPER microprocessor, although the case was ended before a court ruling was pronounced [177]. If extravagant claims are made, it is quite possible that a similar case could occur again. The UK MoD 00-55 Interim Defence Standard [186] differentiates between *formal proof* and *rigorous argument*, preferring the former, but sometimes accepting the latter with a correspondingly lower level of design assurance. Definitions in such standards could affect court rulings in the future.

6.6 Education and Professional Issues

Most modern comprehensive standard textbooks on software engineering aimed at computer science undergraduate courses now include information on real-time and safety-critical systems (e.g., see [233]). However there are not many textbooks devoted solely to these topics, although they are becoming available (e.g., see [167, 240]). Real-time and safety-critical issues are seen as specialist areas, although this is becoming less so as the importance of safety-critical systems increases in the field of software engineering.

Undergraduate computer science courses normally includes a basic introduction to the relevant mathematics (e.g., discrete mathematics such as set theory and predicate logic [204, 99]), which is needed for accurate reasoning about computer-based systems (see, for example, [65, 86]). This is especially important for safety-critical systems where all techniques for reducing faults should be considered [135]. This will help improve matters in the future, although there is a long lag time between education and practical application. It is important to combine the engineering aspects with the mathematical underpinning in courses [205, 207, 208, 87]. Unfortunately, this is often not the case.

In the past, it has been necessary for companies to provide their own training or seek specialist help for safety-critical system development, although relevant courses are quite widely available from both industry and academia in some countries. For example, see a list of formal methods courses using the Z notation in the UK as early as 1991 [193]. Particular techniques such as formal methods may be relevant for the highest level of assurance [227, 244, 256].

There are now more specialized advanced courses (e.g., at Masters level) specifically aimed at engineers in industry who may require the addition of new skills for application in the development of safety-critical systems. For example, see the modula MSc in safety-critical systems engineering at the University of York in the UK [248]. Engineers can take a number of intensive modules, each typically of a week in length. When enough have been undertaken, an MSc degree can be awarded. It is normally easier for working engineers to take a full week off work every so often rather than individual days for an extended period.

Accreditation of courses by professional societies is increasingly important. For example, in the UK, the British Computer Society (BCS) insists on certain subject areas being covered in an undergraduate computer science course to gain accreration (and hence eased membership of the society by those who have undertaken the course through exemption from professional examinations). Most universities are keen for their courses to comply if possible, and will normally adapt their course if necessary to gain accreditation. This gives professional bodies such as the BCS considerable leverage in what topics are included in the majority of undergraduate computer science courses in a particular country.

As well as technical aspects of computing, computer ethics [29] and related professional issues [89] must also be covered (e.g., see [6]). Liability, safety and reliability are all increasingly important areas to be considered as the use of computers in safety-critical systems becomes more pervasive [235]. Software engineers should be responsible for their mistakes if they occur through negligence rather than genuine error [116] and should normally follow a code of ethics [97] or code of conduct. These codes are often formulated by professional societies and members are obliged to follow them.

There are suggestions that some sort of certification of safety-critical system developers should be introduced. The *licensing* of software engineers by professional bodies has been a subject for discussion in the profession [11]. This is still an active topic for debate. However there are possible drawbacks as well as benefits in introducing tight regulations since suitably able and qualified engineers may be inappropriately excluded and under-qualified engineers may be certified without adequate checks on their continued performance and training.

6.7 Technology Transfer

Technology transfer is often fraught with difficulties and is inevitably (and rightly) a lengthy process. Problems and misunderstandings at any stage can lead to overall failure [211, 228]. A technology should be well established before it is applied, especially in critical applications where safety is of great importance. Awareness of the benefits of relevant techniques [3] must be publicized to a wide selection of both technical and non-technical people, especially outside the research community (e.g., as in [237]). The possibilities and limitations of the techniques available must be well understood by the relevant personnel to avoid costly mistakes. Management awareness and understanding of the effects of a particular technique on the overall development process is extremely important.

Journals and magazines concerned with software engineering in general have produced special issues on safety-critical systems which will help to raise awareness among both researchers and practitioners (for example, see [150, 170]). Awareness of safety issues by the general public is increasing as well [75, 198]. This Part includes two related articles from the former, reporting on a major survey of projects using formal methods [63], many concerned with safety-critical systems. The first article [90] reports on the general experience industry has had in applying formal methods to critical systems. The second article [91] covers four specific instances in more detail. Each has been successful to varying degrees and for various aspects of application. The article provides a useful comparison of some of the possible approaches adopted in each of the presented studies. The third article, by Leveson and Turner, gives a complete account of the investigation into the accidents, and subsequent deaths, caused by the Therac-25 radiation therapy machine. The investigation indicates how testing can never be complete, due to the impact that the correction of one 'bug' can have on other parts of the system.

Organizations such as the *Safety-Critical Systems Club* in the UK [219] have organized regular meetings which are well attended by industry and academia, together with a regular club newsletter for members. Subsequently the *European Network of Clubs for REliability and Safety of Software* (ENCRESS) has been formed to coordinate similar activities through the European Union (e.g., see [101]). The *European Workshop on Industrial Computer Systems, Technical Committee 7* (EWICS TC7) on Reliability, Safety and Security, and the *European Safety and Reliability Association* also have an interest in safety-critical systems. There seems to be less coordinated activity in the US of this nature, although the IEEE provides some support in the area of standards.

Unfortunately, the rapid advances and reduction in cost of computers in recent years has meant that time is not on our side. More formal techniques are now sufficiently advanced that they should be considered for selective use in software development for real-time and safety-critical systems, provided the problems of education can be overcome. It is likely that there will be a skills shortage in this area for the foreseeable future and significant difficulties remain to be overcome.

Software standards, especially those concerning safety, are likely to provide a motivating force for the use of emerging techniques, and it is vital that sensible and realistic approaches are suggested in emerging and future standards. 00-55 [186] provides one example of a forward-looking standard that may indicate the direction of things to come in the development of real-time safety-critical systems.

Formal Methods for the Specification and Design of Real-Time Safety-Critical Systems

Jonathan Ostroff

Summary.

Safety-critical computers increasingly affect nearly every aspect of our lives. Computers control the planes we fly on, monitor our health in hospitals and do our work in hazardous environments. Computers with software deficiencies that fail to meet stringent timing constraints have resulted in catastrophic failures. This paper surveys formal methods for specifying, designing and verifying real-time systems, so as to improve their safety and reliability.

1 Introduction

Computers are increasingly used to monitor and control safety-critical systems. Real-time software controls aircraft, shuts down nuclear power reactors in emergencies, keeps telephone networks running, and monitors hospital patients. The use of computers in such systems offers considerable benefits, but also poses serious risks to life and the environment.

Safety-critical systems must satisfy real-time constraints if they are to effectively perform their intended function. The newsletter *Software Engineering Notes* regularly reports incidents involving malfunctioning of real-time or embedded computer systems. For example, the first flight of the space shuttle was delayed by a subtle timing error, which was traced to an improbable race condition in the flight control software [31]. In another incident, a software error caused a stationary robot to

---

© 1992 Elsevier Science Publishers B.V.. Reprinted by permission.
Reprinted from *Journal of Systems and Software*, 18(1):33–60, April 1992.

move suddenly with impressive speed, to the edge of its operational area. A nearby worker was crushed to death. The firing mechanism of an already deployed ballistic missile system was recently analyzed using methods discussed in this survey. It was discovered that a certain sequence of events, unknown to the design team, would lead to the inadvertent firing of a missile [40].

Real-time software must satisfy not only functional correctness requirements, but also timeliness requirements. For example, consider the following "hard" real-time constraints: if the temperature of a nuclear reactor core is too high, an alarm must be generated within some deadline; spray painting a car on a moving conveyor must be initiated at some suitable time and terminated some time later; when an aircraft enters an air traffic control region, the flight controller must be informed in a timely fashion; once the approach of a train is detected, car and pedestrian traffic at the train intersection must be halted before the train reaches the intersection; if the computer controlling a robot does not command it to stop or turn in time, the robot might collide with another object on the factory floor.

There is general consensus in the software and control systems literature that real-time systems are difficult to model, specify and design [142, 42, 17, 121, 74, 137, 73]. In addition, experience has shown that software components of systems are problematic perhaps even more so than mechanical or other hardware components.

Software is complex (consider the documentation needed for even simple modules), non-robust (small errors have major consequences) and software is notoriously difficult to test (the number of test cases that must be checked becomes unmanageably large even in small systems) [115].

This does not necessarily mean that the software controlling real-time systems is poorly designed. Many companies do as much as is commercially feasible with current design methods to make their products more reliable. However, as the burden of controlling complicated systems is shifted onto the computer, so does the complexity of the resulting software increase. Old-fashioned servo-control systems could be tested in isolation. The new more complex software controllers are more difficult to check exhaustively, no matter how intelligently designed the test suite is.

It has been conjectured that formal, mathematically precise methods should be used to design real-time safety-critical systems. Turning this conjecture into sound practice has proved to be extremely difficult – many practically-oriented software engineers probably consider the hurdles insurmountable.

But what benefits do "theorists" hope to obtain by the use of a formal framework? A list of the benefits include the following:

– In the process of formalizing informal requirements, ambiguities, omissions and contradictions will often be discovered.
– The formal model may lead to hierarchical semi-automated (or even automated) system development methods.
– The formal model can be verified for correctness by mathematical methods (rather than by intractable case-by-case testing).
– A formally verified subsystem can be incorporated into a larger system with greater confidence that it will behave as specified.

– Different designs can be evaluated and compared.

Some researchers think that a specific real-time verification methodology is not needed. Conventional wisdom dictates that programs should be designed to function correctly, independent of hardware speed. One extreme position [138] views introducing time with grave suspicion. Time may be an issue in implementation ("use a faster machine if you miss the deadline") but should never appear in a specification. Furthermore, there is a danger in overspecifying and making the verification task more complex than it ought to be. In contrast, de Roever [22] considers it essential that foundational research be undertaken into formal methods for real-time systems if reliable and safe systems are to be constructed.

If the designer is dealing with fixed schedules on a single processor, then it may be possible to get away with using untimed standard verification methods. Certainly one should abstract out time and use standard techniques wherever it is possible to do so. However, the work discussed in this survey clearly shows that tampering with the speed of the computer will not solve the main problems facing the designers of real-time software.

Time is not just another programming variable. Time is continuous, monotonic and divergent whereas program variables generally do not have such properties. Since time ranges over an infinite domain, all the tools that have been developed for finite state verification cannot be naively applied to real-time systems. With some effort, finite state methods can be made to work for real-time systems, but to do this certainly requires the adoption of specific formalisms to deal with explicit timing constraints. Proof systems for dealing with untimed infinite state systems must be refined if they are to deal safely with timed systems.

If time dependencies are introduced into a design, then there should be good reasons to do so. Mok [92] cites the following cases in which timing constraints play an important role.

– The control surfaces of some modern aircraft must be adjusted at a high rate to prevent catastrophic destruction. This places an upper bound on the response time of the avionics software system. Lower bounds are needed in operating systems which require a potential intruder to wait for some minimum time before retyping a password that has been entered incorrectly. In these cases, the "physics" of the application dictate the timing requirements.
– In the Byzantine Generals problem, the non-faulty processors (generals) must arrive at a consensus to perform some action in the presence of other processors that can exhibit faulty behaviour. There is no asynchronous solution to the Byzantine Generals problem. However, a solution is possible if the generals adopt the synchronous protocol of voting in rounds. In each round of voting the generals must complete a set of communication actions within a real-time deadline. Thus, time is an essential synchronization mechanism for solving certain task coordination problems.
– In the NETBLT protocol proposed by a group at MIT, the receiver guarantees the sender that it will be able to process incoming packets at a certain rate, or alternatively, it will meet the deadline associated with each packet. Since the sender

does not need to wait for an acknowledgment from the receiver, network throughput can be significantly improved, especially for networks where the round-trip transmission time is long compared with the width of a packet (e.g., in fiber optics communication systems). Thus, time is a control mechanism which can be exploited to solve problems more efficiently.

In the rest of this survey, we define more carefully what a real-time system is (section 2). Three increasingly formal techniques are surveyed for dealing with real-time systems: section 3 discusses real-time programming languages, section 4 discusses structured analysis methods and graphical or visual modelling languages, and section 5 discusses logics and algebras. Section 6 speculates on future trends.

2 Defining the Terms

This section describes the important features of real-time systems. The following problems are also posed: the modelling problem, the verification problem, the design development problem and the controller synthesis problem. These are some of the main problems that theorists hope to tackle with formal methods.

An algorithm is usually represented as a *program*. Correctness of the algorithm means that the program *satisfies* some desired *specification* (or property). Therefore, in standard program verification, three concepts are needed. A programming language is needed for representing algorithms, a specification language for expressing properties, and a satisfaction relation (or proof system) for verifying the correctness of the algorithm. An important subjective issue revolves around the choice of *syntax* for the programming and specification languages – does the syntax simplify the expression of algorithms and specifications, or does it get in the way of the designer?

To properly develop the concepts mentioned above, some additional notions must be introduced. A formal *semantics* must be provided so that the behaviour of the program and the meaning of the specifications are clearly defined. The proof system must be shown to be *sound* with respect to the semantics, so that only those programs whose behaviours satisfy the specification can be proven correct. An unsound proof system is dangerous because it can be used to prove anything (papers on the assignment axiom for arrays were, for years, filled with errors). Furthermore, it is useful if the proof system is *complete* so that every correct program can be verified for correctness in the proof system. Other issues such as the expressiveness of the languages and the complexity of decision procedures must be explored.

An algorithm usually takes some data as input, performs a computation and outputs the result of the computation to the user. For real-time programs, the situation is more complex. The environment in which the program operates can no longer be ignored, because of the intensive non-terminating interaction of the program with its environment. Such systems are often called embedded systems, discrete event dynamic systems, reactive systems, or process control systems. We shall refer to all of these as "real-time systems."

Ordinary programming languages are not expressive enough to represent the complex features of real-time systems such as concurrency, nondeterminism, synchronization between processes and real-time constraints on the events of such systems. Programming languages must therefore be extended if they are to deal with real-time systems. A *model* of the intended real-time notions is therefore needed.

A *model* is a representation, often in mathematical terms, of the important features of the system that is being studied. A common modelling technique is to define the *state* of the system (a "snapshot" at an instant in time of all the variables defining the system). A state may persist for some period of time, after which there is some change to a new state (as real-time systems are dynamic). Such a state change is referred to as an *event* or a *transition*. The model may be used to *simulate* possible behaviours of the system which helps the designer understand the system better. A simulation of the system is a sequence of states and events capturing the behaviour of the system. A simulation may show the presence of bugs in the system, but never their absence [23]. *Analysis* of the system behaviour must be undertaken to show the correctness of the system. The system is correct provided that its behaviour satisfies the associated specification.

The terms "model" and "specification" are often used interchangeably. In this survey, a *model* is a *description* of the system, perhaps in great detail, or perhaps at a more abstract level. A *specification* is the list of *requirements* that the system must ideally satisfy. A model describes how the system actually behaves. A specification prescribes how we would like it to behave.

What are the most important features of a real-time system? The *Oxford Dictionary of Computing* defines a real-time system as

> ...any system in which the time at which the output is produced is significant. This is usually because the input corresponds to some movement in the physical world, and the output has to relate to that same movement. The lag from input time to output time must be sufficiently small for acceptable timeliness...

The *IEEE Standard Dictionary of Electrical and Electronic Terms* gives the following definition:

> *Real-Time:* (A) Pertaining to the actual time during which a physical process transpires. (B) Pertaining to the performance of a computation during the actual time that the related physical process transpires in order that results of the computation can be used in guiding the physical process.

In software engineering, the term "real-time system" usually refers to the software or programming code (called the *controller* in this survey). The lag time from input to output in the controller must be sufficiently small. However, there is implicitly always another object that is associated with the controller. That object is the physical world or environment in which the controller finds itself. Since the environment is always implicitly there, let us give it a name and call it the *plant*. Then we can refer to the plant and perhaps even reason about it. In fact, the lag time or response time of the controller is determined by the physical nature of the processes in the plant.

The primary goal of the designer is to ensure the correct behaviour of the plant. This is achieved by designing a controller that will interact and control the plant. We may draw an automatic control diagram that is familiar to control engineers:

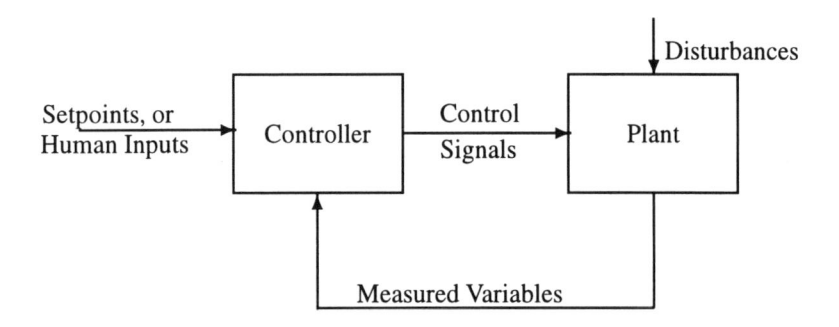

The complete system under development (SUD) is divided into two parts: the controller and the plant. The plant is that part of the system that is to be controlled. It is often a physical or technological process such as a chemical reaction, airplane or robot. The plant is usually a "given"; the designer is not free to change it, although there is usually some kind of "control technology" through which the plant can be controlled (e.g., control valves can be opened or certain plant events can be forced to occur through interlocks). The "open-loop" behaviour of the plant (without the controller) is usually unsatisfactory in some important respect.

It is the task of the controller to ensure that unsatisfactory behaviour in the plant is eliminated. The diagram above indicates the role that feedback plays in the controller. Feedback restores equilibrium after disruptions caused by disturbances to the plant. After measuring the current state of the plant, the controller can take corrective action by issuing appropriate control commands.

There is usually much more freedom in the design of the controller than in that of the plant. In fact, the controller is often implemented by real-time software precisely so that the logic of the controller, or the computation that it performs, can easily be changed if necessary. As a result, the design of a real-time system differs from straight programming (e.g., coding an algorithm) in two important respects:

1. *The plant is part of the overall system.* A real-time system is one in which the *controller* software must synchronize with the *plant* processes whose progress it cannot directly control, so as to ensure that the plant behaves safely and reliably. The design formalism must be flexible enough to represent the plant as an integral part of the complete system. Unsatisfactory plant behaviour can then be examined, and the effect of different control policies on the plant can be evaluated. Potential failures of the plant must be represented in the plant model so that the controller can be checked to see that it functions correctly. A model of the plant will enable the designer to extract the lag and real-time response times that the controller must implement. Furthermore, a deterministic formalism developed for a real-time programming language (to guarantee predictable behaviour),

may be unsuitable for representing nondeterministic and asynchronous event-driven plant behavior.

2. *The plant must be verified for correctness.* The essential concern of the designer is to ensure that the plant behaves in a safe, acceptable fashion. The correctness of the control software is only a means for ensuring correct plant behaviour. If the software of the controller fails (relative to its local specification) in a fashion that has no impact on the plant, then no harm has been done. By contrast, the controller can satisfy all kinds of requirement specifications, but if those requirements do not translate into proper behaviour of the plant, then the verification effort will have been in vain. An important corollary is that a specification of the system must primarily refer to the states, events and properties of the plant (not to the behaviour of the controller software).

Consider the following robot example.[1] The SUD is a robot arm together with position sensors, a force sensor, a camera, a tactile sensor, a gripper, a joystick and keyboard for input, and a computer to control the various parts. Formally, we may write

$$SUD = plant \| controller$$

where $\|$ indicates the parallel composition of plant and controller processes. The plant is further defined by

$$plant = arm \| sensors \| actuators$$

where

$$sensors = positionSensors \| forceSensor \| tactileSensor \| Camera$$

and

$$actuators = gripper \| joystick \| keyboard$$

The model of the plant will have to represent certain timing constraints. The camera works at 30 Hz, and the force sensor at 400 Hz. The robot and position sensors work at 1000 Hz, the joystick at 25 Hz, and the tactile sensor at 120 Hz.

The required specifications are: design a controller that will enable a user to manipulate the arm to perform various tasks at certain speeds, e.g., welding a part to an auto on the assembly line. The sensor measurements must be scanned at the correct rate. The actuators must be activated at the correct time. If an unfamiliar obstacle is encountered stop the arm movement within one second.

The specification S of required behaviour so far only refers to elements of the plant such as the arm, the sensors and actuators. The controller must still be designed, and so its constituent parts cannot yet be referred to in the top level specification.

---

[1] The robot example was used in a discussion on real-time issues on Usenet in 1990 with contributors Duncan Thomson and David Stewart.

Having specified as precisely as possible the plant, and the specification S that it must satisfy, the controller must now be designed. It was necessary to structure the description of the plant with the parallel composition operator. So too, it is often necessary to structure the controller description.

For example, it is possible that only some of the sensors will be used at any one time. A logical way to separate the control functions is by having one task supervise the control signals to the robot and another task read the camera. Other distinct tasks can read the position and force sensors. If only the force sensor is needed for a particular task, and not the camera, then it is simply a matter of starting up the appropriate tasks without the need to change any code.

Without concurrency, the software must be constructed as a single control loop called a cyclic executive. Such a large sequential program with multiple conditional flags such as "if (using camera) do action" is difficult to design robustly because of the different time frames and functions that must be accommodated. The structure of this loop cannot retain the logical distinction between controller modules. It is difficult to ensure that the executive synchronizes in a timely fashion with the plant processes, without the explicit notion of concurrent tasks in the controller software.

In a concurrent controller, each time frame is handled by a different task. The frequency of each task can be specified separately, and the burden of deciding what to run when is placed on the operating system scheduler. Even if the timing changes, there is no need to reprogram the controller. The real-time operating system is designed so as to be capable of adapting to the new requirements. If a large sequential program is used, the entire program would have to be restructured to satisfy the new timing requirements.

The use of concurrency is not without cost. There must be a run-time support system to manage execution of controller tasks or processes. Such run-time schedulers are often not considered in formal verification methods, but should be for a complete treatment of all system issues. Scheduling is treated as one discipline and verification as a different one. Methods that treat, in a unified framework, all aspects of verification and scheduling have not been sufficiently developed.

There is one part of the design process that is informal and intuitive. When the real world (e.g., of valves, pumps, vehicles, and robot arms) is translated into a formal mathematical model *plant* (e.g., of states, events and time bounds), there is no guarantee that the mathematical model properly represents the actual objects to be controlled. Similarly, there is no guarantee that the model *controller* is an accurate representation of all important facets of the actually implemented software (together with the hardware, CPU and run-time system). This translation of real-world objects into mathematical entities is by its very nature informal and intuitive.

As more experience is gained with a particular formalism, and actual designs based on the formal methods are experimentally checked in the field, so the formalism will gain more credibility. This is no different from the methods used in related disciplines. For example, a civil engineer will model the real world of bridges, beams and winds using the formal techniques of Newtonian physics. As more bridges are built and actually succeed in practice, so the Newtonian models gain credibility. In certain cases, the pure Newtonian model must be adjusted with "safety factors" to account for the approximate nature of the models used. It is not clear what constitutes the software equivalent of safety factors.

The fact that one part of the design procedure remains informal and experimental does not in any way detract from the need to use formal design procedures in the rest of the design. Just as the civil engineer uses formal Newtonian models for bridge building, and thereby increases confidence in the design, so too the designer of software uses formal methods to increase confidence in the correctness of the real-time system design. A proof of correctness is always relative to the formal models and specifications provided.

2.1 Major issues that formal theories must address

Formal methods for real-time systems must address the following problems:

- Modelling: Select appropriate models and formal notations for adequately describing plants and controllers. These notations must deal with the dynamic and reactive nature of the plants, and allow for the proper expression of timing properties.
- Verification: The verifier is presented with a formal mathematical model SUD where $SUD = plant \| controller$, and a specification S of how the plant should behave. The *verification problem* involves demonstrating that SUD satisfies the specification S.
- Development: In controller *development* a specification S is given that the *plant* must satisfy (the *controller* is not given). A disciplined method is sought whereby designers can be helped to construct a *controller* so that SUD satisfies S. In development the controller should be built in a modularly structured compositional fashion ("controller architecture").
- Synthesis: If controller development is fully automated, then it is called controller *synthesis*.

There are a few surveys in the literature of formal methods for real-time systems design [60, 22, 133]. This survey uses syntactic categories to classify the various formalisms. There are three main directions that must be distinguished, arranged by increasing formality and hence abstractness of approach. The first category to be dealt with is real-time languages. Then formalisms with visual specification languages are treated. Finally logics and algebras are discussed.

3 Real-Time Programming Languages

Modern real-time languages such as Ada [139], Chill [18], Occam [76] and Conic [65, 79] typically have delay and timeout features for implementing timing constraints. In addition, these languages incorporate features such as task decomposition, abstraction (information hiding), communication and concurrency mechanisms that simplify the description of complex controller software.

For example, in Ada, a module can be decomposed into several tasks. A task can be further divided into two parts: the task specification and the body of the task. During initial program development, only the specification part of the tasks needs to be defined. The specification parts can be compiled to check for overall controller consistency. Later, the task bodies can be specified in more detail. The specification part is done by senior designers, because the specification represents the interface between software components. An error in such code may therefore have more serious ramifications than an error within a task body. A task can then be given to a junior programmer for coding.

Conic implements several useful reconfiguration primitives. The primitives allow for dynamic insertion or deletion of tasks or modules, while the rest of the system continues to run. Thus maintenance to controller software can be implemented without shutting down the plant. Occam has been used as a target language for process algebras (see section 5.2).

The advantage of these languages is that at the end of the design process, the controller is available in directly executable code. However, most real-time programming languages lack an underlying abstract mathematical model. As a result the precise semantics is unspecified or even uncertain, and there is a proliferation of irrelevant detail not needed at the level of abstract specification. Usually the code must be converted into a formal notation (e.g., Petri nets) before the code can be verified. If these languages alone are used, then the plant is not usually represented, although pseudo plant processes can be coded. Thus there is no method to formally verify whether the controller satisfies the requirements specification S.

4 Structured Methods and/or Graphical Languages

4.1 Structured methods

Structured methods for real-time systems [44, 141] originated in systems analysis methods used in industry starting a decade ago. These methods provide a structured set of system (read: controller) requirements. The system requirements specify what problem the controller must solve, and how the controller must be structured.

The system requirements includes various views and layers of the controller such as (a) data flow diagrams to decompose the controller, its functions and its flow of data, (b) control flow diagrams (enhanced state transition diagrams) to represent the system dynamics, (c) a requirements dictionary which is an alphabetical listing of all inputs, outputs, data and control flows, and (d) a table of response times in which the incoming and outgoing events (from and to the plant) are listed with their respective repetition rates or response times. The timing requirements are not particularly well integrated with the rest of the requirements.

These methods have been used with some success in actual industrial applications. However, these methods have no formal semantics. The resulting controller design cannot be executed for simulated behaviour, nor can they be compiled into code (e.g., into Ada or C). There is no support for formal verification. Nondeterministic plant behaviour cannot be suitably modelled.

4.2 Graphical languages with a formally defined semantics

Statecharts and synchronous languages. Statecharts [38] represents an improved version of the structured methods. A graphic tool called "Statemate" [41] exists to implement the formalism. Methods similar to Statecharts may be found in Gabrielian and Franklin [29].

In Statecharts, the normal state transition diagram is enhanced with hierarchical and compositional features. For example, states can be clustered into superstates with the possibility of "zooming in" and "zooming out" of states. In AND decomposition, states are split into orthogonal (concurrent) subcomponents that communicate via broadcasting. OR decomposition decomposes a state into substates such that control resides in exactly one substate.

Statemate is formally based on a precisely defined (although rather complex) semantics. As an important consequence, there is an automated simulation tool which allows the user to execute the model. Exhaustive checking of all possible behaviours (for small systems) is supported. Models (e.g., of the controller) can be compiled into a target environment, although this tool is not yet fully developed. Formal verification is not yet supported, nor are time constraints treated in sufficient detail.

According to [86], the real-time aspects of Statecharts semantics is underdeveloped. A notation is needed for periodic timing functions, and for the specification of timing exceptions without the need to introduce additional states.

Recently, some progress has been made in providing formal analysis techniques for Statecharts. A fully abstract compositional semantics of Statecharts has been presented [53].

The simplest kind of semantics uses the operational notion of the set of all observable behaviours of a program or system. A behaviour may be defined as an infinite sequence of states that the system computes in one run. Such an operational semantics cannot usually be used to deliver a compositional (modular) semantics. In a compositional semantics, a compound system $M_1 \| M_2$ is described in terms of the semantics of the component systems M_1 and M_2. A fully abstract semantics defines the behaviour of the system in sufficient detail without violating the principle of compositionality, i.e., such a semantics does not distinguish between more systems than is necessary to provide a compositional semantics.

The importance of compositionality is that structured program verification can be undertaken. Components of the system can be checked independently, and then combined to provide a verifiably correct compound program.

In addition to the abstract semantics of Statecharts presented in [53], there is an alternative version of Statechart semantics. Pnueli and Shalev [119] present a semantics that uses micro and macrosteps. Observable macrosteps are decomposed into a number of microsteps. If event A triggers B, then these events occur in subsequent microsteps within the same macrostep. Thus a chain of causality inside one macrostep is modelled by a sequence of microsteps. This avoids some of the causal paradoxes that occur in synchronous languages such as Statecharts.

The "synchrony hypothesis" assumes that a program instantly reacts to external events. In practice this means that the reaction time of the controller is always shorter than the minimum delay separating two successive external events in the plant. In addition to Statecharts, the languages Esterel [11], Signal [9] and Lustre [16] have been designed with the synchrony hypothesis in mind. The synchrony hypothesis must be applied with care as it can lead to causal paradoxes such as events disabling their own cause. This hypothesis is not always realistic, as the plant usually involves spontaneous behaviour that may occur at any moment of time. Languages such as Esterel do not allow for nondeterminism which is also not realistic for representing plants.

Petri nets. Petri net theory [116, 129] was one of the first formalisms to deal with concurrency, nondeterminism and causal connections between events. According to [91] it was the first unified theory, with levels of abstraction, in which to describe and analyze all aspects of the computer in the context of its environment (computer + program + aircraft). Such a method must perforce contain a theory of concurrency, because of the three ingredients, at most one – the program – is sequential. Previously the various components of the total system had to be described in diverse and unrelated ways. The computer hardware would be described by low level automata theories, the program by code in a sequential programming language, and the interaction of the program with its environment by narrative prose.

The classic Petri net model is a 5-tuple (P,T,I,O,M). P is a finite set of places (often drawn as circles) representing conditions. T is a finite set of transitions (often drawn as bars) representing events. I and O are sets of input and output functions mapping transitions to bags of places (the incidence functions). M is the set of initial markings.

Places may contain zero or more tokens (often drawn as black circles). A marking (or state) of the Petri nets is the distribution of tokens at a moment in time (i.e., $M:P \to N$ where N is the nonnegative integers). Tokens in Petri nets model dynamic behaviour of systems. Markings change during execution of the Petri nets as the tokens "travel" through the net (modelling flow of materials, for example).

The execution of the Petri nets is controlled by the number and distribution of the tokens (the "state"). A transition is enabled if each of its input places contains at least as many tokens as there exist arcs from that place to the transition. When a transition is enabled it may fire. When a transition fires, all enabling tokens are removed from its input places, and a token is deposited in each of its output places.

Given an initial state (distribution of tokens), the reachability set is the set of all states that result from executing the Petri net. Properties such as boundedness, liveness, safety and freedom from deadlock can be checked by analyzing the reachability graph. The reachability graph is usually constructed using an interleaving operational semantics.

Boundedness means that the number of tokens which any place in the net can accumulate is bounded. Boundedness implies that the system is finite state. In a Petri net, a transition is said to be *live* if it is potentially fireable in all reachable markings. Liveness in the program verification sense is a different concept, meaning that the transition must eventually occur.

In Petri nets causal dependencies and independencies in some set of events are explicitly represented. It is therefore easy to provide a nonrestrictive partial order semantics. Events which are independent of each other are not projected onto a linear timescale. Instead a non-interleaving partial order relation of concurrency is introduced. In an interleaved execution, one cannot differentiate whether two events occur one after the other because the first is a prerequisite of the second, or because this order in time occurs by chance [129].

There are also some structural analysis techniques that use linear algebra to check for invariants. Every marking can be represented as a vector, and the net can therefore be modelled as a set of linear algebraic equations. An example of an invariant is a place-invariant, in which every place in the net is assigned a weight, so that the weighted token count remains constant during the execution of the net. The dual of the place-invariant is the transition-invariant. Since invariants are the characteristic solutions of the net equations, it is possible to compute them by well known techniques in linear algebra. These invariants are useful in the analysis of net liveness properties or of facts (propositional formulas that are true in all cases).

For large nets it is hard to compute the invariants. Usually, there are infinitely many invariants (a linear combination of invariants is also an invariant). Therefore it is often difficult to obtain the interesting ones. If the user supplies the invariant, it is somewhat easier to check automatically that the invariant holds true. If it does not hold, it is relatively easy to see where the net or the invariant must be modified.

Generic "health" checks such as the absence of deadlock can be performed. Such checks are not always useful as some kinds of deadlock may be allowed (e.g., program termination).

Controllers are specified by augmenting the plant net with additional places and transitions to model the required controlled behaviour. For example, let the plant be a Petri net *elevator*, and suppose it is required that the elevator be allowed to be disabled for possible maintenance work. A new place must be added to *elevator*, representing the emergency stop request. A new transition, representing the stop event, is also inserted into the net. The stop event is connected to the place in *elevator* that controls the elevator movement. Short of introducing a specification logic, there is no way (other than by modifying the details of the net) to specify the abstract requirement that "if the stop event is requested then the elevator must eventually come to a halt and be disabled."

Ordinary Petri nets have been criticized for not being able to deal with fairness and data structures (e.g., the data in a message header) [62, 94], although the number of tokens at a particular place in the net can simulate a local program variable. Structuring mechanisms such as composition operators are not inherently part of the theory, and there is no calculus to transform a net into a real-time programming language. Unlike state machines, a "place" in a Petri net cannot easily be identified with a place in the corresponding program code. A further problem is that the reachability graph suffers from state explosion as Petri nets become larger, thus impacting on the ability to scale up analysis to larger systems.

Ordinary Petri nets are still an object of intense research aimed at putting Petri net theory on firm mathematical grounds. However, practically speaking, such standard nets are not up to the task of modelling complex systems. For this reason, higher level nets (coloured nets) and stochastic nets have been introduced to extend the modelling power of Petri nets [13].

In coloured nets, the main idea is that the tokens themselves may have values (or colours). Coloured nets allow for a more concise, manageable representation of systems. They can be used to model data and resources that reside in the system. As long as the number of colours is finite, a coloured net is equivalent to a (much larger) ordinary Petri net. An infinite number of colours allow for the expressive power of Turing machines so that most general questions become undecidable.

Petri net theory was one of the first concurrent formalisms to deal with real-time. Two basic timed versions of Petri nets have been introduced: time Petri nets [88] and time *d* Petri nets [124]. Both have been used in recent work [145, 125, 87, 72, 12, 27]. There are two questions that arise when time is introduced to net theory: (a) the location of the time delays (at places or at transitions), and (b) the type of the delay (fixed delays, intervals or stochastic delays) [140].

Timed Petri nets are derived from classical Petri nets by associating a firing finite duration (a delay) with each transition of the net. The transition is prevented from occurring for the delay period, but is fired immediately after becoming enabled. These nets are used mainly in performance evaluation.

Time Petri Nets (TPNs) are more general than timed Petri nets. A timed Petri net can be simulated by a TPN, but not vice versa. Both a lower and an upper bound are associated with each transition in a TPN. A state in the reachability graph is a tuple consisting of a marking, and a vector of possible firing intervals of enabled transitions in that marking. Since transitions may fire at any time in the allowed interval, states in the reachability graphs may have an unbounded number of successors (if continuous time is used). This adds complexity to the next-state function. Various techniques such as state classes and enumerative analysis techniques [12] have been introduced to overcome this problem. There are no necessary and sufficient conditions for boundedness (finiteness of the reachability graph); however, some sufficient conditions have been provided.

Perhaps the most general Petri nets available for real-time problems are the interval timed colour Petri net (ITCPN) models of Van der Aalst [140]. These nets are higher level nets, and an interval is used to specify the timing characteristics, by attaching a timestamp to every token. The resulting semantics is quite elegant because both the timing and the colour are attributes of tokens. A software tool called *ExSpect* is available for performing analyses on ITCPNs.

In Leveson and Stolzy [72], safety properties of TPNs are analyzed without the need to necessarily generate the entire reachability graph. The idea is to work backwards from high-risk states to determine if these hazardous states are reachable. This backward method uses the inverse Petri net (reversed input and output functions), and is practical only when a small number of unsafe states is considered. The idea is to work backwards from unsafe states to all critical states (i.e., states having at least two successors). When a critical state is reached, interlocks can be used to force the system to take those paths that do not lead to unsafe states.

A similar backward method is employed in the real-time temporal logic approach to controller design [103, 107] (see section 5.1.1). Instead of dealing with unsafe states one at a time, a predicate (characterizing a possibly infinite set of unsafe states) is used. Weakest preconditions are used to work backwards to critical predicates. The advantage of using predicates (rather than individual states) is that much larger systems can be treated. The method has been semi-automated. The backward method is an example in which the same basic idea is applicable in two very different computational models.

5 Logics and Algebras

Logics and algebras provide the most abstract approach to the analysis of real-time systems. These approaches typically consist of several elements. One element is a high-level, formal specification language in which the requirements that the system must satisfy can be specified. A second element is a proof system (or finite state decision procedures) in which the correctness of the system relative to the specification can be verified. Another important element (that is not always provided) is a set of heuristics and general guidelines for using the approach on systems larger than the standard "textbook" examples.

Some researchers have investigated the general properties that any specification formalism must satisfy [55]. This is in contrast to the development of specific frameworks for doing verification. In [114], the relations that must hold between plant (environmental) variables and controller (software) variables are specified. These relations are used to express under what conditions a design is feasible, and what formal functional or relational properties a software requirements document must satisfy.

The current rigorous approaches to real-time systems are:

- Real-time temporal logics,
- Algebraic approaches (process algebras),
- RTL (real-time logic) and event/action models, and
- Assertional calculi

In this survey, a syntactic classification has been used based on the style of specification. The same underlying semantic model may often be applied to different syntactic specification styles. For example, both process algebras and temporal logics may be endowed with a discrete time semantics. Alternatively, in each case, a dense time semantics may be chosen. The classification of formal approaches could also have been performed on the basis of semantic models rather than syntactic specification styles.

There are a variety of timed transition systems (e.g., the timed automata discussed in Lynch and Vaandrager [77]) that are being promoted as general models of real-time systems. These timed transition systems are not discussed in this survey as an independent group, but are treated individually where they relate to a particular specification language.

Some of the specification approaches are complementary. For example, temporal logic is good at describing properties that pertain to the complete system such as safety, liveness, fairness, and real-time response. However, temporal logic specifications are relatively unstructured, and could benefit from the more structured notions of processes algebras [22]. Process algebras are not good at specifying inherently global properties such as fairness which involve the complete computation. There is currently no theory that combines the best features of each formalism.

The following areas of research are listed below for the sake of completeness. They do not at present deal with real-time issues. However, they may be extended in the future to deal with real-time constraints.

- VDM [59] and Z [136] are specification languages based on set theory and predicate logic. These methods have been found useful for specifying large commercial systems [36], but are weak in their ability to deal with concurrency and real-time. They use concepts from classical programming logics such as Hoare's triples [49], and Dijkstra's weakest precondition calculus [23, 35]. Owicki and Gries [113] provided the first extension of Hoare triples to concurrent systems.
- Control theoretic approaches based on algebraic methods and formal language theory have been developed for complex discrete event dynamic systems [123, 122, 54, 15, 75]. These methods are good at modular synthesis of controllers. They have, on the whole, not yet been extended to deal with real-time constraints, nor do they deal with data structures. Also noteworthy are the synthesis methods proposed [84, 24], and the automata based methods [80, 1].
- UNITY [19] is a specification and verification framework that uses extended state-transition systems to model plants and controllers (abstract programs). A logic, which is similar to temporal logic (but simpler), is used for specification and verification. A UNITY program describes *what* should be done. A *mapping* to a particular architecture is concerned with implementation details such as the type of machine that should be used. For example, the same abstract program can be mapped to a set of concurrent processors, to a single CPU using multiprogramming, or to a systolic array. This leads to a separation of concerns. Correctness is concerned with verifying the abstract program. Complexity is computed from the mapping to an implementation.

5.1 Real-time temporal logic

The following discussion is taken from [104]. Temporal logic has its origins in philosophy, where it was used to analyze the structure or topology of time [130]. In recent years, it has found application in computer science, especially in the areas of software verification and knowledge-based systems [30, 117, 70, 112, 69, 67, 28, 66].

In physics and mathematics, time has traditionally been represented as just another variable. First order predicate calculus is used to reason about expressions containing the time variable, and there is thus apparently no need for a special *temporal* logic.

Philosophers found it useful to introduce special temporal operators, such as □ (henceforth) and ◇ (eventually), for the analysis of temporal connectives in language. The new formalism was soon seen as a potentially valuable tool for analyzing the topology of time. For example, various types of semantics can be given to the temporal operators depending on whether time is linear, parallel or branching. Another question that may be asked is whether time is discrete or continuous.

The temporal operators have been found useful for specifying program behaviour. A *structure* of states (e.g., a sequence or tree of states) is the key concept that makes temporal logic suitable for program specification. A formula, containing temporal logic operators, is interpreted over a structure of states.

In programming languages, the structures represent the computations executed by a program. Such a computation may be used to interpret a temporal formula. In this way, a programming language is said to be endowed with a temporal semantics.

The different types of temporal semantics include:

- *Interval semantics* [134, 95, 96]. The semantics is based on intervals of time, thought of as representing finite chunks of system behaviour. An interval may be divided into two contiguous subintervals, thus leading to the *chop* operator.
- *Point semantics*, in which temporal formulas are interpreted as requiring some system behaviour with respect to a certain reference point in time. *Past* operators refer to the time prior to the reference point. *Future* operators refer to the time after the reference point. Obviously, a point cannot be divided, and there is thus no simple definition of a *chop* operator.

Point semantics may be further divided[2] into three classes:

1. *Linear semantics* [83, 120, 81]. In linear semantics, each moment has only one possible future corresponding to the history of the development of the system.
2. *Branching semantics* [25, 20]. In branching time semantics, time has a tree-like nature in which, at each instant, time may split into alternative courses representing different choices made by a system.
3. *Partial order semantics*. Partial order semantics has been explored only recently. The reader is referred to [81] and other articles in the same volume for further information.

Once the type of *structure* to be used for interpreting temporal formulas is selected, there is still a further decision to be made. How are the structures to represent program executions or computations? There are at least two possibilities:

---

[2] Ron Koymans has pointed out [61] that interval semantics may also be coupled with linear/branching/partial orders – in practice interval semantics has tended to use linear time orders. However, in theory these are orthogonal issues.

- *Maximal parallelism* [52, 62]. The number of instructions in concurrent processes that can be executed simultaneously is maximized. Thus, two processes are never both waiting to achieve a shared communication.
- *Interleaved executions.* Concurrent activity of two parallel processes is represented by interleaving their atomic actions [82]. Fairness and time bound constraints are then used to exclude inappropriate interleavings (e.g., a sequence in which an enabled action is never executed).

The various temporal logics can be used to reason about *qualitative* temporal properties. Safety properties that can be specified include mutual exclusion and absence of deadlock. Liveness properties include termination and responsiveness. Fairness properties include scheduling a given process infinitely often, or requiring that a continuously enabled transition ultimately fire.

Various proof systems and decision procedures for finite state systems can be used to check the correctness of a program or system.

In real-time temporal logics, *quantitative* properties can also be expressed such as periodicity, real-time response (deadlines), and delays. Early approaches to real-time temporal logics were reported in [10, 63, 111]. Since then, real-time temporal logics have been explored in great detail.

The TTM/RTTL framework – explicit clock linear logics. The timed transition models/real-time temporal logic (TTM/RTTL) framework was first presented in [111], and in detail in [102]. It includes the following elements: (a) a semantic model of time, (b) a generic computational model (TTM's[3]) for modelling plants and controllers, (c) an abstract specification language (RTTL), (d) verification methodologies including model-checking for finite state systems, and a deductive proof system for infinite state systems, and (e) heuristics for constructing proofs and controller synthesis methods [104, 105, 110, 107, 109, 108]. The first four elements represent an extension of untimed Manna-Pnueli temporal logic [82] to timed systems. Each of these elements is discussed below.

Semantic model of time. The notion of a possible behaviour or *trajectory* σ of a system is given by an infinite sequence of states q_i and events τ_i defined as

$$\sigma \stackrel{\text{def}}{=} q_0 \stackrel{\tau_0}{\rightarrow} q_1 \stackrel{\tau_1}{\rightarrow} q_2 \cdots \stackrel{\tau_{i-1}}{\rightarrow} q_i \stackrel{\tau_i}{\rightarrow}$$

representing a possible run or computation of the system.

A *discrete* notion of time is employed using an external (conceptual) *explicit clock*. There is a distinguished *tick* transition, corresponding to the movement of the clock whose current time is represented by the variable t, with $type(t)$ (the set of all values that t can have) the nonnegative integers. The clock event *tick* occurs infinitely often ("time must make progress") in the trajectory σ. When the clock tick occurs it increments t by one ("time never decreases"). No event other than the clock tick can change the time. The clock ticks are *interleaved* with other system transitions.

---
[3] Originally called Extended State Machines.

Time bounds on events determine when they may occur relative to the clock ticks. A lower time bound l on the event τ means that it may not occur prior to l ticks of the clock. An upper time bound u means that τ must occur no later than u ticks of the clock (unless τ is preempted by some other event). Thus an event that is continuously enabled over an interval of time does not actually occur for l ticks of the clock, but must occur by u ticks of the clock or become disabled.

Many events may occur between two ticks of the clock, in which case the events can only by distinguished by temporal ordering, not by time. A discrete-time domain necessarily sacrifices information about precise times.

A computational model. Timed Transition Models (TTMs) provide an effective representation of realizable systems. Concrete real-time programming languages, Petri nets and Statecharts can be mapped into TTMs. Most real-time features such as delays, timeouts and various scheduling constraints can be represented. True parallel processing, multiprogramming, communication through shared variables as well as message passing over channels can also be modelled.

A TTM M is defined as a 3-tuple $M = (\mathcal{V}, \Theta, \mathcal{T})$, where $\mathcal{V}$ is the set of *activity*[4] and *data* variables (including the clock variable t). Θ is a predicate asserting an initial condition on the variables. $\mathcal{T}$ is the set of all transitions (representing events). Each transition has an enabling condition, transformation function, and lower and upper time bounds.

TTMs may be composed in parallel with each other to obtain more complex TTMs. A *graphical language* such as Statecharts is used to visually represent TTMs to the designer. The visual notation of Statecharts is extended by annotating each transition with its enabling condition, transformation function, and lower and upper time bounds.

For the transition

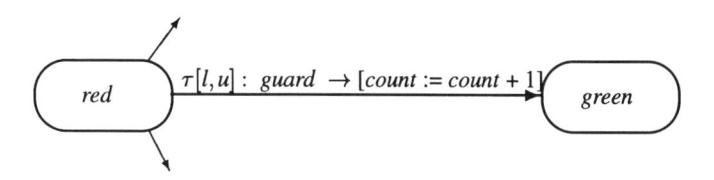

the variable *count* is an example of a data variable that counts the number of times the traffic light has changed from the activity *red* to *green*. The intended operational meaning is as follows: the transition is said to be *enabled* if (a) the guard is true, and (b) the TTM currently resides in activity *red*. The lower time bound l guarantees that once τ becomes enabled, then it may not occur for at least l ticks of the clock. Meanwhile, other enabled transitions may occur and disable τ. After τ has

---

[4] An *activity* variable is also sometimes called a *control* or *location* variable. An *activity* is any particular value that the activity variable may assume. The word "activity" is used rather than "state" as the word "state" is reserved for the global vector of all values of activity and data variables. An activity has persistence as opposed to a transition which occurs instantaneously.

been continuously enabled for more than l ticks of the clock, then the transition τ *may* be taken, instantaneously moving the TTM from red to the activity *green*, and simultaneously incrementing the counter by one. After having been continuously enabled for u ticks of the clock, either τ *must* be taken before the next clock tick or be preempted by the occurrence of some other transition that disables τ.

A *spontaneous* transition $\tau[0,\infty]$ represents an event that may occur at any moment. However, it may also delay occurring forever. Spontaneous transitions are useful for modelling nondeterministic unpredictable behaviour in the plant. Examples include the failure of various devices (e.g., a pump or a valve). Spontaneous transitions can also represent situations where the designer initially has no knowledge of the time bounds.

More than one transition may be enabled and eligible (by virtue of its bounds) to occur at any point in time. In such a case, the order of transitions (in a behaviour) are chosen nondeterministically. This is typical of how the interleaving approach represents a process that must occur along several edges at the same time.

Lawford [71] proposed a set of transformations for taking a given TTM into a new TTM that is bisimulation equivalent. These transformations can be used to show that an implementation TTM is correct with respect to a specification TTM (in the style of process algebras discussed in the next section).

Concise specification language. Real-time temporal logic (RTTL) is used to specify the properties to be verified. Given the timed transition model $SUD \stackrel{\text{def}}{=} plant \| controller$, the objective is to check that SUD satisfies a specification S (which is a formula of RTTL).

An example of an RTTL formula is the *bounded response* time given by

$$\forall T[(red \wedge t = T) \rightarrow \Diamond(green \wedge T+3 \leq t \leq T+5)]$$

In the above formula, the clock variable t is a flexible variable. The quantified variable T is a rigid variable. The clock variable is called flexible because it changes from state to state in the trajectory. By contrast, the rigid variable T retains the same value over all states in the trajectory, and is used to record the time when *red* becomes true. Accordingly, the above formula asserts that if the traffic light is *red* at time T, then eventually within 3 to 5 ticks from T the light must turn *green*. The bounded response property may be *abbreviated* by the formula

$$red \rightarrow \Diamond_{[3,5]} green$$

RTTL is an *explicit clock* logic because an RTTL formula may explicitly use the clock time variable t with any of the arithmetic operators (e.g., $+, -, =, \leq, >$), using arbitrary first-order quantification over rigid time variables. Hence RTTL is very expressive but undecidable (see section 5.1.2). RTTL may be used to: (a) refer to absolute times (e.g., "do some action on January 22nd 1998"), or (b) relate adjacent temporal contexts (e.g., "every stimulus A is followed by a response B, and then by another response C that is within 5 ticks of the original stimulus A").

Verification via model-checking and proof systems. The *model-checking*[5] problem is as follows: check whether all legal trajectories of a *finite state* timed transition model *SUD* satisfy a specification *S*. The challenge is to construct a finite reachability graph, even though the time domain is unbounded.

Algorithms (and an implemented verifier) are provided [105, 109], for checking a subset of RTTL specifications. The verifier represents processes in a fashion close to the mathematical definition of TTMs. All kinds of data variables are treated including booleans, enumerated or numerical types, lists, sets and sequences. If an RTTL property fails to hold, then the failing trajectories are provided, making it possible to debug the system.

Model-checking suffers from exponential explosion in the size of the state space, when dealing with the parallel composition of processes. Model-checking is suitable for checking small core parts of real-time systems. Reduced models, such as the synchronization skeleton of a mutual exclusion protocol, can also be treated. Large systems will often require different techniques.

For large systems (or infinite data domains) a deductive proof system must be used. A sound first-order proof system for RTTL is presented in [104]. The proof system reduces to standard Manna-Pnueli temporal logic if all the upper and lower bounds are zero and infinity respectively.

An advantage of RTTL is that no new temporal operators are introduced. As a result, all the proof rules of Manna-Pnueli temporal logic can be used. In addition, certain rules are added for the real-time part of the reasoning [104, 108]. Systems in which there are mixed fairness and time constraints can also be handled.

Pragmatics – semi-automated proof and synthesis methods. A proof system, with perhaps some small examples to illustrate the method of proof, is not on its own sufficient to make the proof system practically useful for infinite state systems. Additional guidelines and heuristics must provide insight to the design and verification procedures. Automated support tools (beyond model-checking for finite state systems) are needed. Theorem provers must be provided with adequate tacticals (built in heuristics) to support verification.

RTTL has heuristics for doing proofs using proof diagrams and weakest-preconditions [104, 108]. A proof diagram is an abstract view of a state reachability graph. It is not confined to finite state systems because a node in the proof diagram is a predicate that can characterize a possibly infinite set of states. The proof diagram contains the intuition of system executions without the distracting proliferation of states. Most of the reasoning takes place in the ordinary predicate calculus, with temporal or real-time reasoning introduced only where absolutely needed.

Constraint logic programming has been used to semi-automate the heuristics. The language CLP($\Re$) was used initially [106], but more recently the constraint logic language Prolog III [107] has been investigated for providing automated support. Methods of synthesizing controllers (for some infinite state systems) to satisfy

---

[5] The notion of model-checking was first explored by Clarke et al. [20] in the context of (untimed) branching time temporal logics.

given plant specifications are provided in [107] (see also the last paragraph of section 4.2.2).

Koymans [64] claims that explicit clock logics such as RTTL do not "hide" time in accordance with the original philosophy of temporal logic (which was to abstract from time as much as possible). Specifications are not as succinct as hidden clock logics. However, most of the reasoning about time in RTTL involves the use of abbreviated formulas (similar to the bounded operators of hidden clock logic). Explicit time is resorted to only in those instances where needed (e.g., to refer to adjacent time contexts or other properties that hidden clock logics cannot specify).

It has also been claimed [56, 62] that while the interleaving model of computation may be adequate for qualitative analysis of systems, a more realistic model such as maximal parallelism is needed for real-time systems. This claim is refuted by the interleaving model in the TTM/RTTL framework, in which system actions are interleaved with clock ticks. A careful incorporation of time allows for an adequate representation of most real-time phenomena while preserving the simplicity associated with interleaving models, namely, at any one point in time only one transition can occur and has to be analyzed.

The main disadvantage of the framework is its lack of compositional proof methods, although some of the synthesis methods allow for a modular style of controller development. The question of modular specification and verification methods is an active area of research in the field. Manna-Pnueli temporal logic has recently been provided with a compositional proof system [82]. Since RTTL is based on the untimed Manna-Pnueli system, it appears that their compositional methods should also carry over to RTTL.

The TTM/RTTL framework is a state-based, linear discrete time, interleaved, asynchronous, explicit clock logic formalism. It is state-based because states rather than actions are the primitive components of behaviours. State-based approaches may be more general than action-based methods (e.g., process algebras) because state-based methods can easily encode actions as well as histories of actions It is difficult to extract the state from action-based formalisms.

TTM/RTTL uses a discrete-time domain rather than a dense (e.g., the rationals) time domain. If simplicity of use can be preserved, the more general modelling powers of a dense time domain would be preferable. Concurrency is modelled by interleaving rather than a partial order or maximal parallelism. It is asynchronous because a finite number of events can occur between clock ticks. In a synchronous model, all concurrent activity happens in lock-step with the tick of the clock.

Many of the choices made in the TTM/RTTL computational model are independent of each other. For example, RTTL can be defined over dense as well as continuous time domains. It can be given a branching time semantics or be based on time intervals. The choice of semantics is, in principle, independent of the syntax of the specification language [61, 46]. The reader is referred to [118, 46, 47] for other explicit clock logics. In particular, [47] compares explicit clock logics with hidden clock logics.

MTL – hidden clock linear logics and other RTTL fragments. Metric Temporal Logic (MTL) [64] is a fragment of RTTL in which references to time are restricted to bounds on the temporal operators. For example, the formula $A \rightarrow \Diamond_{\leq 5} B$ means that if A occurs then eventually within 5 time units B must occur. No references to an explicit clock are allowed and hence MTL is called a *hidden clock* or *bounded temporal operator* logic.

Interpretations for MTL are metric point structures based on a linearly ordered time domain. A distance function provides a metric for time. Various time constraints can be imposed on the distance function, depending on the notion of time that is used (e.g., transitivity, irreflexibility, and the existence of absolute differences).

In the hidden clock approach, $\Diamond_{\leq 5}$ is a new temporal operator that restricts or bounds the scope of the qualitative operator $\Diamond$. The bounded formula $\Diamond_{\leq 5} B$ predicts the occurrence of B within 5 time units from now. The qualitative formula $\Diamond B$ asserts that B will eventually happen, but puts no bound on when.

Koymans [64] uses a real-valued time domain. This allows MTL to express certain properties of continuous time variables (e.g., temperature and pressure) more succinctly than discrete-time logics. MTL does not allow references to an absolute point in time, nor does it allow the specifier to relate adjacent temporal contexts. A sound proof system for MTL is provided.

An important extension to the literature on MTL is a compositional proof system for Occam style programs [52, 50]. The proof system uses the maximal parallelism model of program execution. Because the proof system is compositional, the properties of a compound system $P_1 \| P_2$ (the parallel composition of two simpler processes $P1$ and P_2) can be deduced from specifications of its constituent parts (P_1 and P_2), without any further information about the internal structure of these parts. Compositionality is important for scaling up the application of the proof system to deal with large systems in a structured fashion.

It is not clear whether the proof system can be extended to reason about complex plant descriptions, which are not always representable in Occam. The extra *chop* operator, needed for compositional proofs, makes the reasoning relatively complex. Nevertheless, once a module's specification is fixed, any implementation of the module with the same specification can be used, without having to redo the proof.

Alur and Henzinger [6] have compared various ways in which to restrict RTTL to obtain decidable fragments of the logic. These fragments are restricted to finite state, propositional temporal properties. There are at least four interesting syntactic fragments of RTTL:

- MTL [7, 64] is a discrete-time propositional version of the bounded operator logic discussed above.
- XCTL [43] is a discrete-time propositional-explicit clock logic. The atomic timing constraints allows the primitives of comparison and addition. XCTL restricts the quantification level. It allows only one outermost level of quantification over rigid time variables. The quantification is, therefore, never explicitly displayed.

On the other hand, it allows general arithmetic timing expressions, including addition and subtraction of variables and constants.
- TPTL [7] is a discrete-time propositional logic whose timing constraints allow comparison and addition (but only of integer constants, i.e., no variables). TPTL uses auxiliary static timing variables to record the value of the clock at different states, but replaces the explicit references to the clock itself by a special type of freezing quantification.
- MITL [5] employs a dense time domain. It has a bounded-operator syntax, but cannot express punctuality properties. A *punctuality* property states that the event B follows A in *exactly* 3 seconds.

All of the above fragments can be interpreted over discrete, dense and continuous time domains. The fragments can then be compared for expressiveness, and complexity of satisfiability and model-checking.

Satisfiability is important in the homogeneous verification case. Let the implementation I and the specification S (that the implementation must satisfy) can both be given as temporal logic formulas F_I and F_S respectively, in the appropriate fragment of RTTL. Then the implementation I meets the specification S iff the implication $F_I \rightarrow F_S$ is valid (or, equivalently, if the conjunction $F_I \wedge \neg F_S$ is unsatisfiable). Only propositional versions of temporal logics are decidable for satisfiability. Decidability depends on the nature of the time domain (discrete, dense etc.) and the operations on the time domain that are permitted.

Model-checking is important in the heterogeneous verification case. The implementation I is given by a timed automaton or timed transition system [4, 5] A_I. The specification S is given by a temporal logic formula F_S. To do the check, a timed automaton $A_{\neg F_S}$ is constructed from the negation of the specification $\neg F_S$. The implementation I satisfies the specification S precisely when the product automaton $A_I \times A_{\neg F_S}$ has no run (timed observation sequence).

Let RTTL($<$,s) denote the restriction of RTTL to propositions and timing constraints containing only ordering ($<$), successor(s), and congruence over time (e.g., all times with an event time difference from the initial state). Thus, RTTL($<$,s) is interpreted over a discrete-time domain, and can be used to specify constant lower and upper time bounds on the time distance between events. The various logics are compared in Table 1 for satisfiability, model-checking, and expressiveness over discrete and dense time domains relative to RTTL.

For any real-time logic that is closed under boolean operations, and that can express punctuality, the satisfiability problem is undecidable for a dense time domain. MITL cannot express punctuality properties, and is thus less expressive than the other logics, but remains decidable even if the time domain is dense.

Harel *et al.* [43] showed that XCTL and TPTL/MTL are incomparable. For each of these logics, there is a property expressible in one which is not expressible in the other. Each of these properties is a reasonable real-time requirement. In the discrete-time case, TPTL and MTL are equally expressive (it is conjectured that this equality does not extend to dense domains [46]).

Discrete Time	Satisfiability	Model-Checking	Expressiveness
RTTL	undecidable	undecidable	
RTTL(<,s)	nonelementary	nonelementary	< RTTL
XCTL	PSPACE-complete	PSPACE-complete	< RTTL
TPTL	EXPSPACE-complete	EXPSPACE-complete	=RTTL(<,s)
MTL	EXPSPACE-complete	EXPSPACE-complete	=RTTL(<,s)
MITL	EXPSPACE-complete	EXPSPACE-complete	< RTTL(<,s)
Dense Time	Satisfiability	Model-Checking	
RTTL	undecidable	undecidable	
RTTL(<,s)	undecidable	undecidable	
XCTL	?	?	
TPTL	undecidable	undecidable	
MTL	undecidable	undecidable	
MITL	EXSPACE-complete	EXPSPACE-complete	

Table 1. Comparison of linear propositional real-time logics

There are doubly-exponential-time decision procedures for both TPTL and MTL. The verification algorithm for MTL depends, exponentially, on the value of the largest time constant involved. It is a little less expensive than the algorithm for TPTL, which depends exponentially on the value of the product of all time constants.

XCTL is not closed under negation, and hence cannot be used to solve the homogeneous verification problem. However, a special model-checking algorithm for XCTL has been given that is doubly exponential in the size of the specification formula and singly exponential in the size of the model.

Branching time temporal logics. Linear time and branching time logics are incomparable. For example, branching time logics cannot express general fairness constraints in the syntax of the language (although certain fairness conditions can be imposed by external constraints on the reachability graphs when doing model-checking for example). Linear time logics can directly specify fairness. On the other hand, branching time logics can express certain existential path conditions (e.g., it is always possible for the system to eventually do some action). Such path constraints cannot generally be expressed in linear time logics.

Although the validity problem for (untimed) branching logics is EXTIME-complete, model-checking is in PTIME. Model-checking is performed with a special purpose algorithm (relabelling of the program reachability graph) and does not use the satisfiability procedure. The algorithm for model-checking branching time logics is linear both in the size of the reachability graph and the size of the formula to be checked.

Linear time logics cannot use this special purpose algorithm, and hence untimed model-checking in the linear case is exponential in the size of the formula. Model-checking for branching time logics has therefore been applied more successfully than that of linear time logics, although additional constructs must be employed to deal with fairness [20].

There is no consensus among researchers as to whether branching time or linear time logics are more suited to verification. In practice, branching time logics are usually used to verify finite state systems by model-checking because of the efficiency of the model-checking algorithms. Linear time logics usually come with a deductive proof system for dealing with the infinite state systems.

Alur and coworkers [2, 3] propose a branching real-time time logic called TCTL. It is based on hidden clock bounded operators. For TCTL, the validity problem for dense time domains is undecidable, yet model-checking is decidable. The complexity of model checking is exponential in the number of clocks (each new process or hardware device needs its own clock), and doubly exponential in the product of the timing constants that appear in the formula. It is linear in the product of program and formula size.

Emerson *et al.* [26] introduced a bounded operator branching time logic called RTCTL. The satisfiability problem in this logic is doubly exponential time complete. Model-checking has a polynomial time algorithm.

Hansson [37] introduced a branching time logic called TPCTL [37]. The logic deals with real-time constraints and reliability. For example, the following property can be specified: "after a request for service there is at least a 98% probability that the service will be carried out in 2 seconds."

Formulas of TPCTL are interpreted over a discrete-time extension of Milner's Calculus of Communicating Systems (see process algebras later) called TPCCS. Probabilities are introduced by allowing two types of transitions, one labelled with actions and the other labelled with probabilities. A probabilistic strong bisimulation for equivalence of processes is defined, which has a sound and complete axiomatization. The model-checking algorithm is exponential in the size of the TPCCS process, and polynomial in the size of the formula and number of arithmetic expressions.

Because of the action-based nature of TPCTL, it is difficult to specify state-based properties such as: "henceforth, if the train is at the crossing then the gate must be down." Propositions such as "the gate is down" must be encoded indirectly through actions that change the state of the model, in which case the specification becomes unnecessarily complicated.

TPCTL is one of the few logics that can express both hard and soft real-time deadlines, a feature useful in the verification of communication protocols in noisy media. Strong assumptions on the behaviour of the medium (e.g., the medium never loses more than three consecutive messages) can be replaced with weaker assumptions (e.g., successful transmission with some probability).

Interval and other temporal logics. Interval-based real-time temporal logic specifications have been developed in [96, 36]. In [36], Moszkowski's ITL [95] is embedded in the theorem-prover higher order logic (HOL). Why not use HOL directly? There are two reasons. First, ITL avoids the proliferation of time variables in specifications, as do all temporal logics. Second, ITL is sufficiently general to express any discrete computation, yet specific enough to have a natural operational interpretation, which HOL does not. Since ITL has an executable subset (called Tempura), programs and their specifications can be expressed using the same notation. Very little is known about the expressiveness and decidability of these logics in comparison to the linear and branching time logics. Interval logics have been used for specification and simulation, but not much work has been done on deductive calculi or model-checking for verification.

TRIO [34] is a first-order logic augmented with temporal operators (similar in style to linear temporal logics). The choice of first-order logic was motivated by reasons of naturalness, simplicity and compactness of specification. The two temporal operators $Futr(A,t)$ and $Past(A,t)$ mean that A holds at a time t in the future (respectively in the past) with respect to the current time. From these two basic operators many other derived temporal properties can be defined such as "always in the future" and "sometime in the past."

TRIO does not have a deductive calculus. Instead a major goal of TRIO is executability of specifications, although this is only done on finite time domains, leaving it up to the user to extrapolate to infinite domains. This method runs the risk of making the user think a formula is true (by a check on a finite time domain) when in actuality the property is false on, say, a dense time domain.

5.2 Process algebras

Untimed process algebras. Algebraic approaches such as CSP [48], CCS [90] and CIRCAL [89] have been important in analyzing concurrent processing. These process algebras provide structured methods for the analysis of discrete-event systems. A few constructs lead to a language capable of expressing the full complexity of parallel or distributed computing. The constructs include sequential and parallel composition, nondeterministic choice, concealment and recursion. Several computational models have been developed giving these algebras a precise denotational semantics. The computational models lead to methods for doing compositional verification.

Algebraic laws relating the algebraic constructs allow for the transformation of one system into another. In CSP, if P is a process and a an event, then $a \to P$ denotes a process that first engages in the event a, and then behaves exactly as described by P. Shared events require simultaneous participation of both the processes involved. A typical example of a shared event is the communication over a channel in which a message is sent by one process and received by another.

If a pair of processes initially engage simultaneously in some shared event c, then the relevant algebraic law is

$$(c \to P) \| (c \to Q) = (c \to (P \| Q))$$

STOP is a process that never engages in any events, but also never terminates. If c and d are both shared events (in the alphabet of both processes), then the law

$$(c \to P \| d \to Q) = STOP \quad \text{if } c \neq d$$

shows how a pair of processes P and Q, running in parallel, deadlock if they disagree on what the first action should be. Non-shared events are events in the alphabet of P but not in that of Q, or vice versa. Non-shared events occur independently of Q whenever P engages in them (and vice versa). Thus the parallel composition operator $\|$ is defined in such a way that events in the alphabet of both operands require simultaneous participation of them both, whereas the remaining actions of the system occur in an arbitrary interleaving.

The *synchronous* nature of interactions simplifies the analysis of concurrent systems. It is then claimed that the asynchronous nature of lower level handshaking via semaphores, monitors and condition queues can be abstracted away. However, broadcasts to the world (as in Ethernet protocols) are not easily modelled by CSP processes.

A common computational model of a process P is a 3-tuple (E, F, D), where E is the alphabet or set of process events, F is the set of *failures* and D the set of *divergent traces*.

A trace is a behaviour of a process. It is a finite sequence of events of the process, recording the actions that the process has engaged in up to some point in time. Divergent traces ("infinite loops") occur when a process engages in an infinite unbroken sequence of internal events invisible to the environment. As a result the environment is left waiting eternally for a response.

A failure is a tuple (tr, X) where tr is a trace of P and X is a set of events offered by the environment of the process. If it is possible for P to deadlock when placed in this environment, then X is said to be a refusal of P. Thus a failure (tr, X) means that P can engage in the sequence of events recorded by tr, and then refuse to do anything more, in spite of the fact that its environment is prepared to engage in any of the events of X. The set of all traces (behaviours) of P can easily be obtained from the failures of P; the domain of the failures relation F is the set of traces of P.

Several constraints are imposed on (E, F, D) to fully capture the behaviour of nondeterministic concurrent processes. The computational model provided a mathematically precise definition of the operators (e.g., sequential or parallel composition). The model is also used to prove the correctness of the algebraic laws. An operator (such as parallel composition) is shown to be well-defined by assuming that the operands satisfy the constraints, and then demonstrating that the composition of the operands also satisfies the constraints.

Olderog and Hoare [100] gave a complete description of a family of increasingly sophisticated models for providing CSP specification semantics. These computational models include the counter model, the trace model, the divergences model, the readiness model, and the failures model (described above).

Most existing proof methods in CSP focus on bottom-up methods, in which each component is proved and compositionally used to develop more complex systems. Recent work has been performed on top-down development (refinement) from abstract high-level system requirements to implemented executable component parts (e.g., as an Occam task). The algebraic rules preserve the meaning and equivalence of the abstract process and its implementation. So far, the refinement methods treat only safety properties of trace-based nondivergent cyclic networks.

A specification S is allowed to be any predicate on behaviours (traces). For example, consider the specification that the process $SUD = controller \| plant$ must never deadlock. Let SUD/tr be the process described by SUD after engaging in the trace tr. Then the specification S is given by:

$$(SUD/tr) \neq STOP \quad \text{for all traces } tr \text{ of } SUD$$

A semantic proof that SUD **satisfies** S proceeds by taking an arbitrary trace tr, and showing that in all cases there is at least one event by which tr can be extended. The use of **satisfies** is compositional, i.e., a proof of a property of a compound process can be constructed from a proof of correctness of its parts.

Another way of doing proofs is to provide a proof system. For example, an axiom for the process $STOP$ is given by $STOP$ **satisfies** $tr = <>$, where $<>$ is the empty trace. An axiom or rule is provided for each operator. A proof that P **satisfies** S is reduced to a number of smaller derivations on the syntactically simpler subcomponents of P. Ultimately, the verification task is reduced to tautology checking of statements written in the specification language. Allowing specifications to be any predicate over traces has the advantage of expressivity, but its generality makes fully formal verification difficult. For this reason, a restricted specification language such as temporal logic is often used [128].

In other frameworks such as CCS, the emphasis is on defining a series of equivalences (bisimulations), each equivalence defining a different model of concurrency. Thus certain processes that might be considered identical in CSP, would be different in CCS. CCS has a form of modal logic to specify the observable behaviour of processes. CSP has a richer set of laws than CCS, allowing for optimizing designs and implementations. CCS concentrates on a minimal set of operators needed for the full expression of nondeterministic concurrency and its resulting equivalences.

In CCS, a system is verified by using the notion of a bisimulation. For example, consider a protocol verification problem where one has a specification S and an implementation I. The main idea is that both are formulated in the same language, namely, as processes in a process algebra. The specification is abstract and high-level. The implementation contains many details, data structures and microcode. One can abstract from the implementation details by renaming certain internal actions to be a silent action. Then, one can apply the axioms of the algebra for proving the equality between the specification and the implementation. Bisimulation on finite state automata can be decided in $O(m \log n)$ time (using the Paige/Tarjan algorithm).

Let $\|$ stand for the parallel composition operator with some hiding of internal actions. Let $\sim$ stand for the bisimulation equivalence between processes. The specification S of required system behaviour is specified as a (simple) process. The object is to find the unknown process *controller* that is the solution to the equation

$$plant \| controller \sim S$$

Thus the notion of correctness is captured by bisimulation. Using equational laws such as $P \| Q \sim Q \| P$, we can try to solve the above equation for *controller*.

Timed process algebras. Untimed process algebras have been extended with timing constructs in several ways including (in alphabetical order):

- ACP_ρ (real-time ACP) [8]. A dense time domain is used.
- ATP (algebra of timed processes) [97].
- CCSR (calculus of communicating shared resources based on CCS) [32, 33]. This algebra also provides a proof system for dealing with priority-based access to scarce resources.
- TCSP (timed CSP) [126, 127, 132, 128]. A dense time domain is used.
- TCCS (temporal CSP) [93]. A complete set of axioms is presented for discrete-time domains, but the semantics can be given as either discrete or dense.
- TCCS (timed CCS) [144]. Discrete or dense time domains can be used.
- TPCCS (timed probabilistic CCS) [37]. TPCCS was already discussed in the context of branching time temporal logic in the previous section. A discrete-time domain is used.
- TPL (temporal process language) [45]. A discrete-time domain is used.
- U-LOTOS (urgent LOTOS) [14]. Discrete or dense time domains can be used.

We mention a few examples illustrating syntactic extensions for timed behaviour and then describe the general principles involved.

In TCSP, the CSP syntax is enriched with the additional process WAIT d, where d is a non-negative unit of time. The wait process terminates successfully after d units of time. All events recorded by processes relate to a conceptual global clock, and a process can only engage in a finite number of events in a bounded period of time.

There is a constant delay δ associated with each action. Consider a user interface of a vending machine *VM*. The insertion of a coin is modelled by the action *coin* and a time t_{drop} is the time allowed for the coin to drop before the event *button* is made available. The user then presses the button and the machine offers a drink *coke* after a short delay t_{coke}. If the operator "; " stands for sequential composition of processes (i.e., *P*; *Q* means do *P* then do *Q*), then the timed behaviour of the vending machine can be specified as [21]

$$\begin{aligned} VM \;=\; & coin \to WAIT(t_{drop} - \delta); \\ & button \to WAIT(t_{coke} - \delta); \\ & coke \to WAIT(t_{reset} - \delta); VM \end{aligned}$$

The vending machine presents the user with no choice of product, so the button is an unnecessary feature of the interface. The hiding operator *VM\button* may be used to conceal the *button* event from the user. Hidden events occur as soon as they become available so using the algebraic rules we obtain

$$\begin{aligned} VM\backslash button \;=\; & coin \to WAIT(t_{drop} + t_{coke} - \delta); \\ & coke \to WAIT(t_{reset} - \delta); VMS \end{aligned}$$

The delays before and after the *button* event are unaffected by the hiding operator.

In TCCS (temporal CCS), the construct $(t).P$ denotes a process that will evolve into process P after exactly t units of time. $\delta.P$ denotes the process that is willing to wait any amount of time before behaving like P.

As an example, consider the alternating bit protocol *ABP*. The process *ABP* is the parallel composition of the sender, the receiver and the medium. Internal events (such as the acknowledgment signal between the medium and the sender) are hidden or projected out.

In the internal behaviour of the sender, r is the time that the sender will wait after sending a message before assuming the message has been lost and retransmitting.

The specification S that *ABP* must satisfy is

$S = \delta.send.(d).receive.(d).S$

i.e., S is a process that after some time sends a message, followed by a transmission delay of d clock units. The transmission delay is the time that it takes to transmit the message and receive an acknowledgment. Once the message is received and acknowledged (this also takes d clock units), the same behaviour is then repeated. The protocol is verified to be correct by showing that if $r > 2d$ then

$ABP = S$

The equality is interpreted in a labelled transition graph semantics. It means that the graph of *ABP* is the same as that of S, modulo the occurrence of any number of internally hidden transitions.

An extended version of CCS called CCSR has been presented in [32, 33]. CCSR deals with timing properties as well as resource sharing based on a priority semantics. Most real-time formalisms capture delays due to synchronization. Resource specific details are abstracted out by assuming idealistic operating environments. The problem with this abstraction is that true parallelism may take place only at the system level where a group of shared resources is executed simultaneously. Each resource, however, is inherently sequential in nature. A resource can only execute a single action at one point in time. This constraint leads naturally to an interleaving notion of concurrency. On the other hand, scheduling algorithms ignore the effect of process synchronization except for simple precedence relations between processes.

The computation model of CCSR treats synchronization and scheduling. It is resource based in that multiple resources execute synchronously, while processes assigned to the same resource are interleaved according to their priorities. CCSR possesses a prioritized equivalence for terms, based on strong bisimilarity. An equational proof system is provided for syntactic manipulation of terms based on resource configuration and priority ordering.

Nicollin and Sifakis [98] presented an overview of the above timed process algebras, as well as a unifying framework for treating them. These authors point out that most timed process algebras implicitly adopt the following view concerning their operation:

– A timed system is the composition of cooperating sequential components or processes. Each component has (semantically) a time variable as part of its state defined on an appropriate domain D with binary operation + (addition on nonnegative numbers). A component modifies its state either by executing some atomic action (atomic actions take no time) or by increasing its time variable (letting time progress).

- The time variable increases synchronously in all processes only if all components accept to do so. (In some timed process algebras this results in the counterintuitive notion that time stops).
- An execution sequence takes place in two phases. In phase 1, components may execute a finite though arbitrarily long sequence of actions either independently or in cooperation with each other. In phase 2, components coordinate to let time progress by some finite (or infinite) amount.

An untimed process algebra is a quadruple $UPA = (O, A, R, \sim)$ where O is a set of operators defining the syntax of the language. L is a set of transition labels (actions). R is a set of rules defining the operational semantics or models, associating with each term of the language a transition system. The relation $\sim$ is a behavioural equivalence (e.g., bisimulation) defined over the models.

A labelled transition system (whose states are process expressions) is the main computational model considered for the sake of comparing the various algebras. $P \xrightarrow{a} Q$ means the process P may perform the atomic and timeless action a and then it behaves like Q. The transition $P \xrightarrow{d} Q$ means that the process P may idle for d time units, after which it behaves like Q. A time domain is a commutative monoid $(D, +, 0)$. As D is usually infinite, models of processes are generally infinitely branching transition systems.

A timed process algebra is obtained from the untimed algebra $(O, A, R, \sim)$ by adding a set O' of time constraining operations. The timed process algebra is then defined as $TPA = (O \bigcup O', A, R', \sim')$. It must then be decided how to obtain the operational semantic rules R' and the strong equivalence $\sim'$ with respect to the labelled transition system.

The two main constraints that must be satisfied are:

Semantics conservation. The untimed process and its timed equivalent should have the same behaviour as long as we observe execution actions only. This means that the untimed rules R remain valid in the corresponding timed process algebra, as far as they are applied on terms of the untimed process algebra.

Isomorphism. For any terms P, Q of untimed process algebra, the equivalence $P \sim Q$ holds iff $P \sim' Q$. This requirement guarantees that any theoretical development in untimed process algebra remains valid in timed process algebra and conversely.

See [98] for a further discussion of how and to what extent these constraints are satisfied in the various timed process algebras.

An important issue that arises is the *finite variability* property (or non-Zeno behaviour) of the algebras. TCSP is the only algebra for which all processes satisfy the finite variability property, namely, that a process can only perform a finite number of actions in a finite time interval. A process that has Zeno behaviours may be unrealizable. In TCSP, non-Zeno behaviour is achieved by enforcing a system delay between two actions of a sequential process. Thus the isomorphism requirement is not satisfied, and hence not all laws of CSP are valid in TCSP. The assumption of a system delay seems to be the only solution that ensures finite variability, but yields instead a complicated theory which also destroys the abstractness of time [98].

In algebras such as TCCS, U-LOTOS and ACP_ρ there exist processes whose models can block the progress of time. For timed systems it is natural to demand that a terminated process does not block time; but then a distinction must be made between termination and deadlock. The designers of algebras that block time admit that such time-locks are counterintuitive. However, they claim that time-locks can detect certain types of timing inconsistencies and unrealizable specifications.

In summary, verifying that a timed process P satisfies a specification S depends on whether a dual language framework is used or a single language framework.

- In a dual language framework the specification S is a formula in a high-level logical language (e.g., S is a predicate over behaviours or a temporal logic formula). The process P is an expression of an algebraic process construction language. A proof system is provided in which there is a rule relating each operator of the algebra to a predicate representing its satisfying behaviours. A formal derivation that P **satisfies** S can then be constructed. This is the main method used for verification in TCSP. The TCSP proof system has been used to prove the correctness of control software for aircraft engines, of realistic telephone switching networks and of a local area network protocol [128]. In TCSP there is also a method of verification called *timewise refinement*. There is a hierarchy of theories from the most abstract untimed theories to the most detailed timed theories. Some specifications may be decomposed into a functional part and a timed part. The functional part of the specification is checked more simply in the untimed model by using correctness-preserving migration between models in the hierarchy. Only the timing part of the specification need be checked in the more complex timed model.
- In a dual language system it is possible to consider automated model-checking of finite state systems. Such model-checking has been investigated for the algebra TPCCS [37]. For ATP [99] processes are translated into timed transition systems [3] which already have available model-checking algorithms (see section on temporal logics).
- In a single language framework both the detailed implementation P of the system and its abstract specification S are terms of the process algebra. A bisimulation is then used to show that the implementation is equivalent to its abstract specification, i.e., $P \sim S$.

Often, the requirement that two specifications be equivalent is too strong. For example, it may not be necessary to prove two processes equally fast, as perhaps "faster" would be sufficient. On the other hand equivalences are interesting tools for abstractions as a larger concrete implementation can be replaced by its smaller high-level specification, and vice versa [37]. The approach of using a bisimulation has been successful in the untimed case. However, some researchers claim that it will not be useful in the timed case owing to the complexity introduced by the timed constructs [21].

The dual language approach of using a specification language such as temporal logic, has the advantage of separation of concerns. Each relevant requirement can be expressed as a separate formula, and each formula can be verified separately [37].

5.3 Real-time logic and event action models

Real-time logic (RTL) is a formal language for reasoning about events and their times of occurrence [56, 57, 92]. An external event, such as an operator pushing a button, is denoted $\Omega BUTTON$. The start and stop phase of a compound sampling event is denoted $\uparrow SAMPLE$ (denoting the beginning the action), and $\downarrow SAMPLE$ (its completion). The time domain is the set of nonnegative integers. Time is captured by the occurrence function @ which assigns time values to event occurrences. This function is defined as

$$@(EVENT, i) = \text{time of the } i\text{-th occurrence of } EVENT$$

The specification which asserts that upon pressing the button the action SAMPLE is executed within 30 seconds is written as follows:

$$\forall x [@(\Omega BUTTON, x) \leq @(\uparrow SAMPLE, x)$$
$$\wedge @(\downarrow SAMPLE, x) \leq @(\Omega BUTTON, x) + 30]$$

Let the system under development SUD be represented by the conjunction of a set of RTL formulas. Let the specification of legal behaviour be another RTL formula S (e.g., specifying a safety property that one plant event must occur 20 seconds after some other event). Then the objective is to prove that $SUD \Rightarrow S$.

Once the syntax of the logic is fixed as above, an underlying computational semantic model is needed. This is provided by the event-action specification, which is a textual language for specifying event ordering that is easier to use (and more readily understandable than RTL). The event action model can be used to generate sequences of event sets indexed by times of occurrences, thus providing an operational semantics for interpreting RTL formulas. $SUD \Rightarrow S$ is valid precisely when the formula F, given by $SUD \wedge \neg S$, is unsatisfiable (has no satisfying sequence of event sets).

Various techniques are provided for showing F to be unsatisfiable. One possibility is to translate F into a corresponding formula F' in quantifier free Pressburger arithmetic extended with uninterpreted integer functions. Pressburger arithmetic is doubly exponential in complexity, and undecidable with even a single uninterpreted function. Therefore, only a semi-decision procedure can be given. The verification is also impractical for large systems. A resolution-based inequality prover (the Bledsoe-Hines algorithm) has been used with slightly better results than the Pressburger procedures.

To improve the decision procedures, two approaches have been used. First, the RTL formulas are limited to safety assertions. Second, the RTL formulas can be better structured, using domain knowledge, into a computation graph. With this improved structuring (and hence better choice of clauses in the resolution theorem prover), an exponential time decision procedure (in the worst case) is obtained. The decision procedure involves checking for positive cycles in the computation graph, and checking for unsatisfiability based on the positive cycles detected.

Jahanian and Stuart [58] introduced a visual formalism called Modecharts. Modecharts bares some similarity to Statecharts. Modecharts specify a decidable fragment of RTL, in a "natural," state-based, visual fashion preferred by design engineers. A method is provided for translating Modecharts into computational graphs, from which the verification can be performed. For modular extensions to RTL and the use of the HOL theorem prover see [78].

RTL's event occurrence function allows for a rich expression of periodic and non-periodic real-time properties. However, unrestricted RTL is undecidable. It does not treat data structures or infinite state systems. RTL formulas impose a partial order on computational actions which is useful for representing high-level timing requirements.

5.4 Assertional and other formal methods

Real-time Hoare logic. Hooman [50] and Hooman and de Roever [51] introduced an assertional style of reasoning about real-time systems is introduced, based on classical Hoare triples $\{q\}P\{r\}$. P is a program, and q and r are first-order predicates [49]. Hoare triples can only express partial correctness (properties that hold *if* the program terminates). This however is not suitable for real-time programs which must deal with non-terminating processes and intensive interaction with the environment.

Therefore Hoare triples are extended with a third assertion C called a *commitment*. This leads to formulas of the form $C: \{q\}P\{r\}$. The commitment expresses the communication interface of the program P (part of the controller) with the environment (the plant or other parts of the controller). The commitment must be satisfied by terminating and non-terminating computations. Communication between processes is by message passing only (there are no shared variables), so C contains no program variables. The special time variable *time* is allowed in the commitment.

The specification asserting that P does not perform any communication on channel c is written

$$(\forall t: \neg comm \text{ via } c \text{ at } t): \{time = 0\}P\{true\}$$

The specification asserting that P terminates after 12 time units, incrementing x by 5, is written

$$time < 12: \{x = v \land time = 0\}P\{x = v + 5\}$$

A sound and relatively complete compositional proof system is provided for Occam-style programs. The first extension of Hoare-style reasoning from sequential to qualitative (non real-time) concurrent reasoning is provided in [113], but the proof system requires the presence of all the code and hence is not compositional. To aid in the development of the proof system, a denotational semantics for Occam is developed. The execution model is based on maximal parallelism and synchronous message passing.

Hooman [50] compares metric temporal logic (MTL) and the assertional Hoare-style proof systems. In general MTL allows for more concise real-time specifications than the more verbose assertional style. The assertional style of reasoning is more suitable for detailed reasoning about sequential program fragments. A combination of both styles of reasoning is recommended. Use concise MTL formulas for top level specifications and the initial design outline. Use the assertional style to perform detailed verification of sequential components. In both cases, compositional proofs of correctness are complex even for simple examples.

Putting time into proof outlines. Schneider *et al.* [131] provide a proof outline logic for concurrent programming with additional rules to perform real-time verification. The logic is defined using the maximal parallelism computational model.

Safety properties assert that something bad does not occur during a run of the system. For example, assume that we wish to prove that $\neg Q$ never occurs during any run of the system. To prove this, the designer typically searches for an invariant I, that characterizes current and possibly past program states, and is not invalidated by system actions. If the invariant I holds in all initial states of the system, and $I \Rightarrow Q$ is valid, then $\neg Q$ never becomes true.

Timing properties can often be formulated as safety properties. For example, in a process control system, the elapsed time between stimulus and response must be bounded by some time d. The "bad thing" (reaching time d before seeing the response) can be specified in terms of times at which various control points in the real-time program are reached.

A logic L to verify untimed safety properties can form the basis of a logic L' to verify timing properties. To do this, constructs must be added so that in L' the designer can specify in the predicates I and Q information about the times at which events of interest occur. It must also be possible to establish that the actions of the system do not invalidate the invariant I. This means that the rules of L have to be refined with information about execution times. Schneider *et al.* [131] develop such a proof outline logic (POL). Knowledge of the execution times of individual actions is needed to reason about timing properties.

POL is similar to the Hoare-style logic in [135], which augments each action with an assignment to a clock variable to keep track of elapsed time. In contrast, POL augments the assertion language with additional terms. This results in a more expressive language.

The assertional logic of Hooman and de Roever [51] (discussed above) deals with synchronous message passing and has no shared variables (which makes compositional reasoning easier). Only certain times can be recorded, e.g. times at which externally visible events (such as communication) can occur, and the times at which program execution starts and terminates. Information about control points cannot be specified because internal activities betray the internal structure of a component, which would destroy compositionality. Certain liveness proofs can also be made. In contrast, POL deals with shared variables, but then relaxes the compositionality requirement. Liveness proofs cannot be given. POL can also be used to represent synchronous communication. The two logics are, therefore, incomparable although both are assertional in style.

Another assertional logic which is being extended to deal with real-time is the temporal logic of actions discussed in [68]. A report on this work was not available at the time this survey article was written.

5.5 Hybrid models

Many of the computational models discussed previously assume that the plant or environment can be modelled as a *discrete-event dynamic system*. This assumption is useful as it allows a symmetrical treatment of controllers (software implemented on a digital computer) and plants. It also encourages structured modular analysis. Many simplifying assumptions can be made that make the analysis much easier. The discrete description of digital logic circuits via boolean functions is an example of where a discrete model simplifies analysis. If the digital circuit is viewed as a continuously changing numerical vector that is a solution to a set of differential equations, then analyzing its behaviour would be much more difficult compared with treating it as a boolean system.

While the discrete-event approach is justified in many situations, there are other contexts in which the assumption of discreteness may lead to unreliable conclusions. A control program driving a robot through a maze is an example where it may be necessary to introduce a continuous variables analysis. Continuous variable dynamic systems have been extensively studied by control theorists [143].

Recently researchers have turned their attention to *hybrid systems theory*, i.e., systems consisting of a non-trivial mixture of discrete and continuous components. It is hoped such systems will obtain just the right kind of computational model in which each kind of analysis (discrete and continuous) can be carried out in its relevant domain but in an integrated fashion.

Maler *et al.* [101] proposed a hybrid formalism based on Statecharts and real-time temporal logic. The underlying semantic model is that of hybrid traces which are mappings from continuous time to system states. A phase transition system is used as the computational model to represent the behaviour of the system. A behaviour is a sequence of phases alternating between continuous and discrete changes. A continuous phase takes some amount of time and allows changes over this time that are governed by differential equations. A continuous phase is followed by a discrete phase. The discrete phase consists of a finite number of discrete transitions, each of which causes a possibly discontinuous change in the value of the variables.

Two specification formalisms are allowed: Statecharts and temporal logic. Statecharts is used to describe the detailed behaviour of the system. An unstructured state (of the Statechart) may be labelled with the appropriate differential equations that describe the system behaviour while in that state. When a discrete event occurs (e.g., the pilot requests a new mode of flight to a higher altitude) then there is a discontinuous change in the variables (e.g., in the set-points), and an instantaneous change to a new state in which some other continuous behaviour is observed.

A modest extension to real-time temporal logic is made, enabling it to refer to continuous change and time. A proof system for safety properties is provided, leaving a more thorough investigation of the subject to subsequent research.

Marzullo et al. [85] used weakest precondition predicate transformers to derive sequential process control programs. Only one extension to Dijkstra's calculus had to be made, involving the use of function-valued auxiliary variables, for reasoning about physical processes during program transitions. A proof system for hybrid systems can thus be obtained with only some modest additions to Dijkstra's calculus. The proof system is limited to sequential real-time programs.

Nicollin et al. [99] proposed a generalization to action timed graphs which allows for the modelling of hybrid systems. A set of timers, and a set of state variables is added to the model. The state variables to do not change linearly with respect to time, but according to a continuous evolution function (e.g. differential equations). No proof system is provided.

6 Future Trends

This survey has shown that formal methods for real-time systems are being energetically explored. The proliferation of formalisms indicates that the field is still in its "adolescence." It would therefore be hazardous to speculate on new developments and trends and their range of applicability. Nevertheless, we summarize below some of the main ideas mentioned in this survey, and also mention further areas of future development [22, 40]:

- Real-time software is part of a greater system. Computational models must be flexible enough to represent both controllers (software) as well as the plant (the environment). Software harms no one. It is the plant (that the software must control) that does the damage. The total system, consisting of controllers and plant, must be modelled and validated.
- Two possible strategies for improving reliability of complex real-time systems have been developed. Industrial institutions have promoted structured, visual design methods and the use of real-time programming languages. In academic institutions, formal analysis and verification methods have been provided. Both strategies need to be further explored and integrated with each other.
- Structured development tools need to be improved to allow for powerful execution and compilation facilities (e.g., into Ada or Occam). Such tools are indispensable in the design of large scale systems. Improved visual methods for structuring systems should be explored. This will make the tools accessible to design engineers. Verification methodologies should be incorporated into these tools. Research into fast algorithms for automatic verification of finite state systems is

already showing some promising results. The problems of state explosion must be dealt with by symbolic techniques and the analysis of reduced-order systems.
- Different formal methods have evolved independently of each other. The best features of each method should be synthesized and incorporated into a more powerful and hierarchical unified theory. The expressiveness of specification methods should be improved without resulting in intractability. It is important to combine existing methods, broaden their scope and investigate their limits of applicability. New formalisms such as hybrid systems theory should be explored. This, and more, will be required to deal with realistic large scale systems.
- Scheduling of processes and the verification of timing properties must be integrated into a comprehensive theory. To do this, it may be necessary to develop new methods for efficient and concise expression of timing constraints. This will result in complex runtime environments that must be dealt with in the new formalisms.
- Totally automated synthesis of controllers that will satisfy arbitrary properties is probably not obtainable. That does not prevent theorists from exploring semi-automated methods and heuristics for disciplined development of controllers from their specifications. In addition, partial verification methods can be explored, either by applying the methods to a small core part of the system (the most critical one), or to an abstraction (simplified representation) of the system. In either case, partial verification methods must be accompanied by a clear explanation of the validity of these partial results to total behaviour, and how these methods can be safely applied to real-world systems.
- Collaboration between industry and researchers on real problems is needed to ensure the right balance of practice and theory. Practical methods often lack a theoretical basis, thereby limiting their analysis capabilities. Theoretical work can be stimulated by the need to deal with practical applications.

There is a need to start using real systems as examples. These examples should be documented and published by industries interested in looking for solutions. Current models and procedures work on tiny examples in research papers, but these methods often carefully leave out anything the model cannot handle, which usually includes most things needed in a real specification. There is, nevertheless, cause for cautious optimism. Recent collaboration has shown some signs of closing the gap between theory and practice [22, 39].

Acknowledgements. I gratefully acknowledge help received from Nancy Leveson, Willem-Paul de Roever, Al Mok, Dave Parnas, Murray Wonham, Jozef Hooman, Ron Koymans, Ben Moszkowski, Mike Gordon, Farnam Jahanian, Insup Lee, Rajeev Alur and Roger Hale. Of course, any errors or misinterpretation of concepts are my sole responsibility.

References

1. B. Alpern and F.B. Schneider. Verifying temporal properties without temporal logic. *ACM Transactions on Programming Language Systems*, 11(1), 1989.

2. R. Alur. *Techniques for Automatic Verification of Real-Time Systems.* PhD Thesis, Dept. of Computer Science, Stanford University, CA 94305, 1991.
3. R. Alur, C. Courcoubetis, and D.L. Dill. Model checking for real-time systems. In *Proceedings 5th Conference on Logic in Computer Science.* IEEE, 1990.
4. R. Alur and D.L. Dill. Automata for modeling real-time systems. In M.S. Paterson, editor, *ICALP 90: Automata, Languages and Programming*, LNCS 443, pages 322–335. Springer-Verlag, 1990.
5. R. Alur, T. Feder, and T.A. Henzinger. The benefits of relaxing punctuality. In *Proceedings of the 10th Annual ACM Symposium on Principles of Distributed Computing*, 1991.
6. R. Alur and T.A. Henzinger. Logics and models of real-time: A survey. In J.W. de Bakker, C. Huizing, W.-P. de Roever, and G. Rozenberg, editors, *Proceedings of the REX Workshop – Real-Time: Theory in Practice*, LNCS 600. Springer-Verlag, 1991.
7. Rajeev Alur and Thomas Henzinger. Real-time logics: Complexity and expressiveness. In *Proceedings of the 5th Annual IEEE Symposium on Logic in Computer Science*, pages 390–401, June 1990.
8. J.C.M. Baeten and J.A. Bergstra. Real Time Process Algebra. Technical Report CS-R9053, Center for Mathematics and Computer Science, Amsterdam, 1990.
9. A. Benveniste and P. LeGuernic. Hybrid dynamical systems theory and the SIGNAL language. *IEEE Trans. on Automatic Control*, 35(5):535–546, May 1990.
10. A. Bernstein and P.K. Harter. Proving real-time properties of programs with temporal logic. In *Proceedings of ACM SIGOPS 8th Annual ACM Symposium on Operating Systems Principles*, pages 1–11, December 1981.
11. G. Berry and G. Gonthier. The Esterel Synchronous Programming Language: Design, semantics, implementation. Technical Report, Ecole Nationale Superieure des Mines de Paris, 1988.
12. B. Berthomieu and Michael Diaz. Modeling and verification of time dependent systems using time petri nets. *IEEE Transactions on Software Engineering*, 17(3):259–273, March 1991.
13. J. Billington, G.R. Wheeler, and M.C. Wilbur-Ham. PROTEAN: a high-level Petri net tool for the specification and verification of communication protocols. *IEEE Transactions on Software Engineering*, 14(3):301–316, March 1988.
14. T. Bolognesi and F. Lucidi. LOTOS- like process algebra with urgent or timed interactions. In J.W. de Bakker, C. Huizing, W.-P. de Roever, and G. Rozenberg, editors, *Proceedings of the REX Workshop – Real-Time: Theory in Practice*, LNCS 600. Springer-Verlag, 1991.
15. K.P. Brand and J. Kopainsky. Principles and engineering of process control with Petri nets. *IEEE Transactions on Automatic Control*, 33(2):138–149, February 1988.
16. P. Caspi, D. Pilaud, N. Halbwachs, and J. Plaice. LUSTRE : a declarative language for programming synchronous systems. In *Proc. 14th ACM Symposium on Programming Languages*, Jan. 1987.
17. J.F. Cassidy, T.Z. Chu, M. Kutcher, S.B. Gershwin, and Y. Ho. Research needs in manufacturing systems. *IEEE Control Systems Magazine*, 5(3):11–13, August 1985.
18. CCIT. CCIT High Level Language CHILL Recommendation z.200, CCIT, Geneva, 1980.
19. K.M. Chandy and J. Misra. *Parallel Program Design.* Addison-Wesley, Reading Massachusetts, 1988.
20. E.M. Clarke, E.A. Emerson, and A.P. Sistla. Automatic verification of finite state concurrent systems using temporal logic. *ACM Transactions on Programming Languages and Systems*, 8(2):244–263, April 1986.
21. J. Davis. *Specification and Proof in Real-Time Systems.* PhD Thesis, Oxford University Computing Laboratory, Oxford, UK, 1991.

22. W.-P. de Roever. Foundations of computer science: Leaving the ivory tower. In *EATCS Bulletin*. EATCS, June 1991.
23. E.W. Dijkstra. *A Discipline of Programming*. Prentice-Hall, Englewood Cliffs, New Jersey, 1976.
24. E.A. Emerson and E.C. Clarke. Using branching time temporal logic to synthesize synchronization skeletons. *Science of Computer Programming*, 2:241–266, 1982.
25. E.A. Emerson and J.Y. Halpern. 'Sometimes' and 'not never' revisited: on branching versus linear time temporal logic. *Journal of the Association for Computing Machinery*, 33(1):151–178, January 1986.
26. E.A. Emerson, A.K. Mok, A.P. Sistla, and J. Srinisvan. Quantitative temporal reasoning. In E.M. Clarke, A. Pnueli, and J. Sifakis, editors, *Proceedings of the Workshop on Automatic Verification Methods for Finite State Systems*. Springer-Verlag, Lecture Notes in Computer Science, 1989.
27. F.S. Etessami and G.S. Hura. Rule based design methodology for solving control problems. *IEEE Transactions on Software Engineering*, 17(3):274–282, March 1991.
28. N. Francez. *Fairness*. Springer-Verlag, 1986.
29. A. Gabrielian and M.K. Franklin. State-based specification of complex real-time systems. In *Proceedings of the 9th Real-Time Systems Symposium*, pages 2–11, December 1988.
30. A. Galton, editor. *Temporal Logics and their Applications*. Academic Press, 1987.
31. J.R. Garman. The bug heard round the world. *ACM SIGSOFT Software Engineering Notes*, 6(5), 1981.
32. R. Gerber and I. Lee. Ccsr: A calculus for communicating shared resources. In *CONCUR'90*, LNCS 458, pages 263–277. Springer-Verlag, August 1990.
33. R. Gerber and I. Lee. A proof system for communicating shared resources. In *Proceedings of the Real-Time Systems Symposium*, 1990.
34. C. Ghezzi, D. Mandrioli, and A. Morzenti. TRIO, a logic language for executable specifications of real-time systems. *Journal of Systems and Software*, 12(2):107–123, May 1990.
35. D. Gries. *The Science of Programming*. Springer-Verlag, 1985.
36. R.W.S. Hale. Using temporal logic for prototyping: The design of a lift controller. In B. Banieqbal, H. Barringer, and A. Pnueli, editors, *Temporal Logic in Specification*, LNCS 398. Springer-Verlag, 1989.
37. H.A. Hansson. *Time and Probability in Formal Design and Distributed Systems*. PhD Thesis, Dept. of Computer Science, Uppsala University, S-751 20 Uppsala, Sweden, 1991.
38. D. Harel. Statecharts: A visual formalism for complex systems. *Science of Computer Programming*, 8:231–274, 1987.
39. D. Harel. Biting the silver bullet: Towards a brighter future for systems development. Technical Report CS90-08, Weizmann Institute, 1990.
40. D. Harel. Biting the silver bullet: Towards a brighter future for system development. *Computer*, 25(1):8–20, January 1992.
41. D. Harel, H. Lachover, A. Naamad, A. Pnueli, M. Politi, R. Sherman, and M. Trachtenbrot. Statemate: a working environment for the development of complex reactive systems. *IEEE Transactions on Software Engineering*, 16:403–414, 1990.
42. D. Harel and A. Pnueli. On the development of reactive systems. In K.R Apt, editor, *Logics and Models of Concurrent Systems*, volume 13 of *NATO ASI*, pages 477–498. Springer-Verlag, 1985.
43. E. Harel, O. Lichtenstein, and A. Pnueli. Explicit clock temporal logic. In *Proceedings of the 5th Annual Symposium on Logic in Computer Science*, pages 402–413, June 1990.
44. Derek J. Hatley and Imitai A. Pirbhai. *Strategies for Real-Time System Specification*. Dorset House Publishing Co., New York, 1988.

45. M. Hennessy and T. Regan. A process algebra for timed systems. Technical Report 5/91, Dept. of Computer Science, University of Sussex, UK, 1991.
46. T.A. Henzinger. *The Temporal Specification and Verification of Real-Time Systems.* PhD Thesis, Dept. of Computer Science, Stanford University, CA, 1991.
47. T.A. Henzinger, Z. Manna, and A. Pnueli. Temporal proof methodologies for real-time systems. In *Proceedings of the 18th ACM Symposium on Principles of Programming Languages*, pages 353–366, January 1991.
48. C.A.R. Hoare. *Communicating Sequential Processes.* Prentice-Hall, 1985.
49. C.A.R. Hoare. An axiomatic basis for computer programming. *Communications of the ACM*, 12(10), October 1969.
50. J. Hooman. *Specification and Compositional Verification of Real-Time Systems.* PhD Thesis, Eindhoven University of Technology, Dep. of Maths and Comp. Sc., Eindhoven, The Netherlands, 1991.
51. J. Hooman and W.-P. de Roever. Design and verification in real-time distributed computing: an introduction to compositional methods. In *Proceedings of of the 9th International Symposium on Protocol Specification, Testing and Verification.* North-Holland, 1989.
52. J. Hooman and J. Widom. A temporal logic based compositional proof system for real-time message passing. In *Proceedings of PARLE89 vol. II*, LNCS 366. Springer-Verlag, 1989.
53. C. Huizing. *Semantics of Reactive Systems: Comparison and Full Abstraction.* PhD Thesis, Technische Universiteit Eindhoven, March 1991.
54. K. Inan and P.P Varaiya. Finitely recursive process models for discrete event systems. *IEEE Transactions on Automatic Control*, 33(7):626–639, July 1988.
55. M.S. Jaffe, N.G. Leveson, M.P.E. Heimdahl, and B.E. Melhart. Software requirements analysis for real-time process control systems. *IEEE Transactions on Software Engineering*, 17(3):241–258, 241 1991.
56. F. Jahanian and A.K. Mok. Safety analysis of timing properties in real-time systems. *IEEE Transactions on Software Engineering*, SE-12(9):890–904, September 1986.
57. F. Jahanian and A.K. Mok. A graph-theoretic approach for timing analysis and its implementation. *IEEE Transactions on Computers*, C36(8), 1987.
58. F. Jahanian and D. Stuart. A method for verifying properties of modechart specifications. In *Proceedings 9th Real-time Systems Symposium*, pages 12–21. IEEE Computer Society, December 1988.
59. C.B. Jones. *Systematic Software Development using VDM.* International Series in Computer Science. Prentice-Hall, 1986.
60. M. Joseph and A. Goswami. Formal Description of Real-Time Systems: A Review. Technical Report RR129, Dep. of Computer Science, University of Warwick, UK, August 1988.
61. R. Koymans. (Real) time: A philosophical perspective. In J.W. de Bakker, C. Huizing, W.-P. de Roever, and G. Rozenberg, editors, *Proceedings of the REX Workshop – Real-Time: Theory in Practice*, LNCS 600. Springer-Verlag, 1991.
62. R. Koymans, R.K. Shyamasundar, W.-P. de Roever, R. Gerth, and S. Arun-Kumar. Compositional semantics for real-time distributed computing. In *Proceedings of Logics of Programs (Brooklyn)*, LNCS 193, pages 167–190. Springer-Verlag, 1985.
63. R. Koymans, J. Vytopil, and W.-P. de Roever. Real-time programming and asynchronous message passing. In *Proc. 2nd Annual Symposium on Principles of Distributed Computing*, pages 187–197, Montreal, August 1983. (An extended version appeared in Information and Computation, Volume 79, Number 3, December 1988).
64. Ron Koymans. Specifying real-time properties with metric temporal logic. *Real-Time Systems*, 2(4):255–299, November 1990.
65. J. Kramer and J. Magee. Dynamic configuration for distributed systems. *IEEE Transactions on Software Engineering*, SE-11(4):424–436, April 1985.

66. F. Kroger. *Temporal Logics of Programs*, volume 8 of *EATCS Monographs on Theoretical Computer Science*. Springer-Verlag, 1987.
67. L. Lamport. What good is temporal logic? In R.E. Mason, editor, *Information Processing 83*, pages 657–668. Elsevier Science Publishers, North Holland, 1983.
68. L. Lamport. The temporal logic of actions. Technical Report, DEC Systems Research Center, Palo Alto, CA, 1991.
69. L. Lamport. Specifying concurrent program modules. *ACM Transactions on Programming Languages and Systems*, 5(2):190–222, April 1983.
70. L. Lamport. 'Sometime' is sometimes 'not never'. *Proceedings of the 7th Annual ACM Symposium on Principles of Programming Languages*, pages 174–185, Jan 1980.
71. M.S. Lawford. Transformational Equivalence of Timed Transition Models. Master's Thesis, Dept. of Electrical Engineering, University of Toronto, Toronto, Canada, 1992. (Available as Systems Control Group Report No. 9202, January 1992.)
72. N.G. Leveson and J.L Stolzy. Safety analysis using Petri nets. *IEEE Transactions on Software Engineering*, SE-13(3):386–397, March 1987.
73. S.-T Levi and A.K. Agrawala. *Real Time System Design*. McGraw-Hill Publishing Company, 1990.
74. A.H. Levis. Challenges to control: a collective view. *IEEE Transactions on Automatic Control*, AC-32(4), April 1987.
75. Y. Li. *Control of Vector Discrete-Event Systems*. PhD Thesis, Dept. of Electrical Engineering, University of Toronto, Toronto, Canada, 1991. (available as Systems Control Group Report No 9106, July 1991).
76. INMOS Limited. *Occam Programming Manual*. International Series in Computer Science. Prentice-Hall, Englewood Cliffs, New Jersey, 1984.
77. N. Lynch and F. Vaandrager. Forward and backward simulations for timing-based systems. In J.W. de Bakker, C. Huizing, W.-P. de Roever, and G. Rozenberg, editors, *Proceedings of the REX Workshop – Real-Time: Theory in Practice*, LNCS 600. Springer-Verlag, 1991.
78. G.H. MacEwen and D.B. Skillicorn. Using higher-order logic for modular specification of real-time distributed systems. In M. Joseph, editor, *Symposium on Formal Techniques in Real-Time and Fault-Tolerant Systems*, LNCS 331, pages 36–66. Springer-Verlag, 1988.
79. J. Magee, J. Kramer, and M. Sloman. Constructing distributed systems in Conic. *IEEE Transactions on Software Engineering*, 15(6):663–675, June 1989.
80. Z. Manna and A. Pnueli. Specification and verification of concurrent programs by $\forall$-automata. In *Proceedings of the 14th ACM Symposium of Principles of Programming Languages*, pages 1–12, 1987.
81. Z. Manna and A. Pnueli. The anchored version of the temporal framework. In J.W. de Bakker, W.-P. de Roever, and G. Rozenburg, editors, *Models of Concurrency: Linear, Branching and Partial Orders*, LNCS. Springer-Verlag, 1989.
82. Z. Manna and A. Pnueli. *The Temporal Logic of Reactive and Concurrent Systems*. Springer-Verlag, 1992.
83. Z. Manna and A. Pnueli. Verification of Concurrent Programs: A Temporal Proof System. Technical Report, Dept. of Computer Science, Stanford University, CA, June 1983. See also Foundations of Computer Science IV, Amsterdam, Mathematical Center Tracts, pages 163-225, 1983.
84. Z. Manna and P. Wolper. Synthesis of communicating processes from temporal logic specifications. *ACM Transactions on Programming Languages and Systems*, 6(1):68–93, January 1984.
85. K. Marzullo, F.B. Schneider, and N. Budhiraja. Derivation of Sequential, Real-Time, Process-Control Programs. Technical Report 91-1217, Dept. of Computer Science, Cornell University, Ithaca, New York 14853, 1991.

86. B.E. Melhart, N.G. Leveson, and M.S. Jaffe. Analysis Capabilities for Requirements Specified in Statecharts. Technical Report, Dept. of Information and Computer Science, University of California, Irvine, California, September 1988.
87. M. Menasche. PAREDE: An automated tool for the analysis of time(d) Petri nets. In *International Workshop on Timed Petri Nets*, pages 162–169. IEEE Computer Society, June 1985.
88. P.M. Merlin and A. Segall. Recoverability of communication protocols - implications of a theoretical study. *IEEE Transactions on Communications*, pages 1036–1043, September 1976.
89. G.J. Milne. CIRCAL and the representation of communication, concurrency and time. *ACM Transactions on Programming Languages and Systems*, 7(2):270–298, April 1985.
90. R. Milner. *A Calculus of Communicating Systems*. LNCS 92. Springer-Verlag, 1980.
91. R. Milner. Some directions in concurrency theory (panel statement). In *Proceedings of the International Conference on Fifth Generation Computer Systems*. ICOT, 1988.
92. A.K. Mok. Towards mechanization of real-time system design. In *Foundations of Real-Time Computing: Formal Specifications and Methods*. Kluwer Press, 1991.
93. F. Moller and C. Tofts. A temporal calculus of communicating systems. In *CONCUR 90*, LNCS 458, pages 401–415. Springer-Verlag, 1990.
94. E.T. Morgan and R.R. Razouk. Interactive state-space analysis of concurrent systems. *IEEE Transactions on Software Engineering*, SE-13(10):1080–1091, October 1987.
95. B. Moszkowski. A temporal logic for multilevel reasoning about hardware. *Computer*, 18(2):10–19, February 1985.
96. K.T. Narayana and A.A. Aaby. Specification of real-time systems in real-time temporal interval logic. In *Proceedings Real-time Systems Symposium*, pages 86–95. IEEE Computer Society, December 1988.
97. X. Nicollin, J.L. Richier, J. Sifakis, and J. Voiron. ATP: an algebra for timed processes. In *Proceedings IFIP Working Group Conference on Programming Concepts and Methods*, pages 402–429, 1990.
98. X. Nicollin and J. Sifakis. An overview and synthesis of timed process algebras. In J.W. de Bakker, C. Huizing, W.-P. de Roever, and G. Rozenberg, editors, *Proceedings of the REX Workshop – Real-Time: Theory in Practice*, LNCS 600. Springer-Verlag, 1991.
99. X. Nicollin, J. Sifakis, and S. Yovine. From ATP to timed graphs and hybrid semantics. In J.W. de Bakker, C. Huizing, W.-P. de Roever, and G. Rozenberg, editors, *Proceedings of the REX Workshop – Real-Time: Theory in Practice*, LNCS 600. Springer-Verlag, 1991.
100. E.R. Olderog and C.A.R. Hoare. Specification oriented semantics. *ACTA Informatica*, 23:9–66, 1986.
101. O. Maler, Z. Manna, and A. Pnuelli. From timed to hybrid systems. In J.W. de Bakker, C. Huizing, W.-P. de Roever, and G. Rozenberg, editors, *Proceedings of the REX Workshop – Real-Time: Theory in Practice*, LNCS 600. Springer-Verlag, 1991.
102. J.S. Ostroff. Real-Time Computer Control of Discrete Event Systems Modelled by Extended State Machines: A Temporal Logic Approach. Technical Report 8618, Systems Control Group, Dept. of Electrical Engineering, University of Toronto, Toronto, Canada, September 1986. Revised January 1987.
103. J.S. Ostroff. Synthesis of controllers for real-time discrete event systems. In *Proceedings of the 28th IEEE Conference on Decision and Control*, December 1989.
104. J.S. Ostroff. *Temporal Logic for Real-Time Systems*. Advanced Software Development Series. Research Studies Press Limited (distributed by John Wiley and Sons), England, 1989.
105. J.S. Ostroff. Deciding properties of timed transition models. *IEEE Transactions on Parallel and Distributed Systems*, 1(2):170–183, April 1990.

106. J.S. Ostroff. Constraint logic programming for reasoning about discrete event processes. *The Journal of Logic Programming*, 11(3&4):243–270, October/November 1991.
107. J.S. Ostroff. Systematic development of real-time discrete event systems. In *Proceedings of the ECC91 European Control Conference*, pages 522–533, Paris, France, July 1991. Hermes Press.
108. J.S. Ostroff. Verification of safety critical systems using TTM/RTTL. In J.W. de Bakker, C. Huizing, W.-P. de Roever, and G. Rozenberg, editors, *Proceedings of the REX Workshop – Real-Time: Theory in Practice*, LNCS 600. Springer-Verlag, 1991.
109. J.S. Ostroff. A verifier for real-time properties. *Real-Time Journal*, 4:5–35, 1992. (In press).
110. J.S. Ostroff and W.M. Wonham. A framework for real-time discrete event control. *IEEE Transactions on Automatic Control*, April 1990.
111. J.S. Ostroff and W.M. Wonham. A temporal logic approach to real time control. In *Proceedings of the 24th IEEE Conference on Decision and Control*, pages 656–657, Florida, December 1985.
112. S. Owicki and L. Lamport. Proving liveness properties of concurrent programs. *ACM Transactions on Programming Languages and Systems*, 4(3):455–495, Jul 1982.
113. S.S. Owicki and D. Gries. Verifying properties of parallel programs: an axiomatic approach. *Communications of the ACM*, 19(5), May 1976.
114. D.L. Parnas and J. Madey. Functional Documentation for Computer Systems Engineering. Technical Report TR 90-287, TRIO, Queen's University, Kingston, Ontario, Canada K7L3N6, 1990.
115. D.L. Parnas, A.J. van Schouwen, and S.P. Kwan. Evaluation standards for safety-critical software. Technical Report TR 88-220, Department of Computer Science, Queen's University, Kingston, Ontario, Canada, May 1988.
116. J.L. Peterson. *Petri Net Theory and the Modelling of Systems*. Prentice-Hall, Englewood Cliffs, N.J., 1981.
117. A. Pnueli. The temporal logic of programs. In *Proceedings of the 18th IEEE Annual Symposium on the Foundations of Computer Science*, pages 46–57, Providence, R.I., November 1977.
118. A. Pnueli and E. Harel. Applications of temporal logic to the specification of real-time systems. In *Formal Techniques in Real-Time and Fault Tolerant Systems*, LNCS 331. Springer-Verlag, 1988.
119. A. Pnueli and M. Shalev. What is in a step? In T. Ito and A.R. Meyer, editors, *Theoretical Aspects of Computer Software*, LNCS 298, pages 244–264. Springer-Verlag, 1991.
120. Amir Pnueli. Applications of temporal logic to the specification and verification of reactive systems: a survey of current trends. In J. de Bakker, W.-P. de Roever, and G. Rozenburg, editors, *Current Trends in Concurrency*, LNCS 244. Springer-Verlag, 1986.
121. W.J. Quirk. *Verification and Validation of Real-Time Software*. Springer-Verlag, Berlin, 1985.
122. P.J. Ramadge and W.M. Wonham. Modular feedback logic for discrete event systems. *SIAM Journal of Control and Optimization*, 25(5):1202–1218, September 1987.
123. P.J. Ramadge and W.M. Wonham. Supervisory control of a class of discrete-event processes. *SIAM Journal of Control and Optimization*, 25(1):206–230, January 1987.
124. C. Ramchandani. Analysis of asynchronous concurrent systems by timed Petri nets. Technical Report MAC TR 120, MIT, February 1974.
125. R.R. Razouk and C.V. Phelps. Performance analysis of timed Petri nets. In *Proceedings of 4th International Workshop on Protocol Verification and Testing*, June 1984.
126. G.M. Reed and A.W. Roscoe. A timed model for communicating sequential processes. In *Proceedings ICALP 86*, LNCS 226. Springer-Verlag, 1986.

127. G.M Reed and A.W. Roscoe. A timed model for communicating sequential processes. *Theoretical Computer Science*, 58:249–261, June 1988.
128. G.M. Reed, A.W. Roscoe, et al. Timed CSP: Theory and practice. In J.W. de Bakker, C. Huizing, W.-P. de Roever, and G. Rozenberg, editors, *Proceedings of the REX Workshop – Real-Time: Theory in Practice*, LNCS 600. Springer-Verlag, 1991.
129. W. Reisig. *Petri Nets: An Introduction*. Springer-Verlag, Berlin, 1985.
130. N. Rescher and A. Urquhart. *Temporal Logic*. Springer-Verlag, Library of Exact Philosophy, 1971.
131. F.B. Schneider, B. Bloom, and K. Marzullo. Putting time into proof outlines. In J.W. de Bakker, C. Huizing, W.-P. de Roever, and G. Rozenberg, editors, *Proceedings of the REX Workshop – Real-Time: Theory in Practice*, LNCS 600. Springer-Verlag, 1991.
132. S. Schneider. *Correctness and Communication in Real-Time Systems*. PhD Thesis, Oxford University Computing Laboratory, Oxford, UK, 1990.
133. D.J. Scholefield. The Formal Development of Real-Time Systems. Technical Report, Dept. of Computer Science, University of York, UK, 1990.
134. R.L. Schwartz and P.M. Melliar-Smith. From state machines to temporal logic: Specification methods for protocol standards. *IEEE Transactions on Communications*, Com-30(12), Dec 1982.
135. A. Shaw. Reasoning about time in higher-level language software. *IEEE Transactions on Software Engineering*, SE-15(7):875–899, July 1989.
136. J.M. Spivey. *The Z Notation: A Reference Manual*. Prentice-Hall, Englewood Cillfs, N.J., 1989.
137. J.A. Stankovic. Misconceptions about real-time computing: a serious problem for next generation systems. *Computer*, 21(10):10–19, October 1988.
138. W.M. Turski. Time considered irrelevant for real-time systems. *BIT*, 28:473–486, 1988.
139. USDOD. *Reference Manual for the Ada Programming Language*. Springer-Verlag, New York, 1983.
140. W.M.P van der Aalst. *Timed Coloured Petri Nets and their Application to Logistics*. PhD Thesis, Eindhoven University of Technology, Eindhoven, The Netherlands, 1992.
141. P. Ward and S. Mellor. *Structural Development for Real-Time Systems*. Yourdon Press, New York, 1985.
142. N. Wirth. Towards a discipline of real-time programming. *Communications of the ACM*, 20(8), August 1977.
143. W.M. Wonham. *Linear Multivariable Control: A Geometric Approach*. Springer-Verlag, 3rd edition, 1985.
144. Wang Yi. CCS + time = an interleaving model for real time systems. In *Proceedings of ICALP'91*, Madrid, Spain, 1991.
145. W.M. Zubrek. Timed Petri nets and preliminary performance evaluation. In *Proceedings 7th Annual Symposium on Computer Architecture*, La Baule, France, 1980.

Experience with Formal Methods in Critical Systems

Susan Gerhart, Dan Craigen and Ted Ralston

Summary.

Although there are indisputable benefits to society from the introduction of computers into everyday life, some applications are inherently risky. Worldwide, regulatory agencies are examining how to assure safety and security. This study reveals applicability and limitations of formal methods.

Several regulatory and standards organizations in North America and Europe are investigating how to certify critical systems, and formal methods are figuring importantly in their studies. Several draft standards and regulations are circulating, covering many application domains and approaches – from the mandatory use of formal methods to provisions that recommend "best practices."

To better understand the contributions of formal methods, we systematically studied 12 cases in which organizations in North America and Europe used formal methods. This six-month study, sponsored by the US National Institute of Science and Technology, the US Naval Research Laboratory, and the Atomic Energy Control Board of Canada, is detailed in Appendix A on pp. 423–425.

We had three main objectives:

- To better inform deliberations within industry and government, especially within the study's sponsors, on standards and regulations.
- To provide an authoritative record on the practical experience of formal methods to date.
- To suggest where more research and technology development are needed.

This article focuses on our findings when formal methods were applied to safety- and security-critical systems within a regulatory environment. We also impart some lessons learned about applying formal methods in other environments.

© 1994 IEEE. Reprinted by permission.
Reprinted from *IEEE Software*, 11(1):21–28, January 1994.

In the context of this article, formal methods are mathematical synthesis and analysis techniques used to develop computer-controlled systems. The overriding reason to develop and use formal methods is to attempt to predict, in a scientific manner, the behavior of computer-controlled systems.

As our study shows, formal methods span requirements capture, reengineering, documentation, testing, and other forms of analysis. We also found that, although formal methods can help develop more predictable systems, developers, regulators, and the public should understand that formal methods – like any technology – have limits when applied to critical applications [1]. There are both practical and theoretical limits and much room for more research.

We also found significant technology-transfer problems. In some cases, the use of formal methods was a one-shot effort, with little follow-on, and nowhere did we find any widespread penetration.

Case Studies

In keeping with our objectives, we provided both experiential data and an analysis of that data. The 12 projects we studied were drawn from commercial, exploratory, and regulatory domains.

- *Commercial cases* involve products that must be commercially viable. We studied five commercial projects, briefly described in Appendix B on pp. 425–427.
- *Exploratory cases* are investigations of the potential use of formal methods in a particular setting. We studied three exploratory projects, also briefly described in Appendix B on pp. 425–427.
- *Regulatory cases* exhibit safety- or security-critical attributes and thereby attract the attention of standards communities and agencies and regulators. These cases are elaborated in the next chapter:
  1. *Darlington Nuclear Generating Station.* At this power plant outside Toronto, developers used formal methods to help achieve certification for the plants shutdown systems, the first software-driven shutdown systems in Canada.
  2. *Paris Metro Signaling System.* This system, designed to reduce the separation between trains in the Paris Metro, is the first safety-critical software system certified by the French railway authority. Its developers used formal methods extensively for verification and validation.
  3. *Traffic Alert and Collision Avoidance System.* To improve an industry-government working groups capability to review this system, which alerts and advises pilots in the event of an impending collision, formal specifications of two major subsystems were developed using a formal, graphical notation.
  4. *Multinet Gateway System.* The use of formal methods was required in developing this security-critical internetwork gateway, to achieve clearance from the US Department of Defense to carry sensitive information.

In addition to the two-volume official report [2–3], we have written of this study elsewhere, to address issues in software engineering [4] and formal methods research and development [5]. Volume 1 of the final report describes the study, formal methods, the cases studied, our approach, and our analysis, findings, and conclusions. Volume 2 provides case-study details.

For each case, we present a description, summarize the information obtained (from interviews and the literature), provide an evaluation of the case, highlight R&D issues pertaining to formal methods, and provide some conclusions.

Together, the volumes total 300 pages. It is impossible to condense such a prodigious amount of technical information into an article of this length and preserve all the subtleties. We have tried to capture the main themes here, but urge that you obtain a full report if you have any questions.

Lessons Learned in Regulatory Cases

Regulators can certify the *product* (as the US Federal Aviation Administration has done with its system to avoid mid-air collisions), the *process* (as is the Atomic Energy Control Board of Canada's usual practice), and the *professional* (as the UK Ministry of Defence's Interim Standard on the Procurement of Safety Critical Systems [6] does).

The organizations charged with developing and applying these standards and regulations are concerned with three issues:

- What is the best policy approach to achieve assurance?
- What should the requirements be and how can they best be achieved reasonably?
- How can conformance with certification requirements best be demonstrated?

In the regulatory cases, organizations seemed to use formal methods primarily to unambiguously and comprehensibly demonstrate to regulators a system's proposed effects (do they satisfy requirements?) and to produce evidence (not only through test plans, but by proof) that the code conforms to its requirements. In addition, if formal mathematical models are used, developers must definitively demonstrate the relationship between the model and the underlying code.

As Appendix A (pp. 423–425) explains, we developed a list of features against which to evaluate the effect of formal methods. For each feature, we asked, "Was the influence of formal methods positive, neutral, or negative (or was there enough information to discern)?" Our full report analyzes the factors that led to our conclusions.

Client satisfaction. *Were clients happier with the product?* We recognize, of course, that happiness is influenced by many factors, including enhanced reliability and reduced cost.

In all four cases, we found that the clients (chiefly the regulatory agencies) were satisfied with the products developed using formal methods. Pivotal to client satisfaction were perceived gains in assurance and comprehension.

We found that mathematical-based modeling made system behavior more comprehensible. Everyone we interviewed on the Multinet project said they better understood its security aspects because formal methods were used. The FAA's working group said the formal description of the Collision-Avoidance Systems Logic subsystem was easier to review and modify than the original pseudocode and natural-language specifications.

Product cost. *Was the overall cost of the product reduced or profit increased?*

We were unable to obtain sufficient information to draw strong conclusions about the cost of using formal methods on these four projects. Regulatory systems are inherently expensive because the products are so important and involve so many organizations. We can say that the cost of using formal methods was, with the exception of Multinet, where they were required, just small change relative to total cost.

We did not find that product costs dramatically increased, but the effects of formal methods were measured in other ways – namely, something was needed to achieve assurance. In Darlington, perhaps the costs of use were higher than they should have been because there were no tools and the methodology was immature. The cost of using formal methods in the TCAS project will be measured over time as it is upgraded.

Product impact. *Was the product important to the company's profit margin or an organization's reputation?*

In general, we found that the surveyed products developed using formal methods positively affected the organizations involved. Perhaps the clearest case is the Paris Metro: Not only did the project achieve its goal of eliminating the need for an additional railway line, but project leader GEC Alsthom is using its newfound expertise to market its services.

For TCAS, independent verification and validation uncovered a handful of consequential problems with the CAS Logic pseudocode, which are being repaired for the next release.

Product quality. *Was the quality of the product improved by the use of formal methods? By "quality," we mean good safety and security properties, enhanced functionality and performance, and fewer errors.*

We found evidence of increased quality, but in different forms. To the Multinet and Paris Metro developers, formal methods helped achieve quality goals. On the Multinet project, mathematical analyses and modeling improved the understanding of the security principles. The Paris Metro system met the Paris regional rail system's quality requirements, even though it had to meet increased functionality requirements.

Darlington is an interesting case because formal methods did improve assurance, but the regulators did not claim an increase in quality. In effect, formal methods were used a posteriori to model what existed and to demonstrate that the code met the requirements.

The CAS Logic formalism illustrated subsystem requirements more clearly than the pseudocode, and independent verification and validation uncovered consequential errors in the pseudocode.

Time to market. *Was the product, or family of products, made available for marketing more rapidly (or at least not delayed further)?*

Time to market does not seem to have been a primary concern in these projects, but the possible effects of failing to complete product development or to achieve licensing can be extensive. This was especially obvious in the Darlington project; the operator of the plant would have had to revert to a hardware solution at a cost of about $1 million and a one-year wait for parts had they not been able to certify the software-based shutdown systems.

On the Paris Metro project, failure to achieve the time-to-market goal would have cost hundreds of millions of dollars for an additional railway line.

Process cost. *This feature measures cost in terms of reduction in effort and is based on the adage "time is money."*

We found the effort to attain assurance and comprehension in regulatory cases to be substantially more than we found in the commercial cases.

Darlington reported that formal methods cost about $4 million; the Paris Metro project invested about 120,000 person-hours. These costs are substantially more than we would expect in future projects. In both cases, developers had to develop not only the product but also the technology. GEC Alsthom has indeed reported that the cost of applying formal methods has been lower on the two projects they undertook after the Paris Metro.

Process impact. *What effect did the formal-methods process have on the organization?*

In two cases, we rated the effect as positive: Both the Paris railway system and the FAA participants have expressed an interest in the continued use of formal methods.

In the other two, the effect was neutral: The developers of the Darlington shutdown systems have acknowledged that formal methods must play an important role in future developments, but some managers now have less enthusiasm for shifting from hardware to software controllers. And the effect of formal methods on the process used by the Multinet developers is lessened by the contract-driven nature of the organization – novelty is not always viewed positively in responding to proposal requests.

Pedagogical. *What did the organization make of this learning opportunity?*

All the organizations reported receiving educational benefits from the formal-methods efforts. They better understand formal methods and research-and-development issues. And, especially in the Darlington and Multinet cases, they better understand what process will satisfy regulators. The Darlington and TCAS projects have produced substantial feedback to research programs.

Tools. *Did formal-methods tools help or hinder the development of the product? Were they reliable?*

We found that there does appear to be a need for automated deduction support, especially to demonstrate consistency of code and specification. There is an apparent dichotomy in that the Multinet and Paris Metro projects used formal-methods tools extensively; whereas, Darlington and TCAS didn't. This dichotomy is more in appearance than in reality, because the developers in the Darlington and TCAS projects voiced no philosophical objections to tools, there simply weren't any available. Tool development is the subject of ongoing research.

Design. *Were the designs produced using formal methods fundamentally better or worse in some respect? For example, were they simpler?*

Formal methods appear to have uniformly improved either the product or the developers' understanding of it. Consequently, they had more faith in its quality than with traditional development methodologies. These improvements appear to be the result of using mathematics to analyze domain theories (Multinet), mathematical arguments to demonstrate code and specification properties (Paris Metro), and mathematical-based notations to describe requirements (TCAS) and specifications (Darlington).

Reusable components. *Did the use of formal methods ease the development or use of reusable hardware, software, designs, or abstractions?*

In the two cases for which we could draw a conclusion, formal methods positively affected reuse. The security and safety models developed as part of the Multinet and Paris Metro projects, respectively, are reusable. The reuse benefits involved models or mathematical theories, not code. However, although we found no evidence of code reuse, we believe formal methods will ultimately help develop reusable code because the resulting specifications will unambiguously describe the codes functionality and because using mathematics will result in sufficiently general code that is more suitable for reuse.

Maintainability. *Is it easier to maintain the product (including incremental updates and error repair)?*

It appears that formal notations to capture specifications and requirements, information hiding, and modularization should increase comprehension and clarify interactions between parts of systems, thereby making maintenance simpler. However, if the benefits are to be ongoing, maintenance and product improvements must use and build on practices already in place.

Requirements capture. *Was it easier to acquire requirements?*

We were told by the people involved in all four cases that formal methods improved intellectual control, clarified requirements, and removed superfluous requirements. For example, the FAA's working group believes that the University of California at Irvine's Statecharts-like notation has allowed them to argue about the technical substance of the formal descriptions, instead of minor grammatical matters. The Multinet developers reported a sharper understanding of the security principles involved in building a heterogeneous network.

Verification and validation. *What effect did formal methods have on overall verification and validation?*

Using formal methods was crucial to achieving assurance in these systems. Proofs played a fundamental role in the Darlington and Paris Metro projects. Some projects also used formal descriptions to generate test cases and to complement other verification-and-validation procedures. We believe strongly that developers must use a spectrum of such techniques to attain adequate assurance.

General Lessons Learned

Because the support and market for formal methods will eventually transcend organizational and application domains, we believe it is instructive to summarize the lessons learned from all 12 case studies.

Wider applicability. Ten years ago, most believed that investing in the technology and know-how to apply formal methods was warranted in only a few domains, like computer security. We found that two major changes have occurred since then:

- Formal methods now encompass not only program verification but also formal specification, formal design, and similar terms that connote the use of a mathematical description and analysis.
- Formal methods are now being used in a range of applications by organizations who require more intellectual control than traditional development methods can offer. We found formal methods being used to develop oscilloscopes, ships, satellites, smart cards, transaction-processing units, floating-point arithmetic units, networks, medical instruments, programming environments, and language processors.

Larger scale. Formal methods are being applied to systems of significant scale and extreme importance, although project success depends on more than formal methods. We learned that lines of code, the most common measure, does not always correlate with scale. Not only is lines of code an awkward measure (because of differences in formats and the inclusion of comments), but it

- *Does not take into account the use of abstraction.* Abstraction lets us express a family of products in a single formal specification, apart from design and code. It is especially important for effective communication among stakeholders (for example, designers to managers, or among designers from different disciplines).
- *Does not adequately reflect the design and verification process.* This process goes from safety studies, through many design iterations, often across several organizational boundaries, culminating in what may be a few thousand lines of critical code. It invariably takes a long time and involves many people.
- *Does not practically represent complexity.* Complexity may have more to do with the environment (rare events, multiple failures, or feature interference) than the code, which could be straight-line but have lots of formulas.

Primary manifestations. We found that formal methods are manifested in many ways

- Specification only, to capture abstractions of product families or requirements models.
- Specification with refinement through multilevel designs.
- Proofs, sometimes of specification properties, sometimes of refinement steps, and in some cases at or close to code level.
- Reviews of specifications and design refinements, both the steps performed and other qualities (complexity and clarity) shown by the formal review process.

As we expected, we found that no single formal method is sufficiently general to cover all the significant characteristics of an application's domain. However, there is generally a weak understanding of how to use different formal methods together or with other methods, like structured analysis.

Use in certification. The first step toward the use of formal methods within a regulatory process is to recognize their potential. The next step is to identify candidate methods – we found that this is very opportunistic. Then the chosen method must evolve to meet the needs of the various stakeholders. The four regulatory cases showed considerable interaction among regulators, developers, and researchers, who are working together to develop practical, effective techniques for system certification.

The long-term effect of this experience will be evident in the standards that emerge and, although no standard has yet been sanctioned on the basis of such cases, de facto standards may arise from high-profile cases like these.

Tool support. To be fully industrialized, formal methods will require computer-based tools, but we found such tools are neither necessary nor sufficient for success. Instead, the dominant drivers are flexibility, mixed modes of communication, and intellectual control. On the other hand, projects that have employed advanced tools (like theorem provers) have not shown inordinately high costs.

One reason current formal methods don't have adequate support technology is that there is no common architecture for the development of scalable tools. There are very large tools and very small ones, and not much in between. Few products enjoy any commercial support in terms of documentation, training, and evolution, but we expect some of the internal tools used in the project we studied may be commercialized in the next few years.

Technology transfer. Several North American organizations and many more European ones have formal-methods technology-transfer efforts in progress. However, even organizations with successful applications and significant technology-transfer efforts show only a small degree of penetration.

We found three specific technology-transfer efforts:

- The LaCoS (Large, Correct Systems) project, funded for the next several years by the European Strategic Program for Research in Information Technology, is specifically designed to encourage technology transfer. It focuses on a specific tool, Raise.

- The Cleanroom method is supported by the IBM Software Technology Center, which is chartered to perform training and demonstrations for other parts of IBM.
- Hewlett-Packard used its Applied Methods Group as its technology-transfer mechanism, but did not achieve critical mass and subsequent support within its developer shop.

In addition, some security applications have been successful, but their results were sensitive and hence not widely reported. Many tools developed under the auspices of security organizations have been prohibited from transfer.

We observed four important factors in transferring formal methods:

- Sometimes, projects enjoyed greater success when they packaged formal methods as part of a larger methodology. In some cases, the other aspects were more successful than the formal methods, which served as a "carrier" of modern concepts.
- Successful projects usually had a guru or some form of sustained guidance.
- Management support at the right time is key.
- Sometimes the impetus for the adoption of formal methods is a major change in technology (from hardware- to software-based control, for example).

Skill building. Skills are building slowly in organizations that are trying to use formal methods on industrial projects. Of the companies we surveyed, the largest number of persons skilled in using formal methods was at IBM: Between 40 to 50 people at Hursley and about the same at Federal Systems Division.

Most of the projects we studied had fewer than 10 knowledgeable project members, but overall the project members had strong mathematical and engineering backgrounds. Many of those new to the mathematics underlying formal methods (such as predicate calculus) could adapt to formal notations when they were presented suitably. The mathematics involved in most formal methods is elementary, so the greater challenge may lie in teaching users how to model systems properly and carry a design through.

Code-level application. We found that there are limits to applying formal methods at the code level. Most programming languages (and many specification languages) lack adequate semantic bases to fully support formal methods. Developers can use some of the static-analysis and compiler-type tools to complement design refinements down to a level close to code level. However, many aspects of runtime environments and hardware are not treated adequately and must be viewed as holes in the general use of formal methods. Also, refinement is not viewed as cost-effective for commercial applications, although it may be useful in regulatory cases.

Cost modeling. It is difficult to establish the value of formal methods in situations when there are other methods that can increase quality or when time-to-market dominates product goals. We did not have adequate metrics to perform the cost and cost-benefit analyses that would capture the effect of formal methods on the development process.

Some of the cases we studied attempted to collect performance data using accepted metrics, but we found these to be inadequate. First, the metrics rely heavily on comparisons with previous data collected using the same metrics, which, with one exception, had not been kept. Second, formal methods, as practiced in most cases, require substantial change to the development process as compared to other, informal methods. The metrification methods did not seem to account for these changes.

We believe the 12 cases we studied demonstrate that formal methods are applicable to industrial software development and should not be ignored by industry. Our study found that formal methods are used primarily for

- *Assurance.* Some projects that require a high degree of confidence, with auditable information, have explicit targets of low or zero error rates.
- *Domain analysis.* Some projects use formal methods to better understand an application domain.
- *Communication.* When communication among system stakeholders is the primary need, the use of formal methods is not so much for mathematical analysis, but to supplement informal notations with formal notations.
- *Evidence of best practice.* Sometimes the use of formal methods bestows a competitive advantage or is simply required.
- *Reengineering.* Formal methods can be used on products undergoing long-term upgrades and on those that require structure recovery or function enhancement.

The transfer of formal-methods technology from academia to industry (and vice versa) is slowly proceeding. The industrial application of the technology is constrained by the sophisticated nature of the technology, negative connotations, and the small cadre of experts.

We would also like to see this kind of systematic study, which focuses on both technical and organizational facets, applied to other technological areas. Such studies – we might call them research-usage feedback studies – provide useful, pragmatic feedback and could serve as another model of research activity [7].

Acknowledgements. This study was sponsored by the US National Institute for Standards and Technology, the US Naval Research Laboratory, and the Atomic Energy Control Board of Canada. The US National Science Foundation also provided independent research time for Gerhart for work initiated by Applied Formal Methods, Inc. Previous studies of trends in commercial and regulatory applications of formal methods were performed in conjunction with the organization of the FM89 conference and the Microelectronics and Computer Technology Corp.'s Formal Methods Transition Study. Gerhart's work on this article was done under US National Aeronautics and Space Administration cooperative agreement 9-16.

We thank the interviewees for their time, professional information, and openness. Robin Bloomfield participated in many of the Darlington interviews. The advisory committee – Adele Goldberg, John Marciniak, Morven Gentleman, Lorraine Duvall, and John Gannon – and the sponsors' review teams were especially helpful.

References

1. *Formal Methods for Trustworthy Computer Systems*, D. Craigen and K. Summerskill, eds., Springer-Verlag, London, 1990.
2. D. Craigen, S. Gerhart, and T. Ralston, "An International Survey of Industrial Applications of Formal Methods, Volume 1 Study Methodology," Tech. Report PB93-178556/AS, National Technical Information Service, Springfield, Va.; Tech. Report 5546-93-9581, US Naval Research Laboratory, Washington, DC; Tech. Report Info-0474-1, Atomic Energy Control Board of Canada, Ontario, 1993.
3. D. Craigen, S. Gerhart, and T. Ralston, "An International Survey of Industrial Applications of Formal Methods, Volume 2 Case Studies," Tech. Report PB93-178564/AS, National Technical Information Service, Springfield, Va.; Tech. Report 5546-93-9582, US Naval Research Laboratory, Washington, DC; Tech. Report Info-0474-2, Atomic Energy Control Board of Canada, Ontario, 1993.
4. S. Gerhart, D. Craigen, and T. Ralston, "Observations on Industrial Applications of Formal Methods," *Proc 15th Intl. Conference on Software Engineering*, IEEE CS Press, Los Alamitos, Calif., 1993, pp. 24–33.
5. D. Craigen, S. Gerhart, and T. Ralston, "Formal Methods Reality Check: Industrial Usage," *Proc. Formal Methods Europe*, Springer-Verlag, Berlin, 1993, pp. 250–268.
6. *The Procurement of Safety Critical Software in Defence Equipment (Part 1: Requirements, Part 2: Guidance)*, Interim Defence Standard 00-55, Issue 1, Ministry of Defence, Glasgow, Scotland, 1991.
7. C. Potts, "Software-Engineering Research Revisited," *IEEE Software*, Sept. 1993, pp. 19–28.

Appendix A
Our Approach to Studying Formal-Methods Experience

Previous studies, some of which we have worked on, have uncovered anecdotal evidence of a significant increase in the use of formal methods [1–2]. We decided to team up and further investigate this evidence. Under Ted Ralston's leadership, we found sponsors and began our survey, which took about 1.5 person-years.

Information acquisition. Our general procedure was to

1. Send an initial questionnaire to the interview subjects.
2. Study relevant project literature.
3. Interview project participants using a second questionnaire to structure the interviews. We conducted 23 interviews, which involved about 50 individuals in North America and Europe (we interviewed at least two and as many as five

project participants). Each interview took anywhere from 30 minutes to one and a half days.
4. Produce raw notes on the interview. These notes, along with information gathered from the literature, supplemented the initial and interview questionnaires. The study team wrote a report on each case, using a reasonably consistent framework. We sent the individual case reports to project participants for comment and corrections.
5. Analyze the cases. As we went along, we developed an analytic framework.

Questionnaires. Both questionnaires had six categories:

- *Organizational context.* We were intentionally vague as to the meaning of "organization" because we wanted respondents to define the environment they felt had the greatest impact on them.
- *Project content and history.* We asked for a description of the application, its evolution, and the resources used. Other questions in this category also helped us compare organizational and project compositions.
- *Application goals.* We asked why the application was developed and the major influences that led to or affected development.
- *Formal-methods factors.* These questions elicited the "why" and "what" of the projects formal-method selection process.
- *Formal methods and tool use.* We asked what processes and tools were used to support the chosen formal method.
- *Results.* We asked for general conclusions about the project and the effect of formal methods.

Analytic framework. For each case, we produced vectors pertaining to important product features and process activities. Relative to the organization's usual approach to development (and this may be a subjective measurement), we characterized whether the use of formal methods played a positive, neutral, or negative role. When no information on a product feature or process characteristic was obtainable, we did not make an entry.

The features and activities included as part of our vectors, described in the main text, are not necessarily independent of each other. For example, client satisfaction depends on product cost and quality. What we are trying to measure is the relative effect of using formal methods.

We also included an analysis of how the project started, the types of events that either helped or hindered it, and its status.

Biases and limits. As experts in formal methods, each of us, to differing extents, have vested interests in the technology. One way we addressed this was to form a committee who reviewed and commented on the interim reports. This also gave us input from individuals who have expertise that complements ours.

Our methodology was a common-sense approach – as opposed to a specific social-scientific approach – driven by the need to discover both the general context of how formal methods are used and specific aspects of how a method was selected and how it was used. Many variables affected the success or failure of the cases, so our ability to reach purely scientific conclusions is limited.

Other limits were

- We did not have much time or money.
- We did not study some important classes of methods (for example, standard protocol languages like Specification Design Language and Lotos) and some important domains.
- Although every project we studied was successful to various degrees and in different ways, we did not seek examples of outright failure. Such cases – there are probably dozens of them – would probably be manifested in drop-outs and personnel turnover.

References

1. *Formal Methods for Trustworthy Computer Systems*, D. Craigen and K. Summerskill, eds., Springer-Verlag, London, 1990.
2. S. Gerhart et al., *Formal Methods Transition Study Final Report and Videotape*, Tech. Report TR STP-FT-322/323-91, MCC Software Technology Program, Austin, Tex., 1991; available from RICIS, University of Houston at Clear Lake.

Appendix B
Commercial and Exploratory Cases

In addition to the four regulatory projects that are the focus of this article, we studied five commercial projects and three exploratory projects.

SSADM tool set. The British firm Praxis developed a computer-aided systems-engineering tool set to support the use of the Structured Systems Analysis and Design Method [1]. Praxis used Z to formally specify the tool set's infrastructure. Later, the project team developed guidelines for the use of Z with object-oriented design. The project resulted in 37,000 lines of Objective C and a 350-page, annotated Z specification.

Customer Information Control System. CICS is a large transaction-processing system developed by IBM. Developers at IBM Hursley, UK, reengineered a major portion of CICS Version 3 Release 1 and subsequent releases using the Z method and tools. CICS is approximately 800,000 lines of source code; of the approximately 50,000 lines of new or modified code, 37,000 were completely specified using Z and about 11,000 were partially specified using Z. IBM claims that using Z reduced both development cost and error rates [2].

Cleanroom applications. To better understand the Cleanroom methodology, we investigated two industrial applications: one at the US National Aeronautics and Space Administration's Goddard Space Flight Center and another at IBM Federal Systems Division. The Goddard application was a system to provide attitude ground support for NASA's International Solar Terrestrial Physics Satellite. The IBM application, the focus of our Cleanroom study, was the development of a Cobol Structuring Facility to convert old Cobol programs to a semantically equivalent "structured-programming" form [3]. Cobol/SF comprises 80,000 lines of code and required 70 person-months. It demonstrated to IBM management the potential of the Cleanroom methodology.

Software architecture for oscilloscopes using Z. Tektronix, in Beaverton, Oregon, used Z to develop a reusable software architecture for several new oscilloscope products [4]. Developers used Z to explore design ideas through mathematical models, which were viewed as nonexecutable prototypes. Their intent was not formal correctness; they used Z as a design aid. The software architecture consists of 200,000 lines of code and 30 pages of Z.

Inmos transputers. Inmos, in Bristol, England, makes a transputer family of 32-bit VLSI circuits that have a unique architecture designed for concurrent, multiprocessor applications (the processor, memory, and communication channels are self-contained on each transputer chip). In 1985, a small group of Inmos designers began exploring how to use formal program specification, transformation, and proof techniques to design microprocessors. We studied three related projects, all of which use formal methods in some aspect of the design or development of components of three generations of the Inmos transputer: the use of Z to specify the IEEE floating-point standard which was applied to two successive generations of transputer (a software and a hardware implementation) [5]; the use of Z and Occam to design a scheduler for the T800 transputer; and the use of Communicating Sequential Processes and Calculus of Communicating Systems plus a "refinement checker" in the design and verification of a new feature of the T9000 transputer, the Virtual Channel Processor.

Large correct systems. The LaCoS project seeks to transfer the Raise (Rigorous Approach to Industrial Software Engineering) language and tool set into practice. Raise, which evolved from the Vienna Development Method, is being commercialized by Computer Resources International of Denmark – the producer partner. We interviewed one consumer partner at length and a second briefly. The first, Lloyd's Register, is evaluating Raise (as well as other methods) for a data-acquisition and equipment-management system. The second, Matra Transport, builds railway and other systems. Both are building consultancies in formal methods and assessment. Because LaCoS is a large, on-going, technology-transfer project, it is an important one to follow for the remaining three years of ESPRIT funding and beyond.

Token-Based Access Control System. TBACS is a smartcard access-control system with cryptographic authentication being developed at the US National Institute of Standards and Technology. One group at NIST had been developing a series of prototype smartcards for cryptographic authentication for network access. A second group was looking at new technology to support open systems and other commercial standards. A member of the second group, looking for an application on which to base an experiment in formal methods, chose the smartcard application. In this case, the researchers chose a tool set and approach that followed the standard process in trusted-system certification, using a theorem-prover to verify that a design meets the requirements of a security-policy model [6].

Hewlett-Packard medical instruments.. Although this was a large, important project, we consider it to be exploratory because its primary objective was technology transfer. The product is a real-time database, the Analytical Information Base, of patient-monitoring information. Using an HP-developed specification language (a VDM variant), a formal-methods transfer group and a developer produced a specification. The transfer effort failed because time-to-market was the key feature, and formal methods offered little beyond the high quality already achievable by other means that were consistent with the culture of the organization [7].

References

1. D. Brownbridge. "Using Z to Develop a CASE Toolset," *Proc. Z User Workshop*, Springer-Verlag, London, 1989, pp. 142–149.
2. I. Houston and S. King, "CICS Project Report: Experiences and Results from the use of Z," *Proc. VDM 91*, Volume 551, Springer-Verlag, Berlin, 1991, pp. 588–596.
3. R. Linger and H. Mills. "A Case Study in Cleanroom Software Engineering: the IBM COBOL Structuring Facility," *Proc. Compsac*, IEEE CS Press, Los Alamitos, Calif., 1988, pp. 10–17.
4. D. Garlan and N. Delisle. "Formal Specifications as Reusable Frameworks," *Proc. VDM 92*, Springer-Verlag, Berlin, 1990, pp. 150–163.
5. G. Barrett, "Formal Methods Applied to a Floating Point Number System," *IEEE Trans. Software Eng.*, 1989, pp. 611–621.
6. D.R. Kuhn and J.F. Dray. "Formal Specification and Verification of Control Software for Cryptographic Equipment," *Proc. Computer-Security Applications Conf.*, IEEE CS Press, Los Alamitos, Calif., 1990, pp. 32–43.
7. *Hewlett-Packard Journal* special issue on HP-SL, Dec. 1991, pp. 24–65.

Regulatory Case Studies

Susan Gerhart, Dan Craigen, and Ted Ralston

1. Case Study: Darlington Nuclear Generating Station

Summary.

At this power plant outside Toronto, developers used formal methods to help achieve certification for the plant's shutdown systems, the first software-driven shutdown systems in Canada.

Darlington is a four-reactor nuclear plant east of Toronto. It is operated by Ontario Hydro, the provincial power utility owned by the province of Ontario, and licensed by the Atomic Energy Control Board of Canada.

Each reactor has two independent shutdown systems. The first, SDS1, drops neutron-absorbing rods into the core; the second, SDS2, injects liquid poison into the moderator. Both are safety-critical and require high levels of confidence.

Confidence in the shutdown system is of major importance in the licensing of any nuclear plant. At Darlington, concern about the shutdown systems was compounded because in 1982 Ontario Hydro, with the concurrence of AECB, had decided to fully implement the shutdown systems' decision-making logic on computers. This was to be the first Canadian instance of such a system, so there were questions about what procedures to follow, both in developing and licensing the system.

In this case, formal methods were applied to convince the AECB that the code was of acceptable quality and in accordance with specifications. Formal methods, applied only when serious concerns about the adequacy of the software and documentation arose, took the form of a formal-model-based inspection.

System evolution

Ontario Hydro, along with Atomic Energy of Canada Ltd., which is owned by the Canadian government, began work on the shutdown systems in early 1983. Most of the people involved had engineering degrees, but only limited software-engineering training. In fact, the first two versions of the system were developed by experts in

---

© 1994 IEEE. Reprinted by permission.
Reprinted from *IEEE Software*, 11(1):30–39, January 1994.

safety-system engineering and control systems. It was only during the development of the second version and throughout the third version that individuals with software backgrounds were hired. These later hires did not have extensive backgrounds in nuclear engineering.

Although applying formal methods to the control logic constituted substantial effort, the actual amount of code was small: There are 6,000 lines of assembly distributed over SDS1 and SDS2. In addition, SDS1 has 7,000 lines of Fortran and SDS2 has 13,000 lines of Pascal. Eventually, the specification code, and proofs for each system filled 25 three-inch binders.

By the end of the project, the software had gone through unit testing, integration testing, validation testing, in-situ trajectory-based random testing, software assessment, and software-hazard analysis.

In early 1987, an AECB review of the second version of the software uncovered discrepancies and raised doubt as to whether the software implemented the requirements correctly.

In mid 1987, AECB hired David Parnas, then at Queen's University and now at McMaster University, as the principal investigator on a research contract to recommend how to improve and gain confidence in the software.

Formal methods

Parnas identified areas of concern and in January 1989 proposed a walkthrough (a formal mathematical) to break the licensing impasse.

Before Darlington, neither Ontario Hydro nor AECL had any exposure to formal methods. Their main reason for agreeing to use formal methods was the recognition that AECB was listening carefully to Parnas (and others). In the view of the developers, the formal inspection was an alternative to reimplementing the shutdown-system logic. Consequently, the project was primarily a reverse-engineering exercise – code already existed when the formal specifications were written.

By May 1989, there was general agreement to proceed with a formal inspection based on technology originally developed at the US Naval Research Laboratory, now called Software Cost Reduction. Work began on SDS1 in the fall of 1989 and on SDS2 in early 1990.

SCR/Darlington method. SCR, as applied at Darlington, has three main components:

– formalize informal requirements by generating specification tables,
– use the existing code to develop program-function tables for it, and
– demonstrate that the code is consistent with the specifications.

The specification and program-function tables consist of mathematical formulas that express the effects of the relevant routines. The proof consisted of manually transforming and comparing these tables. Linkage tables helped identify dependencies, ease navigation, and support modularity. Interaction among asynchronous processes was treated as interprocess I/O occurring via shared data objects. Each process had its own set of specifications and program-function tables; processes were analyzed separately, as were process interactions.

Three separate teams applied the SCR/Darlington method, one for each component: One team used the informal requirements documentation to generate a process's specification table. A second team generated the program-function tables, without any access to either the formal or informal specification. A third team used the resulting tables to demonstrate that, under suitable transformations, the specification and program-function tables were equivalent. This last team recorded discrepancies and reported them to the other teams.

For the most part, the developers felt that the process worked well, although they had no specialized formal-methods tools. Instead, the proving team did the analysis manually; Microsoft Excel was used to produce the program-function tables.

This process was labor-intensive. At one point, as many as 30 people were working on different aspects of the verification. When Ontario Hydro began to perceive the licensing impasse might delay start-up (and revenue generation) of the multibillion-dollar plant, the head of the proving team was given his pick of the best staff.

The SDS1 inspection was completed in November 1989, and AECB issued a license for one-percent power operation (the plant could run up to one percent of its rated capacity). Shortly thereafter, in January 1990, formal verification inspection of SDS2 began and was completed one month later. In February 1990, AECB issued a license for full-power operation of the Darlington generating station.

Evaluation

Although AECB declared that the shutdown systems were no longer an impediment to licensing, it also stated that the software would have to be redesigned for long-term use. As a consequence, Ontario Hydro, AECL, and AECB are designing a new set of standards for future software developments.

An analysis of the results obtained for each relevant feature is marginally positive (the exact definition of these features is in the previous chapter *Experience with Formal Methods in Critical Systems*):

– *Client satisfaction.* AECB was finally convinced by the arguments produced with formal methods that the code was adequately correct and safe.
– *Product cost.* It's unclear if formal methods had any effect on cost. It could be argued on the one hand that formal methods delayed licensing; on the other hand, licensing may not have been achievable without them.
– *Product impact.* With the development of the product and the successful demonstration that the code was adequately correct and safe, the shutdown system was no longer an impediment to plant licensing.
– *Product quality.* Safety-related discrepancies were found in an earlier version of the software; none are known in the present version. However, AECB does not believe that the quality of the software was improved.

- *Time to market.* Again, it is unclear if formal methods affected time to market. Did formal methods delay licensing or make licensing achievable?
- *Process cost.* Formal-methods technology evolved as the project progressed; a fixed process was not in place at the start of the effort. Hence, tool support was absent and efforts had to be directed at developing the technology, not solely applying it.
- *Process impact.* Ontario Hydro and AECL management have a greater awareness of software issues. Also, new standards and processes are being developed for safety-critical software. Conversely, some managers have been delaying replacing hardware systems with computers because of the experiences with the shutdown system.
- *Pedagogical.* Everyone involved learned and is responding to those lessons. Parnas found interesting research areas; Ontario Hydro, AECL and AECB are more aware of formal methods and software engineering and are working on new standards and procedures.
- *Tools.* No special tools were used, so no evaluation is possible. We believe the developers at Darlington could have found tools to use, but had no time to investigate availability or to customize what they might have found.
- *Design.* Although the design did not change, the increased precision and readability of the formal documents were deemed advantageous. Hence, there was an increased ability to review the system for licensing.
- *Requirements capture.* The procedures clarified the requirements and removed some safety-related ambiguities.
- *Verification and validation.* Without the formal methods there would have been no proofs of the correspondence between specification and program-function tables. The formalism was also extensively used in review and led to increased confidence in the system.

As this case study illustrates, the SCR/Darlington method was successfully used to demonstrate that code conformed to its specification, though perhaps at a high cost – it was estimated that software verification cost about $4 million Canadian and reverting to a hardware solution would have meant a one-year delay and would have cost about $1 million Canadian. The methodology improved reviewability and helped increase assurance. However, this effort was hindered by lack of tool support. Ontario Hydro and AECL are developing and experimenting with tools.

To our knowledge, the collection of techniques described here has been used only by Ontario Hydro and AECL [1]. Parnas and his colleagues (including researchers with the NRL) continue to enhance SCR and are also considering the development of tool support [2].

References

1. G. Archinoff et al., "Verification of the Shutdown System Software at the Darlington Nuclear Generating Station," *Proc. Int'l Conf. Control and Instrumentation in Nuclear Installations*, Inst. Nuclear Eng., London, 1990.
2. T. Alspough et al., "Software Requirements for the A-7E Aircraft," Tech. Report NRL/FR/5530-92-9194, US Naval Research Laboratories, Washington, DC, 1992.

2. Case Study: Paris Metro Signaling System

Summary.

This system, designed to reduce the separation between trains in the Paris Metro, is the first safety-critical software system certified by the French railway authority. Its developers used formal methods extensively for verification and validation.

The developers of this signaling system sought to reduce the separation between trains in the Paris rapid-transit system by 30 seconds, to two minutes. They were required to convince the RATP (the Paris rapid-transit authority) that the system met safety requirements. This was the first use of safety-critical software in a French railway system.

The new system, called SACEM, allows for 60,000 passengers per hour. Its successful deployment has eliminated the need for another railway line (and the associated rail cars and labor), a saving of hundreds of millions of dollars.

Questions of proof

There were three developers: GEC Alsthom, Matra Transport, and CSEE (Compagnie de Signaux et Entreprises Électriques). GEC Alsthom was the project leader. The project was conceptualized in 1979, funded in early 1982, and a prototype system was complete by the end of 1985. The system was fully deployed in May 1989.

SACEM is a system of moderate complexity: It consists of 9,000 lines of verified code. All SACEM hardware and software was entirely new.

The developers chose to use formal methods to enhance the credibility of the validation. At first, they used Hoare's proof-of-program method [1] because they knew of no other techniques available in 1982. By 1987, the SACEM project had three sets of proven software using the Hoare approach, without knowing if these were consistent.

They then hired mathematician and consultant Jean-Raymond Abrial to help perform an external evaluation. There was apparently some question about what had actually been proved. They didn't know of any proofs of the scale they were attempting or what process to follow. They decided to do a top-to-bottom respecification and refinement along with a bottom-to-top respecification and verification (using the Hoare approach), hoping to meet somewhere in the middle.

The goal was to go down to assertions following the original design structures. They developed a technique for extracting the pre- and postconditions from the design and, when they got to a level close to code, these were matched with the bottom-up effort.

This revalidation by proof reengineering validated both their method and the software product.

The client, RATP, divided its validation into four parts:

- *Validation of the high-level requirements (the "operational need")*. To meet this requirement, the developers used a tool called Grafcet to transform the natural-language specification into a finite-state machine representation and used simulation. They represented and validated the software architecture using Softech's Structured Analysis and Design Techniques product.
- *Verification and testing*. To meet these requirements, the developers had a separate team model the SACEM system, perform tests in the lab, and simulate the system using Asa (a Verilog product that combines SADT with finite-state analysis). The encoded microprocessor was validated by testing only.
- *Operations and maintenance*. To meet these requirements, the developers used a French version of failure-mode and -effects analysis to perform safety studies, and fault-tree analysis to perform hazard studies. They carried out operations and maintenance analysis by physically checking out the layout of the track-side systems and performing on-site tests.
- *Certification*. A 10-person committee was convened because nothing like SACEM had been done before. The committee included members from SNCF (the French national railway), RATP, the French aviation authority, and academic and research experts on safety. It produced a document, *Dossier on Software Safety*. The RATP devised 600 operational scenarios, checked them for completeness, elaborated them into a finite-state automation, and checked for coverage at the transition level.

The RATP team found many specification anomalies through testing. The main problem was in specifying degraded modes. The real-time simulation checked the interleaving of cycles and that variables used in one cycle had been produced properly in a preceding one. This was all done by testing.

Hoare logic

There are numerous variants of Hoare logic; here we present one. Hoare introduced the notation $P\{q1\}Q$, which means that if the predicate P is true of the program state before program fragment $q1$ executes, predicate Q will be true of the program state when $q1$ terminates.

With Hoare logic, developers annotate programs with assertions that specify intended behavior. Generally, procedures will have a precondition, which is a relationship that must be true when it is invoked, a postcondition, which must be true when it terminates, and loop invariants, which specify a relationship that must be true whenever loop execution reaches a state associated with the invariant.

Hoare triples ($P\{q1\}Q$) let you eliminate all code fragments and obtain formulas in (usually) predicate calculus. When you can demonstrate that these formulas hold, you have validated the annotations – and proved the code is consistent with its specification. Thus Hoare logic is one way to provide assurance.

Hoare logic provides a means of demonstrating that a program is consistent with its specifications, but most real programming languages have complex proof rules, so using a method at the code level relies on the quality of the rules and their usability in the process.

Hoare logic and its variants are used in many formal-methods tools. We have known since the early 1970s how to eliminate code fragments automatically and produce a set of predicate-calculus propositions (the verification conditions). Tools that do this, usually called verification-condition generators, are a crucial component of most verification systems.

B method

The B method was developed by Abrial [2] and has been supported by various vendors, including BP International, Sunbury-on-Thames, UK; Edinburgh Portable Compilers, Edinburgh, Scotland; and B-Core, Oxford, UK [3].

The B method uses abstract-machine notation, which lets you describe a state (variables of the abstract machine), an invariant (constraints and relations among variables), and operations (interface with the outside world). You can write B expressions as guarded commands and express the state changes in terms of substitutions.

In the B method, design is defined as the process of identifying appropriate decompositions, refinements, and implementations. Verification is defined as the discharge of all proof obligations, mainly that invariants are maintained. The method does not prescribe how to determine the top-level specification or the number or size of refinements, but there are five main steps:

1. Express specifications in abstract-machine notation and prove that a machine's operations preserve its invariants.
2. Compose machines using, for example, semihiding, parameterization, and removal of duplicated machine specifications.
3. Refine data (make variables more tied to the target machines) and algorithms (make operations closer to target control structures). Prove that the refinement relation is transitive and monotonic.
4. Implement by removing unbounded choice, preconditioning, and parallelism (possibly by automatic translations), with further proof obligations.
5. Import into an implementation of separately defined machines.

B provides an analyzer that generates proof obligations (in effect, a verification-condition generator); a type checker; an animator that symbolically executes abstract machines; a status checker that presents the development path (including discharge of proof obligations); checkpoint, reset, and remake (replays of analyses and proofs after machine modifications); and a prover.

The B method lets you perform and record an entire development. It accommodates change through replay tools. Refinement, implementation, and composition steps have precise notions of correctness and mechanical generation of proof obligations. Tests may be performed using the simulator.

The final implementation step may be partially mechanized for common languages (C and Ada) and for some specification constructs.

However, the B method provides no guidance for making design decisions, recording testing or inspection methodology, or presenting specifications. The tool set is still evolving and, while commercially supported, it has not yet been evaluated by many outside organizations.

Evaluation

The RATP regulators were somewhat skeptical of the formal process, but they report that SACEM has been an eye-opening, instructive effort that has taught them the value of combining formal methods with prototyping, simulation, and testing.

Because RATP is responsible for validation, the ability to read the formal specifications and prove properties is a plus. They would like to see more work on animating specifications and tying formal methods to quality assurance.

An analysis of the results obtained for each relevant feature is positive (the exact definition of these features is in the previous chapter *Experience with Formal Methods in Critical Systems*):

- *Client satisfaction.* RATP has approved the SACEM system and supports its use by the Paris transit system. The system is apparently functioning properly with respect to the ultimate client – the Parisian commuter.
- *Product cost.* Some 120,000 person-hours were spent on formal methods, out of a total development effort of 315,000 person-hours (170,000 on the prototype; 145,000 hours on the commercial system). RATP believes the use of formal methods did not increase product cost, but determining this is a complex function of sociology and technology.
- *Product impact.* SACEM helped RATP improve its subway capacity. GEC Alsthom is now selling additional products that use the same approach.
- *Product quality.* The system meets its quality requirements as established by RATP: increased throughput and certification.
- *Process cost.* Data suggests that the additional activities required to assimilate and use formal methods did not add to the overall process cost, given that RATP accepted the verification as part of the certification.
- *Process impact.* A significant process was established over several years to support the use of software in the context of safety-critical railway systems.

- *Pedagogical.* GEC Alsthom learned to apply the methods they found available – first Hoare logic then B – over the course of a decade.
- *Tools.* Working with only crude tools at the beginning, GEC Alsthom managed to complete significant specification and verification. This led to the creation of their own tools, which they plan to commercialize. The tool set used with SACEM was evolving at the time.
- *Design.* The B abstract machine and refinement approaches have become part of the GEC Alsthom design methodology on two subsequent projects. However, formal methods did not affect the design (only the verification) of SACEM.
- *Reuse.* GEC Alsthom is using the SACEM safety model and process-specification outline in their subsequent railway products.
- *Requirements capture.* Formal specifications help developers understand the requirements and negotiation specifications.
- *Verification and validation.* Although formal methods were not the only means of assurance, they played a major role in certification.

From project start, the SACEM project collected data on hours spent on particular tasks and the resources committed to achieve these tasks. As a result, we know that the formal proof required 32.4 percent of total effort; module testing required 20.1 percent; functional testing 25.9 percent; and respecification 21.6 percent [4].

The RATP regulators found that the formality of the specification helped control the project's coherence. User communication was good when they were writing the specification, but that was late in the process. RATP would have liked direct simulation of the specification.

A few academic groups, including Oxford University, have reported using B, as have some UK government groups.

GEC Alsthom has used B in two subsequent applications: a transportation system in Calcutta, India, and a safety net to protect against driver failure on all the electrified lines operated by the French national railways authority.

References

1. C.A.R. Hoare, "An Axiomatic Basis for Computer Programming," *Comm. ACM*, Oct. 1969, pp. 576–580, 583.
2. J.-R. Abrial et al., "The B Method", *Proc. VDM '91*, Springer Verlag, Berlin, 1991, pp. 398–405.
3. M. Carnot et al., "Error-Free Software Development for Critical Systems using the B-methodology," *Proc. Int'l Symp. On Software Reliability Engineering*, IEEE Press, New York, 1992.
4. G. Guiho and C. Hennebert, "SACEM Software Validation," *Proc. Int'l Conf. Software Eng.*, IEEE CS Press, Los Alamitos, Calif., 1990, pp. 186–191.

3. Case Study: Traffic Alert and Collision-Avoidance System

Summary.

To improve an industry-government working group's capability to review this system, which alerts and advises pilots in the event of an impending collision, formal specifications of two major subsystems were developed using a formal, graphical notation.

In 1987, the US Congress mandated that all aircraft with more than 30 seats install a system to avoid midair collisions by the end of 1991 (later extended to the end of 1993). The mandated system, the Traffic Alert and Collision-Avoidance System, had been under development by the Federal Aviation Administration for several years.

The TCAS family of instruments are air-based, functioning separately from the ground-based air-traffic-control system. The system has two software subsystems: CAS Logic and CAS Surveillance. TCAS II, the subject of our study, provides traffic advisories and recommends vertical escape maneuvers in the event of an impending collision [1]. TCAS II is designed to be used on airliners and larger commuter and business aircraft.

Road to formal methods

RTCA, Inc. (formerly called the Radio Technical Commission for Aeronautics) develops and publishes the Minimum Operational Performance Standards to which TCAS II must conform. In 1983, it published a natural-language specification of TCAS II, which included a pseudocode description of CAS Logic. This specification was to be revised six times in the next six years. RTCA also helped form a working group, SC147, which included pilots, FAA representatives, and other interested parties, to develop the TCAS II specification.

Most of the individuals involved with TCAS II had engineering backgrounds, but with the exception of a few individuals, there was very little in-depth understanding of software-engineering principles and no knowledge of formal methods.

TCAS II was a project of moderate size: CAS Logic comprises 7,000 lines of pseudocode, and the formal specification of its requirements is about the same size.

Formal methods were considered when Nancy Leveson, then at the University of California at Irvine and now at the University of Washington, asked an FAA resource specialist if he knew of a real application to which she could apply her safety analysis techniques. At the time, mid 1990, the FAA and others had become concerned about the apparent loss of intellectual control over the specification and the errors uncovered through simulations of the pseudocode.

The FAA wanted to further clarify the TCAS II requirements and obtain improved confidence in the system. Consequently, in 1991, the TCAS program office (part of the FAA) provided a grant to Leveson and her research group at UCI to formalize CAS Logic and, later, CAS Surveillance. Some months later, the working group adopted Leveson's approach to describing the logic and terminated their own efforts to write a narrative English specification.

In the spring of 1992, the working group stated that the formal specification was ready for independent verification and validation.

According to an informal report to the authors in November 1993, the formal specification of CAS Logic has completed the IV&V process. As part of this process, a simulator for the CAS Logic specification was written and used to run a series of benchmark examples. After a number of discrepancies were resolved, the specification passed all benchmarks and was approved. The IV&V also uncovered consequential problems in the pseudocode. These problems will be resolved in subsequent releases of CAS Logic.

In addition, the intention is to maintain both the pseudocode and the formal specification (with ongoing IV&V). Because of limited resources, the formal specification of the CAS Surveillance system is not playing as significant a role as that of CAS Logic.

Methodology

The TCAS methodology aims to formally analyze requirements for correctness and safety and develop readable, state-based requirements-specification documents. Leveson chose a method based in formal methods because safety analysis requires mathematical modeling and analysis – testing or executing a specification does not provide sufficient assurance for most safety-critical applications.

In general, the TCAS methodology [2] is directed at process-control systems, which are designed to maintain a relationship between a system's inputs and outputs in light of disturbances to a process. A controller uses a model of the process it is controlling and its environment to determine what corrective actions are required.

The relationship between the real-world process state and the internal model must be explicit in the requirements specification and reviewable. To achieve this, the TCAS methodology uses black-box behavioral specifications, provides as much information as possible so that the context for state transitions is clear (*information exposure*), and *uses hierarchies*, which relate a specification component to other components on which its behavior depends.

From her theoretical work on safety, Leveson decided that a state-machine-based specification methodology was the most practical model to use. Among the existing reactive-system specification languages based on state machines, she decided that Statecharts [3] was the most useful for real, complex systems that involve large numbers of states.

Leveson's group changed the Statecharts language to meet their specific need to emphasize the transition logic of the TCAS subsystems and generate specifications that were amenable to formal mathematical analysis and suitably abstract.

As part of changing the Statecharts language, the group used a tabular representation of *disjunctive normal form* formulas to specify transition conditions. Essentially, these formulas are an "or-ing" of clauses, each clause being an "and-ing" of terms. Experience with TCAS II demonstrated that this representation of predicate-calculus formulas is easier for both engineers and nonengineers to comprehend than the usual predicate-calculus formulas.

Finally, the group modified Statecharts so that it could accommodate their approach to describing TCAS II as a set of parallel, communicating state machines. Communication among system components occurs over directed communication links.

During the early TCAS II specification and specification-language development, which were occurring in parallel, Leveson and her students wrote most of the specification, and the domain experts reviewed it. As the process continued, however, the responsibility for evolving and correcting the specification shifted to the domain experts.

The only tools used by the group were LaTeX, to help produce readable documents, and some configuration-management tools. In the future, Leveson intends to experiment with automated deduction tools.

Evaluation

Although the techniques used are based on a state-machine representation, there are several research issues pertaining to scalability, presentation style, and modifications to the Statecharts language.

An analysis of the results obtained for each relevant feature is neutral (the exact definition of these features is in the previous chapter *Experience with Formal Methods in Critical Systems*):

- *Client satisfaction.* The FAA and the SC147 committee appear to be happy with the formal specification.
- *Process impact.* The FAA and the working group found the formalism easier to comprehend because it was presented in a style analogous to approaches used in their own engineering discipline. However, the FAA has not abandoned its old method entirely, keeping the pseudocode as well as the formal specification.
- *Pedagogical.* Members of the FAA and working group have readily adopted the ideas. Some members not only reviewed but wrote parts of the formal specification.
- *Tools.* In TCAS, a variant of Statecharts was used, hence the existing Statemate tool set was not usable. However, the one tool they did use, LaTeX, was in support of their primary goal to produce a readable, reviewable specification. Careful consideration was given to the presentation of the specification and to cross-referencing between related concepts.
- *Design.* The formalism was reviewable and led to intellectual control of the specification. The formal description is generally conceded to be more tractable because it excludes design information that is incorporated into the pseudocode.
- *Requirements capture.* The formalism helped clarify requirements because it made the specification more reviewable and tractable than the pseudocode.

– *Verification and validation.* The CAS Logic has completed IV&V and has been approved.

In this case, formal methods resulted in at least one significant change in the way the working group operated – it eliminated the development of an informal natural-language specification. To date, feedback on the modified Statecharts language has been positive. Engineers and others not trained in formal methods can review and modify the specification.

The method is limited by a lack of tool support and as yet is used only by Leveson's research group and some members of the working group, though the ideas are being disseminated [2].

References

1. *Introduction to TCAS II*, Federal Aviation Administration, US Dept. of Transportation, Washington DC, 1990.
2. N. Leveson et al. "Requirements Specification for Process-Control Systems," *IEEE Trans. Software Eng.*, to appear.
3. D. Harel, "Statecharts: A Visual Formalism for Complex Systems", *Science of Computer Programming, Volume 8*, M. Sintzoff, ed., North Holland, Amsterdam, 1987, pp. 231–274.

4. Case Study: Multinet Gateway System

Summary.

The use of formal methods was required in developing this security-critical network gateway, to achieve clearance from the US Department of Defense to carry sensitive information.

The Multinet Gateway System is a protocol-based service that delivers datagrams to Internet hosts. In addition to the delivery service, MGS provides mechanisms, in accordance with the US Department of Defense's security criteria, to protect sensitive information. It is the major computer-security case we studied.

A main aspect of the MGS project was to achieve certification from the US National Computer Security Center. In December 1985, the DoD published a set of criteria and a hierarchy of evaluation classes for security-related products [1]. The more confidence a developer could demonstrate, the higher the product's evaluation class.

There are four classes: D, minimal protection; C, discretionary; B, mandatory; and A, verified. The highest class requires the developer to use formal security-verification methods to assure that the system can effectively protect classified or other sensitive information it stores or processes. It also requires extensive documentation to demonstrate that the *trusted computer base* (the hardware and software used to enforce security policies, required for a B rating) meets the security requirements in all aspects of design, development, and implementation.

Novel project

The developer of MGS, Ford Aerospace (now Loral), wanted to achieve an A-class certification. With Mitre Corp. performing oversight, Ford Aerospace designed and refined MGS between 1981 and 1984, building the first development models (for both hardware and software components) in 1984 and 1985.

Many things about MGS were novel. While there had been some experience with formal methods within Ford, it certainly had not been applied to networks. Although Ford had experience with networks, the security requirements were a new wrinkle. In addition this was a first attempt to distribute protocols over separate processors and to use microcomputer boards.

Ford Aerospace operates through matrix management (organizational units versus projects). Most Ford Aerospace employees have only bachelor's degrees, but three of the formal-methods personnel had doctorates.

MGS was a project of moderate complexity: The specification comprises about 10 pages of mathematics and 80 pages of Gypsy specification; the underlying operating system was about 6,000 lines of code.

Security policy. In some ways, the MGS security-policy model is simple. There are several security assertions, but the main three are

- the system accepts data only from input wires and only if the data is consonant with the security levels of the input wires;
- the system delivers data to an output wire only if it is "derived" from data received at input wires and the security levels of this data are the same as the output wire; and
- the system delivers data only to output wires and only if the data is consonant with the security levels of the output wires.

Development model. The MGS developers tried to adhere to standard DoD procedures: They used structured design methods, dataflow diagrams, program-description languages, and walkthroughs.

The project did not use independent verification and validation, although Mitre, the National Computer Security Center, and Computational Logic (the company that supports the formal-methods environment) did closely analyze its formal methods and security aspects.

The MGS development had two phases. In the first phase, developers used formal methods and prototyping to develop their understanding of MGS. In the second phase, they implemented MGS, using mathematical modeling and the Gypsy Verification Environment [3] to identify 50 axioms that must be true of the MGS implementation before it could meet security requirements.

The team used several tools, including a system for source-code control, GVE, and Unix utilities to help manage, manipulate, and coordinate the source code and Gypsy.

One of the main problems was integrating formal methods with the standard life cycle and developing a documentation tree that would be useful for certification.

For example, a system-security document describes the system and security architecture in implementation, functional, trust-domain, and GVE documents and how these documents correspond. A trust-domain document describes the MGS security policy without using a formal specification language (it seems to have been used, in part, to hide the mathematics from those unfamiliar with Gypsy and mathematical notations). Finally, a GVE document summarized the MGS specification, focusing on security attributes.

Gypsy verification environment

GVE is one of two verification systems endorsed by the US National Computer Security Center for use in the development of security-critical applications. It can be used to develop and explore formal specifications and prove that the resulting code is consistent with them. GVE was used in this case because there was a mandate to use an "endorsed tool" to achieve an A-class certification.

The Gypsy specification language is strongly typed, first-order predicate calculus that has, at times, been used as a design language. The programming language is a Pascal derivative that includes a form of modularization (scopes), concurrency (processes communicate through buffers), exception handling, and abstract data types.

Most projects that have used Gypsy have used its specification component to model security properties. For example, some applications have described security in terms of noninterference: A process output cannot depend on a process that has a higher security classification.

But GVE offers more than support for specification. It also supports the expression of domain concepts, proofs of derived properties, using domain concepts to specify programs, and proofs that programs are consistent with their specifications (using a variant of Hoare logic [2]). These steps are iterative, as the developer's understanding of the application domain increases.

GVE provides an interface to external text editors to create and revise Gypsy text; a parser to check the static semantics of Gypsy text; a verification-condition generator to generate formulas that are adequate to establish correspondence between code and specifications; a mechanical proof checker to assist in the verification or in constructing proofs; an information-flow analyzer for establishing certain information-security properties of special Gypsy specifications; and utilities like a pretty printer and an algebraic simplifier.

The resulting artefacts include Gypsy descriptions of domain theories, specifications, and code; and proofs of domain theorems and verification conditions (the propositions produced by the verification-condition generator).

Evaluation

Because they used formal methods, developers could better understand the system and improve performance. In 1985, the MGS project was awarded a certification contract, which resulted in the creation of an advanced development model and supporting evidence. In 1988, MGS was deployed.

Although MGS did not achieve an A-class certification (probably because its low commercial potential did not warrant the effort an A-class certification would have required), the US government seems to be generally satisfied with the development and the chief architect has more confidence and assurance in MGS than in systems of similar size and complexity.

An analysis of the results obtained for each relevant feature is neutral (the exact definition of these features is in the previous chapter *Experience with Formal Methods in Critical Systems*):

- *Client satisfaction.* Both the developers and assessors of MGS feel that the system is of high quality and that their confidence is based, partly, on the clarifications arising from using formal methods.
- *Product impact.* MGS has been fielded and is being used to transmit sensitive data.
- *Product quality.* Both the developers and assessors feel that the product's reliability was enhanced by the application of formal methods.
- *Process impact.* We did not determine any long-term effects on Ford Aerospace's development process from using formal methods.
- *Pedagogical.* The GVE was not easy to learn. With respect to formal methods, the developers learned that you should try to understand what you are modeling, express that understanding, and learn the ethos of the tools and methods you are to use before proceeding with development. This project yielded new approaches for describing the security functions in communication networks.
- *Tools.* One reviewer commented that the GVE proofs did not add to his understanding of the application domain. In addition, the GVE technology, which was developed in the 1970s, provides little automated deduction power and does not fully support Gypsy's concurrency and abstract data-type features. From our current perspective, the proof checking capabilities of the GVE are weak and are surpassed by a number of existing systems (primarily in North America).
- *Design.* The team leader felt that the use of rigorous mathematics helped clarify underlying concepts and resulted in a nicely modular system.
- *Reuse.* MGS resulted in the development of a reusable security-policy model that could be applied to other Internet devices.
- *Requirements capture.* Formalism helped clarify the security requirements for networks that are to comply with DoD security policies.
- *Verification and validation.* Formalism helped raise the confidence of the developers and assessors. The V & V team could use formal specifications to generate tests that uncovered coding errors.

Part of the reason the MGS team chose GVE was its ability to keep track of proof developments. However, the GVE also imposed some restrictions. For example, it did not support generic data structures.

GVE was sufficiently robust, but it was complex and not of production quality. The project team had concerns about the soundness of GVE, but felt that the part of it they used was reliable.

The team also found that communicating formal ideas to implementers is difficult. The implementers, who are used to having more latitude in interpreting functionality, did not appreciate the need for precision. Also, the team reported that integrating formal methods into a contract-driven organization like Ford Aerospace was difficult because it had to fulfil contracts in a conservative manner.

For the most part, the developers would not have proceeded much differently. They would have liked to have more tool support and would like to better understand how to integrate formal methods with standard development processes.

References

1. "Trusted Computer System Evaluation Criteria," Tech. Report DoD 5200.28.-STD, US Department of Defense, Washington DC, 1985.
2. "Mechanical Proofs about Computer Programs," in *Mathematical Logic and Programming Languages*, C.A.R. Hoare and J.C. Shepherdson, eds., Prentice-Hall, Englewood Cliffs, N.J., 1985.
3. D. Good, "Mechanical Proofs about Computer Programs," in *Mathematical Logic and Programming Languages*, C.A.R. Hoare and J.C. Sheperdson, eds., Prentice-Hall, Englewood Cliffs, N.J., 1985.

Medical Devices: The Therac-25 Story

Nancy G. Leveson

Summary.

A thorough account of the Therac-25 medical electron accelerator accidents reveals previously unknown details and suggests ways to reduce risk in the future.

1 Introduction

Between June 1985 and January 1987, a computer-controlled radiation therapy machine, called the Therac-25, massively overdosed six people. These accidents have been described as the worst in the 35-year history of medical accelerators [6].

A detailed accident investigation, drawn from publicly available documents, can be found in Leveson and Turner [4]. The following account is taken from this report and includes both the factors involved in the overdoses themselves and the attempts by the users, manufacturers, and governments to deal with them. Because this accident was never officially investigated, some information on the Therac-25 software development, management, and quality control procedures are not available. What is included below has been gleaned from law suits and depositions, government records, and copies of correspondence and other material obtained from the U.S. Food and Drug Administration (FDA), which regulates these devices.

2 Background

Medical linear accelerators (linacs) accelerate electrons to create high-energy beams that can destroy tumors with minimal impact on the surrounding healthy tissue.

© 1995 Addison-Wesley Publishing Company Inc. Reprinted by permission of Addison Wesley Longman.
Reprinted from N. Leveson, *Safeware: System Safety and Computers*, pages 515–553.

Relatively shallow tissue is treated with the accelerated electrons; to reach deeper tissue, the electron beam is converted into X-ray photons.

In the early 1970s, Atomic Energy of Canada Limited (AECL)[1] and a French company called CGR went into business together building linear accelerators. The products of this cooperation were (1) the Therac-6, a 6 million electron volt (MeV) accelerator capable of producing X-rays only and later (2) the Therac-20, a 20 MeV, dual-mode (X-rays or electrons) accelerator. Both were versions of older CGR machines, the Neptune and Sagittaire, respectively, which were augmented with computer control using a DEC PDP-11 minicomputer. We know that some of the old Therac-6 software routines were reused in the Therac-20 and that CGR developed the initial software.

Software functionality was limited in both machines: The computer merely added convenience to the existing hardware, which was capable of standing alone. Industry-standard hardware safety features and interlocks in the underlying machines were retained.

The business relationship between AECL and CGR faltered after the Therac-20 effort. Citing competitive pressures, the two companies did not renew their cooperative agreement when scheduled in 1981.

In the mid-1970s, AECL had developed a radical new "double pass" concept for electron acceleration. A double-pass accelerator needs much less space to develop comparable energy levels because it folds the long physical mechanism required to accelerate the electrons, and it is more economical to produce. Using this double-pass concept, AECL designed the Therac-25, a dual-mode linear accelerator that can deliver either photons at 25 MeV or electrons at various energy levels.

Compared with the Therac-20, the Therac-25 is notably more compact, more versatile, and arguably easier to use. The higher energy takes advantage of the phenomenon of *depth dose*: As the energy increases, the depth in the body at which maximum dose build-up occurs also increases, sparing the tissue above the target area. Economic advantages also come into play for the customer, since only one machine is required for both treatment modalities (electrons and photons).

Several features of the Therac-25 are important in understanding the accidents. First, like the Therac-6 and the Therac-20, the Therac-25 is controlled by a PDP-11 computer. However, AECL designed the Therac-25 to take advantage of computer control from the outset; they did not build on a stand-alone machine. The Therac-6 and Therac-20 had been designed around machines that already had histories of clinical use without computer control.

In addition, the Therac-25 software has more responsibility for maintaining safety than the software in the previous machines. The Therac-20 has independent protective circuits for monitoring the electron-beam scanning plus mechanical interlocks for policing the machine and ensuring safe operation. The Therac-25 relies

---

[1] AECL was an arms-length entity, called a crown corporation, of the Canadian government. Since the time of the incidents related in this paper, AECL Medical, a division of AECL, was privatized and is now called Theratronics International, Ltd.. Currently, the primary business of AECL is the design and installation of nuclear reactors.

more on software for these functions. AECL took advantage of the computer's abilities to control and monitor the hardware and decided not to duplicate all the existing hardware safety mechanisms and interlocks.

Some software for the machines was interrelated or reused. In a letter to a Therac-25 user, the AECL quality assurance manager said, "The same Therac-6 package was used by the AECL software people when they started the Therac-25 software. The Therac-20 and Therac-25 software programs were done independently starting from a common base" [4]. The reuse of Therac-6 design features or modules may explain some of the problematic aspects of the Therac-25 software design. The quality assurance manager was apparently unaware that some Therac-20 routines were also used in the Therac-25; this was discovered after a bug related to one of the Therac-25 accidents was found in the Therac-20 software.

AECL produced the first hardwired prototype of the Therac-25 in 1976, and the completely computer-controlled commercial version was available in late 1982.

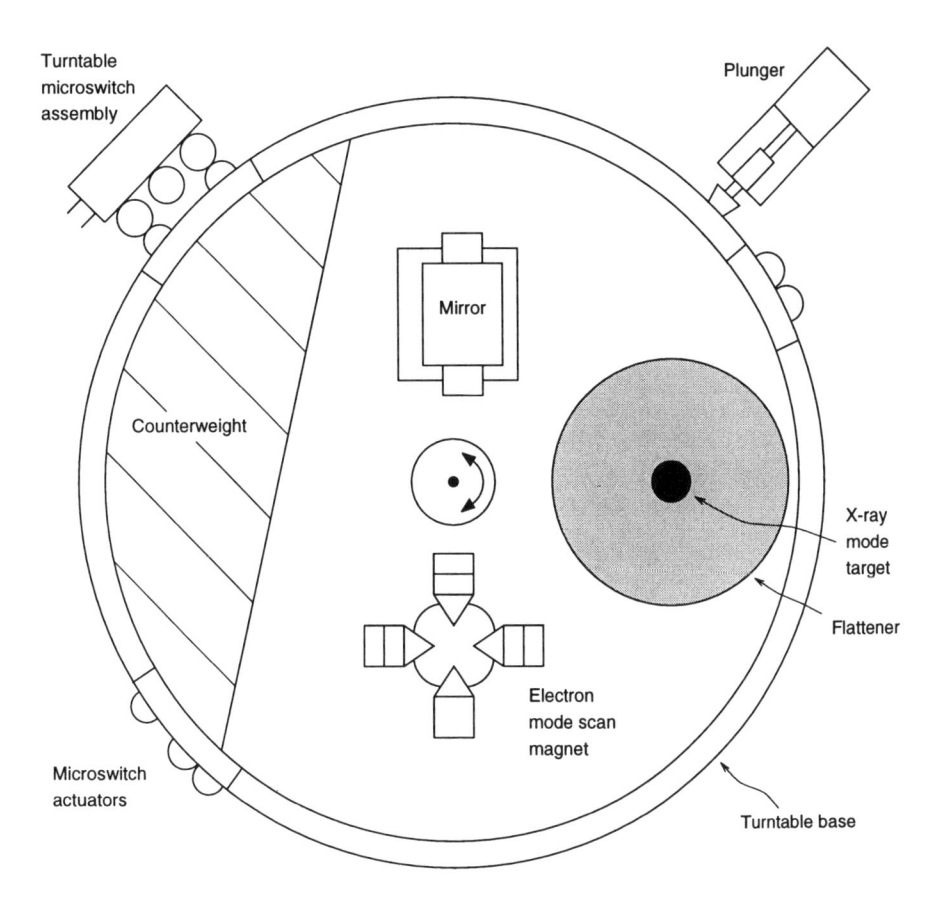

Figure 1. Upper turntable assembly.

Turntable positioning. The Therac-25 turntable design plays an important role in the accidents. The upper turntable (see Figure 1) rotates accessory equipment into the beam path to produce two therapeutic modes: electron mode and photon mode. A third position (called the field light position) involves no beam at all, but rather is used to facilitate correct positioning of the patient. Because the accessories appropriate to each mode are physically attached to the turntable, proper operation of the Therac-25 is heavily dependent on the turntable position, which is monitored by three microswitches.

The raw, highly concentrated accelerator beam is dangerous to living tissue. In electron therapy, the computer controls the beam energy (from 5 to 25 MeV) and current, while scanning magnets are used to spread the beam to a safe, therapeutic concentration. These scanning magnets are mounted on the turntable and moved into proper position by the computer. Similarly, an ion chamber to measure electrons is mounted on the turntable and also moved into position by the computer. In addition, operator-mounted electron trimmers can be used to shape the beam if necessary.

For X-ray (or photon) therapy, only one energy level is available: 25 MeV. Much greater electron-beam current is required for X-ray mode (some 100 times greater than that for electron therapy) [6] to produce comparable output. Such a high dose-rate capability is required because a "beam flattener" is used to produce a uniform treatment field. This flattener, which resembles an inverted ice cream cone, is a very efficient attenuator; thus, to get a reasonable treatment dose rate out of the flattener, a very high input dose rate is required. If the machine should produce a photon beam with the beam flattener not in position, a high output dose to the patient results. This is the basic hazard of dual-mode machines: If the turntable is in the wrong position, the beam flattener will not be in place.

In the Therac-25, the computer is responsible for positioning the turntable (and for checking the turntable position) so that a target, flattening filter, and X-ray ion chamber are directly in the beam path. With the target in place, electron bombardment produces X-rays. The X-ray beam is shaped by the flattening filter and measured by the X-ray ion chamber.

No accelerator beam is expected in the third or field light turntable position. A stainless steel mirror is placed in the beam path and a light simulates the beam. This lets the operator see precisely where the beam will strike the patient and make necessary adjustments before treatment starts. There is no ion chamber in place at this turntable position, since no beam is expected.

Traditionally, electromechanical interlocks have been used on these types of equipment to ensure safety – in this case, to ensure that the turntable and attached equipment are in the correct position when treatment is started. In the Therac-25, software checks were substituted for many of the traditional hardware interlocks.

The operator interface. The description of the operator interface here applies to the version of the software used during the accidents. Changes made as a result of an FDA recall are described later.

The Therac-25 operator controls the machine through a DEC VT100 terminal. In the general case, the operator positions the patient on the treatment table, manually sets the treatment field sizes and gantry rotation, and attaches accessories to the machine. Leaving the treatment room, the operator returns to the console to enter the patient identification, treatment prescription (including mode or beam type, energy level, dose, dose rate, and time), field sizing, gantry rotation, and accessory data. The system then compares the manually set values with those entered at the console. If they match, a *verified* message is displayed and treatment is permitted. If they do not match, treatment is not allowed to proceed until the mismatch is corrected. Figure 2 shows the screen layout.

```
PATIENT NAME    : TEST
TREATMENT MODE : FIX    BEAM TYPE: X    ENERGY (MeV): 25

                          ACTUAL   PRESCRIBED
    UNIT RATE/MINUTE         0        200
    MONITOR UNITS          50 50      200
    TIME (MIN)             0.27       1.00

GANTRY ROTATION (DEG)       0.0         0      VERIFIED
COLLIMATOR ROTATION (DEG)  359.2       359     VERIFIED
COLLIMATOR X (CM)          14.2       14.3     VERIFIED
COLLIMATOR Y (CM)          27.2       27.3     VERIFIED
WEDGE NUMBER                 1          1      VERIFIED
ACCESSORY NUMBER             0          0      VERIFIED

DATE  : 84-OCT-26   SYSTEM : BEAM READY   OP.MODE : TREAT   AUTO
TIME  : 12:55:8     TREAT  : TREAT PAUSE          : X-RAY   173777
OPR ID : T25V02-R03 REASON : OPERATOR     COMMAND :
```

Figure 2. Operator interface screen layout.

When the system was first built, operators complained that it took too long to enter the treatment plan. In response, AECL modified the software before the first unit was installed: Instead of reentering the data at the keyboard, operators could simply use a carriage return to copy the treatment site data [5]. A quick series of carriage returns would thus complete the data entry. This modification was to figure in several of the accidents.

The Therac-25 could shut down in two ways after it detected an error condition. One was a *treatment suspend*, which required a complete machine reset to restart. The other, not so serious, was a *treatment pause*, which only required a single key command to restart the machine. If a *treatment pause* occurred, the operator could press the Ⓟ key to "proceed" and resume treatment quickly and conveniently. The previous treatment parameters remained in effect, and no reset was required. This feature could be invoked a maximum of five times before the machine automatically suspended treatment and required the operator to perform a system reset.

Error messages provided to the operator were cryptic, and some merely consisted of the word MALFUNCTION followed by a number from 1 to 64 denoting an analog/digital channel number. According to an FDA memorandum written after one accident:

> The operator's manual supplied with the machine does not explain nor even address the malfunction codes. The Maintance [sic] Manual lists the various malfunction numbers but gives no explanation. The materials provided give no indication that these malfunctions could place a patient at risk.
>
> The program does not advise the operator if a situation exists wherein the ion chambers used to monitor the patient are saturated, thus are beyond the measurement limits of the instrument. This software package does not appear to contain a safety system to prevent parameters being entered and intermixed that would result in excessive radiation being delivered to the patient under treatment.

An operator involved in one of the accidents testified that she had become insensitive to machine malfunctions. Malfunction messages were commonplace and most did not involve patient safety. Service technicians would fix the problems or the hospital physicist would realign the machine and make it operable again. She said,

> "It was not out of the ordinary for something to stop the machine.... It would often give a low dose rate in which you would turn the machine back on.... They would give messages of low dose rate, V-tilt, H-tilt, and other things; I can't remember all the reasons it would stop, but there was a lot of them."

A radiation therapist at another clinic reported that an average of 40 dose-rate malfunctions, attributed to underdoses, occurred on some days.

The operator further testified that during instruction she had been taught that there were "so many safety mechanisms" that she understood it was virtually impossible to overdose a patient.

Hazard analysis. In March 1983, AECL performed a safety analysis on the Therac-25. This analysis was in the form of a fault tree and apparently excluded the software. According to the final report, the analysis made several assumptions about the computer and its software:

1. Programming errors have been reduced by extensive testing on a hardware simulator and under field conditions on teletherapy units. Any residual software errors are not included in the analysis.
2. Program software does not degrade due to wear, fatigue, or reproduction process.
3. Computer execution errors are caused by faulty hardware components and by "soft" (random) errors induced by alpha particles and electromagnetic noise.

The fault tree resulting from this analysis does appear to include computer failure, although apparently, judging from the basic assumptions above, it considers hardware failures only. For example, in one OR gate leading to the event of getting the wrong energy, a box contains "Computer selects wrong energy," and a probability of 10^{-11} is assigned to this event. For "Computer selects wrong mode," a probability of 4×10^{-9} is given. The report provides no justification of either number.

3 Events

Eleven Therac-25s were installed: five in the United States and six in Canada. Six accidents occurred between 1985 and 1987, when the machine was finally recalled to make extensive design changes. These changes include adding hardware safeguards against software errors.

Related problems were found in the Therac-20 software, but they were not recognized until after the Therac-25 accidents because the Therac-20 includes hardware safety interlocks. Thus, no injuries resulted.

3.1 Kennestone Regional Oncology Center, June 1985

Details of this accident in Marietta, Georgia, are sketchy because it was never investigated. There was no admission that the injury was caused by the Therac-25 until long after the occurrence, despite claims by the patient that she had been injured during treatment, the obvious and severe radiation burns the patient suffered, and the suspicions of the radiation physicist involved.

After undergoing a lumpectomy to remove a malignant breast tumor, a 61-year-old woman was receiving follow-up radiation treatment to nearby lymph nodes on a Therac-25 at the Kennestone facility in Marietta. The Therac-25 had been operating at Kennestone for about six months; other Therac-25s had been operating, apparently without incident, since 1983.

On June 3, 1985, the patient was set up for a 10 MeV electron treatment to the clavicle area. When the machine turned on, she felt a "tremendous force of heat...this red-hot sensation." When the technician came in, she said, "You burned me." The technician replied that that was impossible. Although there were no marks on the patient at the time, the treatment area felt "warm to the touch."

It is unclear exactly when AECL learned about this incident. Tim Still, the Kennestone physicist, said that he contacted AECL to ask if the Therac-25 could operate in electron mode without scanning to spread the beam. Three days later the engineers at AECL called the physicist back to explain that improper scanning was not possible.

In an August 19, 1986 letter from AECL to the FDA, the AECL quality assurance manager said, "In March of 1986 AECL received a lawsuit from the patient involved... This incident was never reported to AECL prior to this date, although some rather odd questions had been posed by Tim Still, the hospital physicist." The physicist at a hospital in Tyler, Texas, where a later accident occurred, reported, "According to Tim Still, the patient filed suit in October 1985 listing the hospital, manufacturer and service organization responsible for the machine. AECL was notified informally about the suit by the hospital, and AECL received official notification of a law suit in November 1985."

Because of the lawsuit (filed November 13, 1985), some AECL administrators must have known about the Marietta accident – although no investigation occurred at this time. FDA memos point to the lack of a mechanism in AECL to follow up reports of suspected accidents [4].

The patient went home, but shortly afterward she developed a reddening and swelling in the center of the treatment area. Her pain had increased to the point that her shoulder "froze," and she experienced spasms. She was admitted to a hospital in Atlanta, but her oncologists continued to send her to Kennestone for Therac-25 treatments. Clinical explanation was sought for the reddening of the skin, which at first her oncologist attributed to her disease or to normal treatment reaction.

About two weeks later, the Kennestone physicist noticed that the patient had a matching reddening on her back as though a burn had gone right through her body, and the swollen area had begun to slough off layers of skin. Her shoulder was immobile, and she was apparently in great pain. It was now obvious that she had a radiation burn, but the hospital and her doctors could provide no satisfactory explanation.

The Kennestone physicist later estimated that the patient received one or two doses of radiation in the 15,000 to 20,000 rad (radiation absorbed dose) range. He did not believe her injury could have been caused by less than 8,000 rads. To understand the magnitude of this, consider that typical single therapeutic doses are in the 200 rad range. Doses of 1,000 rads can be fatal if delivered to the whole body; in fact, 500 rads is the accepted figure for whole-body radiation that will cause death in 50 percent of the cases. The consequences of an overdose to a smaller part of the body depend on the tissue's radio-sensitivity. The director of radiation oncology at the Kennestone facility explained their confusion about the accident as due to the fact that they had never seen an overtreatment of that magnitude before [7].

Eventually, the patient's breast had to be removed because of the radiation burns. Her shoulder and arm were paralyzed, and she was in constant pain. She had suffered a serious radiation burn, but the manufacturer and operators of the machine refused to believe that it could have been caused by the Therac-25. The treatment prescription printout feature of the computer was disabled at the time of the accident, so there was no hardcopy of the treatment data. The lawsuit was eventually settled out of court.

From what we can determine, the accident was not reported to the FDA until *after* further accidents in 1986. The reporting requirements for medical device incidents at that time applied only to equipment manufacturers and importers, not users. The regulations required that manufacturers and importers report deaths, serious injuries, or malfunctions that could result in those consequences, but health-care professionals and institutions were not required to report incidents to manufacturers. The comptroller general of the U.S. Government Accounting Office (GAO), in testimony before Congress on November 6, 1989, expressed great concern about the viability of the incident-reporting regulations in preventing or spotting medical device problems. According to a 1990 GAO study, the FDA knew of less than 1 percent of deaths, serious injuries, or equipment malfunctions that occurred in hospitals [2]. The law was amended in 1990 to require health-care facilities to report incidents to the manufacturer and to the FDA.

At this point, the other Therac-25 users were also unaware that anything untoward had occurred and did not learn about any problems with the machine until after subsequent accidents. Even then, most of their information came through personal communication among themselves.

3.2 Ontario Cancer Foundation, July 1985

The second in this series of accidents occurred about seven weeks after the Kennestone patient was overdosed. At that time, the Therac-25 at the Ontario Cancer Foundation in Hamilton, Ontario (Canada), had been in use for more than six months. On July 26, 1985, a forty-year-old patient came to the clinic for her twenty-fourth Therac-25 treatment for carcinoma of the cervix. The operator activated the machine, but the Therac shut down after five seconds with an HTILT error message. The Therac-25's console display read NO DOSE and indicated a TREATMENT PAUSE.

Since the machine did not suspend and the control display indicated no dose was delivered to the patient, the operator went ahead with a second attempt at treatment by pressing the Ⓟ key (the *proceed* command), expecting the machine to deliver the proper dose this time. This was standard operating procedure, and Therac-25 operators had become accustomed to frequent malfunctions that had no untoward consequences for the patient. Again, the machine shut down in the same manner. The operator repeated this process four times after the original attempt – the display showing NO DOSE delivered to the patient each time. After the fifth pause, the machine went into treatment suspend, and a hospital service technician was called. The technician found nothing wrong with the machine. According to a Therac-25 operator, this scenario also was not unusual.

After the treatment, the patient complained of a burning sensation, described as an "electric tingling shock" to the treatment area in her hip. Six other patients were treated later that day without incident. She came back for further treatment on July 29 and complained of burning, hip pain, and excessive swelling in the region of treatment. The patient was hospitalized for the condition on July 30, and the machine was taken out of service.

AECL was informed of the apparent radiation injury and sent a service engineer to investigate. The U.S. FDA, the then Canadian Radiation Protection Bureau (RPB),[2] and users were informed that there was a problem, although the users claim

---

[2] On April 1, 1986, the Radiation Protection Bureau and the Bureau of Medical Devices were merged to form the Bureau of Radiation and Medical Devices (BRMD).

that they were never informed that a patient injury had occurred. Users were told that they should visually confirm the proper turntable alignment until further notice (which occurred three months later).

The patient died on November 3, 1985, of an extremely virulent cancer. An autopsy revealed the cause of death as the cancer, but it was noted that had she not died, a total hip replacement would have been necessary as a result of the radiation overexposure. An AECL technician later estimated the patient had received between 13,000 and 17,000 rads.

Manufacturer's response. AECL could not reproduce the malfunction that had occurred, but suspected a transient failure in the microswitch used to determine the turntable position. During the investigation of the accident, AECL hardwired the error conditions they assumed were necessary for the malfunction and, as a result, found some turntable positioning design weaknesses and potential mechanical problems.

The computer senses and controls turntable position by reading a 3-bit signal about the status of three microswitches in the turntable switch assembly. Essentially, AECL determined that a 1-bit error in the microswitch codes (which could be caused by a single open-circuit fault on the switch lines) could produce an ambiguous position message to the computer. The problem was exacerbated by the design of the mechanism that extends a plunger to lock the turntable when it is in one of the three cardinal positions: The plunger could be extended when the turntable was way out of position, thus giving a second false position indication. AECL devised a method to indicate turntable position that tolerated a 1-bit error so that the code would still unambiguously reveal correct position with any one microswitch failure.

In addition, AECL altered the software so that the computer checked for "in transit" status of the switches to keep further track of the switch operation and turntable position and to give additional assurance that the switches were working and the turntable was moving.

As a result of these improvements, AECL claimed in its report and correspondence with hospitals that "analysis of the hazard rate of the new solution indicates an improvement over the old system by at least *5 orders of magnitude* [emphasis added]." However, in its final incident report to the FDA, AECL concluded that they "cannot be firm on the exact cause of the accident but can only suspect ...," which underscored their inability to determine the cause of the accident with any certainty. The AECL quality assurance manager testified that they could not reproduce the switch malfunction and that testing of the microswitch was "inconclusive." The similarity of the errant behavior and the patient injuries in this accident and a later one in Yakima, Washington, provide good reason to believe that the Hamilton overdose was probably related to software error rather than to a microswitch failure.

Government and user response. The Hamilton accident resulted in a voluntary recall by AECL, and the FDA termed it a Class II recall. Class II means "a situation in which the use of, or exposure to, a violative product may cause temporary or medically reversible adverse health consequences or where the probability of serious adverse health consequences is remote." The FDA audited AECL's subsequent modifications, and after the modifications were made, the users were told they could return to normal operating procedures.

As a result of the Hamilton accident, the head of advanced X-ray systems in the Canadian RPB, Gordon Symonds, wrote a report that analyzed the design and performance characteristics of the Therac-25 with respect to radiation safety. Besides citing the flawed microswitch, the report faulted both hardware and software components of the Therac's design. It concluded with a list of four modifications to the Therac-25 necessary for compliance with Canada's Radiation Emitting Devices (RED) Act. The RED law, enacted in 1971, gives government officials power to ensure the safety of radiation-emitting devices.

The modifications specified in the Symonds report included redesigning the microswitch and changing the way the computer handled malfunction conditions. In particular, treatment was to be terminated in the event of a dose-rate malfunction, giving a treatment "suspend." This change would have removed the option to proceed simply by pressing the Ⓟ key. The report also made recommendations regarding collimator test procedures and message and command formats. A November 8, 1985 letter, signed by the director of the Canadian RPB, asked that AECL make changes to the Therac-25 based on the Symond's report "to be in compliance with the RED act."

Although, as noted above, AECL did make the microswitch changes, they did not comply with the directive to change the malfunction pause behavior into treatment suspends, instead reducing the maximum number of retries from five to three. According to Symonds, the deficiencies outlined in the RPB letter of November 8 were still pending when the next accident happened five months later.

Immediately after the Hamilton accident, the Ontario Cancer Foundation hired an independent consultant to investigate. He concluded in a September 1985 report that an independent system (beside the computer) was needed to verify the turntable position and suggested the use of a potentiometer. The RPB wrote a letter to AECL in November 1985 requesting that AECL install such an independent interlock on the Therac-25. Also, in January 1986, AECL received a letter from the attorney representing the Hamilton clinic. The letter said that there had been continuing problems with the turntable, including four incidents at Hamilton, and requested the installation of an independent system (potentiometer) to verify the turntable position. AECL did not comply: No independent interlock was installed by AECL on the Therac-25s at this time. The Hamilton Clinic, however, decided to install one themselves on their machine.

3.3 Yakima Valley Memorial Hospital, December 1985

In this accident, as in the Kennestone overdose, machine malfunction was not acknowledged until after later accidents were understood.

The Therac-25 at Yakima, Washington, had been modified by AECL in September 1985 in response to the overdose at Hamilton. During December 1985, a woman treated with the Therac-25 developed erythema (excessive reddening of the skin) in a parallel striped pattern on her right hip. Despite this, she continued to be treated by the Therac-25, as the cause of her reaction was not determined to be abnormal until January 1986. On January 6, her treatments were completed.

The staff monitored the skin reaction closely and attempted to find possible causes. The open slots in the blocking trays in the Therac-25 could have produced such a striped pattern, but by the time the skin reaction was determined to be abnormal, the blocking trays had been discarded, so the blocking arrangement and tray striping orientation could not be reproduced. A reaction to chemotherapy was ruled out because that should have produced reactions at the other treatment sites and would not have produced stripes. When the doctors discovered that the woman slept with a heating pad, they thought maybe the burn pattern had been caused by the parallel wires that deliver the heat in such pads. The staff X-rayed the heating pad but discovered that the wire pattern did not correspond to the erythema pattern on the patient's hip.

The hospital staff sent a letter to AECL on January 31, and they also spoke on the phone with the AECL technical support supervisor. On February 24, the AECL technical support supervisor sent a written response to the director of radiation therapy at Yakima saying, "After careful consideration we are of the opinion that this damage could not have been produced by any malfunction of the Therac-25 or by any operator error." The letter goes on to support this opinion by listing two pages of technical reasons why an overdose by the Therac-25 was impossible, along with the additional argument that there have "apparently been no other instances of similar damage to this or other patients." The letter ends, "In closing, I wish to advise that this matter has been brought to the attention of our Hazards Committee as is normal practice."

The hospital staff eventually ascribed the patient's skin reaction to "cause unknown." In a report written on this first Yakima incident after another Yakima overdose a year later, the medical physicist involved wrote:

> At that time, we did not believe that [the patient] was overdosed because the manufacturer had installed additional hardware and software safety devices to the accelerator.
>
> In a letter from the manufacturer dated 16-Sep-85, it is stated that "Analysis of the hazard rate resulting from these modifications indicates an improvement of at least five orders of magnitude"! With such an improvement in safety (10,000,000%) we did not believe that there could have been any accelerator malfunction. These modifications to the accelerator were completed on 5,6-Sep-85.

Even with fairly sophisticated physics support, the hospital staff, as users, did not have the ability to investigate the possibility of machine malfunction further. They were not aware of any other incidents and, in fact, were told that there had been none, so there was no reason for them to pursue the matter. No further investigation of this incident was done by the manufacturer or by any government agencies (who did not know about it).

About a year later (February 1987), after the second Yakima overdose led the hospital staff to suspect that this first injury had been due to a Therac-25 fault, the staff investigated and found that the first overdose victim had a chronic skin ulcer, tissue necrosis (death) under the skin, and was in continual pain. The damage was surgically repaired, skin grafts were made, and the symptoms relieved. The patient is alive today with minor disability and some scarring related to the overdose. The hospital staff concluded that the dose accidentally delivered in the first accident must have been much lower than in the second, as the reaction was significantly less intense and necrosis did not develop until six or eight months after exposure. Some other factors related to the place on the body where the overdose occurred also kept her from having more significant problems.

3.4 East Texas Cancer Center, March 1986

More is known about the Tyler, Texas, accidents than the others because of the diligence of the Tyler hospital physicist, Fritz Hager, without whose efforts the understanding of the software problems may have been delayed even further.

The Therac-25 had been at the East Texas Cancer Center (ETCC) for two years before the first serious accident, and more than 500 patients had been treated. On March 21, 1986, a male patient came into ETCC for his ninth treatment on the Therac-25, one of a series prescribed as followup to the removal of a tumor from his back.

This treatment was to be a 22 MeV electron beam treatment of 180 rads on the upper back and a little to the left of his spine, for a total of 6,000 rads over six and a half weeks. He was taken into the treatment room and placed face down on the treatment table. The operator then left the treatment room, closed the door, and sat at the control terminal.

The operator had held this job for some time, and her typing efficiency had increased with experience. She could quickly enter prescription data and change it conveniently with the Therac's editing features. She entered the patient's prescription data quickly, then noticed that she had typed "x" (for X-ray) when she had intended "e" (for electron) mode. This was a common mistake as most of the treatments involved X-rays, and she had gotten used to typing this. The mistake was easy to fix; she merely used the ↑ key to edit the mode entry.

Because the other parameters she had entered were correct, she hit the return key several times and left their values unchanged. She reached the bottom of the screen, where it was indicated that the parameters had been VERIFIED and the terminal displayed BEAM READY, as expected. She hit the one-key command, Ⓑ for *beam on*, to begin the treatment. After a moment, the machine shut down and the console displayed the message MALFUNCTION 54. The machine also displayed a TREATMENT PAUSE, indicating a problem of low priority. The sheet on the side of the machine explained that this malfunction was a "dose input 2" error. The ETCC did not have any other information available in its instruction manual or other Therac-25 documentation to explain the meaning of MALFUNCTION 54. An AECL technician later testified that "dose input 2" meant that a dose had been delivered that was either too high or too low. The messages had been expected to be used only during internal company development.

The machine showed a substantial underdose on its dose monitor display – 6 monitor units delivered whereas the operator had requested 202 monitor units. She was accustomed to the quirks of the machine, which would frequently stop or delay treatment; in the past, the only consequences had been inconvenience. She immediately took the normal action when the machine merely paused, which was to hit the Ⓟ key to proceed with the treatment. The machine promptly shut down with the same MALFUNCTION 54 error and the same underdose shown by the dosimetry.

The operator was isolated from the patient, since the machine apparatus was inside a shielded room of its own. The only way that the operator could be alerted to patient difficulty was through audio and video monitors. On this day, the video display was unplugged and the audio monitor was broken.

After the first attempt to treat him, the patient said that he felt as if he had received an electric shock or that someone had poured hot coffee on his back: He felt a thump and heat and heard a buzzing sound from the equipment. Since this was his ninth treatment, he knew that this was not normal. He began to get up from the treatment table to go for help. It was at this moment that the operator hit the Ⓟ key to proceed with the treatment. The patient said that he felt like his arm was being shocked by electricity and that his hand was leaving his body. He went to the treatment room door and pounded on it. The operator was shocked and immediately opened the door for him. He appeared visibly shaken and upset.

The patient was immediately examined by a physician, who observed intense reddening of the treatment area, but suspected nothing more serious than electric shock. The patient was discharged and sent home with instructions to return if he suffered any further reactions. The hospital physicist was called in, and he found the machine calibration within specifications. The meaning of the malfunction message was not understood. The machine was then used to treat patients for the rest of the day.

In actuality, but unknown to anyone at that time, the patient had received a massive overdose, concentrated in the center of the treatment location. After-the-fact simulations of the accident revealed possible doses of 16,500 to 25,000 rads in less than 1 second over an area of about 1 cm.

Over the weeks following the accident, the patient continued to have pain in his neck and shoulder. He lost the function of his left arm and had periodic bouts of nausea and vomiting. He was eventually hospitalized for radiation-induced myelitis of the cervical cord causing paralysis of his left arm and both legs, left vocal cord paralysis (which left him unable to speak), neurogenic bowel and bladder, and paralysis of the left diaphragm. He also had a lesion on his left lung and recurrent herpes simplex skin infections. He died from complications of the overdose five months after the accident.

User and manufacturer response. The Therac-25 was shut down for testing the day after this accident. One local AECL engineer and one from the home office in Canada came to ETCC to investigate. They spent a day running the machine through tests, but could not reproduce a Malfunction 54. The AECL engineer from the home office reportedly explained that it was not possible for the Therac-25 to overdose a patient. The ETCC physicist claims that he asked AECL at this time if there were any other reports of radiation overexposure and that AECL personnel (including the quality assurance manager) told him that AECL knew of no accidents involving radiation overexposure by the Therac-25. This seems odd since AECL was surely at least aware of the Hamilton accident that had occurred seven months before and the Yakima accident, and, even by their account, learned of the Georgia law suit around this time (which had been filed four months earlier). The AECL engineers then suggested that an electrical problem might have caused the problem.

The electric shock theory was checked out thoroughly by an independent engineering firm. The final report indicated that there was no electrical grounding problem in the machine, and it did not appear capable of giving a patient an electrical shock. The ETCC physicist checked the calibration of the Therac-25 and found it to be satisfactory. He put the machine back into service on April 7, 1986, convinced that it was performing properly.

3.5 East Texas Cancer Center, April 1986

Three weeks later, on April 11, 1986, another male patient was scheduled to receive an electron treatment at ETCC for a skin cancer on the side of his face. The prescription was for 10 MeV. The same technician who had treated the first Tyler accident victim prepared this patient for treatment. Much of what follows is from the operator's deposition.

As with her former patient, she entered the prescription data and then noticed an error in the mode. Again she used the edit (↑) key to change the mode from X-ray to electron. After she finished editing, she pressed the RETURN key several times to place the cursor on the bottom of the screen. She saw the BEAM READY message displayed and turned the beam on.

Within a few seconds the machine shut down, making a loud noise audible via the (now working) intercom. The display showed MALFUNCTION 54 again. The operator rushed into the treatment room, hearing her patient moaning for help. He began to remove the tape that had held his head in position and said something was wrong. She asked him what he felt, and he replied, "fire" on the side of his face. She immediately went to the hospital physicist and told him that another patient appeared to have been burned. Asked by the physicist to described what had happened, the patient explained that something had hit him on the side of the face, he saw a flash of light, and he heard a sizzling sound reminiscent of frying eggs. He was very agitated and asked, "What happened to me, what happened to me?"

This patient died from the overdose on May 1, 1986, three weeks after the accident. He had disorientation, which progressed to coma, fever to 104°F, and neurological damage. An autopsy showed an acute high-dose radiation injury to the right temporal lobe of the brain and the brain stem.

User and manufacturer response. After this second Tyler accident, the ETCC physicist immediately took the machine out of service and called AECL to alert them to this second apparent overexposure. The physicist then began a careful investigation of his own. He worked with the operator, who remembered exactly what she had done on this occasion. After a great deal of effort, they were eventually able to elicit the MALFUNCTION 54 message. They determined that data entry speed during editing was the key factor in producing the error condition: If the prescription data was edited at a fast pace (as is natural for someone who has repeated the procedure a large number of times), the overdose occurred. It took some practice before the physicist could repeat the procedure rapidly enough to elicit the MALFUNCTION 54 message at will.

The next day, an engineer from AECL called and said that he could not reproduce the error. After the ETCC physicist explained that the procedure had to be performed quite rapidly, AECL could finally produce a similar malfunction on its own machine. Two days after the accident, AECL said it had measured the dosage (at the center of the field) to be 25,000 rads. An AECL engineer explained that the frying sound heard by the patients was the ion chambers being saturated.

In one law suit that resulted from the Tyler accidents, the AECL quality control manager testified that a "cursor up" problem had been found in the service (maintenance) mode at other clinics in February or March of 1985 and also in the summer of 1985. Both times, AECL thought that the software problems had been fixed. There is no way to determine whether there is any relationship between these problems and the Tyler accidents.

Related Therac-20 problems. The software for both the Therac-25 and Therac-20 "evolved" from the Therac-6 software. Additional functions had to be added because the Therac-20 (and Therac-25) operate in both X-ray and electron mode, while the Therac-6 has only X-ray mode. CGR modified the software for the Therac-20 to handle the dual modes. When the Therac-25 development began, AECL engineers adapted the software from the Therac-6, but they also borrowed software routines from the Therac-20 to handle electron mode, which was allowed under their cooperative agreements.

After the second Tyler, Texas, accident, a physicist at the University of Chicago Joint Center for Radiation Therapy heard about the Therac-25 software problem and decided to find out whether the same thing could happen with the Therac-20. At first, the physicist was unable to reproduce the error on his machine, but two months later he found the link.

The Therac-20 at the University of Chicago is used to teach students in a radiation therapy school conducted by the center. The center's physicist, Frank Borger, noticed that whenever a new class of students started using the Therac-20, fuses and breakers on the machine tripped, shutting down the unit. These failures, which had been occurring ever since the school had acquired the machine, might happen three times a week while new students operated the machine and then disappear for months. Borger determined that new students make many different types of mistakes and use "creative methods" of editing parameters on the console. Through experimentation, he found that certain editing sequences correlated with blown fuses and determined that the same computer bug (as in the Therac-25 software) was responsible. The physicist notified the FDA, which notified Therac-20 users [3].

The software error is just a nuisance on the Therac-20 because this machine has independent hardware protective circuits for monitoring the electron beam scanning. The protective circuits do not allow the beam to turn on, so there is no danger of radiation exposure to a patient. While the Therac-20 relies on mechanical interlocks for monitoring the machine, the Therac-25 relies largely on software.

The software "bug". A lesson to be learned from the Therac-25 story is that focusing on particular software "bugs" is not the way to make a safe system. Virtually all complex software can be made to behave in an unexpected fashion under some conditions. The basic mistakes here involved poor software engineering practices and building a machine that relies on the software for safe operation. Furthermore, the particular coding error is not as important as the general unsafe design of the software overall. Examining the part of the code blamed for the Tyler accidents is instructive, however, in demonstrating the overall software design flaws. First the software design is described and then the errors believed to be involved in the Tyler accidents and perhaps others.

Therac-25 software development and design. AECL claims proprietary rights to its software design. However, from voluminous documentation regarding the accidents, the repairs, and the eventual design changes, we can build a rough picture of it.

The software is responsible for monitoring the machine status, accepting input about the treatment desired, and setting the machine up for this treatment. It turns the beam on in response to an operator command (assuming that certain operational checks on the status of the physical machine are satisfied) and also turns the beam off when treatment is completed, when an operator commands it, or when a malfunction is detected. The operator can print out hardcopy versions of the CRT display or machine setup parameters.

The treatment unit has an interlock system designed to remove power to the unit when there is a hardware malfunction. The computer monitors this interlock system and provides diagnostic messages. Depending on the fault, the computer either prevents a treatment from being started or, if the treatment is in progress, creates a pause or a suspension of the treatment.

There are two basic operational modes: treatment mode and service mode. Treatment mode controls the normal treatment process. In service mode, the unit can be operated with some of the operational and treatment interlocks bypassed, and additional operational commands and characteristics may be selected. Service mode is entered only through the use of a password at the service keyboard.

The manufacturer describes the Therac-25 software as having a stand-alone, real-time treatment operating system. The system does not use a standard operating system or executive. Rather, the real-time executive was written especially for the Therac-25 and runs on a 32K PDP-11/23. Cycles are allocated to the critical and noncritical tasks using a preemptive scheduler.

The software, written in PDP-11 assembly language, has four major components: stored data, a scheduler, a set of critical and noncritical tasks, and interrupt services. The stored data includes calibration parameters for the accelerator setup as well as patient-treatment data. The interrupt routines include

- A clock interrupt service routine
- A scanning interrupt service routine
- Traps (for software overflow and computer hardware generated interrupts)
- Power up (initiated at power up to initialize the system and pass control to the scheduler)
- Treatment console screen interrupt handler
- Treatment console keyboard interrupt handler
- Service printer interrupt handler
- Service keyboard interrupt handler

The scheduler controls the sequencing of all noninterrupt events and coordinates all concurrent processes. Tasks are initiated every 0.1 second, with the critical tasks executed first and the noncritical tasks executed in any remaining cycle time. Critical tasks include the following:

- The treatment monitor (Treat) directs and monitors patient setup and treatment via eight operating phases. These are called as subroutines, depending on the value of the Tphase control variable. Following the execution of a particular subroutine, Treat reschedules itself. Treat interacts with the keyboard processing task, which handles operator console communication. The prescription data is cross-checked and verified by other tasks (such as keyboard processor or parameter setup sensor) that inform the treatment task of the verification status via shared variables.
- The servo task controls gun emission, dose rate (pulse repetition frequency), symmetry (beam steering), and machine motions. The servo task also sets up the machine parameters and monitors the beam-tilt-error and the flatness-error interlocks.
- The housekeeper task takes care of system status interlocks and limit checks and displays appropriate messages on the CRT display. It decodes some information and checks the setup verification.

Noncritical tasks include

- Checksum processor (scheduled to run periodically)
- Treatment console keyboard processor (scheduled to run only if it is called by other tasks or by keyboard interrupts). This task acts as the communication interface between the other software and the operator.
- Treatment console screen processor (run periodically). This task lays out appropriate record formats for either CRT displays or hard copies.
- Service keyboard processor (run on demand). This task arbitrates non-treatment-related communication between the therapy system and the operator.
- Snapshot (run periodically by the scheduler). Snapshot captures preselected parameter values and is called by the treatment task at the end of a treatment.
- Hand control processor (run periodically).

– Calibration processor. This task is responsible for a package of tasks that let the operator examine and change system setup parameters and interlock limits.

It is clear from the AECL documentation on the modifications that the software allows concurrent access to shared memory, that there is no real synchronization aside from data that are stored in shared variables, and that the "test" and "set" for such variables are not indivisible operations. Race conditions resulting from this implementation of multitasking played an important part in the accidents.

Specific design errors. The following explanation of the specific software problems found at this time is taken from the description AECL provided to the FDA, but clarified somewhat. The description leaves some unanswered questions, but it is the best that can be done with the information available.

The treatment monitor task (Treat) controls the various phases of treatment by executing its eight subroutines. The treatment phase indicator variable (Tphase) is used to determine which subroutine should be executed (Figure 3). Following the execution of a particular subroutine, Treat reschedules itself.

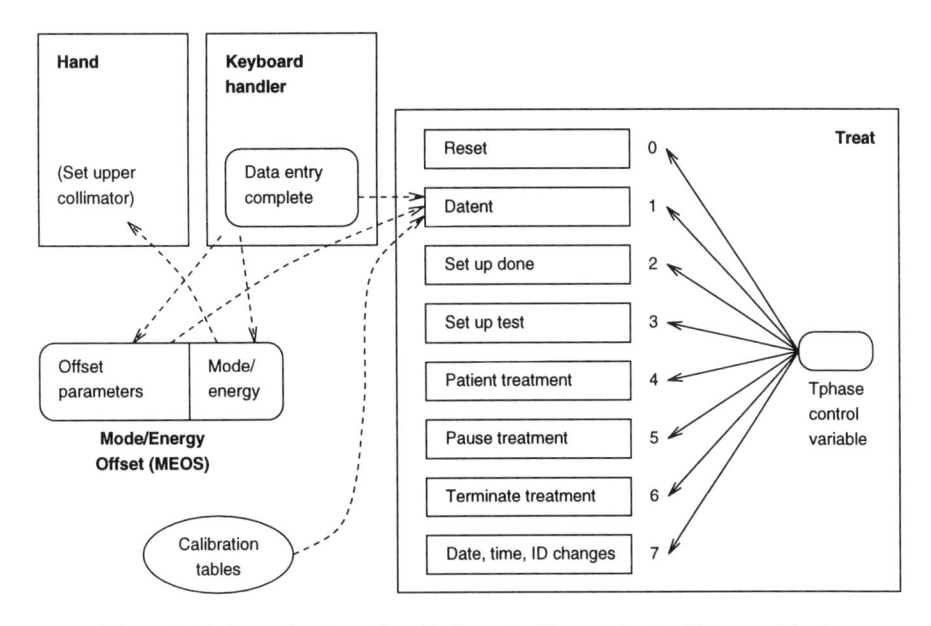

Figure 3. Tasks and subroutines in the code blamed for the Tyler accidents.

One of Treat's subroutines, called Datent (data entry), communicates with the keyboard handler task (a task that runs concurrently with Treat) via a shared variable (Data Entry Complete flag) to determine whether the prescription data has been entered. The keyboard handler recognizes the completion of data entry and changes the Data Entry Complete variable to denote this. Once this variable is set, the Datent subroutine detects the variable's change in status and changes the value of Tphase from 1 (Datent) to 3 (Set Up Test). In this case, the Datent subroutine exits back to the Treat subroutine, which will reschedule itself and begin execution of the Set Up Test subroutine. If the Data Entry Complete variable has not been set, Datent leaves the value of Tphase unchanged and exits back to Treat's mainline. Treat will then reschedule itself, essentially rescheduling the Datent subroutine.

The command line at the lower right-hand corner of the screen (see Figure 2) is the cursor's normal position when the operator has completed all the necessary changes to the prescription. Prescription editing is signified by moving the cursor off the command line. As the program was originally designed, the Data Entry Complete variable by itself is not sufficient because it does not ensure that the cursor is located on the command line; under the right circumstances, the data entry phase can be exited before all edit changes are made on the screen.

The keyboard handler parses the mode and energy level specified by the operator and places an encoded result in another shared variable, the 2-byte Mode/Energy Offset variable (MEOS). The low-order byte of this variable is used by another task (Hand) to set the collimator/turntable to the proper position for the selected mode and energy. The high-order byte of the MEOS variable is used by Datent to set several operating parameters.

Initially, the data-entry process forces the operator to enter the mode and energy except when the photon mode is selected, in which case the energy defaults to 25 MeV. The operator can later edit the mode and energy separately. If the keyboard handler sets the Data Entry Complete flag before the operator changes the data in MEOS, Datent will not detect the changes because it has already exited and will not be reentered again. The upper collimator (turntable), on the other hand, is set to the position dictated by the low-order byte of MEOS by another concurrently running task (Hand) and can therefore be inconsistent with the parameters set in accordance with the information in the high-order byte. The software appears to contain no checks to detect such an incompatibility.

The first thing Datent does when it is entered is to check whether the keyboard handler has set the mode and energy in MEOS. If so, it uses the high-order byte to index into a table of preset operating parameters and places them in the digital-to-analog output table. The contents of this output table are transferred to the digital-to-analog converter during the next clock cycle. Once the parameters are all set, Datent calls the subroutine Magnet, which sets the bending magnets. The following shows a simplified pseudocode description of relevant parts of the software:

 Datent:
   if mode/energy specified **then**
    begin
     calculate table index
     repeat
      fetch parameter
      output parameter
      point to next parameter
     until all parameters set

>   **call** Magnet
>   **if** mode/energy changed **then return**
>   **end**
>   **if** data entry is complete **then** set Tphase to 3
>   **if** data entry is not complete **then**
>   **if** reset command entered **then** set Tphase to 0
>   **return**

Magnet:
>   Set bending magnet flag
>   **repeat**
>   Set next magnet
>   **call** Ptime
>   **if** mode/energy has changed, **then** exit
>   **until** all magnets are set
>   **return**

Ptime:
>   **repeat**
>   **if** bending magnet flag is set **then**
>   **if** editing taking place **then**
>   **if** mode/energy has changed **then** exit
>   **until** hysteresis delay has expired
>   Clear bending magnet flag
>   **return**

Setting the bending magnets takes about eight seconds. Magnet calls a subroutine called Ptime to introduce a time delay. Since several magnets need to be set, Ptime is entered and exited several times. A flag to indicate that the bending magnets are being set is initialized upon entry to the Magnet subroutine and cleared at the end of Ptime. Furthermore, Ptime checks a shared variable, set by the keyboard handler, that indicates the presence of any editing requests. If there are edits, then Ptime clears the bending magnet variable and exits to Magnet, which then exits to Datent. But the edit change variable is checked by Ptime only if the bending magnet flag is set. Because Ptime clears it during its first execution, any edits performed during each succeeding pass through Ptime will not be recognized. Thus, an edit change of the mode or energy, although reflected on the operator's screen and the mode/energy offset variable, will not be sensed by Datent so it can index the appropriate calibration tables for the machine parameters.

Recall that the Tyler error occurred when the operator made an entry indicating the mode and energy, went to the command line, then moved the cursor up to change the mode or energy and returned to the command line all within eight seconds. Because the magnet setting takes about eight seconds and Magnet does not recognize edits after the first execution of Ptime, the editing had been completed by the return to Datent, which never detected that it had occurred. Part of the problem was fixed after the accident by clearing the bending magnet variable at the end of Magnet (after *all* the magnets have been set) instead of at the end of Ptime.

But this is not the only problem. Upon exit from the Magnet subroutine, the data entry subroutine (Datent) checks the Data Entry Complete variable. If it indicates that data entry is complete, Datent sets Tphase to 3 and Datent is not entered again. If it is not set, Datent leaves Tphase unchanged, which means it will eventually be rescheduled. But the Data Entry Complete variable only indicates that the cursor has been down to the command line, not that it is still there. A potential race condition is set up. To fix this, AECL introduced another shared variable controlled by the keyboard handler task that indicates the cursor is not positioned on the command line. If this variable is set, then prescription entry is still in progress and the value of Tphase is left unchanged.

The government and user response. The FDA does not approve each new medical device on the market: All medical devices go through a classification process that determines the level of FDA approval necessary. Medical accelerators follow a procedure called pre-market notification before commercial distribution. In this process, the firm must establish that the product is substantially equivalent in safety and effectiveness to a product already on the market. If that cannot be done to the FDA's satisfaction, a pre-market approval is required. For the Therac-25, the FDA required only a pre-market notification. After the Therac-25 accidents, new procedures for approval of software-controlled devices were adopted.

The agency is basically reactive to problems and requires manufacturers to report serious ones. Once a problem is identified in a radiation-emitting product, the FDA is responsible for approving the corrective action plan (CAP).

The first reports of the Tyler incidents came to the FDA from the State of Texas Health Department, and this triggered FDA action. The FDA investigation was well under way when AECL produced a medical device report to discuss the details of the radiation overexposures at Tyler. The FDA declared the Therac-25 defective under the Radiation Control for Health and Safety Act and ordered the firm to notify all purchasers, investigate the problem, determine a solution, and submit a corrective action plan for FDA approval.

The final CAP consisted of more than twenty changes to the system hardware and software, plus modifications to the system documentation and manuals. Some of these changes were unrelated to the specific accidents, but were improvements to the general safety of the machine. The full CAP implementation, including an extensive safety analysis, was not complete until more than two years after the Tyler accidents.

AECL made their accident report to the FDA on April 15, 1986. On that same date, AECL sent out a letter to each Therac user recommending a temporary "fix" to the machine that would allow continued clinical use. The letter (shown in its complete form) stated:

SUBJECT: CHANGE IN OPERATING PROCEDURES FOR THE THERAC 25 LINEAR ACCELERATOR

Effective immediately, and until further notice, the key used for moving the cursor back through the prescription sequence (i.e., cursor 'UP' inscribed with an upward pointing arrow) must not be used for editing or any other purpose.

To avoid accidental use of this key, the key cap must be removed and the switch contacts fixed in the open position with electrical tape or other insulating material. For assistance with the latter you should contact your local AECL service representative.

Disabling this key means that if any prescription data entered is incorrect then a 'R' reset command must be used and the whole prescription reentered.

For those users of the Multiport option it also means that editing of dose rate, dose and time will not be possible between ports.

On May 2, 1986, the FDA declared the Therac defective, demanded a CAP, and required renotification of all the Therac customers. In the letter from the FDA to AECL, the Director of Compliance, Center for Devices and Radiological Health, wrote:

We have reviewed [AECL's] April 15 letter to purchasers and have concluded that it does not satisfy the requirements for notification to purchasers of a defect in an electronic product. Specifically, it does not describe the defect nor the hazards associated with it. The letter does not provide any reason for disabling the cursor key and the tone is not commensurate with the urgency for doing so. In fact, the letter implies the inconvenience to operators outweighs the need to disable the key. We request that you immediately renotify purchasers.

AECL promptly made a new notice to users and also requested an extension to produce a CAP. The FDA granted this request.

About this time, the Therac-25 users created a user's group and held their first meeting at the annual conference of the American Association of Physicists in Medicine. At the meeting, users discussed the Tyler accident and heard an AECL representative present the company's plans for responding to it. AECL promised to send a letter to all users detailing the CAP.

Several users described additional hardware safety features that they had added to their own machines to provide additional protection. An interlock (that checked gun current values), which the Vancouver clinic had previously added to their Therac-25, was labeled as redundant by AECL; the users disagreed. There were further discussions of poor design and other problems that caused a 10- to 30-percent underdosing in both modes.

The meeting notes said

There was a general complaint by all users present about the lack of information propagation. The users were not happy about receiving incomplete information. The AECL representative countered by stating that AECL does not wish to spread rumors and that AECL has no policy to 'keep things quiet'. The consensus among the users was that an improvement was necessary.

After the first user's group meeting, there were two user's group newsletters. The first, dated fall 1986, contained letters from Tim Still, the Kennestone physicist, who complained about what he considered to be eight major problems he had experienced with the Therac-25. These problems included poor screen-refresh subroutines that leave trash and erroneous information on the operator console and some tape-loading problems upon startup that he discovered involved the use of "phantom tables" to trigger the interlock system in the event of a load failure instead of using a checksum. He asked the question, "Is programming safety relying too much on the software interlock routines?" The second user's group newsletter, in December 1986, further discussed the implications of the phantom table problem.

AECL produced its first CAP on June 13, 1986. The FDA asked for changes and additional information about the software, including a software test plan. AECL responded on September 26 with several documents describing the software and its modifications but no test plan. They explained how the Therac-25 software evolved from the Therac-6 software and stated that "no single test plan and report exists for the software since both hardware and software were tested and exercised separately and together over many years." AECL concluded that the current CAP improved "machine safety by many orders of magnitude and virtually eliminates the possibility of lethal doses as delivered in the Tyler incident."

An FDA internal memo dated October 20 commented on these AECL submissions, raising several concerns:

> Unfortunately, the AECL response also seems to point out an apparent lack of documentation on software specifications and a software test plan.
>
> ...concerns include the question of previous knowledge of problems by AECL, the apparent paucity of software quality assurance at the manufacturing facility, and possible warnings and information dissemination to others of the generic type problems.
>
> ...As mentioned in my first review, there is some confusion on whether the manufacturer should have been aware of the software problems prior to the ARO's [Accidental Radiation Overdoses] in Texas. AECL had received official notification of a law suit in November 1985 from a patient claiming accidental over-exposure from a Therac-25 in Marietta, Georgia.... If knowledge of these software deficiencies were known beforehand, what would be the FDA's posture in this case?
>
> ...The materials submitted by the manufacturer have not been in sufficient detail and clarity to ensure an adequate software quality assurance program currently exists. For example, a response has not been provided with respect to the software part of the CAP to the CDRH's [FDA Center for Devices and Radiological Health] request for documentation on the revised requirements and specifications for the new software. In addition, an analysis has not been provided, as requested, on the interaction with

other portions of the software to demonstrate the corrected software does not adversely affect other software functions.

The July 23 letter from the CDRH requested a documented test plan including several specific pieces of information identified in the letter. This request has been ignored up to this point by the manufacturer. Considering the ramifications of the current software problem, changes in software QA attitudes are needed at AECL.

AECL also planned to retain the malfunction codes, but the FDA required better warnings for the operators. Furthermore, AECL had not planned on any quality assurance testing to ensure exact copying of software, but the FDA insisted on it. The FDA further requested assurances that rigorous testing would become a standard part of AECL's software modification procedures.

We also expressed our concern that you did not intend to perform the protocol to future modifications to software. We believe that the rigorous testing must be performed each time a modification is made in order to ensure the modification does not adversely affect the safety of the system.

AECL was also asked to draw up an installation test plan to ensure that both hardware and software changes perform as designed when installed.

AECL submitted CAP Revision 2 and supporting documentation on December 22, 1986. They changed the CAP to have dose malfunctions suspend treatment and included a plan for meaningful error messages and highlighted dose error messages. They also expanded their diagrams of software modifications and expanded their test plan to cover hardware and software.

3.6 Yakima Valley Memorial Hospital, January 1987

On Saturday, January 17, 1987, the second patient of the day was to be treated for a carcinoma. This patient was to receive two film verification exposures of 4 and 3 rads plus a 79-rad photon treatment (for a total exposure of 86 rads.)

Film was placed under the patient and 4 rads were administered. After the machine paused to open the collimator jaws further, the second exposure of 3 rads was administered. The machine paused again.

The operator entered the treatment room to remove the film and verify the patient's precise position. He used the hand control in the treatment room to rotate the turntable to the field light position, which allowed him to check the alignment of the machine with respect to the patient's body in order to verify proper beam position. He then either pressed the *set* button on the hand control or left the room and typed a SET command at the console to return the turntable to the proper position for treatment; there is some confusion as to exactly what transpired. When he left the room, he forgot to remove the film from underneath the patient. The console displayed "beam ready," and the operator hit the Ⓑ key to turn the beam on.

The beam came on, but the console displayed no dose or dose rate. After five or six seconds, the unit shut down with a pause and displayed a message. The message "may have disappeared quickly"; the operator was unclear on this point. However, since the machine merely paused, he was able to push the Ⓟ key to proceed with treatment.

The machine paused again, this time displaying FLATNESS on the reason line. The operator heard the patient say something over the intercom, but could not understand him. He went into the room to speak with the patient, who reported "feeling a burning sensation" in the chest. The console displayed only the total dose of the two film exposures (7 rads) and nothing more.

Later in the day, the patient developed a skin burn over the entire treatment area. Four days later, the redness developed a striped pattern matching the slots in the blocking tray. The striped pattern was similar to the burn a year earlier at this same hospital, which had first been ascribed to a heating pad and later officially labeled by the hospital as "cause unknown."

AECL began an investigation, and users were told to confirm the turntable position visually before turning on the beam. All tests run by the AECL engineers indicated that the machine was working perfectly. From the information that had been gathered to that point, it was suspected that the electron beam had come on when the turntable was in the field light position. But the investigators could not reproduce the fault condition.

On the following Thursday, AECL sent in an engineer from Ottawa to investigate. The hospital physicist had, in the meantime, run some tests himself. He placed a film in the Therac's beam and then ran two exposures of X-ray parameters with the turntable in field light position. The film appeared to match the film that was left (by mistake) under the patient during the accident.

After a week of checking the hardware, AECL determined that the "incorrect machine operation was probably not caused by hardware alone." After checking the software, AECL engineers discovered a flaw (described below) that could explain the erroneous behavior. The coding problems explaining this accident are completely different from those associated with the Tyler accidents.

Preliminary dose measurements by AECL indicated that the dose delivered under these conditions – that is, when the turntable is in the field light position – is on the order of 4,000 to 5,000 rads. After two attempts, the patient could have received 8,000 to 10,000 instead of the 86 rads prescribed. AECL again called users on January 26 (nine days after the accident) and gave them detailed instructions on how to avoid this problem. In an FDA internal report on the accident, the AECL quality assurance manager investigating the problem is quoted as saying that the software and hardware changes to be retrofitted following the Tyler accident nine months earlier (but which had not yet been installed) would have prevented the Yakima accident.

The patient died in April from complications related to the overdose. He had a terminal form of cancer, but a lawsuit was initiated by his survivors alleging that he died sooner than he would have and endured unnecessary pain and suffering due to the radiation overdose. The suit, like all the others, was settled out of court.

The Yakima software "bug". The software problem for the second Yakima accident is fairly well-established and different from that implicated in the Tyler accidents. There is no way to determine what particular software design errors were related to the Kennestone, Hamilton, and first Yakima accidents. Given the unsafe programming practices exhibited in the code, unknown race conditions or errors could have been responsible for them. There is speculation, however, that the Hamilton accident was the same as this second Yakima overdose. In a report of a conference call on January 26, 1987, between the AECL quality assurance manager and Ed Miller of the FDA discussing the Yakima accident, Miller notes

> This situation probably occurred in the Hamilton, Ontario accident a couple of years ago. It was not discovered at that time and the cause was attributed to intermittent interlock failure. The subsequent recall of the multiple microswitch logic network did not really solve the problem.

The second Yakima accident was again attributed to a type of race condition in the software – this one allowed the device to be activated in an error setting (a "failure" of a software interlock). The Tyler accidents were related to problems in the data-entry routines that allowed the code to proceed to Set Up Test before the full prescription had been entered and acted upon. The Yakima accident involved problems encountered later in the logic after the treatment monitor Treat reaches Set Up Test.

The Therac-25's field light feature allows very precise positioning of the patient for treatment. The operator can control the machine right at the treatment site using a small hand control that offers certain limited functions for patient setup, including setting gantry, collimator, and table motions.

Normally, the operator enters all the prescription data at the console (outside the treatment room) before the final setup of all machine parameters is completed in the treatment room. This gives rise to an UNVERIFIED condition at the console. The operator then completes patient setup in the treatment room, and all relevant parameters now VERIFY. The console displays a message to PRESS SET BUTTON while the turntable is in the field light position. The operator now presses the *set* button on the hand control or types "set" at the console. That should set the collimator to the proper position for treatment.

In the software, after the prescription is entered and verified by the Datent routine, the control variable Tphase is changed so that the Set Up Test routine is entered (Figure 4). Every pass through the Set Up Test routine increments the upper collimator position check, a shared variable called Class3. If Class3 is nonzero, there is an inconsistency and treatment should not proceed. A zero value for Class3 indicates that the relevant parameters are consistent with treatment, and the software does not inhibit the beam.

After setting the Class3 variable, Set Up Test next checks for any malfunctions in the system by checking another shared variable (set by a routine that actually handles the interlock checking) called F$mal to see if it has a nonzero value. A nonzero value in F$mal indicates that the machine is not ready for treatment, and the Set Up Test subroutine is rescheduled. When F$mal is zero (indicating that everything is ready for treatment), the Set Up Test subroutine sets the Tphase variable equal to 2,

474   High-Integrity System Specification and Design

Hkeper

Lmtchk

If Class3 = 0
    Then do not enter Chkcol

If Class3 is not 0
    Then enter Chkcol

Chkcol

If upper collimator
inconsistent with
treatment then set
bit 9 of F$mal

Treat

Tphase → 0, 1, 2, 3

Set Up Test

During set
    Increment Class3 on
    each cycle

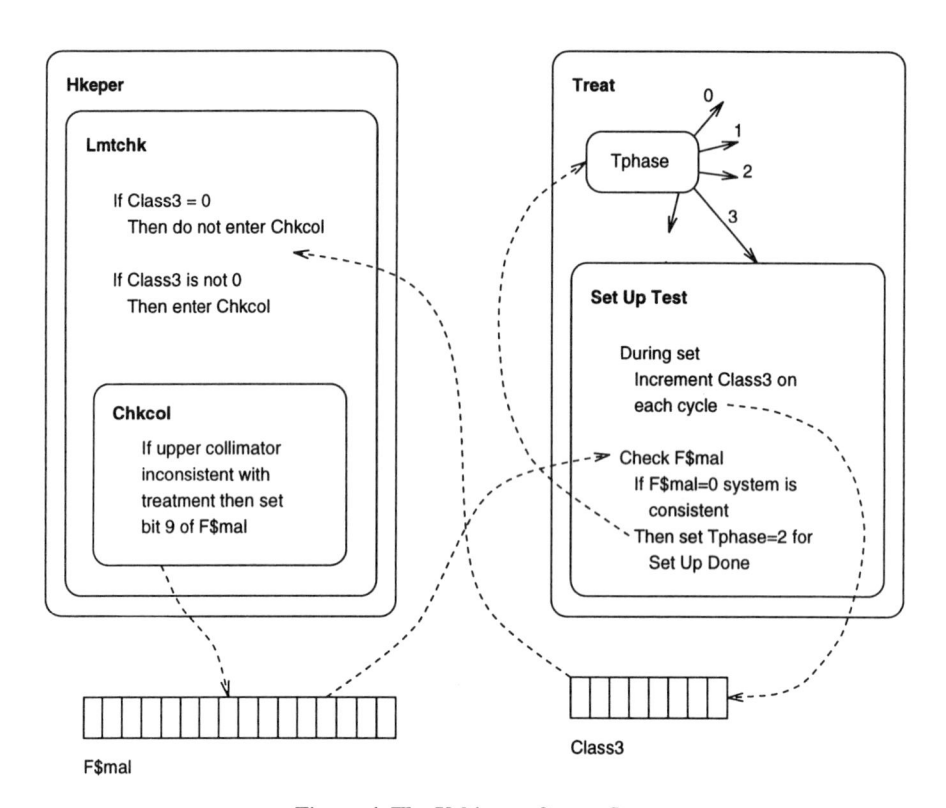

Check F$mal
    If F$mal=0 system is
    consistent
    Then set Tphase=2 for
    Set Up Done

F$mal

Class3

Figure 4. The Yakima software flaw.

which results in next scheduling the Set Up Done subroutine and the treatment is allowed to continue.

The actual interlock checking is performed by a concurrent Housekeeper task (Hkeper). The upper collimator position check is performed by a subroutine of Hkeper called Lmtchk (analog-to-digital limit checking). Lmtchk first checks the Class3 variable. If Class3 contains a non-zero value, Lmtchk calls the Check Collimator (Chkcol) subroutine. If Class3 contains zero, Chkcol is bypassed and the upper collimator position check is not performed. The Chkcol subroutine sets or resets bit 9 of the F$mal shared variable, depending on the position of the upper collimator – which in turn is checked by the Set Up Test subroutine of Treat to decide whether to reschedule itself or to proceed to Set Up Done.

During machine setup, Set Up Test will be executed several hundred times because it reschedules itself waiting for other events to occur. In the code, the Class3 variable is incremented by one in each pass through Set Up Test. Since the Class3 variable is one byte, it can only contain a maximum value of 255 decimal. Thus, on every 256th pass through the Set Up Test code, the variable will overflow and have a zero value. That means that on every 256th pass through Set Up Test, the upper collimator will not be checked and an upper collimator fault will not be detected.

The overexposure occurred when the operator hit the "set" button at the precise moment that Class3 rolled over to zero. Thus, Chkcol was not executed and F$mal was not set to indicate that the upper collimator was still in the field-light position. The software turned on the full 25 MeV without the target in place and without scanning. A highly concentrated electron beam resulted, which was scattered and deflected by the stainless steel mirror that was in the path.

The technical "fix" implemented for this particular software flaw is described by AECL as simple: the program is changed so that the Class3 variable is set to some fixed nonzero value each time through Set Up Test instead of being incremented.

Manufacturer, government, and user response. On February 3, 1987, after interaction with the FDA and others, including the user's group, AECL announced to its customers

1. A new software release to correct both the Tyler and Yakima software problems
2. A hardware single-pulse shutdown circuit
3. A turntable potentiometer to independently monitor turntable position
4. A hardware turntable interlock circuit

The second item, a hardware single-pulse shutdown circuit, essentially acts as a hardware interlock to prevent overdosing by detecting an unsafe level of radiation and halting beam output after one pulse of high energy and current. This interlock effectively provides an independent way to protect against a wide range of potential hardware failures and software errors. The third item, a turntable potentiometer, was the safety device recommended by several groups after the Hamilton accident.

After the second Yakima accident, the FDA became concerned that the use of the Therac-25 during the CAP process, even with AECL's interim operating instructions, involved too much risk to patients. The FDA concluded that the accidents demonstrated that the software alone could not be relied upon to assure safe operation of the machine. In a February 18, 1987, internal FDA memorandum, the Director of the Division of Radiological Products wrote:

> It is impossible for CDRH to find all potential failure modes and conditions of the software. AECL has indicated the "simple software fix" will correct the turntable position problem displayed at Yakima. We have not yet had the opportunity to evaluate that modification. Even if it does, based upon past history, I am not convinced that there are not other software glitches that could result in serious injury.
>
> ... We are in the position of saying that the proposed CAP can reasonably be expected to correct the deficiencies for which they were developed (Tyler). We cannot say that we are reasonable [sic] confident about the safety of the entire system to prevent or minimize exposure from other fault conditions.

On February 6, 1987, Ed Miller of the FDA called Pavel Dvorak of Canada's Health and Welfare to advise him that the FDA would recommend that all Therac-25s be shutdown until permanent modifications could be made. According to Miller's notes on the phone call, Dvorak agreed and indicated that Health and Welfare would coordinate their actions with the FDA.

AECL responded on April 13 with an update on the Therac CAP status and a schedule of the nine action items pressed by the users at a user's group meeting in March. This unique and highly productive meeting provided an unusual opportunity to involve the users in the CAP evaluation process. It brought together all concerned parties in one place and at one time so that a course of action could be decided upon and approved as quickly as possible. The attendees included representatives from

- The manufacturer (AECL)
- All users, including their technical and legal staffs
- The FDA and the Canadian Bureau of Radiation and Medical Devices
- the Canadian Atomic Energy Control Board
- the Province of Ontario
- the Radiation Regulations Committee of the Canadian Association of Physicists

According to Gordon Symonds, from the Canadian BRMD, this meeting was very important to the resolution of the problems, since the regulators, users, and manufacturer arrived at a consensus in one day.

At this second user's meeting, the participants carefully reviewed all the six known major Therac-25 accidents to that date and discussed the elements of the CAP along with possible additional modifications. They came up with a prioritized list of modifications they wanted included in the CAP and expressed concerns about the lack of independent evaluation of the software and the lack of a hardcopy audit trail to assist in diagnosing faults.

The AECL representative, who was the quality assurance manager, responded that tests had been done on the CAP changes, but that the tests were not documented and that independent evaluation of the software "might not be possible." He claimed that two outside experts had reviewed the software, but he could not provide their names. In response to user requests for a hard copy audit trail and access to source code, he explained that memory limitations would not permit including such options and that source code would not be made available to users.

On May 1, AECL issued CAP Revision 4 as a result of the FDA comments and the user's meeting input. The FDA response on May 26 approved the CAP subject to submission of the final test plan results and an independent safety analysis, distribution of the draft revised manual to customers, and completion of the CAP by June 30, 1987. The FDA concluded by rating this a Class I recall: a recall in which there is a reasonable probability that the use of, or exposure to, a violative product will cause serious adverse health consequences or death [1].

AECL sent more supporting documentation to the FDA on June 5, 1987, including the CAP test plan, a draft operator's manual, and the draft of the new safety analysis. This time the analysis included the software in the fault trees but used a "generic failure rate" of 10^{-4} for software events. This number was justified as being based on the historical performance of the Therac-25 software. The final report on the safety analysis states that many of the fault trees had a computer malfunction as a causative event, and the outcome for quantification was therefore dependent on the failure rate chosen for the software. Assuming that all software errors are equally likely seems rather strange.

A close inspection of the code was also conducted during this safety analysis to "obtain more information on which to base decisions." An outside consultant performed the inspection, which included a detailed examination of the implementation of each function, a search for coding errors, and a qualitative assessment of the software's reliability. No information is provided in the final safety report about whether any particular methodology or tools were used in the software inspection or whether someone just read the code looking for errors.

AECL planned a fifth revision of the CAP to include the testing and final safety analysis results. Referring to the test plan at this, the final stage of the CAP process, an FDA reviewer said,

> Amazingly, the test data presented to show that the software changes to handle the edit problems in the Therac-25 are appropriate prove the exact opposite result. A review of the data table in the test results indicates that the final beam type and energy (edit change) has no effect on the initial beam type and energy. I can only assume that either the fix is not right or the data was entered incorrectly. The manufacturer should be admonished for this error. Where is the QC [Quality Control] review for the test program? AECL must: (1) clarify this situation, (2) change the test protocol to prevent this type of error from occurring, and (3) set up appropriate QC control on data review.

A further FDA memo indicated:

[The AECL quality assurance manager] could not give an explanation and will check into the circumstances. He subsequently called back and verified that the technician completed the form incorrectly. Correct operation was witnessed by himself and others. They will repeat and send us the correct data sheet.

At the American Association of Physicists in Medicine meeting in July 1987, a third user's meeting was held. The AECL representative described the status of the latest CAP and explained that the FDA had given verbal approval and that he expected full implementation by the end of August 1987. He went on to review and comment on the prioritized concerns of the last meeting. Three of the user-requested hardware changes had been included in the CAP. Changes to tape load error messages and checksums on the load data would wait until after the CAP was done. Software documentation was described as a lower priority task that needed definition and would not be available to the FDA in any form for over a year.

On July 6, 1987, AECL sent a letter to all users to update them on the FDA's verbal approval of the CAP and to delineate how AECL would proceed. Finally, on July 21, 1987, AECL issued the final and fifth CAP revision. The major features of the final CAP are these:

- All interruptions related to the dosimetry system will go to a treatment suspend, not a treatment pause. Operators will not be allowed to restart the machine without reentering all parameters.
- A software single-pulse shutdown will be added.
- An independent hardware single-pulse shutdown will be added.
- Monitoring logic for turntable position will be improved to ensure that the turntable is in one of the three legal positions.
- A potentiometer will be added to the turntable. The output is used to monitor exact turntable location and provide a visible position signal to the operator.
- Interlocking with the 270-degree bending magnet will be added to ensure that the target and beam flattener are in position if the X-ray mode is selected.
- Beam-on will be prevented if the turntable is in the field light or any intermediate position.
- Cryptic malfunction messages will be replaced with meaningful messages and highlighted dose-rate messages.
- Editing keys will be limited to *cursor up*, *backspace*, and *return*. All other keys will be inoperative.
- A motion-enable footswitch (a type of deadman switch) will be added. The operator will be required to hold this switch closed during movement of certain parts of the machine to prevent unwanted motions when the operator is not in control.
- Twenty-three other changes will be made to the software to improve its operation and reliability, including disabling of unused keys, changing the operation of the *set* and *reset* commands, preventing copying of the control program on site, changing the way various detected hardware faults are handled, eliminating errors in the software that were detected during the review process, adding several

additional software interlocks, disallowing changes in the service mode while a treatment is in progress, and adding meaningful error messages.
- The known software problems associated with the Tyler and Yakima accidents will be fixed.
- The manuals will be fixed to reflect the changes.

Figure 5 shows a typical Therac-25 installation after the CAP changes were made.

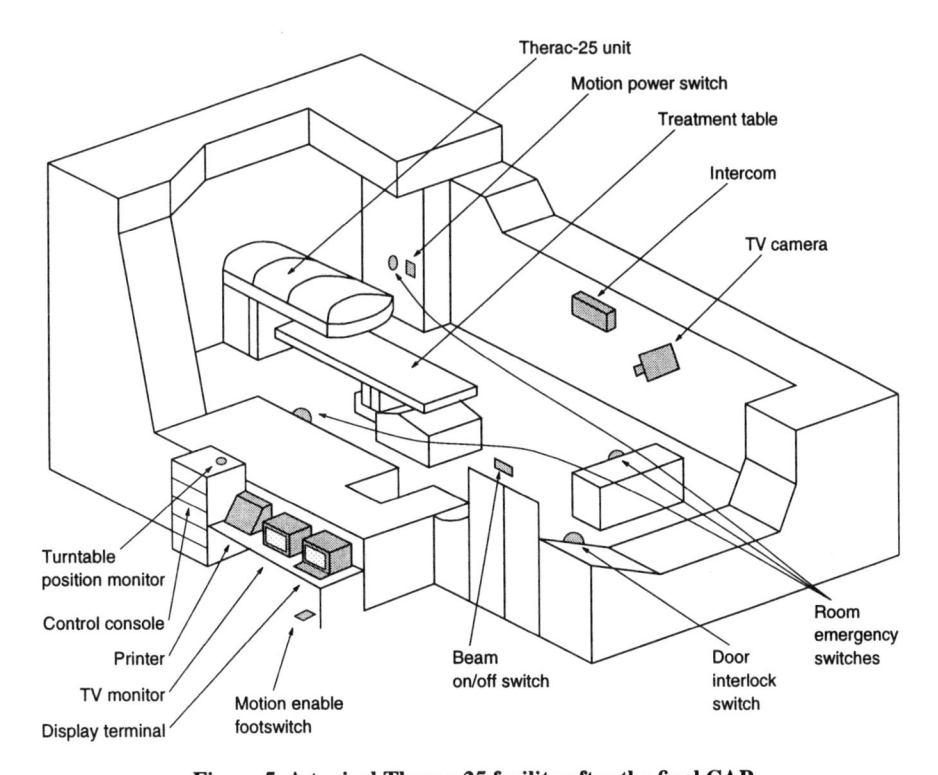

Figure 5. A typical Therac-25 facility after the final CAP.

Ed Miller, the director of the Division of Standards Enforcement, Center for Devices and Radiological Health at the FDA, wrote in 1987:

> FDA has performed extensive review of the Therac-25 software and hardware safety systems. We cannot say with absolute certainty that all software problems that might result in improper dose have been found and eliminated. However, we are confident that the hardware and software safety features recently added will prevent future catastrophic consequences of failure.

No Therac-25 accidents have been reported since the final corrective action plan was implemented.

4 Causal Factors

Many lessons can be learned from this series of accidents. A few are considered here.

Overconfidence in software. A common mistake in engineering, in this case and in many others, is to put too much confidence in software. There seems to be a feeling among nonsoftware professionals that software will not or cannot fail, which leads to complacency and overreliance on computer functions.

A related tendency among engineers is to ignore software. The first safety analysis on the Therac-25 did not include software – although nearly full responsibility for safety rested on it. When problems started occurring, it was assumed that hardware had caused them, and the investigation looked only at the hardware.

Confusing reliability with safety. This software was highly reliable. It worked tens of thousands of times before overdosing anyone, and occurrences of erroneous behavior were few and far between. AECL assumed that their software was safe because it was reliable, and this led to complacency.

Lack of defensive design. The software did not contain self-checks or other error-detection and error-handling features that would have detected the inconsistencies and coding errors. Audit trails were limited because of a lack of memory. However, today larger memories are available and audit trails and other design techniques must be given high priority in making tradeoff decisions.

Patient reactions were the only real indications of the seriousness of the problems with the Therac-25; there were no independent checks that the machine and its software were operating correctly. Such verification cannot be assigned to operators without providing them with some means of detecting errors: The Therac-25 software "lied" to the operators, and the machine itself was not capable of detecting that a massive overdose had occurred. The ion chambers on the Therac-25 could not handle the high density of ionization from the unscanned electron beam at high beam current; they thus became saturated and gave an indication of a low dosage. Engineers need to design for the worst case.

Failure to eliminate root causes. One of the lessons to be learned from the Therac-25 experiences is that focusing on particular software design errors is not the way to make a system safe. Virtually all complex software can be made to behave in an unexpected fashion under some conditions: There will always be another software bug. Just as engineers would not rely on a design with a hardware single point of failure that could lead to catastrophe, they should not do so if that single point of failure is software.

The Therac-20 contained the same software error implicated in the Tyler deaths, but this machine included hardware interlocks that mitigated the consequences of the error. Protection against software errors can and should be built into both the system and the software itself. We cannot eliminate all software errors, but we can often protect against their worst effects, and we can recognize their likelihood in our decision making.

One of the serious mistakes that led to the multiple Therac-25 accidents was the tendency to believe that the cause of an accident had been determined (e.g., a microswitch failure in the case of Hamilton) without adequate evidence to come to this conclusion and without looking at all possible contributing factors. Without a thorough investigation, it is not possible to determine whether a sensor provided the wrong information, the software provided an incorrect command, or the actuator had a transient failure and did the wrong thing on its own. In the case of the Hamilton accident, a transient microswitch failure was assumed to be the cause even though the engineers were unable to reproduce the failure or to find anything wrong with the microswitch.

In general, it is a mistake to patch just one causal factor (such as the software) and assume that future accidents will be eliminated. Accidents are unlikely to occur in exactly the same way again. If we patch only the symptoms and ignore the deeper underlying causes, or if we fix only the specific cause of one accident, we are unlikely to have much effect on future accidents. The series of accidents involving the Therac-25 is a good example of exactly this problem: Fixing each individual software flaw as it was found did not solve the safety problems of the device.

Complacency. Often it takes an accident to alert people to the dangers involved in technology. A medical physicist wrote about the Therac-25 accidents:

> In the past decade or two, the medical accelerator "industry" has become perhaps a little complacent about safety. We have assumed that the manufacturers have all kinds of safety design experience since they've been in the business a long time. We know that there are many safety codes, guides, and regulations to guide them and we have been reassured by the hitherto excellent record of these machines. Except for a few incidents in the 1960's (e.g., at Hammersmith, Hamburg) the use of medical accelerators has been remarkably free of serious radiation accidents until now. Perhaps, though we have been spoiled by this success [6].

This problem seems to be common in all fields.

Unrealistic risk assessments. The first hazard analyses initially ignored software, and then they treated it superficially by assuming that all software errors were equally likely. The probabilistic risk assessments generated undue confidence in the machine and in the results of the risk assessment themselves. When the first Yakima accident was reported to AECL, the company did not investigate. Their evidence for their belief that the radiation burn could not have been caused by their machine included a probabilistic risk assessment showing that safety had increased by five orders of magnitude as a result of the microswitch fix.

The belief that safety had been increased by such a large amount seems hard to justify. Perhaps it was based on the probability of failure of the microswitch (typically 10^{-5}) AND-ed with the other interlocks. The problem with all such analyses is that they typically make many independence assumptions and exclude aspects of the problem – in this case, software – that are difficult to quantify but which may have a larger impact on safety than the quantifiable factors that are included.

Inadequate investigation or followup on accident reports. Every company building safety-critical systems should have audit trails and incident analysis procedures that are applied whenever any hint of a problem is found that might lead to an accident. The first phone call by Tim Still should have led to an extensive investigation of the events at Kennestone. Certainly, learning about the first lawsuit should have triggered an immediate response.

Inadequate software engineering practices. Some basic software engineering principles that apparently were violated in the case of the Therac-25 include the following:

- Software specifications and documentation should not be an afterthought.
- Rigorous software quality assurance practices and standards should be established.
- Designs should be kept simple and dangerous coding practices avoided.
- Ways to detect errors and and get information about them, such as software audit trails, should be designed into the software from the beginning.
- The software should be subjected to extensive testing and formal analysis at the module and software level; system testing alone is not adequate. Regression testing should be performed on all software changes.
- Computer displays and the presentation of information to the operators, such as error messages, along with user manuals and other documentation need to be carefully designed.

The manufacturer said that the hardware and software were "tested and exercised separately or together over many years." In his deposition for one of the lawsuits, the quality assurance manager explained that testing was done in two parts. A "small amount" of software testing was done on a simulator, but most of the testing was done as a system. It appears that unit and software testing was minimal, with most of the effort directed at the integrated system test. At a Therac-25 user's meeting, the same man stated that the Therac-25 software was tested for 2,700 hours. Under questioning by the users, he clarified this as meaning "2700 hours of use." The FDA difficulty in getting an adequate test plan out of the company and the lack of regression testing are evidence that testing was not done well.

The design is unnecessarily complex for such critical software. It is untestable in the sense that the design ensured that the known errors (there may very well be more that have just not been found) would most likely not have been found using standard testing and verification techniques. This does not mean that software testing is not important, only that software must be designed to be testable and that simple designs may prevent errors in the first place.

Software reuse. Important lessons about software reuse can be found in these accidents. A naive assumption is often made that reusing software or using commercial off-the-shelf software will increase safety because the software will have been exercised extensively. Reusing software modules does not guarantee safety in the new system to which they are transferred and sometimes leads to awkward and dangerous designs. Safety is a quality of the system in which the software is used; it is not a quality of the software itself. Rewriting the entire software in order to get a clean and simple design may be safer in many cases.

Safe versus friendly user interfaces. Making the machine as easy as possible to use may conflict with safety goals. Certainly, the user interface design left much to be desired, but eliminating multiple data entry and assuming that operators would check the values carefully before pressing the return key was unrealistic.

User and government oversight and standards. Once the FDA got involved in the Therac-25, their response was impressive, especially considering how little experience they had with similar problems in computer-controlled medical devices. Since the Therac-25 events, the FDA has moved to improve the reporting system and to augment their procedures and guidelines to include software. The input and pressure from the user group was also important in getting the machine fixed and provides an important lesson to users in other industries.

References

1. C.A. Bowsher. Medical device recalls: Examination of selected cases. Technical Report GAO Report GAO/PEMD-90-6, U.S. Government Accounting Organization, October 1990.
2. C.A. Bowsher. Medical devices: The public health at risk. Technical Report GAO Report GAO/T-PEMD-90-2, U.S. Government Accounting Organization, 1990.
3. M. Kival, editor. *Radiological Health Bulletin*, volume XX:8. Center for Devices and Radiological Health, Food and Drug Administration, Rockville, Maryland, December 1986.
4. Nancy G. Leveson and Clark S. Turner. An investigation of the Therac-25 accidents, *IEEE Computer*, 26(7):18–41, July 1993.
5. Ed Miller. The Therac-25 experience. In *Conference of State Radiation Control Program Directors*, 1987.
6. J.A. Rawlinson. Report on the Therac-25. In *OCTRF/OCI Physicists Meeting*, Kingston, Ontario, May 1987.
7. R. Saltos. Man killed by accident with medical radiation. *Boston Globe*, June 20, 1986.

Safety-Critical Systems, Formal Methods and Standards

Jonathan Bowen and Victoria Stavridou

Summary.

Standards concerned with the development of safety-critical systems, and the software in such systems in particular, abound today as the software crisis increasingly affects the world of embedded computer-based systems. The use of formal methods is often advocated as a way of increasing confidence in such systems. This paper examines the industrial use of these techniques, the recommendations concerning formal methods in a number of current and draft standards, and comments on the applicability and problems of using formal methods for the development of safety-critical systems of an industrial scale. Some possible future directions are suggested.

1 A Brief Historical Perspective

Lives have depended on mathematical calculations for centuries. In the 19th century, the scientific community was facing the 'tables crisis' [144] due to the problem of errors in numerical tables such as logarithms and navigation tables, calculated by human 'computers'. It was rumoured that ships had been wrecked as a result of such errors. Charles Babbage was so concerned that he decided to try to alleviate the situation by attempting to mechanize the process of generating such tables using 'difference engines' and later more versatile and programmable 'analytical engines', the forerunners of modern computers.

The first true 'real-time' computer to be developed was on the Whirlwind project at MIT [5]. Started in 1944, the project produced an embryonic (military) air traffic

---

© 1993 The Institution of Electrical Engineers. Reprinted by permission.
Reprinted from *Software Engineering Journal*, 8(4):189–209, July 1993.
Winner of the 1994 IEEE Charles Babbage Premium award.

control system in 1951. The short lifetime of the large number of vacuum tubes used in the computer was a considerable problem. Initially, the mean time between failures was about 20 minutes. Fault-tolerance was achieved by detecting weak tubes before they failed and redirecting signals to other components, thus enabling continued operation even in the event of partial hardware failure [149]. At this time, such failures were a dominant feature of the system.

Computer-based industrial process control followed by the late 1950s. The problems of software development and revision became recognized, but the solutions remained ad hoc and unreliable [134]. Even in the mid 1950s, the cost of producing software had already outstripped that of the computers themselves.

The physical hardware became increasingly reliable. The problem of frequent breakdowns, bulkiness and high power consumption of vacuum tubes was alleviated by the invention of the transistor. Despite considerable improvement, the connections between components (e.g., 'dry joints' between soldered wires) remained a serious source of failure. The advent of integrated circuits in 1959, while helping with this problem, was initially not cost-effective. However the US space programme demanded low-weight and high-reliability components – almost irrespective of cost – for the (safety-critical) computer required on board the space craft. This enabled the US to gain the lead in the microelectronics world at the time; subsequently the price of integrated circuits dropped and the number of transistors per chip increased dramatically year by year. Similar advances were not forthcoming for software that also became more complex but less reliable.

As computers became physically smaller, it was more and more feasible to embed them within the systems that they controlled. In 1971, Intel announced the first complete microprocessor on a single chip, little realising what an enormous impact such an idea would have on the world of computing. At the beginning of the 1980s, embedded software had still not really been considered seriously by theoretical computer science researchers (but see [156]), despite the fact that it is capable of inflicting physical damage [14]. However in the last decade, such systems have come under more and more scrutiny as computers pervade all areas of our lives, especially in embedded applications.

The software currently used in computers has itself become so complex that it is not trustworthy and has caused human injury and death as a result. Neumann [108] provides a list of incidents that is updated annually. Until relatively recently it has not been considered feasible to use formal techniques to verify such software in an industrial setting [61]. Now that some case studies and examples of real use are available, formal methods are becoming more acceptable in industrial circles. Even populist accounts of the computing industry are mentioning the problems of software errors in relation to critical systems and the possibility of applying mathematical techniques to reduce such errors in a wide variety of forums [90, 106, 112, 141].

This paper briefly discusses safety-critical systems, examines the use of formal methods as a possible technique for increasing safety and reliability, and surveys some standards in this area. The objectives of the paper are to provide information on the current safety issues, particularly with regard to software, as reflected by a number of current and emerging standards and to examine ways in which formal methods technology can and has been used to improve system safety. It should be noted that formal methods are only one of a gamut of important techniques, including many classical safety analysis methods, that can be applied in safety-related software development; the scope of this paper excludes many of these other techniques.

This is a fast moving area in which rapid change is the norm; therefore, this paper should be seen as representative snapshot rather than as a comprehensive and definitive guide.[1] It is also our contention that the subject of software safety and the contribution of formal methods is in its infancy; we will, therefore, conclude this paper with a summary of open research questions. A substantial list of references is included at the end of the paper, with a list of relevant standards, to enable interested readers to investigate the issues further.

2 Safety-Critical Computer Systems

Safety is closely coupled to the notion of risk. Charette [28] defines risk as an event or action:

- *Having a loss associated with it.*
- *Where uncertainty or chance is involved.*
- *Some choice is also involved.*

Safety can then be defined as the freedom from exposure to danger, or the exemption from hurt, injury or loss. But in most situations, one is concerned with the *degree* of safety and therefore safety is a subjective measure which makes safety provision and measurement extremely difficult and contentious tasks.

Safety concerns in computer systems are even more confusing. Such systems consist of many subcomponents which are tightly coupled and have highly complex interactions. The binding of application to operating system to architecture is a prime example of a tightly coupled system. When such a system is further embedded within larger contexts, such as command and control systems, the probability of failure quickly approaches unity. Myers [103] estimates that there are approximately 3.3 software errors per thousand lines of code in large software systems. This figure is not surprising given that there are as many as 10^{20} unique end-to-end paths in a moderate-sized program [137]. What is worse is that not all errors in software are created equal, as small errors do not necessarily have small effects. The picture becomes much bleaker when the software/hardware interactions in computer systems are taken into account. In two studies [48, 70], nearly 10% of all software errors and 35% of all software failures identified were later found to be hardware-related, such

---

[1] Probably the best survey paper of the 1980s in the area of software safety is provided by Leveson [84]. However this is now somewhat out of date because of recent developments. For an update, work by Leveson [85] and Parnas *et al.*[113] is recommended.

as transient faults corrupting data. In fact, it appears that hardware can fail three times as often as software under some circumstances [6].

The most effective means to avoid accidents during a system's operation is to eliminate or reduce dangers *during* the design and development, not afterwards when the complexity becomes overwhelming. Safety cannot be considered as an add-on after the system has been developed, in much the same way that it does not make sense to design an aircraft and then think about its weight. We strongly believe that *safety must be designed in a system and dangers must be designed out*. We also feel that software and hardware safety are inextricably intertwined and must be considered as a whole with special attention paid to the interfaces.

2.1 Dependable computer systems

Despite these considerable problems, the advantages of the added versatility and flexibility provided by digital systems as opposed to other means are overwhelming and, therefore, insufficiently understood software and hardware are often used. However implemented, we require that safety-critical systems are *dependable*. There are many terms associated with dependability, and considerable international effort has been expended to standardize these [83]. The accepted definition of the overall concept is [82]:

dependability *is that property of a computing system which allows reliance to be justifiably placed on the service it delivers.*

The life of a system is perceived by its users as an alternation between proper and improper service. Delivery of proper service (service which adheres to specified requirements) is normally termed *correctness*. Therefore a "correct" system is not necessarily a dependable system. Dependability is an overall property which has other measures such as safety, reliability and availability. Laprie [82] defines these terms as follows:

safety *is a measure of the continuous delivery of service free from occurrences of catastrophic failures.*
reliability *is a measure of the continuous delivery of proper service (where service is delivered according to specified conditions) or equivalently of the time to failure.*
availability *is a measure of the delivery of proper service with respect to the alternation of proper and improper service.*

Formal methods address correctness issues and these will be considered in the remainder of this paper. We do not address other dependability measures here although safety, reliability and availability should be modelled and measured independently of verification, using probabilistic techniques and testing. However, it is worth pointing out that confusion often arises between the above concepts which are, in fact, distinct. For instance, a safe system is not necessarily reliable (an airplane in flight may be safe for only some of the time), a reliable system is not necessarily correct (the autopilot may reliably compute an incorrect course) and a safe system is not necessarily available (the safest airplane is one that never leaves the ground).

The key notion in dependability is that reliance must be justifiable [82]. This means that we need explicit and testable requirements and specifications which are refined to a system using rigorous or formal development techniques, as well as credible analytical and experimental evidence demonstrating the satisfaction of the requirements by the system. We believe that if no such evidence can be obtained, the wise developer will use human or purely hardware resources instead of software or software/hardware systems.

There are four approaches to achieving system dependability [82]:

- **fault-avoidance:** How to prevent, by construction, fault occurrence or introduction.
- **fault-tolerance:** How to provide, by redundancy, a service complying with the specification in spite of faults.
- **fault removal:** How to minimize, by verification, the presence of faults.
- **fault forecasting:** How to estimate, by evaluation, the presence, the creation and the consequences of faults.

It is commonly agreed that a combination of these approaches must be used in order to achieve ultra-high dependability. Software testing (fault removal) alone may be able to reduce the failure rate of a program to about 10^{-4} per hour (approximately 1 failure per year) and faster more complex computers can only make matters worse. It has been suggested that only an improvement factor of about 10 may be achievable using fault-tolerance approaches such as N-version programming [101]. In fact, the benefits of these techniques are still a matter of some contention [78]. Combining these gives a figure of around 10^{-5} but most safety-critical situations demand a figure of nearer 10^{-9} or even 10^{-10} (e.g., see [S6]). This leaves us with an enormous gap between what is desired and what is attainable with current practice. A viable means of narrowing this gap in the future is the use of fault-avoidance in the form of formal methods in conjunction with the other techniques, although the quantification of dependability improvements obtained by such combinations is an open research issue. It is particularly fortunate that existing formal methods technology is sufficiently developed and well suited for use during the crucial requirements and specification stages of development when the system is still relatively abstract and therefore less complex than the final implementation. Later in this paper, a number of examples of realistically-sized uses of formal methods for the verification of (parts of) safety-critical systems are briefly outlined and discussed.

2.2 Formal methods

Formal methods have been a topic of research for many years; however they are rarely used in commercial contexts [34]. Although industrial research laboratories are investigating formal methods, there are relatively few examples of real use in the computing industry. Even in companies where formal methods are used, it is normally only to a limited extent and is often resisted (at least initially) by engineers, programmers and managers. This situation is hardly surprising since formal methods technology is largely perceived to consist of a collection of prototype notations and tools which are difficult to use and do not scale up easily; there are many widely held misconceptions about the use of formal techniques [56]. It may be fair to say that formal methods research has to some extent been dominated by the fundamental scientific aspects rather than by problems in application.

Even if we knew how to fit formal methods with current development techniques there is still the problem that a lot of software is currently produced by "chaotic" processes (as defined by the Software Engineering Institute's process maturity metrics [68]). The use of formal methods is no substitute for good software production management. Furthermore, the adoption of these techniques requires up-front committal of resources to projects which runs contrary to industrial practice where most projects consume the bulk of their resources toward the end of system development (testing and debugging). Additionally, present management practice may be entirely inadequate for management of the early stages of full formal development. For example, the simplification and reduction in size of a formal specification is certainly progress, but it is measured by a reduction in the amount of paper produced.

Finally, the use of formal methods requires mathematical expertise which is simply not currently available in industry where most practitioners have little or no formal computer science training. In this paper, we will argue that it is possible, and in the case of safety-critical systems highly desirable, to obtain benefits from formal methods even in constrained contexts.

It is often said that the use of formal techniques in the production of systems should be viewed as a means of delivering enhanced quality rather than establishing correctness. This difference of perception is crucial and is particularly highlighted in the case of safety-critical systems. Formal methods can deliver correctness – i.e., adherence to some requirements – and therefore enhanced quality; but correctness is not the end of the story.

As pointed out by Cohn [32], correctness involves two or more models of a system (designer intentions and software/hardware system), where the models bear a tentative but uncheckable and possibly imperfect relation to both the user requirements and the final implementation. Even under the best possible circumstances, when we have an accurate interpretation of the requirements, at best we can assert that the model of the implementation satisfies these requirements. Whether the system will work satisfactorily *in situ* also depends on factors ranging from communication, training, and behaviour to the performance of mechanical, electrical and chemical components both within the system and its operational environment.

Formal methods may be characterized at a number of levels of use and these provide different levels of assurance for the software developed by such methods [151]. At a basic level, they may simply be used for specification of the system to be designed. The development process itself may be informal, but benefits are still gained since many bugs can be removed by formalizing and discussing the system at an early stage. Proofs may be undertaken to confirm properties of the system that are required or assumed to be true. Such proofs help to increase the design team's understanding of the system and this is an important component of the increased confidence that such validation provides. The Z notation [139] is often used in this manner, and has proved to be beneficial.

The next level of use is to apply formal methods to the development process, using a set of rules or a design calculus that allows stepwise refinement of the specification to an executable program. For example, VDM [76] was specifically designed for the development of programs, as opposed to just their specification or proof in general.

At the most rigorous level, the whole process of proof may be mechanized. Hand proofs or design inevitably lead to human errors occurring for all but the simplest systems. Checking the process by computer reduces the possibility of error, although it never eliminates it since the program that does the checking may itself be incorrect. In addition, it is always possible that the basic underlying axioms may themselves be inconsistent.

Mechanical theorem provers such as HOL [52] and the Boyer-Moore theorem prover [19] have been used to verify significant implementations [32, 100], but need to be operated by people with skills that very few engineers possess today. Such tools are difficult to use, even for experts, and significant improvements will need to be made in their usability before they can be widely accepted in the computing industry. However, proof tools are now becoming commercially available (e.g., the B tool [1, 2] and Lambda [98]). Thus commercial pressures will hopefully improve such tools, which up until now have mainly been used in research environments. In particular, the user interface and the control of proofs using strategies or 'tactics' are areas that require considerable further research and development effort. Despite the present inadequacies, safety-critical software is the one application domain where the added confidence of mechanical proofs may be justifiable if feasible, even though the development cost of such an approach (of which more later) is high. Lindsay [87] provides a good snapshot of what is currently available.

Perhaps an indication of the seriousness with which the UK formal methods community now takes safety-critical computer systems is that the first article of the first volume of the relatively recently introduced journal *Formal Aspects of Computing* is devoted to this subject [146]. This gives an authoritative, reasoned and balanced account of the state of the safety-critical industry. Many workshops specifically concerned with safety-critical systems and formal methods are now being held (e.g., [36, 38]). Safety concerns are considered an important part of state-of-the-art software engineering (e.g., [10, 142]) and formal methods promise to help with some aspects of the problems encountered. Safety-related journals also consider how formal methods can help [12]. There are now entire books on the use of formal methods in safety-critical systems [132], and most more general books at least address the subject [89, 123]. The work by McDermid [99] is especially recommended for further reading; it includes several case studies using different formal notations. Further recent and relevant work includes that by Barroca and McDermid [7], Bowen and Stevridou [18], Knight and Kienzle [79], and Ostroff [110].

2.3 The cost of software safety

Thoreau, in *Walden* [28], wrote that:

> *'the cost of a thing is the amount of what I will call life which is required to be exchanged for it, immediately or in the long run'.*

In other words, the cost of safety is determined, ultimately, by what people are willing to pay. Table 1 – adapted from [77] – illustrates the wide range of amounts of money spent on trying to save a human life in various situations. Although various methods for calculating the objective cost of safety have been proposed [15, 58], the problem is largely unresolved. One cannot ever be certain, when an accident *does not* occur, whether it is because of the safety devices or because the system was designed "well enough" so that the safety devices are superfluous. On the other hand, when accidents *do* occur, the penalties for ignoring software safety can be very severe.

Hazard	Safety measure	Cost (in 1985)
Car crashes	Mandatory seat belts	$500
Cervical cancer	Screening	$75,000
Radiation	Reduce exposure & leaks	$75,000,000
Toxic air	Reduce emissions	$5,880,000,000

Table 1. Cost of saving a life in US dollars.

Reprinted with permission from [77]. Copyright CRC Press, Boca Raton, Florida.

A recent report [125] values "a statistical life" at £2–3M (around $4M) in that this is the sort of amount of money that should be spent on saving one life. However the value placed on a human life varies widely from country to country, and even within a single country depending on the situation and the people involved.

The overall system safety cost includes a multitude of factors and components. From this point on, we will concentrate on the cost of software defects for the *producer* of the software; some of these will affect safety and others will not. We will attempt to estimate how much it costs to eliminate software defects at large since the proportion of safety-critical defects to benign ones cannot be quantified for all systems. Note that we do not take into account the liability costs incurred by producers of safety-critical software that has failed causing accidents.

Software defect costs can be investigated using a variety of approaches. Ward [153] uses data focused on the cost per prerelease software defect that is found and fixed during the integration through to the release phases of project development. The calculation of the cost is based on the formula

Software defect cost = Software defect rework cost + Profit loss

Based on data from an extensive software project database maintained at the Hewlett-Packard Waltham Division for product releases over the past five years,

Ward has produced software defect costs for typical software projects which give an average cost of around $10,000 per *corrected* defect.

The figures supplied by Ward give us an approximation of the cost of software defects in projects where current practice is used. We are interested in a similar cost approximation when fault-avoidance techniques, and in particular formal methods, are used. Calculations based on a substantial railway system of around 70 man years' effort [54], which will be deliberated upon further in the next section, have been made, using similar assumptions to Ward [17]. These result in an estimated order of magnitude greater cost per *avoided* defect. On the other hand, only about half the total effort of the development was devoted to proofs.

One reason for high costs may be the necessity of training, which could be amortized over several projects if formal methods are adopted on a permanent basis. Other substantial industrial examples [63] have demonstrated that formal methods *can* be the most cost-effective technology if used in an appropriate manner. Some of these are mentioned later in the paper. In particular, full verification may not be worthwhile in many cases, but may be helpful for the most critical parts of an application; formal *specification* alone may be more appropriate for the rest of the system, with *rigorous* rather than formal development of implementation.

Such conflicting evidence on the cost-effectiveness of formal methods makes the need for proper deployment and quantification of the technology even more pressing. It is hoped that an international ongoing study of the industrial applications of formal methods [120] will help shed light on this issue.

3 Industrial-Scale Examples of Use

Although safety-critical systems may have the most to gain from the use of formal methods, such techniques are in fact being used in a wide variety of application areas in industry, although still in very few projects overall [8]. Formal methods have been used to improve the quality of software in a number of non-safety-critical areas. They have been shown to have the potential to both reduce the development cost (e.g., the IBM CICS project [67] where a saving of 9% in costs – which runs into millions – has been claimed) and to reduce the time to market (e.g., the Inmos T800 transputer floating-point unit [97], where a saving of 12 months' development time is claimed).

A notable example of the application of formal methods to a number of related levels of abstraction is provided by the work at CLInc., in Austin, Texas. The Boyer-Moore theorem prover [19] has been used to verify a compiler, assembler, kernel and microprocessor (that has since been fabricated) [100]. Most of these components form a 'stack' of verified parts that link together to form several related levels in a verified system [51]. This is the first such effort in the world and although the work is very much based around the Boyer-Moore theorem prover, and thus perhaps difficult to generalize directly, further work in Europe is now building on these foundations along similar lines [11].

It is worth noting that Europe (and in particular the UK) has a leading position in formal methods research and use [145]. These techniques have not gained an equal foothold in North America, even in the safety-critical sector. The notable exception is the security field where most US formal methods work has concentrated. This work is primarily championed by CLInc., ORA Corporation and SRI International.

Safety-critical systems make up a minority of industrial applications using formal methods [8]. Despite the fact that such systems have the most to gain potentially, industry is wisely cautious in adopting new untried techniques in this area [106]. The following sections give a brief overview of some companies and significant projects involved in the development of safety-critical systems that have used formal methods over the past few years. In general the results have been successful, but comments concerning individual cases are included below. Table 2 summarizes these experiments.

For a recent comprehensive market study of safety-related computer-controlled systems in general, resulting from a survey of many businesses and other relevant organizations concerned with safety-critical systems in the UK, see [44]. The formal specification technique most often quoted as being used was Z [139], but HOL [52] and OBJ [49] were also mentioned. Software houses often referred to the potential of formal methods. In many cases the main pressure to use formal techniques was coming from the defence sector, following the publication of Standard 00-55 [S15]. They are seen as one way of providing greater assurance that errors have been minimized in both software and hardware design. In practice few suppliers, especially outside the software houses and consultancies, make use of formal methods. This is mainly because formal methods are relatively new to industry and there is little experience in their use. The cost of training is seen as prohibitive.

Application	Notation	Specification	Verification	Machine Support
Aviation	STP/EHDM	•	•	•
	Spectool/Clio	•	•	•
Railway systems	B	•	•	•
Nuclear power plants	VDM	•		•
Medical systems	HP-SL & Z	•		
Ammunition control	VDM	•	•	•
Embedded micros	HOL	•	•	•

A bullet under a column heading indicates whether a particular activity was undertaken as part of the project. The machine support heading indicates whether machine support was used in this particular case for either specification or verification or both, *not* whether the whole method is supported by tools.

Table 2. Applications of formal methods to safety-critical systems.

3.1 Aviation

An early example of the application of formal methods to real life systems, was the SIFT project, which probably represents the most substantial US experiment in the safety-critical sector. SIFT [155] is an aircraft control computer which was commissioned by NASA in the mid-seventies. The safety requirements proposed by NASA and the FAA (Federal Aviation Administration) are extremely stringent; they permit a probability of life-threatening failure of less than 10^{-10} per hour during a ten hour flight [S6]. Formal methods were used in the SIFT project in order to try and bridge the gap between this failure rate and the 10^{-5} which can be achieved with other techniques such as testing and fault-tolerance [101].

SIFT is designed to operate safely in the presence of hardware faults by replication of processors and adaptive majority voting. In contrast to other majority voted systems, the voting mechanism that detects and masks hardware faults is implemented entirely in software. It is this software, or rather its design, that was subjected to formal verification. The verification was conducted in two stages. The first involved verifying the I/O specification against the pre/post specification and was done initially using the Boyer-Moore theorem prover [19] and subsequently the STP (Shostak Theorem Prover) system [133]. The second, more substantial, proof additionally dealt with the transition specification as well as the fault model specification. This proof was done using the specially built EHDM system [128] and involved approximately one man year of effort.

The SIFT system was delivered to the NASA Langley Research Center AIR-LAB facility where it has formed the basis for other evaluation projects. It has been found to be a very reliable system but as [101] points out this was the result of the simplification of the design rather than the design verification exercise (which was done after code development). This same simplification of the system has led to a number of criticisms of the SIFT project; it was widely felt that the verification exercise involved oversimplification which eventually rendered the system "unfit for purpose" [104]. So, although the SIFT episode was a successful research exercise, it was a failure as far as subsequent actual deployment of the processor was concerned.

More recently, NASA commissioned work involving the application of formal methods to support fault-tolerance in digital flight control systems (DFCS). Rushby [127] contains the formal specification and verification of a model for fault masking and transient recovery in DFCS applications. Rushby and Von Henke [129] describes the formal verification of the interactive convergence algorithm for Byzantine fault-tolerant clock synchronization. Srivas and Bickford [140] discusses the formal verification of the FtCayuga fault-tolerant microprocessor system. It appears that NASA has found this line of investigation fruitful and preferable to experimental quantification of software reliability [23]. Another recent project for the FAA, undertaken by Leveson *et al.*, has been working to produce a formal specification of the TCAS collision avoidance system [S20].

3.2 Railway systems

In 1988 GEC Alsthom, MATRA Transport and RATP started working on a computerized signalling system for controlling RER commuter trains in Paris. Their objective was to increase traffic movement by 25% while maintaining the safety levels of the conventional system. The resulting SACEM system (partly embedded hardware and software) was delivered in 1989 and has since been controlling the speed of all trains on the RER Line A in Paris. The dependability of SACEM has obvious safety implications for 800,000 passengers per day.

The SACEM software consists of 21,000 lines of Modula-2 code. 63% of the code is deemed as safety-critical and has been subjected to formal specification and verification [54]. The specification was done using Abrial's B language [2] and the proofs were done manually using automatically generated verification conditions for the code. The validation effort for the entire system (including non safety-critical procedures) was of the order of 100 man years and therefore, this experiment represents a substantial investment in formal methods technology.

The authors of [54] believe that the system is safer as a result of the formal specification and verification exercise. It is certainly instructive to observe that even within the current constraints, mature formal methods technology can contribute to system safety. The SACEM work has primarily benefited from formal specification which enabled precise and unambiguous statements about the system to be made. It is interesting to note that a difficult problem which the project team had to resolve was communication between the verification personnel and the signalling experts who were not familiar with the formal notations employed. They overcame this problem by providing the engineers with a natural language description derived manually from the formal specification. Similar techniques are now being applied to other train control systems [27] using the B-tool [1].

3.3 Nuclear power plants

Rolls-Royce and Associates have been applying formal methods (mainly VDM) to the development of software for safety-critical systems, and nuclear power plants in particular, for a number of years [62, 63]. This approach has proved very successful and has produced the following conclusions based on practical experience [63]:

- The main problem is the system as a whole, rather than the software alone.
- A combination of modern techniques, including formal methods, can help in the development of safety-critical software, even though their scope may be limited at present.
- There are many myths and few facts concerning software engineering methods [56]. Hill [63] lists some myths and facts concerning the use of formal methods in the development of software.
- Improvements in time-scales, costs and quality are possible in practice using such techniques.

In a (subjective) table giving the contribution of 11 (not necessarily incompatible) software development methods, formal methods are considered the most helpful option. Formal methods are also considered important for the demonstration of software (using animation techniques) and for subsequent changes, although structured methods and documentation configuration control are considered more important for the latter. Some approaches, such as the use of independent project teams or the use of diverse software are considered of little or no help.

Tests are still undertaken, but it is noted that these have normally found mistakes in the test software rather than the software under test, since the former has not been developed rigorously, whereas the latter has.

A comparison of cost-effectiveness of different methods has been made (see Table 3 [63]). Using formal methods has doubled the specification and analysis stage, but eliminated the redevelopment stage. Since the latter can constitute in the order of half the costs whereas the former is a much smaller percentage, the overall saving is up to half the cost. One problem which project managers face is that a project using formal methods may be two-thirds complete without any sign of the final software in sight. This can be unnerving the first time round, and may be one reason for the lack of uptake of formal methods in general; unfortunately people have a proclivity towards wanting to see some actual running results, even if they are the wrong results. An answer to this problem is to use rapid prototyping tools (perhaps through the use of executable specifications) for parts of the system that must be demonstrated to the customer before development of the actual software begins.

Approach	Specification & Analysis	Development	Testing	Redevelopment	Validation & Correction	Total
Development without formal methods or diversity applied	·07	·12	·36	·48	·38	1·31
Development with formal methods and no diversity	·14	·12	·36	0	·38	1·0
Development with two-channel diversity and no formal methods	·07	·24	·72	·96	0	1·99

Table 3. Comparison of cost-effectiveness of approaches at Rolls-Royce and Associates.

© 1991 Elsevier Science Publishers Ltd. Reproduced from [63, page 114] with kind permission of Kluwer Academic Publishers.

Parnas et al.[114] provide an approach to the design, documentation and evaluation of computer-based safety-critical systems that have been used by the Atomic Energy Control Board (AECB) of Canada to assess the safety of software in a nuclear power station. Ontario Hydro and AECB are advocating the use of systematic mathematical verification techniques and rigorous arguments of correctness [75]. Indeed, they have already applied formal methods in the analysis of the shutdown system for the Darlington Nuclear Reactor plant [4].

3.4 Medical systems

A number of medical instruments have life-critical functionality and require a high degree of dependability. Two Hewlett-Packard divisions have used formal specification in order to enhance the quality of a range of cardiac care products. In both cases the formal notation used was HP-SL [9].

The first instance [81] involves a bedside instrument which is used to monitor vital signs of patients in intensive care units and operating rooms. Formal specification was used in a product enhancement involving monitoring a segment of the patient's electrocardiogram (ECG) which can be clinically significant since a change in that segment can indicate reduced blood flow which can be asymptomatic and hence difficult to detect. The team found that using formal specification resulted in higher precision in the development process which helped uncover a number of problems and ambiguities in the informal product specification. They believe that the use of formal notation played a significant role in realising a high quality product. Although they found it difficult to quantify the benefits of formal specification, they do report improved defect densities as shown in Table 4 (reproduced from [81]).

Project	KNCSS	Test Hours	Defect Density
This project	16.1	20.3	0.06
Project X	81.8	61.2	0.20

Table 4. Comparison of some Hewlett-Packard project metrics.

© 1991 Hewlett-Packard. Reproduced with permission.

The second example [41] relates to an instrument involving approximately 16 Kbytes of safety-critical code in ROM. In this case, the formal specification provided a process model of the system, specifying the relationship of inputs and outputs over time. The specification was subsequently used to produce SA/SD diagrams (structured analysis/structured design) from which the code was derived. The team again found that using formal specification helped them to uncover and resolve a number of ambiguities in the informal product definition. They also found that although they had an increased design time, the effort paid back in terms of shorter coding times.

It is interesting to note that both teams were particularly concerned with the impact of formal specification on their project schedules. Notwithstanding the significant benefits that were realised during development, they felt that adoption of formal techniques would have been very difficult if they had not introduced the approach very early on in the project and had they not had managerial commitment and support from the expert HP-SL team in Hewlett-Packard Research Laboratories, Bristol, UK. They found that retrospective specification of existing products was problematic and not very successful.

Tektronix in Oregon, USA, are also producing software for safety-critical applications involving medical equipment (as well as developing oscilloscopes) and have started applying formal methods in both areas. Real-time kernels can often be particularly tricky and error prone. Attempts have been made to formalize existing kernels and this has drawn attention to possible problem areas [138]. In particular, it is possible to calculate the preconditions (prior assumptions) of operations and if these are not vacuously true (i.e., the operation can be called at any time) it is possible that an error may be caused by activating that part of the software at an inappropriate time. These potential error conditions may not be a problem in the initial release of the software since they never occur in practice; however, if they have been inadequately documented (which is often the case), then subsequent maintenance of the software (quite often by a different team) could result in catastrophic failure.

Deaths due to software in medical equipment have been documented elsewhere (e.g., the Therac 25 radiotherapy machine [72, 86, 112, 142], where the dosage editor was poorly designed) and as a result others are also resorting to formal techniques in this area. Jacky [71, 73] discusses formal specification and verification issues regarding a clinical cyclotron control system which is currently under development at the University of Washington Hospital Cancer Treatment Center.

3.5 Ammunition control

The control of operations concerning the storage and use of explosive articles is an area with obvious safety-critical implications. In fact, the Ordnance Board of the UK Ministry of Defence (MoD) contributed substantially to the impetus towards the standardization of safety-critical software by articulating the problems inherent in using software in fusing applications such as torpedoes and missiles. Explosives safety concerns are not however limited to weapons delivery systems. Over the years, the variety of explosive substances and articles has increased significantly and the MoD has a continuing problem with the storage of explosives which is driven by the increasing complexity and variety of weapon systems. Although the MoD does not publish its internal directives, these are known to be consistent with publicly available regulations such as the United Nations Regulations for the Transport of Dangerous Goods ("Orange Book") [S23]. Similar arrangements operate in other NATO countries.

The ammunition holdings of a number of MoD ranges in the UK are managed by an ammunition control software (ACS) system which has been subjected to extensive validation as well as formal specification [102]. Although ACS is not a real-time system, it is nonetheless safety-critical since incorrect storage combinations can lead to massive explosions. The ACS software became more safety-critical as experienced technical staff were replaced by operators who needed to rely implicitly on the computer output. It is therefore vital that the system correctly implements the appropriate MoD regulations since human intervention is not a feasible backup option.

As an example of what can be done, Mukherjee and Stavridou [102] have produced a formal specification of the safety requirements in the Orange book and related it to the operations performed and controlled under ACS in VDM. In particular, they address additions of explosives to magazines and extensions to facilities by means of additional magazines. They have found a number of contradictions in the UN rules.[2] The formal specification is significant because the MoD can now generate a formal specification of their own regulations which when verified by the regulation authority can be incorporated into the Operational Requirement for a planned ACS replacement in accordance with Def Stan 00-55. Furthermore, the work has demonstrated that the use of formal methods can be successfully extended to areas such as planning and prediction as well as a "change facilitator".

3.6 Embedded microprocessors

The Viper (Verifiable Integrated Processor for Enhanced Reliability) is a microprocessor that has been specifically developed for safety-critical applications [39]. The HOL (Higher Order Logic) mechanized theorem prover [52] has been used to verify parts of the processor. However the methods used and the (sometimes misinterpreted) claims about the correctness of this processor have caused some controversy in industrial and even the formal methods communities [20, 33].

Viper was the first "real" microprocessor subjected to formal verification and intended for serious use. This fact, coupled with its Ministry of Defence parentage, makes Viper a high profile hardware verification experiment in the UK. In [37], Cullyer outlines the reasons behind the chip's development, namely MoD control of chip design, manufacture and marketing. The constraints on the architecture and manufacture of Viper can be summarized under the heading of "simplicity". This is understandable as simplicity is a very sensible requirement for systems used in safety-critical applications; it is also fortunate because in this instance it made formal verification experiments possible. Simplicity coupled with the need for quality are potentially fertile ground for the use of formal methods.

In [31, 32], Cohn presents proofs in HOL [52] relating the top specification with the host machine (state machine) and the block level description of Viper (register transfer level description). The block level itself, is still very abstract as one has to go through the gate and electronic levels before arriving at the manufactured chip. The proof relating the top-level functional specification with the host machine revealed a type error, a confused definition and an incomplete check [31] while the (only partially completed) block-level proof did not reveal any problems. Neither proof was of direct concern to the fabricators of Viper chips and indeed, the fact that the first batch of chips from one of the manufacturers contained errors cannot

---

[2] The UN rules are currently being redrafted, independently of the work described above [102]. It is expected, however, that the findings above findings will be incorporated in the revised regulations.

be attributed to the flaws discovered by Cohn. The chips and the manufacturer literature appeared a long time before the conclusion of the formal verification work. It is clearly therefore the case that formal verification in the case of Viper was a *design quality assurance* exercise. The associated costs were prohibitive and therefore the next generation of the chip, Viper2, was not subjected to similar hardware verification (although other verification techniques have been used[3]).

The lessons from the Viper experiment can be summarized as follows:

- The dependability of the chip was enhanced at a price, although no statistics are available.
- Formal methods can certainly help deliver *slower* chips because efficient but complex structures are hard to verify.
- Although no comparative figures are available, it is difficult to imagine that the formal verification produced a cheaper chip.
- The formal verification work was not directly utilized in the development of Viper2 (which is very similar to the original with the addition of a multiply instruction) so there is no evidence of the work aiding design backtracking.
- The experiment has certainly shown that HOL is scalable even if painfully so [32].

Some of the ensuing controversy as to what exactly constitutes a proof is discussed from a sociological viewpoint in [91, 92].

4 Areas of Application of Formal Methods

As has just been illustrated, formal methods are applicable in a wide variety of contexts to both software and hardware, even within the confines of safety-critical systems. They are useful at a number of levels of abstraction in the development process ranging from requirements capture, through to specification, design, coding, compilation and the underlying digital hardware itself. Some examples of current research work in these areas are given in this section. An example of a suggested overall approach to project organization using formal methods is provided by [122].

The Cleanroom approach is another technique that incorporates the use of rigorous methods to produce highly reliable software by means of non-execution-based program development that is establishing itself as an effective means of drastically reducing the number of errors in software [131, 45]. The rigorous development stage is clearly split from the certification stage, that replaces the normal testing phase, and is used to check for the absence of errors rather than for correcting them. The combination of this approach with the use of formal notations such as Z would be a useful area of study that IBM is starting to investigate [109].

In 1991 the UK Department of Trade and Industry (DTI) instituted the 'SafeIT' initiative in order to establish a unified approach to the assurance of software-based

---

[3] Logica Cambridge was contracted to develop and use Meta-Morph, a tool for reasoning about functional language specifications.

safety-critical systems by encouraging and financing collaborative projects in the area [S21]. This sponsors industrial (and to a lesser extent academic) organizations to undertake collaborative projects in this area. A second phase of the initiative was launched in 1992 [94]. An associated Safety Critical Systems Club has been formed and judging by the attendance of 255 delegates at the inaugural meeting, interest in this area is very strong in the UK. A club newsletter includes articles on the application of mathematical methods to safety-critical systems (e.g., see [3]) as well as issues concerning standards. The research effort in the area is gathering momentum and a number of interesting projects are currently under way. The SafeIT MORSE and SafeFM projects aim to build models for analyzing safety requirements and find practical ways of using formal methods in the development of safety-critical systems. The SafeIT initiative is particularly interested in safety standards and has produced a framework for such standards [S22].

The European ESPRIT programme is sponsoring two research projects that have a particular interest in the safety of computer-based systems. The ProCoS (Provably Correct Systems) [11] and PDCS (Predictably Dependable Computing Systems) [80] Basic Research Actions are examining different approaches to safety, the former concentrating on qualitative and the latter on quantitative aspects.

The upsurge of interest in the area is also evident from the emphasis placed on criticality by major international conferences. The ACM SIGSOFT '91 Conference was devoted to safety-critical software and the 1992 International Conference on Software Engineering is concentrating on trusted systems.

4.1 Requirements capture

Accurate requirements capture is very important in the design of any system. A mistake at this stage will be carried through the entire development process and will be very expensive to correct later. Studies have shown that a modification in service can cost up to 1,000 times more than a modification at the requirements stage [26]. Even worse, two-thirds of all errors are made at the requirements stage [26]. So it is hardly surprising that the US Government Accounting Office has calculated requirements defects cost $6·5 million on 9 projects alone. It clearly makes sense to ensure that the requirements are correct before proceeding with development. When formalizing requirements, there is nothing to validate them against except the real world. Thus it is important that the requirements language is simple enough to be easily understandable, but expressive enough to describe the desired requirements fully. This is a difficult balance to achieve, and the language used will vary from project to project depending on which aspects of the system need to be captured.

There is now a considerable interest in this aspect of design in the formal methods community (see, for example, [50]); it forms, for example, a major goal of both the SafeFM and MORSE projects. For safety-critical systems, timing is often of great importance. This has proved to be a difficult area to formalize in a manner that is usable in practice. However research in this area is gathering momentum (e.g., using the Duration Calculus [161]) [59, 121].

4.2 Design

The design process refines a specification down to a program using (possibly) provably correct transformations or some other kind of rigorous refinement method. In general this must involve input from the engineer since there are many programs that meet a particular specification. Most formal methods until now have not considered the problem of timing issues in these transformations, partly because of its intractability. However research is active in this area (e.g., [93]). It is crucial to keep things as simple as possible while still addressing the problems that actually matter. In a *hard real-time* system (which includes most safety-critical systems), a missed response is as bad as functional failure, whereas in a *soft real-time* system the occasional delay in response is tolerable. In the former type of system, it is very important to prove that the desired response time will be met under all circumstances.

Research into real-time formalisms such as Timed CSP (Communicating Sequential Processes) [42] is currently very active and is being applied in the area of robotics, for example, to help ensure correctness of the design [118]. Student textbooks for real-time formalisms are also now appearing [96]. However, there are a number competing formalisms to reason about real-time aspects of systems [130]; there are many problems yet to be solved and it remains to be seen which of the existing formalisms will be most useful in practice. Recently interest in *hybrid systems* [95] has increased, in which continuous variables (as well as time) are considered. The best interface between the differential equations of the control engineer that define the overall system and the controlling computer program of the software engineer has yet to be determined.

4.3 Compilation

Compilers produce code that it is notoriously difficult to analyze, particularly as far as timing aspects are concerned. They themselves may be unreliable and introduce an extra unknown into the development process. The development of the compiler needs to be as strictly controlled and reliable as the development of the high-level safety-critical code itself. Thus in the past, software safety standards and directives have normally insisted that all software is written in an assembler program that can be transliterated almost directly into machine code. Since this is the actual code that is executed, this is the code that needs to be verified [29]. However, this simply shifts the burden of responsibility, since the programmer must ensure that the assembler program meets its specification, and this is more difficult than the equivalent process for a high-level program.

Nowadays, safety standards are recognizing that programmers can produce high-level programs much more reliably than low-level programs and thus some are even insisting that high-level languages are used, a complete reversal of the previous guidance issued to engineers. Recent research has demonstrated that it is possible to verify compiling specifications elegantly and even produce a rapid prototype compiler that is very close to the original specification in the form of a logic program [66]. Other related research is investigating methods to verify an actual compiler, including the bootstrap process, but significant barriers remain before such an approach can become viable in practice [24, 40].

Since the machine code itself is the final program that actually matters, decompilation is sometimes used to ensure that it is correct. Decompilation can be tricky, but very similar (or even identical) programs for compilation and decompilation can be used if a declarative approach is adopted [16].

4.4 Programmable hardware

Programmable Logic Controllers (PLCs) are often used in process control and work has been undertaken to formalize the design process for these devices [55]. Another relatively new digital hardware technology, which may be of interest to safety-critical engineers who currently use embedded computer systems, is the *Field Programmable Gate Array* (FPGA, e.g., [159]). This allows the possibility of directly programming hardware almost as easily as general purpose computers are programmed today. A memory within the FPGA contains a pattern of bits (similar to the object code of a program) that determines the interconnections of a number of digital components such as boolean gates and latches within the chip.

Compilers from high-level programming languages down to a *'netlist'* of components are now being produced [111], and it seems a realistic goal that such compilers could be formally proved correct. A particularly attractive feature of this direct implementation in hardware for safety-critical systems is that the timing aspects of the program can be considerably simplified if synchronous circuits are used. For example, in [111] all assignment statements take one clock cycle and (perhaps surprisingly) all control statements take no clock cycles since the control operates between the clock edges. Additionally, the natural parallelism of hardware can be used to great advantage. Parallel programs can run truly concurrently and parallel assignments of several variables (up to the entire state of the program) still only take one clock cycle.

This looks like a very promising research area for the 1990s and it is foreseen that programmable hardware will be used increasingly during the coming years. Formal verification of the overall system will be simplified since the high-level program is related directly to gate-level hardware without the complexity of an intermediate instruction set.

4.5 Documentation

An important part of a designed system is its documentation, particularly if subsequent changes are made. Formalizing the documentation leads to less ambiguity and thus less likelihood of errors. In the case of safety-critical systems, timing issues become significant and methods for documenting these are especially important [115].

Formal methods provide a precise and unambiguous way of recording expected/delivered system functionality and can therefore be used as a powerful documentation aid. The normal expectation would be that the system documentation contains both the requirements and the system specification in a suitable formal notation, accompanied where appropriate with English narrative. The latter is particularly important for conveying information on system aspects which are not formally specified for various reasons.

4.6 Human-computer interface

The human-computer interface (HCI) is an important part of most software systems. In safety-critical systems, it becomes ever more important that the interface is both dependable [22] and ergonomically sound.[4] Formalizing HCI in a realistic and useful manner is a difficult task since the problem has widely divergent facets such as task allocation and cognition, but progress is being made in categorizing features of interfaces that may help to ensure their reliability in the future. However, as it is recognized by the technical workplan of the second phase of the UK SafeIT research programme [94], there seems to be considerable scope for work in this area. Investigation of human errors [124] and how computers can help to avoid them is now being undertaken in a formal context [60].

4.7 Object-oriented methods

Object-oriented approaches to software development have been advocated as a way to improve the design and reusability of software components, and hence increase their reliability. Recently there has been much discussion on combining object-oriented and formal methods, especially in critical applications [43]. Much research work has been undertaken in extending formal notations such as Z and VDM to include object-oriented concepts (e.g., see [143]). Currently there are many variants, and it remains to be seen which if any will emerge to be used in practice.

4.8 Artificial intelligence

Despite the complexities and difficulty of understanding the exact nature of AI, there is interest in including artificial intelligence in safety-critical systems. In particular, *blackboard systems* are being used as a method of communication within AI systems, for example in the area of robotics [118]. Blackboard systems have previously been rather vaguely described, but this problem is now being recognized and an attempt to formalize them has been undertaken [35]. The formal verification of AI software is further discussed in [126, 150].

---

[4] Consider, for example, the HCI issues surrounding the fly-by-wire A320 Airbus. Some pilots have consistently criticized the ergonomics of the cockpit instrument layout which they have identified as a possible contributory factor to the pilot errors that have caused at least two crashes so far.

4.9 Static analysis

Static analysis techniques and tools such as MALPAS and SPADE are used in industry for the rigorous checking of program code. Such techniques are sometimes used for *post hoc* validation of (safety-critical) code. It is a matter of engineering judgement as to how much effort should be expended to design the system correctly in the first place and how much checking should be undertaken after the design has been implemented. The identification and the discharging of proof obligations are two phases of the design process [30].

5 Safety Standards

There are a wide variety of standards bodies – perhaps too many[5] – throughout the world concerned with software development. The IED/SERC funded SMARTIE project is investigating a standards assessment framework [46] and [57] gives an overview of existing standards. Many have emerged or are currently emerging in the area of software safety, because this is now of such widespread importance and public concern. Formal methods are being increasingly mentioned in such standards as a possible method of improving dependability. This section gives some examples of such standards.

In addition, formal specification languages and their semantics are themselves being standardized (e.g., LOTOS [S14], VDM [S2] and Z [S24]). Formal notations are also becoming increasingly accepted in standards as it is realized that many existing standards using informal natural language descriptions alone (e.g., for programming language semantics) are ambiguous and can easily be (and often are) misinterpreted.

An important trigger for the exploitation of research into formal methods could be the interest of regulatory bodies or standardization committees (e.g., the *International Electrotechnical Commission* [S10, S11], the *European Space Agency* [S4], and the UK *Health and Safety Executive* [S7, S8]). Many emerging standards are at the discussion stage (e.g., [S18, S12]). A major impetus has already been provided in the UK by promulgation of the Ministry of Defence interim standard 00-55 [S15], which mandates the use of formal methods and languages with sound formal semantics. Previous guidelines [S5] have been influential in the contents of safety standards and a standards framework [S22] may help to provide a basis for future standards.

5.1 Formal methods in standards

Until relatively recently there have been few standards concerned specifically with software in safety-critical systems. Often software quality standards such as the

---
[5] During the December 1991 ACM SIGSOFT Conference on safety-critical software, Mike De Walt of the US Federal Aviation Administration mentioned that a recent count revealed 146 different standards relevant to software safety.

ISO9000 series have been used instead since these were the nearest relevant guidelines. Now a spate of standards in this area have been or are about to be issued. [135] gives a good overview (in 1989) and also covers a number of formalisms such as VDM, Z and OBJ. Many standards do not mention a formal approach specifically (e.g., MIL-STD-882B [S3]) although most are periodically updated to incorporate recent ideas (e.g., a draft version of MIL-STD-882C is currently under discussion).

The software engineering community became acutely aware of the introduction of formal methods in standards in the late 1980s and particularly since the introduction of the UK MoD DefStan 00-55 which will be commented upon later in this section. Although the debate on the exact formal methods content of standards like 00-55 is bound to continue, we feel that there are certain aspects such as formal specification which cannot sensibly be ignored by standardizing bodies.

This section introduces the recommendations concerning the use of formal methods in a number of software safety standards. The selection, which is summarized in Table 5, is somewhat eclectic, but demonstrates the range of areas and organizational bodies that are involved. Overviews of current standards concerned with software safety from an American point of view are provided by [152, 158].

The US and Europe are the major sources of software safety standards and research in this area. In Canada, [S1, S17] have been produced in relation to the nuclear industry. Standards Australia is recommending adoption of the IEC Draft Document 65A [S10]. Natsume and Hasegawa [105] provide a rare overview of dependability and safety issues in Japan, including details of an abortive attempt to produce their own JIS standard sponsored by MITI in this area, although guideline reports exist.

Country	Body	Sector	Name	FMs content	FMs mandated	Status (May 1993)	Year
US	DoD	Defence	MIL-STD-882B	No	N/A	Standard	1985
			MIL-STD-882C	No	N/A	Due	1993
US	RTCA	Aviation	DO-178A	No	N/A	Guideline	1985
			DO-178B	Yes	No	Guideline	1992
Europe	IEC	Nuclear	IEC880	No	N/A	Standard	1986
UK	HSE	Generic	PES	No	N/A	Guideline	1987
Europe	IEC	Generic	IEC65A WG9	Yes	No	Draft	1989
			IEC65A 122	Yes	No	Proposed	1991
Europe	ESA	Space	PSS-05-0	Yes	No	Standard	1991
UK	MoD	Defence	00-55	Yes	Yes	Interim	1991
US	IEEE	Generic	P1228	No	No	Draft	1993
UK	RIA	Railway	–	Yes	No	Draft	1991
Canada	AECB	Nuclear	2.234.1	Yes	Yes	Report	1992

Table 5. Summary of software-related standards.

RTCA DO-178. The US *Radio Technical Commission for Aeronautics* (RTCA) produced a guideline on software considerations in airborne systems and equipment certification (DO-178A) in 1985 [S19]. This does not explicitly recognize formal methods as part of accepted practice. However a new guideline (DO-178B) is currently under consideration by a committee and is likely to include a brief section on *Guidelines for the Use of Formal Methods*.

UK HSE. The UK *Health and Safety Executive* issued an introductory guide [S7] and some general technical guidelines [S8] concerning Programmable Electronic Systems (PES) in safety-related applications in 1987. Two pages are devoted to software development (pp. 31–32) and a further two to software change procedures (pp. 32–33). No mention is made of formal methods; it simply states that software should be of high quality, well documented, match its specification and be maintainable. It does list the necessary phases of software development and includes in these requirements specification, software specification, design, coding and testing, and system testing. It goes on to state that modifications to the software should be strictly controlled.

IEC. The *International Electrotechnical Commission* has issued two standards in the area of safety-critical system development [S10, S11]. These documents were originally issued in 1989, but have recently been updated and reissued. The former deals specifically with software for computers in the application of industrial safety-related systems, while the latter is concerned with the functional safety of programmable electronic systems in general. These are generic international standards designed to be applied in many different industrial sectors. An example of a particular instantiation of the IEC65-WG9 standard is included below.

The "formal methods" CCS, CSP, HOL, LOTOS, OBJ, Temporal Logic, VDM and Z are specifically mentioned in [S10] (with a brief description and bibliography for each) as possible techniques to be applied in the development of safety-critical systems in an extensive section (B.30, pp. B-14–18) under a *Bibliography of Techniques*. A shorter section on "formal proof" (B.30, p. B-18) is also included.

ESA. The *European Space Agency* has issued guidelines for software engineering standards [S4]. This suggests that formal notations such as Z or VDM should be used for specifying software requirements in safety-critical systems (p. 1–27). A natural language description should accompany the formal text. A short section on formal proof (p. 2–25) suggests that proof of the correctness of the software should be attempted if practicable. Because of the possibility of human error, proofs should be checked independently. Methods such as formal proof should always be tried before testing is undertaken.

UK RIA. The *Railway Industry Association*, consisting of a number of interested organizations and industrial companies in the UK, has produced a consultative document on safety-related software for railway signalling [S18]. It is a draft proposal for an industry-specific standard that has yet to be ratified. It makes extensive reference to the IEC65-WG9 standard [S10]. Formal methods are mentioned briefly in several places in the document. Rigorous correctness argument is advocated as a less detailed and formal proof method to demonstrate the correctness of a program by simply outlining the main steps of the proof. In general, formal techniques are only recommended or mandated when the very highest levels of safety are required.

MoD 00-55 and 00-56. The UK Ministry of Defence has recently published two interim standards concerning safety. 00-55, on the procurement of safety-critical software in defence equipment [S15] is split into two parts, on requirements and guidance. The 00-56 standard is concerned with hazard analysis and safety classification of the computer and programmable electronic system elements of defence equipment [S16]. These standards, and particularly 00-55, mention and mandate formal methods extensively and have, therefore, created many ripples in the defence software industry as well as the software engineering community in the UK.[6] The standards are currently in interim form. The MoD, which had previously set 1995 as the goal date for the introduction of fully mandatory standards [21], has now withdrawn a specific introduction date.

00-55 mandates the expression of safety-critical module specifications in a formal language notation. Such specifications must be analyzed to establish their consistency and completeness in respect to all potentially hazardous data and control flow domains. A further fundamental requirement is that all safety-critical software must be subject to validation and verification to establish that it complies with its formal specification over its operating domain. This involves static and dynamic analysis as well as formal proofs and informal but rigorous arguments of correctness.

AECB, Canada. The Atomic Energy Control Board (AECB) in Canada has commissioned a proposed standard for software for computers in the safety systems of nuclear power stations [S1]. This has been prepared by David Parnas who is well known in the fields of both software safety and formal methods. The standard formalizes the notions of the environment ('nature'), the behavioural system requirements, and their feasibility with respect to the environment. It is based on the IEC Standard 880 [S9]. AECB have not, at the time of writing, decided to adopt Parnas's proposal and discussions are continuing.

IEEE P1228. The P1228 Software Safety Plans Working Group, under the Software Engineering Standards Subcommittee of the IEEE Computer Society, is preparing a standard for software safety plans. This is an unapproved draft that is subject to change. The appendix of [S12] includes headings of *"Formal/Informal Proofs"* and *"Mathematical Specification Verification"* under techniques being discussed for inclusion. The latest version of the draft (Draft G of January 1992) omits all mention of formal methods so it is unclear what the final position will be.

5.2 Education, certification and legislation

Standards are a motivating force that *pull* industry to meet a minimum level of safety in the development of critical systems. Another complementary force that could be seen to *push* industry is the education of engineers in the proper techniques that should be applied to such systems. A safety-critical software engineer should have

---

[6] Tierney [147] provides a very interesting account of the evolution of 00-55 and the associated debate in the UK.

an an appreciation of far more areas than the average programmer. Such engineers must typically interface with control and hardware engineers for example.

Despite the above, safety-critical software is still either not mentioned at all, or mentioned in passing as being too specialized for inclusion, in many standard textbooks on software engineering, although formal methods are being included more now (e.g., see [136]). Gries [53] bemoans the lack of mathematical content in many software engineering courses. Wichmann [157] includes a recent report on education and training with respect to safety-related software. Professional bodies can provide assistance in the form of up-to-date information aimed at practicing engineers [69].

It is a paradox of current avionics practice that the engineer who fixes bolts on airframes must be accredited whereas the programmer who writes the autopilot software needs no such qualification. [119] discusses the accreditation of software engineers by professional institutions. It is suggested that training is as important as experience in that *both* are necessary. In addition, (software) engineers should be responsible for their mistakes if they occur through negligence rather than genuine error. Safety-critical software is identified as an area of utmost importance where such ideas should be applied first because of the possible gravity of errors if they do occur.

Currently a major barrier to the acceptance of formal methods is the fact that many engineers and programmers do not have the appropriate training to make use of them and many managers do not know when and how they may be applied. This is gradually being alleviated as the necessary mathematics (typically set theory and predicate calculus) is being taught increasingly in computing science curricula. Educational concerns in the UK are reflected in the SafeIT strategy document [S21]. The UK Department of Trade and Industry has commissioned a special study to stimulate the development of education and training in the area. In addition, the British Computer Society and the Institution of Electrical Engineers have established working groups which are aiming to produce proposals on the content of courses aimed at safety-critical systems engineers.

Some standards and draft standards are now recognizing the problems and recommending that appropriate personnel should be used on safety-critical projects. There are suggestions that some sort of certification of developers should be introduced. This is still an active topic of discussion [107], but there are possible drawbacks as well as benefits by introducing such a 'closed shop' since suitable able engineers may be inappropriately excluded (and vice versa).

The education/accreditation debate has been particularly active in the UK, in the wake of Def Stan 00-55. The MoD, having commissioned a report on training and education to support 00-55 [160], has chosen to withdraw from the consequent controversy stating that it is beyond the remit of the standard to set a national training agenda. Perhaps the central issue here is not formal methods education *per se*, but the identity of the whole software engineering profession; in other words, what precisely *is* a software engineer is a question that will no doubt be debated for some time to come.[7]

Finally, legislation is likely to provide increasing motivation to apply appropriate techniques in the development of safety-critical systems. For example, a new piece of European Commission legislation, the Machine Safety Directive, is effective in the UK from 1st January 1993 [106]. This encompasses software and if there is an error in the machine's logic that results in injury then a claim can be made under civil law against the supplier. If negligence can be proved during the product's design or manufacture then criminal proceedings may be taken against the director or manager in charge. There will be a maximum penalty of three months in jail or a large fine. Suppliers will have to demonstrate that they are using best working practice. This could include, for example, the use of formal methods.

6 Discussion

This section offers a discussion of the current situation and some possible ways forward in research. It represents the opinions of the authors as opposed to an impartial and objective survey.

The subject of software safety has profound technical, business, professional and personal aspects for the individuals who research, develop, sell, use and rely upon computer-controlled systems. So it is hardly surprising that the introduction and use of a technology such as formal methods in this context is accompanied by vigorous if not heated debate. What is at stake ranges from substantial industrial investment, to 'closed shop' interests and professional pride in the job, and ultimately to our very lives. The arguments surrounding the value and use of formal methods for safety-critical systems are a prime example of the potential for controversy.[8]

The complexity of critical systems is rising as more and more functionality is provided by software solutions. The gap between the dependability requirements and what we can achieve in terms of delivering and measuring such dependability is huge. We believe that, on the evidence of past experiments, formal methods technology deployed in conjunction with other techniques can help narrow this gap. The factors that diminish the effectiveness of formal methods in this context are:

- Some aspects of the technology, such as formal specification, have been widely used and are relatively well understood. Other practices, however, such as machine-supported theorem proving, have not benefited from real-world use and are correspondingly less well developed.
- Formal methods can be expensive when compared with traditional defect removal techniques. It is naive to assume that "money is no object" given that the cost of safety is highly subjective, varies from system to system even within the same

---

[7] Tierney [148] discusses the drift of many kinds of professionals into software engineering.
[8] Pelaez [117] discusses the 'radical' and 'reformist' factions in software engineering.

sector and depends on the perception and the politics of risk [116].[9] Clearly the cost-effectiveness of formal methods will need to be established on a case by case basis. The UK SafeIT DATUM project [88] is currently investigating this issue.
– Although it is accepted that the use of formal methods increases dependability margins, we cannot measure by how much. In fact, even if we could, we would not be able to measure global dependability since we do not know how to combine formal methods assurance with metrics collected from other techniques such as fault-tolerance.

In spite of these problems, we feel that *mature* formal methods can and should be used to produce safer software because benefits can be obtained without wholesale adoption. The mere act of writing a formal specification, for instance, can help to clarify system design and requirements; it can be used to improve or simplify a design; it can even be used to produce a rapid prototype in order to evaluate the projected system behaviour. However, in the context of safety-critical systems, it is profoundly important to recognize the limitations of any technology. Formal methods cannot do much, for example, in a chaotic software production environment.

If the issues surrounding the applicability of formal methods to critical systems are so complicated, it is hardly surprising that educational provision and standardization are equally complex matters. Currently, there is no universally agreed curriculum for safety-critical software professionals. On the contrary, there is a plethora of standards and this domain is beginning to look surprisingly similar to the state of the art in formal methods; too many standards that are not industrially used and assessed.

In this paper, we have tried to present an objective account of the state of the art of formal methods as reflected by recent industrial practice and standardization activities. In our opinion, the areas that need to be addressed in the future are research, technology, education/accreditation and standardization for the use of formal methods in the development of safety-critical software.

Formal methods research

Research in formal methods to date has largely addressed the functional and/or temporal correctness of system. We believe that as well as continuing to strive for better formal models [64] there is a need to interface formal models with safety engineering techniques such as hazard analysis and risk engineering. We also believe that research needs to focus more on safety-critical system issues which we collectively call *provable dependability*. This viewpoint affords many research dimensions, including amongst others:

– Dependability requirements analysis/capture. Integrity, reliability, security, safety, functional behaviour, temporal behaviour.

---

[9] For example, the MoD in the UK places different criticality on the importance of saving a life threatened by military aircraft in flight depending on whether the individual is a civilian, a pilot in flight in peacetime and a pilot in flight in wartime.

- Dependability specification. Can dependability requirements be formally stated? Is it possible to develop problem-specific calculi for the different aspects of dependability (such as fault-tolerance and security)?
- Development of dependable systems. Can we develop the necessary theories for refinement/transformation? If not, how should high-integrity systems be built?
- Machine-aided formal verification of dependability properties. To what extent can we use theorem-proving tools for verifying the dependability properties of systems? Which existing technologies are relevant?
- Qualitative and quantitative analysis of the dependability that can be achieved using the combination of formal verification and fault-tolerance. Can we increase confidence in systems by combining assurance methods?
- Case studies drawn from a wide spectrum of high-integrity systems. Real-time embedded systems, distributed systems, high-integrity transaction processing systems, theorem-proving systems.

Formal methods technology

Formal methods research is abundant, although we believe that focusing on safety-critical systems is important since provable dependability has not been sufficiently addressed in the field. We must distinguish between the issues relating to technology and those relating to research. By *technology* we mean the transition from research results to methods and tools which are "fit for purpose" with regard to the needs of industry. Understanding the difference between technology and research results is crucial and can go some way in explaining the reluctance of industry to adopt formal methods. The fact that a highly trained expert proves the correctness of a simple computer-based system in a research environment does not imply that a real safety-critical developer will use a theorem prover. Suitable technology must be produced before the process is enabled and as with any other endeavour the users as opposed to the research community must be the driving force.

In summary, in order to strengthen the technology and contribute to its maturity, the following are desirable:

- An engineering approach to formal specification and verification.
- Better tools.
- Investment in technology transfer.
- Unification and harmonization of the engineering practices involved in building safety-critical systems.
- More practical experience of the industrial use of the methods.
- Assessment and measurement of the effectiveness of formal methods.

Education and accreditation

The educational debate is also set to continue. It is likely that there will be a skills shortage in this area for the foreseeable future, although most computer science degree programs now contain at least elements of discrete mathematics and formal methods. The contentious issue is the education of the safety-critical software professional; work in this area is currently undertaken by the professional institutions and learned societies. Although, even for those of us teaching in higher education, there is no established consensus on this issue, it seems to us that software engineering education must be widened with safety engineering and dependability issues at the very least. The most fundamental question that has to be answered is whether the professionals writing the safety-critical software of the future should have a software or hardware or systems education. It is precisely the multidisciplinary nature of most safety-critical systems that makes educational provision such a thorny issue.

A closely related issue is the accreditation of such professionals. In our view, future accreditation is inevitable because of the massive stakes in resources and human lives involved in safety-critical systems. Happily, the professional institutions are actively examining this issue in conjunction with the educational requirements. Although the outcome of these deliberations is uncertain, any reasonable accreditation procedure can hardly fail to take into account a combination of educational qualifications coupled with training and responsible experience requirements.

It appears that Europe is leading the US and the rest of the world in the field of formal methods education, so this may be a good sign for the long-term development and reliability of safety-critical software in Europe.

Standards

The role of standards for safety-related software has critical implications for all the aspects that we have discussed above. Witness the impact of the MoD Def Stan 00-55 both in terms of research and development, and education in the United Kingdom [147, 148]. The current level of standardization activity is encouraging. We note, however, that the proliferation of standards is not in itself sufficient to ensure the production of safer software. These standards need to be used and their impact on software safety assessed and quantified. Moreover, research is needed in order to establish precisely what standards should contain and how various sector-specific standards interact when they are used simultaneously on a system. Work in this direction is reported in [46].

It is important that standards should not be over-prescriptive, or that prescriptive sections are clearly separated and identified as such (perhaps as an appendix or even as a separate document). These parts of a standard are likely to date much more quickly that its goals, and thus should be monitored and updated more often. Dependability goals should be set and the onus should be on the software supplier to ensure that the methods used achieve the required level of confidence. If particular methods are recommended or mandated, it is possible for the supplier to assume that the method will produce the desired results and blame the standards body if it does not. This reduces the responsibility and accountability of the supplier and may also result in a *decrease* of safety.

Standards have the dual effect of reflecting current best practice and normalizing procedures to the highest commonly acceptable denominator. As such, a significant number of software safety standards (at least half in this study) reflect the importance and relative maturity of formal methods. We believe that this trend is set to continue and standards will increasingly provide more motivation for the research, teaching and use of formal methods. We hope that this will eventually lead to some improvement in the safety of people and resources that depend upon computer software.

Acknowledgements. The European ESPRIT Basic Research Action **ProCoS** project (BRA 3104) and the UK Information Engineering Directorate safemos project (IED3/1/1036) provided financial support. Members of these projects provided intellectual support, encouragement and advice. We are particularly indebted to Prof. Tony Hoare (Oxford, UK) and Anders Ravn (DTH, Denmark). The following have also helped by supplying advice, information, papers, standards and feedback on earlier drafts which have been used as input to this survey: G.J.K. Asmis, Steve Bear, Steve Cha, Simon Chadwick, Bernie Cohen, Derek Coleman, Dan Craigen, Ben Di Vito, Susan Gerhart, Pat Hall, Guenter Heiner, Jill Hill, Jim Horning, Jonathan Jacky, Paul Joannou, Nancy Leveson, John McDermid, Peter Neumann, David Parnas, Ted Ralston, John Rushby, Debra Sparkman, Richard Stein, Martyn Thomas, Brian Wichmann, Geoff Wilson, Cynthia Wright, Janusz Zalewski, Tony Zawilski. Finally, the anonymous reviewers provided helpful suggestions and references that have been incorporated here.

References

Standards, draft standards and guidelines

S1. 'Proposed Standard for Software for Computers in the Safety Systems of Nuclear Power Stations'. Final Report for contract 2.117.1 for the Atomic Energy Control Board, Canada, March 1991 (By David L. Parnas, TRIO, Computing and Information Science, Queen's University, Kingston, Ontario K7L 3N6, Canada. Based on IEC Standard 880 [S9].)

S2. 'VDM Specification Proto-Standard'. Draft, ISO/IEC JTC1/SC22/WG19 IN9, 1991

S3. 'Military Standard: System Safety Program Requirements'. MIL-STD-882B, Department of Defense, Washington DC 20301, USA, 30 March 1984

S4. 'ESA Software Engineering Standards'. ESA PSS-05-0 Issue 2, European Space Agency, 8–10 rue Mario-Nikis, 75738 Paris Cedex, France, ESA PSS-05-0 Issue 2, February 1991

S5. REDMILL, F. (Ed.): 'Dependability of Critical Computer Systems 1 & 2'. European Workshop on Industrial Computer Systems Technical Committee 7 (EWICS TC7), Elsevier Applied Science, London, 1988/1989

S6. 'System Design Analysis'. US Department of Transportation, Federal Aviation Administration, Washington DC, USA, Advisory Circular 25.1309 2, September 1982

S7. 'Programmable Electronic Systems in Safety Related Applications: 1. An Introductory Guide'. Health and Safety Executive, HMSO, Publications Centre, PO Box 276, London SW8 5DT, UK, 1987
S8. 'Programmable Electronic Systems in Safety Related Applications: 2. General Technical Guidelines'. Health and Safety Executive, HMSO, Publications Centre, PO Box 276, London SW8 5DT, UK, 1987
S9. 'Software for Computers in the Safety Systems of Nuclear Power Stations'. International Electrotechnical Commission, IEC 880, 1986
S10. 'Software for Computers in the Application of Industrial Safety Related Systems'. International Electrotechnical Commission, Technical Committee no. 65, Working Group 9 (WG9), IEC 65A (Secretariat) 122, Version 1.0, 1 August 1991
S11. 'Functional Safety of Programmable Electronic Systems: Generic Aspects'. International Electrotechnical Commission, Technical Committee no. 65, Working Group 10 (WG10), IEC 65A (Secretariat) 123, February 1992
S12. 'Standard for Software Safety Plans'. Draft P1228, Software Safety Plans Working Group, Software Engineering Standards Subcommittee, IEEE Computer Society, USA, Draft J, 11 February 1991
S13. 'JTC1 Statement of Policy on Formal Description Techniques'. ISO/IEC JTC1 N145 and ISO/IEC JTC1/SC18 N13333, International Standards Organization, Geneva, Switzerland, 1987
S14. 'ISO 8807: Information Processing Systems – Open Systems Interconnection – LOTOS – A Formal Description Technique Based on the Temporal Ordering of Observational Behaviour'. First edition, International Organization for Standardization, Geneva, Switzerland, 15 February 1989
S15. 'The Procurement of Safety Critical Software in Defence Equipment' (Part 1: Requirements, Part 2: Guidance). Interim Defence Standard 00-55, Issue 1, Ministry of Defence, Directorate of Standardization, Kentigern House, 65 Brown Street, Glasgow G2 8EX, UK, 5 April 1991
S16. 'Hazard Analysis and Safety Classification of the Computer and Programmable Electronic System Elements of Defence Equipment'. Interim Defence Standard 00-56, Issue 1, Ministry of Defence, Directorate of Standardization, Kentigern House, 65 Brown Street, Glasgow G2 8EX, UK, 5 April 1991
S17. 'Standard for Software Engineering of Safety Critical Software'. 982 C-H 69002-0001, Ontario Hydro, 700 University Avenue, Toronto, Ontario M5G 1X6, Canada, 21 December 1990
S18. 'Safety Related Software for Railway Signalling'. BRB/LU Ltd/RIA technical specification no. 23, Consultative Document, Railway Industry Association, 6 Buckingham Gate, London SW1E 6JP, UK, 1991
S19. 'Software Considerations in Airborne Systems and Equipment Certification'. DO-178A, Radio Technical Commission for Aeronautics, One McPherson Square, 1425 K Street N.W., Suite 500, Washington DC 20005, USA, March 1985

S20. 'Minimum Operational Performance Standards for Traffic Alert and Collision Avoidance System (TCAS) Airborne Equipment – Consolidated Edition'. DO-185, Radio Technical Commission for Aeronautics, One McPherson Square, 1425 K Street N.W., Suite 500, Washington DC 20005, USA, 6 September 1990

S21. BLOOMFIELD, R.E. (Ed.): 'SafeIT1 – The Safety of Programmable Electronic Systems'. Safety-Related Working Group (SRS-WG), Interdepartmental Committee on Software Engineering (ICSE), Department of Trade and Industry, ITD7a – Room 840, Kingsgate House, 66–74 Victoria Street, London SW1E 6SW, UK, June 1990

S22. BLOOMFIELD, R.E., and BRAZENDALE, J. (Eds.): 'SafeIT2 – A Framework for Safety Standards'. Safety-Related Working Group (SRS-WG), Interdepartmental Committee on Software Engineering (ICSE), Department of Trade and Industry, ITD7a – Room 840, Kingsgate House, 66–74 Victoria Street, London SW1E 6SW, UK, June 1990

S23. UN Committee for the Transport of Dangerous Goods, Technical Report, 1964

S24. 'Z Base Standard'. Draft ISO/IEC JTC1/SC22, 1993

Other references

1. ABRIAL, J.R.: 'The B reference manual', Edinburgh Portable Compilers, 17 Alva Street, Edinburgh EH2 4PH, UK, 1991
2. ABRIAL, J.R., LEE, M.K.O., NEILSON, D.S., SCHARBACH, P.N., and SØRENSEN, I.H.: 'The B-method', *in* PREHN, S., and TOETENEL, W.J. (Eds.): 'VDM '91, Formal Software Development Methods', Volume 2: Tutorials (Springer-Verlag, *Lecture Notes in Computer Science*, 1991) **552**, pp. 398–405
3. ANDERSON, S., and CLELAND, G.: 'Adopting mathematically-based methods for safety-critical systems production', *in* REDMILL, F. (Ed.): 'Safety Systems: The Safety-Critical Systems Club Newsletter', Centre for Software Reliability, University of Newcastle upon Tyne, UK, January 1992, **1**, (2), p. 6
4. ARCHINOFF, G.H., HOHENDORF, R.J., WASSYNG, A., QUIGLEY, B. and BORSCH, M.R.: 'Verification of the shutdown system software at the Darlington nuclear generating station'. International Conference on Control and Instrumentation in Nuclear Installations, The Institution of Nuclear Engineers, Glasgow, UK, May 1990
5. AUGARTEN, S.: 'The Whirlwind project' *in* 'Bit by Bit: An Illustrated History of Computers', chapter 7 (Ticknor & Fields, New York, 1984) pp. 195–223
6. BABEL, P.S.: 'Software integrity program'. Aeronautical Systems Division, Airforce, U.S., April 1987

7. BARROCA, L., and MCDERMID, J.: 'Formal methods: use and relevance for the development of safety critical systems', *The Computer Journal*, **35**, (6), December 1992
8. BARDEN, R., STEPNEY, S., and COOPER, D.: 'The use of Z', *in* NICHOLLS, J.E. (Ed.): 'Z User Workshop, York 1991' (Springer-Verlag, Workshops in Computing, 1992) pp. 99–124
9. BEAR, S.: 'An overview of HP-SL', *in* PREHN, S., and TOETENEL, W.J. (Eds.): 'VDM '91, Formal Software Development Methods' (Springer-Verlag, *Lecture Notes in Computer Science*, 1991) **551**, pp. 571–587
10. BENNETT, P.A.: 'Safety', *in* McDERMID, J.A. (Ed.): 'Software Engineer's Reference Book', chapter 60 (Butterworth-Heinemann Ltd., Oxford, 1991)
11. BJØRNER, D. *et al.* 'A ProCoS project description: ESPRIT BRA 3104', *Bulletin of the EATCS*, 1989, **39**, pp. 60–73
12. BLOOMFIELD, R.E., FROOME, P.K.D., and MONAHAN, B.Q.: 'Formal methods in the production and assessment of safety critical software', *Reliability Engineering & System Safety*, **32**, (1), 1989, pp. 51–66 (Also in [89].)
13. BLYTH, D., BOLDDYREFF, C., RUGGLES, C., and TETTEH-LARTEY, N.: 'The case for formal methods in standards', *IEEE Software*, September 1990, **7**, (5), pp. 65–67
14. BOEBERT, W.E.: 'Formal verification of embedded software', *ACM SIGSOFT Software Engineering Notes*, July 1980, **5**, (3), pp. 41–42
15. BOEHM, B.: 'Software risk management tutorial'. TRW-ACM Seminar, April 1988
16. BOWEN, J.P., and BREUER, P.T.: 'Decompilation', *in* VAN ZUYLEN, H. (Ed.): 'The REDO Compendium of Reverse Engineering for Software Maintenance', chapter 10 (John Wiley, 1992) pp. 131–138
17. BOWEN, J.P., and STAVRIDOU, V.: 'Formal methods and software safety', in [47], 1992, pp. 93–98
18. BOWEN, J.P., and STAVRIDOU, V.: 'The industrial take-up of formal methods in safety-critical and other areas: a perspective', *in* WOODCOCK, J.C.P., and LARSEN, P.G. (Eds.): 'FME'93: Industrial Strength Formal Methods', 1st International Symposium of Formal Methods Europe, Odense, Denmark, 19–23 April 1993 (Springer-Verlag, *Lecture Notes in Computer Science*, 1993) **670**, pp. 183–195
19. BOYER, R.S., and MOORE, J.S.: 'A computational logic handbook' (Academic Press, Boston, 1988)
20. BROCK, B., and HUNT, W.A.: 'Report on the formal specification and partial verification of the VIPER microprocessor'. Technical Report No. 46, Computational Logic Inc., Austin, Texas, USA, January 1990
21. BROWN, M.J.D.: 'Rationale for the development of the UK defence standards for safety-critical computer software'. Proc. COMPASS '90, Washington DC, USA, June 1990
22. BURNS, A.: 'The HCI component of dependable real-time systems', *Software Engineering Journal*, July 1991, **6**, (4), pp. 168–174

23. BUTLER, R.W., and FINELLI, G.B.: 'The infeasibility of experimental quantification of life-critical software reliability'. Proc. ACM SIGSOFT '91 Conference on Software for Critical Systems, *Software Engineering Notes*, ACM Press, December 1991, **16**, (5), pp. 66–76
24. BUTH, B., BUTH, K-H., FRÄNZLE, M., VON KARGER, B., LAKHNECHE, Y., LANGMAACK, H., and MÜLLER-OLM, M.: 'Provably correct compiler development and implementation', *in* 'Compiler Construction '92', 4th International Conference, Paderborn, Germany (Springer-Verlag, *Lecture Notes in Computer Science*, 1992) **641**
25. BUXTON, J.N., and MALCOLM, R.: 'Software technology transfer', *Software Engineering Journal*, January 1991, **6**, (1), pp. 17–23
26. CANNING, A.: 'Assessment at the requirements stage of a project'. Presented at '2nd Safety Critical Systems Club Meeting', Beaconsfield, UK, October 1991 (Available from Advanced Software Department, ERA Technology Ltd, Cleeve Rd, Leatherhead KT22 7SA, UK.)
27. CHAPRONT, P.: 'Vital coded processor and safety related software design', in [47], 1992, pp. 141–145
28. CHARETTE, R.N.: 'Applications strategies for risk analysis' (McGraw Hill, Software Engineering Series, 1990)
29. CLUTTERBUCK, D.L., and CARRÉ, B.A.: 'The verification of low-level code', *Software Engineering Journal*, May 1988, **3**, (3), pp. 97–111
30. COHEN, B., and PITT, D.H.: 'The identification and discharge of proof obligations' *in* 'Testing Large Software Systems', Wolverhampton Polytechnic, UK, 1990
31. COHN, A.J.: 'A proof of correctness of the Viper microprocessor: the first level' *in* 'VLSI Specification, Verification and Synthesis' (Kluwer Academic Publishers, 1988)
32. COHN, A.J.: 'Correctness properties of the Viper block model: the second level'. Proc. 2nd Banff Workshop on Hardware Verification (Springer-Verlag, 1988)
33. COHN, A.J.: 'The notion of proof in hardware verification', *Journal of Automated Reasoning*, May 1989, **5**, (2), pp. 127–139
34. COLEMAN, D.: 'The technology transfer of formal methods: what's going wrong?'. Proc. 12th ICSE Workshop on Industrial Use of Formal Methods, Nice, France, March 1990
35. CRAIG, I.: 'The formal specification of advanced AI architectures' (Ellis Horwood, AI Series, 1991)
36. CRAIGEN, D. (Ed.): 'Formal methods for trustworthy computer systems (FM89)' (Springer-Verlag, Workshops in Computing, 1990)
37. CULLYER, W.J.: 'Hardware integrity', *Aeronautical Journal of the Royal Aeronautical Society*, September 1985, **89**, pp. 263–268
38. CULLYER, W.J.: 'High integrity computing', *in* JOSEPH, M. (Ed.): 'Formal Techniques in Real-time and Fault-tolerant Systems' (Springer-Verlag, *Lecture Notes in Computer Science*, 1988) **331**, pp. 1–35

39. CULLYER, W.J., and PYGOTT, C.H.: 'Application of formal methods to the VIPER microprocessor' *in* 'IEE Proceedings, Part E, Computers and Digital Techniques' May 1987, **134**, (3), pp. 133–141
40. CURZON, P.: 'Of what use is a verified compiler specification?', Technical Report No. 274, Computer Laboratory, University of Cambridge, UK, 1992
41. CYRUS, J.L., BLEDSOE, J.D., and HARRY, P.D.: 'Formal specification and structured design in software development', *Hewlett-Packard Journal*, December 1991, (6), pp. 51–58
42. DAVIES, J.: 'Specification and proof in real-time systems'. Technical Monograph PRG-93, Programming Research Group, Oxford University Computing Laboratory, April 1991
43. DE CHAMPEAUX, D. *et al.* 'Formal techniques for OO software development'. OOPSLA'91 Conference in Object-Oriented Programming Systems, Languages, and Applications, *SIGPLAN Notices*, ACM Press, November 1991, **26**, (11), pp. 166–170
44. 'Safety related computer controlled systems market study', Review for the Department of Trade and Industry by Coopers & Lybrand (HMSO, London, 1992)
45. DYER, M.: 'The Cleanroom approach to quality software development' (Wiley Series in Software Engineering Practice, 1992)
46. FENTON, N., and LITTLEWOOD, B.: 'Evaluating software engineering standards and methods'. Proc. 2èmes Rencontres Qualiteé Logiciel & Eurometrics '91, March 1991, pp. 333–340
47. FREY, H.H. (Ed.).: 'Safety of computer control systems 1992 (SAFECOMP'92)', Computer Systems in Safety-critical Applications, Proc. IFAC Symposium, Zürich, Switzerland, 28–30 October 1992 (Pergamon Press, 1992)
48. GLASS, R.L.: 'Software vs. hardware errors', *IEEE Computer*, December 1980, **23**, (12)
49. GOGUEN, J., and WINKLER, T.: 'Introducing OBJ3'. Technical Report SRI-CSL-88-9, SRI International, Menlo Park, California, USA, August 1988
50. GOLDSACK, S.J., and FINKELSTEIN, A.C.W.: 'Requirements engineering for real-time systems', *Software Engineering Journal*, May 1991, **6**, (3), pp. 101–115
51. GOOD, D.I., and YOUNG, W.D.: 'Mathematical methods for digital system development', *in* PREHN, S., and TOETENEL, W.J. (Eds.): 'VDM '91, Formal Software Development Methods', Volume 2: Tutorials (Springer-Verlag, *Lecture Notes in Computer Science*, 1991) **552**, pp. 406–430
52. GORDON, M.J.C.: 'HOL: A proof generating system for Higher-Order Logic', *in* BIRTWISTLE, G., and SUBRAMANYAM, P.A. (Eds.): 'VLSI Specification, Verification and Synthesis' (Kluwer, 1988) pp. 73–128
53. GRIES, D.: 'Influences (or lack thereof) of formalism in teaching programming and software engineering', *in* DIJKSTRA, E.W. (Ed.): 'Formal Devel-

opment of Programs and Proofs', chapter 18 (Addison Wesley, University of Texas at Austin Year of Programming Series, 1990) pp. 229–236
54. GUIHO, G., and HENNEBERT, C.: 'SACEM software validation'. Proc. 12th International Conference on Software Engineering (IEEE Computer Society Press, March 1990) pp. 186–191
55. HALANG, W.A., and KRÄMER, B.: 'Achieving high integrity of process control software by graphical design and formal verification', *Software Engineering Journal*, January 1992, **7**, (1), pp. 53–64
56. HALL, J.A.: 'Seven myths of formal methods', *IEEE Software*, September 1990, **7**, (5), pp. 11–19
57. HALL, P.A.V.: 'Software development standards', *Software Engineering Journal*, May 1989, **4**, (3), pp. 143–147
58. HAMMER, W.: 'Handbook of system and product safety' (Prentice-Hall Inc., Englewood Cliffs, New Jersey, USA, 1972)
59. HANSEN, K.M., RAVN, A.P., and RISCHEL, H.: 'Specifying and verifying requirements of real-time systems'. Proc. ACM SIGSOFT '91 Conference on Software for Critical Systems, *Software Engineering Notes*, ACM Press, December 1991, **16**, (5), pp. 44–54
60. HARRISON, M.D.: 'Engineering human error tolerant software', *in* NICHOLLS, J.E. (Ed.): 'Z User Workshop, York 1991' (Springer-Verlag, Workshops in Computing, 1992) pp. 191–204
61. HELPS, K.A.: 'Some verification tools and methods for airborne safety-critical software', *Software Engineering Journal*, November 1986, **1**, (6), pp. 248–253
62. HILL, J.V.: 'The development of high reliability software – RR&A's experience for safety critical systems'. Second IEE/BCS Conference, Software Engineering 88, Conference Publication No. 290, July 1988, pp. 169–172
63. HILL, J.V.: 'Software development methods in practice', *in* CHURCHLEY, A. (Ed.): Proc. 6th Annual Conference on Computer Assurance (COMPASS), 'Microprocessor Based Protection Systems' (Kluwer Academic Publishers B.V., 1991)
64. HOARE, C.A.R.: 'Algebra and models', *in* BJØRNER, D., LANGMAACK, H., and HOARE, C.A.R. (Eds.): 'Provably Correct Systems', ProCoS Project Report, January 1993, chapter 1, pp. 1–13 (Available from Department of Computer Science, Technical University of Denmark, Building 3440, DK-2800, Lyngby, Denmark.)
65. HOARE, C.A.R., and GORDON, M.J.C. (Eds.): 'Mechanized reasoning and hardware design' (Prentice Hall International Series in Computer Science, UK, 1992)
66. HOARE, C.A.R., HE Jifeng, BOWEN, J.P., and PANDYA, P.K.: 'An algebraic approach to verifiable compiling specification and prototyping of the ProCoS level 0 programming language', *in* DIRECTORATE-GENERAL OF THE COMMISSION OF THE EUROPEAN COMMUNITIES (Ed.): 'ES-

PRIT '90 Conference Proceedings', Brussels (Kluwer Academic Publishers B.V., 1990) pp. 804–818
67. HOUSTON, I., and KING, S.: 'CICS project report: experiences and results from the use of Z in IBM', *in* PREHN, S., and TOETENEL, W.J. (Eds.): 'VDM '91, Formal Software Development Methods' (Springer-Verlag, *Lecture Notes in Computer Science*, 1991) **551**, pp. 588–603
68. HUMPHREY, W.S., KITSON, D.H., and CASSE, T.C.: 'The state of software engineering practice: a preliminary report'. Proc. 11th International Conference on Software Engineering, Pittsburgh, USA, May 1989, pp. 277–288
69. 'Safety-related systems: A professional brief for the engineer'. The Institution of Electrical Engineers, Savoy Place, London WB2R 0BR, UK, January 1992
70. IYER, R.K., and VERLARDI, P.: 'Hardware-related software errors: measurement and analysis', *IEEE Transactions on Software Engineering*, February 1985, **SE-11**, (2)
71. JACKY, J.: 'Formal specifications for a clinical cyclotron control system', *in* MORICONI, M. (Ed.): 'Proc. ACM SIGSOFT International Workshop on Formal Methods in Software Development', *Software Engineering Notes*, ACM Press, September 1990, **15**, (4), pp. 45–54
72. JACKY, J.: 'Safety-critical computing: hazards, practices, standards and regulation', *in* DUNLOP, C., and KLING, R. (Eds.): 'Computerization and controversy', chapter 5 (Academic Press, 1991) pp. 612–631
73. JACKY, J.: 'Verification, analysis and synthesis of safety interlocks'. Technical Report 91-04-01, Department of Radiation Oncology RC-08, University of Washington, Seattle, WA 98195, USA, April 1991
74. JAFFE, M.S., LEVESON, N.G., HEIMDAHL, M.P., and MELHART, B.E.: 'Software requirements analysis for real-time process-control systems', *IEEE Transactions on Software Engineering*, March 1991, **SE-17**, (3), pp. 241–258
75. JOANNOU, P.K., HARAUZ, J., TREMAINE, D.R., ICHIYEN, N. and CLARK, A.B.: 'The Canadian nuclear industry's initiative in real-time software engineering'. Ontario Hydro, 700 University Avenue, Toronto, Ontario M5G 1X6, Canada, 1991
76. JONES, C.B.: 'Systematic software development using VDM', 2nd edition (Prentice Hall International Series in Computer Science, 1990)
77. KANDEL, A., and AVNI, E.: 'Engineering risk and hazard assessment', Volume I (CRC Press, Boca Raton, Florida, USA, 1988)
78. KNIGHT, J.C., and LEVESON, N.G.: 'A reply to the criticisms of the Knight & Leveson experiment', *ACM SIGSOFT Software Engineering Notes*, January 1990, **15**, (1), pp. 25–35
79. KNIGHT, J.C., and KIENZLE, D.M.: 'Preliminary experience using Z to specify a safety-critical system', *in* BOWEN, J.P. and NICHOLLS, J.E. (Eds.): *in* 'Z User Workshop, London 1992' (Springer-Verlag, Workshops in Computing, 1993) pp. 109–118
80. KOPETZ, H., ZAINLINGER, R., FOHLER, G., KANTZ, H., and PUSCHNER, P.: 'The design of real-time systems: from specification to imple-

mentation and verification', *Software Engineering Journal*, May 1991, **6**, (3), pp. 73–82
81. LADEAU, B.R., and FREEMAN, C.: 'Using formal specification for product development', *Hewlett-Packard Journal*, December 1991, (6), pp. 62–66
82. LAPRIE, J.C.: 'Dependability: a unifying concept for reliable computing and fault tolerance', *in* ANDERSON, T. (Ed.): 'Dependability of Resilient Computers', chapter 1 (Blackwell Scientific Publications, Oxford, 1989) pp. 1–28
83. LAPRIE, J.C. (Ed.): 'Dependability: basic concepts and terminology' (Springer-Verlag, 1991)
84. LEVESON, N.G.: 'Software safety: why, what and how', *ACM Computing Surveys*, June 1986, **18**, (2), pp. 125–163
85. LEVESON, N.G.: 'Software safety in embedded computer systems', *Communications of the ACM*, February 1991, **34**, (2), pp. 34–46
86. LEVESON, N.G., and TURNER, C.T.: 'An investigation of the Therac-25 accidents', UCI Technical Report #92-108 (& University of Washington TR #92-11-05), Information and Computer Science Dept., University of California, Irvine, CA 92717, USA, 1992
87. LINDSAY, P.A.: 'A survey of mechanical support for formal reasoning', *Software Engineering Journal*, 1988, **3**, (1), pp. 3–27
88. LITTLEWOOD, B.: 'The need for evidence from disparate sources to evaluate software safety', *in* REDMILL, F. and ANDERSON, T. (Eds.): 'Directions in Safety-Critical Systems', Proc. Safety-critical Systems Symposium, Bristol, UK, February 1993 (Springer-Verlag, 1993)
89. LITTLEWOOD, B., and MILLER, D. (Eds.): 'Software reliability and safety' (Elsevier Applied Science, London and New York, 1991) (Reprinted from *Reliability Engineering & System Safety*, **32**, (1)–2, 1989.)
90. LITTLEWOOD, B., and STRIGINI, L.: 'The risks of software', *Scientific American*, November 1992, **267**, (5), pp. 38–43
91. MACKENZIE, D.: 'The fangs of the VIPER', *Nature*, 8 August 1991, **352**, pp. 467–468
92. MACKENZIE, D.: 'Negotiating arithmetic, constructing proof: the sociology of mathematics and information technology', Programme on Information & Communication Technologies, Working Paper Series, No. 38, Research Centre for Social Sciences, University of Edinburgh, 56 George Square, Edinburgh EH8 9JU, UK, November 1991
93. MAHONY, B., and HAYES, I.J.: 'A case-study in timed refinement: a mine pump', *IEEE Transactions on Software Engineering*, September 1992, **18**, (9), pp. 817–826
94. MALCOLM, R.: 'Safety critical systems research programme: technical workplan for the second phase', *in* REDMILL, F. (Ed.): 'Safety Systems: The Safety-Critical Systems Club Newsletter', Centre for Software Reliability, University of Newcastle upon Tyne, UK, January 1992, **1**, (2), pp. 1–3
95. MALER, O, MANNA, Z., and PNUELI, A.: 'From timed to hybrid systems', *in* DE BAKKER, J.W., HUIZING, C., DE ROEVER, W.-P., and

ROZENBERG, W. (Eds.): 'Real-Time: Theory in Practice, REX Workshop' (Springer-Verlag, *Lecture Notes in Computer Science*, 1992) **600**, pp. 447–484

96. MANNA, Z., and PNUELI, A.: 'The temporal logic of reactive and concurrent systems: specification' (Springer-Verlag, 1992)
97. MAY, D.: 'Use of formal methods by a silicon manufacturer', *in* HOARE, C.A.R. (Ed.): 'Developments in Concurrency and Communication', chapter 4 (Addison-Wesley, University of Texas at Austin Year of Programming Series, 1990) pp. 107–129
98. MAYGER, E.M., and FOURMAN, M.P.: 'Integration of formal methods with system design'. Proc. Conference on Very Large Scale Integration (VLSI '91), Edinburgh, UK, 1991, pp. 3a.2.1–3a.2.11
99. McDERMID, J.A.: 'Formal methods: use and relevance for the development of safety critical systems', *in* BENNETT, P.A.: 'Safety Aspects of Computer Control' (Butterworth-Heinemann, 1991)
100. MOORE, J.S. *et al.*, 'Special issue on system verification', *Journal of Automated Reasoning*, 1989, **5**, (4), pp. 409–530
101. MOSER, L.E., and MELLIAR-SMITH, P.M.: 'Formal verification of safety-critical systems', *Software — Practice and Experience*, August 1990, **20**, (8), pp. 799–821
102. MUKHERJEE, P., and STAVRIDOU, V.: 'The formal specification of safety requirements for the storage of explosives'. Technical Report No. DITC 185/91, National Physical Laboratory, Teddington, Middlesex TW11 0LW, UK, August 1991
103. MYERS, W.: 'Can software for the strategic defense initiative ever be error-free?', *IEEE Computer*, November 1986, **19**, (11)
104. 'Peer review of a formal verification/design proof methodology'. NASA Conference Publication 2377, July 1983
105. NATSUME, T., and HASEGAWA, Y.: 'A view on computer systems and their safety in Japan', in [47], 1992, pp. 45–49
106. NEESHAM, C.: 'Safe conduct', *Computing*, 12 November 1992, pp. 18–20
107. NEUMANN, P.G. (Ed.): 'Subsection on certification of professionals', *ACM SIGSOFT Software Engineering Notes*, January 1991, **16**, (1), pp. 24–32
108. NEUMANN, P.G.: 'Illustrative risks to the public in the use of computer systems and related technology', *ACM SIGSOFT Software Engineering Notes*, January 1992, **16**, (1), pp. 23–32
109. NORMINGTON, G: 'Cleanroom and Z', *in* BOWEN, J.P. and NICHOLLS, J.E. (Eds.): 'Z User Workshop, London 1992' (Springer-Verlag, Workshops in Computing, 1993) pp. 281–293
110. OSTROFF, J.S.: 'Formal methods for the specification and design of real-time safety critical systems', *Journal of Systems and Software*, 1992, **18**, (1), pp. 33–60
111. PAGE, I., and LUK, W.: 'Compiling Occam into field-programmable gate arrays', *in* MOORE, W., and LUK, W. (Eds.): 'FPGAs', Oxford Workshop

on Field Programmable Logic and Applications (Abingdon EE&CS Books, 15 Harcourt Way, Abingdon OX14 1NV, UK, 1991) pp. 271–283
112. PALFREMAN, J., and SWADE, D.: 'The dream machine' (BBC Books, London, 1991)
113. PARNAS, D.L., VON SCHOUWEN, A.J., and SHU PO KWAN 'Evaluation of safety-critical software', *Communications of the ACM*, June 1990, **33**, (6), pp. 636–648
114. PARNAS, D.L., ASMIS, G.J.K., and MADEY, J.: 'Assessment of safety-critical software in nuclear power plants', *Nuclear Safety*, April–June 1991, **32**, (2), pp. 189–198
115. PARNAS, D.L., and MADEY, J.: 'Functional documentation for computer systems engineering'. Version 2, CRL Report No. 237, TRIO, Communications Research Laboratory, Faculty of Engineering, McMaster University, Hamilton, Ontario, Canada L8S 4K1, September 1991
116. PASQUINE, A., and RIZZO, A.: 'Risk perceptions and acceptance of computers in critical applications', in [47], 1992, pp. 293–298
117. PELAEZ, E.: 'A gift from Pandora's box: the software crisis'. PhD Thesis, Edinburgh University, UK, 1988
118. PROBERT, P.J., DJIAN, D., and HUOSHENG HU: 'Transputer architectures for sensing in a robot controller: formal methods for design', *Concurrency: Practice and Experience*, August 1991, **3**, (4), pp. 283–292
119. PYLE, I.: 'Software engineers and the IEE', *Software Engineering Journal*, March 1986, **1**, (2), pp. 66–68
120. RALSTON, T.J.: 'Preliminary report on the international study on industrial experience with formal methods', *in* 'COMPASS '92: 7th Annual Conference on Computer Assurance', Gaithersburg, Maryland, USA, 15–18 June 1992.
121. RAVN, A.P., and RISCHEL, H.: 'Requirements capture for embedded real-time systems'. Proc. IMACS-MCTS Symposium, Lille, France, Volume 2, May 1991, pp. 147–152
122. RAVN, A.P., and STAVRIDOU, V.: 'Project organisation', *in* BJØRNER, D., LANGMAACK, H., and HOARE, C.A.R. (Eds.): 'Provably Correct Systems', ProCoS Project Report, January 1993, chapter 9, pp. 109–112 (Available from Department of Computer Science, Technical University of Denmark, Building 3440, DK-2800, Lyngby, Denmark.)
123. READE, C., and FROOME, P.: 'Formal methods for reliability', *in* ROOK, P. (Ed.): 'Software Reliability Handbook', chapter 3 (Elsevier Applied Science, 1990) pp. 51–81
124. REASON, J.: 'Human error' (Cambridge University Press, UK, 1990)
125. 'Risk: analysis, perception and management'. The Royal Society, 6 Carlton House Terrace, London SW1Y 5AG, UK, 1992
126. RUSHBY, J., and WHITEHURST, R.A.: 'Formal verification of AI software'. Contractor Report 181827, NASA Langley Research Center, Hampton, Virginia, USA, February 1989

127. RUSHBY, J.: 'Formal specification and verification of a fault-masking and transient-recovery model for digital flight control systems'. Technical Report SRI-CSL-91-3, SRI International, Menlo Park, California, USA, January 1991 (Also available as NASA Contractor Report 4384.)
128. RUSHBY, J., VON HENKE, F., and OWRE., S.: 'An introduction to formal specification and verification using EHDM'. Technical Report SRI-CSL-91-02, SRI International, Menlo Park, California, USA, February 1991
129. RUSHBY, J., and VON HENKE, F.: 'Formal verification of algorithms for critical systems'. Proc. ACM SIGSOFT 91 Conference on Software for Critical Systems, *Software Engineering Notes*, ACM Press, December 1991, **16**, (5), pp. 1–15
130. SCHOLEFIELD, D.J.: 'The formal development of real-time systems: a review'. Technical Report YCS 145, Dept. of Computer Science, University of York, UK, 1990
131. SELBY, R.W., BASILI, V.R., and BAKER, F.T.: 'Cleanroom software development: an empirical evaluation', *IEEE Transactions on Software Engineering*, September 1987, **SE-13**, (9), pp. 1027–1037
132. SENNETT, C.T.: 'High-integrity software' (Pitman Computer Systems Series, 1989)
133. SHOSTAK, R.E., SCHWARTZ, R., MELLIAR-SMITH, P.M.: 'STP: a mechanized logic for specification and verification' *in* '6th International Conference on Automated Deduction (CADE-6)' (Springer-Verlag, *Lecture Notes in Computer Science*, 1982) **138**
134. SMITH, C.L.: 'Digital control of industrial processes', *ACM Computing Surveys*, 1970, **2**, (3), pp. 211–241
135. SMITH, D.J., and WOOD, K.B.: 'Engineering Quality Software: a review of current practices, standards and guidelines including new methods and development tools', 2nd edition (Elsevier Applied Science, 1989)
136. SOMMERVILLE, I.: 'Software engineering', 3rd edition (Addison Wesley, 1989)
137. 'Special issue on reliability', *IEEE Spectrum*, October 1981, **18**, (10)
138. SPIVEY, J.M.: 'Specifying a real-time kernel', *IEEE Software*, September 1990, **7**, (5), pp. 21–28
139. SPIVEY, J.M.: 'The Z notation: a reference manual', 2nd edition (Prentice Hall International Series in Computer Science, 1992)
140. SRIVAS, M., and BICKFORD, M.: 'Verification of the FtCayuga fault-tolerant microprocessor system, vol 1: a case study in theorem prover-based verification'. Contractor Report 4381, NASA Langley Research Centre, Hampton, Virginia, USA, July 1991 (Work performed by ORA corporation.)
141. STEIN, R.M.: 'Safety by formal design', *BYTE*, August 1992, (8), p. 157
142. STEIN, R.M.: 'Software safety' *in* 'Real-time Multicomputer Software Systems', chapter 5 (Ellis-Horwood, 1992) pp. 109–133
143. STEPNEY, S., BARDEN, R., and COOPER, D. (Eds.): 'Object orientation in Z' (Springer-Verlag, Workshops in Computing, 1992)

144. SWADE, D.: 'Charles Babbage and his calculating engines' (Science Museum, London, UK, 1991)
145. THOMAS, M.C.: 'The future of formal methods', *in* BOWEN, J.P. (Ed.): 'Proc. 3rd Annual Z Users Meeting', Oxford University Computing Laboratory, UK, December 1988, pp. 1–3
146. THOMAS, M.C.: 'Development methods for trusted computer systems', *Formal Aspects of Computing*, 1989, **1**, pp. 5–18
147. TIERNEY, M.: 'The evolution of Def Stan 00-55 and 00-56: an intensification of the "formal methods debate" in the UK'. Proc. Workshop on Policy Issues in Systems and Software Development, Science Policy Research Unit, Brighton, UK, July 1991
148. TIERNEY, M.: 'Some implications of Def Stan 00-55 on the software engineering labour process in safety critical developments'. Research Centre for Social Sciences, Edinburgh University, 1991
149. VON NEUMANN, J.: 'Probabilistic logics and synthesis of reliable organisms from unreliable components' *in* 'Collected Works', Volume 5 (Pergamon Press, 1961)
150. WALDINGER, R.J., and STICKEL, M.E.: 'Proving properties of rule-based systems'. Proc. 7th Conference on Artificial Intelligence Applications, IEEE Computer Society, February 1991, pp. 81–88
151. WALLACE, D.R., KUHN, D.R., and CHERNIAVSKY, J.C.: 'Report of the NIST workshop of standards for the assurance of high integrity software'. NIST Special Publication 500-190, Computer Systems Laboratory, National Institute of Standards and Technology, Gaithersburg, MD 20899, USA, August 1991 (Available from the Superintendent of Documents, Government, U.S. Printing Office, Washington, DC 20402, USA.)
152. WALLACE, D.R., KUHN, D.R., and IPPOLITO, L.M.: 'An analysis of selected software safety standards', *IEEE AES Magazine*, August 1992, (8), pp. 3–14
153. WARD, W.T.: 'Calculating the real cost of software defects', *Hewlett-Packard Journal*, October 1991, pp. 55–58
154. WEBB, J.T.: 'The role of verification and validation tools in the production of critical software', *in* INCE, D. (Ed.): 'Software Quality and Reliability: Tools and Methods', Unicorn Applied Info Technology Report 6, chapter 4 (Chapman & Hall, London, 1991) pp. 33–41,
155. WENSLEY, J. *et al.* 'SIFT: design and analysis of a fault-tolerant computer for aircraft control', *Proc. IEEE*, 1978, **60**, (10), pp. 1240–1254
156. WIRTH, N.: 'Towards a discipline of real-time programming', *Communications of the ACM*, August 1977, **20**, (8), pp. 577–583
157. WICHMANN, B.A. (Ed.): 'Software in safety-related systems' (Wiley, 1992) Also published by BCS
158. WRIGHT, C.L., and ZAWILSKI, A.J.: 'Existing and emerging standards for software safety'. The MITRE Corporation, Center for Advanced Aviation System Development, 7525 Colshire Drive, McLean, Virginia 22102-3481,

USA, MP-91W00028, June 1991 (Presented at the IEEE Fourth Software Engineering Standards Application Workshop, San Diego, California, USA, 20–24 May 1991.)
159. XILINX, Inc.: 'The programmable gate array data book'. San Jose, California, USA, 1991
160. YOULL, D.P.: 'Study of the training and education needed in support of Def Stan 00-55'. Cranfield IT Institute Ltd, UK, September 1988 (Can also be found as an appendix of the April 1989 00-55 draft.)
161. ZHOU ChaoChen, HOARE, C.A.R., and RAVN, A.P.: 'A calculus of durations', *Information Processing Letters*, 1991, **40**, (5), pp. 269–276

7. Integrating Methods

7.1 Motivation

In general, no one method is the best in any given situation. Often it is advantageous to use a combination of methods for a particular design, applying each technique in a manner to maximize its benefits [53]. It is possible to integrate the use of formal methods with other less formal techniques. Indeed, often, formal methods provide little more than a mathematical notation, perhaps with some tool support. Combining such a notation with a methodological approach can be helpful in providing a rigorous underpinning to system design.

A number of successful applications of to real-life problems (see, for example, papers in [125]), have helped to dispel the myth that formal methods are merely an academic exercise with little relevance to practical system development. Increasingly, the computer industry is accepting the fact that the application of formal methods in the development process (particularly when used with safety-critical systems) can ensure an increase in levels of confidence regarding the 'correctness' of the resulting system, while improving complexity control, and in many cases reducing development costs (again, see [125]).

Formal methods have now been used, to some extent at least, in many major projects. This trend seems set to continue, as a result of decisions by the UK Ministry of Defence, and other government agencies, to mandate the use of formal methods in certain classes of applications [37].

That is not to say that formal methods have been universally accepted. Many agree that formal methods are still not employed as much in practice as they might be, or as they *should* be [182, 191]. A lot of software development is still conducted on a completely *ad hoc* basis. At best it is supported by various structured methods; at worst it is developed using a very naïve approach – i.e., the approach taken by many undergraduates when they first learn to program: 'write the program and base the design on this afterwards'.

Structured methods are excellent for use in requirements elicitation, and interaction with system procurers. They offer notations that can be understood by non-specialists, and which can be offered as a basis for a contract. In general, they support all phases of the development life-cycle, from requirements analysis, through specification, design, implementation, and maintenance. However, they offer no means of reasoning about the validity of a specification – i.e., whether all requirements are satisfied by the specification, or whether certain requirements are mutually exclusive. Unsatisfied requirements are often only discovered post-implementation; conflicting requirements may be detected during implementation.

Formal methods, on the other hand, allow us to reason about requirements, their completeness, and their interactions. They also enable *proof of correctness* – that is, that an implementation satisfies its specification. The problem is that formal methods are perceived to be difficult to use due to their high dependency on mathematics. Certainly personnel untrained in mathematics and the techniques of formal methods will be loath to accept a formal specification presented to them without a considerable amount of additional explanation and discussion. But, as Hall [105] points out, one does not need to be a mathematician to be able to use and understand formal methods. Most development staff should have a sufficient grounding in mathematics to enable them to understand formal specifications and indeed to write such specifications. Formal proofs and refinement (the translation of a specification into a lower level implementation) do require a considerable degree of mathematical ability, however, as well as a great deal of time and effort.

7.2 Integrating Structured and Formal Methods

In the traditional (structured) approach to software development, problems are analyzed using a collection of diagrammatic notations, such as *Data-Flow Diagrams* (DFDs), *Entity-Relationship-Attribute Diagrams* (ERADs) and *State-Transition Diagrams* (STDs). In general, these notations are informal, or, at best, semi-formal, although work on making them more formal is in progress [7]. Only after the problem has been analyzed sufficiently are the possible sequences of operations considered, from which the most appropriate are chosen.

When using formal specification techniques, however, personnel must begin to think in terms of the derivation of a model of reality (either explicit or implicit – depending on the formal specification language being used, and the level of abstraction of the specification). In the specification of a functional system (one in which output is a relation over the current state and the input) this involves relating inputs to outputs by means of predicates over the state of the system. In reactive systems, of which concurrent, real-time and distributed systems are representative, the specification is complicated by the need to consider side-effects, timing constraints, and fairness. In either case, the mismatch, or 'gap' between the thought processes that are required at the analysis stage and those needed to formally specify a system is significant, and has been termed the *Analysis–Specification Semantic Gap* [214].

In traditional software development, a high-level specification is translated to a design incrementally, in a process known as *stepwise refinement*. This process continues until the design is couched in such terms that it can be easily implemented in a programming language. Effectively what the system designer is doing is deriving an implicit tree of possible implementations, and performing a search of the possibilities, eliminating those which are infeasible in the current development environment, and selecting the most appropriate of the rest. The tree is potentially (and normally) infinite (up to renaming) and so an explicit tree is never derived.

In implementing a formal specification, however, the developer must change from the highly abstract world of sets, sequences and formal logic, to considering their possible implementations in terms of a programming language. Very few programming languages support such constructs, and certainly not efficiently. As a result, this requires determining the most appropriate data structures to implement the higher level entities (*data refinement*), and translating the operations already defined to operate on arrays, pointers, records, etc., (*operation refinement*).

The disparity here has been termed the *Specification–Implementation Semantic Gap*, and is clearly exacerbated by the lack of an intermediate format. Such a 'gap' represents a major difficulty for the software engineering community. Suggestions for its elimination vary greatly ... from the introduction of programming languages supporting higher-level primitives [138], to the use of specification languages which have executable subsets [84], e.g., CSP [129, 127] with Occam [139], OBJ [94], or with inherent tool support, e.g., Larch [103], Nqthm [48], B [2], PVS [201]. The ProCoS project [43] on 'Provably Correct Systems' has been exploring the formal foundations of the techniques to fill in these gaps from requirements through specification, design, compilation [118, 239], and ultimately down to hardware [33, 155], but many problems remain to be solved, especially those concerning scaling.

A means by which structured and formal methods are integrated to some extent could help in systems of an industrial scale [100]. A method based on such an integration would offer the best of both worlds:

- it offers the structured method's support for the software life cycle, while admitting the use of more formal techniques at the specification and design phases, supporting refinement to executable code, and proof of properties;
- it presents two different views of the system, allowing different developers to address the aspects that are relevant to them, or of interest to them;
- it provides a means of formally proving the correctness of an implementation *with respect to its specification*, while retaining a structured design that will be more acceptable to non-specialists;
- the formal method may be regarded as assigning a formal semantics to the structured method, enabling investigations of its appropriateness, and the study of possible enhancements;
- the structured design may be used as the basis for insights into the construction of a formal specification.

The final point above is quite contentious. A number of people have cited this as a disadvantage of the approach and something that should not be encouraged. The view is that such an approach severely restricts levels of abstraction and goes against many of the principles of formal specification techniques. On the other hand, there is a valid argument that such an approach is often easier for those unskilled in the techniques of formal specification to follow, and can aid in the management of size and complexity, and provide a means of structuring specifications.

7.3 An Appraisal of Approaches

A number of experiments have been conducted in using formal methods and structured methods in parallel. Leveson [165], Draper [72] and Bryant [5] all report successes in developing safe and reliable software systems using such techniques. In such cases, non-specialists were able to deal with more familiar notations, such as DFDs (Data-Flow Diagrams), while specialists concentrated on more formal investigations, highlighting ambiguities and errors admitted by more conventional methods.

There is a severe restriction, however, in that the conventional specification and design, and the formal approach will be engaged upon by different personnel. With differing levels of knowledge of the system and implementation environment, and lack of sufficient feedback between the two groups, it is unlikely that the benefits of such an approach will be adequately highlighted. In fact, Kemmerer [148] warns of potential negative effects.

A more integrated approach, whereby formal methods and more traditional techniques are applied in a unified development method, offers greater prospects for success. A number of groups have been working on such integrated methods, their approaches varying greatly – from transliterations of graphical notations into mathematical equivalents, to formalizing the transformations between both representations.

Semmens, France and Docker, in their paper *Integrated Structured Analysis and Formal Specification Techniques* (reprinted here) give an excellent and very complete overview of the various approaches to method integration, both in academia and in industry [229].

Integrated Structured Analysis and Formal Specification Techniques

Lesley Semmens, Robert France and Tom Docker

Summary.

The last decade has seen a large increase in the use of 'structured' methods of software development. They grew out of their predecessors which consisted of a toolkit of techniques with little method of how and when to apply them. Methods such as Yourdon Structured Analysis [38] and SSADM [34] provide means of managing the complexity of large systems. They provide techniques and associated procedures for the development of such systems. In parallel with this, and almost entirely independently, formal specification languages and methods have been developed. Both approaches have their strengths and weaknesses. Recently it has been recognised that benefits can be gained from integrating the two.

A number of researchers have reported progress towards the successful integration of formal and structured methods. This paper reports on a selection of this work[1]. The aim in each case has been to develop specifications which are both structured and formal, and so combine the proven advantages of both approaches. We believe that such integrated methods remove some of the 'culture shock' associated with the introduction of mathematically formal languages and make their use more acceptable to managers and engineers in software development organisations. There is some evidence for the feasibility and cost-effectiveness of this approach when used in an industrial setting; developers at Rolls Royce and Associates [17] have reported the successful combined use of VDM and Yourdon.

Work has also started on the integration of formal notations and graphical techniques for Object-Oriented Analysis and Design but this is all at a very early stage and little has been reported formally.

© 1992 British Computer Society. Reprinted by permission.
Reprinted from *The Computer Journal*, 35(6):600–610, December 1992.

[1] Some of the work was presented at a workshop on *Methods Integration* [1] at Leeds in 1991.

1 Strengths and Weaknesses of Structured and Formal Methods

Structured analysis methods use techniques such as Entity Relationship Modelling (ERM), Data Flow Diagrams (DFD) and State Transition Diagrams (STD) to represent the static and dynamic properties of systems. These are usually underpinned by a Data Dictionary which will contain information such as the attributes associated with a particular entity in the ERM and the attributes associated with data flows on the DFD. These methods provide not only techniques but a structured approach to the development process. They are good for analysing and structuring systems and are relatively easily understood by the customer. They also have the advantage of being well tried and understood and are used by the more conscientious developers of systems. However, some of the techniques lack formality. In particular, because of the variety of notations (diagrams and text) used it is not possible to reason about specifications.

Formal notations have the advantage that they can be reasoned about. They are concise and unambiguous. One major drawback is that they lack structure and thus make it difficult to manage the development of large systems. Most so-called formal 'methods' offer little more than a mathematically based notation and a modelling technique. The use of such notations and techniques must be situated within a software development method.

The advantages of the two approaches would seem to be complimentary. Structured methods assist in the management of size and complexity and provide a means to structure a specification. Formal notations provide a means by which developers can make precise, unambiguous statements about systems and use those statements as a basis for reasoning about the system.

2 Approaches to Integration

There are several possible approaches to integrating structured methods and formal notations. The first is to use the two side by side and not attempt to show any formal link. Approaches of this kind include that used at Rolls-Royce & Associates [17] and proposed by the SAZ project [26] the first of which will be outlined below. The second is to formalise the link between the structured notations and the target formal notation. This is the approach proposed by Goldsmith [16] and taken by Tse [35], France & Docker [13], Semmens & Allen [31], Larsen *et al.* [24], Redmond-Pyle & Josephs [29] and Fencott *et al.* [9] all of which are outlined below.

Much of the work has focussed on Yourdon Structured Analysis (and related methods such as deMarco [6] and SA [15]) perhaps because this is more often used on non-DP systems than other structured methods such as SSADM and its relatives. However Redmond-Pyle & Josephs have done work on LBMS SE which is related to SSADM and there has been some (unpublished) work at BT [30] which has been applied mainly to DP systems.

There is also the question of which type of formal notation to use. The approaches we discuss fall into three categories: model-based specification, algebraic specification and process algebra. We will discuss each separately.

3 Model-Based Specification Techniques

Research relating to the integration of structured analysis and model-based specification techniques began in the late eighties. The first proposals were made by Goldsmith [16] who proposed the integration of Yourdon [38] and VDM [21] and Bryant [3] who proposed the integration of SSADM and Z [33]. Practical pilot studies were being undertaken at Rolls Royce & Associates using Yourdon and VDM. The earliest detailed work was reported at the 1990 Z User Group Workshop [25] where Semmens & Allen [31] and Randell [27, 28] presented their work. These both dealt with the translation of structured notations into Z.

Integration takes two forms. There is the relatively loose approach taken by Rolls Royce where Yourdon and VDM are used side by side and the more formal approach of performing a direct translation of the structured notations into the target language, thus providing a formal semantics for the diagrams.

In the following sections the work at Rolls Royce, that of Larsen *et al.*, of Semmens & Allen and Redmond-Pyle & Josephs will be outlined.

3.1 Yourdon/VDM (Rolls Royce)

The approach taken at Rolls Royce & Associates [17] involves using a Yourdon-based analysis to capture the structure of the requirements. The structure of the specification is that of Yourdon, but the detailed process specifications and the data structures are described in VDM, with explanatory English text. Care is taken that implicit specification is used; this ensures that the specification states what is to be done rather than how.

This approach has utilised the power and usability of the analysis method to ensure that complete and consistent requirements are captured. The structured method makes it easier to capture the essential details of what is wanted rather than how to do it. The precision and rigour of the formal language contributes to this at the detailed level by imposing discipline on the analysis.

The designers need to be able to read the formal specification but the usability of the structured specification means that this is much easier to do.

The approach was found to be cost-effective even in non-critical projects. The slight increase in the estimates for producing the specification was recovered in reducing the contingency in the development costs from then on. In critical projects program proving was made easier by the close mapping of the structure of the specification and the code. Modularity also made the proving of parts of a system feasible.

They have found that structured methods make formal specifications much more approachable. They recognise that in requirements capture it is not practical to work from the top down; that structured methods allow analysts to iterate between top-down, bottom-up and middle-out, gradually improving the analysis until it is complete and can be presented in a top-down fashion; and that used in conjunction with structured methods, formal methods provide much-needed discipline and clarity, and can be introduced without major restaffing or retraining, and without increasing costs. Whether or not the final software is to be proved, they believe that the formal specification justifies itself in the quality and maintainability of the system.

3.2 SA/SD and VDM

Researchers at TU Delft propose a method SVDM [24]. This method provides the graphical notations from SA/SD [15], the methodological guidelines from the SA phase of SA/SD and the formal aspects of VDM. The combined method, illustrated in Figure 1, comprises the following steps:

1. Analyse the problem and develop a context diagram, representing the system boundaries.
2. Decompose the context diagram by splitting the high-level data transformer into several lower-level data transformers. Each of these data transformers is subsequently decomposed until an acceptably complete hierarchy of DFDs has been produced.
3. Provide type information for all data stores and data flows. This type information may be supplied either textually, by means of VDM domain definitions, or if they are more complex, graphically by means of entity-relationship diagrams. It is now possible to (automatically) derive a first VDM specification. (The *level 0 VDM specification.*) This document is considered to be a secondary document, of little use to the designer, but which can be used to perform a consistency check on the system specified so far. It essentially gives a semantics to the hierarchy of DFDs.
4. Complete the analysis phase by specifying all primitive data transformers. These specifications are called mini-specifications and must be described either as function or operations definitions in VDM. It is now possible to (automatically) generate a VDM specification where the mini-specifications are taken into account. (The *level 1 VDM specification.*)
5. For each DFD containing two or more data transformers, control information must be provided defining the order in which the data transformers should be combined. Again it is possible to (automatically) generate a VDM specification using the control information provided in this step. (The *level 2 VDM specification.*) It is also now possible to generate (automatically) *level 1 structure charts* for the designed system.
6. Refine the mini-specifications into explicit function and operation definitions. It is now possible to generate (automatically) a textual representation of the design in the form of a VDM specification. (The *level 3 VDM specification.*) At the same time it is possible to generate a level 2 structure chart description.

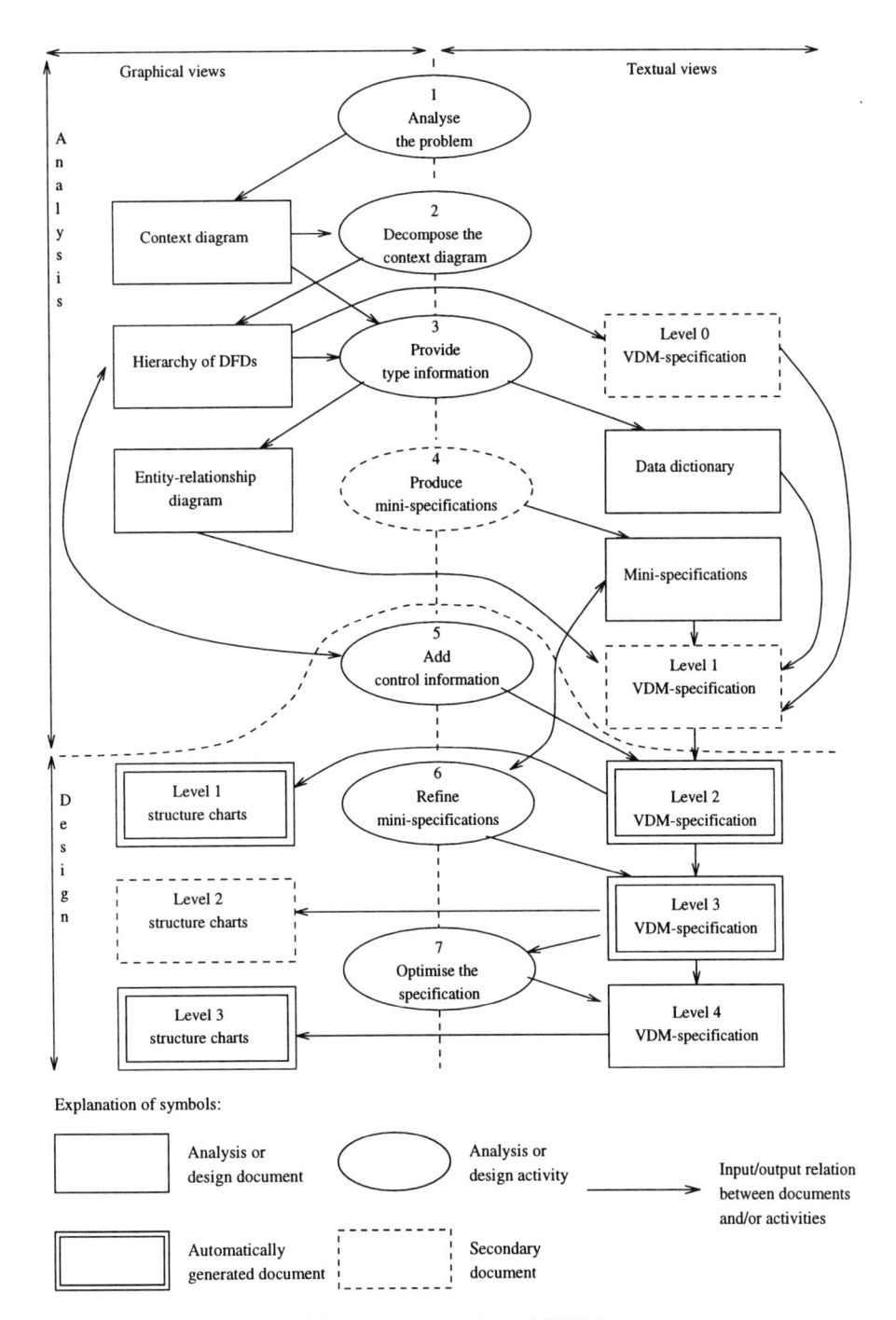

Semmens, France & Docker   Structured Analysis and Formal Specification   537

Figure 1. An overview of SVDM.

7. Optimise the formal specification. In this (optional) step the level 3 VDM specification is changed such that it better reflects the non-functional requirements of the problem to be solved. (The *level 4 VDM specification*.) Structure charts which also reflect these changes can be constructed as well. (The *level 3 structure charts*.)

3.3 Yourdon and Z

Semmens and Allen [31, 32] have done extensive work on integrating Yourdon and Z. The approach they have taken is to define a formal syntax, in Z, for the diagrams and data dictionary. This formal syntax together with a set of well-formedness rules provides the specification for a Yourdon tool which comprises the graphical notations (ERD, DFD and STD) and an underlying data dictionary. They have defined functions (in Z) mapping the Z representations of the diagrams to type definitions, state and operation schemas. The formal specification of the system state is generated automatically from the diagrams and the underlying data dictionary, as are the signatures of the operation schemas. A prototype tool [8] is being built which incorporates the Yourdon techniques and the translation rules which generate the (partial) Z specification. The developer then adds pre- and post-conditions to the operation schemas which are then syntax- and type-checked. The tool will eventually incorporate a proof assistant enabling a completely formal development to proceed.

An example of the relationship between the diagrammatic representation and the Z representation is shown below.

```
  ┌────────┐  N          1  ┌────────┐
  │ Manual ├──○──<loaned to>──○──┤  User  │
  └────────┘                     └────────┘
```

| Manual | ::= | @MANNO + TITLE + SUBJECT |
| User | ::= | @USERNO + NAME + LOCATION |

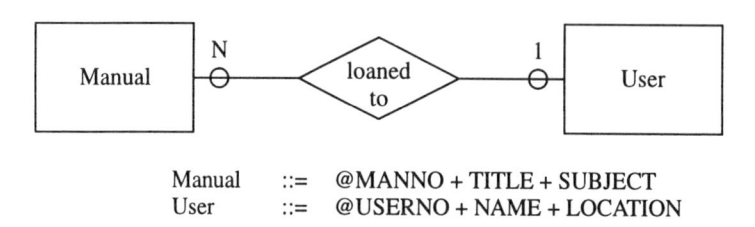

Figure 2. Entity Relationship Diagram and Data Dictionary.

Z basic types are defined for each distinct attribute type:

[*MANNO, TITLE, SUBJECT*]
[*USERNO, NAME*]
[*LOCATION*]

Schemas define the entity types:

$\begin{array}{|l}\hline \textit{Manual} \\ \textit{manno} : MANNO \\ \textit{title} : TITLE \\ \textit{subject} : SUBJECT \\ \hline \end{array}$

$\begin{array}{|l}\hline \textit{User} \\ \textit{userno} : USERNO \\ \textit{name} : NAME \\ \textit{location} : LOCATION \\ \hline \end{array}$

Data store schemas represent the instances of each entity, and include an injection from the entity type to its key attribute (unique identifier):

$\begin{array}{|l}\hline \textit{Manual\_ds} \\ \textit{manual\_set} : \mathbb{P}\,Manual \\ \textit{manual\_id} : \\ \quad Manual \rightarrowtail MANNO \\ \hline \mathrm{dom}\,\textit{manual\_id} = \textit{manual\_set} \\ \forall\,m : \textit{manual\_set} \bullet \\ \quad \textit{manual\_id}(m) = m.manno \\ \hline \end{array}$

$\begin{array}{|l}\hline \textit{User\_ds} \\ \textit{user\_set} : \mathbb{P}\,User \\ \textit{user\_id} : \\ \quad User \rightarrowtail USERNO \\ \hline \mathrm{dom}\,\textit{user\_id} = \textit{user\_set} \\ \forall\,u : \textit{user\_set} \bullet \\ \quad \textit{user\_id}(u) = u.userno \\ \hline \end{array}$

The relationships are declared

$\begin{array}{|l}\hline \textit{Loaned\_to\_ds} \\ \textit{loaned\_to} : Manual \rightarrow User \\ \hline \end{array}$

The complete state is then:

$\begin{array}{|l}\hline \textit{ManualLoans} \\ \textit{Manual\_ds} \\ \textit{User\_ds} \\ \textit{Loaned\_to\_ds} \\ \hline \mathrm{dom}\,\textit{loaned\_to} \subseteq \textit{manual\_set} \\ \mathrm{ran}\,\textit{loaned\_to} \subseteq \textit{user\_set} \\ \hline \end{array}$

If there are any additional constraints on the state they can be added to the entity, data store or state schemas.

Operations schema signatures are generated from the DFD which provides an operation name, the names of the updated data stores and the names of data flows. The type of the data flow is first specified using a schema.

$$\begin{array}{l}\textit{ManInput} \\ \hline title : TITLE \\ subject : SUBJECT \end{array}$$

$$\begin{array}{l}\textit{AddManual} \\ \hline \Delta ManualLoans \\ \Xi User\_ds \\ \Xi Loaned\_to\_ds \\ \hline man\_input? : ManInput \end{array}$$

Pre- and post-conditions are then added by the developer. The main elements of the method incorporating the transformation from Yourdon to Z are illustrated in Figure 3.

3.4 SE/Z

Work on the integration of LBMS SE and Z [29] takes as its starting point the assumption that the use of structured methods as a front end to formal development is a useful approach. They have also examined the scope for enrichment of a structured method by integrating it with a formal notation. The two main aspects of enrichment considered are – enrichment of the method's representational ability (i.e. the notations and their meaning) and enrichment of its transformational ability (i.e. the development process).

The basic mapping of the entity relationship model used in SE is similar to that used by Semmens and Allen, and described above. However the translation is done at a slightly earlier stage in the development process, before any decisions about which attribute(s) will form the primary key. An abstract identifier is used for each entity. So using the example of a user entity above,

[No, Name, Location]

$$\begin{array}{l}\textit{UserRecord} \\ \hline userNo : No \\ userName : Name \\ location : Location \end{array}$$

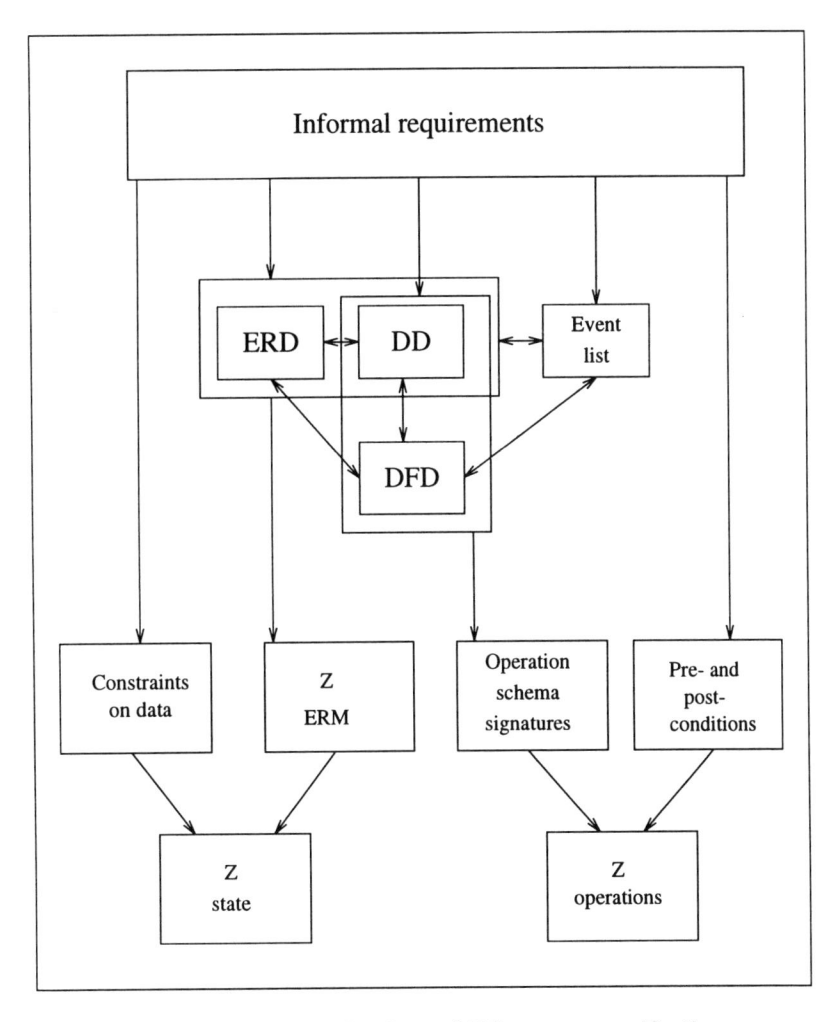

Figure 3. Combining Yourdon and Z for system specification.

a table schema is defined:

[*UserId*]

```
┌─ UserTable ─────────────────────────────
│ knownUser : 𝔽 UserId
│ tableUser : UserId ↛ UserRecord
│ ────────────────────────────────────────
│ knownUser = dom tableUser
└─────────────────────────────────────────
```

Database operations are then defined using operations schemas.

What has been done is to take the specification constructs used in structured methods (e.g. entity, one-to-many relationship) and use them as building blocks of a Z specification. This is seen as directly analogous to the way that the standard building blocks in the mathematical toolkit (functions, sequences etc) are used in Z. To integrate these additional specification constructs they have defined a library of Z generics [23]. These generic schemas define the common semantics of each type of construct.

Enrichment of representation. Natural extensions have been made to the existing specification constructs. Entity invariants, which in most structured specifications are no more than natural language comments, can be captured formally. The subtyping mechanism used in many structured methods is not in any sense rigorous. The use of a formal notation allows their semantics to be defined precisely, which in turn has led to the development of a richer graphical notation which can be used with the confidence that it is semantically sound.

Enrichment of the development process. Four possible ways of enriching the development process are being researched:

- derivation of preconditions
- derivation of consequences
- data refinement
- consequential operation refinement

4 Algebraic Specification Techniques

4.1 Introduction

Research related to the integration of the structured analysis (SA) method and algebraic specification techniques started on two fronts in the early to mid-eighties. The work of Tse [35] was aimed primarily at providing a common formal framework for structured methods, including the SA method, to facilitate the translation of artifacts among the methods. On the other hand, the work of Docker and France

[13, 10, 11, 12], focused on providing an integrated prototyping and formal specification framework for SA tools to create a flexible and formal specification environment based on SA.

Tse's emphasis on the ability to translate specification products across methods meant that his work focused more on the *syntactic structure* of specification artifacts, while France and Docker's emphasis on formally stating and investigating behavioural properties modeled by SA artifacts meant that their work focused more on the *semantic aspects* of SA artifacts. In fact, the algebraic characterization of the syntax of data flow diagrams (DFDs) presented in France [10] is close to Tse's algebraic characterization of DFD structure (there are differences in the notations used), but the characterization itself plays a very insignificant part in the specification framework of France and Docker.

In the next section we discuss the work of France and Docker. This is followed by a brief overview of Tse's approach.

4.2 Formally specifying the semantics of DFDs with algebraic specifications

In this section we describe two frameworks for associating DFDs with formal specifications characterizing their behaviour, developed as part of the research carried out by France and Docker. One framework supports the formal specification of sequential systems [12] while the other also supports the formal specification of non-sequential systems [11]. Both frameworks facilitate formal investigation of application properties, and provide bases for formal decomposition and refinement, and formal verification. The framework supporting the specification of sequential systems is more suited to formally specifying requirements, since one is not too concerned about the details of interactions among processing components at that stage. The other framework is suited to the specification of designs, especially designs of complex systems. In what follows a DFD associated with a formal specification is called a *semantically-Extended DFD* (ExtDFD). We conclude with a brief account of a tool SAME (Structured Analysis Modelling Environment) which provides a front end to the formal system.

Specifying the semantics of sequential systems. In the framework supporting the formal specification of sequential systems, a DFD is interpreted as a system of atomic operations accessing instances of shared data structures, where shared data structures are depicted by data stores, and atomic operations by data transforms. The specification characterizing the intended semantics of a DFD in this framework is called an *Atomic-level Specification* (ASpec). An ExtDFD in this framework is thus a DFD associated with an ASpec characterizing its intended semantics. We shall use the DFD in Figure 4 to illustrate the specification technique outlined below.

The ASpec of a DFD consists of two parts: a *data domain definition* part and an *operation specification* part. The data domain definition part is made up of three parts (see Figure 5):

Data definition: This part contains type definitions for all data elements depicted in the DFD. The *Data definition* part is analogous to the data dictionary of SA.

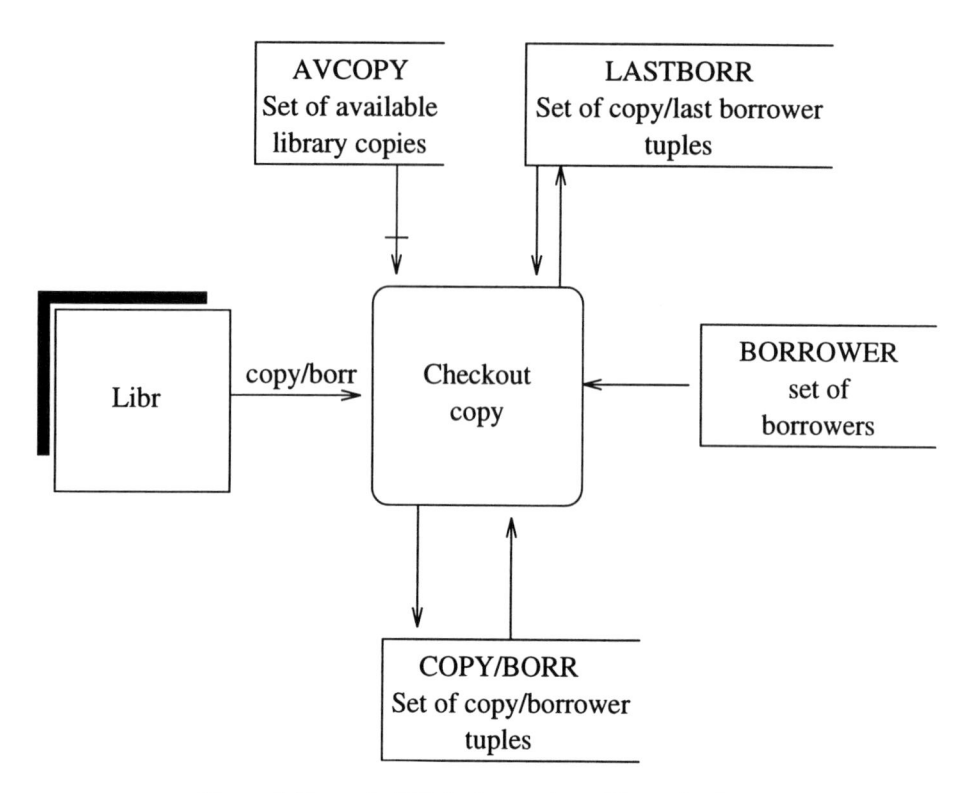

Figure 4. Example DFD for borrowing a library book.

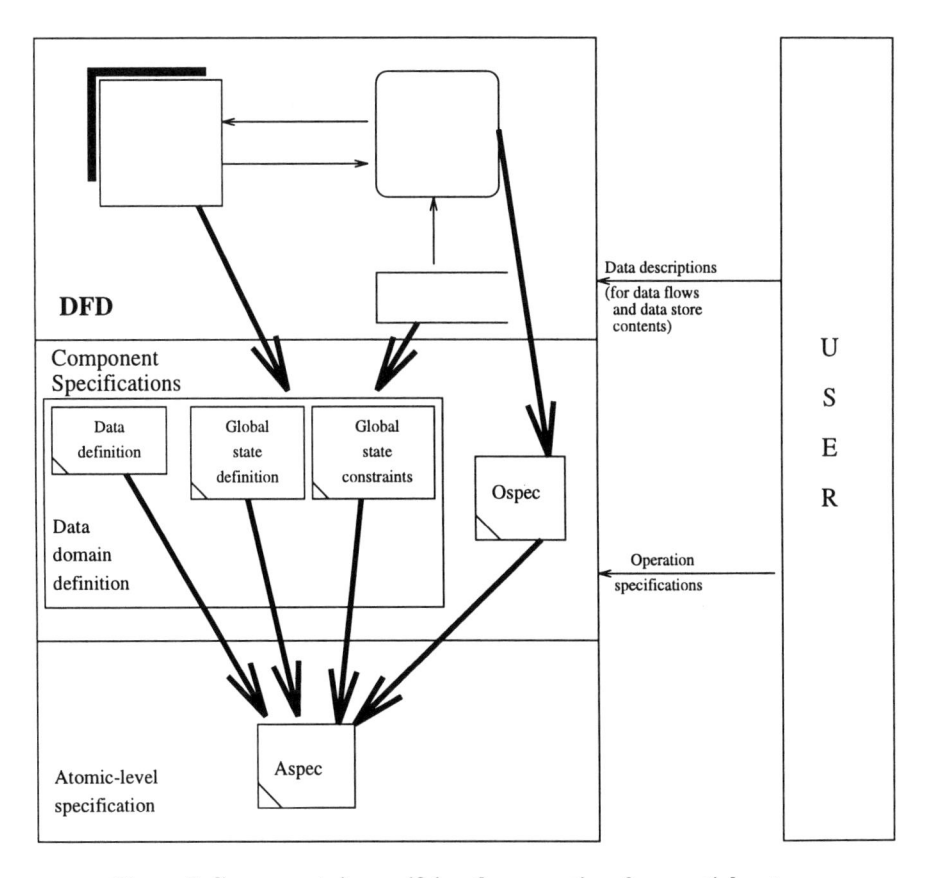

Figure 5. Components in specifying the semantics of sequential systems.

Type definitions are stated in a *Data Description* (DD) language which provides functions for constructing data types from elementary and pre-defined, parameterized data types. Each type definition is actually an (hierarchical) algebraic specification which defines the type in terms of operations that create and manipulate instances of the type defined. The input/output effects of data transforms are expressed solely in terms of the operations defined in the type definitions. An (partial) example of an algebraic specification corresponding to a type definition is given in Figure 6.

Global state definition: This part consists of declarations of the data structures associated with the data stores in the DFD. An instance of the data structure associated with a data store is called a *state* of the data store. France uses *sets* to model data stores, thus a state of a data store is simply a set whose elements represents the contents of the data store. This part also contains definitions of the states associated with external entities whose behaviour affect how the application responds to its stimuli. State definitions are representations of algebraic specifications which define states in terms of operations that create and manipulate their instances. State modifications by data transforms must be expressed solely in terms of the operations in these specifications. An example of a state specification for a data store is given in Figure 7.

Global state constraints: This part stipulates the relationships that must be maintained among the states of data stores and specified external entities. The constraints are stated in first-order predicate logic.

Data Specification is Set
Using *NatNum*
With Parameter Data (sort *data*)
sort *set*
Constructors
$\emptyset :\to set$
insert : $data\ set \to set$
Operations
$count : set \to natnum$
— Counts number of elements in a set.
. . .
Operation axioms
. . .

Figure 6. Algebraic specification associated with the pre-defined type set.

A *global state* of a DFD is a set consisting exactly of a state for each data store depicted in the DFD and for each external entity associated with states in the *Global state definition* part. A global state that satisfies the *global state constraints* is said to be *valid*, otherwise it is said to be *invalid*.

The *operation specification* part of an ASpec consists of specifications called *OSpecs*, each uniquely associated with an operation depicted by a data transform.

A data store state specification. The data store *COPY/BORR* stores 2-tuples of sort $copy/borr = <copy, borrower>$, where *copy* is the type of a library book copy and *borrower* is the type of a library borrower.

$COPY/BORR : set(copy/borr)$
  Access Operations
  Signature
    $get: set(copy/borr)\ borrower \rightarrow set(copy)$
    — Returns the copies currently checked out by a borrower.
    ...
  Axioms
  For all $c : copy/borr;\ S : set(copy/borr);\ b : borrower$
    1. $get(\emptyset, b) = \emptyset$
    2. $c \cdot borrower = b \Rightarrow get(insert(c, S), b) = insert(c \cdot copy, get(S, b))$
    3. $c \cdot borrower \neq b \Rightarrow get(insert(c, S), b) = get(S, b)$
    ...

Figure 7. State specification for a data store.

An OSpec characterizes the desired pre- and post-conditions of an operation and is analogous to a process specification in SA [6]. The pre- and post-conditions stipulated by an OSpec determine the effect a data transform has on the global state of a DFD. An example of an OSpec is given in Figure 8.

An OSpec is said to be consistent with respect to the global constraints of an ASpec if and only if its pre-conditions do not preclude all valid global states, and an execution starting in a valid global state ends in a valid global state. This consistency condition is formally stated in Ref. [12]. Details of how the above framework can be used to verify refinements of ASpecs can also be found there.

Specifying the semantics of non-sequential systems. In the framework supporting the specification of non-sequential systems, DFDs with control extensions, similar to those used in [18, 37], are associated with algebraic specifications characterizing their behaviour. In this framework a control-extended DFD is interpreted as a system of communicating processes (which can also be viewed as a single process), where a process is an entity defined by a set of *states* and *events*, and a class of *behaviours*. The behaviour of a process is defined by a *state transition system* which is characterized by an algebraic specification, using a technique developed by Astesiano et al. [2]. The form of an algebraic specification characterizing a process's state transition system (called an *algebraic state transition system* or ASTS) is given below:

  Transition Specification is *SpecName*
  State Specification is *StateSpec*
  Label Specification is *LabelSpec*
  Transition relation is $\_ \longrightarrow \_ : state\ label\ state$
  Transition axioms *Axioms*

The OSpec for a 'checkout copy' operation in a library application is given below.

OSpec CheckOutCopy

input
  $c : copy/borr$; $AVCOPY_{in} : set(copy)$; $BORROWER_{in} : set(borrower)$;
  $LASTBORR_{in} : set(copy/borr)$; $COPY/BORR_{in} : set(copy/borr)$

output
  $AVCOPY_{out} : set(copy)$; $LASTBORR_{out} : set(copy/borr)$;
  $COPY/BORR_{out} : set(copy/borr)$

Operation I/O definition
  $c \cdot copy \in AVCOPY_{in}, c \cdot borrower \in BORROWER_{in}$,
  $count(get(COPY/BORR_{in}, c \cdot borrower)) < max \Rightarrow$
    $COPY/BORR_{out} = insert(c, COPY/BORR_{in})$,
    $AVCOPY_{out} = delete(AVCOPY_{in}, c \cdot copy)$,
    $LASTBORR_{out} = updatelb(LASTBORR_{in}, c)$

PreCondition. The copy to be checked out ($c \cdot copy$) must be available for checkout, the borrower ($c \cdot borrower$) must be a registered borrower, and the number of copies currently checked out by the borrower must be strictly less than *max*.
PostCondition. The input c is stored in $COPY/BORR$, the copy checked out ($c \cdot copy$) is made unavailable, and the last borrower relation for the copy is updated to reflect the new last borrower of the checked-out copy.

Figure 8. An Ospec for the data transform CheckOutCopy.

where *StateSpec* is the name of an algebraic specification defining the states of the process, *LabelSpec* is the name of the algebraic specification defining the labels of the transition and *Axioms* are first-order axioms of the form $C \Rightarrow s_i \xrightarrow{l} s_j$, where s_i, s_j are states defined in *StateSpec*, and l is a label defined in *LabelSpec*.

The semantics of a control-extended DFD (C-DFD) are characterized by an ASTS created in a bottom-up manner from ASTSs characterizing the semantics of individual DFD components in the following way (see Figure 9, where TS1 to TS4 are ASTSs):

1. Derive ASTSs characterizing the behaviour of each C-DFD component from specifier-supplied descriptions. The resulting set of ASTSs together with the C-DFD is called the *Basic Interpreted C-DFD*.
2. Derive an ASTS characterizing the synchronous interactions that can take place among C-DFD components from the Basic Interpreted C-DFD. This ASTS is called the *Synchronous Interaction Specification* (SIS). The SIS together with the C-DFD is called the *Basic ExtDFD*.
3. Derive an ASTS characterizing the permissible time-dependent relationships among the synchronous interactions specified in the SIS from the Basic ExtDFD. The resulting ASTS is called the *Behavioural Specification* (BS).

In phase 1 of the specification generation method, ASTSs characterizing semantic models of C-DFD components are created from specifier-supplied descriptions and specification schemas. The specifier-supplied descriptions are analogous

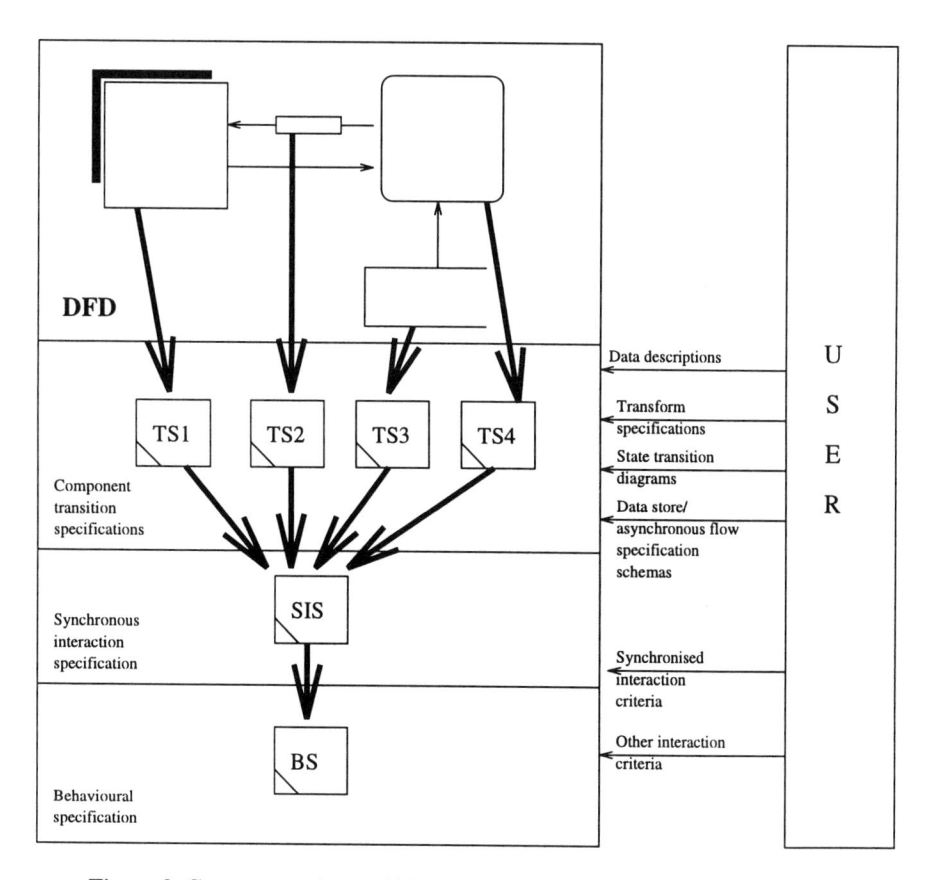

Figure 9. Components in specifying the semantics of non-sequential systems.

to the traditional structured analysis (SA) data dictionary definitions and data transform specifications [6, 15]. For data flow and data store components, specification schemas are instantiated with algebraic specifications derived from the specifier's descriptions of transmitted or stored data to produce algebraic specifications characterizing their structure and data access behaviour.

In phase 2 it is determined which process actions defined in phase 1 are to be synchronized. For example, a read from a data store action of a data transform must be synchronized with a read action of the data store. A specification defining the effects of *synchronous transitions*, that is, transitions caused by synchronizing actions, is derived from the data and control relationships depicted in the control-extended DFD using rules which state what type of interactions depicted in a control-extended DFD result in synchronous transitions. The ASTS resulting from this phase consists of transition axioms that define the effect of synchronized events. For example, given that the transitions $p_1 \xrightarrow{l_1} p_1', \ldots, p_j \xrightarrow{l_j} p_j'$ can take place in an application state $< p_1, \ldots, p_j, p_{j+1}, \ldots, p_n >$, then the synchronized effect of the actions labeled $l_1, \ldots, l_j$, is defined by the axiom:

$$p_1 \xrightarrow{l_1} p_1', \ldots, p_j \xrightarrow{l_j} p_j', l = SYNCH(l_1, \ldots, l_j) \Rightarrow$$
$$< p_1, \ldots, p_j, p_{j+1}, \ldots, p_n > \xrightarrow{l} < p_1', \ldots, p_j', p_{j+1}, \ldots, p_n >$$

In phase 3 constraints on when the synchronous interactions can take place are specified. The ASTS derived in this step (the BS) is an extension of the ASTS derived in phase 2, where the extensions concern definitions of the effects of actions represented by parallel action labels. A more detailed account of the activities in each phase can be found in Ref. [11].

SAME (Structured Analysis Modelling Environment). The research of Docker and France extends beyond a formal interpretation of structured analysis. SAME provides a front-end to the formal system which provides:

- the graphical specification of DFDs
- the definition of data
- an executable dictionary (repository) which stores the DFDs and data definitions, and allows the execution of application models (as prototypes)
- the definition and execution of incomplete models
- a 'soft-fail' environment, in which errors are trapped and analysed and in which the user is generally able to correct the error and continue from the point of failure.

The major features of SAME have been described in some detail elsewhere [7], and will not be discussed further here. The models defined in SAME can be translated into the formal specifications outlined in this paper. Effort is currently being spent on this translation, and on the reporting back of the essential details of the results of the translation through the SAME interface.

4.3 Tse's unifying framework for structured analysis

To facilitate translation of products among structured systems development models, Tse developed a unifying formal framework for the models. The framework is based on an abstract model which captures the common structures of the structured methods. This unifying model is the initial term algebra of an algebraic specification characterizing the common structures. Structured development models can then be translated to the unifying model, which in turn can be translated to other structured systems models (via the unique homomorphism property of initial algebras), thus effecting translation among the models.

In his work Tse focuses on three structured development tools, DeMarco type data flow diagrams [6], Yourdon Structure Charts (SCs) [39], and Jackson's Structure Text (JST) [19].

5 Process Algebras

Some work has been done on the integration of structured methods and process algebras. Some research at Oxford [22] has looked at JSD [20] and CSP while recent work at Teeside Polytechnic has examined the link between Yourdon and CCS. It is the second of these which we will describe.

5.1 Yourdon/CCS

An integrated method using Yourdon and CCS for the specification of real-time systems has been developed at Teeside Polytechnic [9].

The method proceeds thus:

1. Derive context diagram. In the case of real-time systems the externals will tend to be devices which are controlled by the system rather than people who interact with the system. Externals may also, of course, include other systems.
2. Derive system properties in English. In order to (automatically) check the formal model against the requirements it is necessary to formalise the requirements themselves. To achieve this, desirable properties of the system are identified from the user and user requirements.
3. Specify system properties formally. The required properties are then translated into Hennessey-Milner Logic which is supported by the concurrency workbench. This step also continues to define the vocabulary for the intercommunication components which was begun in step 2.
4. Derive DFD explosions. Break the transforms down into as many levels as necessary. It is helpful if the data and control aspects of the system can be separated without compromising the model. The behaviour of the data transforms can be defined either during this step or the next one. It is possible, by allocating a control transform to each device (a device controller), to develop Ward/Mellor data and control flow diagrams which are equivalent to CCS flow graphs (see [9] for a detailed discussion of this approach).

5. Derive State Transition diagrams. There should in fact be two STDs for each control transform, one for the active state initiated by the enable action and the other for the inactive state initiated by the disable. In practice the inactive state is defined by implication.
6. Convert STDs to CCS. This is done automatically but some constructs produce complex alternative behaviours. It may be necessary to manually refine some agents; ideally this would be done via the STDs to maintain the continuity and revisability of the entire model.

The behaviour of a Ward/Mellor control transform is defined as an STD. This diagram documents, for each state the transform can attain, the event flows it will respond to (transitions), the event flows it will create (actions) and the states it will attain as a result. Similarly, in CCS an agent's behaviour is defined as the possible sequences of input and output actions it may take part in and the agent(s) it will become as a result.

An example of the translation of an STD into CCS is given in Figure 10. There is one CCS agent for each state in the STD and one for the STD itself. The latter agent is required to handle the *enable* signal (the unlabelled arrow) which every control transform must have.

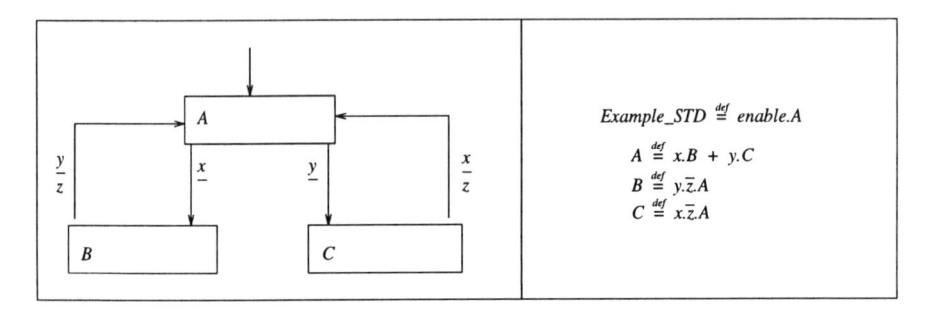

$$Example\_STD \stackrel{def}{=} enable.A$$
$$A \stackrel{def}{=} x.B + y.C$$
$$B \stackrel{def}{=} y.\bar{z}.A$$
$$C \stackrel{def}{=} x.\bar{z}.A$$

Figure 10. Example translation of an STD into CCS.

7. Check functioning of model. Ensure that the model can behave in the desired manner. This entails using the Concurrency Workbench to find deadlocks and to animate the model in various ways.
8. Change model. Any changes required to get the model to function as required must be performed on the structured model. At best this means changing the flow in an STD (step 5) and at worst soliciting new requirements from the customer (step 1).
9. Check properties against model. When it has been established that the model can behave as required, use the Concurrency Workbench to validate the model against the properties expressed formally in HML. Changes may again result from this step.

The work at Teeside is continuing and they are exploring the possible use of LOTOS [36] in place of CCS. They are also working on the interface between their own structured methods tool 'Ascent' and the Concurrency Workbench so as to underpin the method.

6 Other Related Research

Work at BT [30] has led to the development of a rigorous review technique where the products of structured analysis are transformed into a formal system specification. This transformation process has been used to review a number of relatively complex specifications. The process reveals many errors in the structured specification which have not been found during the normal review process. It is hoped to publish the results of this work in the near future.

The problem of comprehending large formal specifications is being looked at by some researchers. Graphical notations are being developed which correspond to the detailed structure of the formal specification. These notations are being developed for VDM using Software Through Pictures [5] and for Z by Randell [27].

7 Conclusion

This paper has outlined some of the current approaches to integrating structured methods of software development with formal notations. Most of this research is at a relatively early stage, although there is evidence that the approach is workable. The integration of structured methods and formal notations aims to overcome some of the problems encountered when formally specifying large systems. Users of structured methods have found that without tool support the methods become unmanageable. It would therefore seem evident that if the integrated methods discussed here are to be of practical use on large systems then tools are essential. Many of the researchers are aware of this and we can soon expect to see reports and demonstrations of their efforts.

Postscript

Since this paper was first published interest has grown in what has come to be known as Methods Integration. Interested readers can refer to the proceedings of a further workshop held in Leeds in 1996 [4].

References

1. P. Allen, A. Bryant and L. Semmens (eds.), *Proceedings of the Methods Integration Workshop, Leeds, September 1991*. Springer-Verlag, Heidelberg (1992).
2. E. Astesiano, A. Giovini and G. Reggio, Data in a concurrent environment. In *International Conference on Concurrency*. Springer-Verlag, Heidelberg (1988).
3. A. Bryant, Structured methodologies and formal notations: developing a framework for synthesis and investigation. In *Z User Workshop, Oxford 1989*, edited J. E. Nicholls. Springer-Verlag, Heidelberg (1990).
4. A. Bryant and L. Semmens (eds.), *Methods Integration, Leeds 1996*. Springer-Verlag, London, eWiCS series (1996).
5. J. Dick and J. Loubersac, Integrating structured and formal methods: a visual approach to VDM. In *Proceedings of ESEC '91 Milan* (October 1991).
6. T. DeMarco, *Structured Analysis and System Specification*. Prentice Hall, Englewood Cliffs, New Jersey (1978).
7. T. W. G. Docker, SAME – a structured analysis tool and its implementation in Prolog. In *Logic Programming, Proceedings of the Fifth International Conference and Symposium*. MIT Press, Cambridge, Mass. (1988).
8. A. S. Evans, *A Prototype Tool for Yourdon and Z*. MSc Dissertation, Sheffield Polytechnic (January 1992).
9. P. C. Fencott, M. A. Lockyer and P. Taylor, Experiences in integrating structured and formal notations for real-time systems. In *Proceedings of the Methods Integration Workshop, Leeds, September 1991*, edited P. Allen, A. Bryant and L. Semmens. Springer-Verlag, Heidelberg (1992).
10. R. B. France, *A Formal Framework for Data Flow Diagrams with Control Extensions*. Massey University, New Zealand (1990).
11. R. B. France, *Semantically Extended Data Flow Diagrams: A Formal Specification Tool*. UMIACS, University of Maryland at College Park (1991).
12. R. B. France, Semantically extended data flow diagrams: a formal specification tool. *IEEE Transactions on Software Engineering*, 18(4):329–346 (1992).
13. R. B. France and T. W. G. Docker, A formal basis for structured analysis. *Software Engineering 88* (1988).
14. R. B. France and T. W. G. Docker, Flexibility and rigour in structured analysis. In *Information Processing 89*. Elsevier Science, Amsterdam (1989).
15. C. Gane and T. Sarson, *Structured Systems Analysis: Tools and Techniques*. Prentice Hall, Englewood Cliffs, New Jersey (1977).
16. S. Goldsmith, Using the Yourdon Structured Method (YSM) and the Vienna Development Method (VDM) together during the system lifecycle. *BCS CASE TOOLS seminar*, IEE (November 1989).
17. V. Hamilton. Experience of combining Yourdon and VDM. In *Proceedings of the Methods Integration Workshop, Leeds, September 1991*, edited P. Allen, A. Bryant and L. Semmens. Springer-Verlag, Heidelberg (1992).
18. D. Hatley and I. Pirbhai, *Strategies for Real-Time System Specification*. Dover Press (1987).
19. M. A. Jackson, *Principles of Program Design*. Academic Press, London (1975).
20. M. A. Jackson, *System Development*. Prentice Hall, Englewood Cliffs, New Jersey (1981).
21. C. B. Jones, *Systematic Software Development using VDM*, Prentice Hall, Englewood Cliffs, New Jersey (1986).
22. M. B. Josephs, JSD and CSP. Programming Research Group, Oxford University (1989).
23. M. B. Josephs and D. A. Redmond-Pyle, *A Library of Z Schemas for use in Entity Relationship Modelling*. Programming Research Group, Oxford University (1991).

24. P. G. Larsen, J. van Katwijk, N. Plat, K. Pronk and H. Toetenel, SVDM: an integrated combination of SA and VDM. In *Proceedings of the Methods Integration Workshop, Leeds, September 1991*, edited P. Allen, A. Bryant and L. Semmens. Springer-Verlag, Heidelberg (1992).
25. J. E. Nicholls (ed.), *Proceedings of the Fifth Z User Workshop, Oxford, 17–18 December 1990*. Springer-Verlag, Heidelberg (1991).
26. F. Polack, M. Whiston and P. Hitchcock, Structured Analysis – A draft method for writing Z specifications. In *Proceedings of the Sixth Z User Workshop, York, 16–17 December 1991*, edited J. E. Nicholls. Springer-Verlag, Heidelberg (1992).
27. G. P. Randell, *Translating Data Flow Diagrams into Z (and vice versa)*. RSRE Report 90010 (October 1990).
28. G. P. Randell, *Improving the Translation from Data Flow Diagrams into Z by Incorporating the Data Dictionary*. RSRE Report 92004 (January 1992).
29. D. Redmond-Pyle and M. B. Josephs, Enriching a structured method with Z. In *Proceedings of the Methods Integration Workshop, Leeds, September 1991*, edited P. Allen, A. Bryant and L. Semmens. Springer-Verlag, Heidelberg (1992).
30. L. Renshaw and P. Davies, *TELSTAR Rigorous Review Technique*. BTRL Martlesham, Internal Report (1992). (To appear: L. Semmens and T. Bryant, Rigorous review technique. In *Industrial-Strength Formal Methods*, edited J. P. Bowen and M. G. Hinchey. Academic Press, London.)
31. L. T. Semmens and P. M. Allen, Using Yourdon and Z: An approach to formal specification. In *Proceedings of the Fifth Z User Workshop, Oxford, 17–18 December 1990*, edited J. E. Nicholls. Springer-Verlag, Heidelberg (1991).
32. L. T. Semmens and P. M. Allen, Formalising Yourdon. In *Proceedings of the Methods Integration Workshop, Leeds, September 1991*, edited P. Allen, A. Bryant and L. Semmens. Springer-Verlag, Heidelberg (1992).
33. J. M. Spivey, *The Z Notation: A Reference Manual*, 2nd edition, Prentice Hall, Englewood Cliffs, New Jersey (1992).
34. *SSADM Version 4 Reference Manual*. NCC/Blackwell, Oxford (1990).
35. T. H. Tse, *A Unifying Framework for Structured Analysis and Design Models*. Cambridge University Press (1991).
36. K. J. Turner, LOTOS – a practical formal description technique for OSI. In *Proceedings, International Conference on Open Systems, London* (March 1987).
37. P. T. Ward and S. J. Mellor, *Structured Development for Real-Time Systems*. Yourdon Press (1981).
38. E. Yourdon, *Modern Structured Analysis*. Prentice Hall, Englewood Cliffs, New Jersey (1989).
39. E. Yourdon and L. Constantine, *Structured Design: Fundamentals of a Discipline of Computer Program and Systems Design*. Prentice Hall, Englewood Cliffs, New Jersey (1979).

8. Implementation

8.1 Refinement

As we discussed in earlier Parts, formal specifications are expressed at high levels of abstraction and in terms of abstract mathematical objects, such as sets, sequences and mappings, and with an emphasis on clarity rather than efficiency. But we want our programs to be efficient and since most programming languages do not support these abstract data types, how do we use the formal specification in system development?

Just as in traditional design methods, such as SSADM and Yourdon, we gradually translate our formal specification into its equivalent in a programming language. This process is called *refinement* (or *reification* in VDM). *Data refinement* involves the transition from abstract data types to more concrete data types such as record-structures, pointers and arrays, and the verification of this transition.

All operations must then be translated so that they now operate on the more concrete data types. This translation is known as *operation refinement* or *operation modeling*, and gives rise to a number of *proof obligations* that each more concrete operation is a *refinement* of some abstract equivalent. By 'refinement', we mean that it performs *at least* the same functions as its more abstract equivalent, but is in some sense 'better' – i.e., more concrete, more efficient, less non-deterministic, terminating more often, etc.

These proof obligations may be discharged by constructing a *retrieve function* for each operation which enables us to return from an operation to its more abstract equivalent. In VDM, we must also construct an *abstraction function* which does the opposite, and brings us from the abstract operation to the more concrete one. More generally there may be a retrieve relation [257].

The refinement process is an iterative one, as shown in Figure 8.1. Except for simple problems, we would never go straight from an abstract specification directly to code. Instead, we translate our data types and operations into slightly more concrete equivalents at each step, with the final step being the translation into executable code.

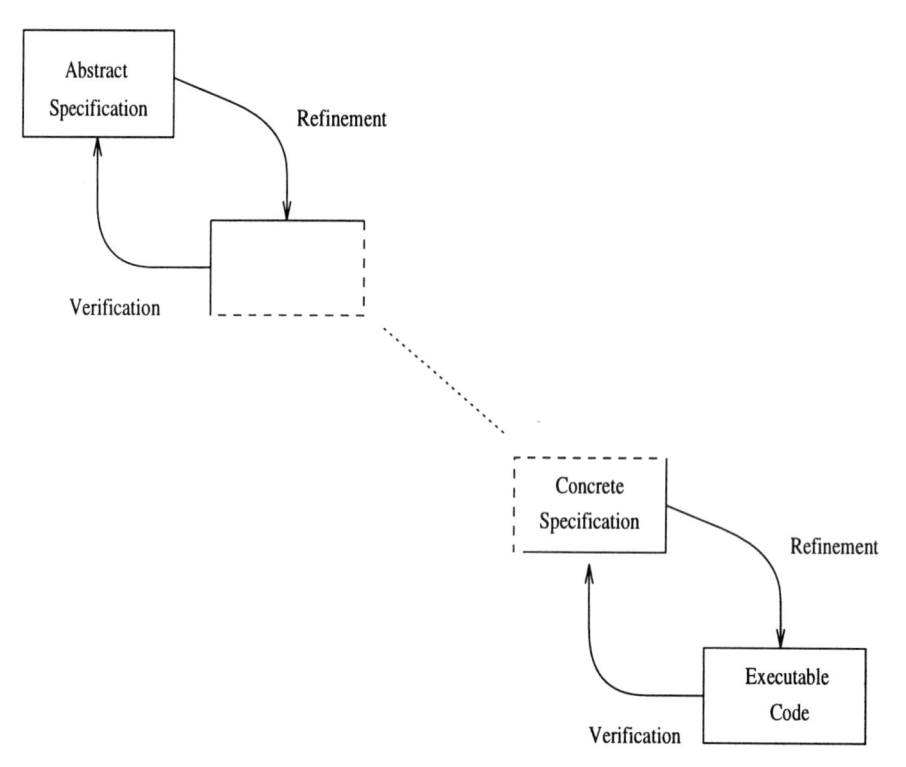

558   High-Integrity System Specification and Design

Figure 8.1. The refinement process

8.2 Rapid Prototyping and Simulation

Rapid System Prototyping (RSP) and simulation have much in common in the sense that both involve the derivation and execution of an incomplete and inefficient version of the system under consideration. They do, however, have different aims (although these are certainly not incompatible), and are applied at different stages in the system life-cycle.

Prototyping is applied at the earlier stages of system development as a means of *validating* system requirements. It gives the user an opportunity to become *au fait* with the 'look-and-feel' of the final system, although much of the logic will still not have been implemented. The aim is to help in determining that the developer's view of the proposed system is coincident with that of the users. It can also help to identify *some* inconsistencies and incompatibilities in the stated requirements. It cannot, for example, be used to determine whether the requirements of efficiency of operation and requirements of ease of maintenance are mutually satisfiable. The prototype will in general be very inefficient, and will not necessarily conform to the stated design objectives.

Best practice holds that the code for a prototype should be discarded before implementation of the system. The prototype was merely to aid in eliciting and determining requirements and for *validation* of those requirements; that is, determining that we are building the 'right' system [19]. It may have a strong *bias* towards particular implementations, and using it in future development is likely to breech design goals, resulting in an inefficient implementation that is difficult to maintain. Retaining a prototype in future development is effectively equivalent to the transformational or evolutionary approach described above, with a certain degree of circumvention of the specification and design phases.

Simulation fits in at a different stage of the life-cycle. It is employed after the system has been specified, to *verify* that an implementation may be derived that is consistent both with the explicitly stated requirements, and with the system specification; in other words, that we are building the system 'right' [19]. While prototyping had the aim of highlighting inconsistencies in the requirements, simulation has the aim of highlighting requirements that are left unsatisfied, or only partly satisfied.

Both rapid prototyping and simulation suffer from one major drawback. Like testing, which can only highlight the presence of software bugs, but not their absence [70], prototyping and simulation can only demonstrate the existence of contradictory requirements or the failure to fully satisfy particular requirements. They cannot demonstrate that no contradictory requirements exist, nor that all specified requirements are satisfied, respectively [126]. That is why attention has begun to be focused on the use of formal methods in both Rapid System Prototyping and simulation, as formal methods can actually augment both of these areas with *proof* [121].

The use of executable specification languages and the animation of formal specifications are clearly two means of facilitating prototyping and simulation, while retaining the ability to prove properties.

8.3 Executable Specifications

We make a distinction between the concept of executable specifications and that of specification , although many authors consider them to be identical.

In our view, specifications are 'executable' when the specification language inherently supports explicit execution of specifications. While the means by which executions of such specifications are performed are varied and interesting in themselves, they are not of concern to us here.

An executable specification language offers one distinct advantage – it augments the conceptual model of the proposed system, derived as part of the system specification phase, with a behavioral model of that same system. As Norbert Fuchs points out in his paper *Specifications are (Preferably) Executable* (reprinted in this Part), this permits validation and verification (as appropriate) at earlier stages in the system development than when using traditional development methods [84].

There is a fine line between executable specifications and actual implementations – that of resource management [266]. While a good specification only deals with the functionality and performance properties of the system under consideration, implementations must meet performance goals in the execution environment through the optimal use of resources.

In their paper *Specifications are not (Necessarily) Executable* (also reprinted in this Part), Ian Hayes and Cliff Jones criticize the use of executable specifications on the grounds that they unnecessarily constrain the range of possible implementations [117]. While specifications are expressed in terms of the problem domain in a highly abstract manner, the associated implementation is usually much less 'elegant', having, as it does, to deal with issues of interaction with resources, optimization, meeting timing constraints, etc. Hayes and Jones claim that implementors may be tempted to follow the algorithmic structure of the executable specification, although this may still be far from the ideal, producing particular results in cases where a more implicit specification would have allowed a greater range of results.

They also claim that while executable specifications can indeed help in early validation and verification, it is easier to prove the correctness of an implementation with respect to a highly abstract equivalent specification rather than against an implementation with different data and program structures. This is crucial; it indicates that executable specifications, while permitting prototyping and simulation, in the long run may hinder *proof of correctness*.

8.4 Animating Formal Specifications

While executable specifications incorporate inherent support in the specification language, animation applies to specification languages which are not normally executable. In this category we include the animation of Z in Prolog [252] (logic programming [85]) and Miranda [49] (functional programming), and the direct translation of VDM to SML (Standard ML) [197], as well as the interpretation and compilation of Z as a set-oriented programming language [249], etc.

Specification languages such as VDM and Z are not *intended* to be directly executable, but by appropriately restating them directly in the notation of a declarative programming language, become so. And, as Fuchs illustrates in his paper *Specifications are (Preferably) Executable*, with appropriate manipulations such animations can be made reasonably efficient.

This approach seems preferable to executable specification languages. It too provides a behavioral model of the system, but without sacrificing abstraction levels. It supports rapid prototyping and even more powerful simulation, but prototypes and simulations are not used in future development. The refinement of the specification to a lower-level implementation, augmented with the discharge of various *proof obligations* ensures that the eventual implementation in a conventional (procedural) programming language satisfies the original specification.

Specifications are not (Necessarily) Executable

I.J. Hayes and C.B. Jones

Summary.

Specifications can be written in languages which have formal semantics. Their very formality, and the similarities with some aspects of implementation languages, invites the idea that specifications might be executed. This paper presents a number of arguments against that idea. The aim is to warn of the dangers of limiting specification languages to the point where all of their constructs can be executed. While conceding the difficulties of relating specifications to an understanding of the "requirements" for a system, it is argued that other solutions should be sought than "executable specification languages".

1 Introduction

For the development of software, the starting point is usually a set of requirements typically given informally in natural language. The informal nature of the requirements means that misunderstandings are possible and that formal verification of an implementation is not possible. To overcome this problem the development process can be viewed as being split into phases. In fact, the so-called phases have to be iterated at least when changes to the requirements occur: it is however useful to view the required project documentation as being created by a series of idealised phases. Initially, a detailed functional[1] specification of what the system should do can be developed from the requirements. The specification can then be validated[2] against the requirements early in the development of the software. By

---

© 1989 The Institution of Electrical Engineers. Reprinted by permission.
Reprinted from *Software Engineering Journal*, 4(6):330–338, November 1989.

[1] In the normal sense of the word and not in the more restricted sense as used in *functional programming*.

[2] We use the term *(formal) verification* to indicate that an implementation has been proved to satisfy a specification, and the more general term *validate* to indicate some form of check of satisfaction.

this process many of the initial errors and misunderstandings can be detected when the cost of correction is low.

Currently specifications are most commonly written in a natural language. However, using a natural language leads to specifications that are vague and ambiguous. While such specifications do aid in detecting errors early in the development process, the imprecision of an informal specification leads to misunderstandings both in validating the specification against the requirements, and the implementation against the specification. For this reason many people have argued that a more formal approach to specification is required. Once a specification has been formalised there is a precise document against which further implementation can be verified; in fact, only then is it possible to formally verify that an implementation satisfies a specification.

There are three more-or-less distinct ways in which software design can be based on a formal specification: the "transformational" approach (e.g., [3, 4]), the "constructive mathematics" approach (e.g., [2]), and those methods where designs are posited and then justified at each development step. The arguments presented in this paper apply to all of these approaches, however, this presentation focuses on the third – posit and prove – approach.

Even when using a formal specification, one is left with the problem of validating the specification against the informal requirements. One approach that has been advocated is to use an executable specification and perform the validation by a series of tests on the specification. (A full discussion of notions of executability and specification can be found in [15] which studies the use of symbolic execution for validating specifications.) Although considering individual test cases is useful, it is not as powerful as proving general properties about a specification. Requiring a specification notation to be directly executable restricts the forms of specification that can be used. In developing specifications of computing systems it is necessary to be able to precisely and concisely specify its desired properties. Any formalism that is applicable should be available to specify the properties of the system: one does not wish to be restricted to a notation that can be executed.

In general, a specification written in a notation that is not directly executable will contain less implementation detail than an executable one. The process of directly matching a specification to a set of requirements will be more straightforward with a specification phrased in terms of desirable properties of the system as opposed to one containing the algorithmic details necessary to make it directly executable. Similarly, it will be easier to verify that an implementation meets the more abstract specification than to try to match an executable specification against an implementation for which different data and program structure may have been chosen.

In fact, executable specifications tend to overspecify the problem. Firstly, because the implementor is tempted to follow the algorithmic structure of the specification (although this may not be desirable for efficiency or other reasons), and secondly because the executable specification will produce particular results in cases where a more implicit specification might allow a number of different results. The latter point is all the more important because of the danger of unnecessarily constraining the choice of possible implementations.

As well as their role at the top level of the system, specifications play an important part in defining the interfaces of modules internal to the system. The validation of a module specification is done with respect to a higher-level specification, or more likely a higher-level design that meets the higher-level specification. As both the higher-level specification and design can be formalised, the validation of the internal modular design can also be formalised; here one does not have the same problem of working from informal requirements that motivated the use of executable specifications.

2 Deterministic Operations

A deterministic specification requires a unique result to be produced for a given input, whereas a non-deterministic specification allows a number of possible alternative results. In Section 3 we explore the subject of non-determinism. This section argues that the aim of executability offers unnecessary constraints even for deterministic specifications.

Most of what is said in this paper could be presented either in a declarative or an imperative framework. The latter has been chosen and a program – or part thereof – which changes a state is referred to as an *operation*.

2.1 Specifying in terms of known functions

The authors and readers of any specification can be assumed to share an understanding of a set of "known" available functions (or operators) that may be used in a specification.

The expressive power of a language required to succinctly specify a problem varies considerably with the complexity of the problem itself. Simple problems can be adequately specified in conventional (efficiently executable) programming languages. For example, using multiple assignment, an operation to swap two values may be specified thus:

$i, j := j, i.$

(This also has the virtue that it solves the so-called *frame problem* by making it clear that no variables other than i and j are to be changed.)

A very high-level language (e.g., SETL [7]) expands the range of problems that can be succinctly specified by providing a richer set of available functions that can be used. A powerful technique is the use of functions that are available for objects which are more abstract than those of the final implementation language. For example, if s_1 and s_2 are sets, then

$s_1, s_2 \cdot = s_1 \cap s_2, s_1 \cup s_2$

defines a functional behaviour which might – when working on representations in terms of linked lists – have to be implemented in several procedures.

Apart from the lack of available functions, there is a more subtle problem with such specifications. If the functions used are *partial*, the assignment style of specification does not really provide a suitable way of recording a *pre-condition*. Such assumptions are often crucial in specifying a system.

As a larger example of an operation that can be specified in a functional manner consider a text file update: given a text file consisting of a sequence of lines, it is to be updated both by deleting a set of numbered lines and by adding sequences of lines after given line numbers in the original file. Let *Line* be the type of a line and *Lines*, a sequence of lines:

Lines = seq of *Line*.

Then a text file update can be defined abstractly as a function

$update: Lines \times (\text{set of } \mathbf{N}_1) \times (\mathbf{N} \to Lines) \to Lines,$

where the first parameter is the initial file (a sequence of lines); the second parameter is the set of line numbers of lines to be deleted; the third parameter is the additions, which are modelled as a mapping from a line number to the text that is to be added after that line number; and the result is the updated file.

There is, here, an important pre-condition. For an update $update(f,d,a)$, the lines to be deleted must be in the original file: $d \subseteq \text{dom} f$; and the additions must go after line numbers in the original file or after the pseudo line number zero to insert text at the beginning of the file: $\text{dom} a = \{0\} \cup \text{dom} f$. (Additions at every point in the file have been required – typically many of these will be empty.) These two assumptions are the pre-condition to be able to successfully apply the *update* function.

Each line in the original file is replaced by a sequence of lines in the output; this sequence consists of either the empty sequence if the line is deleted, or just the original line if that line is unaffected by the update; in either case it is augmented with additions. If n is a line number then the sequence of lines that it will be replaced by in the output file is given by

$(\text{if } n \in d \text{ then } [] \text{ else } [f(n)]) \frown a(n),$

where $s \frown t$ is the concatenation of the sequences s and t.

To specify *update*, for each line in the original file the sequence of lines it is replaced by is constructed and all of these sequences are concatenated to form the output:

$update(f,d,a) \triangleq$
$\quad a(0) \frown \text{conc} \{n \mapsto (\text{if } n \in d \text{ then } [] \text{ else } [f(n)]) \frown a(n) \mid n \in \text{dom} f\},$

where conc ss forms the concatenation of all the sequences in the sequence of sequences ss.

Although the above is written in a very high-level fashion, it is still quite close to an executable program in a functional programming language. Such a high-level program could be executed and such programs can tempt one to consider requiring specifications to be executable. Although this particular specification could be executed, the approach does not generalise to all specifications as is shown in Section 3.1 for a specification closely related to this one. In addition, it is crucial to specify a pre-condition for *update*, otherwise it does not make sense for all possible inputs; such pre-conditions are not usually part of an executable language but are essential in a specification.

2.2 Specifying by inverse

The next question is how to specify operations where no known function is available. Notice that writing something like

$$i := gcd(i,j)$$

only shifts the problem, unless *gcd* is already fully understood.

Some specifications of novel concepts can be constructed by using a known function to constrain the *inverse* of the operation. Suppose, for example, that (integer) square root is both unfamiliar and to be specified, but that squaring is known. It is possible to fix r as the largest integer square root of n ($r, n \in \mathbf{N}$) by writing

$$r^2 \leq n < (r+1)^2.$$

Although this example is very small, the general approach of specifying via an inverse function should not be dismissed. It is, for example, convenient (see [11]) to express the task of constructing a parse tree by stating *inter alia* that collecting the terminal strings from the wanted tree should yield the string given as input. There is, in general, no way of executing such an inverse specification. Even where a search happens to be possible, it is likely to be enormously inefficient. The point is not that it is impossible to write the required operation but rather that a clear (inverse) specification should not be disallowed because it cannot be executed.

2.3 Combining clauses in a specification

Although the technique of the previous section extends the repertoire of specifiable operations, there are many specifications which can be built up only from a combination of properties. It is widely accepted that such combinations can be built up using the operators of predicate calculus. A standard example is to specify a *SORT* operation on sequences without duplicates. Let *Useq* be the set of all sequences without duplicates:

$$Useq = \{s \in \text{seq of } \mathbf{N} \mid \forall i,j \in \text{dom} \, s \cdot i \neq j \Rightarrow s(i) \neq s(j)\}.$$

The *SORT* operation transforms a sequence *in* without duplicates to another sequence *out* without duplicates as follows:

$in, out \in Useq$
$\text{is-ordered}(out) \land \text{is-permutation}(in, out),$

where

$\text{is-ordered} : Useq \to \mathbf{B}$
$\text{is-ordered}(s) \triangleq \forall i, j \in \text{dom}\, s \cdot i < j \Rightarrow s(i) < s(j)$

$\text{is-permutation} : Useq \times Useq \to \mathbf{B}$
$\text{is-permutation}(s_1, s_2) \triangleq \text{rng}\, s_1 = \text{rng}\, s_2.$

This version of the sorting (cf. *is-permutation*) problem is simplified by the assumption that the sequences (*Useq*) do not contain duplicate elements. (The general case is considered in Section 3.1.) But even here several interesting observations can be made. Most importantly, the conjunction of the ordering and permutation properties shows a specification technique which is just not available in an implementation language: it is essentially defining the valid outputs of *SORT* to be the intersection of the results of two processes one of which yields a very large set of permutations of *in* and the other of which can be thought of as yielding an infinite set of ordered sequences. In general, conjunction is not a construct of executable languages. With care, such conjunctions can *sometimes* be reformulated as Prolog programs. Another point about *is-permutation* is the way it is made concise by shifting between data types (here, sequences to sets). This technique can be useful in a range of specifications.

Even where a specification does not explicitly use a conjunction, the technique may be used implicitly. In both Z [8, 19] and VDM [12], *data type invariants* are considered to be conjoined to other properties over types using them.

An example of the use of conjunction in a non-trivial specification appears in work on *unification*: see chapters by Fitzgerald and Vadera in [14].

2.4 Negation in specifications

Specifications can be built up using any expressions of predicate calculus. But, just as conjunction provides a particularly powerful extension to notions of executable languages, negation is also worthy of special mention. Consider, for example, the function to calculate the greatest common divisor (highest common factor). If one defines a common factor by the following predicate:

$\text{is-cd} : \mathbf{N}_1 \times \mathbf{N} \times \mathbf{N} \to \mathbf{B}$

$\text{is-cd}(d, i, j) \triangleq d \text{ divides } i \land d \text{ divides } j,$

then one can specify the greatest common divisor as follows:

$gcd: \mathbf{N}_1 \times \mathbf{N}_1 \to \mathbf{N}_1$
$gcd(i,j) = d \Leftrightarrow$
$\quad is\text{-}cd(d,i,j) \wedge \neg(\exists e \in \mathbf{N}_1 \cdot is\text{-}cd(e,i,j) \wedge e > d).$

This specification makes use of both conjunction and negation. The structure of the specification does not lead directly to the structure of a program to calculate greatest common divisors. Although it is straightforward to implement the common divisor check *is-cd* from its specification, the same cannot be said for implementing *gcd* based directly on the structure of the specification.

If one treats the two conjuncts as each generating possible sets of results[3] (d's) then the value of the *gcd* must satisfy both constraints and hence must be in the intersection of the two sets. To calculate the second set based on the structure of the specification, one should calculate the finite set of d's that satisfy

$$\exists e \in \mathbf{N}_1 \cdot is\text{-}cd(e,i,j) \wedge e > d,$$

and then take the complement of this set relative to the natural numbers, giving an infinite set. As use has been made of an intermediate infinite set, this approach is not executable. One needs to reason about the problem and realise that the first set is finite so one can use it to generate possibilities, while the second predicate is used to check these possibilities; even this approach has problems as one then has to perform similar reasoning to limit the search space for possible values of e. Note that although it is possible to rewrite the negated existential quantification as the universal quantification

$$\forall e \in \mathbf{N}_1 \cdot \neg is\text{-}cd(e,i,j) \vee e \leq d,$$

this only moves the problem; it does not resolve it.

All this reasoning about the problem is not necessary to just specify the task. Such reasoning is part of the process of coming up with an implementation, and in performing such reasoning one would hope to come up with a more efficient implementation than that based directly on the structure of the specification. To produce an executable specification it would be necessary both to make the specification more complicated than necessary, and to perform reasoning that would be better done at the time of designing an actual implementation.

The reader might like to consider the structurally similar specification of determining the least common multiple given below; this example is further complicated by the fact that the set of common multiples of two numbers is infinite, and – while the second conjunct generates a finite set – the set generated by the existentially quantified predicate before it is negated is infinite. Hence one cannot use either conjunct in an evaluation based on the structure of the specification without running into infinite sets.

Defining a common multiple by the predicate:

---

[3] This use of a Boolean function is actually an example of using the inverse of a function as discussed in Section ?.? – some of the arguments to the Boolean function and the desired result (namely *true*) are supplied, and the other argument is generated.

$is\text{-}cm : \mathbf{N} \times \mathbf{N}_1 \times \mathbf{N}_1 \to \mathbf{B}$

$is\text{-}cm(m,i,j) \triangleq i \text{ divides } m \land j \text{ divides } m,$

one can specify the least common multiple as follows:

$lcm: \mathbf{N}_1 \times \mathbf{N}_1 \to \mathbf{N}_1$
$lcm(i,j) = m \Leftrightarrow$
$\quad is\text{-}cm(m,i,j) \land \neg(\exists n \in \mathbf{N}_1 \cdot is\text{-}cm(n,i,j) \land n < m).$

2.5 Quantifiers

Consider the following simple specification:

$is\text{-}perfect\text{-}square(i) \triangleq \exists j \in \mathbf{N} \cdot i = j^2.$

A straightforward attempt to directly execute the above specification would probably enumerate the natural numbers testing each to see if i is a perfect square. If it is, this will terminate; but if it is not, it will not terminate. We can guarantee termination in all cases by stopping when the enumeration gets to i, however, this relies on the property that the square of a natural number is always greater than or equal to the number itself.

Even this simple example involving a quantifier leads to problems for direct execution. In general, the property of the problem that is used to control the enumeration is not as simple as above; and one is required to reason about the problem (preferably in the mathematical system associated with the application area) in order to determine such properties before one can attempt execution.

2.6 Non-computable clauses in specifications

The problem of calculating the so-called Hamming numbers is found in [6]. The Hamming numbers are those whose only prime factors are 2, 3, and 5. The problem is to generate the sequence of Hamming numbers in increasing order. This sequence, *ham*, can be specified by

$ham: \mathbf{N}_1 \to \mathbf{N}$
$ordered(ham) \land$
$\quad \text{rng } ham = \{n \in \mathbf{N} \mid \forall p \in Primes \cdot p \text{ divides } n \Rightarrow p \in \{2,3,5\}\},$

where *Primes* is the set of all prime numbers. As this sequence is infinite, it cannot be computed in its entirety; but its prefixes can (e.g., the first 100 Hamming numbers). This can be done by stating that the output should be the prefix of *ham* of length 100. Note that if the first conjunct (*ordered(ham)*) is used to generate possibilities, all of the ordered infinite sequences would have to be generated: this is not possible. However, by adding the condition that only the first 100 items are required, an implementation of the whole specification becomes possible.

In the paper entitled "Functional programs as executable specifications", Turner [20, pages 43–44] makes use of the following non-executable specification for the problem of computing the Hamming numbers (given in Turner's notation):

$$ham = SORT\{2^a \times 3^b \times 5^c \mid a, b, c \leftarrow [0..]\}$$

where the notation in braces generates a sequence with no duplicates containing the given expression for a, b and c taking natural number values greater than or equal to zero. Note that, although this specification looks formal, it is not since *SORT* on infinite sequences cannot be defined as a recursive function; the above use of *SORT* is informal and the above specification is not directly executable as it involves sorting an infinite sequence. By relying on properties of the Hamming numbers, however, it can be transformed into a program that merges already ordered sequences and is executable, although as specified it never terminates.

Specifications can contain clauses that are not computable; when these clauses are conjoined with additional constraints the whole may be computable. However, the structure of the specification does not lead directly to the structure of an implementation as a component is not computable. The specification must be transformed (typically, by taking into account not necessarily obvious properties of the problem) to a form that has a different structure and is amenable to implementation.

A specification language should be expressive enough to specify non-computable problems such as the halting problem. If it is not, one cannot use the single specification notation to cover both theoretical aspects of computing and practical ones. It is possible to build a specification of implementable systems where a component of the specification is itself not computable. For example, if one takes the specification of the halting problem and adds the condition that the program being examined to determine whether or not it halts contains no loops or recursion, then the problem is trivially implementable.

One can also specify problems such as the following one related Fermat's last theorem: given $n \in \mathbf{N}$ can three natural numbers x, y and z be found such that

$$x^n + y^n = z^n.$$

Whether or not this is computable, at the time of writing nobody has been able to determine whether or not this theorem holds. Again a specification notation should be able to specify such problems irrespective of these issues.

3 Non-Deterministic Operations

We hope the reader is by now aware of some of the expressive advantages of specifications which are not (necessarily) executable. The case against executable specifications changes from one of convenience to necessity when non-determinism is considered.

3.1 External non-determinism

There are some computer systems where even their external behaviour should not be too closely determined by the specification. Section 2.3 considers a simplified *SORT* problem without duplicate keys. One specification where it is reasonable to have a complete specification which does not determine a unique result is for sorting where records (*Rec*) can contain duplicate keys. The components of the records can be obtained using selector functions:

$key: Rec \to \mathbf{N}$
$data: Rec \to Data.$

SORT can then be specified by

$in, out \in$ seq of *Rec*
$\text{is-ordr}(out) \land \text{is-permr}(in, out),$

where

$\text{is-ordr} :$ seq of $Rec \to \mathbf{B}$
$\text{is-ordr}(s) \;\triangleq\; \forall i, j \in \text{dom}\, s \cdot i < j \;\Rightarrow\; key(s(i)) \leq key(s(i)),$

and

$\text{is-permr} :$ seq of $Rec \times$ seq of $Rec \to \mathbf{B}$
$\text{is-permr}(s_1, s_2) \;\triangleq\; bagof(s_1) = bagof(s_2),$

where a sequence is converted into a *bag* (or multi-set) representation by

$bagof :$ seq of $Rec \to (Rec \to \mathbf{N}_1)$
$bagof(s) \;\triangleq\; \{r \mapsto \text{card}\,\{i \in \text{dom}\, s \mid s(i) = r\} \mid r \in \text{rng}\, s\},$

where card gives the cardinality of a set: in this case the frequency of occurrence of *r* in the sequence. Notice, here again, the advantage of finding a convenient operator (=) in another type – in this case bags.

In this example a deterministic executable sort algorithm, no matter how abstract and high-level, will yield a unique result for any given input. Such a "specification" would put a restriction on all implementations that they produce exactly the same ordering although this may not be a requirement as far as the user is concerned. Thus one cannot write a deterministic specification of the above sorting problem that allows the implementor to choose either a Quicksort or an insertion sort to implement it: an insertion sort is stable – records with identical keys retain their original order – while Quicksort is not stable. In fact, a deterministic specification may allow neither Quicksort nor an insertion sort as implementations.

Another example is the specification of a differential file comparison, *diff*, which can be obtained by inverting the specification of *update* given in Section 2.1. The operation *diff* takes two files (f_1, f_2: *Lines*) as input and outputs a set of deletions

(d: set of $\mathbf{N}$) and additions ($a: \mathbf{N} \to \textit{Lines}$) that will change the first file into the second. This can be specified by making use of the *update* function:

$$d \subseteq \text{dom} f_1 \land \text{dom}\, a = \{0\} \cup \text{dom} f_1 \land f_2 = update(f_1, d, a)$$

Given any two input files the output deletions and additions are not, in general, uniquely determined. For example, if the first file contains two consecutive identical lines and the second file contains just one copy of the line in the same place, *diff* may either delete the first line or the second line; both choices will satisfy the specification. Hence it is not possible to use a functional program to specify *diff* without selecting a particular output and hence overconstraining the space of implementations. More importantly, the specification of *diff* above clearly describes **what** *diff* should do; it gives no indication of **how** it should do it. Any description of *diff* that can be executed will contain considerably more detail about how to go about computing the differences.

A particularly interesting specification which embodies such external non-determinism is given in [17]. One of the tasks considered is the constraints which must be put on the representation of lines on a raster display. It is obvious that the limitations of the pixel grid prevent, in general, a completely accurate portrayal of a line; the problem of "staircasing" is a well-known corollary of this limitation. Marshall proposes a series of consistency conditions which any acceptable implementation must fulfill. These conditions do not uniquely determine the output.

There are many examples of non-deterministic specifications for numerical algorithms; these specifications often contain constructs which are not representable in decimal (or binary) notation. Let $\mathbf{R}$ be the set of mathematical real numbers; these cannot be represented on a machine and hence we need a set *Float* of floating point approximations to real numbers which are available on the machine. Consider the example of finding the square root of a real number. Given a positive floating point number, x: *Float*, we wish to calculate its square root, r, so that $r^2 = x$. For positive x, r is an element of $\mathbf{R}$ but it is not necessarily an element of *Float*. Hence the result of this operation may not be representable as an element of *Float* as the accuracy of the machine is limited. We must augment our specification to allow for the actual result to be an approximation to the square root

sqrt: *Float* $\to$ *Float*

can be defined by

$$x \geq 0 \land sqrt(x) = r_1 \;\Rightarrow\; \exists r \in \mathbf{R} \cdot r^2 = x \;\land\; |r_1 - r| < 0 \cdot 01.$$

This is an example where we combine a deterministic clause ($r^2 = x$) involving an unrepresentable value r with an additional clause that makes the actual result required not as well determined but representable as a *Float*. As the above specification contains an unrepresentable component we cannot consider the specification notation used to be directly executable.

The specification of *sqrt* does not give any indication of how to compute the square root. A possible implementation is one based on Newton's method of successive approximation. This method is based on deeper mathematical results than anything immediately obvious in the specification. In addition, it is based on the theory of the real numbers rather than *Floats*.

3.2 Internal non-determinism

The preceding section begins with a hint that non-determinism is more important than the frequency of genuinely under-determined systems might suggest. Even where the external behaviour of a system is defined to be deterministic, non-deterministic specifications of its components can arise in design. This is obvious in the case of parallelism: components whose behaviour is influenced by interference can be composed in a way which yields a deterministic system. Obvious examples of this permeate the whole of our operating systems. For example, the non-deterministic paging behaviour of programs must not be allowed to influence the outcome of user's programs.

It is at first sight surprising – but is a very important fact – that non-deterministic specifications of sub-components of deterministic systems can be useful even where the eventual implementation is also deterministic. The resolution of this apparent paradox comes from the usefulness of non-deterministic specifications to leave freedom to the implementor. Thus it is possible to make and record some design decisions but postpone other decisions to later phases of development. An example of this would be a design which can be realised by introducing, say, a buffer pool manager. The essential properties of such a manager are easy to describe whilst leaving open the question of the algorithm which chooses which free buffer to allocate on the next request. The design decision involving the manager can be verified before work commences on the choice of a particular (deterministic!) algorithm. This use of non-deterministic specifications has been shown to be very useful in the design of larger systems.

3.3 Under-determined versus non-determinism

The discussion in the preceding section might lead the reader to the suspicion that under-determined (but deterministic) behaviour is all that is required. Obviously, this does not work in the presence of parallelism. Intriguingly, it can even fail in its absence. In fact, a semantics needs to cover the genuinely non-deterministic case even where the final implementation language is deterministic. The important fact is the way in which levels of abstraction influence the notion of "behaviour". Consider specifying a module with an abstract state, s, consisting of a set of natural numbers. The module has an operation, *ADD*, to add an element to the set. A second operation, *ARB*, selects an arbitrary element, i, from the set: i is returned by the operation as well as being deleted from s. The choice of the value of i returned is nondeterministic. It would seem reasonable to accept an implementation of the module based on a state consisting of a sequence of natural numbers. Adding an element to the set is implemented by appending it to the sequence, provided that value is not already in the sequence, and the operation *ARB* is implemented by choosing i to be the head of the sequence and removing the head from the sequence. We call the implementations of *ADD* and *ARB* on lists ADD_l and ARB_l, respectively.

The behaviour of ARB_l is thus non-deterministic when viewed at the set level. The actual choice can be determined from the history of operations *ADD* and *ARB* performed, but insufficient of this history is stored in the abstract (set) state to determine the choice. This is an example where the principle of information hiding leads to the abstract level of the system appearing to be non-deterministic while the implementation is deterministic.

In the following we need to be precise about what is meant by a mathematical function: a function has only one possible result for any given argument, and two calls on a function with the same argument must always return the same result. This definition of a function is the one used in mathematics and is consistent with that used in purely functional programming languages. This means, for example, that if $S = T$, then $ARB(S)$ must equal $ARB(T)$.

Often *ARB* is taken to be the specification of a class of mathematical functions all of which satisfy the specification and any of which can be used as an implementation. This interpretation is restrictive since it does not allow the operation ARB_l to be used as an implementation of *ARB*. The implementation ARB_l is a mathematical function at the sequence level: any two calls with the same sequence return the same result; but it is not a function when viewed at the set level: two different sequences can represent the same set (with the elements in different orders) and hence two different calls on ARB_l with the same set (but different representations of that set) can return different results.

The above argues that considering a specification as determining a set of possible (deterministic) functions is too restrictive. An approach that avoids this restriction while still using functions is to use a function that returns a set of possible results (see, for example [20, page 31]). In fact, for our purposes this is theoretically equivalent to using a relational approach; however, a function returning a set is more complicated to deal with in practice. Consider, for example, whether deterministic functions should be treated specially or whether they should just be functions returning singleton sets, and whether functional composition should be redefined or whether the function should take sets of possible inputs as well as producing sets of possible outputs. In addition, if the functions return sets of possible results then we cannot use a function as a value in an expression and we cannot use the law of substitution which is the major reason put forward for the simplicity of reasoning using a functional model. Another problem when considering executable specifications is that the set of all possible results of an operation may be infinite; this would preclude computing the complete set, but it does not preclude computing one element of the set as is required of an implementation.

Another interesting example is a non-deterministic merge as required in operating systems or transaction processing systems. For example, we have streams of commands coming from a number of different terminals and we wish to merge these into a single stream to be executed. An implementation can be considered deterministically at the level where we know about the time at which the commands arrive from the terminals, but at the abstract level (where we hide information about arrival times) non-deterministic behaviour is apparent. See [9, especially page 190] for a discussion of this with respect to purely functional operating systems.

A subtle example of the use of non-determinism occurs in giving the semantics of programming languages. The goal is to leave the implementor free to allocate storage addresses to variables. Thus, a language description should not dictate a particular stack implementation for Pascal. In, for example, [1] the choice of locations (*Loc*) is under-determined for precisely this reason. This example manifests the problem of something being essentially non-deterministic at the level of abstraction of the specification in spite of its being deterministic in terms of the representation chosen for an implementation.

This raises the question of the semantics which can be used, for example, to verify proof rules in the presence of "true non-determinacy". This subject is pursued in [13] and [18].

4 Other Issues

4.1 Specification variables

In the specifications that we have given up to this point the specification variables have stood for the values of program variables (or abstractions thereof). However, it is useful to use specification variables that one would never think of implementing as program variables. These variables do not play a part in the actual execution of the program, rather they are used to specify the required behaviour.

In specifying a real-time system we need to be able to specify real-time constraints on operations. For example, to specify that an operation must be completed in less than two seconds we can introduce variables into the specification that represent the time before (t) and after (t') an operation and specify that $t' - t < 2$. Such mathematical variables are used for specification and are not directly reflected in the variables of the program. They are part of the specification that an implementation has to satisfy, but will an executable specification satisfy such a constraint? Can such a specification be considered to be valid if it does not satisfy the constraint when we execute it? The point here is that we should clearly distinguish a specification and an implementation. An executable specification tends to confuse the two issues.

In specifying concurrent systems such as communications protocols it is necessary to introduce specification variables that contain histories of messages on communication channels. For example, to specify a simple communication channel we can introduce specification variables:

in, *out*: seq of *Message*

which record the histories of messages passed in to and out of the channel, respectively. We require that the output is always a prefix of the input:

$\exists b \in$ seq of $Message \cdot out \frown b = in$.

The variables *in* and *out* do not correspond directly to any variables that would be found in a typical implementation, rather they are used purely to specify the desired operation of the channel in terms of observable histories. In an implementation, we are likely to have a buffer plus indices and counters. Here again we run into a problem if we insist on executable specifications, as history variables are used to help specify the problem and are not intended to be reflected by program variables.

4.2 Inferences from specifications

Being able to reason about a specification is important for two reasons: firstly, one needs to be able to validate user requirements by inferring that the specification has the properties desired by the user; and secondly, one needs to be able to verify that an implementation meets the specification or alternatively derive the implementation from the specification via a sequence of refinement steps.

While an executable specification allows straightforward validation of individual test cases, it may be more difficult to validate more general properties of the system. Using a specification phrased as the conjunction of the desired properties of the system, the validation of a property may well be trivial if it is one of those used in the specification. If the particular property to be validated is not one of those used in the specification, it will typically be more difficult to derive the property from a specification complicated by the necessary algorithmic detail to make it executable.

For the task of verifying an implementation against a specification, executability of the specification is of little value. For a deterministic specification it may be possible to check that the implementation produces the same results as an executable specification for particular test cases. To verify that the implementation is correct it will typically be simpler to show that it satisfies a property-oriented specification, rather than show that it is equivalent to a more detailed executable specification. In fact, the algorithmic structures for the executable specification and the implementation may be quite different. For example, it is easier to show that Quicksort and an insertion sort both satisfy the deterministic specification given in Section 2.3 than to show that either satisfies the other, and for the non-deterministic case given in Section 3.1 neither satisfies the other: they are both over specifications of the problem.

To derive an efficient implementation from a specification, the fact that the specification is (inefficiently) executable is not usually a benefit. The process of refining to an efficient implementation typically starts by inferring additional properties of the problem from the properties given in the specification. From these properties an algorithmic structure is developed that may be widely variant from the structure of the specification. For the example of calculating the square root of a real given in Section 3.1 the most interesting part of deriving the solution using Newton's method is done in the theory of real numbers; once this is done it remains to be approximated using floating point representations.

In general the structure of a specification does not correspond to the structure of an efficient implementation. System designers have to be careful to consider other, possibly more efficient structures than that of the specification before committing themselves. With an executable specification there is a greater temptation to stay with the structure of the specification and to improve its efficiency, rather than starting from the properties of the problem and deriving an alternative more efficient solution. With a property-oriented specification, although the specification may be structured, that structure has not been chosen to enable execution and hence one is encouraged to consider alternative structures.

5 Summary

Software can be specified in terms of a relationship between inputs and outputs. In many cases the software not only produces an explicit output but also modifies an (implicit) state of the system; such operations can also be specified in terms of a relationship between inputs and outputs, if we consider the state before the operation as an input and the state after the operation as an output.

Programs do precisely define a relationship between inputs and outputs and hence can be considered to be specifications. Indeed for many systems the program code is the only precise specification of what the system does. There are two problems, however, with using a program as a specification. Firstly, the relationship between inputs and outputs that a program specifies is typically more restrictive than is required, and secondly, the way in which the relationship is specified tends to be complicated by algorithmic details of how to compute the result.

At the level of a relationship between inputs and outputs, programs typically restrict the allowable results when compared to the results that would satisfy the real requirements of the users of the system.

Specifications are intended for human consumption – they provide a communication link between the specifier and the user, and the specifier and the implementor. For this role programs have too much detail of *how* to solve the problem, rather than specifying *what* problem is to be solved. Programs are only suitable for very simple problems where the specification of the problem is as easily expressed in a programming language as in any other medium.

We can supply a program with a legal input – just how the legality of the input is determined is not clear unless the specification includes a pre-condition and pre-conditions are not generally regarded as part of a programming language – and determine what output it returns. If the programming language is deterministic then any implementation should return the same result. If the language is not deterministic – for example, Dijkstra's guarded command language [6, 5] or languages with concurrency constructs – then that output may be one of a number of possible outputs for that input, but it is not necessarily the output that will be produced by another implementation or even a second run on the same implementation. Running a non-deterministic program with a particular input will not allow us to determine all possible outputs for the given input. If the output is not what was required we know the program is not correct, but if it is suitable it still does not guarantee that the program will always produce suitable results for that particular input. "Testing shows the presence of bugs not their absence" – in the case of non-deterministic programs even testing a particular input does not guarantee that the program is correct for that input! Readers who are familiar with bugs in operating systems will be well aware of this problem.

To determine that a program meets a user's requirements one has to examine the program itself as opposed to runs of the program. Using knowledge of the meaning of the programming language constructs (i.e., the semantics of the programming language) one can determine the possible outputs of a program for a particular input, or classes of input, even the class of all legal inputs. However, any reasoning about a program is difficult as the program is not concise nor is it expressed in a notation suitable for reasoning. A specification should provide the properties of the desired system, from which a program is developed to implement the system.

Specifications also play an important role for component modules of a system. Even if an implementation of a module exists, it is desirable to have a precise and concise specification of the module to avoid users of the module having to read the more complex code of the implementation and to avoid users making unwarranted assumptions about the function of the module. These aspects are further reinforced if the module implements a data abstraction; in this case, the specification is given in terms of the abstract data type, while the implementation involves more detailed programming language data structures. In a situation where an implementation exists, it is clear that the important property of a specification is that it communicate the function of the module to the users as clearly as possible; executability of a specification provides no benefit.

Both functional and logic-programming have been suggested as possible bases for executable specifications [10, 16]. While these have the advantage of being formal and of being higher-level than most programming languages, they are too restrictive when compared to using the full power of whatever mathematical systems are applicable to the problem.

There is another – more psychological – argument against attempts to use specifications as prototypes. It has been argued above that the restriction of a specification notation so that it be executable is bound to result in less clear specifications; an actual executable specification is open to the further injury of "tuning" for increased performance. The resulting destruction of the clarity of the "specification" would lose what the current authors believe is the principal benefit of the construction of a formal specification: its ability to make the essential concepts of the specified system clear.

A wide-spectrum language [3, 4] is one which includes facilities for specification as well as an executable subset. This approach has advantages for program refinement as a single notation can be used throughout the development process. Care has to be taken, however, with the use of such a language to avoid the pitfall of confusing the objectives of specification and prototyping.

It is relevant to draw a distinction between specification and prototyping. For user interface decisions a mock up (not necessarily a full implementation) is useful to give the user a feel for the system. Here executability is important but the function is that of a prototype rather than a specification. However, the executable prototype is typically considerably more detailed in describing *how* to compute, as opposed to the specification's *what* to compute.

Our final suggestion is that perhaps much of what is described in the literature as executable specifications would be better classified as rapid prototyping – a valuable area in its own right. The plea in this paper is that the positive advantages of specification should not be sacrificed to the separable objective of prototyping.

Acknowledgements. The authors are grateful to many people for discussions on this topic. In particular meetings of IFIP WG 2.3 and members of the (ESPRIT-funded) RAISE project have stimulated one of the authors. We would also like jointly to thank Ralf Kneuper, Ketil Stølen and Carroll Morgan for constructive comments on drafts of this paper. Cliff Jones is grateful to SERC for support both via research grants and his Senior Fellowship and to the Wolfson Foundation for financial support.

References

1. D. Bjørner and C. B. Jones. *Formal Specification and Software Development*. Prentice Hall International, 1982.
2. R. L. Constable et al. *Implementing Mathematics with the NuPRL Proof Development System*. Prentice-Hall, 1986.
3. CIP Language Group. *The Munich Project CIP—Volume I: The Wide Spectrum Language CIP-L*, volume 183 of *Lecture Notes in Computer Science*. Springer-Verlag, 1985.
4. CIP System Group. *The Munich Project CIP—Volume II: The Program Transformation System CIP-S*, volume 292 of *Lecture Notes in Computer Science*. Springer-Verlag, 1987.
5. E. W. Dijkstra. Guarded commands, nondeterminacy and formal derivation of programs. *Communications of ACM*, 18(8):453–457, August 1975.
6. E. W. Dijkstra. *A Discipline of Programming*. Prentice-Hall, 1976.
7. S.M. Freudenberger, J.T. Schwartz, and M. Sharir. Experience with the SETL optimizer. *ACM Transactions on Programming Languages and Systems*, 5(1):26–45, January 1983.
8. I. J. Hayes, editor. *Specification Case Studies*. Prentice-Hall International, second edition, 1993.
9. P. Henderson. Purely functional operating systems. In J. Darlington, P. Henderson, and D. A. Turner, editors, *Functional Programming and its Applications*, pages 177–192. Cambridge University Press, 1982.
10. P. Henderson. Functional programming, formal specification, and rapid prototyping. *IEEE Transactions on Software Engineering*, SE-12(2):241–250, February 1986.
11. C. B. Jones. *Software Development: A Rigorous Approach*. Prentice Hall International, 1980.
12. C. B. Jones. *Systematic Software Development Using VDM*. Prentice Hall International, second edition, 1990.
13. C. B. Jones. Program specification and verification in VDM. In M. Broy, editor, *Logic of Programming and Calculi of Discrete Design — NATO ASI Series F: Computer and Systems Sciences, Vol. 36*, pages 149–184. Springer-Verlag, 1987.
14. C. B. Jones and R. C. F. Shaw, editors. *Case Studies in Systematic Software Development*. Prentice Hall International, 1990.
15. R. Kneuper. *Symbolic Execution as a Tool for Validation of Specifications*. PhD thesis, Department of Computer Science, University of Manchester, 1989.

16. R. Kowalski. The relation between logic programming and logic specification. In C. A. R. Hoare and J. C. Shepherdson, editors, *Mathematical Logic and Programming Languages*, pages 11–27. Prentice Hall, 1985.
17. L. S. Marshall. A formal specification of straight lines on graphics devices. *Lecture Notes in Computer Science*, 186:129–147, Springer-Verlag, March 1985.
18. T. Nipkow. Non-deterministic data types: Models and implementations. *Acta Informatica*, 22:629–661, 1986.
19. J. M. Spivey. *The Z Notation: A Reference Manual*. Prentice Hall International, second edition, 1992.
20. D. A. Turner. Functional programs as executable specifications. In C. A. R. Hoare and J. C. Shepherdson, editors, *Mathematical Logic and Programming Languages*, pages 29–54. Prentice-Hall, 1985.

Specifications are (Preferably) Executable

Norbert E. Fuchs

Summary.

The validation of specifications with respect to user requirements is extremely difficult. To ease the validation task and to give users immediate feedback on the behaviour of the future software, it was suggested that specifications should be made executable. However, Hayes and Jones [18] argue that executable specifications should be avoided because executability can restrict the expressiveness of specification languages, and can adversely affect implementations. We argue for executable specifications by showing that non-executable formal specifications can be made executable on almost the same level of abstraction, and without essentially changing their structure. No new algorithms have to be introduced to get executability. Furthermore, we show that declarative specification languages combine high expressiveness and executability.

1. Introduction

Specifications play a central role in software development in more than one way. They define all required characteristics of the software to be implemented, and thus form the starting point of any software development process. Specifications are also an important means of communication between users and developers; they can even be contracts. As formalised expressions of the requirements, specifications stand at the borderline between informal and formal descriptions of an application area.

To define the required characteristics precisely and concisely, specifications must be written in formal and highly expressive languages [39]. For an immediate reflection of the consequences of the specifications and for an early validation, it has been suggested that specifications should furthermore be executable [1].

Hayes and Jones [18] however, argue that the demands for high expressiveness and executability are mutually exclusive, and that executable specifications should

---

© 1992 The Institution of Electrical Engineers. Reprinted by permission.
Reprinted from *Software Engineering Journal*, 7(5):323–334, September 1992.

be avoided. They also state that executable specifications can negatively affect implementations. They support their arguments by a detailed and exhaustive discussion of specification problems which, in their opinion, cannot adequately be handled by executable specification languages.

We dissent for two reasons. First we consider the lack of correctness in software the most serious problem of software development, and not (as Hayes and Jones do) the possible lack of expressive power of specification languages. Since the correct behaviour of the software is defined by the requirements, and since the specifications are the basis for software development, all applicable means should be available to validate the specifications with respect to explicit and implicit requirements. Executable specifications can be crucial for this because, in addition to formal reasoning about the specification, they allow immediate validation by execution, and they provide users and developers with the *touch-and-feel* experience necessary to validate non-functional behaviour, e.g. user interfaces. Excluding executability from specification languages therefore means depriving oneself of a powerful method for validation.

Secondly, as we show in this paper, high expressiveness and executability need not exclude each other if specifications are written in declarative languages.

2. Software Specifications

2.1 Executable software specifications

A software specification should describe the required behaviour of a future software system in problem-oriented terms, i.e. the specification should form a conceptual model of the system. The description should be as abstract as the requirements permit. This is only possible if the specification language is sufficiently powerful to express the required behaviour adequately.

Traditionally, specifications have been written in natural language, but today more and more specifications are written in formal specification languages [39]. Compared with specifications in natural language, formal specifications have many advantages [14]. Since a formal language has a well-defined syntax and a well-defined semantics, all details of a specification must be stated explicitly; thus missing, ambiguous, or inconsistent information can be found more easily. In addition, formal reasoning about the specification is possible, especially verification and validation with respect to the requirements. In the context of this paper, we will only consider specifications in formal languages. Descriptions in natural language are called requirements.

If the formal specification language is executable, there is an additional advantage; an executable specification represents not only a conceptual, but also a behavioural model of the software system to be implemented [9]. The behaviour of the system interacting with its environment can be demonstrated and observed before it actually exists in its final form.

This quality of executable specifications promises to remedy the most serious problem of software, its lack of correctness and reliability. In the traditional software development one of the main reasons for this problem is the large time lag between the specification of a system and its validation. Since the implementation is the first formal (and executable) version of the system, validation is only possible after design decisions were made. This means that validation has to deal with the enormous amount of detail in the implementation. Design decisions may also have to be made again. Executable specifications, however, allow early validation on an abstract level and in terms of the problem. This will increase the correctness and the reliability of the software, and reduce development costs and time.

Furthermore, executable specifications can serve as prototypes which allow us to experiment with different requirements or to use an evolutionary approach for software development. This is especially important as, in many projects, the requirements cannot initially be stated completely and precisely.

Their very executability makes executable specifications an optimal communication vehicle between users and developers in their discussion of the intended system behaviour. Even those uncomfortable with formality can experience the behaviour generated by executing the specifications, and check whether it conforms to their intentions [9].

Executable specifications can be embedded in various software development paradigms. Particularly attractive are the combinations with prototyping, and with the operational and the transformational approaches [1]. If we combine executable specifications with the transformational approach the executable specification forms the only relevant document for all phases of software development.

2.2 Hayes' and Jones' [18] critique of executable specifications

Hayes and Jones argue that executable specifications should be avoided. Their arguments against executable specifications can be summarised as follows.

- All applicable formalisms should be used to specify the desired properties of a system. Executability inevitably limits the expressive power of a specification language and restricts the forms of specifications that can be used. Specifications should be phrased in terms of required properties of the system. They should not contain the algorithmic details necessary to make them directly executable.
- Although executable specifications permit early validation with respect to the requirements by executing individual test cases, proving general properties about a specification is much more powerful.
- Executable specifications can unnecessarily constrain the choice of possible implementations. Implementors can be tempted to follow the algorithmic structure of the specification although that may not be desirable. Executable specifications can produce particular results in cases where a more implicit specification may allow a number of different results.

– It is easier to verify that an implementation meets a more abstract specification, than to match an executable specification against an implementation for which possibly different data and program structures have been chosen.

In the main part of their paper, Hayes and Jones elaborate on their arguments against executable specifications by addressing in detail particular aspects and problems of specifications. In each case, they argue that executable specifications are not able, or not adequate, to represent the pertinent aspect, or to solve the pertinent problem. They illustrate their arguments by a number of example specifications.

2.3 Logic specification languages

Declarative languages, e.g. the functional language ML [27] or the logic language Prolog [32], state *what* is to be computed in a form that is largely independent of *how* the computation is performed. Declarative languages are based on sound mathematical foundations, have well-defined semantics, permit descriptions at a very high level of abstraction, and are referentially transparent. Thus, declarative languages are especially suitable as specification languages.

Traditionally, logic has been used as a powerful, concise, and declarative language for software specifications. The restriction to Horn clause logic and the mechanisation of proofs, which led to logic languages such as Prolog, makes these specifications executable [22]. Logic specification languages have received much research interest [10, 16, 17, 24, 31, 35, 36, 38].

In the following, we express example specifications in a logic specification language (LSL) based on the extended Horn clause syntax proposed by Lloyd and Topor [26]. LSL can be considered a subset of the logic programming language Gödel [19].

A specification consists of a finite number of LSL statements of the form

$H \leftarrow B.$

where the head H is an atomic formula and the body B is a (not necessarily closed) first-order formula containing the usual connectives and quantifiers. For each free variable in H and in B there is an implicit universal quantifier in front of the statement. The body B can be absent.

An example specification is the subset predicate $\subseteq$, defined by the statement

$X \subseteq Ys \leftarrow \forall Z(Z \in X \rightarrow Z \in Y).$

The computation rule of LSL is similar to that adopted for Gödel. The left-most literal that can safely be executed is selected for execution. Specifically, negated literals are only executed when they are ground. The execution of literals can be delayed until explicit conditions are fulfilled. This permits us to specify co-routining, and thus to increase efficiency.

The greater expressiveness of LSL facilitates the formulation of specifications in two ways. First, LSL statements are closer to statements in natural language than

Horn clauses. This makes it easier to translate software requirements, which are typically expressed in natural language, into specifications written as LSL statements. Second, the readability of the specifications is increased because LSL statements allow us to state facts more directly and more concisely.

Despite their greater expressiveness, LSL statements remain within the Horn clause subset of predicate logic. In fact, Lloyd and Topor [26] demonstrated that statements can easily be transformed into equivalent Horn clauses, provided that negation as failure is safe. The above LSL statement for the subset predicate can be transformed into the Horn clauses

$X \subseteq Y \leftarrow not\, p(X,Y).$

$p(X,Y) \leftarrow Z \in X \wedge not\, Z \in Y.$

The connective *not* stands for (safe) negation as failure.

3. Hayes' and Jones' example specifications

Hayes and Jones request that specifications should abstractly define properties of systems by all available means of expression, and should not restrict possible implementations. Their central argument is that these requests are jeopardised if specifications are executable.

We refute their argument by showing that their example specifications can be directly translated into executable form on almost the same level of abstraction, and without essentially altering their structure.

As is seen below, the translation of non-executable specifications into executable ones is made possible by reformulating them in a declarative specification language (in this case LSL) and by adding constructive elements. Since no new algorithms need to be introduced to achieve executability many of the executable specifications are based on search. The executable specifications remain property-oriented and have a declarative semantics.

3.1 Specifying in terms of available functions

Hayes and Jones observe that very often specifications can be constructed as combinations of simpler properties or operations, especially if these are already available in the specification language. They state that the operators of predicate calculus can be used to build up the combinations.

Hayes and Jones further point out that to specify a problem concisely the specification language must provide an adequate level of functionality and the necessary expressive power. They state that simple problems can be specified in conventional programming languages, whereas for the adequate specification of complex problems we need an expressive power which is usually not available in executable languages.

We counter their arguments by showing that declarative languages, specifically LSL, provide the functionality and the expressiveness to adequately represent their example specifications in executable form.

Following Hayes and Jones, and as usual in mathematics, we assume that some simple predicates are available. We do not indicate in each case whether these predicates are predefined in LSL or can be constructed from more elementary predicates.

3.1.1 Set union and intersection: Hayes and Jones specify the *union* and *intersection* of two sets, $S1$ and $S2$, in a language that makes the functions $\cup$ and $\cap$ available.

$Union := S1 \cup S2$

$Intersection := S1 \cap S2$

In logic languages these two functions are not usually available, but they can easily be specified starting from their basic definitions. Functions are represented as predicates with an additional last argument which stands for the value of the function. Sets are represented as ordered lists without duplicates, the empty set as the empty list. The predicates *union* and *intersection* can then be specified by the following LSL statements:

$union(S1, S2, Union) \leftarrow$
  $set(Element, (member(Element, S1) \lor$
  $member(Element, S2)), Union).$

$intersection(S1, S2, Intersection) \leftarrow$
  $set(Element, (member(Element, S1) \land$
  $member(Element, S2)), Intersection).$

The predicates *set* and *member* are assumed to be available. The predicate *set* is a set constructor. The atom

$set(X, p(X), Xs)$

constructs the set

$Xs = \{X \mid p(X)\}$

Note that the LSL predicate *set* returns the empty list for the empty set, while Prolog's standard predicate *setof* fails.

As the predicates *union* and *intersection* are now available we can specify the *union* and *intersection* of two sets as abstractly as Hayes and Jones.

3.1.2 Update of text file: In the next example, Hayes and Jones specify the update of a text file. Although they state that their specification could eventually be made executable, we believe that it is instructive to redevelop the specification in a logic language. A file consists of a sequence of lines represented as the list

$File = [Line \mid Lines]$

Lines to be deleted are modeled as a set of line numbers, which is represented as a list

$Deletes = [LineNumber \mid LineNumbers]$

and a sequence of lines to be added is represented as a list of lines

$Adds = [Line \mid Lines]$

Lines can be added before the first line of the file and after each line of the file. The list of lines *AddBefore* will be added before the first line. *AddsAfter* is a list of lists of lines. For every line of the file, it contains a list of lines to be added after that line, i.e. line numbers are mapped to lists of lines. Many of these lists will be empty since no lines have to be added.

The updated file is defined by Hayes and Jones as

$UpdatedFile = AddBefore\&$
$\quad\&\&\{(\text{if } N \in Deletes \text{ then } [] \text{ else } File(N))$
$\quad\quad \& AddsAfter(N) \mid N \in domain(File)\}$

where & denotes the concatenation of two sequences and && the concatenation of all the sequences in the sequence of sequences of lines. Two preconditions

$Deletes \subseteq domain(File)$

$domain(AddsAfter) = domain(File)$

state that lines to be deleted have to be in the original file, and that additions must go after every line of the original file.

In LSL, we specify the update operation by the predicate *update*. The predicate is defined as an implication of the conjunction of its pre- and postconditions [11], and thus completely reflects Hayes' and Jones' original non-executable definition.

$update(File, Deletes, AddBefore, AddsAfter, UpdatedFile) \leftarrow$
$\quad domain(File, DomainOfFile) \wedge \quad\quad\quad\quad\quad \% \ domain(File)$
$\quad subset(Deletes, DomainOfFile) \wedge \quad\quad\quad\quad \% \ Deletes \subseteq domain(File)$
$\quad domain(AddsAfter, DomainOfFile) \wedge \% \ domain(AddsAfter) = domain(File)$
$\quad delete\_add(File, DomainOfFile, Deletes, AddsAfter, IntermediateFile) \wedge$
$\quad concatenate(IntermediateFile, ConcatenatedIntermediateFile) \wedge$
$\quad append(AddBefore, ConcatenatedIntermediateFile, UpdatedFile).$

The operations & and && are represented by the predicates *append* and *concatenate*, respectively. The predicate *delete_add*

$delete\_add([LineN \mid Lines], [N \mid Ns], Deletes, [AddN \mid Adds],$
$\quad [NewLinesN \mid NewLines]) \leftarrow$
$\quad (\text{if } member(N, Deletes) \text{ then } NewLineN = [] \text{ else } NewLineN = [LineN]) \wedge$
$\quad append(NewLineN, AddN, NewLinesN) \wedge$
$\quad delete\_add(Lines, Ns, Deletes, Adds, NewLines).$

$delete\_add([], \_, \_, \_, []).$

calculates the sequence of sequences of lines

$$\{(\text{if } N \in \textit{Deletes} \text{ then } [] \text{ else } \textit{File}(N)) \& \textit{AddsAfter}(N) \mid N \in \textit{domain}(\textit{File})\}$$

by a recursive loop over the domain of the file.

The predicates *domain*, *subset*, *concatenate*, *append*, *member*, and the operator notation of *if–then–else* are assumed to be available.

The example update operation

$$update([f1,f2],[2],[a0],[[a1],[]], \textit{UpdatedFile})$$

results in

$$\textit{UpdatedFile} = [a0, f1, a1]$$

3.1.3 Sorting sequences without duplicate elements: Hayes and Jones specify the *sort* operation for sequences of natural numbers without duplicates using the simpler *permutation* and *ordered* properties. The *sort* operation transforms a sequence X satisfying the precondition

$$\textit{sequence\_of\_natural}(X)$$

into a sequence Y which satisfies the postcondition

$$\textit{permutation}(X, Y) \wedge \textit{ordered}(Y)$$

If we assume (like Hayes and Jones) that the predicates *sequence_of_natural*, *permutation* and *ordered* are available, we can immediately specify the predicate *sort* in LSL as an implication of the conjunction of its pre- and postconditions

$$\textit{sort}(X,Y) \leftarrow \textit{sequence\_of\_natural}(X) \wedge \textit{permutation}(X,Y) \wedge \textit{ordered}(Y).$$

This well-known *slow sort* algorithm is in the form of a generate-and-test solution. The executable specification is as property-oriented and declarative as the non-executable one.

3.1.4 Greatest common divisor and least common multiple: Hayes and Jones specify the greatest common divisor of two natural numbers by

$$gcd(I,J) = D \Leftrightarrow$$
$$\quad \textit{common\_divisor}(D,I,J) \wedge$$
$$\quad \neg\, (\exists E \in N(\textit{common\_divisor}(E,I,J) \wedge E > D))$$

$$\textit{common\_divisor}(D,I,J) \Leftrightarrow \textit{divides}(D,I) \wedge \textit{divides}(D,J)$$

and state that the structure of the specification does not lead directly to the structure of a program to calculate the greatest common divisor. They further state, that to make the specification executable, it would be necessary to complicate the specification and to reason about the problem.

We show that the specification can be made executable without changing its structure, without complicating it, and with only some reasoning about termination.

To transform this specification into an executable one we represent the function *gcd* by the predicate *gcd* defined by the LSL statement

$gcd(I,J,D) \leftarrow$
  $D \in N \wedge$
  $common\_divisor(D,I,J) \wedge not(E \in N \wedge$
  $common\_divisor(E,I,J) \wedge E > D).$

We introduced the precondition $D \in N$ that is implicit in the original specification and replaced the logical negation ¬ by the negation as failure *not*. We also omitted the existential quantifier for E since all free variables in LSL statements are implicitly quantified.

In order to make the specification of *gcd* executable we represent the predicate $\in$ by the executable predicate *limited_natural_number(Natural, Limit)*, which recursively generates natural numbers *Natural* up to *Limit*. Since the largest integer divisor of an integer is the integer itself, the domains of the variables D and E are finite. The generator uses these obvious upper limits to enforce termination of the generate-and-test cycle. We get the executable specification

$gcd(I,J,D) \leftarrow limited\_natural\_number(D,I) \wedge common\_divisor(D,I,J) \wedge$
  $not(limited\_natural\_number(E,I) \wedge common\_divisor(E,I,J) \wedge E > D).$

$common\_divisor(D,I,J) \leftarrow divides(D,I) \wedge divides(D,J).$

which directly reflects the original specification.

In the same way we translate the specification of the *least common multiple*

$lcm(I,J) = M \Leftrightarrow$
  $common\_multiple(M,I,J) \wedge$
  $\neg (\exists L \in N(common\_multiple(L,I,J) \wedge L < M))$

$common\_multiple(M,I,J) \Leftrightarrow divides(I,M) \wedge divides(J,M)$

into the LSL statements

$lcm(I,J,M) \leftarrow$
  $limited\_natural\_number(M,I*J) \wedge$
  $common\_multiple(M,I,J) \wedge$
  $not(limited\_natural\_number(L,I*J) \wedge$
  $common\_multiple(L,I,J) \wedge L < M).$

$common\_multiple(M,I,J) \leftarrow divides(I,M) \wedge divides(J,M).$

In the definition of *lcm*, we use the fact that the least common multiple of two integers is not larger than their product. As a consequence, the generated set of common multiples is finite.

The results show that non-executable specifications of the *greatest common divisor* and of the *least common multiple* can directly be translated into LSL. The resulting executable specifications are based on the generate-and-test technique and remain declarative.

During the translation we replaced the predicate ∈ by a recursive generator which generates natural numbers up to a given limit, i.e. we used a specific property of the problem to control the enumeration and to enforce termination. Hoare uses the same reasoning [20]. Hayes and Jones doubt the generality of this approach. They argue that it can be difficult to find such a property and, if found, the property is possibly not as simple as in the example.

This can actually be the case. On the other hand, it is always possible to enforce the termination of an enumeration by an educated guess. Similar guess-work is used in limited depth-first search. Iterative deepening shows how the guessing can even be automated [28].

3.2 Specifying by inverse

Sometimes it is impossible to specify an unknown function directly in terms of given functions. Hayes and Jones state that, in this case, the function may be specified indirectly by constraining its inverse by available functions. They emphasise that inverse functions are not generally executable, or if executable, that the execution is usually very inefficient.

We show that LSL allows specification by inverse. Contrary to Hayes' and Jones' supposition, the inverse specifications are executable, but they are based on search and can indeed be rather inefficient.

3.2.1 Integer square root: Hayes and Jones define the unknown function *integer square root* by its known inverse *square*. The natural number R, as the largest integer square root of the natural number I, is defined by the constraints

$$R^2 \leq I < (R+1)^2$$

We define the predicate *integer_square_root* again as an implication of the conjunction of its pre- and postconditions

    integer_square_root$(I, R) \leftarrow$
        $R \in N \wedge R**2 \leq I \wedge I < (R+1)**2.$

Next, we introduce a representation for the predicate ∈. Since termination is guaranteed by the constraints, we represent ∈ by the recursive generator *natural_number*, which enumerates all natural numbers.

    integer_square_root$(I, R) \leftarrow$
        natural_number$(R) \wedge R**2 \leq I \wedge I < (R+1)**2.$

This executable specification defines *integer square root* declaratively by its properties, and generates solutions by a simple generate-and-test approach.

3.2.2 Parse tree: Hayes and Jones observe that it can be convenient to express the task of constructing a parse tree by demanding that the concatenation of the terminal strings of the wanted tree yields the input string. They point out that, if this inverse specification is executable at all, it leads to enormously inefficient search.

Like Prolog, LSL provides definite clause grammars in the form of grammar rules, e.g.

> sentence $\rightarrow$ noun_phrase, verb_phrase.
>
> noun_phrase $\rightarrow$ determiner, noun.
>
> verb_phrase $\rightarrow$ verb, noun_phrase.
>
> determiner $\rightarrow$ [the].
>
> noun $\rightarrow$ [cat] | [dog].
>
> verb $\rightarrow$ [sees] | [bites].

The grammar rule

> sentence $\rightarrow$ noun_phrase, verb_phrase.

is understood as the LSL statement

> $sentence(S0, S) \leftarrow noun\_phrase(S0, S1) \wedge verb\_phrase(S1, S)$.

As a consequence a grammar given in the form of grammar rules is executable; it is already a recursive-descent parser for the language it defines. The grammar is reversible; it allows to parse given sentences and to generate non-deterministically all sentences that can be derived from the grammar.

By adding to the non-terminals arguments that represent the respective subtrees, it is possible to construct the parse tree automatically during the parsing, e.g.

> sentence(s(NP, VP)) $\rightarrow$ noun_phrase(NP), verb_phrase(VP).
>
> noun_phrase(np(DET, N)) $\rightarrow$ determiner(DET), noun(N).
>
> verb_phrase(vp(VP, NP)) $\rightarrow$ verb(VP), noun_phrase(NP).

...

Parse trees are then represented as compound terms, e.g. the parse tree of the sentence

> *the dog sees the cat*

by the term

> $s(np(det(the), n(dog)), vp(v(sees), np(det(the), n(cat))))$

Following Hayes' and Jones' proposal, we can construct the parse tree *P0* of a given sentence *S0*, by requiring that the concatenation of the terminals of *P0* equals *S0*. In the conjunction

$$sentence(P, S, [\,]) \land S = S0$$

sentence(P, S, [ ]) generates (by virtue of the reversibility of the grammar) all possible sentences *S* with their respective parse trees *P*, while $S = S0$ tests whether *S* equals the given sentence *S0*. If the test succeeds *P* is the wanted parse tree *P0*.

As Hayes and Jones point out, this generate-and-test approach is enormously inefficient because many possible sentences with their respective parse trees are generated before the correct sentence and parse tree are found. Fortunately, it is not necessary to specify the construction of the parse tree indirectly since (as we saw above) it can be specified directly with no more search involved than required by recursive-descent parsing.

3.3 Non-computable clauses in specifications

Hayes and Jones argue that a specification language should be expressive enough to specify in the same notation, computable problems, non-computable problems (e.g. the halting problem), and problems that are not known to be computable (e.g. Fermat's last theorem). Especially interesting are specifications containing components that are not computable by themselves. When these components are combined with constraints, the whole can become computable. Hayes and Jones state that, in this case, the structure of the specification does not lead directly to the structure of the implementation, as components are not computable.

Using their example we show that their non-executable specification leads directly to an executable one.

3.3.1 Hamming numbers: Hamming numbers are those natural numbers whose only prime factors are 2, 3, and 5 [6]. The problem is to generate the sequence of Hamming numbers in increasing order. Hayes and Jones specify the sequence by

$$ordered(Hamming) \land Hamming = \{H \in N \mid PdividesH \rightarrow P \in \{2,3,5\}\}$$

The sequence of Hamming numbers is infinite and cannot be computed, but (as Hayes and Jones point out) finite prefixes of the sequence are computable.

The predicate *hamming_number* is true if *H* is an individual Hamming number.

$hamming\_number(H) \leftarrow$
 $natural\_number(H) \land has\_primefactors\_2\_3\_5(H)$.

We represent the pre- and postconditions by the executable predicates *natural_number* and *has_primefactors_2_3_5*. Based on this definition, the predicate *hamming_numbers* calculates the ordered sequence *Hamming* of Hamming numbers represented as a list.

hamming_numbers(Hamming) ←
    set(H, (natural_number(H) ∧
    has_primefactors_2_3_5(H)), Hamming).

As the sequence *Hamming* is infinite, this predicate does not terminate. By replacing the predicate *natural_number* by *limited_natural_number*, we obtain the predicate *prefix_of_hamming_numbers(Limit, Hamming)*, which calculates the finite sequence of Hamming numbers *Hamming* that are smaller than or equal to *Limit*.

prefix_of_hamming_numbers(Limit, Hamming) ←
    set(H, (limited_natural_number(H, Limit) ∧
    has_primefactors_2_3_5(H)), Hamming).

The postcondition *ordered(Hamming)* is automatically fulfilled. For completeness it should nevertheless appear in the specification as a comment.

With the help of the predicate *prefix_of_hamming_numbers* we can, for example, calculate the Hamming numbers up to 20

2, 3, 4, 5, 6, 8, 9, 10, 12, 15, 16, 18, 20

The predicate *hamming_numbers* directly reflects the structure of the non-executable definition which is not changed besides representing a sequence by a list. Thus, our specification stays much closer to the original definition than Turner's specification [37], which introduces additional algorithmic details by generating and merging three streams of numbers. A recursive solution for the Hamming problem can be constructed by induction [11].

3.4 Non-deterministic operations

Non-deterministic operations can produce more than one result for a given input. Hayes and Jones emphasise that the semantics of a specification language needs to cover non-determinism, even if the final implementation is deterministic. They believe that executable specification languages do not have the required semantics, so that executable specifications can restrict the range of possible implementations by producing particular results in cases where a non-executable specification might allow a number of different results.

Logic languages are based on relations, and can thus be used to express non-deterministic operations.

3.4.1 Sorting sequences with duplicate elements: as an example of a system that shows external non-determinism, Hayes and Jones generalise the sorting problem of Section 3.1.3 by allowing duplicate elements, e.g. records with duplicate keys. Thus the sorting operation is no longer deterministic. Hayes and Jones demand that the specification respects this non-determinism and does not overly restrict the implementation (e.g. insertion sort will leave records with identical keys in the given order, while quicksort will not necessarily do this).

We represent records as (*key*, *value*) pairs. It is easy to generalise the LSL specification of the sorting operation (see Section 3.1.3) so that it sorts sequences with duplicate elements. In fact, if we represent sequences as lists and define the predicate *ordered* as

ordered([]).
ordered([X]).
ordered([(*Key1*, *Value1*), (*Key2*, *Value2*) | *Xs*]) ←
    Key1 < *Key2* ∧ *ordered*([(*Key2*, *Value2*) | *Xs*]).

the only change necessary to allow for records with duplicate keys is the replacement of the comparison operator < by ≤. Hayes and Jones introduce the same change in their non-executable specifications.

Sorting the sequence

$$[(2,b),(2,c),(1,a)]$$

gives the two possible results:

$$[(1,a),(2,b),(2,c)]$$
$$[(1,a),(2,c),(2,b)]$$

3.4.2 Differential files: Hayes and Jones resume the file update problem of Section 3.1.2. Given two files, they define a differential file as the sets of deletions and additions that transform the first file into the second. In general, the differential file is not unique. For example, if the original file contains two consecutive identical lines, and the updated file only one of these lines, either line could have been deleted.

Hayes and Jones point out that the specification of the differential file is an inversion of the specification of the update problem, and that considerable detail must be supplied to make the specification of the differential file executable. We show that this need not be the case.

The LSL specification of the update problem is in the form of a relation of its arguments. Once some arguments are sufficiently instantiated, other arguments can be determined. Calling *update* with instantiated *File* and *UpdatedFile* will determine the differential file consisting of *Deletes*, *AddBefore*, and *AddsAfter*. Solutions are found non-deterministically by generate-and-test.

Using Hayes' and Jones' example of a file with two identical lines

update([*f*1,*f*1], *Deletes*, *Before*, *After*, [*f*1])

we obtain the expected two differential files

Deletes = [1]   *Before* = []   *After* = [[], []]
Deletes = [2]   *Before* = []   *After* = [[], []]

In fact, the degree of non-determinism is even larger, since there are three additional differential files that delete both lines, and subsequently add one of them in a different place.

3.4.3 Internal non-determinism: even if the external behaviour of a system is defined to be deterministic, components can internally behave non-deterministically. A well-known example is a system of concurrent, co-operating processes. Hayes and Jones emphasise that specifications which define externally deterministic behaviour by internal non-determinism are extremely useful since they leave great freedom for the implementation.

The specifications of the greatest common divisor and the least common multiple (Section 3.1.4) demonstrated that logic languages, specifically LSL, can specify externally deterministic behaviour with non-deterministic components. This especially applies to solutions that rely on the generate-and-test technique. In addition, other approaches, e.g. those based on the simple but powerful concept of non-deterministic finite automata, can generate deterministic behaviour from a non-deterministic one.

Yet another form of internal non-determinism and external determinism arises when we interpret the literals *permutation*(X,Y) and *ordered*(Y) of the statement

$$sort(X,Y) \leftarrow sequence\_of\_natural(X) \land permutation(X,Y) \land ordered(Y).$$

as parallel processes that communicate via the shared variable Y. This interpretation forms the basis of concurrent logic languages and of co-routining available in LSL, in Gödel, and in some Prolog implementations.

4. All Things Considered

After demonstrating that expressiveness and executability of logic specification languages are not mutually exclusive, we now discuss various other aspects of executable specifications. Some of these aspects are also addressed by Hayes and Jones.

4.1 From non-executable to executable specifications

In the preceding section, we demonstrated that non-executable specifications can be made executable by reformulating them in a logic specification language, and by adding a small number of *constructive elements*.

Specifically, the constructive elements were representation of sets and sequences by lists; construction of sets and sequences by recursion; partial instantiation of variables; and representation of the predicate ∈ by generators of elements of the respective domains. Generators are usually recursively defined, although for a finite domain its extension could be used. Some recursive generators need upper limits to ensure termination of the specification. Transformations that make non-executable specifications executable are also discussed by Partsch [29].

Executable specifications generated in this way are direct translations of their non-executable counterparts. Since they are built from available powerful predicates they are property oriented, declarative, and highly abstract, although the addition of constructive elements results in a level of abstraction slightly lower than that of non-executable specifications. The structure of the non-executable specifications is also not essentially changed, since no new algorithms have to be introduced to achieve executability. In many cases the combination of property-orientation and backtracking results in specifications based on the generate-and-test technique.

This means that the transformation of non-executable into executable specifications is accompanied by a minimum of design decisions. However, even these design decisions are revisable, they need not restrict possible implementations.

We want to emphasise that the translation of non-executable specifications into executable ones on a high level of abstraction is only possible because we use a declarative specification language, in this case the logic specification language (LSL). Declarative languages are especially suitable for specifications because they provide the degree of functionality and the expressiveness to adequately formulate conceptual, as well as behavioural, models.

Logic languages like LSL are basically relational languages and, as shown in the preceding section, can be used to specify non-deterministic operations (even if they have an infinite number of solutions) or to specify deterministic operations by constraining the non-determinism. Both non-determinism and determinism are available at any level of abstraction.

4.2 Efficiency of the derived executable specifications

Many of the derived executable specifications are based on generate-and-test, i.e. on potentially inefficient search. Although the purpose of this paper is not to advocate generate-and-test solutions in general, but to show that non-executable specifications can be transformed into equivalent executable ones, it is nevertheless interesting to show how generate-and-test solutions can be made more efficient.

For preciseness we use the specification of *sort* (see Section 3.1.3)

$$sort(X,Y) \leftarrow sequence\_of\_natural(X) \wedge permutation(X,Y) \wedge ordered(Y).$$

as an example.

As specified, the generator *permutation* will generate complete permutations Y, even if the first few elements of Y are not ordered. This suggests the following co-routining, which will reduce the runtime of *sort* considerably; let *permutation* generate the first two elements of Y, then execute *ordered*. If these elements are ordered let *permutation* generate the next element and continue testing; otherwise let *permutation* generate another couple of elements. As a result of this interleaving of generator and tester, failure branches of the search tree are pruned much earlier, and the program becomes significantly more efficient than without co-routining.

Whereas co-routining interleaves the generator and tester at runtime, program transformations based on unfold/fold rules [13] lead to a form of interleaving at compile-time. Unfolding *sort* on *permutation* and *ordered*, and folding the resulting conjunction *permutation*$(X,Y) \wedge$ *ordered*(Y), produces an equivalent, recursive program for *sort*. This program is considerably more efficient because a number of proof steps are performed before the actual execution, and constraints between arguments are already taken into account.

4.3 A constructive approach to executable specifications

Hayes and Jones specify the square root r_1 of a floating point number x by

$$x \geq 0 \wedge sqrt(x) = r_1 \Leftrightarrow \exists r \in R(r^2 = x \wedge |r_1 - r| < 0.01)$$

The symbol r represents a real number, r_1 its floating point approximation.

The specification postulates the existence of the square root, but is not constructive; there is no indication how the square root should be calculated. The specification cannot even be used to test a hypothetical solution.

Actually, the specification as given is incomplete. Hayes and Jones point out that, to find an implementation for this specification, programmers have to refer to their knowledge of the theory of real numbers. Thus the real numbers in the specification do not serve any direct functional purpose; they have to be understood as specification variables (see Section 4.5) meaning 'use the theory of real numbers', and constraining possible solutions.

This implicit reference to a body of knowledge seems to pose no problem since we are dealing with the well-known and well-defined theory of real numbers. In our opinion, this approach cannot be generalised. In ill-defined situations, e.g. if we develop expert systems, the implicit reference to knowledge has turned out to be very problematic. Furthermore, the reference to the theory of real numbers is so much taken for granted that we tend to overlook the fact that, in other situations, there may be no indication where and how to acquire the knowledge. As experience shows, these problems of knowledge acquisition become even worse when several people are involved since everyone may have different ideas about the undocumented information.

We can explicitly acknowledge that an application field is ill-defined and use an evolutionary approach to develop a system [33]. We start by implementing only a part of the system, and let users work with this partial system. From the experience gained we derive further requirements and augment the system until we are satisfied. Even in this approach, however, the specifications of the initial system and of the additions must be clear and complete. Thus, the problem of knowledge acquisition persists, although on a somewhat smaller scale.

As we have seen, formal specifications just as mathematical definitions can postulate the existence of an object without telling us how to construct it. We are convinced that a specification, as an abstract definition of something that will have to be concretely realised, must be constructive in the sense of *constructive mathematics*. Quine [30] defines as constructive a mathematics that is intolerant of methods affirming the existence of things of some sort without showing how to find them.

Constructive methods, especially constructive logics, are also proposed by other researchers [2, 3, 5, 7, 8, 23].

4.4 Degree of abstraction of the specification

Borrowing a saying from Einstein, we maintain that specifications should be as abstract as possible, but not more abstract. We see three limitations to the degree of abstraction.

First, a specification as an adequate formalisation of the requirements cannot be more abstract than the requirements themselves. If a specific algorithm is required, this algorithm must be specified. This argument applies as well to non-functional requirements constraining possible implementations. Some constraints can appear as comments in specifications, e.g. the requirement that a specific language should be used for the implementation. Other constraints, however, must be concretely specified, e.g. the requirement that the future software system has to adhere to the data structures of a given interface.

The second limitation to abstraction arises when we make formal specifications executable. Even if the degree of abstraction of the data structures and the algorithms stays the same, we have to add constructive elements to the executable specifications which are not present in the non-executable specifications.

User interfaces often account for a large percentage of the functionality of software systems. Their specification poses a third limitation to abstraction since they have to be specified in great detail. This limitation can be partially removed if, in addition to the usual predefined functions, powerful I/O functions are available to specify user interfaces abstractly. Fromherz [10] proposes an object-oriented specification framework providing default I/O operations that can be used as defaults, tailored to the required functionality or replaced by custom operations.

We distinguish between property-oriented and model-oriented specifications [39]. A property-oriented specification defines the behaviour of a system indirectly by a set of properties in the form of axioms that the system must satisfy. A model-oriented specification defines the behaviour of a system directly by constructing a model of the system.

Often the level of abstraction determines whether a specification can be called property-oriented or model-oriented. If we specify the sorting algorithm by the two concurrent processes *permutation* and *ordered* as

$sort(X,Y) \leftarrow permutation(X,Y), ordered(Y).$

the specification can be called property-oriented. If we introduce explicit details of the process synchronisation and of the data exchange, the specification could be called model-oriented. Since LSL allows us to formulate both property-oriented and model-oriented specifications in the same language there does not seem to be a clear-cut boundary between them.

4.5 Specification of non-functional requirements by specification variables

How do we specify non-functional requirements like efficiency, reliability, modularity, maintainability, ease-of-use, or constraints on resources? Many of these non-functional requirements define emerging properties of the implementation, others constrain possible implementations, and all can lead to demands on the software development process.

Traditionally, non-functional requirements are specified informally as comments, which are to be used by developers during the design and implementation phases. However, there are other ways.

Hayes and Jones state that it is useful to introduce into the specification variables that do not stand for implementation variables. These *specification variables* do not play a part in the execution of the implementation; instead they can serve to formalise comments or directives for the development process, or they can be used to reason about the specification. In particular, specification variables allow us to formalise non-functional requirements and to validate them by formal proofs. However, it must be emphasised that some non-functional requirements defy formalisation, e.g. ease-of-use of user interfaces. Their correct implementation can only be tested and must be validated by the user.

Hayes and Jones question the role of specification variables for executable specifications. Must executable specifications already fulfill constraints expressed by specification variables? How are specification and implementation variables related when specifications are executable?

In our opinion, specification variables can play an important role in executable specifications. We suggest that specification variables partake in the execution of the specification in the same way as other variables. The specification may or may not fulfill the specified constraints. In either case, valuable information will be gained that can help to validate and to verify the specification. This information is especially valuable if the executable specification is used for explorative prototyping. It can also result in guidelines for the development of the implementation.

4.6 Validation of the specification

Correctness of a software system means correctness with respect to the requirements, i.e. with respect to explicit and implicit user intentions and needs. This implies that users must be involved in the validation of the system, since only they know what they want. Users prefer to think in problem-oriented terms; they are usually not interested in implementation details. This suggests that the conceptual level provided by specifications is the appropriate level for the user involvement, and that validation should preferably take place in the specification phase.

Validation means checking the correspondence between informal requirements and formal specifications. Principally, there can be no formal method to check this correspondence [20]. This means that we have to rely on other means to convince ourselves of the correctness of the specifications with respect to the requirements, i.e. inspection, reasoning and execution.

Formal, non-executable specifications can be validated by reasoning. Unfortunately, this does not apply to user interfaces, where the direct experience of operations and timing is the major criterion for acceptability. Most specification examples, e.g. the ubiquitous greatest common divisor, or the standard stack example, emphasise the algorithmic aspect of specifications, i.e. the functional behaviour. Considering that a growing percentage of the code of current programs pertains to input and output, i.e. nonfunctional behaviour, the emphasis on functional behaviour seems most unfortunate. There are other, still relatively small, specification examples, like the library database [21], that could provide a more realistic point of view.

Since validation cannot go beyond the conviction that the specifications are correct, we believe that it is extremely important to have available all means that can be used for validation, i.e. in addition to inspection and reasoning, the execution of specifications. Executable specifications can contribute enormously to the validation because they give users the necessary *touch-and-feel* experience. Even if an executable specification is so inefficient that it cannot be executed for all values, the information gained from 'partial execution' remains valuable.

Executable specifications result in greater involvement by the users. Users can participate in the formulation of the specifications and in the immediate validation. The involvement of users and the immediate reflection of the consequences of the specifications back to the users are of utmost importance because they contribute to the correctness of the software, to the reduction of the costs, and to the adherence to the schedules.

4.7 Inferences from specifications

Hayes and Jones emphasise the relevance of being able to reason about a specification. Reasoning helps to validate the specification with respect to user requirements by inferring that the specification has the required properties. Reasoning also helps to verify that an implementation meets the specification, or to derive the implementation from the specification via transformations or refinement steps. Hayes and Jones maintain that, in both cases, the reasoning does not usually benefit from the fact that the specification is executable.

We concur with Hayes' and Jones' statement that traditional validation of software by individual test cases has inherent limitations. There is no way of predicting the general behaviour of a software system from the observed behaviour of a finite number of test cases and, for non-deterministic systems, test results are not necessarily reproducible.

However, we want to emphasise that testing of executable specifications, although basically subject to the same limitations, differs from testing implementations in three ways.

- Test results are of much greater relevance because they are available at the very beginning of software development; costly mistakes can be avoided.
- Testing executable specifications is more efficient since it is done in terms of the application domain, and on a much higher, much more abstract level.
- If a logic specification language is used, executing a test case is actually a proof; testing and inference become identical. Some proofs have the same limited meaning as testing, whereas other proofs are more meaningful; e.g. if a predicate has a finite number of solutions, we can enumerate them, and prove that there are no other solutions.

Other forms of reasoning are available to prove properties of the specification and to verify it, e.g. to show its consistency. Meta-interpreters can derive information that is not directly related to specified properties or can provide alternative proof methods. Declarative debugging [25] can locate the exact cause of errors. These forms of reasoning are only available because the specification is executable.

Reasoning as a means for validation also has its limitations. Usually, non-functional behaviour cannot be validated by inference; it can only be tested. This applies particularly to user interfaces, which often form a large part of the requirements.

We agree with Hayes and Jones that the executability of a specification contributes little to the derivation of an implementation or to the verification of the implementation with respect to the specification. It is usually not feasible to check that an executable specification and an implementation produce exactly the same results (see Section 4.8 for a discussion of the transformational approach which constructively solves the verification problem).

4.8 Executable specifications versus implementations

Logic languages can be used to formulate executable specifications and implementations. Both uses must be clearly distinguished.

Primarily, there is a distinction by intention. Executable specifications form the basis for implementations; they are not themselves implementations. Problem-oriented and implementation-oriented phases of the software development should be clearly separated.

Executable specifications and implementations have different commitments to specific algorithms, specific data structures and efficiency. If we remain on the abstraction level of non-executable specifications and do not introduce additional algorithms, executable specifications are often based on generate-and-test, i.e. on search [11, 24]. As a consequence the execution of an executable specification is usually much less efficient than the execution of an implementation, although it may appear to be similar. Implementations, on the other hand, should efficiently generate the specified behaviour in the targeted environment, using all available algorithms and data structures.

This view is shared by Zave and Yeh [40, 41], who state that the borderline between executable specifications and implementations is resource management. Specifications should only specify the functional and performance properties of the proposed system. Implementations, however, have to meet performance goals in the intended environment by an optimal use of resources.

The separation into problem-oriented and implementation-oriented phases is also reflected in another aspect. Specifications should be expressed in terms of the problem domain, and they should be abstract, concise, and extremely readable. Implementations, on the other hand, are usually much less readable because of their amount of detail and their optimised structure.

The transformational approach [1] is an especially attractive way to generate an implementation. With the help of transformations we can gradually introduce refinements and details into an executable specification, and in this way transform it step by step into the implementation. We may even start with an incomplete specification. If the transformation steps preserve the meaning of the specification, the verification of the implementation becomes unnecessary, i.e. the approach is constructive. For declarative languages the unfold/fold transformations [4, 13, 34] can be used. These source-to-source transformations can change data structures and algorithms, and generate implementations that are orders of magnitude more efficient than the specification. If we succeed in automating the transformations, to a large extent [12] the executable specifications will form the only relevant document for software development.

In this context it is worthwhile to briefly discuss prototypes. Many people consider executable specifications as prototypes. Although executable specifications can be used as prototypes, there is again a distinction of intention which is reflected in the importance given to different attributes. Prototypes serve to explore ideas and to verify decisions. Usually they generate only a part of the functionality of the future system, in whatever way seems appropriate. Executable specifications, on the other hand, form the basis for implementations. They must describe the complete functionality of the software system to be implemented, and they have to be as abstract as possible.

5. Summary and Conclusions

The following statements summarise our arguments for the use of executable specifications written in declarative languages.

- Executable specifications allow us to demonstrate the behaviour of a software system before it is actually implemented. This has three positive consequences for software development.
  - Executable components are available much earlier than in the traditional lifecycle. Therefore, validation errors can be corrected immediately, without incurring costly redevelopment.
  - Requirements that are initially unclear can be clarified and completed by hands-on experience with the executable specifications.
  - Execution of the specification supplements inspection and reasoning as means for validation. This is especially important for the validation of non-functional behaviour.
- Declarative languages, especially logic languages, combine high expressiveness with executability. They allow us to write both property-oriented and model-oriented executable specifications on the required level of abstraction. Logic specification languages permit us to express non-determinism in a natural way.
- Executable specifications are constructive, i.e. they do not only demand the existence of a solution, they actually construct it.
- Non-executable specifications that are constructive can be transformed into executable ones on almost the same level of abstraction. The resulting executable specifications are often based on search. It is not necessary to introduce new algorithms to achieve executability.

- Executable specifications do not necessarily constrain the choice of possible implementations because only minimal design and implementation decisions are necessary to get executability. In addition, these decisions are revisable.
- Verification of an implementation against the specification becomes superfluous if we use the transformational approach.

Acknowledgements. The author would like to thank I.J. Hayes and C.B. Jones whose paper inspired him to critically review the arguments for and against executable specifications; P. Baumann and M. Fromherz for stimulating discussions; and F. Bry, P. Flener, M. Fromherz, Ch. Draxler, J. Lloyd, L. Popelinsky, R. Stadler, and G. Wiggins for helpful comments on an earlier draft of this paper.

This research has been partially supported by the Swiss National Science Foundation under the contract 2000-5.449.

References

1. W. W. Agresti (Ed.), *New Paradigms in Software Development*, IEEE Computer Society Press, 1986
2. F. Bry, Logic Programming as Constructivism: A Formalization and its Application to Databases, Proc. 8th ACM SIGACT-SIGMOD-SIGART Symposium on Principles of Database Systems (PODS), pp. 34–50, 1989
3. A. Bundy, A. Smaill, G. Wiggins, The Synthesis of Logic Programs from Inductive Proofs, in J. W. Lloyd (Ed.), Computational Logic, Symposium Proceedings, Brussels November 1990, Springer Verlag, 1990
4. R. M. Burstall, J. Darlington, A Transformation System for Developing Recursive Programs, *Journal of the ACM*, Vol. 24, No. 1, pp. 44–67, January 1977
5. Y. Deville, *Logic Programming, Systematic Program Development*, Addison-Wesley Publishing Company, 1990
6. E. W. Dijkstra, *A Discipline of Programming*, Prentice Hall, 1976
7. P. Flener, Towards Stepwise, Schema-Guided Synthesis of Logic Programs, in: K.-K. Lau, T. Clement (Eds.), Proc. LOPSTR '91, Manchester, UK, Springer Verlag, 1992
8. L. Fribourg, Extracting Logic Programs from Proofs that Use Extended Prolog Execution and Induction, in: Proc. 7th International Conference on Logic Programming, MIT Press, 1990
9. M. P. J. Fromherz, A Survey of Executable Specification Methodologies, Technical Report 89.05, Department of Computer Science, University of Zurich, Switzerland, 1989
10. M. P. J. Fromherz, A Methodology for Executable Specifications – Combining Logic Programming, Object-Orientation and Visualization, PhD thesis, Department of Computer Science, University of Zurich, Switzerland, 1991
11. N. E. Fuchs, Hoare Logic, Executable Specifications, and Logic Programs, *Structured Programming*, Vol. 13, pp. 129–135, 1992; also: Technical Report 92.02, Department of Computer Science, University of Zurich, Switzerland, 1992
12. N. E. Fuchs, M. P. J. Fromherz, Schema-Based Transformations of Logic Programs, in T. Clement, K.-K. Lau (Eds.), Logic Program Synthesis and Transformations, Proc. LOPSTR '91, Manchester, UK, Springer Verlag, 1992
13. P. A. Gardner, J. C. Shepherdson, Unfold/Fold Transformations of Logic Programs, PM-89-01, School of Mathematics, University of Bristol, UK, 1989

14. N. Gehani, Specifications: Formal and Informal – A Case Study, *Software – Practice and Experience*, Vol. 12, pp. 433–444, 1982; reprinted in [15]
15. N. Gehani, A. D. McGettrick (Eds.), *Software Specification Techniques*, Addison-Wesley Publishing Company, 1986
16. C. Ghezzi, D. Madrioli, A. Morzenti, TRIO: A Language for Executable Specifications of Real-Time Systems, Journal of Systems and Software, 12, pp. 107–123, 1990
17. J. A. Goguen, One, None, A Hundred Thousand Specification Languages, in: H.-J. Kugler (Ed.), Information Processing 86 (IFIP), Elsevier Science Publisher, pp. 995–1003, 1986
18. I. J. Hayes, C. B. Jones, Specifications are not (Necessarily) Executable, *Software Engineering Journal*, Vol. 4, No. 6, pp. 330–338, November 1989
19. P. M. Hill, J. W. Lloyd, The Gödel Report, TR-91-02, Computer Science Department, University of Bristol, March 1991
20. C. A. R. Hoare, An Overview of Some Formal Methods for Program Design, *IEEE Computer*, Vol. 20, No. 9, pp. 85–91, September 1987; reprinted in C. A. R. Hoare, C. B. Jones (Ed.), Essays in Computing Science, Prentice-Hall, 1989
21. R. A. Kemmerer, S. White, A. Mili, N. Davis, Problem Set for the Fourth Int. Workshop on Software Specification and Design, in: IEEE, ACM, Proc. Fourth Int. Workshop on Software Specification and Design, Monterey, California, April 1987, pp. ix–x
22. R. A. Kowalski, The Relation Between Logic Programming and Logic Specification, in: C. A. R. Hoare, J. C. Shepherdson (Eds.), Mathematical Logic and Programming Languages, Prentice-Hall International, 1985
23. K.-K. Lau, S. D. Prestwich, Synthesis of a Family of Recursive Sorting Procedures, in: V. Saraswat, K. Ueda (Eds.), Proc. 1991 International Symposium on Logic Programming, MIT Press, 1991
24. G. Levi, New Research Directions in Logic Specification Languages, in: H.-J. Kugler (Ed.), Information Processing 86 (IFIP), Elsevier Science Publisher, pp. 1005–1008, 1986
25. J. W. Lloyd, Declarative Error Diagnosis, *New Generation Computing*, Vol. 5, No. 2, pp. 133–154, 1987
26. J. W. Lloyd, R. W. Topor, Making Prolog More Expressive, *Journal of Logic Programming*, Vol. 1, No. 3, pp. 225–240, 1984
27. R. Milner, M. Tofte, R. Harper, *The Definition of Standard ML*, MIT Press, 1990
28. R. A. O'Keefe, The Craft of Prolog, MIT Press, 1990
29. H. A. Partsch, *Specification and Transformation of Programs, A Formal Approach to Software Development*, Springer Verlag, 1990
30. W. V. O. Quine, *Philosophy of Logic*, Prentice-Hall, 1970
31. R. Stadler, Ausführbare Beschreibung von Directory-Systemen – Prolog-basierte Spezifikation der Architektur von Directory-Systemen, PhD thesis, Department of Computer Science, University of Zurich, Switzerland, 1990
32. L. Sterling, E. Shapiro, *The Art of Prolog – Advanced Programming Techniques*, MIT Press, 1986
33. M. Stolze, M. Gutknecht, R. Pfeifer, Integrated Knowledge Acquisition: Toward Adaptive Expert System Design, Technical Report 91.04, Department of Computer Science, University of Zurich, Switzerland, 1991
34. H. Tamaki, T. Sato, Unfold/Fold Transformation of Logic Programs, in: Proc. Second Int. Conference on Logic Programming, S.-Å. Tärnlund (Ed.), pp. 127–138, 1984
35. R. B. Terwilliger, An Overview and Bibliography of ENCOMPASS, an Environment for Incremental Software Development Using Executable, Logic-Based Specifications, *ACM SIGSOFT, Software Engineering Notes*, Vol. 15, No. 1, pp. 93–94, January 1990
36. R. B. Terwilliger, R. H. Campbell, PLEASE: Executable Specifications for Incremental Software Development, Journal of Systems and Software, 10, pp. 97–112, 1989

37. D. A. Turner, Functional Programs as Executable Specifications, in: C. A. R. Hoare, J. C. Shepherdson (Eds.), Mathematical Logic and Programming Languages, Prentice-Hall International, 1985
38. H. Ural, Specifications of Distributed Systems in Prolog, *Journal of Systems and Software*, Vol. 11, pp. 143–154, 1990
39. J. M. Wing, A Specifier's Introduction to Formal Methods, *IEEE Computer*, Vol. 7, No. 5, pp. 8–24, September 1990
40. P. Zave, An Operational Approach to Requirements Specification for Embedded Systems, *IEEE Transactions on Software Engineering*, Vol. SE-8, No. 3, pp. 250–269, May 1982; reprinted in [1] and [15]
41. P. Zave, R. T. Yeh, Executable Requirements Specification for Embedded Systems, Proc. 5th Int. Conf. on Software Engineering, pp. 295–304, San Diego, 1981; reprinted in [15]

9. CASE

Just as mechanization made the Industrial Revolution in Britain possible at the beginning of the 19th century, so too is mechanization in system development seen as a means to increased productivity and a 'Systems Revolution'.

Indeed, in Part 1 we saw Harel's criticism of Brooks' view [50] of the state of the software development industry due to his failure to adequately acknowledge developments in CASE (Computer-Aided Software Engineering) technology and visual formalisms [109]. In addition, in Part 2 we saw the originators of various structured methods recognize the fact that certain levels of automated support are vital to the successful industrialization of their respective methods [100].

9.1 What is CASE?

CASE is a generic term used to mean the application of computer-based tools (programs or suites of programs) to the software engineering process.

This loose definition serves to classify compilers, linkers, text editors, etc., as 'CASE tools', and indeed these should be classified in these terms. More usually, however, the term 'CASE' is intended to refer to a CASE workbench or CASE environment – an integrated suite of programs intended to support a large portion (ideally all) of the system development life-cycle.

To date, most CASE workbenches have focused on information systems and on supporting diagrammatic notations from various structured methods (DFDs, ERDs, etc.) rather than any specific methodology. In their article *CASE: Reliability Engineering for Information Systems* (reprinted in this Part), Chikofsky and Rubenstein provide an excellent overview of the motivation for the use of CASE workbenches in the development of reliable information systems, and of the advantages of such an approach [57].

That is not to say that the application of CASE is limited to the domain of information systems. CASE workbenches have been applied successfully to components of real-time and safety-critical systems, and some provide support for State-Transition Diagrams (STDs), Decision Tables, Event-Life History Diagrams, and other notations employed by various 'real-time' structured methods such as SART [251], DARTS [96] and Mascot [222].

9.2 CASE Workbenches

As was previously pointed out, commercially available CASE workbenches generally do not support any particular methodology (although there are exceptions) but rather a range of differing notations that may be tailored to a particular (standard or 'home-grown') methodology. They differ greatly in the degree to which they support various methodologies and, as one might expect, in the levels of functionality that they provide. We can, however, determine a minimal set of features that we would expect all realistic CASE workbenches to support:

- a consistent interface to various individual tools comprising the workbench, with the ability to exchange data easily between them;
- support for entering various diagrammatic notations with a form of syntax-directed editor (that is, that the editor can aid the user by prohibiting the derivation of syntactically incorrect or meaningless diagrams);
- an integrity checker to check for the consistency and completeness of designs;
- the ability to exchange data with other tools (perhaps using CDID, the CASE Data Interchange Format);
- report generation facilities;
- text editing facilities.

9.3 Beyond CASE

We can see from the above that CASE workbenches concentrate primarily on the early stages of system development. A number of workbenches, however, incorporate tools to generate skeleton code from designs as an aid to prototyping. Indeed, some vendors claim code that is of a sufficiently high quality that it may be used in the final implementation. Generally such workbenches are referred to as *application generators*.

From our discussion of the system life-cycle in this and previous Parts, it should be clear that we ideally require a CASE workbench that will support all aspects of system development from requirements analysis through to post-implementation maintenance. A workbench supporting all aspects of the software engineering process is generally termed a *Software Engineering Environment*, or SEE. A useful SEE can reasonably be expected to support an implementation of some form of software metric, project costing, planning, scheduling and evaluation of progress.

Realistically, large-scale system development involves a large number of personnel, working on various aspects of the development. Different personnel may modify the same software components [264], or may be modifying components required by others, perhaps due to changing requirements, or as a result of errors highlighted during unit testing. Therefore, co-ordination between developers and control over modification to (possibly distributed) software components is required, and software configuration management is desirable in a system development support environment. Such support is provided by an *Integrated Project Support Environment* or IPSE.

9.4 The Future of CASE

We see tool support becoming as important in formal development as it has been in the successful application of more traditional structured methods. In *Seven More Myths of Formal Methods* (reprinted in Part 3), we described some widely available tools to support formal development, and emphasized our belief that such tools will become more integrated, providing greater support for project management and configuration management [39]. In essence, we foresee the advent of Integrated Formal Development Support Environments (IFDSEs), the formal development equivalent of IPSEs.

As we also saw in Part 8, method integration is also an area auguring great potential. As a first step towards IFDSEs, visual formalisms offer great promise; in his paper *On Visual Formalisms* (reprinted in this Part) David Harel realizes the great importance of visual representations and their relationship to underlying formalisms [108].

His paper describes his own works on Statecharts, supported by the STATEMATE tool [110, 111], whereby an intuitive graphical notation that may be used in the description of reactive systems is given a formal interpretation in terms of 'higraphs', and for which support environments covering most phases of the life-cycle already exist. The approach has proven to be very popular and very successful in practice, and indeed many see visual formalisms as providing the basis for the next generation of CASE tools.

CASE: Reliability Engineering for Information Systems

Elliot J. Chikofsky and Burt L. Rubenstein

Summary.

You can use CASE environments in new ways to support the entire software life cycle, including reliability engineering, maintenance, documentation, and auditing.

Developers of information systems have historically been the last to apply computer-based tools to improve the quality, reliability, and productivity of their own work – a phenomenon known as the "shoemaker's children" syndrome, from the story of the shoemaker whose children never had new shoes because all new shoes were made for others. This tradition is changing as organizations involved in both commercial data processing and embedded real-time applications review their heavy investment in software and information systems. Having recently identified information systems as a capital resource, they now realize their need for surer design and reliability. By introducing new CASE technology, they can achieve greater system development productivity while providing a new approach to engineering information systems reliably.

As early as 1973, Barry Boehm projected that software costs would, by 1985, reach or exceed 90 percent of the total cost of data processing (the combined hardware and software costs) [1,2], as Figure 1 shows. It was clear that hardware costs were rapidly falling and that personnel costs in the labor-intensive software development arena were rising. The projection has turned out to be all too true.

Today, the rapid pace at which hardware innovations are announced, particularly in the area of microprocessor technology, now well exceeds the capabilities of our software-development technology. Consider, for example, the Intel 80286 processor, which can support multitasking operations. At the time of its introduction, the existing general-purpose operating systems for IBM PCs (such as MS-DOS and Xenix)

© 1988 IEEE. Reprinted by permission.
Reprinted from *IEEE Software*, 5(2):11–16, March 1988.

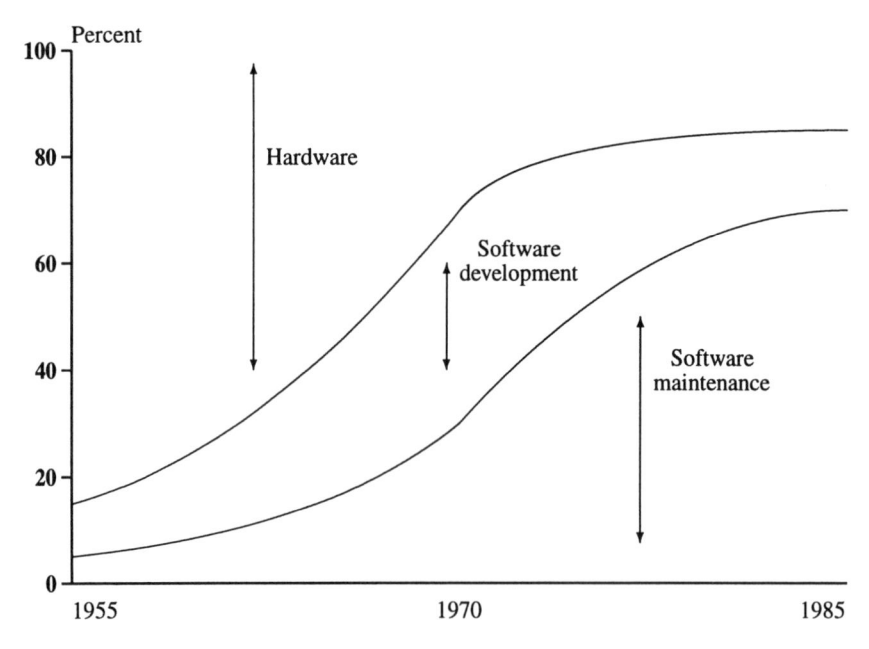

Figure 1: Evolution of system-development costs (*y*-axis is percent of total cost).

had no way to use its capabilities. And then, before the first operating system (OS/2) was available to take full advantage of the 286, the 80386 processor made its debut with even greater capabilities. An entire generation of processor hardware technology has arrived and been superseded without any software to support it reaching the marketplace!

Further, the ability to develop software to meet new needs is rapidly losing ground to software maintenance. The US Air Force's F-16 jet fighter, for example, has an $85-million budget for software development. On top of this, the Air Force is expecting to spend about $250 million in software maintenance – almost three times the development cost [3].

Organizations are now recognizing how the software crisis affects them. Randall Jensen of Hughes Aircraft, for example, has identified six key software problems resulting from systems-development approaches as commonly applied [4]:

– products exceeding cost estimates,
– late delivery,
– inadequate performance,
– impossible maintenance,
– prohibitive modification costs, and
– unreliability.

More than ever before, organizations are looking for workable solutions to increase the productivity of their systems-development staff, to improve the cost-effectiveness of the development process, and to ensure the reliability and quality of systems produced.

1. Development Approaches

Since the mid-1970s, the approach to developing information systems has evolved with the growth of methods to aid both project management and specification. Organizations have turned to more formal methods of system development and, most recently, to automated tools to support these methods.

Classical methods. The development of information systems and software has long been viewed as an art rather than a science. The programmer or analyst would wade through a loose collection of user wants and needs. Some time later, through some arcane and mystical process, a system would appear that, even though it did not meet all the user's needs, was usually considered better than what existed before. This classical approach was characterized by informal guidelines, lack of standardization, and minimal documentation (usually produced as an afterthought).

Some order was introduced in the early 1970s in the form of project-management methods based on models of the system-development life-cycle. Since then, many packaged life-cycle methods – incorporating directions, forms, and acceptance standards – have been marketed commercially. Military standards for specification and documentation practices in use today are examples of content-based life-cycle methods. These methods try to manage the development process by requiring that documents be produced at specific checkpoints, according to prescribed forms or document-content guidelines.

The effectiveness of life-cycle methods has been limited by two key problems: lack of formality, resulting in inconsistency, and lack of maintainability. Most life-cycle methods stress the capture of documentation during the development process but do not adequately provide for the continued usefulness of the documents produced. The result is often notebooks full of completed forms or a set of Victorian novel-like narrative specifications, both of which are destined to sit on bookshelves gathering dust. The specifications produced are often incomplete, inconsistent, and incorrect, and are seldom updated with changes to the system.

Formal methods. The need for greater productivity in the system-development life cycle led to the introduction of more formal methods in the late 1970s and early 1980s. Most methods were aimed at specific stages of the life cycle and were based on different user viewpoints about the target information systems.

Structured analysis, introduced popularly by Tom DeMarco [5], applied some of the decomposition techniques that improve programming to the front-end requirements and analysis phases of the systems life cycle. Structured analysis grew out of structured design, which itself had grown out of structured programming. Through the use of structured dataflow diagrams and descriptions of data, the analyst could build up a systematic description of the information system's logical (functional) and physical (implementation) aspects. Management procedures provided manual validation of the dataflow diagrams via walkthroughs, and diagrams and data descriptions became deliverable parts of system documentation.

Many variations of formal methods now exist. Well-known versions of structured analysis include the Yourdon/DeMarco and Gane/Sarson methods. Recent adaptations of structured analysis to specific needs of real-time systems development include the Ward/Mellor and Hatley methods. Data-oriented methods, applying similar principles to both data-centered design and data administration, include the Warnier/Orr, Holland, Bachman, and Martin's information-engineering approaches. The realm of structured design has the Yourdon/Constantine and Jackson methods.

Much fanfare accompanied the introduction of formal methods, but their manual nature has limited their general use and acceptance. Dataflow diagrams developed manually are difficult to modify and are seldom maintained with the system they represent. The effort and cost to develop complete and useful descriptions of an evolving system are hard to justify when the information is clearly not a lasting part of maintenance.

2. What CASE Offers

With the spread of desktop computers, the mid-1980s have seen the introduction of automated environments and tools that make it practical and economical to use formal system-development methods. This technology, known as CASE, lets systems analysts document and model an information system from its initial user requirements through design and implementation and lets them apply tests for consistency, completeness, and conformance to standards.

These techniques for software engineering apply equally well to modeling hardware and human interfaces, so the acronym also refers to computer-aided *systems* engineering. Integrated in this field are models, tools, and techniques that open new areas for applying reliability engineering to information systems.

Much like the children of the shoemaker who were always the last to get new shoes, computer professionals have traditionally been the last ones to apply the benefits of computer technology to the improvement of their own work. Now, however, with personal workstations becoming a common resource, CASE environments let computer professionals develop and validate system designs and specifications, automating and enhancing the manual methods of the 1970s and 1980s.

Features. A CASE environment provides the analyst or systems developer with facilities for drawing a system's architectural diagrams, describing and defining functional and data objects, identifying relationships between system components, and providing annotations to aid project management.

The user's various work products are stored in an integrated, nonredundant form in a central repository or dictionary on the workstation or on a central server or host system. The system definition as a whole can be checked for consistency and completeness. Analysis can be performed on the information collected or defined to date, thus supporting incremental development and the detection of inconsistencies and errors early in the life cycle. Documentation required by organizational or deliverable standards, such as DoD-Std 2167, can be generated from the system description in the dictionary. Also, generators for database schemes and program code are being incorporated in, or interfaced to, CASE environments to provide a step toward automated system generation. Figure 2 shows key elements in a CASE system.

Tools. A comprehensive CASE development environment for the front end of the life cycle integrates several component tools and facilities:

- The system developer can choose from at least seven basic diagram types, including dataflow diagrams (Yourdon/De Marco or Gane/Sarson notations), structure charts (Yourdon/Constantine or Jackson), entity-relationship diagrams, logical data models, and presentation graphs. Additional diagram types are available for real-time system development, including transformation graphs, state-transition diagrams, and decision matrices. The user can directly create diagrams with the graphics-editing facilities on the workstation and then produce those diagrams for system documentation. Figures 2 and 3 demonstrate these graphics capabilities.
- Information about the user's target system, entered incrementally via diagrams and form screens, is integrated in a central dictionary.
- End-user screens and reports can be developed for the system under design with screen-paint facilities tied to the central dictionary. These form functional prototypes on the workstation that can be demonstrated to end users for evaluation and validation.
- Analysis facilities provide checks for consistency and completeness. Entity-list query capabilities combined with a general report writer allow user-definable analysis that can be tailored to meet project or organizational needs. Extended analysis utilities provide advanced conclusions about the integrity of a proposed design, including validation of data normalization and traceability of data elements through activities in the target-system description.
- Deliverable documentation can be organized graphically and can incorporate diagrams and text from the central dictionary. This facility lets the user generate documentation that is internally consistent and true to the system design. The environment provides links to desktop-publishing, page-layout, and Postscript output facilities.
- An open architecture for access to the central dictionary allows the integration of the CASE environment with other tools of the project or the organization. Import/export facilities let you bridge to other programs, transfer information among multiple analysts, and access other information resources, such as the corporate data dictionary (Figure 3 shows data-dictionary integration). In addition, a programmer interface lets you access the system description in the central dictionary from application programs to allow transfer of data, broader analysis, and specialized documentation.
- Established bridges and integrated packages connect the front-end environment to many tools used in later stages of the life cycle. Links to code-generation tools

and fourth-generation languages, as well as to other types of development tools, give users a wide variety of options.

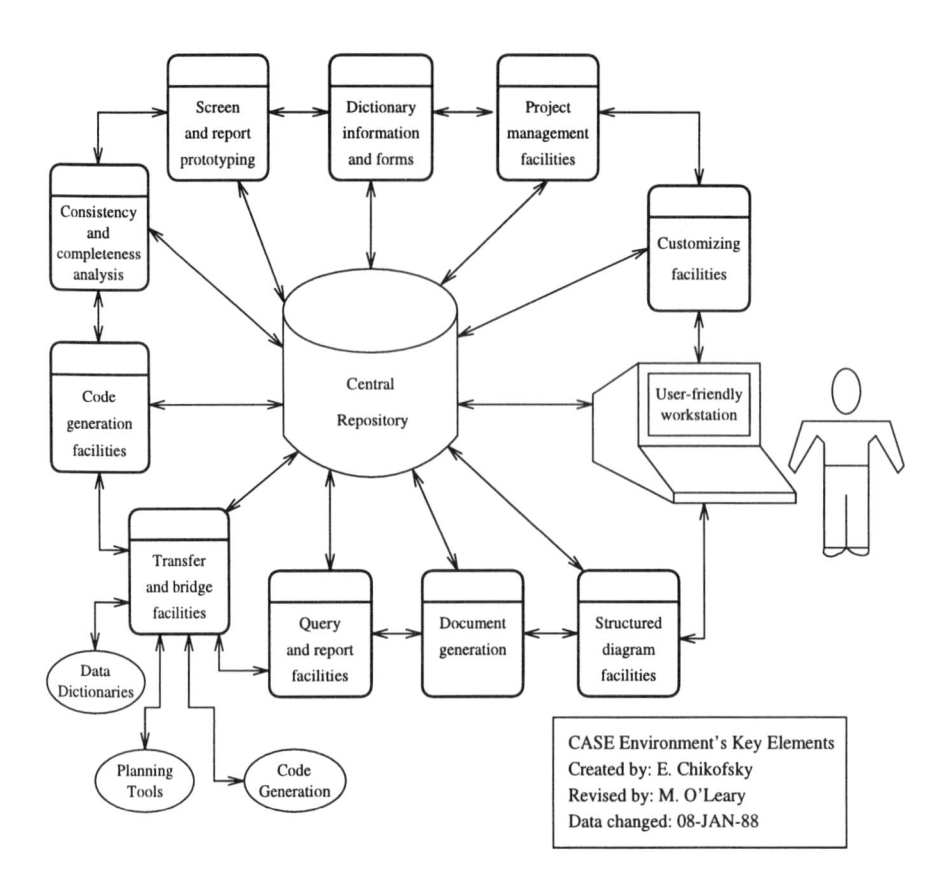

Figure 2: Key elements in a CASE system. This figure was generated from Index Technology's Excelerator CASE system and represents current CASE graphics capabilities.

Adaptability. A key feature of a well-developed CASE environment is adaptability. To be successful in a wide range of organizations and projects, the environment must be able to operate on many hardware configurations in a consistent and user-friendly manner. To serve today's development organizations, the same base environment should be available on IBM PC-class and PS/2-class machines, on engineering workstations from Sun, Apollo, and Digital Equipment Corp., and on a variety of local-area networks.

Another important aspect of adaptability is how well the CASE environment can conform to an organization and project, rather than how much it makes the

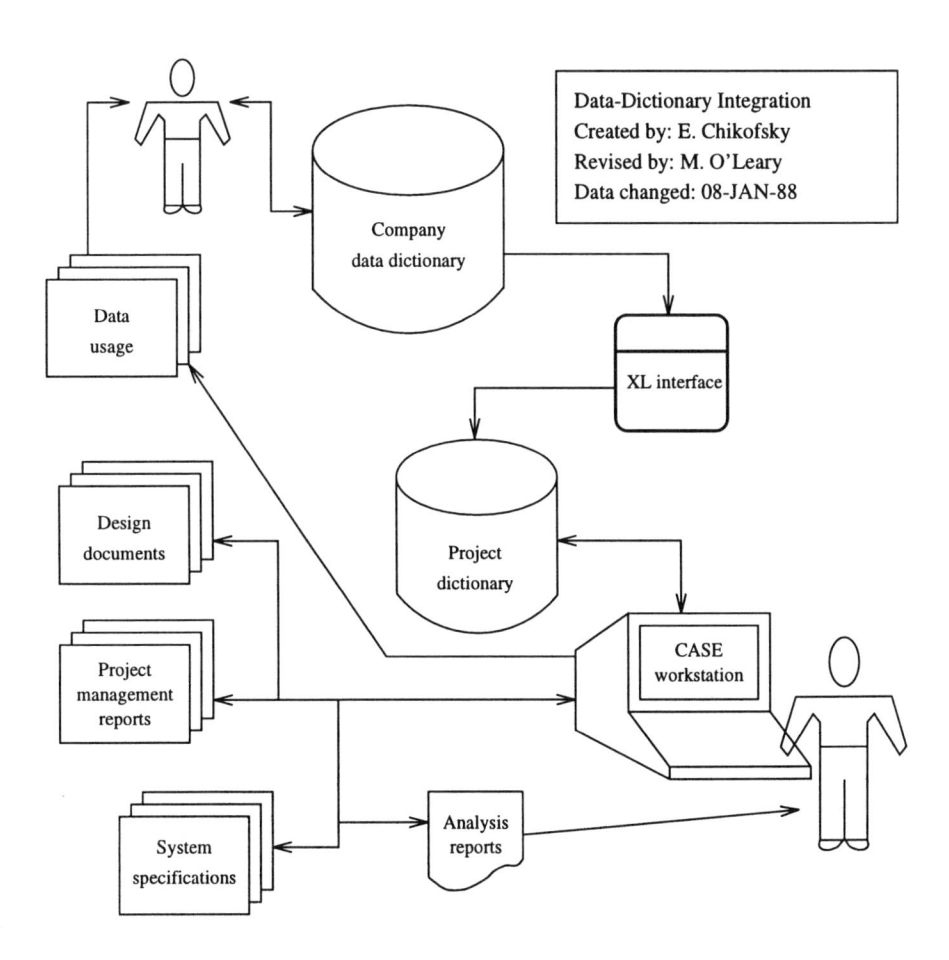

Figure 3: Data-dictionary integration. This figure was generated from Index Technology's Excelerator CASE system and represents current CASE graphics capabilities.

project conform to the idiosyncrasies of the tool. The CASE environment needs to be customizable so the user can adapt it to closely fit the organization's development method, project-management standards, and information requirements. This versatility lets a single CASE environment support the organization even as projects, standards, and contractual obligations change.

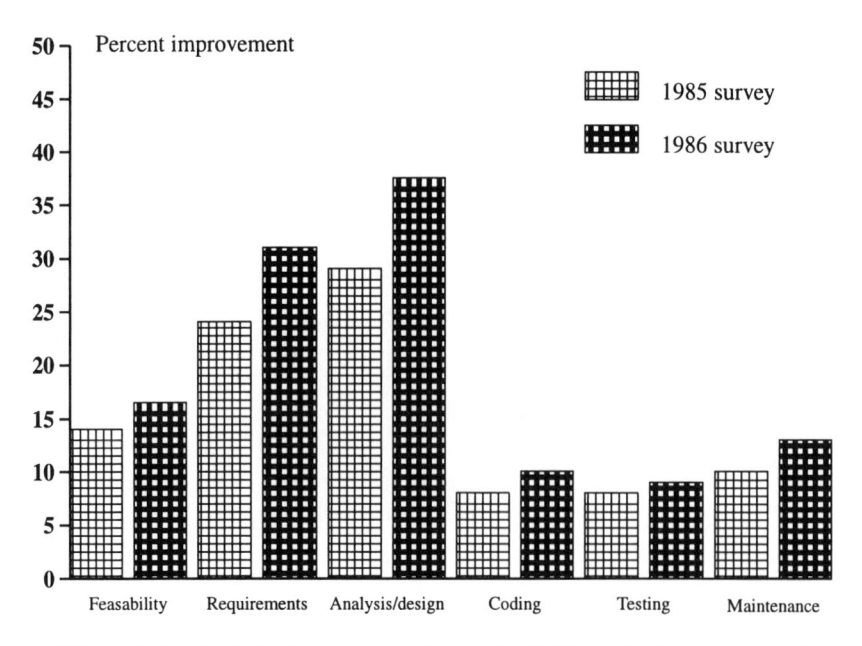

Figure 4: Productivity improvement in a system's life-cycle phases when using a CASE tool (sources are two surveys of users of Index Technology's Excelerator product).

Benefits. Organizations using CASE environments have experienced various degrees of improvement in productivity. Users of Index Technology's Excelerator environment, for example, have reported in surveys an average of 30- to 40-percent improvement in the life cycle's analysis and design phases (see Figure 4). But many of the user organizations also report that their key gain is in the quality of the systems being developed, principally because they can detect errors and inconsistencies and refine specifications easily to reflect their own customer's needs.

3. Reliability Engineering

Besides serving as productivity aids to support the capture of system-design information, CASE environments provide new opportunities to use analysis techniques to assess the reliability of information systems before they are implemented. They also help audit a completed system against its design and maintain the system description as accurate documentation.

Analysis. A CASE environment stores the systems description in an integrated form in a central repository or dictionary. It provides native facilities for inspecting and analyzing aspects of the system description, particularly in support of standard development methods such as structured analysis.

With the system description in the dictionary, other forms of inspection can be made using database query techniques. For example, if the correctness of timing factors is important to a system's success, an analyst can target those portions of the description that affect timing. The dictionary can provide information not only about the specific timing attributes but also about all other components that affect these attributes.

An analyst can also discover secondary effects, where the impact of an attribute was not explicitly defined but was implicit in the design of other parts of the system. The CASE environment thus forms a vehicle for reliability assessment as well as for system description.

The CASE environment can help standardize quality assurance and test processes for systems under development. By using the available system description for test planning, aided by automated CASE facilities, an organization can develop more rigorous coverage for test cases and can better determine if the features and components being tested match important paths in the system.

Maintenance. When a system description has been completed, the CASE environment can continue to serve as an active repository and reference encyclopedia for the system's builders and maintainers. The ease of making changes to the system description lets the documentation be maintained with the system. When maintenance staff can use an up-to-date system description as a source of information on the system architecture, they are encouraged to update it for their own benefit as they make system modifications. The result is more shoemaker's children with new and valuable shoes.

Audit. The same principle applies to auditing. With an up-to-date system description supported by a CASE environment, the dictionary can serve as a key resource and record-keeping vehicle. Various system components and their operation can be compared to their intended function in the system description, and notes can be made in an auditor's copy of the dictionary. The completed system can be more effectively evaluated against its design, and automated assistance can be provided to trace requirements through design and into the finished system. Thus, the CASE environment also becomes an auditor's tool. This advantage can be further enhanced by customizing the CASE environment to handle the specific attributes required of the auditing or reliability evaluation task at hand.

Emerging technology in CASE provides new and potentially invaluable support to aspects of systems work throughout the system's life cycle. There are broad opportunities for automating reliability-engineering tasks for information systems. As this technology matures, we can look forward to the incorporation of meaningful expert-system and artificial-intelligence capabilities to help the systems analyst, libraries of reusable system designs, and automated prototyping of systems to help determine reliability.

Existing developments in CASE put these possibilities within our grasp and offer a bright future for the entire area of information-systems reliability.

References

1. B. Boehm, "Software and Its Impact: A Quantitative Assessment," in *Writings of the Revolution*, Yourdon Press, New York, 1982, pp. 267–289.
2. B. Boehm, *Software Engineering Economics*, Prentice-Hall, Englewood Cliffs, N.J., 1981.
3. W. Suydam, "CASE Makes Stride toward Automated Software Development," *Computer Design*, Jan. 1, 1987, pp. 49–70.
4. R. Jensen, "Predicting and Controlling Software Development Costs: Metrics for Managers," *Proc. Second Ann. Excelerator Users' Conf.*, XL Group, Cambridge, Mass., 1986.
5. T. DeMarco, *Structured Analysis and System Specification*, Yourdon Press, New York, 1978.

On Visual Formalisms

David Harel

Summary.

The higraph, a general kind of diagramming object, forms a visual formalism of topological nature. Higraphs are suited for a wide array of applications to databases, knowledge representation, and, most notably, the behavioral specification of complex concurrent systems using the higraph-based language of statecharts.

Visualizing information, especially information of complex and intricate nature, has for many years been the subject of considerable work by many people. The information that interests us here is nonquantitative, but rather, of a structural, set-theoretical, and relational nature. This should be contrasted with the kinds of quantitative information discussed at length in [43] and [46]. Consequently, we shall be interested in diagrammatic paradigms that are essentially topological in nature, not geometric, terming them *topovisual* in the sequel.

Two of the best known topo-visual formalisms have their roots in the work of the famous Swiss mathematician Leonhard Euler (1707–1783). The first, of course, is the formalism of graphs, and the second is the notion of *Euler circles*, which later evolved into *Venn diagrams*. Graphs are implicit in Euler's celebrated 1736 paper, in which he solved the problem of the bridges of Königsberg [12]. (An English translation appears in [3]). Euler circles first appear in letters written by Euler in the early 1760s [13], and were modified to improve their ability to represent logical propositions by John Venn in 1880 [48, 49]. (See [19, chap. 2] for more information.[1])

A graph, in its most basic form, is simply a set of points, or nodes, connected by edges or arcs. Its role is to represent a (single) set of elements S and some binary relation R on them. The precise meaning of the relation R is part of the application and has little to do with the mathematical properties of the graph itself. Certain restrictions on the relation R yield special classes of graphs that are of particular interest, such as ones that are connected, directed, acyclic, planar, or bipartite. There

---

© 1988 Association for Computing Machinery, Inc. Reprinted by permission.
Reprinted from *Communications of the ACM*, 31(5):514–530, May 1988.

[1] Interestingly, both these topo-visual achievements of Euler were carried out during the period in which he could see with one eye only. (Euler lost sight in his right eye in 1735, and in the left around 1766.) It is tempting to attribute this in part to the fact that the lack of stereoscopic vision reduces one's ability to estimate size and distance, possibly causing a sharper awareness of topological features.

is no need to elaborate on the use of graphs in computer science – they are used extensively in virtually all branches of the field. The elements represented by the nodes in these applications range from the most concrete (e.g., physical gates in a circuit diagram) to the most abstract (e.g., complexity classes in a classification schema), and the edges have been used to represent almost any conceivable kind of relation, including ones of temporal, causal, functional, or epistemological nature. Obviously, graphs can be modified to support a number of different kinds of nodes and edges, representing different kinds of elements and relationships.

A somewhat less widely used extension of graphs is the formalism of *hypergraphs* (see, e.g., [1]), though these are also finding applications in computer science, mainly in database theory (see [14], [15], and [31]). A hypergraph is a graph in which the relation being specified is not necessarily binary; in fact, it need not even be of fixed arity. Formally, an edge no longer connects a pair of nodes, but rather a subset thereof. This makes hypergraphs somewhat less amenable to visual representation, but various ways of overcoming this difficulty can be conceived (see Figure 1). In analogy with graphs, several special kinds of hypergraphs are of particular interest, such as directed or acyclic.

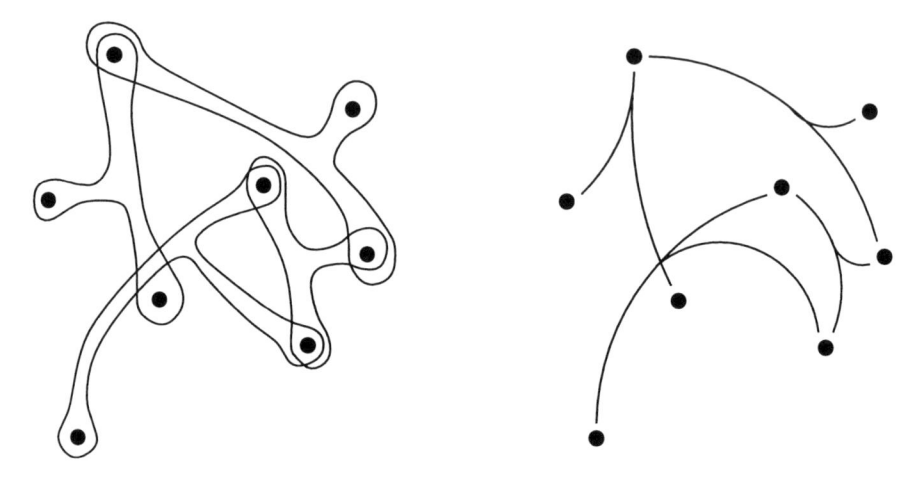

Figure 1. Graphical representation of hypergraphs

It is important to emphasize that the information conveyed by a graph or a hypergraph is nonmetric and captured by the purely topological notion of *connectedness* (a term taken from [18]); shapes, locations, distances, and sizes, for example, have no significance.

Although not quite as widely used as graphs, Euler circles, or Venn diagrams, are often used to represent logical propositions, color charts, etc. (see Figure 2). The basic idea is to appeal to the two-dimensional case of the Jordan curve theorem (e.g., [11, 30]), which establishes that simple closed curves partition the plane into disjoint inside and outside regions. A set is then represented by the inside of such

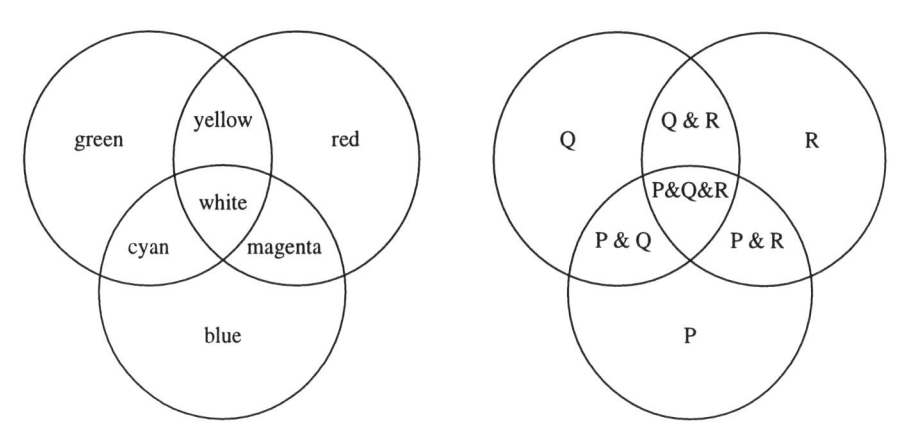

Figure 2. Applications of Euler circles, or Venn diagrams

a curve,[2] giving the topological notions of *enclosure*, *exclusion*, and *intersection* of the curves their obvious set-theoretic meanings: being a subset of, being disjoint from, and having a nonempty intersection with, respectively.[3]

The bottom line is that, whereas graphs and hypergraphs are a nice way of representing a set of elements together with some special relation(s) on them, Euler/Venn diagrams are a nice way of representing a *collection* of sets, together with some *structural* (i.e., set-theoretical) relationships between them. The difference between the two types of relationships is obvious. The structural ones are uniformly interpreted in the obvious set-theoretic fashion, in much the same way as the = symbol in logical formalisms is uniformly interpreted as the equality predicate, whereas the edge relations of graphs and hypergraphs attain different meanings in different applications.

The main observation motivating the present work is that in numerous computer-related applications the complexity of the objects, systems, or situations under consideration is due in large part to the fact that *both* capabilities are needed. We have a (usually large) number of sets that are interrelated in nontrivial set-theoretic ways, but they are also related via one or more additional relationships of special nature, depending on the application at hand. Furthermore, among the structural, set-theoretic relationships it is often desirable to identify the *Cartesian product* of some of the sets – an action that can be crucial in preventing certain kinds of representations from growing exponentially in size. In line with these observations, which will be supported by examples in the sequel, the purpose of this article is to extend and combine Euler's two topo-visual formalisms into a tool suitable for dealing with such cases.

---

[2] Venn himself was not always consistent in this respect: see [49, p. 117] or [19, p. 43] for a description of his five-set diagram.

[3] The topological paradigm used here is termed *insideness* in [18].

In the next section, we introduce *higraphs*,[4] first modifying Euler/Venn diagrams somewhat, then extending them to represent the Cartesian product, and finally connecting the resulting curves by edges or hyperedges. (The appendix contains the formal syntax and semantics of simple higraphs.) We will then illustrate the power of the formalism by briefly discussing higraph-based versions of such graphical languages as entity-relationship diagrams, semantic and associative networks, and dataflow diagrams. Later we will detail a less obvious application called *statecharts* [21], which are essentially a higraph-based version of finite-state machines and their transition diagrams.

Higraphs

Let us start with a simple example of Euler circles (Figure 3). As can be seen, we prefer to use rounded rectangles, or rounded rectilinear shapes (*rountangles*?), rather than circles or unrestricted curves, and shall call the areas, or zones, they enclose *blobs* in the sequel. Second, as the formal definition supplied in the appendix shows, we regard each blob as denoting a certain kind of set, with the nesting of curves denoting set inclusion, not set membership. Thus, Figure 3 can be seen to contain several cases of inclusion, disjointness, and intersection of sets.

For our first real departure from Euler and Venn's treatment, we now require that every set of interest be represented by a unique blob, complete with its own full contour. One of the reasons for this is the desire to provide every set with its own area (e.g., for naming or labeling purposes). For example, does the A in Figure 3 represent the difference between the sets represented by the two large blobs, or the entire set on the upper left? The answer, following Venn's notational conventions, would appear to be the former; but then how do we label the upper set itself?

Our solution is illustrated in Figure 4, where the two large intersecting blobs are clearly labeled A and D, the intersection $A \cap D$ is labeled C, and the difference $A - D$ is called B. In fact, had we left out B and its contour we could not refer to $A - D$ at all. More precisely, with this "unique-contour" convention, the only real, identifiable sets are the *atomic* sets, that is, those represented by blobs residing on the bottom levels of the diagram, containing no wholly enclosed blobs within. Any other blob merely denotes the compound set consisting of the union of all sets represented by blobs that are totally enclosed within it. The atomic blobs of Figure 4 are thus B, C, E, G, H, I, K, L, M, N, O, Q, S, and, significantly, also T. The fact that T, as a Jordan curve, intersects R in Figure 4 does not necessarily mean that the sets represented by[5] T and R really intersect or that $T - R$ is nonempty. In fact, in our formalism, the intersection of two curves does not, in itself, mean anything since unless internal

---

[4] This is not a particularly successful choice of term, but was chosen nevertheless to be reminiscent of *high graphs* or *hierarchical graphs*, though our diagrams are not limited to being stratified in the way the word *hierarchical* might imply.

[5] In the sequel, we shall often blur the distinction between a curve, its associated blob, and the set it depicts.

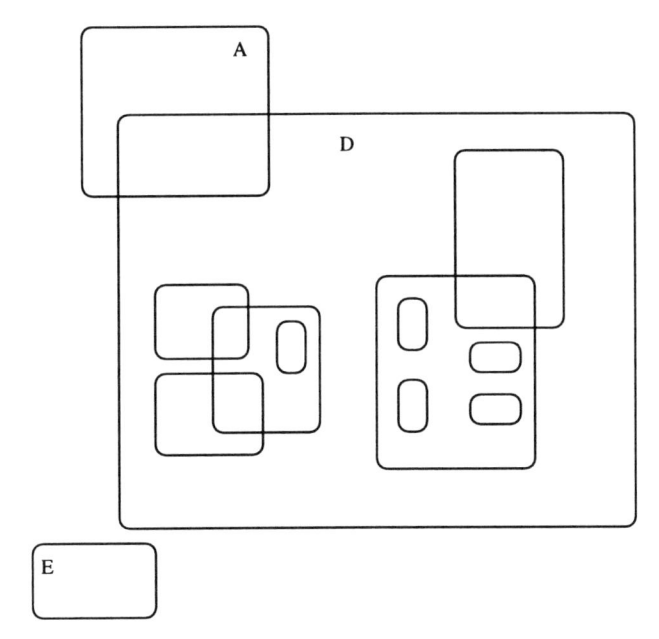

Figure 3. Simple blobs

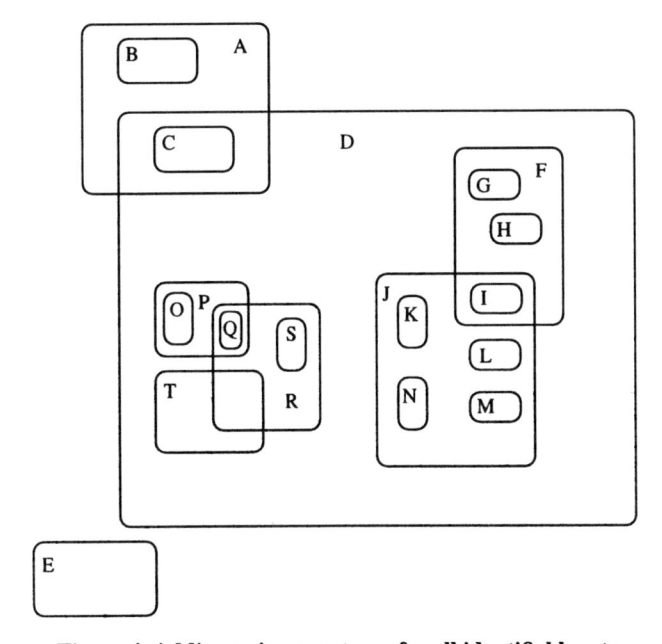

Figure 4. Adding unique contours for all identifiable sets

blobs appear in the appropriate places neither the difference nor the intersection of the sets they represent is itself identifiable. Thus, as far as the information present in Figure 4, T could just as well have been drawn completely disjoint from R, since R is defined by the figure to be the union of Q and S, whether T's curve intersects it or not. Of course, if T had been entirely enclosed within R, things would have been quite different, with R then being the union of Q, S, and T. All this might sound a little strange, but it is not really restrictive, since one can always let T and R intersect and simply add extra blobs representing $T \cap R$ and $T - R$, as is done in Figure 5.

Thus, one might say that empty space in our diagrams always represents nothing at all, except if it is the area of an atomic blob, which is one that contains no enclosed blobs. An atomic blob always represents some identifiable set, though clearly such a set might just happen to be an empty one.

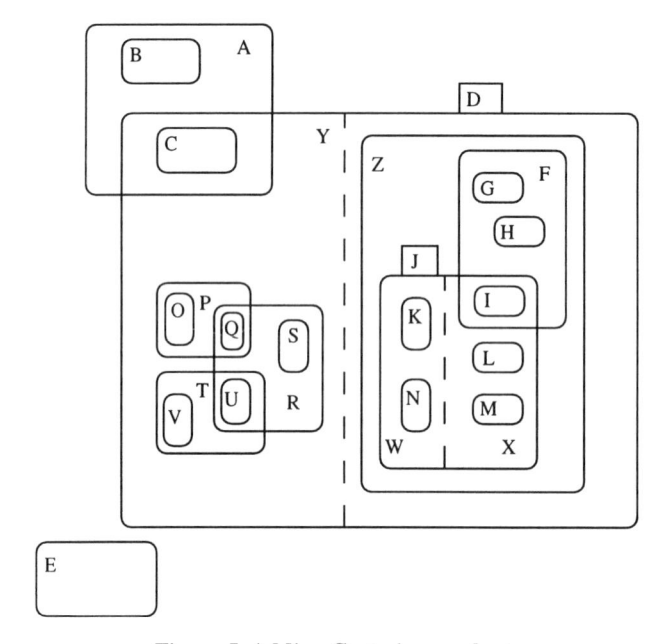

Figure 5. Adding Cartesian products

We now add the ability to represent the *Cartesian product*. Figure 5 shows the notation used – a *partitioning* by dashed lines. In it J, for example, is no longer the union of K, N, I, L, and M, but, rather, the product of the union of the first two with the union of the last three. Symbolically,

$$J = W \times X = (K \cup N) \times (I \cup L \cup M).$$

We shall call the operands of the product, W and X in this case, the *orthogonal components* of blob J. Actually, the Cartesian product is *unordered*, in the sense that $A \times B$ is always the same as $B \times A$, so that J is really a set of unordered pairs of elements. Thus, our $\times$ operator is symmetric, and in fact, in the appendix we use the symbol $\otimes$, instead of $\times$, to denote it. Another consequence of this, and of our previous convention regarding set inclusion versus set membership, is that the product is also associative. In this way, if $c \in C$, $k \in K$, and $m \in M$, then the unordered triple $\{c, k, m\}$ would be a legal element of the set D of Figure 5, without the need to distinguish it from $\{c, \{k, m\}\}$. To make this idea work, it helps to assume that all atomic sets are pairwise disjoint (i.e., no element appears in any two of these sets).

Decomposing a blob into its orthogonal components by topologically partitioning the inner area of a Jordan curve yields a unique unambiguous area for each such component. Thus, the labels, Y, W, and X in Figure 5 label the appropriate components unambiguously. On the other hand, as we shall see, there is another reason for wanting sets to have their own blob contours, and if so desired an orthogonal component can be enclosed in one of its own, as is Z in Figure 5. Notice the somewhat awkward location for the labels D and J. There are a couple of other possibilities for locating the label of a product blob, among which is the one illustrated in Figure 6, but we shall remain with that of Figure 5.

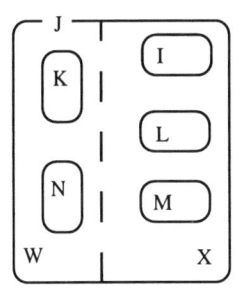

Figure 6. An alternative for labeling partitioned blobs

Now that we have a formalism for representing the sets we are interested in and their structural, set-theoretic relationships, it is time to add edges. A *higraph* is obtained by simply allowing edges, or more generally, hyperedges, to be attached to the contour of *any* blobs. As in graphs, edges can be directed or undirected, labeled or unlabeled, of one type or of several, etc. In Figure 7 we have allowed for a single kind of unlabeled directed hyperedge of arity between 2 and 3. Most of the arrows in the figure are simple binary edges, such as the very high-level one connecting E to A, the very low-level one connecting N to K, and the interlevel one connecting U to E. Others are directed three-way hyperedges, such as the one connecting E to both J and T, and the one connecting both R and M to D. Clearly there is nothing to prohibit self-directed or partially self-directed edges, such as the one connecting A to its subblob B. The formal meaning of such edges (see the appendix) in the graph-theoretic spirit simply associates the target blobs with the source blobs via

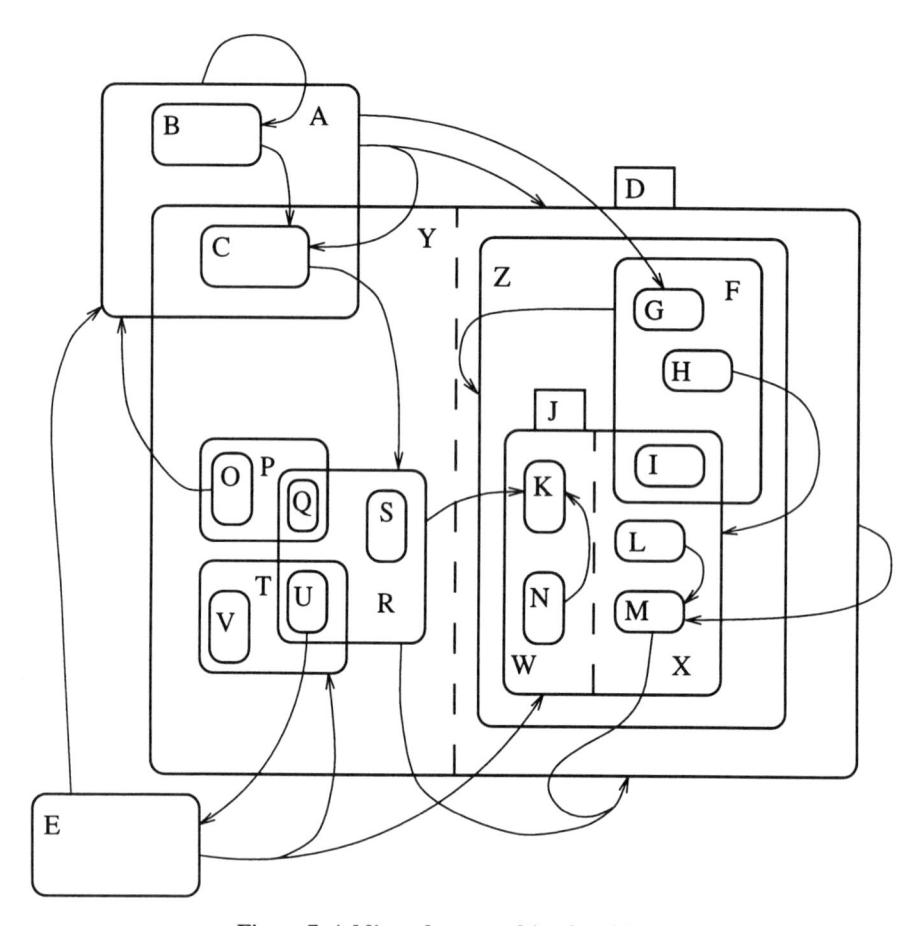

Figure 7. Adding edges, resulting in a higraph

the particular relationship the edges represent. Here, then, is the other reason for wanting each set of interest to have its own contour: to enable it to be connected to others via the edges.

In the sequel the term *higraph* will be used in a very liberal sense, making no real distinction between the various possibilities, for example, the edge-based or hyperedge-based cases.

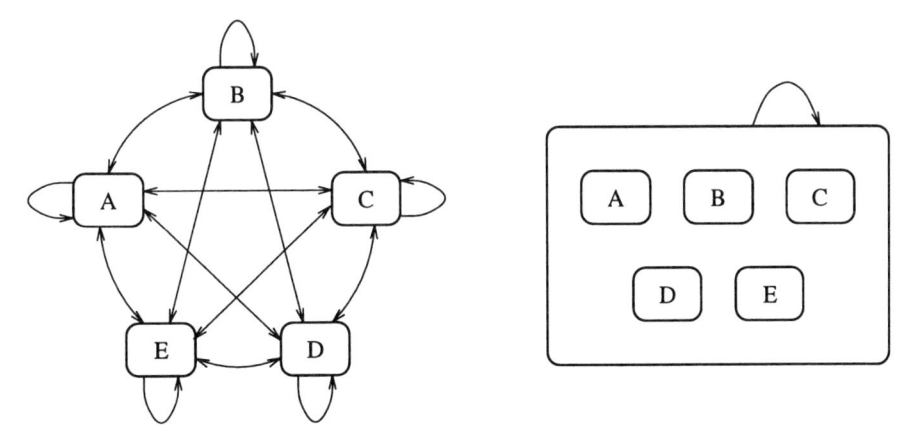

Figure 8. Two representations of a 5-clique

Some Immediate Applications

The first thing to notice when attempting to apply higraphs is that edges connect sets to sets, not elements to elements as in graphs. The most common way of interpreting a higraph edge is as a collection of regular edges, connecting each element in one set with each element in the other. In this way, for example, it is possible to represent a 5-clique, as in Figure 8. This all-to-all semantics is not mandatory, however, since the bare meaning of a higraph edge is that the relationship it represents holds between the *sets* it connects. Hence, we are free to attach any meaning at all to the relationship itself and to the way (if any) that it extends downwards to the elements of those sets. Thus, if we take the relationship R represented by ordinary arrows in a higraph to mean "each element in the source set is related to *some* element in the target set by relationship T," then the information conveyed by Figure 9, for example, cannot really be captured by an ordinary graph with with T-edges, since one would be forced to decide which element in the target set is meant, thus causing an overspecification.

The computer science literature is full of uses of graphs, and it appears that many of these can benefit from the extensions offered by higraphs. Consider the *entity-relationship (E-R) diagrams* used in the conceptual specification of databases [7].

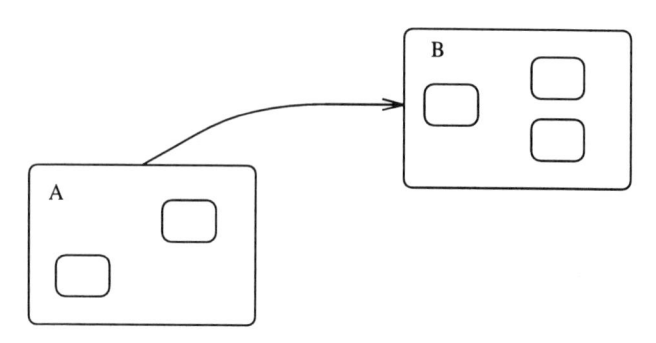

Figure 9. A simple higraph

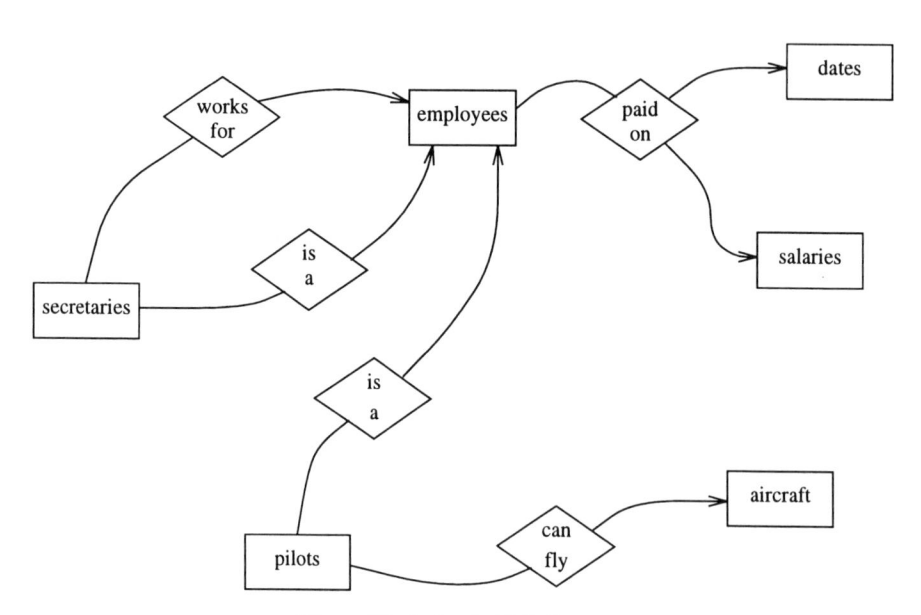

Figure 10. A simple E-R diagram

These are really hypergraphs with a single type of node that is depicted by a rectangle and denotes an entity in the described pool of data. The hyperedges, whose labels are written in small diamond-shaped boxes (that should not be regarded as nodes), capture the intended relationships between entities. Figure 10 shows a simple example of such a diagram, representing a small part of the data used by an airline company.[6] Its information content is clear: pilots can fly aircraft, secretaries work for employees and employees are paid salaries on certain dates (the latter being a three-way relationship). Notice, however, the is-a edges, informing us that pilots and secretaries are really employees too. These are conveying information of a totally different kind. Indeed, they capture precisely the kind of structural, set-theoretic relations discussed earlier. Using the very same "flat" diagrammatic representation for both kinds of relationships can cause a lot of confusion, especially in large and intricate cases, as a glance at some of the examples in the literature shows.

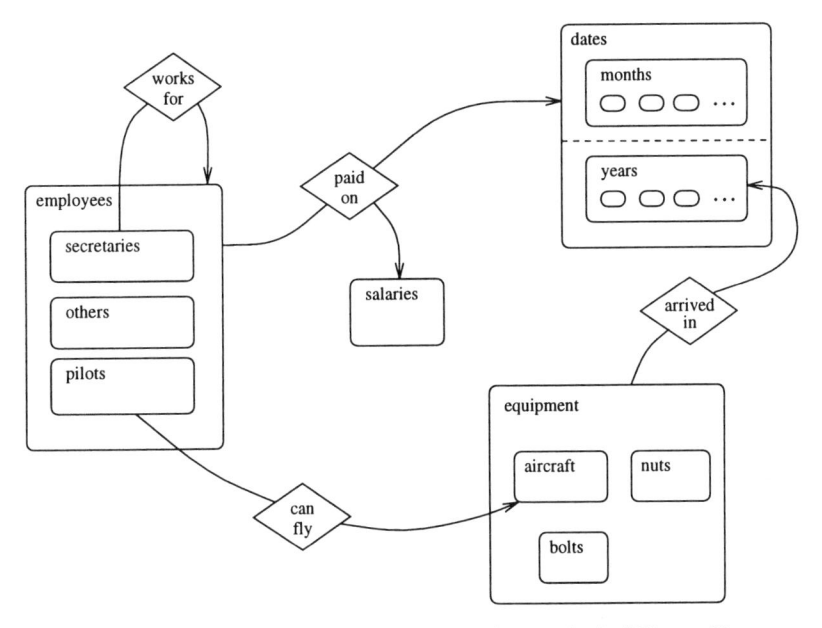

Figure 11. A higraph-based version (and extension) of Figure 10

Figure 11 shows the way such information can be represented in a higraph-based extension of E-R diagrams. The set of employees is divided into the sub-

---

[6] Actually, Figure 10 does some injustice to the E-R formalism, as it is sometimes called, by ignoring the additional features that the formalism supports, such as attributes for both entities and relationships, and the classification of relationships as one-one, many-one, etc. Throughout, we shall have to be satisfied with describing only those features of a formalism that are directly relevant to our discussion.

sets of interest, secretaries and pilots (with an additional blob for all others, if so desired). The paid-on edge emanates from the employees blob, while the can-fly edge emanates from the pilots blob only – exactly what one would expect. The work-for edge rightly connects the secretaries blob with its parent blob – employees. The new information has been quite easily added: aircraft are now just part of the overall equipment, which is related to years by the relationship received-on, while the dates on which salaries are received have been specified as consisting of pairs from the orthogonal components month and year. Moreover, independent divisions can be represented by overlapping blobs, as illustrated in Figure 12, which shows how a new breakup of the employees by sex can be added to the previous figure with a couple of additional details. In it we might have reason to relate the female pilots or the male secretaries to other entities. In practice, overlaps should probably be used somewhat sparingly, as overly overlapping blobs might detract from the clarity of the total diagram, an observation that is in line with the often-made claim that a hierarchy is by far the way humans prefer to structure things (see [45, chap. 1]). This opinion is not universally accepted, however, so the human-factors aspects of formalisms like higraphs would appear to require careful experimental research, such as those carried out in [18] and [20].

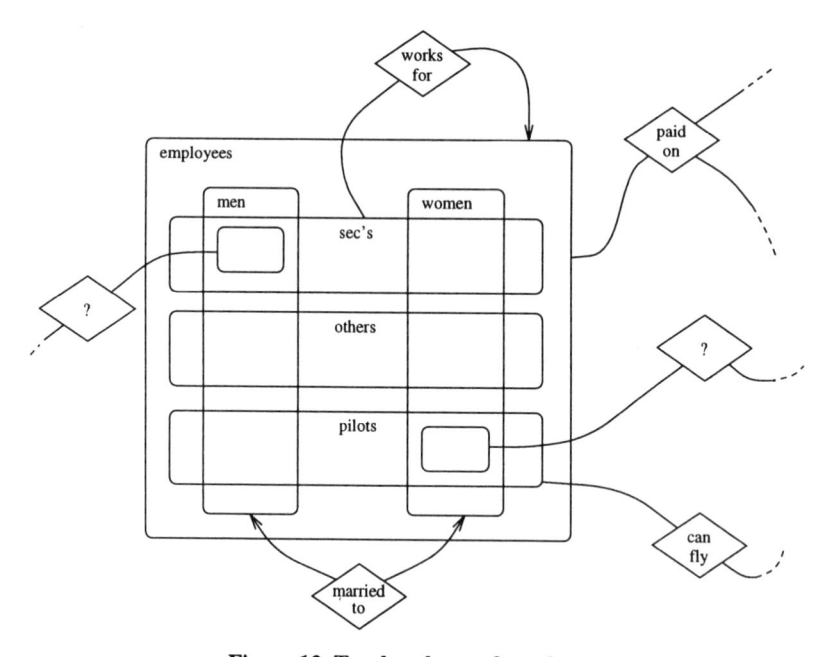

Figure 12. Two breakups of employees

Occasionally, authors have used other labels to capture is-a relationships, typically ones that try to describe the special nature of the breakup into subsets. As

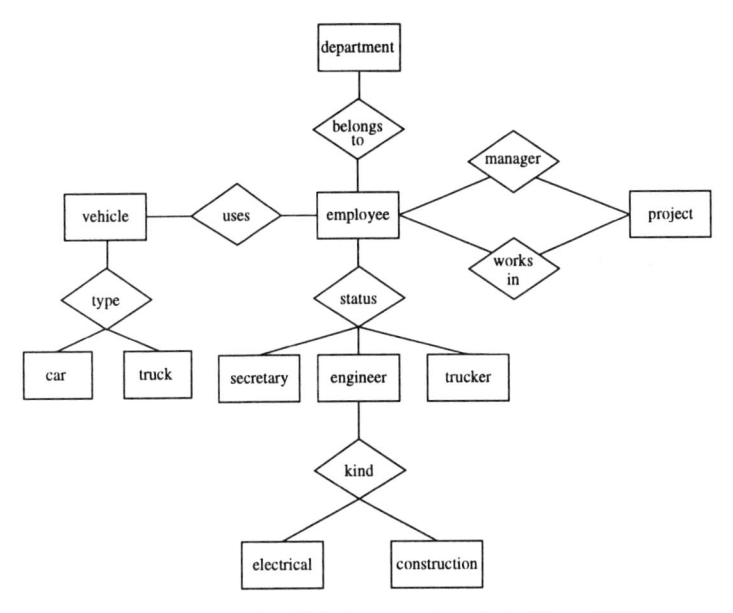

Figure 13. Another E-R diagram (reprinted from [42])

©1979, with permission from Elsevier Science.

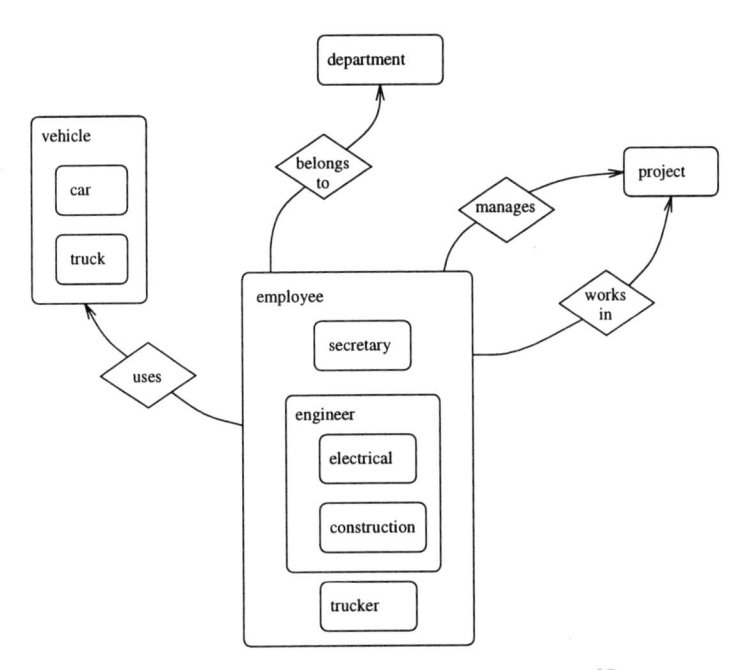

Figure 14. A higraph-based version of Figure 13

an example consider Figure 13, which is Figure 9 of [42] almost verbatim, and our higraph-based Figure 14, which contains the same information.

A formalism that is very similar to that of E-R diagrams, and actually predated it by a number of years (see [40]), is that of *semantic*, or *associative*, *networks*. These graph-based structures are used widely in artificial intelligence for natural language processing and knowledge representation, and are discussed in numerous books and papers. (A good survey and history appears in [4], and more examples can be found in [6], [37], [44], and [50] and in the collection of papers in [17].) Semantic networks can actually be thought of as *concept-relationship diagrams*, with much of the research in the area concerned with the association of rich semantic meaning with the various types of nodes and edges. Here, too, is-a edges are used in abundance resulting in large, and at times incomprehensible, diagrams. Often, semantic networks contain more than one distinct type of is-a edges, corresponding to set inclusion, set membership, a physical "being-part-of" relationship, etc.[7] The way higraphs can be used here is exactly as in E-R diagrams, and the advantages become all the more significant if such different shades of structural is-a relationships can be made visually distinct (see the section called "Possible Variations on the Theme"). Clearly, it would be naive to claim that the profound problematics of knowledge representation can be overcome by diagrammatic considerations alone. Nevertheless, every little improvement helps.

In both E-R diagrams and semantic networks, people have observed that often the relationships, not only the entities and concepts, have to be stratified by levels of detail. This is typically done by considering the diamond-shaped relationship labels to be nodes of a second kind, and involving them also in structural is-a relationships with others. Although some people are opposed to this visual blurring of the distinction between entities and relationships, there is nothing to prevent those who are not from transferring this idea to the higraph framework. This would yield a blob structure also for the relationships, with the edges now serving to connect the entities and concepts to their relevant real, nonstructural relationships.

It is noteworthy that the area of the blobs in a higraph can be further exploited in these applications. Full E-R diagrams and semantic networks are typically laden with attributes, or properties, that are attached as additional "stump" nodes to the various entities. These attributes are often of the kind that are "inherited down" the is-a hierarchy, as the phrase goes. (In fact, there are many interesting issues associated with the very notion of inheritance; see [5], [45].) In a higraph-based representation, the area inside a blob would appear to be an ideal place to list, attach, or otherwise identify any properties, attributes, or explanations that are relevant to that blob and anything enclosed therein. Thus, simple inheritance is made possible quite naturally by the insideness approach to representing the subset relationship.

We should remark that some papers on semantic networks and the E-R model have indeed suggested the use of insideness and interblob edges to represent high-

---

[7] A variety of names have been attached to these, such as isa and inst in [6], SS and EL in [37] (standing for *is a, instance, subset,* and *element,* respectively), and many others elsewhere, such as a-kind-of, group-of, is-part-of, etc.

level entities and relationships, though the ideas do not seem to have been pursued to their full potential (see [10], [16], [25], [34], and [36]). Also, the idea of basing the decomposition of sets on Cartesian products and OR's is consistent with much of the literature on types. (For example, see [5] where these two features are captured by the notions of a *record* and a *variant*, respectively.)

Among the other graph-based formalisms for which higraphs appear to be useful are data-flow diagrams. A higraph-based version of such diagrams, called *activity-charts*, is one of the graphical languages supported by the STATEMATE system of ILogix@I-Logix and is described in [24] and [28]. In activity charts the blobs denote functions, or activities, with the subset relation representing the subfunction relationship. The edges denote the possible flow of data. (Cartesian product is not used.) Consider the activity-chart of Figure 15, which is a simple part of the functional decomposition of an automatic teller machine. One of the edges therein means that the customer's account-number might possibly flow (following, perhaps, a read or write instruction) from the identify activity to the update-account activity, or to anywhere in the serve-customer activity, that is, to either (or all) of the deposit, withdraw, or balance-query subactivities. Another of the edges in Figure 15 means that the new amount with which the customer's balance should be adjusted might flow from any one of the deposit or withdraw activities to the update-account activity.

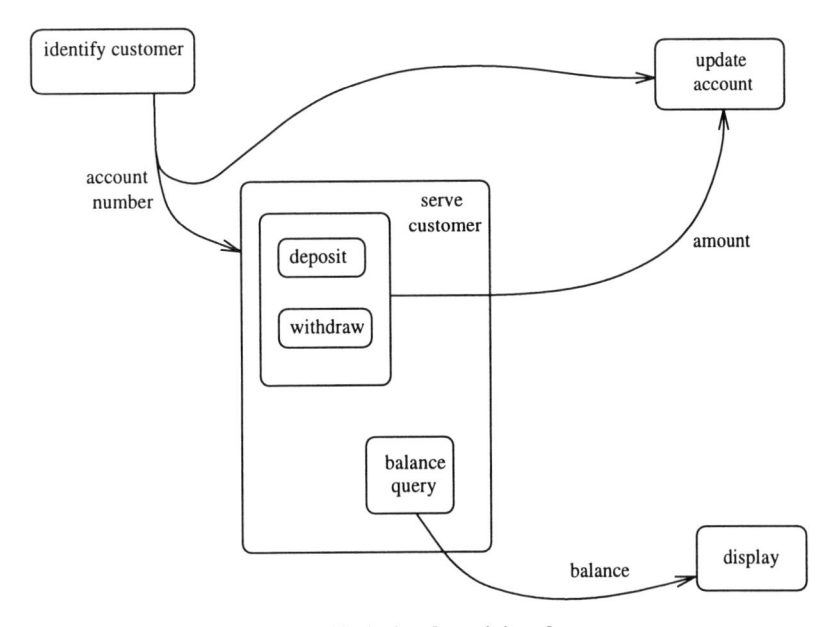

Figure 15. A simple activity-chart

Higraphs also form the basis of a recent paper [47], in which a visual language for specifying security constraints in operating systems is presented. The formalism represents access rights and exceptions thereof as distinct kinds of edges in a higraph, the blobs of which represent groups of users, files, and other entities. Cartesian product is used to represent the breakup of files into their components. Reference [47] also contains a number of interesting special-purpose extensions to the basic higraph formalism. Another use of higraph-like ideas appears in [32] and [38] in the form of proof diagrams for verifying concurrent programs, and there is a simple way of using higraphs as the basis of a hypertext system rather than conventional graph. In part, many issues that arise in the context of hypertext systems, such as multiple hierarchies, superconcepts, and composite nodes are treated naturally in the higraph formalism. (See [8].) One can also conceive of additional applications in visualizing interrupt-driven flowcharts and certain kinds of model-collapsing constructions in model theory.

Statecharts: A Less Obvious Application

The previous section notwithstanding, it would appear that the most beneficial application of higraphs lies in extending state-transition diagrams to obtain the *statecharts* of [21]. It was actually in the process of trying to formulate the underlying graphical concepts embodied in (the earlier) statecharts that higraphs emerged. This section contains a brief description of the statechart formalism; the reader is referred to [21] for further details.

To motivate the discussion, there appears to be agreement in the literature on software and systems engineering as to the existence of a major problem in the specification and design of large and complex *reactive systems*. A reactive system (see [22] and [39]), in contrast with a *transformational system*, is characterized by being event driven, continuously having to react to external and internal stimuli. Examples include telephones, communication networks, computer operating systems, avionics systems, VLSI circuits, and the man-machine interface of many kinds of ordinary software. The problem is rooted in the difficulty of describing reactive behavior in ways that are clear and realistic, and at the same time formal and rigorous, in order to be amenable to precise computerized analysis. The behavior of a reactive system is really the set of allowed sequences of input and output events, conditions, and actions, perhaps with some additional information such as timing constraints.

Most notable among the solutions proposed for this problem are Petri nets [41], communicating sequential processes (CSP) [26], the calculus of communicating systems (CCS) [35], the sequence diagrams of [51], ESTEREL [2], and temporal logic [39]. Statecharts constitute yet another attempt at solving this problem, but one that is aimed at reviving the classical formalism of finite-state machines (FSMs) and their visual counterpart, state-transition diagrams, trying to make them suitable for use in large and complex applications. Indeed, people working on the design of really complex systems have all but given up on the use of conventional FSMs and their state diagrams for several reasons:

(1) State diagrams are "flat." They provide no natural notion of depth, hierarchy, or modularity, and therefore do not support stepwise, top-down, or bottom-up development.
(2) State diagrams are uneconomical when it comes to transitions. An event that causes the very same transition from a large number of states, such a high-level interrupt, must be attached to each of them separately, resulting in an unnecessary multitude of arrows.
(3) State diagrams are extremely uneconomical, indeed quite infeasible, when it comes to states (at least when states are interpreted in the usual way as "snapshots" of the situation at a given point in time). As the system under description grows linearly, the number of states grows exponentially, and the conventional FSM formalism forces one to explicitly represent them all.
(4) Finally, state diagrams are inherently sequential in nature and do not cater for concurrency in a natural way.[8]

There have been attempts to remove some of these drawbacks, mostly by using various kinds of hierarchical or communicating state machines. Typically, however, these hierarchies provide little help in reducing the size of the resulting description, as they do not condense any information. Moreover, the communication between FSMs is usually one-to-one, being channel or processor based, and allows for only a single set of communicating machines on the highest level of the description. Furthermore, for the most part such extensions are not particularly diagrammatic in spirit, and hence one loses the advantages a visual medium might offer.

Statecharts are a higraph-based extension of standard state-transition diagrams, where the blobs represent states and arrows represent transitions. (For additional statechart features, the reader is again referred to [21].)[9] As to the basics, we might say that

statecharts = state diagrams + depth
+ orthogonality + broadcast communication.

Depth is represented by the insideness of blobs, as illustrated in Figure 16, where 16b may replace 16a. The symbols e, f, g, and h stand for events that trigger the transitions, and the bracketed c is a condition. Thus $g[c]$ triggers the transition from A to C if and when g occurs, but only if c is true at that time. The fact that A and C do not overlap and are completely inside D means that the latter is the *exclusive-or (XOR)* of the former, so that being in D is tantamount to being in either A or C, but not in both. The main point here is that the f-arrow, which leaves the contour of D, applies to both A and C, as in 16a. This simple higraph-based principle, when applied to large collections of states with many levels, helps overcome points (1) and (2) above (flatness and multilevel events). The idea of exploiting this kind of insideness in describing levels in a state-transition diagram appears also in [20]. It

---

[8] Here, modeling a highly concurrent system by its global states only is considered unnatural.

[9] Some encouraging experimental evidence as to the appropriateness of statecharts for system description is discussed in [21, sect. 9].

should be noted that the small *default arrows* depend on their encompassing blobs. In Figure 16a state A is singled out as being the default, or start state, of the three, a fact represented in 16b by the top default arrow. The bottom one, however, states that C is default among A and C if we are already in D and hence alleviates the need for continuing the h-arrow beyond D's boundary.

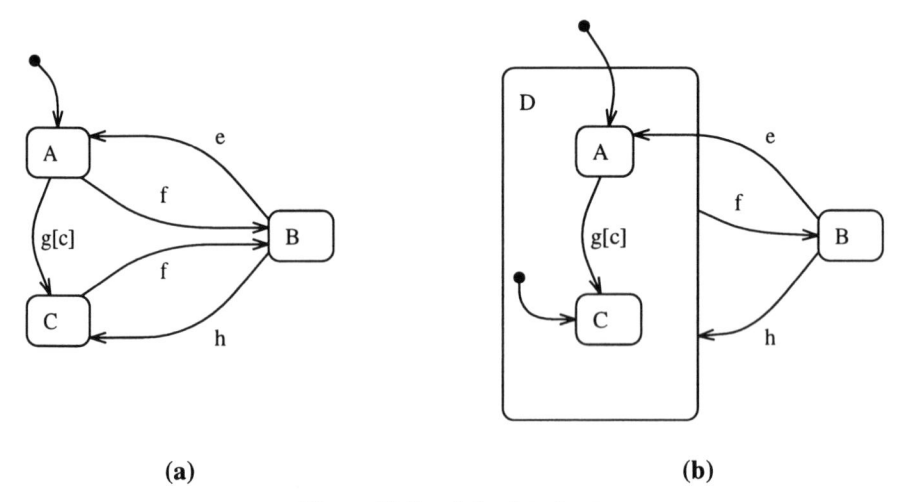

Figure 16. Depth in statecharts

Orthogonality is the dual of the *XOR* decomposition of states, in essence an *AND* decomposition, and is captured by the partitioning feature of higraphs, that is, by the unordered Cartesian product. In Figure 17b state Y consists of two *orthogonal components*, A and D, related by *AND*: To be in Y is tantamount to being in both A and D, and hence the two default arrows. The intended semantics of 17b is given by its equivalent "flat" version 17a, which represents a sort of automata product. Notice the simultaneity of transitions that takes place when event e occurs in state configuration (B, F), and the merging and splitting transitions that lead to and from Y. Note also the special condition $[\text{in}(G)]$ attached to the f-transition from C, and the way it is reflected in Figure 17a. Figure 17 illustrates the heart of the exponential blowup problem, the number of states in the explicit version of Y being the product of the numbers of states in the orthogonal components of its higraph version. If orthogonality is used often and on many levels, the state explosion and sequentiality difficulties (points (3) and (4)) are also overcome in a reasonable way. This can be further observed by studying the examples and references in [21]).

Figures 16 and 17 do not contain any outputs, and hence, orthogonal components can synchronize so far only through common events (like e in Figure 17) and can affect each other only through $[\text{in }(state)]$ conditions. A certain amount of subtlety is added to the way statecharts model concurrency by allowing *output* events. Here, statecharts can be viewed as an extension of Mealy machines (see [27]), since

Harel On Visual Formalisms 641

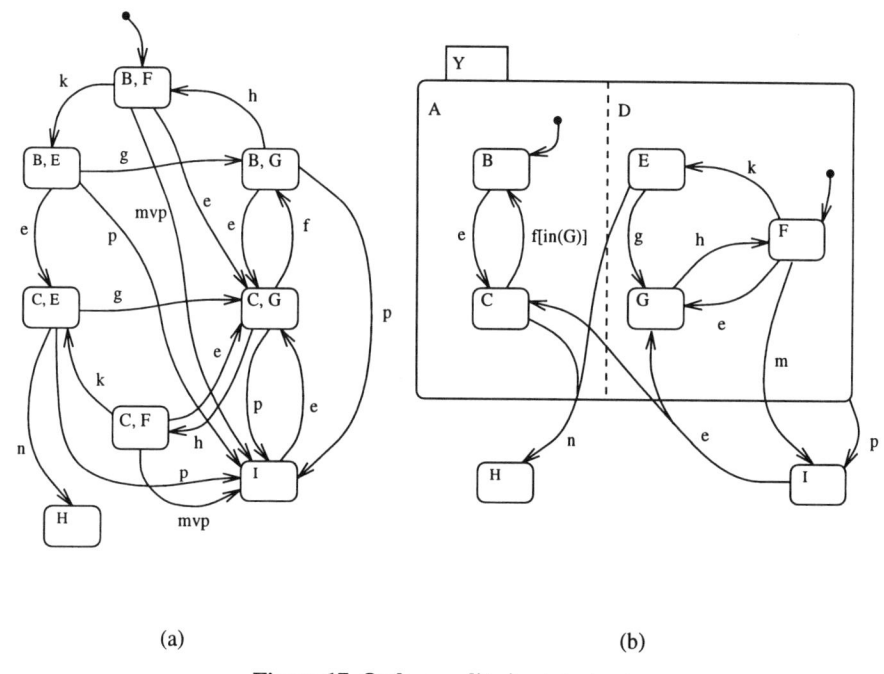

(a)

(b)

Figure 17. Orthogonality in statecharts

output events, which are called *actions*, can be attached optionally to the triggering event along a transition. In contrast with conventional Mealy machines, however, an action appearing along a transition in a statechart is not merely sent to the "outside world" as an output. Rather, it can affect the behaviour of the statechart itself in orthogonal components. This is achieved by a simple broadcast mechanism: Just as the occurrence of an external event causes transitions in all components to which it is relevant (see Figure 17), if event e occurs and a transition labeled e/f is taken, the action f is immediately activated, and is regarded as a new event, possibly causing further transitions in other components.

Figure 18 shows a simple example of this. If we are in (B,F,J) and along comes the external event m, the next configuration will be (C,G,I), by virtue of e being generated in H and triggering the two transitions in components A and D. This is a *chain reaction* of length 2. If no external event n occurs, the new configuration will be (B,E,J), by virtue of a similar chain reaction of length 3.

This concludes our brief account of the basic features of statecharts, and we now illustrate the formalism with a rather simplified version of the digital watch described in [21]. The watch has four external control buttons, as well as a main display that can be used to show the time (hour, minutes, and seconds) or the date (weekday, day of month, and month). It has a chime that can be enabled or disabled, beeping on the hour if enabled. It has an alarm that can also be enabled or disabled, and beeps for 2 minutes when the time in the alarm setting is reached unless any one

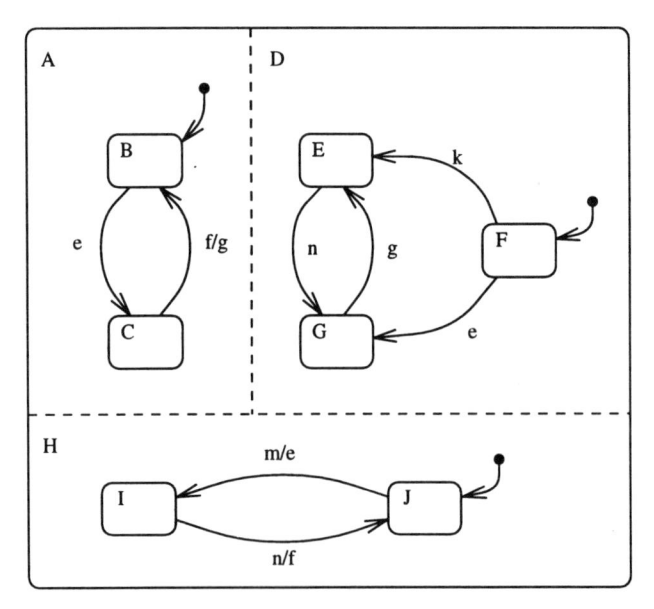

Figure 18. Broadcasting in statecharts

of the buttons is pressed earlier. It has a stopwatch with two display modes (regular and lap), a light for illumination, and a weak-battery blinking indication.

Some of the external events relevant to the watch are a, b, c, and d, which signify the pressing of the four buttons, respectively, and b-up, for example, which signifies the release of button b. Another event we shall be using, 2-min, signifies that 2 minutes have elapsed since the last time a button was pressed. (We choose not to get involved here in a syntax for the event expressions themselves. In a language of compound events that includes a time-out construct, such as that of [24] and [28], this last event can be expressed easily.)

Statecharts can be used to describe the behavior of the watch in terms of its human interface; namely, how the user's operations, such as pressing buttons, influence things. It should be noted, however, that the descriptions that follow do not specify the activities carried out internally by the watch, only their control. Thus, nothing is said here about the time elapsing activity itself, or the technicalities of the beeping, the blinking, or the displays. These aspects of a system can be described using other means, and should be incorporated into the overall specification together with the statecharts. (See [24] for one approach to this incorporation.)

Figure 19 shows the basic displays state of the watch. Notice that time is the default state, and there is a cycle of pressings of a leading from time through the alarm, chime, and stopwatch states back to time. There is a general update state, and a special state for updating the alarm's internal setting. The 2-min event signifies return to time if 2 minutes have elapsed in any state other than stopwatch and no button has been pressed.

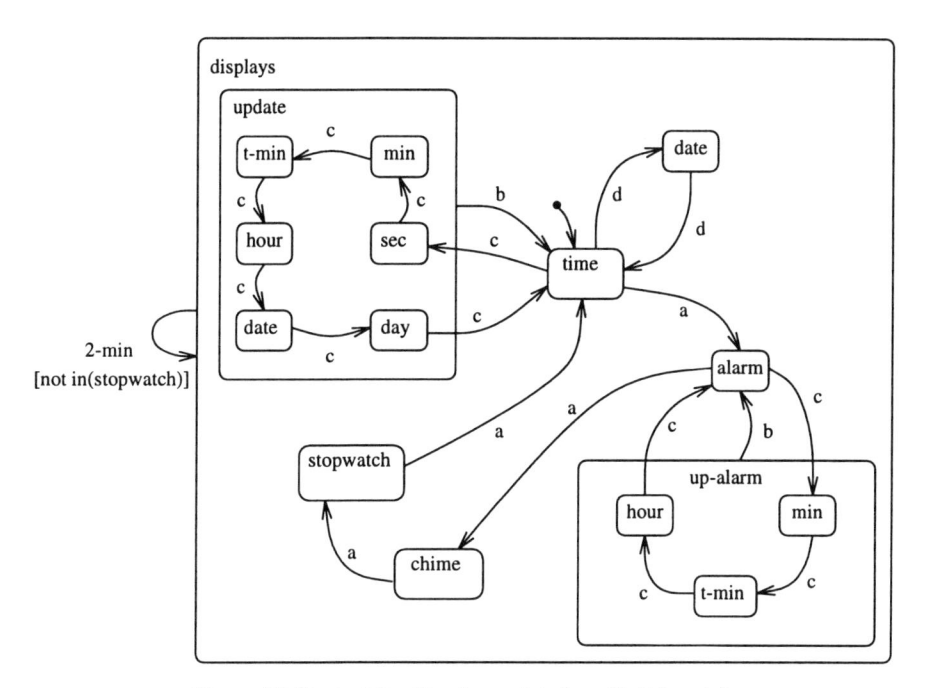

Figure 19. Part of the `displays` state in a digital watch

The specification of the watch contains examples of orthogonal states on various levels. We should first consider the `stopwatch` state, detailed in Figure 20. It has two substates, `zero` and {`disp`, `run`}, the first being the default. Pressing b takes the stopwatch from the former to the latter causing it to start running with a regular display. Repeatedly pressing b causes it to stop and start alternately. Pressing d can be seen to cause the display to switch to `lap` and back to `reg`, or to leave the orthogonal state and return to `zero` depending, as illustrated, on the present state configuration. The encircled and starred H is one of the additional notations described in [21], and prescribes that, upon entering `stopwatch` from `chime` by pressing a, the state actually entered will be the one in which the system was in most recently. Thus, we are entering the `stopwatch` state by "history" – hence, the H. The default will be used if this is the first time `stopwatch` is entered, or if the history has been cleared.

The description of the high levels of the watch also uses orthogonality. In Figure 21 the watch is specified as being either `dead` or `alive`, with the latter consisting of five orthogonal components. (Notice where the `displays` state fits in.) In this figure the events `bt-in`, `bt-rm`, `bt-dy` and `bt-wk` signify, respectively, the insertion, removal, expiration, and weakening (below a certain level) of the battery. We use `t-hits-tm` to signify that the internal time of the watch has reached the internal time setting of the alarm, and `t-hits-hr` to signify that it has reached a whole hour. Also, `beep-rt` occurs when either any button is pressed or 2 minutes have

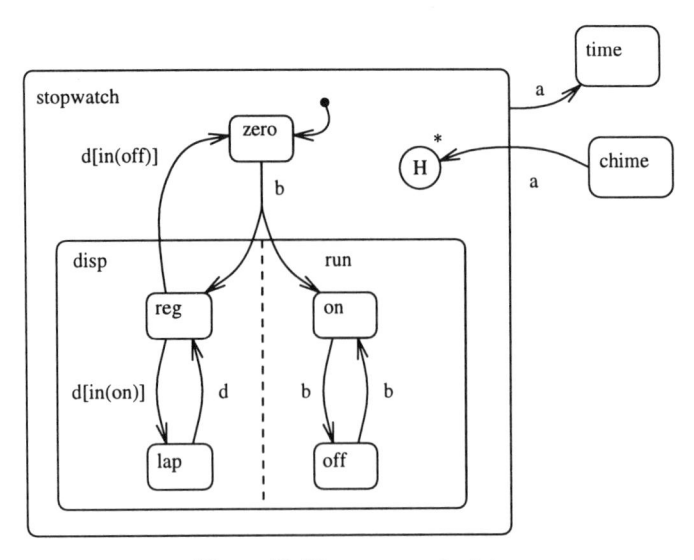

644   High-Integrity System Specification and Design

Figure 20. The `stopwatch` **state**

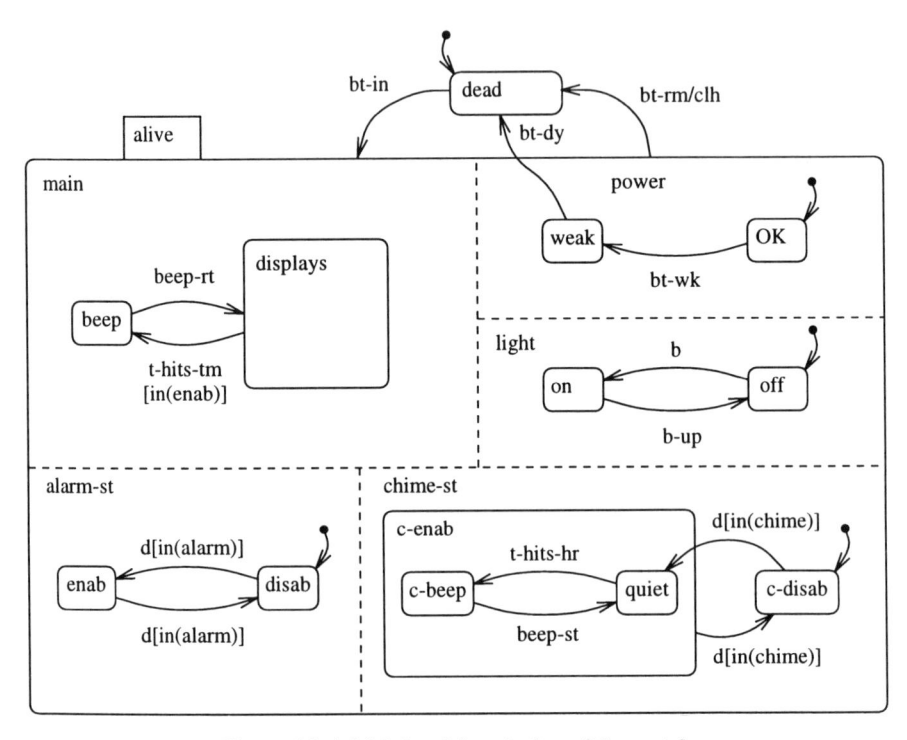

Figure 21. A high-level description of the watch

elapsed since entering beep, and beep-st occurs 2 seconds after entering c-beep. (As mentioned, these events should also be written formally as compound event expressions in a language involving time-outs, disjunctions, and so on; see [28].)

The first of the five components in Figure 21, main, specifies the transitions between displaying and beeping, where displays is simply the state described earlier (see Figure 19). (In actuality, the displaying activities themselves do not shut off when the watch is beeping, but cannot be changed until control returns to the displays state.) The alarm-st component describes the status of the alarm, specifying that it can be changed using d when control is in the alarm display state. The chime-st state is similar, with the additional provision for beeping on the hour given within. The power state is self-explanatory, where the activity that would take place in the weak state would involve the displays blinking frantically.

In considering the innocent-looking light state, the default is off, and depressing and releasing b causes the light to switch alternately between on and off. What is interesting is the effect these actions might have elsewhere. If the entire statechart for the parts of the watch described so far is contemplated (see Figure 22), one realizes that pressing b for illumination has significant side effects: It will cause a return from an update state if we happen to be in one, the stopping of the alarm if it happens to be beeping, and a change in the stopwatch's behavior if we happen to be working with it. Conversely, if we use b in displays for any one of these things the light will go on, whether we like it or not. These seeming anomalies are all a result of the fact that the light component is orthogonal to the main component, meaning that its scope is very broad. One can imagine a far more humble light component, applicable only in the time and date states, which would not cause any of these problems. Its specification could be carried out by attaching it orthogonally, not to main, but to a new state surrounding time and date, as in Figure 23.

As mentioned earlier, this section has only described the "no-frills" version of the statecharts. A more complete treatment appears in [21], and a formal syntax and semantics appear in [23]. The reader may have noticed that we have not used intersecting states in the statecharts. While intersecting blobs in higraphs do not cause any serious semantic problems (see the appendix), intersecting states in statecharts do. In fact, since not all syntactically legal higraphs make sense as statecharts, it is not even clear how to define an appropriate syntax for statecharts with intersecting states (see [21, sect. 6.2]). A preliminary approach to these problems appears in [29].

Possible Variations on the Theme

The higraph formalism can be enriched and extended in various ways. We shall point to a few of these possibilities briefly and informally.

At times it becomes useful to base a formalism on a three-valued, rather than a two-valued, underlying model. For example, in certain uses of graphs in databases and artificial intelligence there arises a need to state not only that a certain relationship R holds or does not hold between two objects, but also to capture the situation

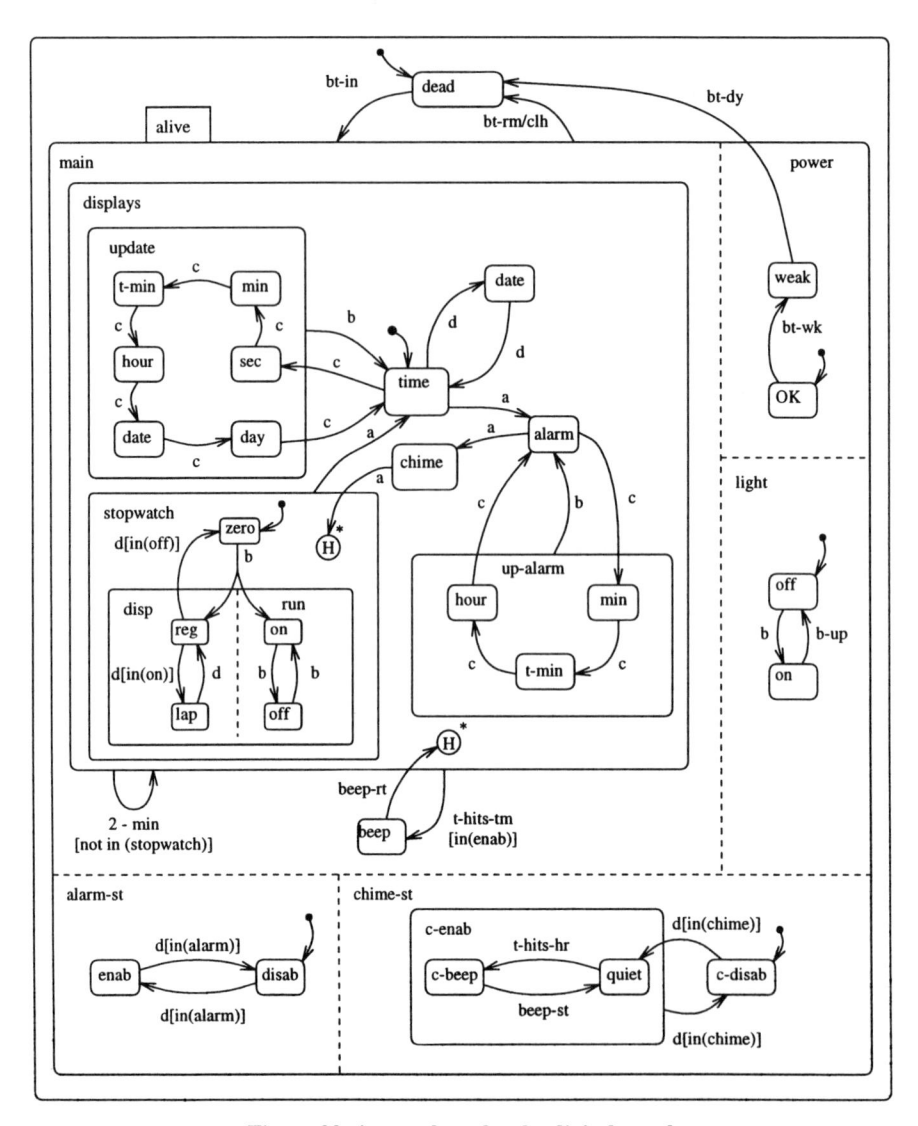

Figure 22. A statechart for the digital watch

Harel On Visual Formalisms 647

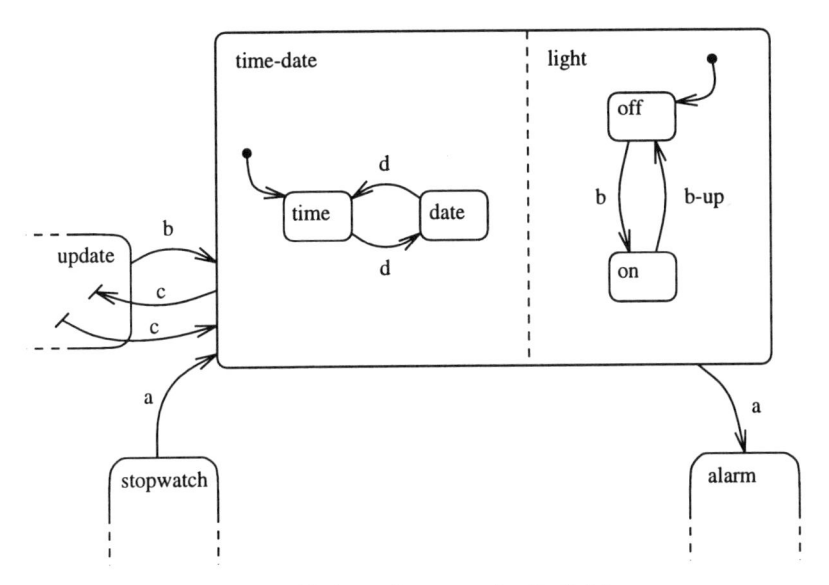

Figure 23. A smaller scope for the light

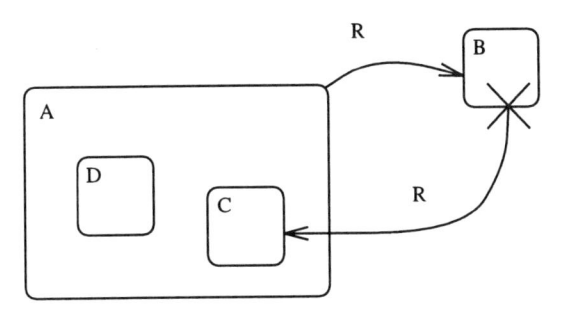

Figure 24. Negative arrows

whereby we do not know which of these is the case. One possibility is to reinterpret the absence of an *R* arrow as denoting the don't-know situation, and have a new kind of arrow representing the *negative information* that *R* definitely does *not* hold. This simple idea can be adopted in higraphs too, as in Figure 24, which is supposed to indicate that *R* holds between *A* and *B* and does not hold between *B* and *C*, and that all other possibilities (including whether or not *R* holds between *C* and *B*)[10] are left open.

Often a don't-know option is needed not only for arrows, but for blobs as well. That is, we might want to represent uncertainty as to the presence or absence of identifiable sets, rather than relationships. Accordingly, we can use a new blob notation (e.g., one with a dashed contour) to denote a set that we are not sure actually exists (here one assumes that all regular blobs stand for nonempty sets). Figure 25 asserts our uncertainty as to whether $A - B$ is empty or not, and also states that if it is not empty then the difference is called *E* and is related to *F* via relationship *R*.

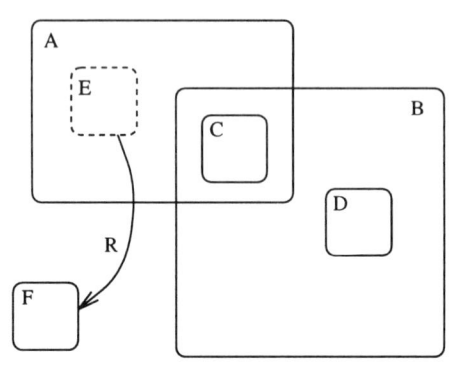

Figure 25. "Not-quite-sure" blobs

When higraphs are used in practice (see [21], [24], [28], and [47]), it is useful to be able to "zoom out" of a particular view, suppressing low-level details. A good example would be going from Figure 22, the detailed statechart description of the watch, to the less detailed Figure 21. In such cases there arises a problem with edges connected to subblobs that are omitted from the new, less detailed view. If we decide to zoom out of the likes of Figure 26 by suppressing blobs *B* and *C*, it might be a mistake to consider Figure 27a as the correct new version, since the two are clearly inconsistent. Figure 27b is better, with its stubs that represent relationships to unspecified subblobs. For example, since a statechart arrow whose target is a high-level state *A* prescribes entrance to none other than the default substate of *A*, Figure 21 is somewhat inconsistent with Figure 22. In the present context, a better version would have shown the beep-rt arrow crossing the contour of the displays

---

[10] This is not determined by the arrow from *A* to *B*, since, as discussed earlier, the fact that *R* holds between *A* and *B* says nothing about what the case is for *A*'s subsets.

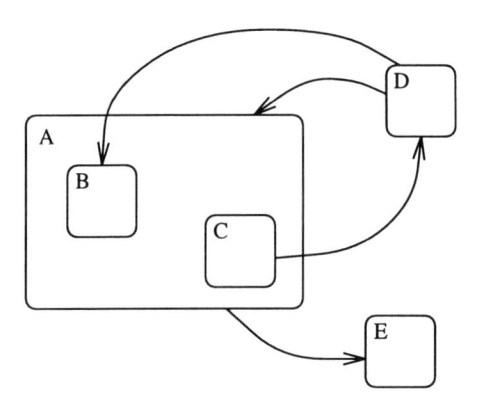

Figure 26. Another simple higraph

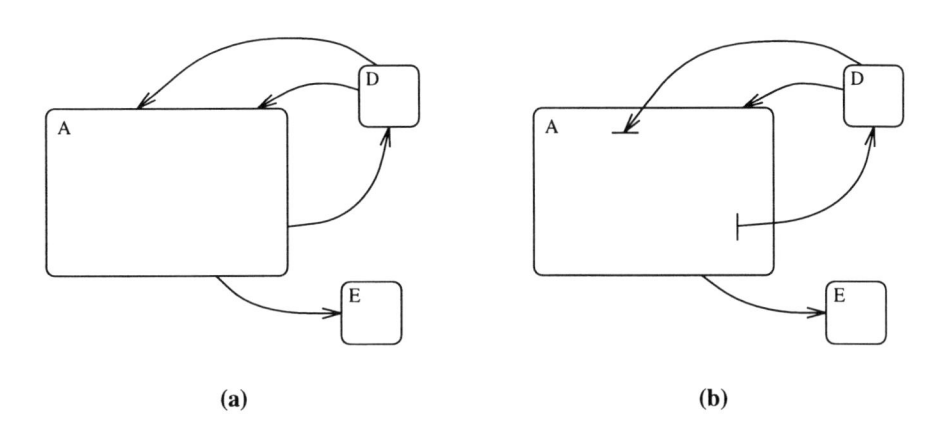

(a) (b)

Figure 27. Two possible zoom outs for Figure 26

state and ending with a stub indicating entrance to a substate (as of now unspecified) that is possibly different from the default substate, time.

One weakness of the higraph formalism is its inability to specify both set inclusion and set membership. We have chosen to adopt the former as the meaning of blob enclosure, although we could probably have chosen the latter too without causing too many problems. This weakness is all the more apparent when higraphs are contrasted with their graph-based equivalents, in which set inclusion is depicted by is-a edges (see Figure 10). In the latter, one need only use an additional type of edge, labeled elmnt-of, for instance, to be able to represent set membership. We would like to claim that this is not much more than a notational problem that requires a topo-visual way of distinguishing between two different kinds of insideness. Most of the solutions to this notational problem that come to mind are somewhat unsatisfactory, with the exception of the one that calls for a three-dimensional basis for higraphs, in which the third dimension is responsible for such distinctions (e.g., by having set inclusion take place in the same plane and set membership be reflected by different levels of planes).[11]

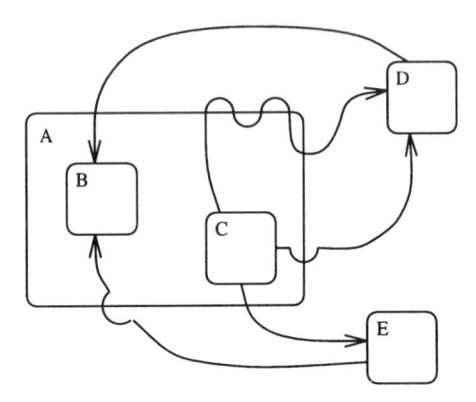

Figure 28. Skipping and multiple crossovers

An additional possible extension to higraphs is to make arrows mean more than a simple connection between source and target. (We are assuming ordinary directed binary edges here, not, say, hyperedges). Since higraph arrows in general cut across blob contours, we might want to say something more about the *sequence* of crossovers that the edge takes on its way from the source to the target. This can be achieved trivially by drawing the arrow through the appropriate contours in the desired order (assuming this order is indeed possible, given the basic topology of

---

[11] Visual formalisms that are predominantly two-dimensional in nature, but make some use of a third dimension, are far from being out of the question, even if we are not willing to wait for quality holographic workstations to show up. If all we need, as in this case, is the ability to tell when two nested blobs are on the same plane or not, then a simple graphical simulation of a dynamic left-right shift in point of view would do the job.

the blobs). The interesting case occurs when we want to omit from such a sequence one or more of the contours that, topologically speaking, must be crossed by any line from the source to the target. We would like the *D*-to-*B* arrow in Figure 26, for example, to enter *B*, but *not* to enter *A* in the process. Statecharts with intersections give rise to one interesting motivation for such cases, whereby one wants the system to enter only one of two intersecting states: again, the reader is referred to [21, sect. 6.2] for details. This richer notion of an edge can be represented visually by simply allowing arrows to skip edges as in Figure 28. Multiple crossovers, if desired, can also be represented as illustrated in the figure. Clearly, the formal semantics would be more elaborate, since a finite sequence of blobs, rather than an ordered pair, is the interpretation of a directed edge, and a finite set thereof, rather than an unordered pair, is the interpretation of an undirected edge.

Conclusion and Future Work

Higraphs seem to give rise to several interesting mathematical notions adapted to a large extent from graphs and hypergraphs. For example, one can provide reasonable definitions of connectivity, transitive closure, planarity, and acyclicity in higraphs, as well as a couple of different notions of "hitrees." For each of these, we may ask for upper and lower bounds on the computational complexity of the corresponding algorithmic problems. In some cases algorithms and bounds can be carried over from the work on graphs and hypergraphs, but one gets the feeling that in other cases these bounds can be improved by utilizing the special structure of higraphs. Some of these algorithmic problems have indeed arisen during the implementation of the STATEMATE system [24, 28], which supports three higraph-based formalisms. It would appear that the algorithmics of higraphs forms a fruitful avenue for further research.

The main thesis underlying this paper is that the intricate nature of a variety of computer-related systems and situations can, and in our opinion should, be represented by *visual formalisms*: visual, because they are to be generated, comprehended, and communicated by humans; and formal, because they are to be manipulated, maintained, and analyzed by computers. (This thesis is consistent with the study in [9], which argues for a more visual, nonverbal approach toward mathematics.)

Part of our motivation in stressing this point, despite the fact that it might appear to be so obvious, is the rather different approach that one occasionally finds elsewhere. For example, [33] is a compendium of many computer-related diagrammatic methods (virtually all of which are based on graphs). In our opinion, [33] is quite inadequate, since it accepts the *visual*, but apparently rejects the *formal*. For the most part, the methods and languages appearing in [33] are described in a manner that is devoid of semantics, and can therefore be used at best as informal aids when working with some other, hopefully more rigorous, nonvisual medium.

One of the implicit points we have tried to make in this article is that a considerable amount of mileage can be gotten out of basing such formalisms on a small number of simple diagrammatic notions, first and foremost among which are those that are topological in nature, not geometric. A lot can be gained by using topo-visual formalisms based on insideness, connectedness, and partitioning, with the semantics as given here, before one attempts to attach special significance to, for example, shapes, colors, and sizes.

We are entirely convinced the future is "visual." We believe that in the next few years many more of our daily technical and scientific chores will be carried out visually, and graphical facilities will be far better and cheaper than today's. The languages and approaches we shall be using in doing so will not be merely iconic in nature (e.g., using the picture of a trash can to denote garbage collection), but inherently diagrammatic in a conceptual way, perhaps also three-dimensional and/or animated. They will be designed to encourage visual modes of thinking when tackling systems of ever-increasing complexity, and will exploit and extend the use of our own wonderful biological visual system in many of our intellectual activities.

Appendix. Formal Definition of Higraphs

In what follows we present a formal (nongraphical) syntax and semantics for higraphs with simple binary directed edges. The reader should have no difficulty in extending the edge set E to represent, say, hyperedges.

A *higraph* is a quadruple

$$H = (B, \sigma, \pi, E),$$

where B is a finite set of elements, called *blobs*, and E, the set of *edges*, is a binary relation on B:

$$E \subseteq B \times B.$$

The *subblob* function σ is defined as

$$\sigma : B \to 2^B.$$

It assigns to each blob $x \in B$ its set $\sigma(x)$ of subblobs and is restricted to being cycle free. Thus, if we define

$$\sigma^0(x) = \{x\}, \quad \sigma^{i+1}(x) = \bigcup_{y \in \sigma^i(x)} \sigma(y),$$

and $\quad \sigma^+(x) = \bigcup_{i=1}^{\infty} \sigma^i(x),$

then σ is restricted so that $x \notin \sigma^+(x)$.

The *partitioning* function π is defined as

$$\pi : B \to 2^{B \times B},$$

associating with each blob $x \in B$ some equivalence relation $\pi(x)$ on the set of subblobs, $\sigma(x)$. This is really just a rigorous way of specifying the breakup of x into its orthogonal components, which are now defined simply to be the equivalence classes induced by the relation $\pi(x)$. Indeed, for $x \in B$ let us denote these classes by $\pi_1(x),\ldots,\pi_{k_x}(x)$. For the orthogonal division into components to be representable graphically (and in order to make the semantics cleaner), we shall require that blobs in different orthogonal components of x are disjoint. Formally, for each x we require that no two elements y and z of $\sigma(x)$ can intersect – that is, can satisfy $\sigma^+(y) \cap \sigma^+(z) \neq \emptyset$ – unless they are in the same orthogonal component – that is, unless the relation $\pi(x)$ renders them equivalent. Clearly, $k_x = 1$ means x is not partitioned into components at all.

This concludes the syntax of higraphs; now for the semantics. Two notations are useful. Given a higraph H, define the set of *atomic blobs* to be

$$A = \{x \in B \mid \sigma(x) = \emptyset\}.$$

(Obviously, the finiteness of B and the cycle-freeness restriction on σ imply A is nonempty.) The *unordered Cartesian product* of the two sets S and T is defined as

$$S \otimes T = \{\{s,t\} \mid s \in S, t \in T\}.$$

Given a higraph H, a *model* for H is a pair

$$M = (D, \mu),$$

where D is a set of unstructured elements[12] called the *domain* of the model M and μ assigns disjoint subsets of D to the atomic blobs of H. Thus,

$$\mu : A \to 2^D,$$

where if $x \neq y$ then $\mu(x) \cap \mu(y) = \emptyset$. We now have to show how to extend the association of atomic blobs with sets over D to an association of all blobs with more complex objects over D. Accordingly, extend μ by defining, inductively, for each $x \in B$,

$$\mu(x) = \otimes_{i=1}^{k_x} \left(\bigcup_{y \in \pi_i(x)} \mu(y) \right),$$

the intuition being that to calculate the semantics of a blob x we form the unordered Cartesian product of the meanings of its orthogonal components, each of which, in turn, is simply the union of the meanings of its constituent blobs. In particular, of course, if $k_x = 1$, no product is taken, and we really have

$$\mu(x) = \bigcup_{y \in \sigma(x)} \mu(y),$$

as expected.

---

[12] We want to avoid situations in which, say, x and $\{x\}$ are both elements of D.

To complete the semantics, note that the edge set E induces a semantic relation E_M on the $\mu(x)$s, defined by

$$(\mu(x), \mu(y)) \in E_M \quad \text{iff} \quad (x, y) \in E.$$

Acknowledgements. Thanks are due to Ton Kalker, Doug Tygar, and Jeanette Wing for comments on the appendix, and to an anonymous referee for a very detailed and thoughtful report.

References

1. Berge, C. *Graphs and Hypergraphs.* North-Holland, Amsterdam, 1973.
2. Berry, G., and Cosserat, I. The ESTEREL synchronous programming language and its mathematical semantics. In *Seminar on Concurrency*, S. Brookes and G. Winskel, Eds. Lecture Notes in Computer Science, vol. 197. Springer-Verlag, New York, 1985, pp. 389–448.
3. Biggs, N.L., Lloyd, E.K., and Wilson, R.J. *Graph Theory: 1736–1936.* Clarendon Press, Oxford, 1976.
4. Brachman, R.J. On the epistemological status of semantic networks. In *Associative Networks: Representation and Use of Knowledge by Computer*, N.V. Findler, Ed. Academic Press, New York, 1979, pp. 3–50.
5. Cardelli, L.A. Semantics of multiple inheritance in semantics of data types. Kahn. G. et al. Lecture Notes in Computer Science, vol. 173. Springer-Verlag, 1984, pp. 51–67.
6. Charniak, E., and McDermott, D. *Introduction to Artificial Intelligence.* Addison-Wesley, Reading, Mass., 1985.
7. Chen, P.P.-S. The entity-relationship model – toward a unified view of data. *ACM Trans. Database Syst. 1*, 1 (Mar. 1976). 9–36.
8. Conklin, J. Hypertext: An introduction and survey. *IEEE Computer 20*, 9 (Sept. 1987), 17–41.
9. Davis, P.J., Anderson, J.A. Nonanalytic aspects on mathematics and their implication on research and education. *SIAM Review 21*, 1 (Jan. 1979), 112–127.
10. dos Santos, C.S., Neuhold, E.J., and Furtado, A.L. A data type approach to the entity-relationship model. In *Entity-Relationship Approach to Systems Analysis and Design*, P.P. Chen, Ed. North-Holland, Amsterdam, 1980, pp. 103–119.
11. Dugundji, J. *Topology.* Allyn and Bacon, Boston, Mass., 1966.
12. Euler, L. Solutio problematis ad geometriam situs pertinentis. *Comm. Acad. Sci. Imp. Petropol. 8* (1736), 128–140.
13. Euler, L. *Lettres à une Princesse d'Allemagne.* Vol. 2. 1772 (letters 102–108).
14. Fagin, R. Degrees of acyclicity for hypergraphs and relational database schemes. *J. ACM 30*, 3(July 1983), 514–550.

15. Fagin, R., Mendelzon, A., and Ullman, J. A simplified universal relation assumption and its properties. *ACM Trans. Database Syst. 7*, 3 (Sept. 1982), 343–360.
16. al-Fedaghi, S.S. An entity-relationship approach to modelling petroleum engineering database. In *Entity-Relationship Approach to Software Engineering*, C.G. Davis et al., Eds. Elsevier Science Publishers, Amsterdam. 1983. pp. 761–779.
17. Findler, N.V., Ed. *Associative Networks: Representation and Use of Knowledge by Computer*. Academic Press, New York, 1979.
18. Fitter, M., and Green, T.R.G. When do diagrams make good computer languages? *Int. J. Man-Mach. Stud. 11*, 2 (March 1979). 235–261.
19. Gardner, M. *Logic Machines and Diagrams*. 2nd ed. University of Chicago Press, Chicago, Ill., 1982.
20. Green, T.R. Pictures of programs and other processes, or how to do things with lines. *Behav. Inf. Technol. 1*, 1 (1982), 3–36.
21. Harel, D. Statecharts: A visual formalism for complex systems. *Sci. Comput. Program. 8*, 3 (June 1987), 231–274.
22. Harel, D., and Pnueli, A. On the development of reactive systems. In *Logics and Models of Concurrent Systems*. NATO, ASI Series, vol. 13, K.R. Apt, Ed. Springer-Verlag, New York, 1985, pp. 477–498.
23. Harel, D., Pnueli, A., Schmidt, J.P., and Sherman, R. On the formal semantics of statecharts. In *Proceedings of the 2nd IEEE Symposium on Logic in Computer Science* (Ithaca, N.Y., June 22–24). IEEE Press, New York, 1987, pp. 54–64.
24. Harel, D., Lachover, H., Naamad, A., Pnueli, A., Politi, M., Sherman, R., and Shtul-Trauring, A. STATEMENT: A working environment for the development of complex reactive systems. In *Proceedings of the Tenth IEEE International Conference on Software Engineering* (Singapore, April 13–15). IEEE Press, New York, 1988. [Published by *IEEE Trans. Soft. Eng. 16* (1990), 403–414.]
25. Hendrix, G.G. Expanding the utility of semantic networks through partitioning. In *Proceedings of the 4th International Conference on Artificial Intelligence* (Tbilisi, Georgia, USSR, Sept. 3–8). International Joint Council on Artificial Intelligence, Cambridge, Mass., 1975, pp. 115–121.
26. Hoare, C.A.R. Communicating sequential processes. *Commun. ACM 21*, 8 (Aug. 1978), 666–677.
27. Hopcroft, J.E., and Ullman, J.D. *Introduction to Automata Theory, Languages, and Computation*. Addison-Wesley, Reading, Mass., 1979.
28. Harel, D., and Politi, M. *Modelling Reactive Systems with Statecharts: The STATEMATE Approach*, McGraw-Hill, New York, 1998. [Revised and published version of the technical report listed here originally.]
29. Kahana, C.A. Statecharts with overlapping states. M.S. thesis, Dept. of Mathematics and Computer Science, Bar-Ilan University, Ramat Gan, Israel, 1986 (in Hebrew). [Published in *ACM Trans. Soft. Eng. Method. 1* (1992), 399-421.]
30. Lefschetz, S. *Introduction to Topology*. Princeton University Press, Princeton, N.J., 1949.

31. Maier, D., and Ullman, J.D. Connections in acyclic hypergraphs. In *Proceedings of the ACM Symposium on Database Systems* (Los Angeles, Calif., March 29–31). ACM, New York, 1982, pp. 34–39.
32. Manna, Z., and Pnueli, A. Specification and verification of concurrent programs by ∀-automata. In *Proceedings of the 14th ACM Symposium on Principles of Programming Languages* (Munich). ACM, New York, 1987, pp. 1–12.
33. Martin, J., and McClure, C. *Diagramming Techniques for Analysts and Programmers.* Prentice-Hall, Englewood Cliffs, N.J., 1985.
34. McSkimin, J.R., and Minker, J. A predicate calculus based semantic network for deductive searching. In *Associative Networks: Representation and Use of Knowledge by Computer*, N.V. Findler, Ed. Academic Press, New York, 1979, pp. 205–238.
35. Milner, R. *A Calculus of Communicating Systems.* Lecture Notes in Computer Science, vol. 92. Springer-Verlag, New York, 1980.
36. Nakano, R. Integrity checking in a logic-oriented ER model. In *Entity-Relationship Approach to Software Engineering*, C.G. Davis et al., Eds. Elsevier Science Publishers, Amsterdam, 1983, pp. 551–564.
37. Nilsson, N.J. *Principles of Artificial Intelligence*, Tioga, Palo Alto, Calif., 1980.
38. Owicki, S., and Lamport, L. Proving liveness properties of concurrent programs. *ACM Trans. Program. Lang. Syst. 4*, 3 (July 1982), 455–495.
39. Pnueli, A. Applications of temporal logic to the specification and verification of reactive systems: A survey of current trends. In *Current Trends in Concurrency*, J.W. de Bakker et al., Eds. Lecture Notes in Computer Science, vol. 224, Springer-Verlag, New York, 1986, pp. 510–584.
40. Quillian, M.R. Semantic memory. In *Semantic Information Processing*, M. Minsky, Ed. MIT Press, Cambridge, Mass., 1968, pp. 227–270.
41. Reisig, W. *Petri Nets: An Introduction.* Springer-Verlag, Berlin, 1985.
42. Schiffner, G., and Schuermann, P. Multiple views and abstractions with an extended-entity-relationship model. *Comput. Lang. 4*, 3/4 (1979), 139–154.
43. Schmid, C.F. *Statistical Graphics: Design Principles and Practices.* Wiley, New York, 1983.
44. Shapiro, S.C. A net structure for semantic information storage, deduction, and retrieval. In *Proceedings of the 2nd International Joint Conference on Artificial Intelligence.* 1971, pp. 512–523.
45. Touretzky, D.S. *The Mathematics of Inheritance Systems.* Pitman, London, and Morgan Kaufmann, Los Altos, Calif. 1986.
46. Tufte, E.R. *The Visual Display of Quantitative Information.* Graphics Press, Cheshire, Conn., 1983.
47. Tygar, J.D., and Wing, J.M. Visual specification of security constraints. In *The IEEE Workshop on Visual Languages* (Linköping, Sweden, Aug. 19–21). IEEE Press, New York, 1987.
48. Venn, J. On the diagrammatic and mechanical representation of propositions and reasonings. *Phil. Mag.* (1880), 123.

49. Venn, J. *Symbolic Logic*, 2nd ed. London, 1894. (Reprinted by Chelsea, Bronx, N.Y., 1971.)
50. Woods, W.A. What's in a link? Foundations for semantic networks. In *Representation and Understanding*, D.G. Bobrow and A.M. Collins, Eds. Academic Press, New York, 1975, pp. 35–82.
51. Zave, P. A distributed alternative, to finite-state-machine specifications. *ACM Trans. Program. Lang. Syst.* 7, 1 (Jan. 1985), 10–36.

Glossary

Accreditation: The formal approval of an individual organization's services (e.g., a degree course at a university) by a *professional body* provided that certain specific criteria are met. Cf. *certification*.

Animation: The direct execution of a *specification* for *validation* purposes. This may not be possible in all cases, or may be possible for only part of the specification. Cf. *rapid prototype*.

Availability: A measure of the delivery of proper *service* with respect to the alternation of proper (desirable) and improper (undesirable) service.

Assertion: A *predicate* that should be true for some part of a program *state*.

CASE: Computer-Aided Software Engineering. A programming support environment for a particular method of software production supported by an integrated set of tools.

Class: A form of abstract data type in *object-oriented* programming.

Certification: The formal Indorsement of an individual by a *professional body* provided that certain specific criteria concerning education, training, experience, etc. are met. This is likely to be of increasing importance for personnel working on *high-integrity systems*, especially when *software* is involved. Cf. *accreditation*. The term is also applied to the rigorous demonstration or official written guarantee of a system meeting its *requirements*.

Code: *Executable program software* (normally as opposed to data on which the program operates).

Concurrent system: A *system* in which several processes, normally with communication between the processes, are active simultaneously. Cf. *distributed system*.

Deduction: A system of reasoning in a *logic*, following inference steps to arrive at a desired logical conclusion.

Dependability: A property of a computing system which allows reliance to be justifiably placed on the *service* it delivers. The combined aspects of *safety*, *reliability* and *availability* must normally be considered.

Design: The process of moving from a specification to an executable program, either *formally* or *informally*.

Development: The part of the *life-cycle* where the system is actually produced, before it is delivered to the customer. After this time, maintenance of the system is normally undertaken, and this is often far more costly than the originally development.

Distributed system: A system that is implemented on a number of physically separate computer systems, with communication, normally via a network. Cf. *concurrent system*.

Embedded system: A system in which the controlling computer forms an integral part of the system as a whole.

Emulation: A completely realistic imitation of a system by another different system that is indistinguishable from the original via some interface for all practical purposes. Cf. *simulation*.

Error: A mistake in the specification, design or operation of a system which may cause a *fault* to occur.

Executable specification: Thought by some to be an oxymoron, this is a high-level *formal specification* that can be *animated*.

Execution: The running of a *program* to perform some *operation*.

Failure: A condition or event in which a system is unable to perform one or more of its required functions due to a *fault* or *error*.

Fault: An undesirable system state than may result in a *failure*.

Fault avoidance: Prevention by construction of fault occurrence or introduction. For example, *formal methods* help in fault avoidance.

Fault tolerance: The provision by redundancy of a *service* complying with the specification in spite of faults. *N-version programming* is an example of fault tolerance.

Fault removal: The reduction by verification or testing of the presence of pre-existing faults.

Fault forecasting: The estimation by evaluation of the presence, creation and consequences of faults.

Formal methods: Techniques, notations and tools with a mathematical basis, used for *specification* and reasoning in *software* or *hardware* system *development*. The Z notation for *formal specification*) and the B-Method (for formal development) are leading examples of formal methods.

Formal notation: A language with a mathematical semantics, used for *formal specification*, reasoning and *proof*.

Formal specification: A *specification* written in a *formal notation*, potentially for use in *proof of correctness*.

Genericity: A program unit that can accept parameters that are types and subprograms as well as variables and values. Cf. *polymorphism*.

Hardware: The physical part of a computer system. Cf. *software*.

Glossary 661

HCI: The means of communication between a human user or operator and a computer-based system.

High-integrity system: A system that must be trusted to work dependably and may result in unacceptable loss or harm otherwise. This includes *safety-critical systems* and other critical systems where, for example, *security* or financial considerations may be paramount.

Hybrid system: A system which includes a combination of both analogue and digital (e.g., a controlling computer) aspects.

Implementation: An efficiently executable version of a *specification* produced through a *design* process.

Informal: An indication of an absence of mathematical underpinning. E.g., cf. an informal notation like English or diagrams with a *formal notation* like Z.

Information hiding: The encapsulation of data within program components or *modules*, originally proposed by David Parnas, and now widely accepted as a good *object-oriented* programming development principle.

Integrity: A system's ability to avoid undesirable alteration due to the presence of errors.

Life-cycle: The complete lifetime of a system from its original conception to its eventual obsolescence. Typically phases of the life-cycle include *requirements, specification, design,* coding, testing, integration, commissioning, operation, maintenance, decommissioning, etc.

Logic: A scheme for reasoning, *proof,* inference, etc. Two common schemes are propositional logic and *predicate logic* which is propositional logic generalized with quantifiers. Other logics, such a modal logics, including *temporal logics* which handle time – e.g., Temporal Logic of Actions (TLA), Interval Temporal Logic (ITL) and more recently Duration Calculus (DC) – are also available. Schemes may use first-order logic or higher-order logic. In the former, functions are not allowed on predicates, simplifying matters somewhat, but in the latter they are, providing greater power. Logics include a calculus which allows reasoning in the logic.

Method integration: The combination of two or more techniques or notations to improve the development process by benefits from the strengths of each. Typically the approaches may be a combination of *formal* and informal methods.

Methodology: The study of methods. Also sometimes used to mean a set of related methods.

Model: A representation of a system – for example, an abstract *state* of the system and a set of *operations* on that state. The model may not cover all the features of the actual system being modeled.

Module: A structuring technique for programs, etc., allowing the breakdown of a system into smaller parts with well-defined interfaces.

N-version programming: The *implementation* of several programs from a common *specification* with the aim of reducing *faults*. Any variation in the operation of programs points to *errors* that can than be corrected. Also known as *diverse programming*.

Object-oriented: An approach where all component parts (e.g., processes, files, operations, etc.) are considered as objects. Messages may be passed between objects. See also *classes* and *information hiding*.

Operation: The performance of some desired action. This may involve the change of state of a system, together with inputs to the operation and outputs resulting from the operation. To specify such an operation, the *before state* (and inputs) and the *after state* (and outputs) must be related with constraining predicates.

Polymorphism: A high-level programming language feature allowing arguments to procedures and functions to act on a whole *class* of data types rather that just a single type. Cf. *genericity*.

Postcondition: An *assertion* (e.g., a *predicate*) describing the *state* after an *operation*, normally in terms of the state before the operation. Cf. *precondition*.

Precondition: An *assertion* (e.g., a *predicate*) which must hold on the *state* before an *operation* for it to be successful. Cf. *postcondition*.

Predicate: A constraint between a number of variables which produces a truth value (e.g., *true* or *false*). Predicate *logic* extends the simpler propositional logic with quantifiers allowing statements over potentially infinite numbers of objects (e.g., all, some).

Professional body: A (normally national or international) organization that members of a particular profession (e.g., engineers) may join. *Accreditation, certification* and *standards* are activities in which such organizations are involved. Examples include the Association of Computing Machinery (ACM) and the Institute of Electrical and Electronics Engineers (IEEE), based in the USA but with international membership, and the British Computer Society (BCS) and the Institution of Electrical Engineers (IEE), based in the UK.

Program: A particular piece of *software* (either a programming language or its matching executable machine *code*) to perform one or more *operations*.

Proof: A series of mathematical steps forming an argument of the correctness of a mathematical statement or theorem using some *logic*. For example, the *validation* of a desirable property for a formal specification could undertaken by proving it correct. Proof may also be used to perform a formal *verification* or 'proof of correctness' that an implementation meets a specification. A less formal style of reasoning is *rigorous argument*, where a proof outline is sketched informally, which may be done if the effort of undertaking a fully formal proof is not considered cost-effective.

Provably correct systems: A system that has been formally specified and implemented may be proven correct by demonstrating a mathematical relationship between the specification and the implementation in which the implementation is 'better' in some sense (e.g., more deterministic, terminates more often, etc.) with respect to some set of *refinement* laws.

Rapid prototype: A quickly produced and inefficient implementation of a *specification* that can be executed for *validation* purposes. Cf. *animation*.

Real-time: A system where the timing aspects are important (e.g., the timing of external events is of comparable time to that of the computation undertaken by the controlling computer) is known as a real-time system.

Refinement: The stepwise transformation of a specification towards an implementation (e.g., as a program). Cf. *abstraction*, where unnecessary implementation detail is ignored in a specification.

Reliability: A measure of the continuous delivery of proper *service* (where service is delivered according to specified conditions) or equivalently of the time to failure.

Requirements: A statement of the desired properties for an overall system. This may be formal or informal, but should normally be as concise and easily understandable as possible.

Rigorous argument: An informal line of reasoning that could be formalized as a *proof* (given time). This level of checking may be sufficient and much more cost-effective than a fully formal proof for many systems.

Risk: An event or action with an associated loss where uncertainty or chance together with some choice are involved.

Safety: A measure of the continuous delivery of a *service* free from occurrences of catastrophic failures.

Safety-critical system: A system where failure may result in injury or loss of life. Cf. *high-integrity system*.

Safety-related: A system that is not necessarily safety-critical, but nevertheless where safety is involved, is sometimes called a *safety-related system*.

Security: Control of access to or updating of data so that only those with the correct authority may perform permitted operations. Normally the data represents sensitive information.

Service: The provision of one or more *operations* for use by humans or other computer systems.

Simulation: The imitation of (part of) a system. A simulation may not be perfect; for example, it may not run in *real-time*. Cf. *emulation*.

Software: The programs executed by a computer system. Cf. *hardware*.

Specification: A description of *what* a system is intended to do, as opposed to *how* it does it. A specification may be *formal* (mathematical) or *informal* (natural language, diagrams, etc.). Cf. an *implementation* of a specification, such as a program, that actually performs and executes the actions required by a specification.

Standard: An agreed document or set of documents produced by an official body designed to be adhered to by a number of users or developers (or an associated product) with the aim of overall improvement and compatibility. Standards bodies include the International Organization for Standardization (ISO), based in Switzerland but with international authority, and the American National Standards Institute (ANSI), based in the USA.

State: A representation of the possible values that a system may have. In an abstract specification, this may be modeled as a number of sets. By contrast, in a concrete program implementation, the state typically consists of a number of data structures, such as arrays, files, etc. When modeling sequential systems, each operation may include a *before state* and an *after state* which are related by some constraining predicates. The system will also have an *initial state*, normally with some additional constraints, from which the system starts at initialization.

Structured notation: A notation to aid in system analysis. A structured approach aims to limit the number of constructs available to those that allow easy and hence convincing reasoning.

System: A particular entity or collection of related components under consideration.

Temporal logic: A form of modal *logic* that includes operators specifically to deal with timing aspects (e.g., always, sometimes, etc.).

Validation: The checking of a system (e.g., its specification) to ensure it meets its (normally informal) requirements. This helps to ensure that the system does what is expected by the customer, but may be rather subjective. *Animation* or *rapid prototyping* may help in this process (e.g., as a demonstration to the customer). *Proof* of expected properties of a *formal specification* is another worthwhile approach. Cf. *verification*.

Verification: The checking of an implementation to ensure it meets its specification. This may be done formally (e.g., by *proof*) or information (e.g., by testing). This helps to ensure that the system does what has been specified in an objective manner, but does not help ensure that the original specification is correct. Cf. *validation*.

Bibliography

1. M. Abadi & L. Lamport (1993) Composing Specifications. *ACM Transactions on Programming Languages and Systems (TOPLAS)*, 15(1):73–132.
2. J-R. Abrial (1996) *The B Book: Assigning Programs to Meanings.* Cambridge University Press.
3. J-R. Abrial, E. Börger and H. Langmaack (1996) *Formal Methods for Industrial Applications.* Springer-Verlag, Lecture Notes in Computer Science, volume 1165.
4. G.R. Andrews & F.B. Scheider (1983) Concepts and Notations for Concurrent Programming. *ACM Computing Surveys*, 15(1), March 1983. Reprinted in [267], Chapter 2, pp 29–84.
5. S. Aujla, A. Bryant & L. Semmens (1993) A Rigorous Review Technique: Using Formal Notations within Conventional Development Methods. In *Proc. 1993 Software Engineering Standards Symposium (SESS'93)*, IEEE Computer Society Press, pp 247–255.
6. R. Ayres (1999) *The Essence of Professional Issues in Computing.* Prentice Hall, Essence of Computing series, Hemel Hempstead.
7. L. Baresi & M. Pezzè (1998) Towards Formalizing Structured Analysis. *ACM Transactions on Software Engineering and Methology (TOSEM)*, 7(1):80–107, January 1998.
8. J.G.P. Barnes (1997) High Integrity Ada – The SPARK approach. Addison-Wesley.
9. L. Barroca & J.A. McDermid (1992) Formal Methods: Use and Relevance for the Development of Safety Critical Systems. *The Computer Journal*, 35(6):579–599, December 1992.
10. BCS (1996) High Integrity Real-Time Software. Report of the Foresight Defence and Aerospace Panel, British Computer Society, UK.
11. BCS (1998) Licensed to Work. *The Computer Bulletin*, p 18, November 1998.
12. R. Bell & D. Reinert (1993) Risk and System Integrity Concepts for Safety-related Control Systems. *Microprocessors and Microsystems*, 17(1):3–15, January/February 1993.
13. C. Bernardeschi, A. Fantechi, S. Gnesi, S. Larosa, G. Mongardi & D. Romano (1998) A Formal Verification Environment for Railway Signaling System Design. *Formal Methods in System Design*, 12(2):139–161, March 1998.
14. T. Berners-Lee (1996) World Wide Web Past Present and Future. *IEEE Computer*, 29(10):69–77, October 1996.
15. D. Bert, editor (1998) *B'98: Recent Advances in the Development and Use of the B Method.* Springer-Verlag, Lecture Notes in Computer Science, volume 1393.
16. R. Bharadwaj & C. Heitmeyer (1997) *Model Checking Complete Requirements Specifications Using Abstraction.* Technical Report NRL/MR/5540--97-7999, Center for High Assurance Systems, Information Technology Division, Naval Research Laboratory, Washington, DC 20375-5320, USA, November 1997.
17. J.C. Bicarregui (1998) *Proof in VDM: Case Studies.* Springer-Verlag, Formal Approaches to Computing and Information Technology (FACIT) series, London.

18. B.W. Boehm (1975) The High Cost of Software. In E. Horowitz, editor, *Practical Strategies for Developing Large Software Systems*, Addison-Wesley, London.
19. B.W. Boehm (1981) *Software Engineering Economics*, Prentice Hall, Hemel Hempstead and Englewood Cliffs.
20. B.W. Boehm (1988) A Sprial Model of Software Development and Maintenance. *IEEE Computer*, 21(5):61–72, May 1988.
21. E.A. Boiten, H.A. Partsch, D. Tuijnman & N. Völker (1992) How to Produce Correct Software – An Introduction to Formal Specification and Program Development by Transformations. *The Computer Journal*, 35(6):547–554, December 1992.
22. * G. Booch (1986) Object-Oriented Development. *IEEE Transactions on Software Engineering*, 12(2):211–221, February 1986.
(See page 237 in this collection.)
23. G. Booch (1994) *Object-Oriented Analysis and Design with Applications*, 2nd edition. Addison Wesley Longman, Object Technology Series.
24. G. Booch (1996) *Object Solutions: Managing the Object-Oriented Project*. Addison Wesley Longman, Object Technology Series.
25. G. Booch, J. Rumbaugh & I. Jacobson (1999) *The Unified Modeling Language User Guide*. Addison Wesley Longman, Object Technology Series.
26. J.P. Bowen (1993) Formal Methods in Safety-Critical Standards. In *Proc. 1993 Software Engineering Standards Symposium (SESS'93)*, IEEE Computer Society, pp 168–177.
27. J.P. Bowen, editor (1994) *Towards Verified Systems*, Elsevier, Real-Time Safety Critical Systems, Volume 2, 1994.
28. J.P. Bowen (1996) *Formal Specification and Documentation using Z: A Case Study Approach*. International Thomson Computer Press, International Thomson Publishing, London.
29. J.P. Bowen (1997) The Ethics of Safety-Critical Systems. In D. Gritzalis & T. Anderson, editors, *Reliability, Quality and Safety of Software-Intensive Systems: Application experiences, trends and perspectives, and key theoretical issues*. European Commission ESPRIT/ESSI Programme ENCRESS (21542) Project, pp 253–267. Revised version to appear in *Communications of the ACM*.
30. J.P. Bowen, P.T. Breuer & K.C. Lano (1993) Formal Specifications in Software Maintenance: From code to Z^{++} and back again. *Information and Software Technology*, 35(11/12):679–690, November/December 1993.
31. J.P. Bowen, R.W. Butler, D.L. Dill, R.L. Glass, D. Gries, J.A. Hall, M.G. Hinchey, C.M. Holloway, D. Jackson, C.B. Jones, M.J. Lutz, D.L. Parnas, J. Rushby, H. Saiedian, J. Wing & P. Zave (1996) An Invitation to Formal Methods. *IEEE Computer*, 29(4):16–30, April 1996.
32. J.P. Bowen, A. Fett & M.G. Hinchey, editors (1998) *ZUM'98: The Z Formal Specification Notation*. Springer-Verlag, Lecture Notes in Computer Science, volume 1493.
33. J.P. Bowen, M. Fränzle, E-R. Olderog & A.P. Ravn (1993) Developing Correct Systems. In *Proc. Fifth Euromicro Workshop on Real-Time Systems*, Oulu, Finland, 22–24 June 1993. IEEE Computer Society Press, pp 176–187.
34. J.P. Bowen & T. Gleeson (1990) Distributed Operating Systems. In [267], Chapter 1, pp 3–28.
35. J.P. Bowen & J.A. Hall, editors (1994) *Z User Meeting, Cambridge 1994*, Springer-Verlag, Workshops in Computing.
36. J.P. Bowen, He Jifeng, R.W.S. Hale & J.M.J. Herbert (1995) Towards Verified Systems: The SAFEMOS Project. In C. Mitchell and V. Stavridou, editors, *Mathematics of Dependable Systems*, Clarendon Press, Oxford, pp 23–48.
37. J.P. Bowen & M.G. Hinchey (1994) Formal Methods and Safety-Critical Standards. *IEEE Computer*, 27(8):68–71, August 1994.

38. * J.P. Bowen & M.G. Hinchey (1995) Ten Commandments of Formal Methods. *IEEE Computer*, 28(4):56–63, April 1995.
    (See page 217 in this collection.)
39. * J.P. Bowen & M.G. Hinchey (1995) Seven More Myths of Formal Methods. *IEEE Software*, 12(4):34–41, July 1995.
    (See page 153 in this collection.)
40. J.P. Bowen & M.G. Hinchey, editors (1995) *ZUM'95: The Z Formal Specification Notation*. Springer-Verlag, Lecture Notes in Computer Science, volume 967.
41. J.P. Bowen & M.G. Hinchey (1997) Formal Models and the Specification Process. In [246], Chapter 107, pp 2302–2322.
42. J.P. Bowen, M.G. Hinchey & D. Till, editors (1997) *ZUM'97: The Z Formal Specification Notation*. Springer-Verlag, Lecture Notes in Computer Science, volume 1212.
43. J.P. Bowen, C.A.R. Hoare, H. Langmaack, E-R. Olderog and A.P. Ravn (1996) A ProCoS II Project Final Report: ESPRIT Basic Research project 7071. *Bulletin of the European Association for Theoretical Computer Science (EATCS)*, 59:76–99, June 1996.
44. J.P. Bowen & J.E. Nicholls, editors (1993) *Z User Workshop, London 1992*, Springer-Verlag, Workshops in Computing.
45. J.P. Bowen & V. Stavridou (1993) The Industrial Take-up of Formal Methods in Safety-Critical and Other Areas: A Perspective. In [259], pp 183–195.
46. * J.P. Bowen & V. Stavridou (1993) Safety-Critical Systems, Formal Methods and Standards. *Software Engineering Journal*, 8(4):189–209, July 1993.
    (See page 485 in this collection.)
47. J.P. Bowen & V. Stavridou (1994) Formal Methods: Epideictic or Apodeictic? *Software Engineering Journal*, 9(1):2, January 1994 (Personal View).
48. R.S. Boyer & J.S. Moore (1988) *A Computational Logic Handbook*. Academic Press, London.
49. P.T. Breuer & J.P. Bowen (1994) Towards Correct Executable Semantics for Z. In [35], pp 185–209.
50. * F.P. Brooks, Jr. (1987) No Silver Bullet: Essence and Accidents of Software Engineering. *IEEE Computer*, 20(4):10–19, April 1987. Originally published in H.-J. Kugler, editor (1986) *Information Processing '86*, Proc. IFIP Congress, Dublin, Ireland, Elsevier Science Publishers B.V. (North-Holland).
    (See page 11 in this collection.)
51. F.P. Brooks, Jr. (1995) *The Mythical Man-Month: Essays on Software Engineering*, 20th anniversary edition. Addison-Wesley, Reading, Massachusetts.
52. S.D. Brookes, C.A.R. Hoare & A.W. Roscoe (1984) A Theory of Communicating Sequential Processes. *Journal of the Association for Computing Machinery*, 31:560–599, 1984.
53. A. Bryant & L. Semmens, editors (1996) *Methods Integration*, Proc. Methods Integration Workshop, Leeds, 25–26 March 1996. Springer-Verlag, Electronic Workshops in Computing.
    URL: *http://www.springer.co.uk/ewic/workshops/MI96/*
54. R.W. Butler & G.B. Finelli (1993) The Infeasibility of Experimental Quantification of Life Critical Software Reliability. *IEEE Transactions on Software Engineering*, 19(1):3–12, January 1993.
55. * J.R. Cameron (1986) An Overview of JSD. *IEEE Transactions on Software Engineering*, 12(2):222–240, February 1986.
    (See page 77 in this collection.)
56. CCTA (1990) *SSADM Version 4 Reference Manual*, NCC Blackwell Ltd.
57. * E.J. Chikofsky & B.L. Rubenstein (1988) CASE: Reliability Engineering for Information Systems. *IEEE Software*, 5(2):11–16, March 1988.
    (See page 613 in this collection.)

58. E. Clarke, J. Wing *et al.* (1996) Formal Methods: State of the Art and Future Directions. *ACM Computing Surveys*, 28(4):626–643, December 1996.
59. R. Cleaveland, S.A. Smolka *et al.* (1996) Strategic Directions in Concurrency Research. *ACM Computing Surveys*, 28(4):607–625, December 1996.
60. P. Coad & E. Yourdon (1991) *Object Oriented Design*, Yourdon Press/Prentice Hall, New York.
61. D. Coleman, P. Arnold, S. Bodoff, C. Dollin, H. Gilchrist, F. Hayes amd P. Jeremaes. *Object-Oriented Development: The Fusion Method*. Prentice Hall, Object-Oriented Series, Hemel Hempstead.
62. J. Cooke (1998) *Constructing Correct Software: The basics*. Springer-Verlag, Formal Approaches to Computing and Information Technology (FACIT) series, London.
63. D. Craigen, S. Gerhart & T. Ralston (1993) *An International Survey of Industrial Applications of Formal Methods*. NIST GCR 93/626, Atomic Energy Control Board of Canada, U.S. National Institute of Standards and Technology, and U.S. Naval Research Laboratories, 1993.
64. J. Crow & B. Di Vito (1998) Formalizing Space Shuttle Software Requirements: Four Case Studies. *ACM Transactions on Software Engineering and Methology (TOSEM)*, 7(3):296–332, July 1998.
65. C.N. Dean & M.G. Hinchey, editors (1996) *Teaching and Learning Formal Methods*. Academic Press, International Series in Formal Methods, London.
66. B. Dehbonei & F. Mejia (1994) Formal Methods in the Railway Signalling Industry. In M. Naftalin, T. Denvir & M. Bertran, editors, *FME'94: Industrial Benefit of Formal Methods*, Springer-Verlag, Lecture Notes in Computer Science, volume 873, pp 26–34.
67. T. DeMarco (1978) *Structured Analysis and System Specification*. Yourdon Press, New York.
68. J. Dick & E. Woods (1997) Lessons Learned from Rigorous System Software Development. *Information and Software Technology*, 39(8):551–560, August 1997.
69. E.W. Dijkstra (1968) Goto Statement Considered Harmful, *Communications of the ACM*, 11(3):147–148 (Letter to the Editor).
70. E.W. Dijkstra (1981) Why Correctness must be a Mathematical Concern. In R.S. Boyer & J.S. Moore, editors, *The Correctness Problem in Computer Science*, Academic Press, London, pp 1–6.
71. A. Dix, J. Finlay, G. Abowd & R. Beale (1998) *Human-Computer Interaction*, 2nd edition. Prentice Hall, Hemel Hempstead & Englewood Cliffs.
URL: *http://www.hiraeth.com/books/hci/*
72. C. Draper (1993) Practical Experiences of Z and SSADM. In [44], pp 240–254.
73. M. Dyer (1992) *The Cleanroom Approach to Quality Software Development*, John Wiley & Sons, Series in Software Engineering Practice.
74. S. Easterbrook & J. Callahan (1998) Formal Methods for Verification and Validation of Partial Specifications: A case study. *Journal of Systems and Software*, 40(3):199–210, March 1998.
75. The Economist (1997) Fasten your Safety Belts. *The Economist*, pp 69–71, 11–17 January 1997.
76. H.-E. Eriksson & M. Penker (1998) *UML Toolkit*. Wiley Computer Publishing, New York.
77. S.R. Faulk (1995) *Software Requirements: A Tutorial*. Technical Report NRL/MR/-5546--95-7775, Center for High Assurance Systems, Information Technology Division, Naval Research Laboratory, Washington, DC 20375-5320, USA, November 1995.
78. * R.G. Fichman & C.F. Kemerer (1992) Object-Oriented and Conventional Analysis and Design Methodologies: Comparison and Critique. *IEEE Computer*, 25(10):22–39, October 1992.
(See page 261 in this collection.)

79. J.S. Fitzgerald, P.G. Larsen, T. Brookes & M. Green (1995) Developing a Security-Critical System Using Formal and Conventional Methods. In [125], Chapter 14, pp 333–356.
80. R. France, A. Evans & K.C. Lano (1997) The UML as a Formal Modeling Notation. In H. Kilov, B. Rumpe & I. Simmonds, editors, *Proc. OOPSLA'97 Workshop on Object-Oriented Behavioral Semantics (with an Emphasis on Semantics of Large OO Business Specifications)*, TUM-I9737, Institut für Informatik, Technische Universität München, Munich, Germany, pp 75–81, September 1997.
81. M.D. Fraser, K. Kumar & V.K. Vaishnavi (1994) Strategies for Incorporating Formal Specifications in Software Development. *Communications of the ACM*, 37(10):74–86, October 1994.
82. M.D. Fraser & V.K. Vaishnavi (1997) A Formal Specifications Maturity Model. *Communications of the ACM*, 40(12):95–103, December 1997.
83. V. Friesen, Nordwig & M. Weber (1998) Object-Oriented Specification of Hybrid Systems Using UML^h and ZimOO. In [32], pp 328–346.
84. * N.E. Fuchs (1992) Specifications are (Preferably) Executable. *Software Engineering Journal*, 7(5):323–334, September 1992.
(See page 583 in this collection.)
85. N.E. Fuchs, editor (1997) Logic Program Synthesis and Transformation, Springer-Verlag, Lecture Notes in Computer Science, volume 1463.
86. D. Garlan (1995) Making Formal Methods Effective for Professional Software Engineers. *Information and Software Technology*, 37(5/6):261–268, May/June 1995.
87. D. Garlan (1996) Effective Formal Methods Education for Professional Software Engineers. In [65], Chapter 2, pp 11–29.
88. D. Garlan, R. Allen & J. Ockerbloom (1995) Architectural Mismatch: Why Reuse is So Hard. *IEEE Software*, 12(6):17–26, November 1995.
89. C. Gaskell & A.A. Takang (1996) Professional Issues in Software Engineering: The Perspective of UK Academics. *IEE Computing & Control Engineering Journal*, 7(6)287–293.
90. * S. Gerhart, D. Craigen & T. Ralston (1994) Experience with Formal Methods in Critical Systems, *IEEE Software*, 11(1):21–28, January 1994.
(See page 413 in this collection.)
91. * S. Gerhart, D. Craigen & T. Ralston (1994) Regulatory Case Studies, *IEEE Software*, 11(1):30–39, January 1994.
(See page 429 in this collection.)
92. W.W. Gibbs (1994) Software's Chronic Crisis. *Scientific American*, 271(3):86–95, September 1994.
93. G.R. Gladden (1982) Stop the Life Cycle – I Want to Get Off. *ACM Software Engineering Notes*, 7(2):35–39.
94. J.A. Goguen & T. Winkler (1988) *Introducing OBJ3*, Technical Report SRI-CSL-88-9, SRI International, Melo Park, CA, August 1988.
95. J.A. Goguen (1981) More Thoughts on Specification and Verification. *ACM SIGSOFT*, 6(3):38–41.
96. H. Gomaa (1993) *Software Design Methods for Concurrent and Real-Time Systems*, Addison-Wesley, Reading, Massachusetts.
97. D. Gotterbarn, K. Miller & S. Rogerson (1997) Software Engineering Code of Ethics. *Communications of the ACM*, 40(11):110–118, November 1997.
98. J.N. Gray (1986) An Approach to Decentralized Computer Systems. *IEEE Transactions on Software Engineering*, SE-12(6):684–692, June 1986.
99. D. Gries & F.B. Schneider (1993) *A Logical Approach to Discrete Math*. Springer-Verlag, New York.
100. K. Grimm (1998) Industrial Requirements for the Efficient Development of Reliable Embedded Systems. In [32], pp 1–4.

101. D. Gritzalis, editor (1997) *Reliability, Quality and Safety of Software-Intensive Systems*. Chapman & Hall, London, on behalf of the International Federation for Information Processing (IFIP).
102. R.L. Grossman, A. Nerode, A.P. Ravn & H. Rischel, editors (1993) *Hybrid Systems*. Springer-Verlag, Lecture Notes in Computer Science, volume 736.
103. J.V. Guttag & J.J. Horning (1993) *Larch: Languages and Tools for Formal Specification*, Springer-Verlag, Texts and Monographs in Computer Science, New York.
104. W.A. Halang & A.D. Stoyenko (1991) *Constructing Predictable Real Time Systems*. Kluwer Academic Publishers, Boston.
105. * J.A. Hall (1990) Seven Myths of Formal Methods. *IEEE Software*, 7(5):11–19, September 1990.
(See page 135 in this collection.)
106. J.A. Hall (1996) Using Formal Methods to Develop an ATC Information System. *IEEE Software*, 13(2):66–76, March 1996.
107. D. Harel (1987) Statecharts: a Visual Formalism for Complex Systems. *Science of Computer Programming*, 8(3):231–274, June 1987.
108. * D. Harel (1988) On Visual Formalisms. *Communications of the ACM*, 31(5):514–530, May 1988.
(See page 623 in this collection.)
109. * D. Harel (1992) Biting the Silver Bullet: Toward a Brighter Future for System Development. *IEEE Computer*, 25(1):8–20, January 1992.
(See page 29 in this collection.)
110. D. Harel & A. Haamad (1996) The STATEMATE Semantics of Statecharts. *ACM Transactions on Software Engineering and Methology (TOSEM)*, 5(4):293–333, October 1996.
111. D. Harel & M. Politi (1998) *Modeling Reactive Systems with Statecharts: The STATEMATE Approach*. McGraw-Hill, London & New York.
112. M.D. Harrison (1992) Engineering Human Error Tolerant Software. In [194], pp 191–204.
113. L. Hatton (1995) *Safer C: Developing for High-Integrity and Safety-Critical Systems*. McGraw-Hill International Series in Software Engineering, London & New York.
114. L. Hatton (1997) Software Failures – Follies and Fallacies. *IEE Review*, 43(2):49–52.
115. H. Haughton & K.C. Lano (1996) *Specification in B: An Introduction Using the B Toolkit*. World Scientific Publishing Company, Imperial College Press, London.
116. The Hazards Forum (1995) *Safety-Related Systems: Guidance for Engineers*. The Hazards Forum, 1 Great George Street, London SW1P 4AA, UK.
URL: *http://www.iee.org.uk/PAB/safe_rel.htm*
117. * I.J. Hayes & C.B. Jones (1989) Specifications are not (Necessarily) Executable. *Software Engineering Journal*, 4(6):330–338, November 1989.
(See page 563 in this collection.)
118. He Jifeng (1995) *Provably Correct Systems: Modelling of Communication Languages and Design of Optimized Compilers*. McGraw-Hill, International Series on Software Engineering, London & New York.
119. C. Heitmeyer (1997) Formal Methods: A Panacea or Academic Poppycock? In [42], pp 3–9.
120. C. Heitmeyer & D. Mandrioli, editors (1996) *Formal Methods for Real-Time Computing*. John Wiley & Sons, Trends in Software.
121. S. Hekmatpour & D.C. Ince (1989) *System Prototyping, Formal Methods and VDM*, Addison-Wesley, Reading, Massachusetts.
122. A. Heydon, M. Maimone, J.D. Tygar, J. Wing & A.M. Zaremski (1990) Miró: Visual Specification of Security. *IEEE Transactions on Software Engineering*, 16(10):1185–1197, October 1990.

123. J.V. Hill (1991) Software Development Methods in Practice, In A. Church, editor, *Microprocessor Based Protection Systems*, Routledge.
124. M.G. Hinchey (1993) The Design of Real-Time Applications. In *Proc. RTAW'93, 1st IEEE Workshop on Real-Time Applications*, New York City, 13–14 May 1993, IEEE Computer Society Press, pp 178–182.
125. M.G. Hinchey & J.P. Bowen, editors (1995) *Applications of Formal Methods*. Prentice Hall International Series in Computer Science, Hemel Hempstead & Englewood Cliffs.
126. M.G. Hinchey & S.A. Jarvis (1994) Simulating Concurrent Systems with Formal Methods. In *Proc. WMC'94, Winter Multiconference of the Society for Computer Simulation*, Tempe, Arizona, January 1994.
127. M.G. Hinchey & S.A. Jarvis (1995) *Concurrent Systems: Formal Development in CSP*. McGraw-Hill International Series in Software Engineering, London & New York.
128. * C.A.R. Hoare (1978) Communicating Sequential Processes, *Communications of the ACM*, 21(8):666–677, August 1978.
(See page 303 in this collection.)
129. C.A.R. Hoare (1985) *Communicating Sequential Processes*. Prentice Hall International Series in Computer Science, Hemel Hempstead & Englewood Cliffs.
130. * C.A.R. Hoare (1987) An Overview of Some Formal Methods for Program Design. *IEEE Computer*, 20(9):85–91, September 1987.
(See page 201 in this collection.)
131. C.A.R. Hoare (1995) Algebra and Models. In [118], Chapter 1, pp 1–14.
132. C.A.R. Hoare (1996) How did Software get so Reliable Without Proof? In M-C. Gaudel & J. Woodcock, editors, *FME'96: Industrial Benefit and Advances in Formal Methods*, Springer-Verlag, Lecture Notes in Computer Science, volume 1051, pp 1–17.
133. C.A.R. Hoare (1996) The Logic of Engineering Design. *Microprocessing and Microprogramming*, 41(8–9):525–539.
134. C.A.R. Hoare & He Jifeng (1998) *Unifying Theories of Programming*. Prentice Hall International Series in Computer Science, Hemel Hempstead and Englewood Cliffs.
135. G.J. Holzmann (1996) Formal Methods for Early Fault Detection. In B. Jonsson & J. Parrow, editors, *Formal Techniques in Real-Time Fault-Tolerant Systems*, Springer-Verlag, Lecture Notes in Computer Science, volume 1135, pp 40–54.
136. G.J. Holzmann (1997) The Model Checker Spin. *IEEE Transactions on Software Engineering*. 23(5):279–295, May 1997.
137. M.E.C. Hull, A. Zarea-Aliabadi & D.A. Guthrie (1989) Object-Oriented Design, Jackson System Development (JSD) Specifications and Concurrency, *Software Engineering Journal*, 4(3), March 1989.
138. D.C. Ince (1992) Arrays and Pointers Considered Harmful. *ACM SIGPLAN Notices*, 27(1):99–104, January 1992.
139. Inmos Ltd. (1988) *Occam2 Reference Manual*, Prentice Hall International Series in Computer Science, Hemel Hempstead and Englewood Cliffs.
140. International Standards Organization (1989) *Information processing systems – Open Systems Interconnection – LOTOS – A formal description technique based on the temporal ordering of observational behaviour*, Document Number ISO 8807:1989. URL: http://www.iso.ch/cate/d16258.html
141. International Standards Organization (1996) *Information technology – Programming languages, their environments and system software interfaces – Vienna Development Method – Specification Language – Part 1: Base language*, Document Number ISO/IEC 13817-1:1996. URL: http://www.iso.ch/cate/d22988.html
142. M.A. Jackson (1975) *Principles of Program Design*, Academic Press, London.
143. M.A. Jackson (1983) *System Development*. Prentice Hall International Series in Computer Science, Hemel Hempstead and Englewood Cliffs.
144. J. Jacky (1995) Specifying a Safety-Critical Control System in Z. *IEEE Transactions on Software Engineering*, 21(2):99–106, February 1995.

145. J. Jacky (1997) *The Way of Z: Practical Programming with Formal Methods*. Cambridge University Press.
146. C.B. Jones (1991) *Systematic Software Development Using VDM*, 2nd edition. Prentice Hall International Series in Computer Science, Hemel Hempstead and Englewood Cliffs.
147. M. Joseph, editor (1996) *Real-Time Systems: Specification, Verification and Analysis*. Prentice Hall International Series in Computer Science, Hemel Hempstead and Englewood Cliffs.
148. R.A. Kemmerer (1990) Integrating Formal Methods into the Development Process. *IEEE Software*, 7(5):37–50, September 1990.
149. J.C. Knight & D.M. Kienzle (1993) Preliminary Experience Using Z to Specify a Safety-Critical System. In [44], pp 109–118.
150. J. Knight & B. Littlewood (1994) Critical Task of Writing Dependable Software. *IEEE Software*, 11(1):16–20, January 1994.
151. L. Lamport (1978) Time, Clocks and the Ordering of Events in a Distributed System. *Communications of the ACM*, 21(7):558–565, July 1978.
152. * L. Lamport (1989) A Simple Approach to Specifying Concurrent Systems. *Communications of the ACM*, 32(1):32–45, January 1989.
    (See page 331 in this collection.)
153. L. Lamport (1994) The Temporal Logic of Actions. *ACM Transactions on Programming Languages and Systems (TOPLAS)*, 16(3):872–923, May 1994.
154. L. Lamport (1994) *LaTeX: A Document Preparation System User's Guide and Reference Manual*, Addison-Wesley, Reading, Massachusetts.
155. H. Langmaack (1997) The ProCoS Approach to Correct Systems. *Real-Time Systems*, 13:253–275.
156. K.C. Lano (1996) *The B Language and Method: A Guide to Practical Formal Development*. Springer-Verlag, Formal Approaches to Computing and Information Technology (FACIT) series, London.
157. K.C. Lano (1996) *Formal Object-Oriented Development*. Springer-Verlag, Formal Approaches to Computing and Information Technology (FACIT) series, London.
158. K.C. Lano & J. Bicarregui (1998) Formalising the UML in Structured Temporal Theories. In H. Kilov & B. Rumpe, editors, *Proc. Second ECOOP Workshop on Precise Behavioral Semantics (with an Emphasis on OO Business Specifications)*, TUM-I9813, Institut für Informatik, Technische Universität München, Munich, Germany, pp 105–121, June 1998.
159. K.C. Lano & H. Haughton, editors (1994) *Object-Oriented Specification Case Studies*, Prentice Hall, Object-Oriented Series, Hemel Hempstead.
160. P.G. Larsen, J.S. Fitzgerald & T. Brookes (1996) Applying Formal Specification in Industry. *IEEE Software*, 13(3):48–56, May 1996.
161. H.C. Lauer & R.M. Needham (1979) On the Duality of Operating System Structures. *Operating Systems Review*, 13(2):3–19, April 1979.
162. D. Learmount (1992) Airline Safety Review: Human Factors. *Flight International*, 142(4238):30–33, 22–28 July 1992.
163. B. Le Charlier & P. Flener (1998) Specifications are Necessarily Informal: More myths of formal methods. *Journal of Systems and Software*, 40(3):275–296, March 1998.
164. G. LeLann (1981) Motivations, Objectives and Characterization of Distributed Systems. In *Distributed Systems – Architecture and Implementation*, Springer-Verlag, pp 1–9.
165. N.G. Leveson (1991) Software Safety in Embedded Computer Systems. *Communications of the ACM*, 34(2):34–46, February 1991.
166. N.G. Leveson (1993) *An Assessment of Space Shuttle Flight Software Development Processes*. National Academy Press, USA.

167. N.G. Leveson (1995) *Safeware: System Safety and Computers*, Addison-Wesley, Reading, Massachusetts.
168. * N.G. Leveson (1995) Medical Devices: The Therac-25 Story. In [167], Appendix A, pp 515–553.
(See page 447 in this collection.)
169. N.G. Leveson & C.T. Turner (1993) An Investigation of the Therac-25 Accidents. *IEEE Computer*, 26(7):18–41, July 1993.
170. N.G. Leveson & P.G. Neumann (1993) Introduction to Special Issue on Software for Critical Systems. *IEEE Transactions on Software Engineering*, 19(1):1–2, January 1993.
171. B.P. Lientz & E.B. Swanson (1980) *Software Maintenance Management*, Addison-Wesley, Reading, Massachusetts.
172. B. Littlewood & L. Strigini (1992) The Risks of Software. *Scientific American*, 267(5):38–43, November 1992.
173. Luqi & J.A. Goguen (1997) Formal Methods: Promises and Problems. *IEEE Software*, 14(1):73–85, January 1997.
174. J.L. Lyons (1996) *ARIANE 5: Flight 501 Failure*. Report by the Inquiry Board, European Space Agency, 19 July 1996.
URL: *http://www.esrin.esa.it/htdocs/tidc/Press/Press96/ariane5rep.html*
175. D.D. McCracken & M.A. Jackson (1982) Life Cycle Concept Considered Harmful. *ACM Software Engineering Notes*, 7(2):28–32.
176. J.A. McDermid, editor (1992) *Software Engineer's Reference Book*. Butterworth-Heinemann.
177. D. MacKenzie (1992) Computers, Formal Proof, and the Law Courts. *Notices of the American Mathematical Society*, 39(9):1066–1069, November 1992.
178. D. MacKenzie (1995) The Automation of Proof: A Historical and Sociological Exploration. *IEEE Annals of the History of Computing*, 17(3):7–29, Fall 1995.
179. K.L. McMillan (1993) *Symbolic Model Checking*. Kluwer Academic Press, Boston.
180. S. Magee & L.L. Tripp (1997) *Guide to Software Engineering Standards and Specifications*. Artech House, Boston.
181. J.J. Marciniak, editor (1994) *Encyclopedia of Software Engineering*. John Wiley & Sons, Wiley-Interscience Publication, New York (2 volumes).
182. B. Meyer (1985) On Formalism in Specification. *IEEE Software*, 2(1):5–13, January 1985.
183. H.D. Mills (1993) Zero-Defect Software – Cleanroom Engineering. *Advances in Computers*, 36:1–41.
184. H.D. Mills, M. Dyer & R.C. Linger (1987) Cleanroom Software Engineering. *IEEE Software*, 4(5):19–25, September 1997.
185. R. Milner (1989) *Communication and Concurrency*. Prentice Hall International Series in Computer Science, Hemel Hempstead and Englewood Cliffs.
186. Ministry of Defence (1991) *The Procurement of Safety Critical Software in Defence Equipment* (Part 1: Requirements, Part 2: Guidance). Interim Defence Standard 00-55, Issue 1, MoD, Directorate of Standardization, Kentigern House, 65 Brown Street, Glasgow G2 8EX, UK, 5 April 1991.
187. C. Morgan (1994) *Programming from Specifications*, 2nd edition. Prentice Hall International Series in Computer Science, Hemel Hempstead and Englewood Cliffs.
188. L. Moser, Y.S. Ramakrisha, G. Kutty, P.M. Melliar-Smith and L.K. Dillon (1997) A Graphical Environment for the Design of Concurrent Real-Time Systems. *ACM Transactions on Software Engineering and Methology (TOSEM)*, 6(1):31–79, January 1997.
189. S.J. Mullender, editor (1993) *Distributed Systems*. Addison-Wesley, Reading, Massachusetts.
190. R.M. Needham (1993) Cryptography and Secure Channels. In [189], pp 531–541.

191. P.G. Neumann (1989) Flaws in Specifications and What to do About Them. In *Proc. 5th International Workshop on Software Specification and Design, ACM SIGSOFT Engineering Notes*, 14(3):xi–xv, May 1989.
192. P.G. Neumann (1994) *Computer-Related Risks*. Addison-Wesley, Reading, Massachusetts.
193. J.E. Nicholls (1991) A Survey of Z Courses in the UK. In J.E. Nicholls, editor, *Z User Workshop, Oxford 1990*, Springer-Verlag, Workshops in Computing, pp 343–350.
194. J.E. Nicholls, editor (1992) *Z User Workshop, York 1991*. Springer-Verlag, Workshops in Computing.
195. N. Nissanke (1997) *Realtime Systems*. Prentice Hall International Series in Computer Science, Hemel Hempstead and Englewood Cliffs.
196. P. Oman, editor (1994) Computing Practices: Hardware/Software Codesign. *Computer* 27(1):42–55, January 1994.
197. G. O'Neill (1992) Automatic Translation of VDM Specifications into Standard ML Programs. *The Computer Journal*, 35(6):623–624, December 1992 (Short note).
198. T. O'Riordan, R. Kemp & M. Purdue (1988) *Sizewell B: An Anatomy of the Inquiry*. The Macmillan Press Ltd, Basingstoke.
199. * K. Orr, C. Gane, E. Yourdon, P.P. Chen & L.L. Constantine (1989) Methodology: The Experts Speak. *BYTE*, 14(4):221–233, April 1989.
 (See page 57 in this collection.)
200. * J.S. Ostroff (1992) Formal Methods for the Specification and Design of Real-Time Safety-Critical Systems. *Journal of Systems and Software*, 18(1):33–60, April 1992.
 (See page 367 in this collection.)
201. S. Owre, J.M. Rushby & N. Shankar (1992) PVS: A Prototype Verification System. In D. Kapur, editor, *Automated Deduction – CADE-11*, Springer-Verlag, Lecture Notes in Artificial Intelligence, volume 607, pp 748–752.
202. P. Palanque & F. Paternò, editors (1997) *Formal Methods in Human-Computer Interaction*. Springer-Verlag, Formal Approaches to Computing and Information Technology (FACIT) series, London.
203. D.L. Parnas (1972) On the Criteria to be Used in Decomposing Systems. *Communications of the ACM*, 15(5):1053–1058.
204. D.L. Parnas (1993) Predicate Logic for Software Engineering. *IEEE Transactions on Software Engineering*, 19(9):856–862, September 1993.
205. D.L. Parnas (1995) Teaching Programming as Engineering. In [40], pp 471–481.
206. D.L. Parnas (1995) Using Mathematical Models in the Inspection of Critical Software. In [125], Chapter 2, pp 17–31.
207. D.L. Parnas (1996a) Education for Computing Professionals. In [65], Chapter 3, pp 31–42.
208. D.L. Parnas (1996b) Teaching Programming as Engineering. In [65], Chapter 4, pp 43–55.
209. D.L. Parnas (1997a) Software Engineering: An Unconsummated Marriage. *Communications of the ACM*, 40(9):128, September 1997.
210. D.L. Parnas (1997b) Precise Description and Specification of Software. In V. Stavridou, editor, *Mathematics of Dependable Systems II*, Clarendon Press, Oxford, pp 1–14.
211. D.L. Parnas (1998a) "Formal Methods" Technology Transfer Will Fail. *Journal of Systems and Software*, 40(3):195–198, March 1998.
212. D.L. Parnas (1998b) Successful Software Engineering Research. *SIGSOFT Software Engineering Notes*, 23(3):64–68, May 1998.
213. D.L. Parnas, G.J.K. Asmis & J. Madey (1991) Assessment of Safety-Critical Software in Nuclear Power Plants. *Nuclear Safety*, 32(2):189–198.
214. D.A. Penney, R.C. Hold & M.W. Godfrey (1991) Formal Specification in Metamorphic Programming. In S. Prehn & H. Toetenel, editors, *VDM'91: Formal Software Development Methods*. Springer-Verlag, Lecture Notes in Computer Science, volume 551.

215. J.H. Poore & C.J. Trammell, editors (1996) *Cleanroom Software Engineering: A Reader*. Blackwell Publishers.
216. J.P. Potocki de Montalk (1993) Computer Software in Civil Aircraft. *Microprocessors and Microsystems*, 17(1):17–23, January/February 1993.
217. R.S. Pressman (1997) *Software Engineering: A Practitioner's Approach*, 4th edition. McGraw-Hill, New York.
218. RAISE Language Group (1992) *The RAISE Specification Language*. Prentice Hall, BCS Practitioner Series, Hemel Hempstead.
219. F. Redmill & T. Anderson, editors (1993) *Safety-critical Systems: Current Issues, Techniques and Standards*, Chapman & Hall, London.
220. A.W. Roscoe (1998) *The Theory and Practice of Concurrency*. Prentice Hall International Series in Computer Science, Hemel Hempstead and Englewood Cliffs.
221. Royal Society Study Group (1992) *Risk: Analysis, Perception and Management*, The Royal Society, 6 Carlton House Terrace, London SW1Y 5AG, UK.
222. Royal Signals and Radars Establishment (1991) *The Official Handbook of MASCOT, Version 3.1*, Computing Division, RSRE, Malvern, UK.
223. W.W. Royce (1970, 1987) Managing the Development of Large Software Systems. In *Proc. WESTCON'70*, August 1970. Reprinted in *Proc. 9th International Conference on Software Engineering*, IEEE Press, 1987.
224. W.W. Royce (1998) *Software Project Management: A Unified Framework*. Addison Wesley Longman, Object Technology Series.
225. A.R. Ruddle (1993) Formal Methods in the Specification of Real-Time, Safety-Critical Control Systems. In [44], pp 131–146.
226. J. Rumbaugh, I. Jacobson & G. Booch (1999) *The Unified Modeling Language Reference Manual*. Addison Wesley Longman, Object Technology Series.
227. J. Rushby (1995) *Formal Methods and their Role in the Certification of Critical Systems*. Technical Report SRI-CSL-95-01, SRI International, Menlo Park, California, USA, March 1995.
228. H. Saiedian & M.G. Hinchey (1996) Challenges in the Successful Transfer of Formal Methods Technology into Industrial Applications. *Information and Software Technology*, 38(5):313–322, May 1996.
229. * L.T. Semmens, R.B. France & T.W.G. Docker (1992) Integrated Structured Analysis and Formal Specification Techniques. *The Computer Journal*, 36(6):600–610, December 1992.
 (See page 533 in this collection.)
230. E. Sekerenski & K. Sere (1998) *Program Development by Refinement: Case Studies Using the B Method*. Springer-Verlag, Formal Approaches to Computing and Information Technology (FACIT) series, London.
231. M. Shaw & D. Garlan (1996) *Software Architectures: Perspectives on an Emerging Discipline*. Prentice Hall, Englewood Cliffs.
232. M.L. Shooman (1983) *Software Engineering: Design, Reliability and Management*, McGraw-Hill, New York.
233. I. Sommerville (1996) Safety-critical Software. In *Software Engineering*, 5th edition, Addison-Wesley, Harlow, England, Chapter 21, pp 419–442, Part 4: Dependable Systems.
234. I. Sommerville & P. Sawyer (1997) *Requirements Engineering: A good practice guide*. John Wiley & Sons, Chichester.
235. R.A. Spinello (1997) Liability, Safety and Reliability. In *Case Studies in Information and Computer Ethics*. Prentice Hall, Upper Saddle River, New Jersey, Chapter 8, pp 190–232.
236. J.M. Spivey (1992) *The Z Notation: A Reference Manual*, 2nd edition. Prentice Hall International Series in Computer Science, Hemel Hempstead & Englewood Cliffs.
237. R.M. Stein (1992) Safety by Formal Design. *BYTE*, p 157, August 1992.

238. R.M. Stein (1992) *Real-Time Multicomputer Software Systems*. Ellis Horwood, Series in Computers and their Applications, 1992.
239. S. Stepney (1993) *High Integrity Compilation: A Case Study*. Prentice Hall, Hemel Hempstead.
240. N. Storey (1996) *Safety-Critical Computer Systems*. Addison-Wesley, Harlow, England.
241. W. Swartout & R. Balzer (1982) On the Inevitable Intertwining of Specification and Implementation. *Communications of the ACM*, 25(7):438–440, July 1982.
242. A.S. Tanenbaum & R. van Renesse (1988) A Critique of the Remote Procedure Call Paradigm. In R. Speth, editor, *Research into Networks and Distributed Applications – EUTECO 1988*, Elsevier, pp 775–783.
243. M.C. Thomas (1993) The Industrial Use of Formal Methods. *Microprocessors and Microsystems*, 17(1):31–36, January/February 1993.
244. M. Thomas (1996) Formal Methods and their Role in Developing Safe Systems. *High Integrity Systems*, 1(5):447–451. Workshop report 20/3/95, IEE, London, UK. URL: http://www.iee.org.uk/PAB/Safe_rel/wrkshop1.htm
245. I. Toyn, D.M. Cattrall, J.A. McDermid & J.L. Jacob (1998) A Practical Language and Toolkit for High-Integrity Tools. *Journal of Systems and Software*, 41(3):161–173, June 1998.
246. A.B. Tucker, Jr., editor (1997) *The Computer Science and Engineering Handbook*. CRC Press.
247. K.J. Turner, editor (1993) *Using Formal Description Techniques: An Introduction to Estelle, LOTOS and SDL*. John Wiley & Sons, Chichester.
248. The University of York (1998) *Modular MSc in Safety Critical Systems Engineering, 1998/99: Diploma, certificate & short courses*. Department of Computer Science, The University of York, Heslington, York YO1 5DD, UK, 1998. URL: http://www.cs.york.ac.uk/MSc/SCSE/
249. S.H. Valentine (1992) Z- -. In [194], pp 157–187.
250. D.R. Wallace, D.R. Kuhn & L.M. Ippolito (1992) An Analysis of Selected Software Safety Standards. *IEEE AES Magazine*, pp 3–14, August 1992.
251. P.T. Ward & S.J. Mellor (1985) *Structured Development for Real-Time Systems*, Yourdon Press, New York.
252. M.W. West & B.M. Eaglestone (1992) Software Development: Two Approaches to Animation of Z Specifications using Prolog. *Software Engineering Journal*, 7(4):264–276, July 1992.
253. B.A. Wichmann (1998) Can we Produce Correct Programs? *The Computer Forum*, IEE, London, UK, 16 October 1998. URL: http://forum.iee.org.uk/forum/
254. S.P. Wilson, T.P. Kelly & J.A. McDermid (1995) Safety Case Development: Current Practice, Future Prospects. In R. Shaw, editor, *Proc. Twelfth Annual CSR Workshop*, Bruges, Springer-Verlag.
255. * J.M. Wing (1990) A Specifier's Introduction to Formal Methods. *IEEE Computer*, 23(9):8–24, September 1990.
  (See page 167 in this collection.)
256. L.A. Winsborrow & D.J. Pavey (1996) Assuring Correctness in a Safety Critical Software Application. *High Integrity Systems*, 1(5):453–459.
257. J.C.P. Woodcock & J. Davies (1996) *Using Z: Specification, Refinement and Proof*. Prentice Hall International Series in Computer Science, Hemel Hempstead & Englewood Cliffs.
258. J.C.P. Woodcock, P.H.B. Gardiner & J.R. Hulance (1994) The Formal Specification in Z of Defence Standard 00-56. In [35], pp 9–28.
259. J.C.P. Woodcock & P.G. Larsen, editors (1993) *FME'93: Industrial-Strength Formal Methods*. Springer-Verlag, Lecture Notes in Computer Science, volume 670.

260. J.B. Wordsworth (1996) *Software Engineering with B*. Addison-Wesley, Harlow, England.
261. E. Yourdon & L.L. Constantine (1979) *Structured Design*, Prentice Hall, Englewood Cliffs.
262. E. Youdon (1989) *Modern Structured Analysis*, Yourdon Press/Prentice Hall, New York.
263. E. Youdon & C.A. Argila (1997) *Case Studies in Object-Oriented Analysis and Design*. Yourdon Press/Prentice Hall, New York.
264. A.M. Zaremski & J.M. Wing (1997) Specification Matching of Software Components. *ACM Transactions on Software Engineering and Methology (TOSEM)*, 6(4):333–369, October 1997.
265. P. Zave & M. Jackson (1997) Four Dark Corners of Requirements Engineering. *ACM Transactions on Software Engineering and Methology (TOSEM)*, 6(1):1–30, January 1997.
266. P. Zave & R.T. Yeh (1982) An Operational Approach to Requirements Specification for Embedded Systems. *IEEE Transactions on Software Engineering*, SE-8(3):250–269, March 1982.
267. H.S.M. Zedan, editor (1990) *Distributed Computer Systems*. Butterworths, London, 1990.
268. Z Standards Panel (1995) *Z Standard: Z Notation Version 1.2*, ISO Panel JTC1/SC22/WG19 / BSI Panel IST/5/-/19/2, Committtee Draft (CD), 14 September 1995.
    URL: *http://www.comlab.ox.ac.uk/oucl/groups/zstandards/*

References marked * *are reprinted in this collection.*

Author Biographies

Jonathan Bowen studied Engineering Science at Oxford University. Subsequently he worked in the electronics and computing industry at Marconi Instruments and Logica. He then joined Imperial College in London and was employed as a research assistant in the Wolfson Microprocessor Unit.

In 1985 he moved to the Programming Research Group at Oxford University where he initially undertook extended case studies using the formal notation Z on the Distributed Computing Software project. He has been involved with several successful proposals for European and UK projects in the area of formal methods involving collaboration between universities and industry. As a senior research officer he managed the ESPRIT REDO and UK IED SAFEMOS projects at Oxford and and the ESPRIT ProCoS-WG Working Group of 25 European partners associated with the ProCoS project on "Provably Correct Systems".

Bowen has given many presentations at conferences and invited talks at academic and industrial sites around Europe, North America and the Far East. He has authored over 130 publications and has produced eight books in the area of formal methods, especially involving the Z notation. He is Chair of the Z User Group, previously served on the UK Safety Critical Systems Club advisory panel, and was the Conference Chair for the Z User Meetings in 1994, 1995 and 1997. He has served on the program committee for many international conferences, and is a member of the ACM and the IEEE Computer Society. In 1994 he won the Institute of Electrical Engineers Charles Babbage premium award for work on safety-critical systems, formal methods and standards [46, see also pages 485–528 in this volume].

Since 1995, Bowen has been a lecturer at The University of Reading, UK.

Mike Hinchey graduated from the University of Limerick, Ireland *summa cum laude* with a B.Sc. in Computer Science, and was awarded the Chairman's prize. He subsequently took an M.Sc. in Computation with the Programming Research Group at Oxford University, followed by working for a Ph.D. in Computer Science at the University of Cambridge. Until 1998 he was a member of faculty in the Real-Time Computing Laboratory in the Dept. of Computer and Information Science at New Jersey Institute of Technology.

He is an Associate Fellow of the Institute of Mathematics, and a member of the ACM, IEEE, American Mathematical Society and the New York Academy of Sciences.

Hinchey has lectured for the University of Cambridge Computer Laboratory, and taught Computer Science for a number of Cambridge colleges. He is Director of Research for BEST CASE Ltd., and also acts as an independent consultant. Previously, he has been a research assistant at the University of Limerick, a Systems Specialist and Network Specialist with Price Waterhouse, and a Research Engineer with Digital Equipment Corporation.

He serves on the IFAC Technical Committee on Real-Time Software Engineering, and is editor of the newsletter of the IEEE Technical Segment Committee on the Engineering of Complex Computer Systems. He is Treasurer of the Z User Group and was Conference Chair for the 11th International Conference of Z Users (ZUM'98). He has published widely in the field of formal methods, and is the author/editor of several books on various aspects of software engineering and formal methods.

Hinchey is currently a professor at the University of Nebraska at Omaha, USA and the University of Limerick, Ireland.

Index

00-55 Defence Standard, 362, 363, 366, 509
00-56 Defence Standard, 362, 509

A-class certification, 442
A320 Airbus, 505
Abrial, Jean-Raymond, 433
absence of deadlock, 384
abstract classes, 279
Abstract Data Type, 17, 169, 182, 231, 237
abstract satisfies relation, 170
abstract specification, 169
abstraction, 33, 128, 194, 242, 599
abstraction function, 170, 176, 557
access control, 300
access model, 273
accessor process, 273
accident investigation, 447
accreditation, 364, 510, 513, 514, 659
ACL, *see* access control list
ACM, *see* Association for Computing Machinery
ACP_ρ, *see* Real-Time ACP
ACS, *see* ammunition control software
Act One, 132, 179
action diagram, 268
action timed graphs, 404
action-based methods, 388
Action-Dataflow Diagram, 273
actions, 78, 277, 641
activation, 325
active entities, 269
activities, 35
activity variable, 385
activity-chart, 637
actors, 248

Ada language, 9, 16, 128, 233, 237, 238, 243, 375
– for object-oriented development, 250–251
– subprogram, 238
adaptability, 296, 618
adaptive maintenance, 5
ADFD, *see* Action-Dataflow Diagram
adjacency, 37
ADT, *see* Abstract Data Type
AECB, *see* Atomic Energy Control Board
AECL, *see* Atomic Energy of Canada Limited
Affirm tool, 181
agent, 248
AI, *see* Artificial Intelligence
algebra, 205–207, 215, 381–404, *see also* process algebra
Algebra of Timed Processes, 396
algebraic laws, 132
algebraic methods, 132, 179
algebraic specification, 542–551
algebraic state transition system, 547
Algol language, 25, 304
ALPHARD, 304
alternating bit protocol, 397
alternative command, 310
American National Standards Institute, 664
ammunition control, 499
ammunition control software, 499
analysis, 40–50, 178, 371
– object-oriented, 261
– object-oriented versus conventional, 274
– static, 506
– transition to design, 287–288
– using CASE, 621

analysis methodology, 274–278
analysis–specification semantic gap, 530
analytical engine, 485
analytical framework, 424
AND connective, 202
AND decomposition, 377, 640
animation, 148, 559, 560, 659
Anna, 179
ANSI, *see* American National Standards Institute
APL language, 25, 324
architectural design, 278
Aristotle, 12
Artificial Intelligence, 9, 17, 505
Ascent tool, 553
ASpec, *see* Atomic-level Specification
assembly of components, 24
assembly-line diagram, 54, 60
assertional logic, 402
assertional proof methods, 347
assertions, 186, 401, 659
assignment command, 307
Association for Computing Machinery, 662
associative network, *see* semantic network
assurance, 422
ASTS, *see* algebraic state transition system
asynchronous reading and writing, 103
Asynchronous Transfer Mode, 295
ATM, *see* Asynchronous Transfer Mode
atomic action, 299
Atomic Energy Control Board, 161, 413, 429, 509
Atomic Energy of Canada Limited, 430, 448
atomic formula, 586
atomic sets, 626
Atomic-level Specification, 543
ATP, *see* Algebra of Timed Processes
audit, 621
audit trail, 482
authentication, 300
automatic buffering, 325
automatic programming, 9, 19
auxiliary state functions, 355
availability, 296, 488, 659
aviation, 495
avoidance of faults, 489, 660
axiomatic methods, 132, 179
axioms, 548

B-Core, 157
B-Method, 132, 188, 435–436, 531, 660
B-Tool, 491
B-Toolkit, 157

Babbage, Charles, 485
Backus-Naur Form, 131, 169, 306
bag, 572
Bailin object-oriented requirements specification, 269
Basic ExtDFD, 548
Basic Research Action, 502, 515
batch execution, 43
BCS, *see* British Computer Society
behaviour, 547, 574
– modelling, 35
– of a system, 171
– open-loop, 372
behavioural equivalence, 398
behavioural model, 561
Behavioural Specification, 171, 548
benefits of CASE, 620
benefits of formal methods, 141
benefits to society, 413
best practice, 413, 422
Binary Decision Diagrams, 159
bisimulation, 395, 398
biting bullets, 30, *see also* silver bullets
blackboard systems, 505
Bledsoe-Hines algorithm, 400
blobs, 626, 652
BNF, *see* Backus-Naur Form
Booch approach, 234
Booch object-oriented design, 279, 283
Boolean connectives, 202
bounded buffer, 319
bounded response time, 386
bounded temporal operator logic, *see* hidden clock logic
boundedness, 378
Boyer-Moore theorem prover, 181, 491
BRA, *see* Basic Research Action
branching semantics, 383
branching time temporal logic, 391–392
British Computer Society, 364, 510, 662
BRMD, *see* Bureau of Radiation and Medical Devices
broad-spectrum notations, 133
Brooks Jr., Frederick, 8, 29, 30
BS, *see* Behavioural Specification
bubble chart, 268, *see also* Data-Flow Diagram
buffer, bounded, 319
buffering, 325
bugs, 5, 130, 365
Bureau of Radiation and Medical Devices, 455
Byzantine Generals problem, 369

C++, 231
C-DFD, *see* control-extended DFD
CADiZ tool, 157
calculation, 201
calculus, 661
Calculus of Communicating Shared Resources, 396, 397
Calculus of Communicating Systems, 132, 179, 296, 395, *see also* Temporal CCS
– and Yourdon, 551–553
call by result, 314
call by value, 314
CAP, *see* corrective action plan
capability, 300
Capability Maturity Model, 10
cardinality, 71
Cartesian product, 625, 628
– unordered, 653
CAS, *see* Collision-Avoidance System
CAS Logic, 438
CAS Surveillance, 438
CASE, *see also* Computer-Aided Software Engineering
– adaptability, 618
– analysis, 621
– audit, 621
– benefits, 620
– facilities, 616–620
– features, 616
– future, 610
– maintenance, 621
– reliability engineering, 620–622
CASE Data Interchange Format, 610
CASE environment, 609, 613
CASE project, 137
case studies
– formal methods, 414–415
– object-oriented design, 252–257
– safety-critical systems, 414–415, 429–445
CASE tools, 75, 609, 611, 617
CASE workbench, 609, 610
CCS, *see* Calculus of Communicating Systems
CCSR, *see* Calculus of Communicating Shared Resources
CDC 600, 304
CDIF, *see* CASE Data Interchange Format
CDRH, *see* Center for Devices and Radiological Health
Center for Devices and Radiological Health, 470
certification, 364, 420, 429, 509, 510, 659
– A-class, 442

CGR company, 448
chance, 487
changeability, 14
Chill, 375
choice, 487
chop operator, 383
CICS, *see* Customer Information Control System
CIP-S programming environment, 177
CIRCAL, 393
Clascal, 246
class, 233, 248, 289, 304, 659
class and object diagram, 272
class cards, 284
class diagram/template, 283
class specification, 284
classical methods, 615
classification of objects, 263
Cleanroom approach, 130, 223, 426, 501
Clear language, 132, 179
client satisfaction, 415
client-server model, 280
clients, 175, 281
CLInc., *see* Computational Logic, Inc.
Clio, 494
clock, 384
closed systems, 191
CLP, *see* constraint logic programming
CLU language, 233, 246, 304
clusters, 304
CMM, *see* Capability Maturity Model
co-design, 297
co-routining, 586
Coad and Yourdon object-oriented analysis, 270, 272
Cobol language, 25, 324, *see also* JSP-Cobol preprocessor
Cobol Structuring Facility, 426
Cocomo, *see* Constructive Cost Model
Cocomo model, 156
code generation, 46, 47
code of conduct, 364
code of ethics, 364
code, program, 659
codification, 47
cohesion measure, 74
collaborations graph, 284
Collision-Avoidance System, 438
coloured nets, 380
commandments of formal methods, 133
Commercial Subroutine Package, 154
commit, two-phase, 299
commitment, 401

Communicating Sequential Processes, 131, 132, 154, 179, 185, 218, 296, 303–328, 393, *see also* Timed CSP
- example, 187
- STOP process, 393
- traces, 187
communication, 295, 304, 422
communication model, 273
communication primitives, 103
Compagnie de Signaux et Entreprises Électriques, 433
compilation, 46, 160, 503
compilers, 149
complacency, 481
complete specification, 172, 205
completeness, 40, 370
complexity, 12
- computational, 216
complexity measure, 226
component factory, 292
components, 151, 257, 610
composition, 119, 122, 257
- parallel, 373
- sequential, 210
CompuCom Speed Protocol, 154
computation, 295
computational complexity, 216
Computational Logic, Inc., 493
Computer-Aided Software Engineering, 8, 40, 54, 609–611, 613–622, 659, *see also* CASE
computer ethics, 364
Computer Resources International, 157, 426
computer-aided systems engineering, 616
conceptual construct, 30, 33, 40
conceptual model, 35, 36, 584
concurrency, 185
concurrency control, 346–350
concurrency specification, 355–356
Concurrency Workbench, 553
Concurrent Pascal, 304
concurrent systems, 132, 169, 195, 295–302, 338, 659
conditional critical region, 304, 319
conduct, 364
conformity, 13
Conic, 375
conjunction, 202
connectedness, 37, 624
consequence relation, 173
consequences, 148
consistency, 40, 172, 299
- of a specification, 205

- verification, 48
consistent specification, 172
constraint logic programming, 387
constructing software, 22
constructive approach, 599
Constructive Cost Model, 221
constructive elements, 597
constructive mathematics, 564, 599
constructor, 247
context diagram, 67
contract, 168
control activities, 35
Control Switching Point, 154
control technology, 372
control-extended DFD, 548
controller, 371
controller architecture, 375
conventional methodology, 264–267
conversion of semantics, 398
Conway's problem, 314
coroutines, 312–314, 327
corrective action plan, 468
corrective maintenance, 5
correctness, 139, 170, 488, 601
correctness proof, 129, 530, 662
- of an implementation, 354–355
- role of auxiliary state function, 355
cost, 416, 417
cost estimates, 221
cost modelling, 421
cost of safety, 492
counter model, 394
coupling measure, 74
courses, 165
CRI, *see* Computer Resources International
critical region, 304, 319
crossbar switch, 304
CSEE, *see* Compagnie de Signaux et Entreprises Électriques
CSP, *see* Communicating Sequential Processes
Customer Information Control System, 149, 162, 219, 425, 493
customers, 175

DAISTS, *see* Data Abstraction, Implementation, Specification and Testing
danger, 487
Danish Datamatik Center, 149
Darlington nuclear generating station, 429–433
DARTS, 609
data, 36, 659

data abstraction, 194
Data Abstraction, Implementation, Specification and Testing System, 177
data definition, 543
data design, 108
Data Dictionary, 534
data dictionary, 53, 265
data domain definition, 543
data models, 90
data refinement, 216, 531, 557
data representation, 176, 314–318
data type invariant, 568
data variable, 385
data-dependency diagrams, 172
Data-Flow Diagram, 54, 61, 66, 265, 268, 530, 532, 534
– data definition, 543
– global state, 546
– semantics, 543–550
data-model diagram, 268
data-oriented methodologies, 263
data-structure diagram, 268
Data-Structured Systems Development, 54, 58
database, 72, 346–350
database management system, 69
datagrams, 441
DATUM project, 512
DB2 database, 72
dBASE database, 72
DBMS, *see* database management system
DC, *see* Duration Calculus
deadlock, 309, 384
decision table, 53, 609
declarative language, 586, 604
decomposition, 119, 176, 257, 377
deduction, 129, 659
default arrows, 640
Defence Standards, 362, 363
defensive design, 480
definition-use chains, 172
delivery, 201
Department of Defense, 441
Department of Trade and Industry, 501
dependability, 488, 659
depth dose, 448
description, 371
design, 1–10, 201, 503, 529, 659
– architectural, 278
– specification, 5
– transition from analysis, 287–288
– Booch, 234, 279, 283
– case study, 252–257

– co-design, 297
– comparison of methods, 282–287
– data, 108
– defensive, 480
– formal, 158, 176, 418
– hardware/software, 297
– object-oriented, 234, 252–257, 261–262, 278–283, 287
– program, 201–216
– responsibility-driven, 280, 284
– SADT, *see* structured analysis and design technique
– software development, 463
– SSADM, *see* Structured Systems Analysis and Design Methodology
– structured, 53, 73–76, 180, 262, 278, 279
– system, 55, 77, 176
– Wasserman et al., 278, 279
– Wirfs-Brock et al., 280, 284
design errors, 465
design methodology, 77, 282–287
design methods, 158
design quality assurance, 501
designers, 25
deterministic operations, 565–571
development, 3, 53, 375, 660
– evolutionary, 6
– formal, 220
– incremental, 24
– transformational, 6
development approaches, 615–616
development by composition, 122
development costs, 146
development life-cycle, 3–6, 529
development methods, 223
development process, 102
DFCS, *see* digital flight control system
DFD, *see* Data-Flow Diagram
diagramming object, 623
difference engine, 485
differential files, 596
digital flight control system, 495
digrammatic notation, 609
Dijkstra's guarded commands, 304
Dijkstra's weakest precondition calculus, 382
Dijkstra, Edsger, 176, 320, 321, 344
dining philosophers, 320
discrete time, 384
discrete-event dynamic system, 403
disjunction, 202
disjunctive normal form, 439
distributed operating system, 300, 301

distributed systems, 169, 195, 295–302, 660
– models of computation, 297
– naming considerations, 298
divergences model, 394
divergent traces, 394
division with remainder, 315
DO-178, 507
documentation, 177, 224, 504
DoD, *see* Department of Defense
dogmatism, 225
domain analysis, 422
domain chart, 273
domains, 169
DOS, *see* distributed operating system
DSSD, *see* Data-Structured Systems Development
DTI, *see* Department of Trade and Industry
Duration Calculus, 502, 661
dynamic binding, 279
dynamic relationships, 272
dynamic system, 403

E-R diagram, *see* Entity-Relationship Diagram
ECG, *see* electrocardiogram
EDFD, *see* Entity-Dataflow Diagram
education, 363, 509, 510, 513
efficiency, 598
EHDM theorem prover, 495
electrocardiogram, 498
embedded microprocessors, 500
embedded systems, 359, 660
EMC, *see* Extended Model Checker
emulation, 660
enabled transition, 385
enabling predicates, 189
encapsulation, 37, 263
enclosure, 625
ENCRESS, 365
encryption key, 301
Encyclopedia, 268
end-to-end process modelling, 290
endorsed tool, 443
ensembles, 289
enterprise model, 268
entity, 70, 91, 269
entity diagram, 54, 60
entity dictionary, 271
Entity-Dataflow Diagram, 271
entity-process matrix, 268
Entity-Relationship, 69–72
Entity-Relationship Diagram, 54, 66, 265, 271, 631

Entity-Relationship Modelling, 534
Entity-Relationship-Attribute Diagram, 530
entries, PL/I, 304
environment, 21, 191, 609, 613
Environment for Verifying and Evaluating Software, 177
ER, *see* Entity-Relationship
ERAD, *see* Entity-Relationship-Attribute Diagram
Eratosthenes, 322
ERD, *see* Entity-Relationship Diagram
Ergo Support System, 177
ERM, *see* Entity-Relationship Modelling
error, 139, 660
erythema, 457
ESA, *see* European Space Agency
ESPRIT, 426, 502
Esterel language, 378
Ethernet, 295
ethics, 364
Euler circles, 623
Euler, Leonhard, 623
European Safety and Reliability Association, 365
European Space Agency, 508
European Workshop on Industrial Computer Systems, 365
evaluation, 178
event, 371
event action models, 400–401
event models, 90
event partitioning, 67
Event-Life History Diagram, 609
events, 304, 547, *see also* actions
eventually $\Diamond$, 350, 352
evolution, 429
evolutionary development, *see* transformational development
EWICS TC7, 365
example specifications, 587
Excelerator environment, 620
exception handling, 279
exclusion, 625
exclusive-or, 639
executable model, 41
executable specification, 41, 180, 559, 560, 563, 583, 584, 604, 660
– constructive approach, 599
– critique, 585
– efficiency, 598
– versus implementation, 603
execution, 41, 43, 45, 602, 660
execution control language, 44

exhaustive execution, 45
existential quantification ∃, 202
expert, *see* guru
expert system, 9, 18
explicit clock, 384
explicit clock linear logics, 384–388
explicit clock logic, 386
explicit naming, 324
expressiveness, 583
ExSpect tool, 380
ExtDFD, *see* semantically-Extended DFD
Extended ML, 177
Extended Model Checker, 181
external non-determinism, 572
EXTIME-complete, 391

FAA, *see* Federal Aviation Authority
factorial, 316
failure, 660
failures model, 394
fairness, 326
fairness properties, 384
fault, 660
fault avoidance, 489, 660
fault forecasting, 489, 660
fault removal, 489, 660
fault tolerance, 489, 660
FDA, *see* Food and Drug Administration
FDM, *see* Formal Development Method
FDR tool, 157
features of CASE, 616
Federal Aviation Administration, 495
Federal Aviation Authority, 438
Fermat's last theorem, 594
Field Programmable Gate Array, 160, 297, 504
file differences, 596
finite state timed transition model, 387
finite variability, 398
finite-state analysis, 434
finite-state machine, 638
first-order logic, 661
Flavors, 247
floating-point standard, 426
floating-point unit, 149, 159, 221
fly-by-wire aircraft, 362, 505
FM9001 microprocessor, 159
Food and Drug Administration, 447
for all ∀, 202
Ford Aerospace, 442
forecasting of faults, 489, 660
foreign key, 71
Formal Aspects of Computing journal, 491

formal development, 220
Formal Development Method, 177, 181
formal methods, 4, 127–133, 201, 360, 367, 413–427, 430, 489, 529, 559, 615, 660
– acceptability, 148
– analysis, 178
– analytical framework, 424
– application areas, 143, 501–506
– benefits, 141
– biases and limits, 424
– bounds, 189–192
– case studies, 414–415
– certification, 420
– characteristics, 178
– choice, 131–133
– client satisfaction, 415
– code-level application, 421
– commandments, 133
– commercial and exploratory cases, 425–427
– compilers, 149
– correctness, 139
– cost, 146, 221, 421
– courses, 165
– definition, 154
– design, 158, 176, 418
– development, 146, 154, 220
– documentation, 177, 224
– dogmatism, 225
– errors, 139
– examples, 181–189, 198
– facts, 150
– fallibility, 138
– further reading, 194–199
– guru, 222
– Hall's myths, 155
– hardware, 149
– ideal versus real world, 189
– in standards, 506
– industrial use, 149
– information acquisition, 423
– integration, 530–531
– larger scale, 419
– lessons learned, 415–422
– level of formalization, 219
– life-cycle changes, 146
– maintainability, 418
– mathematics, 144
– mistakes, 139
– myths, 130, 131, 135–150, 153–163
– notation, 218
– necessity, 160
– pedagogical impact, 417

- periodicals, 165
- pragmatics, 173–181
- primary manifestations, 420
- process, 417
- product, 416
- program proving, 140
- proof, 142, 363
- quality standards, 224
- questionnaires, 424
- reactor control, 149
- requirements, 176, 418
- research, 512
- resources, 164–165
- reuse, 227, 418
- safety-critical systems, 361–362
- skill building, 421
- software, 149, 159
- specification, *see* formal specification
- strengths and weaknesses, 534
- studying, 423–425
- support, 161
- technology, 513
- technology transfer, 420
- testing, 226
- time to market, 417
- tools, 156, 181, 196, 220, 418, 420
- training, 145
- transaction processing, 149
- use, 162, 173, 175, 420
- use in certification, 420
- validation, 177, 419
- verification, *see* formal verification
- versus traditional development methods, 223
- wider applicability, 419
formal notation, 128, 660
formal proof, 142, 363
formal semantics, 370
formal specification, 128, 140, 196, 219, 660
- animation, 148, 560
- concept of formality defined, 332
- consequences, 148
- definition, 154
- difficulties, 145
- example, 151–152
- function described, 332
- implementation, 142
- natural language, 148
- proof, 142
formal specification language, 167, 168
Formal Systems Europe, 157

formal verification, 127, 177, 196, 220, 419, 563
Formaliser tool, 157
formalism, visual, 37, 41, 609, 611, 651
Fortran language, 25, 304
FPGA, *see* Field Programmable Gate Array
frame problem, 565
free variable, 586
freedom from deadlock, 378
French national railway, 434
FSM, *see* finite-state machine
FtCayuga fault-tolerant microprocessor, 495
function, 269
function, of a specification, 66
functional coroutines, 327
functional programming, 207–209, 215, 560, 563, 586
functional specification, 4
Fusion method, 235
future operators, 383
future state, 186
Fuzz tool, 157

Gane/Sarson approach, 61–65
GAO, *see* Government Accounting Office
garbage collection, 211
GCD, *see* greatest common divisor
GEC Alsthom, 433, 496
generate-and-test cycle, 591
generation of code, 46
generic definitions, 279
genericity, 233, 660
Gist explainer, 176
Gist language, 191
glass cockpit, 362
glitches, 304
global state, 546
Gödel language, 586
goto statement, 54
Government Accounting Office, 455
graphical languages, 377–382
graphical notation, 611
graphical programming, 9, 20
greatest common divisor, 201, 590
Gries, David, 318, 322
guard, 327
guarded command, 304, 310
guidelines, 38
guru, 222
GVE, *see* Gypsy Verification Environment
Gypsy specification language, 181, 442
Gypsy Verification Environment, 442–443

halting problem, 594

Index 689

Hamming numbers, 570, 594
hard real-time, 359, 503
hard real-time constraints, 368
hardware, 149, 297, 660
hardware compilation, 159
hardware description language, 48
hardware/software co-design, 297
harvesting reuse, 288, 291
hazard analysis, 192, 452
HCI, *see* Human-Computer Interface
HDM, *see* Hierarchical Development Method
Health and Safety Executive, 508
health checks, 379
heavy-weight process, 299
henceforth □, 350, 352
Hennessey-Milner Logic, 551
heterogeneity, 300
Hewlett-Packard, 427, 492, 498
hidden clock logic, 389
hidden operations, 279
hierarchical decomposition, 356
Hierarchical Development Method, 177, 181
hierarchical types, 17
hierarchy chart, 53
hierarchy diagram, 265, 284
hierarchy of activities, 35
Hierarchy-Input-Processing-Output, 180
High Integrity Systems journal, 165
high-integrity systems, 127, 661
high-level languages, 15, 16
Higher Order Logic, 177, 181, 392, 491, 500, 661
higraphs, 611, 626–631
– formal definition, 652–654
– model, 653
HIPO, *see* Hierarchy-Input-Processing-Output
hitrees, 651
HML, *see* Hennessey-Milner Logic
Hoare, C.A.R., 176
Hoare logic, 401–402, 434–435
Hoare triples, 401, 435
Hoare's proof-of-program method, 433
HOL, *see* Higher Order Logic
Horn clause, 586
"how", 4, 141, 177, 332, 578, 580, 586
HP, *see* Hewlett-Packard
HP-SL, 498
HSE, *see* Health and Safety Executive
human factors, 192
Human-Computer Interface, 362, 505, 661

hurt, 487
HWP, *see* heavy-weight process
hybrid systems, 403–404, 503, 661
hypergraphs, 624

I/O automata, 179
IBM, 493
IBM CICS project, 162
IBM Federal Systems Division, 426
IBM Hursley, 149, 219, 425
IEC, *see* International Electrotechnical Commission
IED, *see* Information Engineering Directorate
IEE, *see* Institution of Electrical Engineers
IEEE, *see* Institute of Electrical and Electronics Engineers
IEEE floating-point standard, 426
IFDSE, *see* Integrated Formal Development Support Environment
I-Logix, 637
implementation, 5, 142, 170, 201, 529, 557–561, 661
– correctness, 343–346
implementation bias, 173
implementation phase, 5, 107
implementors, 175
implements, *see* satisfies relation
IMS database, 72
Ina Jo, 177, 181
incident analysis procedure, 482
incremental development, 24
Independent Verification and Validation, 439
Index Technology, 620
inequations, 209
inference, 661
– from specifications, 565, 577–578, 602
inference rules, 173
infinite loops, *see* divergent traces
informal, 530, 661
informal methods, 199
information clusters, 279
information engineering, 266, 268
Information Engineering Directorate, 515
information exposure, 439
information hiding, 232, 242, 661
Information Resource Dictionary System, 72
information structure diagram, 273
inheritance, 233, 248, 263
initial conditions, 189
initial state, 378

injury, 487
Inmos, 156, 159, 221, 222, 426, 493
innumerate, 145
input command, 304, 305, 309
input guard, 305, 327
insertion sort, 572
inspection, 430
instantiation, 233, 279
Institute of Electrical and Electronics Engineers, 510
institution, 168
Institution of Electrical Engineers, 510, 662
integer semaphore, 319
integer square root, 592
integrated database, 69
Integrated Formal Development Support Environment, 611
integrated methods, 529–532
Integrated Project Support Environment, 610
integration, *see* method integration
integration testing, 211
integrity, 300, 661
Intel 432, 247
Inter-Process Communication, 298
interactive execution, 43
interface
– defined, 337
– specifying, 337–338, 340, *see also* interface state function
interface action, 339, 349, 353
interface specification, 183, 337
interface state function, 337, 338, 340
interleaved execution, 384
internal non-determinism, 574, 597
internal parallelism, 290
internal state function, 340
International Electrotechnical Commission, 508
International Organization for Standardization, 132, 161, 664, *aka* ISO
Internet, 295
interpretation, 46
intersection ∩, 588, 625
interval semantics, 383
Interval Temporal Logic, 392–393, 661
interval timed colour Petri Net, 380
invariant, 568
inverse, 567
inversion operation, 567
invisibility, 14
Iota, 179
IPC, *see* Inter-Process Communication

IPSE, *see* Integrated Project Support Environment
IRDS, *see* Information Resource Dictionary System
is-a relationship, 271
is-a relationship, 634
ISO, *see* International Organization for Standardization
ISO9000 series, 507
isomorphism, 398
is-part-of relationship, 271
ITCPN, *see* interval timed colour Petri Net
iterative array, 316, 322
iterator, 247
ITL, *see* Interval Temporal Logic
IV&V, *see* Independent Verification and Validation

Jackson Structured Programming, 54, *see also* JSP-Cobol preprocessor
Jackson System Development, 54–55, 77, 244
– combining processes, 109
– communication primitives, 103
– composition, 119
– data design, 108
– decomposition, 119
– examples, 96
– implementation phase, 107
– internal buffering, 114
– managerial framework, 122
– modelling phase, 78
– network phase, 93
– projects, 124
– tools, 124
– with several processors, 116
Jackson's Structure Text, 551
JIS, 507
Jordan curve theorem, 624
JSD, *see* Jackson System Development
JSP, *see* Jackson Structured Programming
JSP-Cobol preprocessor, 124
JST, *see* Jackson's Structure Text

Kate system, 176
key distribution, 301
Königsberg bridges problem, 623

LaCoS project, 426
Lamport, Leslie, 176, 188
LAN, *see* local area network
language
– declarative, 586, 604
– formal, 128

- formal specification, 168
- high-level, 15
- natural, 148, 172
- UML, see Unified Modeling Language
- visual, 179
- Z, see Z notation

Language of Temporal Ordering of Specifications, 132, 179
Larch, 132, 179, 338, 531
- example, 183
- trait, 183

Larch handbook, 185
Larch Prover, 181
Larch specification, 183
Large Correct Systems, see LaCoS project
LATEX document preparation system, 440
LCF, 181
leads to ⤳, 188, 350, 352
least common multiple, 591
legislation, 363, 509, 511
level of formalization, 219
Leveson, Nancy, 438
licensing, 364
life-cycle, 2–6, 57, 77, 146, 158, 529, 661
light-weight process, 299
limits on proofs, 138
linac, see linear accelerator
linear accelerator, 447
linear propositional real-time logics, 391
linear semantics, 383
Lisp language, 246
live transition, 379
liveness, 185
- in transition axiom specification, 350–353

liveness properties, 188, 333, 384
Lloyd's Register, 426
local area network, 295
locking, 299
logic, 381–404, 661
- assertional, 402
- branching time, 391–392
- CAS, 438
- concurrent and distributed systems, 195
- explicit clock, 384–388
- first-order, 661
- Hennessey-Milner, 551
- hidden clock, 389
- higher-order, see Higher Order Logic
- Hoare, 401–402, 434–435
- Interval Temporal, 392–393, 661
  linear propositional, 391
- Metric Temporal, 388–391, 402
- proof outline, 402

- Hoare, 401–402
- real-time, 382–393, 400–401
- temporal, 36, 46, 185, 186, 340, 350, 353, 664
- Temporal Logic of Actions, 297, 661

logic programming, 181, 203–205, 215, 560, 586, see also constraint logic programming
logic specification language, 586
logical inference system, 173
logical modelling, 61
LOOPS, 247
loosely coupled systems, 296
Loral, 442
loss, 487
LOTOS, see Language of Temporal Ordering of Specifications, see also Urgent LOTOS
LSL, see logic specification language
lumpectomy, 453
Lustre language, 378
LWP, see light-weight process

Machine Safety Directive, 511
machine tools, 175
machine-checked proofs, 220
macrosteps, 377
maintainability, 418
maintenance, 5, 119, 201, 529
- using CASE, 621
MALPAS tool, 506
management, 122, 235, 417
many-to-many relationship, 59, 71
mapping, 59, 382
Martin information engineering, 266, 268
Mascot, 4, 609
mathematical reasoning, 201
MATRA Transport, 496
Matra Transport, 426, 433
matrix management, 442
matrix multiplication, 322
maturity model, 10
maximal parallelism, 384
McCabe's Complexity Measure, 226
Mealy machines, 640
measures, 73
medical systems, 427, 447–483, 498
message passing, 272
Meta-Morph tool, 501
metaclass, 248
method integration, 158, 529–532, 661
- approaches, 534–535
methodology, 53, 57, 73, 661

- comparison of analysis methods, 274–278
- comparison of design methods, 282–287
- conventional, 264–267
- object-oriented analysis, 267–274
- object-oriented design, 278–282
- software engineering, 57–76
- TCAS, 439

methods, 38, 53, 57, 75, 158
- action-based, 388
- algebraic, 132, 179
- analysis, 274–278
- assertional proof, 347
- axiomatic, 132, 179
- Booch object-oriented design, 234, 283
- classical, 615
- Cleanroom, 130, 223, 426, 501
- Coad and Yourdon object-oriented analysis, 272
- comparison, 274–278, 282–287
- data-oriented, 263
- design, 73, 158, 278–287
- development, 223, 237
- Entity-Relationship, 69–72
- formal, *see* formal methods
- Fusion, 235
- Gane/Sarson, 61–65
- Hoare's proof-of-program, 433
- informal, 199
- integrated, 529–532
- JSD, *see* Jackson System Development
- Martin information engineering, 268
- metrification, 422
- model-oriented, 178
- object-oriented, 278–282, 505
- partial-lifecycle, 258
- process-oriented, 263
- programming, 216
- proof, 433, 564
- property-oriented, 178
- SAZ, 223
- SCR/Darlington, 430
- semi-formal, 180, 199
- Shlaer Mellor object-oriented analysis, 273
- software, 57–76, 73, 237
- state transition, 336
- state-based, 388
- structured, 4, 53–55, 264–265
- SVDM, 536
- TCAS, 439
- transformational, 6–8
- transition axiom, 188, 331
- UML, *see* Unified Modeling Language

- VDM, *see* Vienna Development Method
- Warnier/Orr, 57–61
- Wasserman et al. object-oriented structured design, 279
- Wirfs-Brock et al. responsibility-driven design, 284
- Yourdon, 65–69

Metric Temporal Logic, 388–391, 402
metrification methods, 422
m-EVES tool, 177, 181
MGS, *see* Multinet Gateway System
Michael Jackson Systems, Ltd., 125
microprocessors, 500
microsteps, 377
MIL-STD-882B standard, 507
million instructions per second, 16, 21
mini-spec, 265
Minimum Operational Performance Standards, 438
MIPS, *see* million instructions per second
Miranda, 560
Miró visual languages, 180
MITI, 507
MITL, 390
Mitre Corp., 442
ML language, 586, *see also* Extended ML
modal operators, 186
Modecharts, 401
model, 73, 273, 371, 661
- analysis, 40–50
- conceptual, 35
- concurrent and distributed systems, 195
- executable, 41
- execution, 41
- hybrid, 403–404
- Newtonian, 375
- physical, 35
- versus specification, 371
- waterfall, 3, 6
model checking, 133, 181, 387
model execution tools, 42
model-oriented method, 178
model-oriented specification, 132, 535–542
modelling, 33–40, 61, 78, 375
modern structured analysis, 266, 271
Modula language, 17, 25, 128, 496
modularity, 356–357
modularization, 232
module, 231, 661
module diagram/template, 280, 283
monitors, 304, 318–321
monoprocessor, 304
MORSE project, 502

MS-DOS, 25
MSA, *see* modern structured analysis
MTL, *see* Metric Temporal Logic
multi-set, *see* bag
Multinet Gateway System, 441–445
multiple entry points, 314
multiple exits, 315, 318
multiple inheritance, 279
Mural system, 157
mutual exclusion, 384
m-Verdi, 181
MVS/370, 25
myelitis, 460
myths of formal methods, 130–131, 135–150, 153–163

N-version programming, 662
naming, 324
NASA, 426, 495
National Computer Security Center, 441
National Institute of Science and Technology, 413
National Institute of Standards and Technology, 426
natural language, 148, 172
Naval Research Laboratory, 413, 430
negation, 568, 587
negative information, 648
NETBLT protocol, 369
netlist, 504
network, 295
network operating system, 302
network phase, 93
neural nets, 33
Newtonian model, 375
next state, 186
NIH syndrome, *see* not-invented-here syndrome
NIST, *see* National Institute of Standards and Technology
non-bullets, 31, *see also* silver bullets
non-computable clause, 570, 594
non-determinism, 304, 576
– external, 572
– internal, 574, 597
non-deterministic operations, 571–576, 595
non-functional behaviour, 192
non-functional requirements, 600
non-strict inheritance, 233
non-Zeno behaviour, *see* finite variability
non-atomic operations, 356
normalization, 64
NOS, *see* network operating system

NOT connective, 202
not-invented-here syndrome, 227
notation, 201, 218, 306–312, 324
– diagrammatic, 609
– formal, 128, 660
– graphical, 611
– informal, 661
– semi-formal, 530
– structured, 53–54
Nqthm, 531
nuclear power plants, 496
null command, 306
numerical algorithms, 573
Nuprl proof tool, 177

OAM, *see* object-access model
OBJ, 132, 179, 181, 531
object, 237
object properties, 246–250
object and attribute description, 273
object clustering, 289
object diagram/template, 283
object paradigm, 231
Object Pascal, 231
object–action model, 297
object-access model, 273
object-communication model, 273
object-orientation, 231–235, 662
object-oriented analysis, 261, 277
– Coad and Yourdon, 270
– methodology, 267–274, 276
– Shlaer and Mellor, 271
object-oriented design, 234, 261, 283, 287
– Booch, 279
– methodology, 278–282, 286
object-oriented development, 237, 242–246
– design case study, 252–257
– using Ada, 250–251
object-oriented methods, 505
object-oriented programming, 17
object-oriented requirements specification, 269
object-oriented structure chart, 279
object-oriented structured design, 262, 278, 279
object-state diagram, 272
Objective C, 137, 247
Occam, 132, 301, 375, 426, 531
Occam Transformation System, 156
OCM, *see* object-communication model
one-to-many relationship, 71
Ontario Hydro, 429, 498
OOS, *see* object-oriented requirements specification

OOSD, *see* object-oriented structured design
open-loop behaviour, 372
operating system, 300, 301
operation, 565, 662
– non-atomic, 356
– deterministic, 565–571
– hidden, 279
– inverse, 567
– non-deterministic, 571–576, 595
operation modelling, 557
operation refinement, 531, 557
operation specification, 543, 546
operation template, 283
operator interface, 450
optimization, 209–210
OR connective, 202
OR decomposition, 377
ORA Corporation, 494
Ordnance Board, 499
orthogonal components, 628, 640
OS, *see* operating system
oscilloscope products, 149, 426
OSpec, 546
output command, 304, 305, 309
output events, 640
output guard, 327
overloading, 234
Oxford University Computing Laboratory, 219

P1228 Software Safety Plans, 509
package, 233, 238
Paige/Tarjan algorithm, 395
PAISley language, 181
parallel command, 304, 306
parallel composition, 373
parallel programming, 216
parallelism, 290, 384
parbegin, 304
Paris Metro signalling system, 433, 437
Paris rapid-transit authority, 433, 496, *aka* RATP
Parnas, David, 17, 19, 29, 161, 179, 430
parse tree, 593
partial execution, 602
partial function, 566
partial order semantics, 383
partial-lifecycle method, 237, 244, 258
partitioning, 628, 652
Pascal language, 25
passive entities, 269
past operators, 383
pattern-matching, 305

PCTE, *see* Portable Common Tools Environment
PDCS project, 502
PDF graphics editor, 124
PDL, *see* program definition language
perfective maintenance, 5
performance, 296
periodicals, 165
PES, *see* Programmable Electronic Systems
Petri Nets, 36, 179, 378–384, *see also* interval timed colour Petri Net, *see also* Time Petri Net
phases, 78, 93, 107
physical model, 35
PL/I language, 25, 304
place, 379
plant, 371
point semantics, 383
POL, *see* proof outline logic
polymorphism, 233, 234, 279, 662
port names, 325
Portable Common Tools Environment, 149
posit and prove approach, 564
postcondition, 662
practicing engineers, 510
precondition, 566, 662
predicate, 662
predicate transformers, 176, 404
Predictably Dependable Computing Systems, 502
Pressburger procedures, 400
prime numbers, 322
privacy, 300
probability, 296
procedural programming, 210–213, 215
procedure unit, 64
procedure-call graphs, 172
procedures, 304
process, 273, 295, 299, 304
process activation, 325
process algebra, 132, 551–553
– timed, 396–397
– untimed, 393–395
process cost, 417
process description, 273
process diagram/template, 283
process impact, 417
process model, 132, 271
process modelling, 290
process templates, 280
process–message model, 297
process-decomposition diagram, 268
process-dependency diagram, 268

process-oriented methodologies, 263
ProCoS project, 163, 502, 515, 531, *see also* provably correct systems
product cost, 416
product impact, 416
product quality, 416
professional institutions, 510, 514, 662
professional issues, 363, 364
program, 662
program code, 659
program definition language, 286
program design, 201–216
program execution, 660
program refinement, 195
program verification, 20
Programmable Electronic Systems, 508
programmable hardware, 297, 504
programmed execution, 43
programming
– automatic, 9, 19
– functional, 207–209
– graphical, 9, 20
– logic, 203–205
– procedural, 210–213, 215
– transformational, 8
programming environments, 16, 21
programming execution, 44
programming in the large, 59
programming languages, 169
– real-time, 375–376
– versus specification languages, 342
programming methodology, 216
project management, 235
Prolog language, 148, 181, 204, 560, 586
Prolog III, 387
proof, 8, 201, 363, 433, 559, 564, 662
– and specification, 142
– limits, 138
– machine-checked, 220
– versus integration testing, 211
proof obligations, 176, 557, 561
proof of correctness, 129, 530
proof outline logic, 402
proof outlines, 402–403
proof system, 129
proof-checking tools, 181
proof-of-program method, 433
ProofPower tool, 157
properties, 151
properties of an object, 246–250
properties of specificands, 173
property-oriented method, 178
property-oriented specification, 132

protection mechanism, 300
prototype code, 47
prototype software system, 24
prototyping, *see* rapid prototyping
provably correct systems, 195, 502, 531, 662, *see also* ProCoS project
PTIME, 391
public key, 301
punctuality property, 390
PVS theorem prover, 531

qualitative temporal properties, 384
quality, 10, 416, 224
quantification, 202, 570, 661
quantitative temporal properties, 384
Queen's Award for Technological Achievement, 221
Quicksort, 572

Radiation Emitting Devices, 457
Radiation Protection Bureau, 455
radiation therapy machine, 447
Radio Technical Commission for Aeronautics, 438, 507
Railway Industry Association, 508
railway systems, 496
RAISE, 132, 157, 179, 426
rapid prototyping, 23, 559, 580, 663
Rapid System Prototyping, 559
RATP, *see* Paris rapid-transit authority
RDD, *see* responsibility-driven design
reachability, 378
reachability tests, 45
reactive systems, 33, 179, 530, 638
reactor control, 149
readiness model, 394
real-time, 296, 359, 503, 663
– constraints, 368
– definition, 371
– future trends, 404–405
– graphical languages, 377–382
– Hoare logic, 401–402
– process algebra, 393–400
– programming languages, 375–376
– structured methods, 376–377
Real-Time ACP, 396
Real-Time Logic, 400–401
real-time systems, 359–360, 367, 370
real-time temporal logic, 382–393
– RTTL($<$,s), 390
reasoning, 201, 661
record, 637
recursive data representation, 317

recursive factorial, 316
RED, *see* Radiation Emitting Devices
reengineering, 422
Refine language, 176
refinement, 5, 129, 130, 176, 195, 394, 531, 557, 663
– data, 216
– timewise, 399
refinement checker, 426
reformatting lines, 314
regulatory agencies, 413
reification, 557
relation, consequence, 173
relationship, 70, 91
relationship model, 273
relative completeness, 172
reliability, 488, 663
– versus safety, 480
reliability engineering, 620–622
remote procedure call, 298
removal of faults, 489, 660
repetitive command, 305, 310
requirements, 1, 201–203, 215, 371, 563, 663
– formal, 176, 418
– non-functional, 600
– object-oriented, 269
requirements analysis, 3, 176, 529
Requirements Apprentice system, 176
requirements capture, 418, 502
requirements elicitation, 3, 158, 529
requirements refinement, 23
RER, 496
response time, 386
responsibility-driven design, 280, 284
responsiveness, 384
retrieve function, 557
retrieve relation, 557
reusable components, 418
reusable software architecture, 426
reusable software components, 257
reuse, 9, 227, 288, 291, 292, 483
Reve, 181
revisability, 552
revolutionaries, 261
Rewrite Rule Laboratory, 181
rewrite rules, 181
RIA, *see* Railway Industry Association
rigorous argument, 362, 363, 663
risk, 481, 487, 663
Rolls-Royce and Associates, 149, 496, 497
rountangles, 179, 626
Royce's model, *see* waterfall model

RPB, *see* Radiation Protection Bureau
RPC, *see* remote procedure call
RRL, *see* Rewrite Rule Laboratory
RSP, *see* Rapid System Prototyping
RTCA, *see* Radio Technical Commission for Aeronautics
RTCTL, 392
RTL, *see* Real-Time Logic
RTTL, *see* real-time temporal logic

SA, *see* structured analysis
SACEM, 433, 496
SADT, *see* structured analysis and design technique
SafeFM project, 502
SafeIT initiative, 501
safemos project, 515
safety, 185, 487, 488, 663
– cost, 492
– property defined, 332
– specification, 334, 336, 339
– versus reliability, 480
safety case, 359
safety factors, 375
safety properties, 188, 384
safety standards, 506–511
safety-critical systems, 1, 359–361, 367, 413–427, 487–493, 663
– case studies, 414–415, 429–445
– commercial and exploratory cases, 425–427
– formal methods, 361–362
– general lessons learned, 419–422
– history, 485–487
– industrial-scale examples, 493–501
– lessons learned, 415–419
Safety-Critical Systems Club, 365, 502
safety-related, 663
SAME, *see* Structured Analysis Modelling Environment
SART, 609
SA/SD, 4, 498
– and VDM, 536–538
satisfaction, 176, 370
satisfiability, 390
satisfiable specification, *see* consistent specification
satisfies relation, 168, 170
SAZ method, 223
SC, *see* Structure Charts
scaffolding, 24
scale, 419
scheduling, 318–321

SCR, *see* Software Cost Reduction
SCR/Darlington method, 430
SDI project, 29
SDIO, *see* Strategic Defense Initiative Organization
SDLC, *see* systems development life-cycle
SDS, *see* shutdown system
SE/Z, 540–542
Secure Multiprocessing of Information by Type Environment, 149
security, 300, 663
security-critical network gateway, 441
security-critical systems, 413
security-policy model, 427
SEE, *see* Software Engineering Environment
SEI, *see* Software Engineering Institute
selector, 247
semantic abstraction function, 170
semantic domain, 168, 169
semantic gap, 530, 531
semantic model of time, 384
semantic network, 636
semantically-Extended DFD, 543
semantics, 131, 370, 398
semaphore, 304, 319
semi-formal methods, 180, 199, 530
sequential composition, 210, 303
sequential programs, 194
serialization 347, *see also* concurrency control
servers, 248, 281
service, 663
service availability, 659
service chart, 272
set operators, 588
SETL language, 565
sets, 317, 631, 626
Shlaer and Mellor object-oriented analysis, 271, 273
shoemaker's children syndrome, 613
Shostak Theorem Prover, 495
shutdown system, 429
sieve of Eratosthenes, 322
SIFT project, 495
Signal language, 378
signoff points, 122
silver bullets, 8–10, 29, 31
SIMULA 67, 246, 248, 304
Simula-67 language, 17, 67, 231, 233, 246, 248, 304
simulation, 559, 663
SIS, *see* Synchronous Interaction Specification

skills, 421
skip, 306
sledgehammer, 335, 337
slow sort algorithm, 590
Smalltalk, 25, 238, 246–248, 250, 251
smartcard access-control system, 426
SMARTIE project, 506
SMITE, *see* Secure Multiprocessing of Information by Type Environment
SML, 560
snapshot, 371
SNCF, *see* French national railway
soft real-time, 359, 503
soft-fail, 550
software, 663
– formal methods, 159
software code, 659
software components, 257, 610
Software Cost Reduction, 430
software development, 3, 237
Software Engineering Environment, 610
Software Engineering Institute, 10, 25
software life-cycle, *see* life-cycle
software methodology, 57–76
software process capability, 10
software quality, 10
Software Requirements Engineering Methodology, 180, 244
software reuse, 9, 483
software specification, 584
software tools, 149
sorting, 568, 572, 590, 595
soundness, 370
SPADE tool, 506
specialization, 233
specificand, 168
specification, 1–10, 24, 168, 371, 529, 663
– algebraic, 542–551
– animation, 560, 659
– behavioural, 171
– by inverse, 567, 592
– combining clauses, 567
– complete, 172
– consistency of, 172
– examples, 587
– executable, 41, 180, 560, 563, 584, 604, 660
– formal, 128, 219, 660
– functional, 4
– inference, 565, 577–578
– model-oriented, 132, 535–542
– negation, 568
– non-computable clause, 570

- proof, 142
- properties, 172
- property-oriented, 132
- protocols, 132
- software, 584
- structural, 172
- system, 4
- two-tiered, 183
- unambiguous, 172
- using known functions, 565
- variables, 576–577
- versus model, 371
specification languages, 128, 131, 132, 168–173
- logic, 586
- versus programming languages, 342
specification validation, 601
specification variables, 600, 601
specification–implementation semantic gap, 531
Spectool, 494
SPEEDBUILDER JSD tools, 124
SPIN tool, 133
spiral model, 6
spontaneous transition, 386
spreadsheets, 23
SQL, *see* System Query Language
square root of -1, 153
SREM, *see* Software Requirements Engineering Methodology
SRI International, 494
SSADM, *see* Structured Systems Analysis and Design Methodology
staircasing, 573
stakeholders, 419
standards, 132, 362–363, 514, 664
- formal methods, 506
- safety, 506–511
Standards Australia, 507
standards organizations, 413
start state, 640
state, 371, 547, 664
- future, 186
- global, 546
- initial, 378
- next, 186
- Petri Net, 378
- structure, 383
- substates, 377, 643
- superstates, 377
- zooming in and out, 377
state diagram, 638
state functions, 189

state model, 271, 273
state transition diagram, 335
state transition methods, 336
state transition system, 547
state vector inspection, 105
state-based methods, 388
State-Transition Diagram, 54, 265, 268, 280, 283, 530, 534, 609
Statecharts, 34, 36, 38, 45, 47, 179, 181, 377–378, 439, 611, 638–645
STATEMATE tool, 34, 42, 45, 181, 377, 440, 611, 637
static analysis, 506
STD, *see* State-Transition Diagram
stepwise refinement, 5, 176
stimulus-response diagrams, 291
STOP process, 393
STP, *see* Shostak Theorem Prover
Strategic Defense Initiative Organization, 29
strict inheritance, 233
structural specifications, 172
Structure Charts, 265, *see also* Yourdon Structure Charts
structured analysis, 53, 542
- modern, 266
- unifying framework, 551
structured analysis and design technique, 434
Structured Analysis Modelling Environment, 543, 550
Structured Design, 53, 73–76, 180, 262, 278, 279
structured English, 53
structured methods, 4, 53–55, 264, 265
- integration, 530–531
- real-time, 376–377
- strengths and weaknesses, 534
structured notation, 53–54, 664
structured programming, 53
Structured Systems Analysis and Design Methodology, 53, 223, 425
structured techniques, 53, 65
style sheet, 168
subprogram, 233, 238
subroutines, 304, 314–318
substates, 377, 643
subsystem, 244, 273, 284
SUD, *see* system under development
sufficient completeness, 172
superstates, 377
support environment, 610, 611, 659
SVDM method, 536
SWARD, 247

Index   699

Synchronous Interaction Specification, 548
synchronous interactions, 394
synchronous languages, 377–378
synchronous transitions, 550
synchrony hypothesis, 36, 378
syntactic domain, 168, 169
syntax, 131, 370
synthesis, 375
synthesists, 261
system, 664
- blackboard, 505
- closed, 191
- concurrent, 296, 659
- dependable, 488
- discrete event, 403
- distributed, 297, 660
- dynamic, 403
- embedded, 660
- high-integrity, 127, 661
- hybrid, 661
- loosely coupled, 296
- provably correct, 662
- rapid prototyping, 559
- reactive, 33, 530, 638
- real-time, 359–360, 663
- safety-critical, 359–361, 487, 663
- transformational, 638
system analysis, 178
system behaviour, 171
system design, 55, 77, 176
system development, 53, 660, *see also* Jackson System Development
system documentation, 177
system evolution, 429
system functions, 66
system maintenance, 5
system modelling, 33–40
system outputs, meaning, 118
system partitioning, 289
System Query Language, 71
system specification, 4, 140
system structure, 171
system testing, 5
system under development, 372
system validation, 177
system verification, 177
systems analysis, 77
systems development life-cycle, 264
systems engineering, 616
systolic arrays, 33

T800 Transputer, 159, 221, 426, 493
T9000 Transputer, 159, 426

tables crisis, 485
tabular representation, 439
task, 238
Task Sequencing Language, 177, 179
TBACS, *see* Token-Based Access Control System
TCAS, *see* Traffic Alert and Collision-Avoidance System
TCCS, *see* Temporal CCS, *see* Timed CCS
TCSP, *see* Timed CSP
TCTL, 392
technology transfer, 365, 420
Tektronix, 149, 426
Temporal CCS, 396, 397
temporal logic, 36, 46, 185, 186, 340, 350, 353, 664
- branching time, 391–392
- interval, 392–393
- real-time, 382–393
Temporal Logic of Actions, 297, 661
temporal operators, 188, 350, 352
Temporal Process Language, 396
temporal properties, 384
temporal verification, 46
Tempura language, 392
termination, 384
testing, 5, 196, 226
Therac-20, 448, 462
Therac-25, 447–483
- design errors, 465
- hazard analysis, 452
- operator interface, 450
- software development and design, 463
- turntable positioning, 449
Theratronics International, Ltd., 448
there exists ∃, 202
Third Normal Form, 71
tick transition, 384
time, 384
Time Petri Net, 380
time to market, 417
time-sharing, 15
time-stamp, 299
Timed CCS, 396
Timed CSP, 396, 503
Timed Probabilistic CCS, 396
timed process algebra, 396–397
Timed Transition Model, 384, 385
timed transition model, 387
timers, 271
timestamp, 380
timewise refinement, 399
timing diagram, 283

TLA, *see* Temporal Logic of Actions
Token-Based Access Control System, 426
tokens, 378
tolerance of faults, 489, 660
tool support, 181
- formal methods, 420
toolbenches, 16
tools, 21, 124, 175
- CASE, 609, 611
- model execution, 42
- formal methods, 156, 196, 220, 418
- proof-checking, 181
top-down, 54
top-down development, 394
topovisual, 623
torpedoes, 499
touch-and-feel experience, 584, 602
TPCCS, 392, *see* Timed Probabilistic CCS
TPCTL, 392
TPL, *see* Temporal Process Language
TPN, *see* Time Petri Net
TPTL, 390
trace model, 394
traces, 187
Traffic Alert and Collision-Avoidance System, 438–441, 495
training, 145, 510
trait, 183
transaction processing, 149
transaction-centered organization, 75
transactions, 299
transform-centered organization, 75
transformation, 195
transformational approach, 6–8, 564, 603
transformational system, 638
transition, 371
- enabled, 385
- live, 379
- spontaneous, 386
- tick, 384
transition axiom method, 188, 331
transition axiom specification, 332
- advantages, 333, 336, 338
- concurrency specification, 355–356
- hierarchical decomposition, 356
- liveness properties, 350
- modularity, 356–357
- non-atomic operations, 356
- programming, 341, 342, 349
- safety specification, 336, 339
- temporal specifications, 354
transition axioms, 185
transition model, 387

transparency, 300
Transputer, 149, 159, 221, 296, 426, 493
TRIO, 393
troika, 73
TSL, *see* Task Sequencing Language
TTM, *see* Timed Transition Model
TTM/RTTL framework, 384–388
tuning, 579
Turing machines, 380
two-phase commit, 299
two-tiered specification, 183
type, 17, 70, 248

U-LOTOS, *see* Urgent LOTOS
UML, *see* Unified Modeling Language
unambiguous specification, 172
unbounded process activation, 325
uncertainty, 487
undecidability, 380
under-determined, 574
unfold/fold transformations, 604
unification, 568
Unified Modeling Language, 235
unified programming environments, 16
union ∪, 588
unit testing, 5
UNITY, 179, 382
universal quantification ∀, 202
UNIX, 16, 25, 298, 299, 304
unordered Cartesian product, 653
untimed process algebra, 393–395
update of text file, 588
Urgent LOTOS, 396
user interface, 483
users of formal methods, 173
uses of formal methods, 175

validation, 129, 177, 559, 563, 601, 664
vanilla approach, 30, 32, 34
variant, 637
VDM, *see* Vienna Development Method
VDM-SL Toolbox, 157
vending machine, 396
Venn diagrams, 284, 623
Venn, John, 623
verification, 20, 127, 129, 177, 195, 196, 375, 563, 664
- formal, 220
- of consistency, 48
- temporal, 46
verification and validation, 419
verification conditions, 435
Verilog, 434

Veritas proof tool, 159
very high-speed integrated circuit, 48
VHDL, *see* VHSIC hardware description language
VHSIC, *see* very high-speed integrated circuit
VHSIC hardware description language, 48
Vienna Development Method, 131, 154, 382, 491
– and SA/SD, 536–538
– and Yourdon, 535–536
– example, 182
– reification, 557
– standard, 132
– VDM-SL Toolbox, 157
views of a specificand, 170
VIPER microprocessor, 363, 500
Virtual Channel Processor, 426
Virtual Device Metafile, 154
Virtual DOS Machine, 154
visibility, 279
visual formalisms, 37, 41, 609, 611, 651
visual languages, 179, 180
visual representation, 37
visual specification, 169

walk through, 430, 616
WAN, *see* wide area network
Ward/Mellor data and control flow diagrams, 551
Warnier/Orr approach, 57–61
Wasserman et al. object-oriented structured design, 278, 279
watchdog, 46
waterfall model, 3, 6
weakest precondition calculus, 382

weakest precondition predicate transformers, 404
well-defined, 169
well-formed sentences, 169, 173
"what", 4, 58, 141, 177, 332, 382, 578, 580, 586
Whirlwind project, 485
why, 58
wide area network, 295
Wirfs-Brock et al. responsibility-driven design, 280, 284
workbench, CASE, 609, 610
workstations, 21
World Wide Web, 295

XCTL, 389
XOR, *see* exclusive-or

Yourdon, 4, 53, 54
– and CCS, 551–553
– and VDM, 535–536
– and Z notation, 538–540
Yourdon approach, 65–69
Yourdon Structure Charts, 551

Z notation, 4, 131, 382, 560, 660
– and LBMS SE, 540–542
– and Yourdon, 538–540
– examples, 151–152, 182
– tools, 157
– standard, 132
Zeno, *see* non-Zeno behaviour
Zola tool, 157
zoom out, 648
ZTC tool, 157